History Theses 1901-70

Historical research for higher degrees in the universities
of the United Kingdom

Compiled by

P. M. Jacobs

University of London

Institute of Historical Research

1976

INTRODUCTION

The list of historical theses published here is not a list of
theses which are necessarily available for consultation, since in
nearly all British universities it is only in relatively recent
years that students have been required to place a copy of their
work on deposit. In order to give as complete a picture as possible
of historical research for higher degrees in the first seventy
years of the twentieth century, the titles of all theses which
can be presumed to have been completed have been included. The
compiler apologises to librarians who may be asked to produce
theses which they do not possess and to scholars frustrated in
their desire to consult them.

A brief account of the method of compilation may give some
indication of certain limitations in the present list. Historians
have been fortunate in that regular printed lists of completed
theses in history have been available from 1920. These were printed
in the journal History from 1920 to 1929 and in the Bulletin of the
Institute of Historical Research from 1930 to 1932. From then until
1966 they were recorded in annual Theses Supplements (Nos. 1-27)
to the Bulletin and from 1967 in a separate publication of the
Institute, Historical Research for University Degrees in the
United Kingdom, beginning with List No. 28. Up-to-date lists, containing titles of theses completed in the previous year, have
obvious advantages but also have disadvantages. Since the information has often to be taken from circulars rapidly corrected in
history departments, errors and omissions are numerous, and
'ghosts', that is, theses completed but not approved, may have been
included. The titles culled from these sources could not therefore
simply be put together to form a consolidated list. Nevertheless
they provided a useful basis for the compilation and were tested
and supplemented in three ways.

The first source used was official printed lists of thesis
titles issued by universities. These are surprisingly few in
number: in many universities there is no documentation of post-
graduate research; in others such printed records as exist are
incomplete. A few universities included such lists in their
Calendars, for some if not all of the period covered.

The second attempt at checking was by an approach to the
library of the university in question. Sometimes it was possible
to obtain a xerox copy of the handlist of theses in a given
library: if a separate handlist did not exist, a list of titles
was submitted to the librarian for checking against the main
library catalogue. In this way many titles and names of authors
were verified, but only when copies of the theses had actually
been deposited.

If these sources were unproductive, a third check was made
from the list of graduates of a university, if one existed. In
this way it could be ascertained whether the degree was in fact
awarded. The complete title, however, could not be checked, and
the one recorded here may not be correct. The registrar's department of certain universities confirmed in some cases that post-
graduate degrees had been awarded, and the archives of the University Registry at Oxford were consulted to prove the completion of
theses at that university before the printed lists began.

The list which follows contains theses completed and approved
for the degree of B.Litt. and for doctor's and master's degrees in
universities of the United Kingdom. A few B.D., B.Phil. and B.Sc.
theses are included, but not dissertations for the B.A. degree or
in partial fulfilment of an M.A. degree. Doctorates awarded for
published work and M.Ed. theses are also excluded.

Theses prepared in history faculties have been included, however unhistorical or surprising their subjects may seem to be. Many theses prepared in other faculties have been listed, but for reasons of space the number of titles in marginal subjects has had to be limited. It is not always possible to deduce from the title of a thesis the exact subject matter or period covered, so that there may be errors in arrangement. A large number of London theses were looked at in cases of doubt, but for other universities only the most difficult queries were submitted to university librarians, who kindly furnished replies.

Where possible the calendar year of the degree is given, though in some cases this could not be ascertained and the academic year is used.

The names of students are normally given in the form used by the university in question. Non-British names often do not appear in their correct indigenous form, nor are they consistently westernised. Women students who, in the process of obtaining their degree, were recorded under their maiden and married names are here entered under both. In the index of authors an attempt has been made to distinguish between students with similar names and initials. Where one person appears to have obtained two or even three degrees, these are separately listed in the index.

It would be impossible to record the names of all the librarians and university registrars who have kindly and patiently replied to queries. Thanks are due to them all, and also to my colleagues at the Institute of Historical Research who have saved me from many blunders. This is also a fitting place to express my gratitude to Mrs. Nicole Mott who has cheerfully and speedily typed the Institute's list of theses for very many years and has now helped to produce the consolidated list. Her accurate typing has again saved hours of correcting time and her expert eye has once more detected errors and inconsistencies.

January 1976   P.M.J.

CONTENTS

PHILOSOPHY OF HISTORY

The nature of historical explanation. P.L. Gardiner.   1
Oxford B.Litt. 1950.
    Historical explanation. C.B. McCullagh. Cambridge Ph.D.   2
1965.
    An analysis of historical knowledge. A.R. Louch. Cam-   3
bridge Ph.D. 1956.
    An idealist conception of history. E.J. Widdows.   4
Bristol M.A. 1922.
    The theory of sovereignty in history. W.D. Handcock.   5
Bristol M.A. 1926.
    Some aspects of explanation and interpretation in history. 6
W.H. Dray. Oxford D.Phil. 1956.
    The language and purpose of narrative history. M.A.   7
Kramer. Oxford D.Phil. 1957.
    History, literature, social science and philosophy of   8
history: some aspects of their interrelations.   N.M.L.
Wharton. Leeds Ph.D. 1967.
    Karl Popper's ideas on history. Cynthia R. MacL. Hay.   9
Edinburgh Ph.D. 1969.

HISTORIOGRAPHY

ANCIENT HISTORIOGRAPHY

    An historical commentary on the <u>Hellenica Oxyrhynchia</u>.   10
I.A.F. Bruce. Sheffield Ph.D. 1963.
    A comparison of the principles and methods of Herodotus   11
and Thucydides as historians. T.B. Davis. Wales M.A. 1901.
    Herodotus as a source for Greek colonisation. P. Slade.   12
Manchester M.A. 1968.
    A historical commentary on Herodotus, Book VII, with a   13
general introduction. O.K. Armayor. Oxford D.Phil. 1969.
    Public opinion in the history of Thucydides. T.J. Quinn. 14
Manchester M.A. 1962.
    Power in Thucydides. H. Konishi. Liverpool Ph.D. 1966.   15
    The validity of the evidence of Diodorus Siculus for the   16
Sicilian history, 413-405 B.C. L.J. Sanders. London M.A.
1966.
    The sources and composition of Livy, books xxxi-xlv.   17
A.H. McDonald. Cambridge Ph.D. 1937/8.
    An historical commentary on Sallust's <u>Bellum Iugurthinum</u>. 18
G.M. Paul. London Ph.D. 1963.
    Historical commentary on Plutarch's Life of Brutus.   19
Frances M. Wilson. London M.A. 1956.
    Plutarch's Life of Crassus, with historical commentary.   20
A.S. Osley. London Ph.D. (Ext.) 1942.
    An edition of Plutarch's Life of Marius. T.F. Carney.   21
London Ph.D. (Ext.) 1957.
    Plutarch's Life of Pericles. W.H. Plommer. Oxford   22
D.Phil. 1948.
    An historical commentary on Plutarch's Life of Pompeius.   23
D.J. Opie. London Ph.D. (Ext.) 1955.
    The Annals of Tacitus. A. Splevins. Nottingham M.A.   24
1966.
    A commentary, mainly, but not exclusively, devoted to   25
its historical aspects, on the <u>Vita divi Vespasiani</u> of C.
Suetonius Tranquillus. A.W. Braithwaite. Oxford B.Litt. 1926.
    A special study of the language and contents of Josephus' 26
'Jewish Antiquities', books xi-xx. R.J.H. Shutt. Durham
Ph.D. 1936.
    Quintus Curtius Rufus: sources and historical value.   27
E.I. McQueen. Cambridge M.Litt. 1969.

28   Cassius Dio. F.G.B. Millar. Oxford D.Phil. 1962.
29   The 'Breviarium' of Festus: a critical edition with
historical commentary. J.W. Eadie. London Ph.D. 1962.
30   Ammianus Marcellinus: a study of his historiography and
political ideas. R.C. Blockley. Nottingham Ph.D. 1970.
31   The histories of Agathias: a literary and historical study.
Mrs. Averil M. Cameron. London Ph.D. 1966.

MUSLIM HISTORIOGRAPHY

32   The development of historical writing among the Moslems in
Spain. S. Goldman. Oxford D.Phil. 1936.
33   An introduction to the Kitâb al-Muhabbar of Muḥammad ibn
Ḥabîb, together with an edition of its first twenty folios,
with indices and explanatory notes. Ilse Lichtenstädter.
Oxford D.Phil. 1937.
34   A study of Abū Zakarīyā's work together with the edition
of the second volume of Tārīkh Al-Mausil. A.H.M. Habiba. Cambridge Ph.D. 1965.
35   Fitnat al Qayrawan: a study of traditional Arabic historiography. M. Brett. London Ph.D. 1970.
36   Sources of the contemporary history of Miskawaih (340-369
A.H.). M.S. Khan. Oxford D.Phil. 1958.
37   The Sīra of al-Mu'ayyad fi'd-Dīn ash-Shīrāzi. A.H. Al-
Hamdani. London Ph.D. 1950.
38   The composition of Ibn al-Athir's History of the Crusades,
A.H. 490-516 = A.D. 1097-1122. C.P. Worlsey. Edinburgh Ph.D.
1954.
39   A critical edition of Münejjim Bāshi's history of the
Saljūqids of Irān (Great Saljūqs), with translation and introduction. S.A. Hasan. Cambridge Ph.D. 1956.
40   Studies on the work of Ibn al-Azraq al-Fāriqī together
with an edition of the section on the Marwānidi dynasty. B.A.
el L. Awad. Cambridge Ph.D. 1955.
41   Ideas of history in the historical literature of early
medieval India. V.S. Pathak. London Ph.D. 1962.
42   The Muslim historians of India, from 1205 to 1259. W.H.
Andalib-i-Shadani. London Ph.D. 1934.
43   Studies on the works of Abu Shama, 599-665 A.H. (1203-67).
M.H.M. Ahmad. London Ph.D. 1951.
44   A study and translation of the first book of the first
volume of the compendium of histories by Rašid al-din Fadl
Allah, concerning the Turkish and Mongol tribes. D.G. Maitland
Muller. London Ph.D. 1957.
45   The treatment of history by medieval Indian Muslim
historians, with special reference to Barni, Afif, Amir Khusrau,
Isami and Yahya bin Ahmad Sihrindi. P. Hardy. London Ph.D.
1953.
46   The Fatawa-i-Jahandari of Zia-ud-din Barni: translation,
with introduction and notes. Afsar Afzaluddin. London Ph.D.
1956.
47   Historical studies on the Inbā' Al-Ghumr of Ibn Hajar.
H. Habashi. London Ph.D. 1955.
48   A survey of the early Ottoman histories, with studies on
their textual problems and their sources. V.L. Ménage. London
Ph.D. 1961.
49   Studies on Maqrizi. A.A.R. Elghawabi. Cambridge Ph.D.
1953.
50   The Histories of Ottoman in Egypt attributed to Abu al-
Surur al-Bakri. F.M. El-Mawi. St. Andrews Ph.D. 1970.

MEDIEVAL EUROPEAN HISTORIOGRAPHY INCLUDING CHRONICLES

51   A commentary on the so-called Opus historicum of Hilary
of Poitiers. J. Fleming. Durham Ph.D. 1952.

A study of the Parker Chronicle (449-597 A.D.) in the   52
light of more recent archaeological, place-name and topographical evidence. G.J. Copley. London Ph.D. 1947.

An edition of the Parker Chronicle. J.B. Wynn. Wales   53
M.A. 1951.

Paul the Deacon and the 'Historia Langobardorum'. Mabel   54
H. Blyton. London M.A. 1935.

The history of the Albanians (Aluank') attributed to   55
Movsēs Kaḷankatuaçi. C.J.F. Dowsett. Cambridge Ph.D. 1953/4.

The chronicle of Aethelweard: with especial reference to   56
the form of Anglo-Saxon Chronicle used by him. E.E. Barker.
London Ph.D. (Ext.) 1969.

A critical study of the sources of the Annals of Winch-   57
combe: Faustina B.1 ff.21-9. E. John. Manchester M.A. 1950.

An edition of annals 1070 to 1154 of the Peterborough   58
Chronicle, with introduction, grammar, commentary and glossary.
Cecily Clark. Oxford B.Litt. 1952.

A critical edition of the Historia Francorum of Raymond   59
of Aguilers. J. France. Nottingham Ph.D. 1967.

The unpublished Annals of Merton and Southwark compared.   60
M. Tyson. Manchester M.A. 1923.

The relationship and chronology of the historical manu-   61
scripts of Matthew Paris. R. Vaughan. Cambridge Ph.D. 1954.

The Old French continuations of the Chronicle of William 62
archbishop of Tyre, to 1232. Mrs. Margaret R. Morgan.
Oxford D.Phil. 1970.

An examination of the historical basis of the 'Roman   63
d'Eustache le Moine'. Gwendolen A. Thorn. Leeds M.A. 1949.

Rhymed chronicles, with special reference to Philippe   64
Mousket (13th century). Juliette W. Jaques. London M.A.
1950.

The French Chronicle by the Anonyme de Béthune: a   65
critical edition. Juliette W. Jaques. London Ph.D. 1955.

An edition of part of the chronicle attributed to Robert 66
of Gloucester, with a study of the original language of the
poem. Anne M. Hudson. Oxford D.Phil. 1964.

French historiography in the later middle ages, with   67
special reference to the 'Grandes Chroniques de France'. Mrs.
Sarah M. Farley. Edinburgh Ph.D. 1969.

A critical edition of the Bury St. Edmunds Chronicle in   68
Arundel MS. 30 (College of Arms). Mrs. Antonia Gransden.
London Ph.D. 1957.

The Anglo-Norman Chronicle of Nicolas Trivet. A. Ruther- 69
ford. London Ph.D. 1932.

Nicholas Trevet: a study of his life and works, with   70
special reference to his Anglo-Norman Chronicle. Ruth J. Dean.
Oxford D.Phil. 1938.

The chronicler of Pedro the Cruel: Pedro Lopez de Ayala. 71
Lilias Taylor. Glasgow Ph.D. 1931.

A contribution to the study of the life, personality and 72
works of Pedro Lopez de Ayala, 1332-1407. E.W. Lloyd. London
Ph.D. 1930.

The chronicle of John Strecche for the reign of Henry V. 73
F. Taylor. Manchester M.A. 1931.

The 'Gesta Henrici Quinti' of Thomas Elmham, prior of   74
Lenton (a re-edition with introduction and notes). F. Taylor.
Manchester Ph.D. 1938.

La Chronique de Mathieu d'Escouchy: an edition of an   75
inedited manuscript of the chronicle of Mathieu d'Escouchy.
G.J. Halligan. Cambridge M.Litt. 1963.

A study of the unpublished 15th-century French prose   76
chronicle: Les anchiennes cronicques de Pise. I.M.P. Raeside.
London Ph.D. 1955.

The influence of Italian humanism on the historiography   77
of Castile and Aragon during the 15th century. R.B. Tate.
Belfast Ph.D. 1955.

78   Late 15th-century French historiography, as exemplified in the <u>Compendium</u> of Robert Gaguin and the <u>De Rebus Gestis</u> of Paulus Aemilius. Katharine L. Davies. Edinburgh Ph.D. 1954.

MODERN HISTORIOGRAPHY

79   The Mémoires of Guillaume and Martin du Bellay - a contribution to the history of French historiography in the 16th century. J.D. Duncannon. London M.A. 1938.

80   A critical edition of <u>Le Lettere Storiche</u> of Luigi da Porto. C.H. Clough. Oxford D.Phil. 1961.

81   A study of 17th-century historiographical literature relating to Wales. D. Watkins. Wales M.A. 1955.

82   English influences on French historians during the 17th century. Ena A.E. Mitchell. Cambridge M.Litt. 1931/2.

83   Early modern historiography, as illustrated by the work of G.J. Vossius, 1577-1649. J.N. Wickenden. Cambridge Ph.D. 1964.

84   A critical commentary on the development of the art of writing history in English between 1603 and 1642. I.G. Jones. Wales M.A. 1950.

85   English constitutional history and political ideas from the death of Oliver Cromwell to the fall of Clarendon. H.N. Mukherjee. Oxford B.Litt. 1933.

86   Clarendon as a historian. D.D. Richards. Wales M.A. 1913.

87   The value of Clarendon as a historian. N.M. Smith. Wales M.A. 1906.

88   Henry de Boulainvilliers: historian and philosopher. J. Grace. Cambridge Ph.D. 1931/2.

89   English historical writing on the English Reformation, 1680-1730. E. Jones. Cambridge Ph.D. 1959.

90   Swift's views on history, and his relation to contemporary historians. M. Jones. Oxford B.Litt. 1954.

91   Swift's works, 1710-15 and contemporary ideas of history and historiography. C.J. Parsons. London Ph.D. 1968.

92   Paul Rapin de Thoyras and the English historiography of his time, 1700-30. D.W.L. Earl. Cambridge M.Litt. 1961.

93   Voltaire's philosophy of history and historical method. J.H. Brumfitt. Oxford D.Phil. 1953.

94   A study of Voltaire's <u>Histoire de Charles XII</u>, with special reference to the author's sources and conception of history. Janina W. Felix. London Ph.D. 1961.

95   A detailed study of Voltaire's <u>Histoire de Russie sous Pierre le Grand</u>. Catherine M. Oakley. Exeter M.A. 1959.

96   The historical writings of William Robertson D.D., 1721-93. H.G. Earnshaw. Bristol M.A. 1951.

97   The attitude of Edward Gibbon towards ecclesiastical history. E.K. Roberts. Edinburgh Ph.D. 1954.

98   Herder's contribution to the romantic philosophy of history, with special reference to the theological implications. G.W. Bromiley. Edinburgh Ph.D. 1943.

99   British historical writing from Alexander Dow to Mountstuart Elphinstone on Muslim India. J.S. Grewal. London Ph.D. 1963.

100   The English historians and the medieval church. R.H. Kiernan. Birmingham M.A. 1928/9.

101   Prosper de Barante: the intellectual biography of a historian. S. Bann. Cambridge Ph.D. 1967.

102   The English historiography of the French Revolution in the 19th century. Hedva Ben-Israel. Cambridge Ph.D. 1955.

103   A study of John Lingard's historical work, with special reference to his treatment of the reign of Elizabeth I. E. Jones. Wales M.A. 1956.

104   Sir Walter Scott and history. J. Anderson. Edinburgh Ph.D. 1965.

A N C I E N T   H I S T O R Y

GENERAL

ANCIENT GREECE

128   The history and nature of the dowry among the ancient
Greeks.   Frances A. Collie.   Wales M.A. 1905.

129   The evolution of religion in Greece from earliest times
to the time of Hesiod.   A. Le Marchant.   Belfast M.A. 1920.

130   Topography, movement and supply in the warfare of ancient
Greece, south of Thessaly and Epirus.   W.W. Cruickshank.
London Ph.D. 1955.

131   Early Greek armour and weapons from the end of the bronze
age to c.600 B.C.   A.McE. Snodgrass.   Oxford D.Phil. 1962.

132   Plundering in war and other depredations in Greek history
from 800 B.C. to 146 B.C.   A.H. Jackson.   Cambridge Ph.D.
1970.

133   The relations between Greek colonies and their mother
cities.   A.J. Graham.   Cambridge Ph.D. 1956.

134   Relations between Greece and the Levant in the archaic
age.   M.M. Austin.   Cambridge Ph.D. 1968.

135   Cults of Boeotia.   A. Schachter.   Oxford D.Phil. 1966.

136   The place of coinage in Greek foreign trade down to the
end of the 5th century B.C.   A.H. Lloyd.   Cambridge Ph.D.
1928/9.

137   Early Corinth.   J.B. Salmon.   Oxford D.Phil. 1970.

138   Athen an propertied families, 600-300 B.C.   J.K. Davies.
Oxford D.Phil. 1965.

139   The Eleusinian mysteries.   R.H. Harte.   Belfast M.A.
1927.

140   A study of the conditions which led to the Athenian and
Spartan tyrannies, and the effect of these tyrannies on the
foreign policy of other states.   Mrs. Margaret O. Wason.
Glasgow Ph.D. 1946.

141   The history of the Peisistratid tyranny at Athens.
Patricia M. Davies.   Wales M.A. 1952.

142   A history of the electrum coinage of Mytilene.   J.F.
Healy.   Cambridge Ph.D. 1954.

143   Greek bronze coinage, c.450-150 B.C., its introduction,
circulation and value, with particular reference to the series
of Corinth.   M.J. Price.   Cambridge Ph.D. 1968.

144   The growth of knowledge among the ancient Greeks of the
Atlantic coast of Europe, with special reference to the
British Isles.   A.J. Sweetland.   London M.A. 1957.

145   Knowledge of India among educated Greeks down to the
time of Arrian.   T.R. Robinson.   Belfast M.A. 1960.

146   The Indo-Greeks: a numismatic and historical study.   A.K.
Narain.   London Ph.D. 1954.

147   History of Samos to 438.   J.P. Barron.   Oxford D.Phil.
1961.

148   The mechanism of the diplomacy of the ancient Greek city-
states to 338 B.C.   D.J. Mosley.   Cambridge Ph.D. 1965.

149   The history of Miletus down to the anabasis of Alexander.
Adelaide G. Dunham.   London M.A. 1913.

150   The history of Thessaly.   R. Williams.   Wales M.A. 1903.

151   The history of Thessaly up to 323 B.C.   E.J. Lloyd.
Wales M.A. 1914.

152   The commercial law of ancient Athens to 323 B.C.   E.S.F.
Ridout.   London Ph.D. 1935.

153   Early Greek ships.   R.T. Williams.   Wales M.A. 1958.

154   Moral and religious education at Athens in the 5th century
B.C.   T.W. Herry.   Liverpool M.A. 1915.

155   The campaign of Xerxes from the Persian side.   J.A. Dodd.
London M.A. 1913.

156   A study of the building inscriptions at Epidauros.
Alison M. Burford.   Cambridge Ph.D. 1963.

157   The political parties in Athens during the Peloponnesian
War.   R.A.E. Prosser.   Bristol M.A. 1926.

158   The Four Hundred and the Thirty.   A.J. Barnett.   Birmingham M.A. 1901.

159   Social organisation in Xenophon's anabasis: the communal
or political organisation of the Army of the Ten Thousand.
G.B. Nussbaum.   Birmingham M.A. 1955.

ROME AND THE ROMAN EMPIRE

General and Political History

184 The Etruscan and Roman town of Sutrim (Sutri), in the light of the archaeological remains in and around it. G.C. Duncan. Cambridge Ph.D. 1963.

185 The history of the governing class at Rome from the beginning of the Republic to 100 B.C., with special reference to the accessibility of that class to those born outside it. E.S. Staveley. Oxford D.Phil. 1951.

186 Kinship and political organisation in regal and republican Rome. Diana M. Evans. Manchester M.A. 1961.

187 The development of the ius municipii and the ius Latii to 90 B.C. J. Pinsent. Oxford D.Phil. 1957.

188 The rise and fall of the Caecilii Metelli, 284-46 B.C. M.G. Morgan. Exeter Ph.D. 1961.

189 The tribunate of the plebs, 287-133 B.C. Monica M. Morgan. Liverpool M.A. 1960.

190 Foreign clientelae in Roman foreign policy and internal politics (264 B.C. - 70 B.C.). E. Badian. Oxford D.Phil. 1956.

191 The history of Sardinia under the Roman Republic. Ellen M. Adams. London M.A. 1917.

192 Family influence in Roman politics from Hannibal's invasion to the battle of Pydna. J.R. Cummings. Oxford B.Litt. 1935.

193 'Vis'. Violence in the city in the last two centuries of the Roman Republic - its development in the light of the inadequacy of means of suppression and of the Roman attitude to the rule of law. A.W. Lintott. London Ph.D. 1963.

194 Politics and policies at Rome, 187-167 B.C. Valerie M. Warrior. London Ph.D. 1968.

195 Italian senators, 139 B.C. - A.D. 14. T.P. Wiseman. Oxford D.Phil. 1967.

196 Studies in pre-Gracchan colonisation. E.T. Salmon. Cambridge Ph.D. 1932/3.

197 The legislation of Caius Gracchus, considered especially in relation to the Order of the Equites. G.A. Le Chavetois. London M.A. 1912.

198 Constitutional speculation in the antiquarians and annalists of the last century B.C., with special reference to the legends of Romulus and Servius Tullius in Livy, Cicero, and Dionysius of Halicarnassus. Mary L.M. Leavitt. Oxford B.Litt. 1966.

199 The life and times of Marcus Licinius Crassus, triumvir. J. Thompson. Edinburgh Ph.D. 1941.

200 A biography of Lucius Licinius Lucullus. W.H. Bennett. Oxford B.Litt. 1969.

201 The political and administrative system of Sulla. J.E. Taylor. Oxford B.Litt. 1924.

202 The political activity of Clodius, particularly in relation to the triumvirs. Muriel D. Whitehouse. London M.A. 1916.

203 The political thought of Sallust. D.C. Earl. Cambridge Ph.D. 1957.

204 Politics at Rome during the social and civil wars. C.M. Bulst. Oxford B.Litt. 1961.

205 Political biography at Rome from its first appearance to Augustus. R.G. Lewis. Oxford B.Litt. 1966.

206 Libertas as a political idea at Rome during the late Republic and early Principate. C. Wirszubski. Cambridge Ph.D. 1946/7.

207 The lost sources of Roman history, 44 B.C. - A.D. 68. J.B. Kenyon, formerly Higginbottom. Liverpool M.A. 1968.

208 A history of the relations between the princeps and the senate during the Julio-Claudian period, with special reference to Augustus and Tiberius. T.J. Cadoux. Oxford D.Phil. 1951.

209 The senatorial opposition to the early Roman empire. Winifred Biggs. Manchester M.A. 1917.

The career of Marcus Antonius until the battle of　　210
Philippi.　C.N. Frank.　Leeds M.A. 1935.

The administrative staff of the Roman emperors at Rome　211
from Augustus to Alexander Severus.　G.R.C. Davis.　Oxford
D.Phil. 1947.

The Monumentum Ancyranum compared with other authorities 212
for the life of Augustus.　M.H. Davies.　Wales M.A. 1912.

The frontiers of the Roman empire under Augustus.　C.M.　213
Wells.　Oxford D.Phil. 1965.

Augustus and the Greek world.　G.W. Bowersock.　Oxford　214
D.Phil. 1962.

Augustus and the gods.　S.O. Esan.　London M.A. 1959.　215

The Roman senate during the reigns of Claudius and Nero. 216
D.A. McAlindon.　Belfast M.A. 1953.

The Roman senate, A.D. 69-193.　J.R. Morris.　London　217
Ph.D. 1953.

The philosophic and aristocratic opposition to the　　218
Flavian emperors.　R.L. James.　London Ph.D. 1938.

The early career, accession and domestic policy of the　219
Emperor Domitian.　R.A. Gillespie.　London M.A. 1937.

Concepts of imperial government in the age of Trajan.　220
J. Warmington.　Southampton M.A. 1964/5.

The emperor Lucius Septimius Severus.　M. Platnauer.　221
Oxford B.Litt. 1914.

A prosopographical investigation into the politics of　222
the reigns of Septimius Severus and Caracalla, 193-217.　J.B.
Leaning.　Manchester M.A. 1968.

The reign of Alexander Severus.　I.H.C. Powell.　Bir-　223
mingham M.A. 1964.

Public disorders in the late Roman empire, their causes　224
and character.　J.R. Martindale.　Oxford B.Litt. 1961.

The influence of the senatorial aristocracy on the　　225
imperial government in the late 3rd and 4th centuries A.D.
M.T.W. Arnheim.　Cambridge Ph.D. 1969.

The chronology of the campaigns of the reign of Dio-　226
cletian.　J.V. Maitland.　Manchester M.A. 1969.

The political consequences of Maxentius's usurpation on　227
the Tetrarchic system of Galerius.　Nicola G. Tailby.　Manchester M.A. 1970.

The family and supporters of the emperor in western　228
society in the age of Theodosius.　J.F. Matthews.　Oxford
D.Phil. 1970.

The imperial notarii of the late Roman empire from the　229
accession of Constantine to the death of Honorius.　Mrs. Carol
H. Moulton.　Birmingham M.A. 1970.

Relations between the Roman and Persian empires from　230
the death of Constantine (337) to the death of Theodosius
(395).　M.H. Dodgeon.　Bristol M.Litt. 1968.

A prosopographical study of the court of Theodosius II. 231
Margaret Priest.　London Ph.D. 1970.

The evidence of Salvian for the causes of the fall of　232
the Roman empire in the west.　W.R. Davies.　Wales M.A. 1941.

The sea and the 5th-century west Roman empire.　J.R.　233
Moss.　London Ph.D. 1970.

Economic and Social History

The social and economic history of Ostia.　F.H. Wilson.　234
Oxford D.Phil. 1935.

A study of the development of social and economic life　235
at Pompeii, with a consideration of how far that development
can be regarded as typical of the towns of Campania in general.
R.C. Carrington.　Oxford D.Phil. 1932/3.

An epigraphic survey of costs in Italy and Africa from　236
the Republic to the Tetrarchy.　R.P. Duncan-Jones.　Cambridge
Ph.D. 1965.

237   Social status and legal privilege in the 2nd and 3rd
centuries of the Roman empire, with special reference to the
curial class.   P.D.A. Garnsey.   Oxford D.Phil. 1967.
238   The state of Roman agriculture in the time of the Gracchi.
Claire A.I. Moore.   London M.A. 1914.
239   The agrarian programme of the Democratic party, B.C. 78-
59. Muriel Auld.   Liverpool M.A. 1905.
240   The condition of Roman agriculture in the time of
Augustus.   W.A. Rhodes.   Leeds M.A. 1932.
241   The social legislation of the Roman empire from Augustus
to Constantine, and the policy of its authors.   J.F. Leddy.
Oxford D.Phil. 1938.
242   The practice of medicine in ancient Rome.   E.M. Bell.
Sheffield M.A. 1969.
243   Women in Roman history from 200 B.C. to A.D. 138.
Gwynneth M.L. Jones.   Wales M.A. 1964.
244   The position of women among the Romans.   Alice M. Holmes.
London M.A. 1932.
245   The slave's 'peculium' in Rome, and the protection
afforded to it by Roman law before the year 180 A.D.   Esmée M.
Thomas.   Wales M.A. 1927.
246   Familia Caesaris: a social study of the slaves and freedmen of the Roman imperial administration.   P.R.C. Weaver.
Cambridge Ph.D. 1965.
247   Roman freedmen during the late Republic.   Mrs. Susan M.
Treggiari, née Franklin.   Oxford B.Litt. 1967.
248   Slavery in the first two centuries of the Roman empire.
R.H. Barrow.   Oxford B.Litt. 1926.
249   Freedmen in the early Roman empire.   A.M. Duff.   Oxford
B.Litt. 1926.
250   Social mobility in the early Roman empire.   H.H. Dalby.
Leicester M.A. 1967.
251   A comparative study of the fora of the Roman empire.
Isabel Purchon.   Wales M.A. 1933.
252   Clothing and its manufacture in the northern Roman provinces (excluding leatherwork).   J.P. Wild.   Cambridge Ph.D.
1967.
253   The development of the mining of lead in the Iberian
peninsula and Britain under the Roman empire until the end of
the 2nd century A.D.   H.D.H. Elkington.   Durham M.A. 1968.
254   The design, structure and organisation of Horrea under
the Roman empire.   G.E. Rickman.   Oxford D.Phil. 1963.
255   The medical profession in the Roman empire from Augustus
to Justinian.   V. Nutton.   Cambridge Ph.D. 1970.
256   Studies in Roman imperial numismatic art.   C.C. Vermeule.
London Ph.D. 1953.
257   The aes coinage of Rome and its subsidiary mints in the
West, A.D. 68-81, with special reference to mint organisation,
to the relative frequency of types and to their consequent
interpretation.   C.M. Kraay.   Oxford D.Phil. 1953.
258   A re-examination and analysis of the coinages of Nero,
with special reference to the aes - coined and current in
Italy and the western provinces of the empire.   D.W. Macdowall.
Oxford D.Phil. 1959.
259   The dating and arrangement of the undated coins from the
mint of Rome, A.D. 98-148.   P.V.B. Hill.   London Ph.D. (Ext.)
1969.
260   Inland transport for civilian purposes in the Roman
empire from the Ciceronian age to the principate of Trajan.
G.P. McKenna.   Manchester M.A. 1962.
261   Urban development in the north-western Roman provinces
in the first two centuries A.D.   C.V. Walthew.   Cambridge Ph.D.
1970.
262   The spice trade under the Roman empire.   J.I. Miller.
Oxford D.Phil. 1964.
263   Commerce in the time of the empire between Italy and
other countries.   W.W. Griffiths.   Wales M.A. 1922.

Some 'voluntary' taxes of the Roman empire. Emily C. 264
Wordsworth. Birmingham M.A. 1912.

The Jews in the city of Rome during the first centuries 265
B.C. and A.D., including a study of the references to them in
Greek and Latin writers. J.H. Michael. Wales M.A. 1913.

The Jewish community in Rome, from its foundation until 266
A.D. 313. Mary E. Jacombs. Birmingham M.A. 1915.

Social life in the Roman empire during the reigns of 267
Constantius and Julian. A.R. Foster. Belfast M.A. 1929.

Religion, Art and Letters

The interrelation of state religion and politics in 268
Roman public life, from the end of the Second Punic War to the
time of Sulla. J.A. North. Oxford D.Phil. 1967.

Some aspects of the acting profession in Rome. E.J. 269
Jory. London Ph.D. (Ext.) 1967.

The history of the schools of rhetoric in the Roman 270
empire from Vespasian to the fall of the empire in the west.
A.O. Gwynn. Oxford B.Litt. 1919.

The chronology of the life and letters of the younger 271
Pliny. R.H. Harte. Belfast Ph.D. 1937.

The cult of Isis in Italy: an account of its external 272
history. M.S. Salem. Liverpool Ph.D. 1937.

The meaning and development of the cult of Mars at Rome. 273
E.H. Clement. Oxford B.Litt. 1939.

The cult of Mars in Britain and Gaul. K.J. Fairless. 274
Newcastle M.A. 1967.

The local cults of ancient Latium outside Rome, with the 275
exception of Ostia. T.G. Thomas. Wales M.A. 1930.

The policy of the Roman government towards non-Roman 276
religions from Augustus to Trajan, with special reference to
the treatment of such religions in Rome and Italy. Una C.
Fitzhardinge. Oxford B.Litt. 1940.

The fall of paganism. Elsie M.C. Hunt. Birmingham M.A. 277
1913.

The fall of paganism. A.E. Wilson. Birmingham M.A. 278
1914.

The attitude of the Roman government to Christianity 279
from Nero to Marcus Aurelius. M.H. Evans. Wales M.A. 1909.

The persecution under Diocletian. G.W. Richardson. 280
London M.A. 1924.

The cult of Apollo from the 4th to the 6th century A.D. 281
Alice Weissbruth. London Ph.D. 1967.

Army

The primipilares of the Roman army. B. Dobson. Durham 282
Ph.D. 1955.

The immunes and principales of the Roman army. D.J. 283
Breeze. Durham Ph.D. 1970.

Roman military book-keeping. G.R. Watson. Durham 284
M.Litt. 1953.

The recruitment of Roman legionaries from 146 B.C. to 30 285
B.C. P.J. Cuff. Oxford D.Phil. 1955.

Peace-time routine in the Roman army. R.W. Davies. 286
Durham Ph.D. 1967.

Some aspects of the political influence of the Roman 287
army as it developed from 133 B.C. to A.D. 14. F. Naylor.
Liverpool M.A. 1963.

Some neglected aspects of Scipio Africanus. H.H. 288
Scullard. London Ph.D. 1930.

The armies of the Triumviral period. W.C.G. Schmitt- 289
henner. Oxford D.Phil. 1958.

Studies in the later Roman army. J.R. Hepworth. Dur- 290
ham Ph.D. 1963.

11

291   A study of the Roman cavalry arm, with special reference to the deployment and use of cavalry in the 2nd century A.D. S.H. Bartle. Durham Ph.D. 1962.

292   The Roman high command from the death of Hadrian to the death of Caracalla, with particular attention to the Danubian wars of Marcus Aurelius and Commodus. A.R. Birley. Oxford D.Phil. 1966.

293   The 3rd-century origins of the 'New' Roman army. P.K. Cooper. Oxford D.Phil. 1968.

294   The settlement of veterans in the Roman empire. J.C. Mann. London Ph.D. 1956.

295   The development of the Roman fleets under the empire. L.F. Fitzhardinge. Oxford B.Litt. 1933.

296   Late Roman military architecture in Britain and northern Gaul, with special reference to the coastal defence system. R.M. Butler. Cambridge Ph.D. 1954.

Provinces

Greece and the East

297   Roman relations with the Greek East, from the earliest contacts to 146 B.C., and their relation to internal political struggles. J. Briscoe. Oxford D.Phil. 1965.

298   The development of trade to the end of the 2nd century A.D. between the eastern provinces of the Roman empire and the countries lying further east. J. Thorley. Durham M.A. 1965.

299   Immigration and settlement in the province of Dalmatia from the first Roman contacts to the death of Commodus. A.J.N. Wilson. Oxford D.Phil. 1949.

300   Studies in the Roman province of Dalmatia. J.J. Wilkes. Durham Ph.D. 1962.

301   Proconsular administration of justice in Asia Minor in the late Republic, with special reference to Cicero in Cilicia. A.J. Marshall. Oxford B.Litt. 1962.

302   Cicero's provincial governorship of Cilicia. J.K. Wilkinson. Birmingham M.A. 1959.

303   Social and economic conditions of the province Achaia from Augustus to Caracalla. A.J. Gossage. London Ph.D. 1951.

304   The trade gilds of the eastern provinces of the Roman empire (exclusive of Egypt) during the first three centuries A.D. Esmée M. Thomas. Oxford B.Litt. 1934.

305   The anti-Roman reaction in Sicily and the eastern provinces, 133 B.C. - 85 B.C. Marianne E. Henderson. Sheffield M.A. 1955.

306   Lycia and Pamphylia under the Roman empire from Augustus to Diocletian. Shelagh A. Jameson. Oxford D.Phil. 1965.

307   Roman colonies in southern Asia Minor with special reference to Antioch - towards Pisidia. Barbara M. Levick. Oxford D.Phil. 1958.

308   Rome and Parthia, 70-29 B.C. A. Sandys-Wood. Oxford B.Litt. 1949.

309   Parthia and her relations with Rome from B.C. 27 to A.D. 228. A.T. Owen. Wales M.A. 1920.

310   The relation between the Jews and the Roman government from 66 B.C. to the foundation of the Christian empire. Edith M. Smallwood. Cambridge Ph.D. 1951.

311   A study of Jewish history from the death of Herod the Great to the destruction of Jerusalem, 4 B.C. - 70 A.D. S.G.F. Brandon. Leeds M.A. 1932.

312   Judaea under the procurators. L. Robinson. Cambridge M.Litt. 1926/7.

313   The Roman province of Judea before A.D. 70. Dorothy D. Fielding. Manchester M.A. 1933.

314   Palestine under Roman administration, 6-66 A.D. M. Aberbach. Leeds M.A. 1947.

Palestinian coins of the centuries immediately preceding 315
and following the Christian era. A. Mallinson. Oxford B.Litt.
1923/4.

Currencies and prices in 3rd- and 4th-century Palestine 316
and their implications for Roman economic history. D.
Sperber. London Ph.D. 1968.

Africa

Social life in Roman Africa. Mary A. Gardiner. Belfast 317
M.A. 1931.

History of Numidia under the Roman Republic. Sybil M. 318
Gates. London M.A. 1917.

A study of the municipal aristocracies of the Roman 319
empire in the west, with special reference to North Africa.
M.G. Jarrett. Durham Ph.D. 1958.

The composition and functions of the local councils of 320
the cities of the province of Africa under the early Roman
empire - up to Constantine. C.V.M. Lucas. London Ph.D. 1937.

Studies in the Roman province of Mauretania Tingitana. 321
J.E.H. Spaul. Durham M.Litt. 1958.

Mauretania Caesariensis: an archaeological and geo- 322
graphical survey. R.I. Lawless. Durham Ph.D. 1969.

Studies in the mosaic pavements of Roman North Africa. 323
Katherine M.D. Dunbabin. Oxford D.Phil. 1970.

The agriculture of Cyrenaica in classical antiquity, 324
with special reference to the Jewish Revolt under Trajan.
S.E. Applebaum. Oxford B.Litt. 1948.

Gaul

The political and economic organisation of Gaul from 325
27 B.C. to A.D. 68. Bernardine M. Humphrey. Liverpool M.A.
1961.

The Gallic empire. C.D. Bishop. Durham M.A. 1965. 326

The political and social organisation of Gaul under the 327
Roman empire. E.J. Rowland. Wales M.A. 1910.

The political and social organisation of Gaul under the 328
Roman empire. J. Hooson. Wales M.A. 1912.

Roman civilisation in the three Gauls during the first 329
three centuries of Roman rule. H.W. Lawton. Wales M.A. 1923.

Roman agricultural organisation in western Europe, with 330
special reference to the Tres Galliae. J. Percival. Oxford
D.Phil. 1967.

The organisation and administration of the 'Tres 331
Galliae', 49 B.C. to A.D. 284. Mary A.J.P. Kerr. Manchester
M.A. 1924.

The social and economic history of Cisalpine Gaul under 332
the early empire to the death of Trajan. G.E.F. Chilver.
Oxford D.Phil. 1936.

Some historical problems arising from the martyrdom of 333
the Christians of Lyons and Vienne in 177 A.D. G. McConville.
Belfast M.A. 1958.

Education in Gaul in the last century of the western 334
empire (350-450 A.D.). T.J. Haarhoff. Oxford B.Litt. 1918.

The Celtic personal names in the Celtic inscriptions of 335
Gaul, the Commentaries on the Gallic War and La Graufesenque
graffiti. D.E. Evans. Oxford D.Phil. 1962.

Germania

A historical and cultural survey of the Roman Limes of 336
Germania Superior and Raetia. Olwen P.F. Kendall. London
M.A. 1931.

The honestiores of the Rhine and Danube provinces of the 337
Roman empire, with particular reference to Noricum. B.L.
Cooke. Durham Ph.D. 1964.

13

338   Roman Trier and the Treveri. Edith M. Wightman. Oxford D.Phil. 1968.

339   The Romans in Württemberg: a study of colonial development. J. Rogan. Durham M.A. 1951.

Britain

340   The geography of Roman Britain and its human relationships. C. Midgley. Sheffield M.Sc. 1927.

341   Some aspects of the Romano-British rural system of the lowland zone. S.E. Applebaum. Oxford D.Phil. 1952.

342   A reassessment of the economic basis of Roman Britain. Ilid E. Anthony. London M.A. 1951.

343   The siting and layout of native settlements in the north of England. P.R. Middleton. Durham M.A. 1967.

344   The coin hoards of Roman Britain. Annie S. Robertson. London M.A. 1936.

345   Municipal and military water supply and drainage in Roman Britain. Julie C. Hanson. London Ph.D. 1970.

346   Stone building materials in Roman Britain. J.H. Williams. Manchester M.A. 1968.

347   Roman villas in Britain. Joan E.A. Liversidge. Cambridge M.Litt. 1949.

348   The villas of Roman Britain, and their place in the life of the province. C.A.F. Berry. London Ph.D. (Ext.) 1949.

349   Roman villas in Britain: their nature and distribution. Mabel G.A. Webster. Liverpool M.A. 1920.

350   Romano-British villa bath-suites and bath-houses. J.M.T.H. Younge. Leeds M.A. 1960.

351   The development and affinities of mosaic decoration in Roman Britain. D.J. Smith. Durham Ph.D. 1952.

352   The crafts of Roman Britain, with special reference to the metal remains at Corstopitum. R.A. Peel. Durham M.A. 1965.

353   Non-military ironwork in Roman Britain. W.H. Manning. London Ph.D. 1969.

354   Objects of jet in Roman Britain. C.E.P. Rosser. Manchester M.A. 1961.

355   The religions of Roman Britain. Judith A.P. Angles. London M.A. 1956.

356   The religions of Roman Britain. Bridgett E.A. Jones. London M.A. 1955.

357   A survey of the indigenous, Celtic and Teutonic cults of Roman Britain. J. Herbert. Wales M.A. 1954.

358   Temples and shrines in Roman Britain: their architecture, chronology and distribution. M.J.T. Lewis. Cambridge Ph.D. 1963.

359   The sculptured decoration on Roman votive altars and pedestals from northern Britain. J. Kewley. Durham Ph.D. 1970.

360   Christian evidence (archaeological and documentary) in Roman and sub-Roman north Britain. J. Wall. Bristol M.A. 1966.

361   The ethnic connections and status of civilians of non-British origin in the Roman province of Britain. A.W. Lingard. Sheffield M.A. 1954.

362   Roman civilians and the frontier region of Roman Britain. P. Salway. Cambridge Ph.D. 1958.

363   The milestones and turrets of Hadrian's Wall and their allocation to legionary construction teams. Mrs. Joyce Moss, née Hooley. Durham M.A. 1969.

364   Pottery from the milecastles and turrets on Hadrian's Wall. J.D. Dockerill. Durham M.A. 1969.

365   Romanisation in south-west Scotland. A. Wilson. Durham M.A. 1966.

366   The archaeology of Roman Durham. K.A. Steer. Durham Ph.D. 1938.

H I S T O R I C A L   G E O G R A P H Y :   B R I T A I N

ENGLAND

South

391   The geographical development of west Cornwall. C.F.W.R.
Gullick.   Oxford B.Litt. 1934.

392   The West Penwith peninsula of Cornwall, considered from
the point of view of archaeological evidences concerning
development of settlements. D.H. Watkins. Wales M.A. 1930.

393   The evolution of settlement in Devon. W.L.D. Ravenhill.
Wales M.A. 1951.

394   A comparative study of Kingsbridge and Totnes. A. Dark.
London M.Sc. 1961.

395   The past agricultural utilisation of Dartmoor. E.G. Fogwill.   London M.A. 1952.

396   A study of rural settlement in Somerset. Beatrice M.
Swainson. London M.A. (Ext.) 1932.

397   The settlement pattern in north central Somerset. J.M.
Jennings. Bristol M.A. 1957.

398   The scarplands of the Wiltshire-Gloucestershire-Somerset
borders - a regional study, with particular reference to urban
and rural settlement. Irene G. Youldon. London M.A. 1945.

399   The evolution of rural settlement in Dorset. L. Pritchard.   Wales M.Sc. 1954.

400   Late medieval Dorset: three essays in historical geography.   B. Reynolds. London M.A. 1958.

401   Southampton: a factor in the economic development of the
Hampshire basin. Katharine C. Boswell. London M.Sc. (Ext.)
1936.

402   The agricultural geography of the Adur basin in its
regional setting. H.C.K. Henderson. London Ph.D. 1935.

403   An analysis of some of the interactions of geography and
history in the Arun and Adur valleys. Alice F.A. Mutton.
London M.A. 1932.

404   A contribution to the historical geography of the western
Weald. E.M. Yates. London M.Sc. 1953.

405   The influence of physical geography upon the history of
settlement and distribution of population in Sussex. W.H.
Parker. Oxford B.Sc. 1939.

406   The Sussex gap towns: a geographical analysis. D. Burtenshaw. London M.A. 1963.

407   The common lands and wastes of Sussex. P.F. Brandon.
London Ph.D. 1963.

408   Horsham: a geographical study. Florence A. Hamblin.
London M.A. 1962.

409   The field systems of Kent. A.R.H. Baker. London Ph.D.
1963.

410   The Medway towns: their settlement, growth and economic
development. H. Rees. London Ph.D. (Ext.) 1955.

411   The origins and changing functions of settlement in south-
east London, with special reference to the flood-plain section
of the borough of Deptford. Gladys M. Hickman. London Ph.D.
1951.

412   The historical geography of Maidstone. Valerie E. Morant.
London M.A. 1948.

413   The manor of Tyburn and the Regent's Park, 1086-1965.
Ann L. Saunders. Leicester Ph.D. 1965.

414   The historical geography of the upper Brent. A.J.
Garrett. London M.A. 1935.

415   The city of St. Albans: a study in urban geography. H.S.
Thurston. London M.Sc. 1951.

416   The geography of Berkshire with special reference to
agriculture. J. Stephenson. London M.A. 1936.

417   The Vale of White Horse area: a regional study of settlement. M.W. Smith. London M.Sc. 1956.

418   Settlement patterns in the Chilterns. J.W.R. Whitehand.
Reading Ph.D. 1964.

419   Studies in Chiltern field systems. D. Roden. London
Ph.D. 1965.

449   The historical geography of the rural landscape of Northumberland. R.A. Butlin. Liverpool M.A. 1961.

450   The older settlements of north Northumberland: a study in geography and history. Constance P.M. Olsen. London M.A. 1947.

451   The historical geography of south-west Lancashire prior to the Industrial Revolution. F. Walker. Liverpool M.A. 1937.

452   Historical geography of the Makerfield district in south Lancashire. H. Fairhurst. Liverpool M.A. 1922.

453   The rural landscape of the Furness peninsula: a study in historical geography. W. Rollinson. Manchester M.A. 1961.

454   The urban geography of Barrow-in-Furness. A.D. Hammersley. Manchester M.A. 1965.

455   Salford (Lancs.): its growth and morphology. E.T. Parham. Manchester M.A. 1957.

456   The history of Standish. T.C. Porteus. Manchester M.A. 1924.

457   Common lands and enclosure in Lancashire. G. Youd. Liverpool M.A. 1958.

458   The origin of settlements in the Cheshire plain - an essay in historical geography. W.J. Varley. Wales M.A. 1934.

459   Rural settlement in east Cheshire: a study in historical geography. Pauline F. Kenworthy. Manchester M.A. 1949.

460   The land utilisation of Cheshire. E.P. Boon. London M.Sc. 1941.

461   The reclamation and agricultural development of the moss-land areas of north Cheshire and south Lancashire. D.B. Hardman. Manchester M.A. 1961.

462   The relationship between the spread of settlement and agricultural changes in south Manchester and north Cheshire. E.L. Naylor. Manchester M.A. 1968.

463   The early historical geography of Chester. G. Conzen. Manchester M.A. 1942.

464   Settlement and economy in a selected area within the Lake District. T.C.F. Darley. Leicester M.A. 1966.

465   The economic and social decline of the Rossendales. Christine M. Birdsall. Manchester M.A. 1968.

West and Midlands

466   The historical geography (ancient) of Northamptonshire and the south-east Midlands. S.B. Harris. London M.Sc. (Ext.) 1945.

467   A study of certain aspects in the cultural landscape of a region around the Malvern Hills. R.M.J. Marshall. Birmingham M.A. 1953.

468   Patterns of rural settlement in Gloucestershire, Herefordshire and Worcestershire. P. Hamilton. Reading M.A. 1960.

469   The historical geography of Worcestershire in the early middle ages. R.J. Cavill. Birmingham M.A. 1936.

470   The development of industry and trade in the middle Severn valley. T.W. Birch. London M.Sc. (Ext.) 1933.

471   The territorial evolution of Warwickshire: a study in historical and administrative geography. G.S. Miles. Wales M.A. 1961.

472   Coventry: a study in urban continuity. R.F. Prosser. Birmingham M.A. 1955.

473   Warwick: a study in urban geography. W.T. Rhys. Wales M.A. 1961.

474   Population and land utilisation in the Warwickshire hundreds of Stoneleigh and Kineton (1086-1300): a study in historical geography. J.B. Harley. Birmingham Ph.D. 1960.

475   The geographical distribution of the agricultural industries of Shropshire. E.J. Howell. London Ph.D. 1941.

476   Geographical aspects of settlement in southern Shropshire. Julia M. Wilkes. Leicester M.A. 1961.

The history of the south Shropshire landscape, 1086-   477
1800. R.T. Rowley. Oxford B.Litt. 1958.
Shrewsbury, historical geography and present survey.   478
G. Joan Fuller. London M.A. (Ext.) 1940.
The evolution of rural settlement in Herefordshire.   479
C.W. Atkin. Liverpool M.A. 1951.
The Leintwardine area of north Herefordshire: its   480
physical geography, land use and distribution of population.
D.G. Bayliss. Manchester M.A. 1957.
The historical geography of the Forest of Dean. F.T.   481
Baber. Wales M.A. 1949.
The Forest of Dean: a study of physical and historical   482
geography. P.R.W. Haunton. London M.Sc. 1950.
The history of the Forest of Dean as a timber-producing   483
forest. C.E. Hart. Leicester Ph.D. 1964.
The history of Scraptoft, Leics. Mrs. Nina K. Freebody. 484
Leicester M.A. 1967.

WALES

The morphology of Welsh border towns - a study in   485
historical geography. P.D. Wood. Wales M.A. 1950.
The development of the boundary between England and   486
Wales. P.D. Wood. Reading Ph.D. 1958.
Rural settlement in south-west Wales and Cornwall.   487
Eluned H. Tropp. London M.A. 1951.
An investigation into human influences on marsh develop- 488
ment in the Burry estuary, South Wales. B.A.G. Plummer.
Wales M.A. 1960.
The evolution of settlement in the Teify valley. E.   489
Jones. Wales M.Sc. 1945.
A study of the character of the main changes in the pro- 490
duction and distribution of agricultural produce in Cardigan-
shire in medieval and modern times. Gertrude M. Lyke. Wales
M.A. 1917.
Changing land utilisation, occupation and ownership in   491
south-west Carmarthenshire. W.S.G. Thomas. London Ph.D.
1965.
The distribution of woodland, present and past, in the   492
Nant Ffrancon valley and other parts of Caernarvonshire. L.M.
Hodgson. Wales M.Sc. 1933.
The growth of settlement in the Swansea valley. J.M.   493
Davies. Wales M.A. 1942.
Rural settlement in the vale of Glamorgan. N.H.   494
Harries. Birmingham M.A. 1956.
The historical geography of the Neath region up to the   495
eve of the Industrial Revolution. C.D.J. Trott. Wales M.A.
1946.
The growth of rural settlement in south-eastern Mon-   496
mouthshire. R.A. Worthington. Wales M.A. 1956.
Settlement patterns and farm units in western Pembroke-   497
shire: a study in historical geography. D.H.C. Bennett.
Wales M.A. 1955.
The evolution of rural settlement and land tenure in   498
Merioneth. C. Thomas. Wales Ph.D. 1966.
Little England beyond Wales as a regional unit. Mrs.   499
Margaret F. Harris. London Ph.D. 1950.

SCOTLAND AND ISLE OF MAN

Some aspects of the early historical geography of Scot-   500
land. H. Fairhurst. Liverpool M.A. 1933.
The early historical geography of south-west Scotland.   501
S.V. Morris. Liverpool M.A. 1935.

502   Land systems and settlement in the Isle of Man. E. Davies. Manchester Ph.D. 1937.

503   The historical geography of the Shetland Islands. A.C. O'Dell. London M.Sc. 1933.

504   The geography of Shetland fisheries. C.A. Goodlad. Aberdeen Ph.D. 1968.

505   Changing cultural landscapes of the Orkney Islands. D.P. Willis. Aberdeen M.Litt. 1967.

506   The political geography of north-east Scotland. R. Muir. Aberdeen Ph.D. 1970.

IRELAND

507   Rundale and its social concomitants. D. McCourt. Belfast M.A. 1947.

508   The Rundale system in Ireland: a study of its geographical distribution and social relations. D. McCourt. Belfast Ph.D. 1950.

509   The evolution of settlement in Co. Antrim down to Norman times. E. Watson. Belfast M.A. 1940.

510   The historical geography of Armagh. H.D.McC. Reid. Belfast M.A. 1954.

511   Land utilisation of Co. Armagh. M.W. Wallace. Belfast M.A. 1951.

512   Settlement and economy in Co. Down from the late bronze age to the Anglo-Norman invasion. V.B. Proudfoot. Belfast Ph.D. 1957.

513   Land uses in Co. Down: a study in geographical analysis. F.W. Boal. Belfast M.A. 1958.

514   The Dalradian highlands: a study of hill land utilisation in Kintyre and north Ulster. L.J. Symons. Belfast Ph.D. 1958.

515   The pattern of farming in Co. Tyrone - a study in land use techniques. B.J. McHugh. Belfast M.A. 1959.

516   The population and settlement in Northern Ireland. R.D. James. Wales M.A. 1948.

517   Transhumance in Ireland, with special reference to its bearing on the evolution of rural communities in the West. Jean M. Graham. Belfast Ph.D. 1954.

518   The history of water-power in Ulster. H.D. Gribbon. Belfast Ph.D. 1967.

M E D I E V A L   E U R O P E   A N D   B Y Z A N T I U M

BYZANTIUM AND THE CRUSADES

519   Municipal life at Antioch in the 4th century A.D., with particular reference to the work of Libanius. J.H.W.G. Liebeschuetz. London Ph.D. 1957.

520   The life of Libanius. A.F. Norman. London Ph.D. 1955.

521   The religious policy of Theodosius the Great, 379-95 A.D. N.Q. King. Nottingham Ph.D. 1954.

522   The relation between church and state in the Byzantine empire under the Heracleian dynasty (A.D. 610-711). Rachel M. Toulmin. Oxford B.Litt. 1955.

523   The frontier problems of the Heracleian dynasty, with special reference to the second half of the 7th century. A. Sharf. London Ph.D. 1954.

524   Cyprus 'betwixt Greeks and Saracens' A.D. 647-965. A.I. Dikigoropoulos. Oxford D.Phil. 1961.

525   Essay on the Byzantine revival, 717-1071. Ethel M. Hale. Birmingham M.A. 1913.

526   The sources of Theophanes for the Heraclian dynasty. Ann S. Proudfoot. London M.A. 1965.

The Doukai from the 9th to the 12th centuries: a contri- 527
bution to Byzantine prosopography. D.I. Polemis. London Ph.D.
1964.

The revival of learning at Constantinople in the 11th 528
century, with special reference to Michael Psellos. Joan M.
Hussey. Oxford B.Litt. 1932.

Church and society in the east Roman empire from the 529
death of Constantine VIII to the rise of Alexius Comnenus.
Joan M. Hussey. London Ph.D. 1934.

The attitude of western churchmen towards the Byzantine 530
empire in the period 1054-1204. I.T. Ebeid. Nottingham Ph.D.
1968.

Bohemond I of Antioch. Margaret P. Brennan. Belfast 531
M.A. 1943.

The western attitude towards Islam before and after the 532
First Crusade. A.-el H. Hamdy Mahmoud. Liverpool Ph.D. 1952.

Michael VII Ducas. R.R.T. Prider. London M.Phil. 1967. 533

Military methods employed by the Latin states in Syria, 534
1097-1192. R.C. Smail. Cambridge Ph.D. 1948.

The Ismailis in Syria at the time of the Crusades. N.A. 535
Mirza. Durham Ph.D. 1963.

The concept of Islam in Latin writers of the middle ages 536
from the beginning of the 12th century to the middle of the
14th. N.A. Daniel. Edinburgh Ph.D. 1956/7.

The intellectual and moral standards of Anna Comnena. 537
Georgina G. Buckler. Oxford D.Phil. 1927.

Saladin's campaign of 1188 in northern Syria, with 538
particular reference to the northern defences of the principality of Antioch. J.W. Hackett. Oxford B.Litt. 1937.

The Knights Hospitallers in Latin Syria. J.S.C. Riley- 539
Smith. Cambridge Ph.D. 1964.

The administration of the Nicaean empire, 1204-61. M.J. 540
Angold. Oxford D.Phil. 1967.

The despotate of Epirus, 1204-61. D.M. Nicol. Cam- 541
bridge Ph.D. 1952.

The chief instruments of papal crusading policy, and 542
crusade to the Holy Land from the final loss of Jerusalem to
the fall of Acre, 1244-91. Sister Maureen P. Purcell. Oxford
B.Litt. 1968.

The Crusades of St. Louis. May B. Thomason. Birmingham 543
M.A. 1913.

Influence of the Crusades on the contemporary religious 544
life in Scotland. T. Low. Glasgow Ph.D. 1932.

England and the Crusades during the 13th century. W.F. 545
Mumford. Manchester M.A. 1924.

The Arsenian controversy in Byzantium, 1265-1320. J.S. 546
Roussos. Oxford D.Phil. 1969.

Urban and rural conditions in the Byzantine empire from 547
the end of the 13th to the middle of the 14th century. C.P.
Kyrris. London M.A. 1961.

The Hesychast controversy, with special reference to the 548
'Byzantina Historia' of Nicephorus Gregoras and the 'Historia'
of John Cantacuzenus. Teresa A. Hart. London M.A. 1949.

Manuel II Palaeologos, emperor of Byzantium during the 549
years 1373-1425, with special reference to his relations with
the Ottoman Turks. Julian Chrysostomides. Oxford B.Litt.
1959.

The crusade of Nicopolis: a study based on eastern and 550
western sources, and an examination of the battlefield and its
approaches. A.S. Atiya. London Ph.D. 1933.

The contribution of the Byzantine despotate of Mystra to 551
the Italian Renaissance, with special reference to Gemistos
Plethon and his disciples. A.G. Keller. Oxford B.Litt. 1956.

Projects of crusade in the 15th century. G.W. Pym. 552
Liverpool M.A. 1925.

553   The survival of the Romano-Austrians. A.F. Singer. Oxford B.Litt. 1948.

554   Diplomatic relations of Umayyad Spain with western Europe (A.H. 138-366/A.D. 755-976): an historical survey. A.A. El-Hajji. Cambridge Ph.D. 1966.

555   The character of Visigothic legislation. P.D. King. Cambridge Ph.D. 1967.

556   The origins of the duchy of Aquitaine (9th century - 1152) Mrs. Jane P. Martindale. Oxford D.Phil. 1965.

557   La vicomté de Béarn: étude historique sur la vicomté de Béarn depuis le 10e siècle jusqu'à l'union avec la France en 1620. Barbara J. Daniel. Birmingham M.A. 1955.

558   A comparison of the local administration and law courts of the Carolingian empire with those of the West Saxon kings. Helen M. Cam. London M.A. 1909.

559   Some historical factors in the formation of the Ukrainian people. J. Jagodzinski. Liverpool M.A. 1942.

560   Russo-Bulgarian relations in the 10th century. A.D. Stokes. Cambridge Ph.D. 1959.

561   Reform and politics in lower Lotharingia in the first half of the 11th century. R.G. King. Manchester M.A. 1968.

562   Rituals of royal inauguration in early medieval Europe: from dux populi to athleta Christi. Mrs. Janet L. Nelson. Cambridge Ph.D. 1967.

563   The effect of the religious movement on the origin and early growth of the Milanese commune during the 11th century. S.M. Brown. Oxford B.Litt. 1929.

564   The antecedents of the political and ecclesiastical ideas of Arnold of Brescia, and his relation to the civic movement in Italy. W.E.F. Ward. Oxford B.Litt. 1923/4.

565   Medieval Orvieto: the political history of an Italian city state, 1157-1334. D.P. Waley. Cambridge Ph.D. 1950.

566   The Order of Santiago, 1170-1275. D.W. Lomax. Oxford D.Phil. 1961.

567   Local administration in France, 1180-1328. B. Schofield. Liverpool Ph.D. 1921.

568   Novgorod and the princes of Suzdal in the 12th and 13th centuries. Sally A. Miles. Birmingham M.A. 1969.

569   Politics and administration in the mainland provinces of the Sicilian kingdom from 1189 to 1198, with a calendar of the diplomas of the Emperor Henry VI concerning the Sicilian kingdom. Dione R. Clementi. Oxford D.Phil. 1951.

570   The importance of the Channel Islands in British relations with the continent during the 13th and 14th centuries: a study in historical geography. D.T. Williams. Wales M.A. 1927.

571   A critical edition, with an historical introduction, of the archives of Cahors, 1203-70. Anita D. Edwards. Southampton M.A. 1965.

572   Augustinus Triumphus and the problem of authority in medieval society, 1250-1350. M.J. Wilks. Cambridge Ph.D. 1958.

573   The philosophy of law of St. Thomas Aquinas. F.H. Hunt. Cambridge Ph.D. 1941.

574   Contemporary influences on some aspects of St. Thomas Aquinas's use of sources in his political writings. F. Devereux. Liverpool M.A. 1967.

575   The last years of the Paduan commune, c.1256-1328. J.K. Hyde. Oxford D.Phil. 1960.

576   The commentaries on the Politics of Aristotle in the late 13th and early 14th centuries, with reference to the thought and political life of the time. C.J. Martin. Oxford D.Phil. 1949.

577   Marsilius of Padua and the papal claim to universal supremacy: a study in 14th-century political thought. A.C. MacLean. St. Andrews Ph.D. 1966.

23

606 'Remonstrances au roy pour la réformation du royaume', by Jean Juvenal des Ursins with introduction and notes. Dorothy Kirkland. Liverpool Ph.D. 1938.

England and France, including the Hundred Years War

607 The English in the south of France from the accession of Henry III to the death of the Black Prince. N.L. Frazer. London M.A. 1906.

608 Gaston de Béarn; a study in Anglo-Gascon relations (1229-90). Jean H. Ellis. Oxford D.Phil. 1952.

609 Gascon appeals to England (1259-1453). P.T.V.M. Chaplais. London Ph.D. 1950.

610 English embassies to France in the reign of Edward I: their personnel, powers, equipment and objects. Mary C.L. Salt. London M.A. 1927.

611 Calais under Edward III. Dorothy Greaves. Manchester M.A. 1912.

612 The colonisation of Calais, 1347-77. L.S. Thorn. Oxford B.Litt. 1953.

613 The provisioning of Calais, 1347-65. S.J. Burley. Leeds M.A. 1952.

614 The establishment of the Calais staple (1365). Anne M. Oakley. Leeds M.A. 1959.

615 The relations between England and the duchy of Brittany, 1360-81. G.W. Jones. Leeds M.A. 1961.

616 John de Montfort, England and the duchy of Brittany, 1364-99. M.C.E. Jones. Oxford D.Phil. 1967.

617 The usages of war in the period of the Hundred Years War. M.H. Keen. Oxford D.Phil. 1963.

618 The part of Castile in the Hundred Years War. A. Christelow. Oxford B.Litt. 1934.

619 The careers of four 14th-century military commanders serving Edward III and Richard II in the Hundred Years War. G.A. Snead. Kent M.A. 1968.

620 A critical analysis of contemporary French description of the English in France in the time of the Black Prince. J.P. Perkins. Bristol M.A. 1965.

621 The position and powers of the king's lieutenants in France during the reign of Edward III. Mrs. Mavis Cunningham, née Walton. Leeds M.A. 1957.

622 The English administration of the county of Ponthieu, 1360-9. Sheila B. Challenger. Leeds Ph.D. 1953.

623 The war with France in 1377. A.F.O'D. Alexander. London Ph.D. (Ext.) 1934.

624 The relations of England and France under Richard II. N.B. Lewis. Manchester M.A. 1922.

625 The Anglo-French peace negotiations, 1386-99. J.J.N. Palmer. London Ph.D. 1967.

626 A view of Anglo-French relations, 1389-99. J. Burr. Liverpool M.A. 1936.

627 War, government and politics in English Gascony, 1399-1453. M.G.A. Vale. Oxford D.Phil. 1967.

628 Henry V as conqueror in France, and the Lancastrian experiment in Normandy. Ethel Wragg. Birmingham M.A. 1916.

629 The relations between the English government, the higher clergy and the papacy in Normandy, 1417-50. C.T. Allmand. Oxford D.Phil. 1963.

630 The English rule of Normandy, 1435-50. Elizabeth M. Burney. Oxford B.Litt. 1958.

631 John, duke of Bedford as regent of France, 1422-55, his policy and administration in the North. Benedicta J.H. Rowe. Oxford B.Litt. 1927.

632 The English rule in France, 1422-35. Annie Hague. Liverpool M.A. 1921.

633 Jean V, duke of Brittany (1399-1442), in relation to England. G.A. Knowlson. Liverpool M.A. 1934.

The congress of Arras, 1435. Joycelyne G. Dickinson.   634
Oxford D.Phil. 1951.
The connexion between England and France in the reign of 635
Louis XI. T.J. Griffiths. Wales M.A. 1917.

ECONOMIC AND SOCIAL HISTORY

A history of academical and legal dress in Europe from   636
classical times to the end of the 18th century. W.N.
Hargreaves-Mawdsley. Oxford D.Phil. 1958.
Lyons as a market of ideas (from B.C. 43 to 1307 A.D.).   637
M. Berryman. London M.A. 1910.
The medieval carpenter and worker in wood. G.J.   638
Eltringham. Sheffield M.A. 1952.
The development of husbandry in Russia down to the   639
Mongol invasion. R.E.F. Smith. London M.A. 1955.
The development of the 'manorial' system ('Grundherr-   640
schaft' and 'Gutsherrschaft') in north-eastern Germany until
the end of the 16th century. F.L. Carsten. Oxford D.Phil.
1942.
The status of women in Spain during the Arab domination. 641
Dorria M. Abdel Al. Cambridge M.Litt. 1955/6.
The influence of the medicine of the western caliphate   642
on the medical system of Europe. D. Campbell. Oxford B.Litt.
1923.
The part played by the aristocracy in the later Caro-   643
lingian empire, with special reference to Germany. Janet H.
Matthews. Cambridge Ph.D. 1949.
A study of the Germanic personal names of Catalonia from 644
800 to 1000 A.D. K.W.J. Adams. London M.A. 1966.
Coinage in the Balkan peninsula, A.D. 1100-1350: a study 645
of colonial monetary affairs. D.M. Metcalf. Cambridge Ph.D.
1959.
An examination of price fluctuations in certain articles 646
in the 12th, 13th and early 14th centuries. D.L. Farmer.
Oxford D.Phil. 1958.
The historical development of heraldic terms, with   647
special reference to armes parlantes. H.E. Tomlinson. Man-
chester M.A. 1942.
Ocean navigation of the middle ages: northern waters.   648
G.J. Marcus. Oxford D.Phil. 1954.
England and the Teutonic Hanse. A. Weiner. Wales M.A. 649
1904.
The building of the Hanseatic League from its earliest   650
days until 1370. Lilian M. Seckler. Birmingham M.A. 1929.
Anglo-Flemish trading relations in the later middle   651
ages. Lilian M. Seckler. London Ph.D. 1932.
The Scottish nation of merchants in Bruges: a contri-   652
bution to the history of medieval Scottish foreign trade. W.H.
Finlayson. Glasgow Ph.D. 1951.
The commercial relations of Holland and Zeeland with   653
England from the late 13th century to the close of the middle
ages. Nelly J.M. Kerling. London Ph.D. 1952.
Anglo-Castilian trade in the later middle ages. Mrs.   655
Wendy R. Childs. Cambridge Ph.D. 1970.
Commercial relations between England and Venice in the   656
13th and 14th centuries. G.F. Shaw. London M.A. 1909.
The wine trade with Gascony under Edward III. F. Sar-   657
geant. Manchester M.A. 1912.
The cult and pilgrimage of St. James of Compostela, Spain, 658
and their effects on the life and thought of the people in the
north-western corner of Spain. H.W. Howes. Wales M.A. 1938.
Studies in the medieval book trade from the late 12th   659
century to the middle of the 14th century, with special reference to the copying of bibles. Mrs. Josephine E. Schnurman.
Oxford B.Litt. 1960.

660   Landownership and rural conditions in the Padovano during the late middle ages. Lesley A. Steer. Oxford D.Phil. 1967.
661   The Malatesta of Rimini. P.J. Jones. Oxford D.Phil. 1950.
662   The evolution of defensive armour in England, France and Italy in the first half of the 14th century. J.G. Mann. Oxford B.Litt. 1922.
663   The development of the rabbinate in central Europe during the years 1348-1648. A. Tobias. London Ph.D. 1945.
664   Life and times of Rabbi Joseph Colon (Kolom), 1420-80. M.H. Rabinowicz. London Ph.D. 1948.
665   French pilgrims to Jerusalem in the 15th century. Lucie L.G. Polak. London M.A. 1954.
666   The pilgrim book of Jehan de Tournay (1488-9), being a critical edition of Valenciennes MS. 493. Lucie L.G. Polak. London Ph.D. 1958.
667   Economy and society in Castile in the 15th century. A.I.K. McKay. Edinburgh Ph.D. 1970.
668   Economic problems of Bohemia in the early 15th century and the Hussite attempts at their solution. K. Kornell. Wales M.A. 1970.
669   The Datin family and Liège in the first half of the 15th century. R.K. Blumenau. Oxford B.Litt. 1950.
670   The trade of Southampton with the Mediterranean, 1428-1547. Alwyn A. Ruddock. London Ph.D. 1940.
671   The Gascon wine trade of Southampton during the reigns of Henry VI and Edward IV. Margaret K. James. Oxford B.Litt. 1948.
672   Monetary problems and policies in the Burgundian Netherlands, 1433-96. P. Spufford. Cambridge Ph.D. 1963.
673   Documents for the history of commercial relations between Egypt and Venice, 1442-1512. J.E. Wansbrough. London Ph.D. 1962.
674   The problem of Paolo Vitelli, condottiere in the service of Florence. Evelyn B. Darke. London M.A. 1909.

ECCLESIASTICAL HISTORY

    General

675   The history of Christian baptism. C.H. Murray. Oxford B.Litt. 1927.
676   The evolution of the Christian year. A.A. McArthur. Aberdeen Ph.D. 1952.
677   The development of the sanctuary and furnishing from early Christian times to the present day. D.M. Chappell. Sheffield M.A. 1963.
678   The religious element in anti-Semitism up to the time of Charlemagne in the West and Leo the Isaurian in the East. J.W. Parkes. Oxford D.Phil. 1934.
679   Studies in Clement of Alexandria. R.P. Casey. Cambridge Ph.D. 1924.
680   The unity of the church and the reunion of the churches: a study of the problem of church unity from the end of the 1st till the close of the 4th century. N. Zernov. Oxford D.Phil. 1931/2.
681   The idea of the unity of the church: a study of its development in the first three centuries. W.N. Jamison. Edinburgh Ph.D. 1948.
681A   The status of women in the life of the church during the first three centuries. C.C. Ryrie. Edinburgh Ph.D. 1954.
682   The influence of Roman law on the history and doctrine of the ancient Christian Church. W. Phillips. Edinburgh Ph.D. 1930/1.

The reciprocal influence of Roman law and Christianity. 683
J.W. Jones. London Ph.D. 1925.

The conception of the <u>civitas christiana</u> in the thought 684
of the early church. E. Langstadt. Cambridge Ph.D. 1938.

The social and economic conditions of the members of the 685
Collegia from Constantine to Theodosius II. Winifred Utley.
London M.A. 1925.

Basil of Caesarea's contribution to the unity of the 686
church from 340 to 380. J. Thomson. St. Andrews M.Th. 1968.

An analysis, with commentary, of St. Augustine of 687
Hippo's treatises on marriage. G.G. Willis. Manchester M.A.
1939.

The social message of those homilies of St. John 688
Chrysostom which were delivered in Constantinople, 398 A.D.
to 404 A.D. I.M. Fouyas. Manchester Ph.D. 1963.

A re-assessment of Julian of Eclanum. E.S.P. Jones. 689
St. Andrews Ph.D. 1965.

The office of <u>comes sacrarum largitionum</u>. J.P.C. Kent. 690
London Ph.D. 1951.

Sidonius Apollinaris and his age. C.E. Stevens. Oxford 691
B.Litt. 1930.

The church and the councils of the early 5th century. 692
H. Spencer. Liverpool M.A. 1915.

Salvian of Marseilles. D.J. Cleland. Oxford B.Litt. 693
1969.

A study of Gregory of Tours and his times. Cynthia M. 694
Begbie. London Ph.D. 1969.

Bishops and the secular power in the writings of Gregory 695
of Tours. Stephanie Mullins. Oxford B.Litt. 1950.

A critical edition of the <u>Prognosticum futuri saeculi</u> of 696
St. Julian of Toledo. J.N. Hillgarth. Cambridge Ph.D. 1957.

The conversion of the Slovenes. A.L. Kuhar. Cambridge 697
Ph.D. 1949.

Liturgical reforms of Charlemagne. H.B. Porter. Oxford 698
D.Phil. 1954.

St. Clement of Ochrida. M. Kusseff. London Ph.D. 1954. 699

A history of Bogomilism in Bulgaria. D. Obolensky. 700
Cambridge Ph.D. 1943.

A study of the 'Vita Sancti Andreae Sali'. J.T. Wort- 701
ley. London Ph.D. 1969.

Neo-Manichaean heresy in Germany and the Low Countries 702
during the 11th, 12th and 13th centuries (with a note on its
infiltration into England during the 12th century). Margaret
A.E. Nickson. London M.A. 1956.

The new eremetical movement in western Europe, 1000- 703
1150. Mrs. Henrietta L.V. Leyser. Oxford B.Litt. 1967.

St. Vladimir of Kiev in the Russian medieval tradition. 704
M. Fortounatto. Oxford B.Litt. 1970.

Adalbero, bishop of Laon. R.T. Coolidge. Oxford 705
B.Litt. 1965.

The archbishops of Rouen, 1037-1110. Anne Brinkworth. 706
Bristol M.Litt. 1967.

The influence of economic factors in the Gregorian 707
reform of the 11th century. D.B. Zema. Cambridge Ph.D. 1939.

Odo, bishop of Bayeux 1049-97. D.R. Bates. Exeter 708
Ph.D. 1970.

Cardinal Humbert of Silva Candida. R.J. Mayne. Cam- 709
bridge Ph.D. 1955.

The political ideas of Cardinal Humbert of Silva Candida 710
(1050-61) with an edition of the 'Diversorum patrum sententiae'. J.T.I. Gilchrist. Leeds Ph.D. 1957.

The history of St. Anselm's theology of the redemption 711
in the 12th and 13th centuries. B.P. McGuire. Oxford D.Phil.
1970.

The doctrine of poverty in its religious, social and 712
political aspects as illustrated by some 12th- and 13th-
century movements. J.L. Flajszer. London Ph.D. 1944.

713 'The mirror of fools': a study in church history chiefly of the 12th century. Rose Sidgwick. Birmingham M.A. 1908.

714 The constitutional position of the church in the Norman kingdom of Sicily, 1130-94, with special reference to the relations between papacy, monarchy, metropolitan and immediate sees. Joan M. Shaxby. Oxford B.Litt. 1933.

715 The Contra Petrobusianos of Peter the Venerable. J.V. Fearns. Liverpool Ph.D. 1964.

716 A critical edition of the letters of Arnulf of Lisieux. F. Barlow. Oxford D.Phil. 1937.

717 The letter collections attributed to Master Transmundus, papal notary and monk of Clairvaux in the late 12th century. Sheila J. Heathcote. Liverpool Ph.D. 1959.

718 The concept of 'Ecclesia' and its development from the mid 12th to the 14th centuries. G.H.W. Parker. Cambridge M.Litt. 1959.

719 The canonistic treatment of heresy and inquisition. Patricia K. Dodds. Cambridge M.Litt. 1955.

720 The nature and extent of the heresy of the Fraticelli. Decima L. Douie. Manchester Ph.D. 1930.

721 Aspects of the development of the doctrine of the absolute poverty of Christ and the apostles in the 13th and 14th centuries. M.D. Lambert. Oxford B.Litt. 1959.

722 The vicarage system in western Europe in the later middle ages, c.1200-1500. R.A.R. Hartridge. London Ph.D. 1929.

723 The history of the Serbian Church from the foundation of its independence to the fall of the Serbian patriarchate in the 15th century. Y. Andritch. Oxford B.Litt. 1919.

724 Studies in the history and administration of the German Church from 1225 to 1275, with special reference to the province of Cologne. F.R. Lewis. Oxford D.Phil. 1936.

725 Chapters in the history of the Albigensian heresy. A. Warne. Leeds M.A. 1937.

726 A critical edition of the treatise on heresy ascribed to Pseudo-Reinerius, with an historical introduction. Margaret A.E. Nickson. London Ph.D. 1962.

727 St. Louis of Toulouse and the process of canonisation up to the 14th century. Margaret R. Toynbee. Manchester Ph.D. 1924.

728 The Council of Lyons, 1274. Ethel M. Woodall. Manchester M.A. 1917.

729 The life and writings of Nicholas de Clamanges: a study in the repercussions of the schism and conciliar movement. Margaret H. Bell. London M.A. 1948.

730 The theories of Cardinal Pierre d'Ailly concerning forms of government in church and state, with special reference to his interest in suggestions made by William of Occam. Agnes E. Roberts. London M.A. 1931.

731 A study of the works attributed to William of Pagula with special reference to the Oculus Sacerdotis and the Summa Summarum. L.E. Boyle. Oxford D.Phil. 1956.

732 The teaching of John Hus concerning the church. J.H.S. Burleigh. Oxford B.Litt. 1922.

733 The influence of John Hus on Europe to the time of the Reformation, with special reference to central and eastern Europe. J. Sedlo. Edinburgh Ph.D. 1943.

734 Gerson and Occam: a study in the origin and development of Gerson's ideas about the reform of religion and the church. Mrs. Zofia Rueger. London Ph.D. 1956.

735 The political and social doctrines of the Unity of the Czech Brethren in the 15th century. P. de B. Brock. Oxford D.Phil. 1954.

736 Thomas à Kempis and the mystical movement: their historical context and place in the later middle ages. C.G. Thorne. St. Andrews B.Phil. 1965.

737 Poland's case against the Teutonic Knights at the Council of Constance, 1414-18. Mrs. Rose U. Goble. Oxford B.Litt. 1958.

The work of the 'deputation of reform' during the early stages of the Council of Basel. R.L.H. Lloyd. Oxford B.Litt. 1936. 738

The Council of Ferrara-Florence, to the union of the Greek and Latin Churches, 6 July 1439. D.E.B. Lutyens. Oxford B.Litt. 1953. 739

The life, works and ideas of Cardinal Margarit. R.B. Tate. Belfast M.A. 1950. 740

Papacy

The patriarchate of Alexandria and the see of Rome: their relations as reflected in the life work of Athanasius. J. Douglas. Edinburgh Ph.D. 1955. 741

Innocent I: his life and letters. J. Macdonald. Oxford B.Litt. 1957. 742

The relations of Pope Gregory the Great with the churches in the Roman empire of the East. W.J. Boast. Birmingham M.A. 1931. 743

The political influence of Pope Gregory the Great in Italy. H.V.W. Lewis. Wales M.A. 1913. 744

Sweden and the papacy, 822-1248. C.J.A. Oppermann. London Ph.D. (Ext.) 1931. 745

The holy see, the Roman nobility and the Ottonian emperors. B.F. Hamilton. London Ph.D. 1960. 746

Petrus-Petra-Ecclesia Lateranensis: a study in the symbolic aspects of papal authority in their bearing on the investiture contest. C.R. Ligota. Cambridge Ph.D. 1956. 747

The elements of Hildebrand's conception of the church. Dorothy Dymond. London M.A. 1915. 748

Pope Eugenius III. Elsie Tesh. Manchester M.A. 1919. 749

Pope and general council in the writings of medieval canonists. B. Tierney. Cambridge Ph.D. 1951. 750

Reform and reaction: the Spanish kingdoms and the papacy in the 13th century. P.A. Linehan. Cambridge Ph.D. 1969. 751

The Emperor Lewis IV and the curia from 1330 to 1347: canon law and international politics in the first half of the 14th century. H.S. Offler. Cambridge Ph.D. 1939. 752

The light thrown by the papal registers on papal provisions: and some ecclesiastical abuses during the pontificate of John XXII, 1316-34. Ann P. Deeley. Manchester M.A. 1927. 753

The government of the states of the church under Martin V. P.D. Partner. Oxford D.Phil. 1955. 754

Pope, council and secular powers, 1431-49: diplomacy and doctrine. A.J. Black. Cambridge Ph.D. 1966. 755

See also MEDIEVAL ENGLAND: ECCLESIASTICAL HISTORY: Relations with Papacy

Monasticism and Religious Orders

The origin, ideal and early history of monachism. Edith H. Humphreys. Bristol M.A. 1925. 756

The rise and earliest development of Christian monasticism, with a study of its origin. J.R.M. Forbes. Edinburgh Ph.D. 1928. 757

The monastery of Vivarium and its historical importance. Mary Stanley. Oxford B.Litt. 1939. 758

The Celtic monastics on the continent. R.R. Lindsay. Glasgow Ph.D. 1927. 759

Monasticism in south Italy from the beginning of the 9th century to the foundation of Grottaferrata (1004). Joyce M. Whale. London M.A. 1958. 760

The Kievo-Pechersky monastery from its origins to the end of the 11th century. Muriel Heppell. London M.A. 1951. 761

762   The _Paterikon of the Kievan Monastery of Caves_ as a source for monastic life in pre-Mongolian Russia. Muriel Heppell. London Ph.D. 1954.

763   The greater Norman monasteries during the first half of the 11th century. Jean Y. Shaw. Bristol M.A. 1952.

764   The Cluniac order under Abbot Hugh, 1049-1109. Noreen Hunt. London Ph.D. 1958.

765   The relations between Abelard and St. Bernard. A.V. Murray. Oxford B.Litt. 1930.

766   The Cistercian movement. Catherine Brien. Birmingham M.A. 1926.

767   Brother Elias and the government of the Franciscan order, 1217-39. Mrs. Rosalind B. Brooke, née Clark. Cambridge Ph.D. 1950.

768   Early Franciscan influence on liturgical services and popular devotional practices. Joan Walker. London Ph.D. (Ext.) 1954.

769   The expansion and provincial organisation of the temple in the 'Corona de Aragon'. A.J. Forey. Oxford D.Phil. 1963.

770   The rise of the Franciscan Observants. H.H. Hill. Leeds M.A. 1922.

771   The convent of San Marco in Florence, 1436-94. Evelyn E. Curtis. London M.A. 1956.

772   The third order of Penitents. C.W. Hutton. Leeds M.A. 1917.

773   Juan Fernández de Heredia, Castellan of Amposta (1347-77), grand master of the Order of St. John at Rhodes (1377-96). A.T. Luttrell. Oxford D.Phil. 1959.

774   The Grand Masters of the Order of the Temple. M.C. Barber. Nottingham Ph.D. 1968.

775   The chapters general of the Knights Hospitaller in the late 14th and 15th centuries from the extant MS. material in the Royal Library at Valletta. Ann Williams. Oxford B.Litt. 1961.

ART AND LEARNING

776   Christianity and education in the first five centuries A.D. J.V. Patton. Oxford B.Litt. 1916.

777   Church architecture in the first four centuries of the Roman empire. G.U.S. Corbett. Cambridge Ph.D. 1953.

778   Studies in the early Christian 'tituli' of wall decoration in the Latin West. R.W. Gaston. London Ph.D. 1970.

779   The development of hierocratic ideas from Gratian to Hostiensis. J.A. Watt. Cambridge Ph.D. 1954.

780   The services of monks to art. R.E. Swartwout. Cambridge M.Litt. 1931/2.

781   The architecture of the Latin gospel books before A.D. 800. P.M. McGurk. London Ph.D. 1954.

782   Late Celtic and Anglo-Saxon influence on continental art of the Carolingian period. G.R. Reitlinger. Oxford B.Litt. 1923.

783   Relations, historical and literary, between Ireland and Scandinavia from the 9th century to the 13th. Jean I. Young. Cambridge Ph.D. 1929/30.

784   Norman illumination at Mont St. Michel in the 10th and 11th centuries. J.J.G. Alexander. Oxford D.Phil. 1964.

785   Illumination at St. Bertin at St. Omer under the abbacy of Odbert. Claire Kelleher. London Ph.D. 1968.

786   The plainsong music-drama of the medieval church. W.L. Smoldon. London Ph.D. (Ext.) 1940.

787   Patriotism in Old French literature - 11th to the 15th century. J. Williams. London Ph.D. (Ext.) 1933.

788   Literary life in England and France between the years 1066 and 1400. J. Scotland. Cambridge M.Litt. 1928/9.

Layman and cleric: an aspect of the literacy of the   789
laity in the middle ages, with special reference to medieval
France. H.H. Mills. Cambridge Ph.D. 1953.

Study of the antecedents of the De Claris Jurisconsultis 790
of Diplovatatius. H. Koeppler. Oxford D.Phil. 1936.

The impact of social change on ideology in the middle   791
ages: the conflict between intellectuals and religious leaders,
1050-1150. J. Ameller Vacaflor. London Ph.D. 1966.

A catalogue of illuminated manuscripts of the Romanesque 792
period from Rheims, 1050-1130. Mrs. M. Marie Montpetit, nee
Farquhar. London Ph.D. 1968.

Peter Abelard's following and the influence of his theo- 793
logy in the early scholastic period. D.E. Luscombe. Cambridge Ph.D. 1964.

The provision of books in the centrally-organised   794
religious orders before 1400. K.W. Humphreys. Oxford B.Litt.
1949.

External influences on west European art in the 12th   795
century, with special reference to Spain and the neighbouring
countries. Mrs. Emmy F. Wellesz. Oxford B.Litt. 1948.

Ornamental motifs on tombstones from medieval Bosnia and 796
surrounding regions. Marian B. Wenzel. London Ph.D. 1966.

An edition of Egerton MS. 3511: a 12th-century missal   797
of S. Peter's in Benevento. Elizabeth Peirce. London Ph.D.
1964.

The methods of the medieval translators of Greek philo- 798
sophical works into Latin. L. Minio-Paluello. Oxford D.Phil.
1947.

The life and works of Honorius Augustodunensis, with   799
special reference to chronology and sources. Valerie I.J.
Flint. Oxford D.Phil. 1969.

The illuminations of Petrus de Ebulo: 'De balneis   800
Puteolanis'. C.M. Kauffmann. London Ph.D. 1957.

A study in student life in a medieval university, with   801
particular reference to Oxford and Paris. Hilda Moyns. Oxford B.Litt. 1931.

The study of rhetoric in the first half of the 12th   802
century, with special reference to the cathedral schools of
northern France. Mary C.G. Dickey. Oxford B.Litt. 1953.

Oxford and Paris University manuscripts of the 13th   803
century. Mrs. Sonia Patterson. Oxford B.Litt. 1970.

The iconography of local saints in Tuscan painting from 804
the 13th to the end of the 15th century. G. Kaftal. Oxford
D.Phil. 1946.

Studies in Tuscan sources for the history of art, c.   805
1300-1550. P.J. Murray. London Ph.D. 1956.

A study of the 'De formatione corporis humani in utero' 806
of Giles of Rome. M.A. Hewson. London M.Phil. 1967.

Soldiers' songs of the 13th and 14th centuries. G.E.   807
Morris. Sheffield M.A. 1947.

Ethical problems as discussed by Masters of Arts and   808
theologians in the 13th-century universities. Mrs. Jean H.
Dunbabin. Oxford D.Phil. 1965.

The Dominican organisation of studies in the middle   809
ages. Mary C. Rixon. Manchester M.A. 1930.

The influence of popes' and cardinals' patronage on the 810
introduction of the Gothic style into Rome and the surrounding
area, 1254-1305. J.R. Gardner. London Ph.D. 1969.

The Cyrurgia Magna of Brunus Longoburgensis: a critical 811
edition. Mrs. Susan P. Hall. Oxford D.Phil. 1957.

The illustrations to the Haggadah (B.M. Add. MS. 27210) 812
and its relation to other Jewish and to Christian biblical
cycles. B. Narkiss. London Ph.D. 1963.

The later history of the Franciscans in the universities 813
of Paris and Oxford. Janet Dykes. Leeds M.A. 1916.

Education in the 14th and 15th centuries with special   814
reference to the development of the universities of northern
Europe. G.R. Potter. Cambridge Ph.D. 1926/7.

815   Domenico di Bandino of Arezzo and his <u>De viris claris</u>.
Ann T. Hankey. London Ph.D. 1955.

816   The letters of Nicholas Poillevillain de Clémanges,
1363(4)-1437. F.J. Moorhead. Liverpool M.A. 1936.

817   Studies in the life, scholarship and educational achievement of Guarino da Verona (1374-1460). I. Thomson. St.
Andrews Ph.D. 1969.

818   Vespasiano da Bisticci, historian and bookseller. Albinia
C. de la Mare. London Ph.D. 1966.

819   Pius II as a patron of art, with special reference to the
history of the Vatican. Mrs. Ruth K. Rubinstein. London
Ph.D. 1957.

820   The Colchester graduale of 1462: a study in north Italian
book illumination in the second half of the 15th century.
Marina A.R. Betts. London M.A. 1959.

M E D I E V A L   E N G L A N D

POLITICAL HISTORY

General

821   Offa of Mercia in history and tradition. A.E. Smith.
Leeds M.A. 1942.

822   The life and times of Egbert, king of Wessex, 809-39.
A. Jean Thorogood. Reading M.A. 1931.

823   The Norse occupation of the Lake District. Marjorie J.
Anderton. London M.A. 1953.

824   The sokemen of the southern Danelaw in the 11th century.
Barbara Dodwell. London M.A. 1936.

825   The harrying of the North by William the Conqueror.
Christine Cordingley. Leeds M.A. 1935.

826   Earl Waltheof of Northumbria in history and tradition.
F.S. Scott. Cambridge M.Litt. 1951.

827   Richard Coeur de Lion before his accession to the throne.
Hilda F.M. Prescott. Manchester M.A. 1921.

828   William de Braose. M. Jones. Wales M.A. 1901.

829   Some aspects of the history of England north of Trent
and Ribble in Stephen's reign. H.A. Cronne. Belfast M.A.
1931.

830   The 'northern' barons under John. J.C. Holt. Oxford
D.Phil. 1952.

831   Aliens in British politics during the reign of King John
and the minority of King Henry III, 1204-24. M.J. Knight.
Nottingham M.A. 1959.

832   William the Marshal. Mary Salmon. Wales M.A. 1909.

833   The relations between Crown and baronage in England
between 1216 and 1232, with especial reference to the
administration of Hubert de Burgh. Gladys Malbon. London
M.A. (Ext.) 1940.

834   Hubert de Burgh. S.H.F. Johnston. Oxford B.Litt. 1933.

835   Hubert de Burgh. C. Ellis. Wales M.A. 1912.

836   Richard Marshal and the rising of 1233-4. R.F. Walker.
Wales M.A. 1950.

837   The early years of Richard, earl of Cornwall. Lillian
W. Kelley. Liverpool M.A. 1913.

838   Richard of Cornwall, king of the Romans (1257-72). F.R.
Lewis. Wales M.A. 1933/4.

839   Edmund, earl of Cornwall, and his place in history.
Laura M. Midgley. Manchester M.A. 1930.

840   Peter of Rievaux. Mary Broxap. Manchester M.A. 1925.

841   The Barons' Wars, 1258-67. R.F. Treharne. Manchester
M.A. 1923.

842   The preliminaries of the Barons' War, 1258-63. R.F.
Treharne. Manchester Ph.D. 1925.

872 Richard the Second's <u>coup d'état</u> of 1397. Lilian B. Meyer. London M.A. 1908.

873 Royal political propaganda in England, 1399-1509. J.W. McKenna. Cambridge Ph.D. 1965.

874 Studies in constitutional ideas in England during the 15th century. S.B. Chrimes. Cambridge Ph.D. 1933.

874A The territorial settlement of the house of Lancaster, 1399-1401. S. Smith. Manchester M.A. 1940.

875 The Crown lands and the parliamentary acts of resumption, 1399-1495. B.P. Wolffe. Oxford D.Phil. 1954.

876 The alienation and resumption of Crown lands and revenues from 1399 to the outbreak of the Wars of the Roses. B.P. Wolffe. Oxford B.Litt. 1950.

877 Rebellion and disaffection in the north of England, 1403-8. P. McNiven. Manchester M.A. 1967.

878 The suppression of Sir John Oldcastle's rebellion in 1414. Hilda Lofthouse. Manchester M.A. 1934.

879 John, 1st duke of Bedford, his work and policy in England, 1389-1435. S.B. Chrimes. London M.A. 1929.

880 English diplomacy in the reign of Henry VI, 1422-61. J.T. Ferguson. Oxford D.Phil. 1967.

881 Humphrey Stafford, 1st duke of Buckingham: an estimate of the significance of his political activities. H. Cole. London M.A. 1945.

882 London and the Wars of the Roses, 1445-61. Margaret I. Peake. London M.A. 1925.

883 John Tiptoft, earl of Worcester. Rosamund J. Mitchell. Oxford B.Litt. 1929.

884 The Herberts of Raglan as supporters of the house of York in the second half of the 15th century. D.H. Thomas. Wales M.A. 1968.

Administration and Royal Household

885 The drafting of royal charters in the reign of King Edgar. R.E.A. Poole. London Ph.D. (Ext.) 1969.

886 Royal provision for clerks to 1272. Cecily Davies. Liverpool M.A. 1952.

887 The office of justiciar in Anglo-Norman England. F.J. West. Leeds Ph.D. 1951.

888 The early history of the English Chapel Royal, <u>c</u>.1066-1327. I.D. Bent. Cambridge Ph.D. 1969.

889 The composition and work of the royal council in the reign of Henry II, 1154-89. Audrey D. Perkyns. London M.A. 1951.

890 The court and household of King Henry II (1154-89). J.E. Lally. Liverpool Ph.D. 1969.

891 The royal family in the reign of Henry II. R.J. Smith. Nottingham M.A. 1961.

892 The English sheriffs in the reign of King John. B.E. Harris. Nottingham M.A. 1961.

893 A study, mainly from royal wardrobe accounts, of the nature and organisation of the king's messenger service from the reign of John to that of Edward III, inclusive. Mary C. Hill. London M.A. 1939.

894 English administrative families in the 12th and 13th centuries with special reference to the Cornhill family. W.R. Powell. Oxford B.Litt. 1952.

895 The justiciarship in England, 1204-32. F.J. West. Cambridge Ph.D. 1956.

896 The position and duties of the king's almoner, 1255-1327. Marguerite E. Lack. London M.A. 1949.

897 The king's government in Yorkshire, 1258-1348. Helen M. Jewell. Leeds Ph.D. 1968.

898 The clerical dynasties from Howdenshire, Lindsey and Nottinghamshire in the royal administration 1280-1340. J.L. Grassi. Oxford D.Phil. 1960.

899 The local administration of the sheriff in the 13th century. Margaret A. Hennings. London M.A. 1916.

The sheriffs and shrievalty of Lancaster in the 14th century. A.D. King. Sheffield M.A. 1953. 900

The sheriffs of Hampshire. P. White. London M.A. (Ext.) 1954. 901

The sheriffs and sheriffdoms under Edward II. J. Wood. Manchester M.A. 1923. 902

The financing and organisation of the household of the queens of England during the first part of the 14th century. Alice M. Best. London M.A. 1916. 903

The chancery in the reign of Edward III. B. Wilkinson. Manchester M.A. 1921. 904

The English chancery under Edward III and Richard II. B. Wilkinson. Manchester Ph.D. 1926. 905

The Exchequer Chamber, being 'the assembly of all the judges of England'. Mary Hemmant. London Ph.D. 1929. 906

The king's secretary and the signet office in the 15th century. Annette J. Otway-Ruthven. Cambridge Ph.D. 1937. 907

The privy seal in the early 15th century. A.L. Brown. Oxford D.Phil. 1955. 908

The great council in the 15th century. T.F.T. Plucknett. London M.A. 1917. 909

The council under Henry IV. Phyllis G. Harvey. Oxford B.Litt. 1932. 910

The royal household of Henry IV. A. Rogers. Nottingham Ph.D. 1966. 911

Some aspects of the king's household in the reign of Henry V, 1413-22. Eileen H. de L. Fagan. London M.A. 1935. 912

The king's council in England during the early years of the minority of Henry VI. J. Kirkland. Manchester M.A. 1940. 913

The activities of household officials in the 15th century, as illustrated by the Hatteclyff family. G.E. Burtt. London M.A. 1955. 914

The finance of the royal household, 1437-60. G.L. Harriss. Oxford D.Phil. 1953. 915

The relations between the Crown and the boroughs in the mid 15th century. A.P.M. Wright. Oxford D.Phil. 1966. 916

The administration of the Yorkist kings. J.R. Lander. Cambridge M.Litt. 1950. 917

The household ordinances of Edward IV. A.R. Myers. London Ph.D. (Ext.) 1956. 918

The later medieval sheriff and the royal household (c. 1437-1547). R.M. Jeffs. Oxford D.Phil. 1961. 919

Law

In pursuit of the merchant debtor and bankrupt: 1066-1732. F.J.J. Cadwallader. London Ph.D. 1965. 920

A comparative study of the language of the Anglo-Norman bills of eyre and similar documents of the Channel Isles, Gloucestershire, London and a northern area (Lancashire). C.J.H. Topping. London Ph.D. 1934. 921

The court leet of Southampton and leet jurisdiction in general. F.J.C. Hearnshaw. London M.A. 1908. 922

The writ of habeas corpus. H.P. Letcher. London LL.D. (Ext.) 1933. 923

Some aspects of local jurisdiction in the 12th and 13th centuries, with special reference to private and county courts. Lorna E.M. Walker. London M.A. 1958. 924

A study of the controversy as to the application of Roman canon law in England during the middle ages. B. Allen. Oxford B.Litt. 1923. 925

Legal aspects of villeinage between Glanvill and Bracton. P.R. Hyams. Oxford D.Phil. 1968. 926

The medieval coroner, 1194-1487, with special reference to the county of Sussex. R.F. Hunnisett. Oxford D.Phil. 1956. 927

The early history of placita coram rege. M. Tyson. Manchester Ph.D. 1927. 928

929   Royal wardship in the reign of King John, with reference to chapters 3-6 of Magna Carta. Mary Renshaw. Manchester M.A. 1947.

930   The problem relating to the maintenance of law and order in 13th-century England, with particular reference to the 'custos pacis'. H. Ainsley. Wales Ph.D. 1968.

931   The roll and writ file of the Berkshire eyre of 1248. M.T. Clanchy. Reading Ph.D. 1966.

932   The Shropshire eyre roll of 1256. A. Harding. Oxford B.Litt. 1957.

933   Judicial investigations under the dictum de Kenilworth. Margery L. Hoyle. Manchester Ph.D. 1934.

934   The judicial proceedings under the dictum of Kenilworth in west Berkshire. Ellen Roberts. Manchester M.A. 1927.

935   The judicial proceedings under the dictum of Kenilworth in east Berkshire. Alys L. Gregory. Manchester M.A. 1927.

936   Judicial proceedings under the dictum of Kenilworth in north Buckinghamshire. J. Lunn. Manchester M.A. 1928.

937   Judicial proceedings under the dictum of Kenilworth in south Buckinghamshire. Margery L. Hoyle. Manchester M.A. 1928.

938   Judicial investigations under the dictum of Kenilworth (Cambridgeshire). C.C. Bayley. Manchester M.A. 1929.

939   Judicial proceedings under the dictum of Kenilworth, Cambridgeshire. Assize Roll 83: membranes 9-16. Sarah Cohen. Manchester M.A. 1929.

940   Judicial proceedings in Cambridgeshire under the dictum of Kenilworth. Assize Roll 83: membranes 17-24d. Kathleen H. Holden. Manchester M.A. 1929.

941   Judicial proceedings under the dictum of Kenilworth in Essex. H. Roberts. Manchester M.A. 1928.

942   Judicial investigations under the dictum of Kenilworth (Northamptonshire). Mary M. Rothwell. Manchester M.A. 1929.

943   Judicial investigations under the dictum of Kenilworth (Northamptonshire). E.H. Graham. Manchester M.A. 1930.

944   Judicial investigations under the dictum of Kenilworth: Northamptonshire. T.W. Byrne. Manchester M.A. 1932.

945   Judicial proceedings under the dictum of Kenilworth in Surrey. Lucy M. Round. Manchester M.A. 1928.

946   The judicial proceedings under the dictum of Kenilworth in Sussex, Surrey and Kent. Annie Buckley. Manchester M.A. 1927.

947   The doctrine of judicial precedent: its history and importance as a source of law. T.E. Lewis. Cambridge Ph.D. 1927/8.

948   Chester pentice and portmote courts under Edward I. A. Hopkins. Liverpool M.A. 1947.

949   Quo warranto proceedings in the reign of Edward I, 1278-94. D.W. Sutherland. Oxford D.Phil. 1956.

950   The quo warranto proceedings for the county of Lancaster, 1292. A. Cantle. London M.A. 1935.

950A   Aspects of the development of the crime of high treason. J.K. Barratt. Manchester LL.M. 1956.

951   The law of treason in England in the later middle ages. J.G. Bellamy. Nottingham Ph.D. 1966.

952   P.R.O. Assize Roll 505, edited with an introduction on the war-time administration of Lincolnshire, 1294-8. W.S. Thomson. Edinburgh Ph.D. 1939.

953   Sir William de Bereford, c.1250-1326. C.P. Cottis. Oxford B.Litt. 1958.

954   A history of the order of the serjeants at law. J.H. Baker. London Ph.D. 1968.

955   Sir Geoffrey Le Scrope, chief justice of the king's bench, 1324-38. E.L.G. Stones. Glasgow Ph.D. 1950.

956   The origin and early history of the office of notary. J.C. Brown. Edinburgh Ph.D. 1934/5.

957   Proceedings in the court of chancery up to c.1460. Margaret E. Avery. London M.A. 1958.

The working of the court of king's bench in the 15th   958
century. Marjorie Blatcher. London Ph.D. 1936.
    The system of gaol delivery as illustrated in the extant 959
gaol delivery rolls of the 15th century. Marguerite E.H.J.
Gollancz. London M.A. 1936.
    Commissions of oyer and terminer in 15th-century Eng-   960
land. Judith B. Avrutick. London M.Phil. 1967.

Parliament

    A study of the knights of the shire returned to parlia- 961
ment by Bedfordshire during the middle ages. Margery A.
Fletcher. London M.A. 1933.
    The parliamentary representation of the county of York   962
from the earliest parliaments to 1601. A. Gooder. Leeds
Ph.D. 1933.
    Aspects of the history of the Commons in the 14th cent- 963
ury. Doris Rayner. Manchester Ph.D. 1934.
    The parliamentary representation of the county of Lan-   964
caster in the reign of Edward II. E. Fox. Manchester M.A.
1956.
    County representatives in the parliaments of Edward III. 965
Kathleen L. Wood-Legh. Oxford B.Litt. 1929.
    Suggestions concerning the date and authorship of the   966
Modus Tenendi Parliamentum. Dorothy K. Hodnett. Bristol M.A.
1918.
    The opening address to parliament, with particular   967
reference to the period 1377-1484. F. Williamson. Manchester
M.A. 1935.
    The parliamentary representation of Northamptonshire and 968
Rutland, 1377-1422. F.A. Clifford. Manchester M.A. 1967.
    The parliamentary representation of Warwickshire and   969
Leicestershire, 1377-1422. Margaret G. Webb. Nottingham
M.A. 1961.
    The parliamentary representation of Essex and Hertford- 970
shire, 1377-1422. Anthea Wade. Manchester M.A. 1967.
    The parliamentary representation of Bedfordshire and   971
Buckinghamshire, 1377-1422. A.E. Goodman. Oxford B.Litt.
1965.
    Parliamentary representation of Norfolk and Suffolk,   972
1377-1422. E.L.T. John. Nottingham M.A. 1959.
    The parliamentary representation of Surrey and Sussex,   973
1377-1422. A. Rogers. Nottingham M.A. 1957.
    The knights of the shire for Worcestershire, 1377-1421. 974
J.T.P. Driver. Liverpool M.A. 1962.
    The parliamentary representation of Nottinghamshire,   975
Derbyshire and Staffordshire during the reign of Richard II.
J.G. Bellamy. Nottingham M.A. 1961.
    Parliament in the reign of Richard II. May McKisack.   976
Oxford B.Litt. 1923/4.
    Parliamentary representation in Derbyshire and   977
Nottinghamshire in the 15th century. Elizabeth A. Ayres.
Nottingham M.A. 1956.
    Petitions in parliament under the Lancastrians from, or 978
relating to, towns. Miriam A. Rose. London M.A. 1926.
    The knights of the shire for the county of Lancaster,   979
1399-1437. J.S. Roskell. Manchester M.A. 1934.
    The personnel of parliament under Henry IV. Janet W.   980
Muir. London M.A. 1924.
    A study of the parliamentary burgesses during the first 981
half of the 15th century, based on the returns of London,
York, Norwich, Bristol and Southampton, between 1413 and 1437.
J. Lawson. Manchester M.A. 1936.
    Some aspects of the history of the Commons in the reign 982
of Henry V and the minority of Henry VI (with special reference to parliamentary petitions). A.R. Myers. Manchester
M.A. 1935.

983   Burgess representation of the county of Wiltshire, 1422–37: a local study of the social composition of the burgess element in parliament. J.T. Driver. Oxford B.Litt. 1951.

984   The personnel of the house of commons in 1422. J.S. Roskell. Oxford D.Phil. 1941.

985   The parliament of 1449–50. R. Virgoe. London Ph.D. 1964.

986   The burgesses in the parliaments of Yorkist England. K.N. Houghton. Liverpool M.A. 1961.

MILITARY AND NAVAL HISTORY

987   The military and naval terms in the Norman and Anglo-Saxon chronicles of the 12th century. G.C. Johnson. Leeds Ph.D. 1949.

988   Military organisation in England, 1124–1254. J.S. Critchley. Nottingham Ph.D. 1968.

989   The place of English castles in the administrative and military organisation 1154–1216, with special reference to the reign of John. R.A. Brown. Oxford D.Phil. 1953.

990   Aspects of military organisation in England under King John: the foreign mercenaries, their place in the royal armies and in feudal society, and their relationship to the household. W.J. Smith. Wales M.A. 1951.

991   Ireland's participation in the military activities of English kings in the 13th and early 14th centuries. J.F. Lydon. London Ph.D. 1955.

992   The Welsh soldier in England's armies of the 13th and 14th centuries. T.L. Williams. Wales M.A. 1915.

993   The Anglo–Welsh wars, 1217–67: with special reference to English military developments. R.F. Walker. Oxford D.Phil. 1954.

994   Edward I's wars and their financing, 1294–1307. M.C. Prestwich. Oxford D.Phil. 1968.

995   The administration of the navy in the reign of Edward III. R.M. Hedley. Manchester M.A. 1922.

996   The employment of naval forces in the reign of Edward III. A.T. Hall. Leeds M.A. 1956.

997   Military system of Edward III. A.E. Prince. Oxford B.Litt. 1929.

998   Berwick upon Tweed in the wars of Edward III. Beryl L. Atkinson. Leeds M.A. 1959.

999   Measures taken by the king to fortify and munition the royal castles of England between the years 1327 and 1345. A.J. Campbell. Durham M.A. 1956.

1000   Naval policy at the end of the 14th century. T. Booth. Leeds M.A. 1932.

1001   Royal administration and the keeping of the seas 1422–85. C.F. Richmond. Oxford D.Phil. 1963.

1002   The armourer and his methods, with some account of individual masters of the craft. C.J. ffoulkes. Oxford B.Litt. 1911.

See also MEDIEVAL EUROPE AND BYZANTIUM: GENERAL AND POLITICAL HISTORY: England and France, including the Hundred Years War.

ECONOMIC AND SOCIAL HISTORY

Finance

1003   Moneyers of the late Anglo-Saxon coinage, 973–1016. Veronica J. Smart. Nottingham M.A. 1963.

1004   The organisation of the currency, c.1180–c.1250. G.K. Tibbo. Reading M.A. 1954.

1005   The great roll of the pipe for the 9th year of the reign of King Richard I, Michaelmas 1197. Helen M. Grace. Reading M.A. 1929.

The carucage of 1200. P.W. Hasler. Reading M.A. 1955. 1006

The great roll of the pipe for the 7th year of the 1007
reign of King John, Michaelmas 1205. S. Smith. Reading Ph.D.
1937.

The great roll of the pipe for the 14th and 16th years 1008
of the reign of King John. Patricia M. Barnes. Reading Ph.D.
1956.

Pipe roll, 2 Henry III. Erica P. Ebden. Reading 1009
M.Phil. 1969.

The great roll of the pipe for the 4th year of the 1010
reign of Henry III. B.E. Harris. Nottingham Ph.D. 1970.

Jewish finance in England, 1216-90, with special refer- 1011
ence to royal revenue. P. Elman. London M.A. 1935.

Plea rolls of the exchequer of the Jews (Michaelmas 1012
Term 1277 - Hilary Term 1279) preserved in the Public Record
Office. Sarah Cohen. London Ph.D. 1951.

The financial relations between the Crown and the City 1013
of London in the reigns of Edward I to Henry VII (excluding
parliamentary taxation). G.J. de C. Mead. London M.A. 1936.

Clerical taxation and consent in the reign of Edward I. 1014
H.S. Deighton. Oxford B.Litt. 1935.

Scutages and aids in England, particularly in the 14th 1015
century. Helena M. Chew. London M.A. 1921.

The Stapeldon-Meldon exchequer reforms and their exec- 1016
ution. Dorothy M. Broome. Manchester M.A. 1920.

The exchequer under Edward III: a preliminary study. 1017
Dorothy M. Broome. Manchester Ph.D. 1922.

The taxation of wool, 1327-48. F.R. Barnes. Man- 1018
chester M.A. 1912.

The London lay subsidy of 1332. Margaret Curtis. Man- 1019
chester M.A. 1912.

Studies in taxation and the development of parliament, 1020
1336-48. W.N. Bryant. Cambridge Ph.D. 1964.

The administration of the subsidies under Edward III, 1021
1336-48. M.V. Gregory. Manchester M.A. 1921.

Edward III's war finance 1337-41: transactions in wool 1022
and credit operations. E.B. Fryde. Oxford D.Phil. 1947.

English government finance, 1399-1413. T. Kido. 1023
London Ph.D. 1966.

Land Tenure

The Anglo-Saxon thegnage from 871 to c.1100, with some 1024
comparison with the pre-feudal Frankish nobility of service.
Mary C. Pinsent. London M.A. 1952.

Agricultural enterprise on the red loams and culm 1025
measures of Devon - an analytical survey. J.R. Blunden.
Exeter Ph.D. 1965.

Studies in the geography of Domesday Book. I.B. 1026
Terrett. Liverpool Ph.D. 1950.

Norman Lincolnshire. G.H. Marshall. Leeds M.A. 1948. 1027

Feudalism in Jersey. Agnes F. Luce. London M.A. 1924. 1028

The eperqueries of the Channel Islands and their ana- 1029
logues. Brenda M. Bolton. Leeds M.A. 1963.

The lands and rights of Harold, son of Godwine, and 1030
their redistribution by William I. R.H. Davies. Wales M.A.
1968.

Aspects of sub-infeudation on some Domesday secular 1031
fiefs. J.F.A. Mason. Oxford D.Phil. 1952.

The king's thegns and serjeants in Domesday Book. Amy 1032
E. Watkinson. London M.A. 1958.

The social structure of English Mercia in Domesday. 1033
Pauline M. Lehmann. London M.A. 1950.

The Domesday survey of Middlesex. T.G. Pinder. London 1034
M.A. 1960.

The Domesday survey of Dorset and the Dorset geld 1035
rolls. E. Ann Williams. London Ph.D. 1964.

1036   The feudal aspect of the Domesday survey of Somerset
and Dorset in connexion with the barony of Moiun (Dunster
castle) and analogous feudal estates, based upon contemporary
public and local records. Margaret F. Moore. London Ph.D.
1930.

1037   The Domesday geography of Somerset and Staffordshire.
P. Wheatley. London M.A. 1951.

1038   A study of the lay fiefs of Norfolk at the time of the
Domesday Survey. P. Carnell. Wales M.A. 1966.

1039   Feudal tenure in 11th-century England: the Norman conquest of Kent. G.R. Duncombe. Exeter M.A. 1967.

1040   The Cartae Baronum of 1166. B.J. Feeney. Belfast M.A.
1970.

1041   Some contributions to 13th-century feudal geography.
I.J. Sanders. Oxford D.Phil. 1938.

1042   English ecclesiastical baronies and knight service,
especially in the 13th and 14th centuries. Helena M. Chew.
London Ph.D. 1926.

1043   Frank almoign: a study of ecclesiastical tenure in
England chiefly in the 14th and 15th centuries. Elisabeth
G. Kimball. Oxford B.Litt. 1927.

1044   The Leicestershire survey, c. A.D. 1130. C.F. Slade.
Reading Ph.D. 1956.

Estates and Forests

1045   A study of the social and economic influence of the
small unit of cultivation. E. Thomas. Oxford B.Litt. 1926.

1046   A contribution to the study of strip lynchets. G.W.
Whittington. Reading Ph.D. 1959.

1047   Anglo-Saxon charters. Agnes J. Robertson. Cambridge
Ph.D. 1933/4.

1048   The role of the Fenland in English history. H.C. Darby.
Cambridge Ph.D. 1930/1.

1049   The Lincolnshire Fenland in the early middle ages: a
social and economic history. H.E. Hallam. Nottingham Ph.D.
1957.

1050   The history of Pershore abbey and its estates. R.A.L.
Smith. London M.A. 1938.

1051   Custodia Essexae: a study of the conventual property
held by the priory of Christ Church, Canterbury, in the
counties of Essex, Suffolk and Norfolk. J.F. Nichols.
London Ph.D. 1930.

1052   The estates of the cathedral church of Hereford, 1066-
1317. Marjorie Jones. Oxford B.Litt. 1958.

1053   The estates of the Clare family, 1066-1317. Jennifer
C. Ward. London Ph.D. 1962.

1054   The family and honour of Mowbray in England and Normandy,
1100-91. Diana E. Greenway. Cambridge Ph.D. 1967.

1055   Some northern royal forests, north of Trent, 1066-1307.
W.H. Liddell. Nottingham M.A. 1961.

1056   The administration and economy of the Forest of Feckenham during the early middle ages. J. West. Birmingham M.A.
1964.

1057   The administration and agrarian policy of the manors of
Durham cathedral priory. Elizabeth M. Halcrow. Oxford
B.Litt. 1949.

1058   The estates of Peterborough abbey, 1086-1310: the Norman
settlement to the Edwardian administration. E.J. King. Cambridge Ph.D. 1968.

1059   Settlement, land use and population in the western
portion of the Forest of Arden, Warwickshire, between 1086
and 1350: a study in historical geography. B.K. Roberts.
Birmingham Ph.D. 1965.

1060   The reclamation of waste in the Forest of Knaresborough:
a study in settlement and enclosure. Margaret Agerskow.
Leeds M.A. 1958.

The Forest of Dean in its relations with the Crown 1061
during the 12th and 13th centuries. Margaret L. Bazeley.
London M.A. 1911.

The estates of Norwich cathedral priory during the 12th 1062
and 13th centuries. E. Stone. Oxford D.Phil. 1956.

Ramsey abbey estates: a study in economic growth and 1063
organisation. J.A. Raftis. Cambridge Ph.D. 1954.

A calendar of the de Hoghton deeds and papers at Pres- 1064
ton Hoghton Towers, Lancs. J.H. Lumby. Liverpool M.A. 1936.

The administration of the royal forests of England 1065
during the 13th century. R.K.J. Grant. Wales Ph.D. 1938.

The forest books of the royal forest of Sherwood. 1066
Helen E. Boulton. Nottingham M.A. 1959.

The monastic grange: a survey of the historical and 1067
archaeological evidence. C.P.S. Platt. Leeds Ph.D. 1966.

The grange system and sheep farming activities of some 1068
Yorkshire Cistercian abbeys. Patricia B. Atkinson. London
M.A. (Ext.) 1953.

The estates of Glastonbury abbey in the later middle 1069
ages. I.J.E. Keil. Bristol Ph.D. 1964.

The Worcestershire peasantry in the later middle ages. 1070
R.K. Field. Birmingham M.A. 1962.

The peasant land market in Berkshire during the later 1071
middle ages. Mrs. Rosamund J. Faith. Leicester Ph.D. 1962.

Agrarian conditions on the Wiltshire estates of the 1072
duchy of Lancaster, the Lords Hungerford and the bishopric of
Winchester in the 13th, 14th and 15th centuries. Mrs.
Richenda C. Scott. London Ph.D. 1940.

English manorial accountancy in the 13th and early 14th 1073
centuries, with special reference to the didactic treatises
on the subject. Dorothea Oschinsky. London Ph.D. 1942.

The machinery of manorial administration, with special 1074
reference to the lands of the bishopric of Winchester, 1208-
1454. Eleanor Swift. London M.A. 1930.

The franchise in 13th-century England, with especial 1075
reference to the estates of the bishopric of Winchester. A.N.
May. Cambridge Ph.D. 1970.

Land and population on the bishop of Winchester's 1076
estates, 1209-1350. J.Z. Titow. Cambridge Ph.D. 1962.

The pipe roll of the bishopric of Winchester, 1210-11: 1077
an edition of the text with an introductory essay on its
value for administrative history. N.R. Holt. Manchester M.A.
1955.

The estates of Titchfield abbey, c.1245 to c.1380. 1078
D.G. Watts. Oxford B.Litt. 1958.

The organisation of the manor, with reference to the 1079
estates of Crowland abbey. Frances M. Page. Cambridge Ph.D.
1929/30.

Accounts and surveys of the Wiltshire lands of Adam de 1080
Stratton, 1269-89. M.W. Farr. Birmingham M.A. 1959.

A geographical study of agriculture on the Kentish 1081
manors of Canterbury cathedral priory, 1272-1379. Ann Smith.
Liverpool M.A. 1961.

The lands of Isabella de Fortibus, countess of Aumale: 1082
a study in 13th-century administration. N. Denholm-Young.
Oxford B.Litt. 1929.

The manorial administration of the bishopric of Win- 1083
chester, 1282-1304. Jean Parke. Manchester M.A. 1947.

The Dean Forest eyre of 1282. C.E. Hart. Bristol M.A. 1084
1956.

Bolton priory, 1286-1325: an economic study. I. Ker- 1085
shaw. Oxford D.Phil. 1969.

Agrarian conditions in Herefordshire and the adjacent 1086
border during the later middle ages. A.J. Roderick. London
Ph.D. 1938.

The abbey of Chertsey and its manors under Abbot John 1087
de Rutherwyk, 1307-47. Elsie Toms. London Ph.D. 1935.

1088   Aspects of the economic development of some Leicester-shire estates in the 14th and 15th centuries. R.H. Hilton. Oxford D.Phil. 1940.

1089   The administration of the estates of Merton College in the 14th century, with special reference to the Black Death and the problems of labour. Mrs. Edith C. Lowry. Oxford D.Phil. 1932/3.

1090   The Woodlands Estate, 1357-1527. P.A. Crowther. Nottingham M.A. 1969.

1091   The lands and servants of the dukes of York to 1415. T.B. Pugh. Oxford B.Litt. 1948.

1092   The Stanley family, c.1385-1651: a study of the origins, power and wealth of a landowning family. B. Coward. Shef-field Ph.D. 1968.

1093   Christ Church, Canterbury, and its lands from the begin-ning of the priorate of Thomas Chillenden to the Dissolution (1391-1540). Mrs. Mary N. Birchall, née Carlin. Oxford B.Litt. 1970.

1094   A study of landowners and their estates in Essex, Kent, Surrey and Sussex at the opening of the 15th century, based on the assessments for the land tax of 1412 (Feudal Aids, VI, p.391 seq.). Mrs. Madeline J. Barber. Oxford B.Litt. 1949.

1095   The estates of the Pelham family in east Sussex before 1500. Marie Clough. Cambridge Ph.D. 1957.

1096   The estates of the Percy family, 1416-1537. J.M.W. Bean. Oxford D.Phil. 1952.

1097   Some Yorkshire estates of the Percies, 1450-1650. E.J. Fisher. Leeds Ph.D. 1955.

1098   An edition of the cartulary of John de Macclesfield. Julia L.C. Bruell. London M.A. (Ext.) 1969.

1099   The economy and administration of the estates of the dean and chapter of Exeter cathedral in the 15th century. D.J.B. Hindley. London M.A. (Ext.) 1958.

For cartularies of religious houses, see under ECCLESIASTICAL HISTORY: Monasticism and Religious Orders

Trade and Industry

1100   The Old English gild system. Mrs. Constance W. Dove. Leeds M.A. 1941.

1101   The growth of the organisation of the Cinque ports con-federation. Katherine M.E. Murray. Oxford B.Litt. 1932.

1102   The Cinque port towns: a comparative geographical study. Marjorie Wright. London Ph.D. 1965.

1103   The location and development of the Hull fishing indus-try. G.S. Clark. Hull M.Sc. 1957.

1104   The history of the port of Hull to the end of the 14th century. W.R. Jones. Wales M.A. 1944.

1105   The pastoral custom and local wool trade of medieval Sussex, 1085-1485. A.M.M. Melville. London M.A. 1931.

1106   Medieval fairs in England. J. Bennison. London M.A. 1911.

1107   Yorkshire fairs and markets to the end of the 18th century. K.L. McCutcheon. Durham M.Litt. 1935.

1108   Historical survey of the Somerset and Bristol fairs. N.F. Hulbert. Bristol M.A. 1935.

1109   A glossary of textile fabrics used in England prior to 1500 A.D., with notes upon their history and application. Marjorie Leaf. Leeds M.A. 1934.

1110   The market for Flemish and Brabantine cloth in England from the 12th to the 14th century. Lorna J. Buyse. London M.A. 1956.

1111   The history of the London Weavers' Company. Frances Consitt. Oxford B.Litt. 1929.

1112   The medieval gilds of Stratford-on-Avon and the timber-framed building industry. T.H. Lloyd. Birmingham M.A. 1961.

The London fur trade in the later middle ages, with   1113
particular reference to the Skinners' Company. Elspeth M.
Veale. London Ph.D. 1953.

The medieval pottery industry in Great Britain. J.W.G. 1114
Musty. Bristol M.A. 1966.

The medieval pottery of the Leicester region and its   1115
interpretation for social and economic history. J.F.O'N.
Russell. Belfast M.A. 1966.

The history of Reading in the later middle ages, con-   1116
sidered with special reference to the importance of the gild
merchant in medieval seignorial boroughs. N.H. Gibbs. Oxford D.Phil. 1935.

The trade and industry of Devonshire in the later   1117
middle ages. Frances A. Mace. London M.A. 1925.

The borough of Droitwich and its salt industry, 1215-   1118
1700. Elizabeth K. Gillan. Birmingham M.A. 1956.

Economic change in Derbyshire in the late middle ages, 1119
1272-1540. I.S.W. Blanchard. London Ph.D. 1967.

A general sketch of the history of the Italian mer-   1120
chants in England, 1272-1399; especially in connexion with
the wool trade. Ada Neild. London M.A. 1914.

The English wool trade in the 13th century. F. Miller. 1121
Oxford B.Litt. 1921.

The medieval wills of Bristol. Mrs. Gillian H. Nicol- 1122
son, née Sutcliffe. Birmingham M.A. 1970.

The rise of the English merchants from the expulsion of 1123
the Jews to the peace of Bretigny. Ann K. Pattison. Liverpool M.A. 1953.

The Wealden iron industry. Margaret Richards. London 1124
Ph.D. 1924.

The import trade in salt into England in the 14th and   1125
15th centuries. A.R. Bridbury. London Ph.D. 1953.

The non-sweet wine trade of England during the 14th and 1126
15th centuries. Margaret K. James. Oxford D.Phil. 1952.

Some aspects of the trade of Newcastle upon Tyne in the 1127
14th century. J.B. Blake. Bristol M.A. 1962.

The port of Chester in the late middle ages: a study of 1128
the customs organisation, the trade and merchant community
of Chester between 1301 and 1558. K.P. Wilson. Liverpool
Ph.D. 1966.

The borough and the merchant community of Ipswich,   1129
1317-1422. G.H. Martin. Oxford D.Phil. 1955.

The legal and economic relations between alien mer-   1130
chants and the central government in England, 1350-77. Alice
Beardwood. Oxford D.Phil. 1928/9.

The position of foreign merchants in England in the   1131
time of Edward III, mainly from the legal standpoint. Alice
Beardwood. Oxford B.Litt. 1924.

The societies of the Bardi and Peruzzi and their deal- 1132
ings with Edward III. E. Russell. Manchester M.A. 1912.

The history of the Staple at Westminster in the reign   1133
of Richard II. Janet S.A. Macaulay. Oxford B.Litt. 1934.

The ship-building industry on the east and south coasts 1134
of England in the 15th century. Mary A.S. Hickmore. London
M.A. 1937.

A study of the merchant class of London in the 15th   1135
century, with special reference to the Company of Grocers.
Sylvia L. Thrupp. London Ph.D. 1931.

The overseas trade of Bristol in the later middle ages: 1136
a study of English commerce, 1399-1485. Eleanora M. Carus-
Wilson. London M.A. 1926.

Women in the textile industries and trade of 15th-   1137
century England. Marian K. Dale. London M.A. 1928.

The port book of Southampton for 1439-40, edited, with 1138
an introduction relating to local port dues and the coastal
trade of Southampton. H.S. Cobb. London M.A. 1957.

1139   The brokage book of Southampton for 1443-4, edited, with an introduction on the Bargate tolls and the overland distribution of goods from Southampton. Olive P. Coleman. London M.A. 1957.

1140   The transactions between the merchants of the Staple and the Lancastrian government, 1449-61. Winifred I. Haward. London Ph.D. 1931.

1141   Prices and wages in England, 1450-1550. Y.S. Brenner. London M.A. 1960.

1142   The financing of trade in the later middle ages, with special reference to English foreign trade in the 15th century. M.M. Postan. London M.Sc. 1926.

1143   Plymouth Haven: a survey of the Haven in relation to the sea manuals and charts used in the home waters of north-west Europe from the late 14th century to 1693. A.E. Stephens. London M.Sc. 1936.

1144   The history of cartographical symbols. Eila M.J. Campbell. London M.A. 1946.

Social History

1145   Kingship and nobility in Anglo-Saxon England to the time of Alfred the Great. H.R. Loyn. Wales M.A. 1949.

1146   The family of de la Pomerai of Beri, 1066-1700 (with appendix post 1720). E.B. Powley. Liverpool M.A. 1941.

1147   The early history of the Davenports of Davenport. T.P. Highet. Manchester M.A. 1953.

1148   The Lacy family in England and Normandy, 1066-1194. W.E. Wightman. Leeds Ph.D. 1960.

1149   The Lacy family of Herefordshire before 1243: their influence on the political history of England, Normandy and Ireland. Barbara Donaldson. Bristol M.A. 1957.

1150   The character and use of domestic furnishings in England as discernible from documentary and archaeological evidence from the 11th to the 15th centuries. Mrs. Penelope Eames. Liverpool M.A. 1969.

1151   The social and economic condition of the unfree classes in England from the 12th to the 14th century, with special reference to the eastern counties. N. Neild. London M.A. 1908.

1152   The acta of John, lord of Ireland and count of Mortain, with a study of his household. Margaret Preen. Manchester M.A. 1949.

1153   The development of West Riding surnames from the 13th to the 20th century. G. Redmonds. Leicester Ph.D. 1969.

1154   The Hungerford family in the later middle ages. J.L. Kirby. London M.A. 1939.

1155   The position and history of the Jews in England in the 13th century. E. Dakin. Wales M.A. 1913.

1156   The house of Bigod in the reign of Henry III. G. Goodall. Manchester M.A. 1925.

1157   The English view of usury and the distribution of wealth in the later middle ages. H.G. Richardson. London M.A. 1912.

1158   The distribution of lay wealth in south-east England in the early 14th century. R.E. Glasscock. London Ph.D. 1962.

1159   The career, lands and family of William Montague, earl of Salisbury, 1301-44. R. Douch. London M.A. (Ext.) 1950.

1160   Medieval administration in the 14th century, with special reference to the household of Elizabeth de Burgh, Lady of Clare. Clare A. Musgrave. London M.A. 1923.

1161   Foreign chivalry at the court of Edward III. F. Schenck. Oxford B.Litt. 1912.

1162   The Lords Grey of Ruthin, 1325 to 1490: a study in the lesser baronage. R.I. Jack. London Ph.D. 1961.

1163   The English nobility in the reign of Edward III. G.A. Holmes. Cambridge Ph.D. 1952.

The Black Death, 1348-9, with special reference to 1164
cathedral registers for the mortality of the clergy. J. Lunn.
Cambridge Ph.D. 1930/1.
Social life in England during the reign of Richard II. 1165
Grace B.C. Newell. Leeds M.A. 1931.
The family of Talbot, Lords Talbot and earls of Shrews- 1166
bury, 1387-1473. A.J. Pollard. Bristol Ph.D. 1968.
Medieval travel, as illustrated by the wardrobe 1167
accounts of Henry, earl of Derby, 1390-3. Grace Stretton.
London M.A. 1924.
The Yorkshire baronage, 1399-1433. C.D. Ross. Oxford 1168
D.Phil. 1950.
East Anglian society in the 15th century: an historico- 1169
regional survey. G.E. Morey. London Ph.D. (Ext.) 1951.
Ralph, Lord Cromwell and his household: studies in rel- 1170
ation to household accounts in the possession of Lord De
l'Isle and Dudley. Evelyn M. Price. London M.A. 1948.
The Bulkeleys of Baron Hill, 1440-1621. D.C. Jones. 1171
Wales M.A. 1958.
The nobility of England, 1453-1558. P.J. Higson. 1172
Liverpool M.A. 1959.
A new edition of the Cely Letters: 1472-88. Mrs. 1173
Alison H. Hanham, née Forester. Bristol Ph.D. 1954.
The Plumpton correspondence: an historical and social 1174
survey. Mrs. Shirley M. Walker, née Thomas. Leeds M.A. 1962.
The status and function of minstrels in England between 1175
1350 and 1400. Margaret A. Price. Birmingham M.A. 1964/5.
Music under the later Plantagenets. B.L. Trowell. 1176
Cambridge Ph.D. 1960.
The royal entry in medieval and early Tudor England. 1177
Caroline L.W. Holt. Manchester Ph.D. 1969.

ECCLESIASTICAL HISTORY

General

A short consideration of the influence of the Roman see 1178
in the conversion of Britain to Christianity. E.M. Swift.
Belfast M.A. 1915.
The archiepiscopal sees in England from St. Augustine 1179
to St. Dunstan. J.W. Lamb. Leeds Ph.D. 1953.
The territorial possessions of St. Wilfrid and their 1180
influence upon his career. M. Roper. Manchester M.A. 1958.
Theodore of Tarsus, archbishop of Canterbury 668-90. 1181
R.H. Whitaker. Edinburgh Ph.D. 1948.
The autonomy of the Anglo-Saxon Church. J.G.M. Howard. 1182
Durham M.A. 1931.
Anglo-Saxon ecclesiastical organisation in the kingdom 1183
of Wessex. P.G. Medd. Oxford B.Litt. 1958.
A correlation of linguistic and archaeological evidence 1184
for Anglo-Saxon heathenism. Audrey L. Savill. Cambridge
Ph.D. 1959.
The Celtic Church in England after the synod of Whitby. 1185
J.L.G. Meissner. Belfast M.A. 1927.
The origin of the parish. M.W. Neilson. Aberdeen 1186
Ph.D. 1928.
Some aspects of Northumbrian history in the 11th cent- 1187
ury, with particular reference to the four last Anglo-Saxon
archbishops of York, 1002-69. Janet M. Cooper. Cambridge
Ph.D. 1968.
The king's government and episcopal vacancies in 1188
England, 11th to 14th century. Margaret E. Howell. London
Ph.D. 1955.
The bishops of Chichester and the administration of 1189
their diocese from the Norman Conquest to 1207, with a col-
lection of acta. H.M.R.E. Mayr-Harting. Oxford D.Phil. 1961.

1190   Church and state during the reign of William I. J.W. Lamb. Leeds M.A. 1933.

1191   The Norman episcopate during the reign of William the Conqueror. P.L. Hull. Bristol M.A. 1954.

1192   The church of Exeter in the Norman period. D.W. Blake. Exeter M.A. 1970.

1193   The parish in Domesday Book: a study of the mother churches, manorial churches and rural chapels in the late Saxon and early Norman periods. Daphne H. Gifford. London Ph.D. 1952.

1194   The English Church under Henry I. M. Brett. Oxford D.Phil. 1969.

1195   Anselm and his circle; a study of the historical importance of his letters. Winifred M. Mitchiner. London M.A. 1945.

1196   The correspondence of Archbishop Lanfranc: a critical edition with notes and a historical introduction. Mrs. V. Helen Clover. Cambridge Ph.D. 1962.

1197   Themes and traditions in saints' legends in Britain and Ireland. B.K. Martin. Cambridge M.Litt. 1958.

1198   English hagiology, 1100-35. D.F.H. Farmer. Oxford B.Litt. 1967.

1199   Jacobean pilgrims from England from the early 12th to the late 15th century. Mrs. Constance M. Storrs. London M.A. 1964.

1200   The activities of rural deans in England in the 12th and 13th centuries. J. Foster. Manchester M.A. 1955.

1201   The statutes of the provincial courts of Canterbury and York. C.E. Welch. Southampton Ph.D. 1968.

1202   The archiepiscopate of William of Corbeil, 1123-36. D.L.T. Bethell. Oxford B.Litt. 1963.

1203   An edition and translation of the 'Vita domini Roberti de Betune Herfordensis episcopi', by William de Wycumba, with introduction and notes. Betty J. Parkinson. Oxford B.Litt. 1951.

1204   The life of Theobald, archbishop of Canterbury. A.A. Saltman. London Ph.D. 1951.

1205   The life and acts of Robert of Chesney, bishop of Lincoln, 1148-66. H.P. King. London M.A. 1955.

1206   Roger, bishop of Worcester, 1164-79. Mary G. Hall. Oxford B.Litt. 1940.

1207   The _acta_ of Archbishops Richard and Baldwin, 1174-90. Bridgett E.A. Jones. London Ph.D. 1964.

1208   Gilbert Glanville, bishop of Rochester, 1185-1214, and the relationship of the see of Rochester to Canterbury to 1238. J. Moule. Manchester M.A. 1954.

1209   An edition of William of Malmesbury's Treatise on the Miracles of the Virgin, with an account of its place in his writings and in the development of Mary legends in the 12th century. P.N. Carter. Oxford D.Phil. 1960.

1210   Contribution to the study of the life of Thomas Becket with special reference to the manuscripts of the poem De Sancto Thoma Archiepiscopo Cantuariensi. H.H. Hodge. London M.A. 1923.

1211   The tradition of St. Thomas of Canterbury in literature, art and religion. A.B. Cottle. Wales M.A. 1947.

1212   Thómas saga Erkibyskups: a new collation. Margaret Orme. London M.A. 1964.

1213   The organisation and administration of the see and diocese of Durham, 1195-1229. P.C. Brooke. Newcastle M.Litt. 1967.

1214   The episcopal constitutions of the diocese of Durham in the century after the Fourth Lateran Council. E. Featherstone. Durham M.A. 1960.

1215   Some aspects of the chantry system in Lancashire. Mary F. Coogan. Manchester M.A. 1944.

The minor corporations of the secular cathedrals of   1216
the province of Canterbury (excluding the Welsh sees) between
the 13th century and 1536, with special reference to the minor
canons of St. Paul's cathedral from their origin in the 12th
century to the visitation of Bishop Gibson in 1724.   A.R.B.
Fuller. London M.A. 1947.

The administrative machinery of the archbishopric of   1217
Canterbury as illustrated chiefly by records at Lambeth and
Canterbury. Irene J. Churchill. Oxford D.Phil. 1930.

Christ Church, Canterbury and the sede vacante juris-   1218
diction of Canterbury during the 13th century. Marjorie M.
Morgan. Oxford B.Litt. 1938.

John de Gray, bishop of Norwich. G.M. Budge. Man-   1219
chester M.A. 1946.

A study of the archiepiscopal household of Stephen   1220
Langton and a collection of his acta. Kathleen Major. Oxford B.Litt. 1931.

The questions of Stephen Langton. Alys L. Gregory.   1221
Manchester Ph.D. 1929.

Stephen Langton as a defender of English liberty. Eva   1222
D. Parry. Wales M.A. 1923.

The Lincoln cathedral chapter under Bishop Hugh of   1223
Wells, 1209-35. G.E. Milburn. Manchester M.A. 1969.

The administration of Hugh of Wells, bishop of Lincoln, 1224
1209-35. D.M. Smith. Nottingham Ph.D. 1970.

An examination of the theory and practice of appoint-   1225
ments in the reigns of Henry III and Edward I (1216-1307),
and of their historical significance. Phyllis H. Scotney.
London M.A. 1927.

Disputes about episcopal elections in England in the   1226
reign of Henry III, with special reference to some unpublished
Durham documents. W.K. Evers. Oxford B.Litt. 1936.

The episcopate in the reign of Henry III. Marion E.   1227
Gibbs. Oxford B.Litt. 1932.

Edition of Liber Albus I of Wells cathedral, fos.9-61.   1228
Alison E. Cavendish. London M.A. 1959.

English preaching, 1221-93. Jennifer M. Sweet. Oxford 1229
B.Litt. 1950.

Ecclesiastical letter-books of the 13th century. Rosa- 1230
lind M.T. Hill. Oxford B.Litt. 1936.

A study of certain letter-books in the possession of   1231
the dean and chapter of Durham as illustrations of the life
of the church in England in the later 13th century. F. Barlow. Oxford B.Litt. 1934.

Anglo-Norman letters and archives from the 13th to the   1232
15th centuries, with especial reference to the archives of
the dean and chapter of Durham. J.L. Freer. Durham M.A.
1956.

The relations of the bishops and citizens of Salisbury 1233
(New Sarum) between 1225 and 1612. Fanny Street. London
M.A. 1915.

An edition of the metrical life of St. Robert of   1234
Knaresborough (together with the other pieces in Middle
English contained in the British Museum MS. Egerton 3143).
Joyce Bazire. Leeds M.A. 1949.

Ralph Neville, bishop of Chichester and chancellor.   1235
Jeanne M.B. Fradin. Oxford B.Litt. 1942.

The Speculum Ecclesie of St. Edmund of Abingdon: a   1236
critical study of the text, with edition. Helen P. Forshaw
(Mother Mary Philomena). London M.A. 1965.

A critical study and edition of the biographies of St. 1237
Edmund of Abingdon, archbishop of Canterbury. C.H. Lawrence.
Oxford D.Phil. 1955.

The life of St. Edmund Rich in the south English   1238
legendary. J.T. Morris. Liverpool M.A. 1963/4.

A critical edition of The Life of St. Edmund, by John   1239
Lydgate. Mrs. Audrey Eccles. London M.A. 1957.

1240   Aspects of the career of Boniface of Savoy, archbishop
of Canterbury, 1241-70. D.T. Williams. Wales Ph.D. 1970.
1241   Ecclesiastical patronage in the diocese of York, 1258-
1316. Joan C. Sinar. Manchester M.A. 1949.
1242   The register of Walter Bronescombe, bishop of Exeter
1258-80. Mrs. Olivia F. Robinson. London Ph.D. 1965.
1243   Edward I and the church. Florence E. Sweetinburgh.
Birmingham M.A. 1917.
1244   The church in the reign of Edward I. Dorothea T. Price.
Wales M.A. 1907.
1245   The church in the reign of Edward I, with special reference to the register of Archbishop Peckham. Blanche E.
Brimson. Wales M.A. 1909.
1246   Archbishop Peckham. T.W. Pay. Leeds M.A. 1917.
1247   The religious policy of Archbishop Peckham. H. Cox.
Leeds M.A. 1911.
1248   Some aspects of the life and work of Archbishop Peckham.
Dorothy Sutcliffe. Manchester M.A. 1919.
1249   The archbishops and province of York, 1279-99. Mrs.
Gwendolen M. Hallas. Leeds M.Phil. 1969.
1250   The metropolitan jurisdiction of the archbishops of York
(1279-96). R.J. Brentano. Oxford D.Phil. 1952.
1251   Tutorial appeal to the archbishops of Canterbury and
York in the 13th century. Priscilla J. Wood. Edinburgh
M.Litt. 1969/70.
1252   Life of Antony Bek, bishop of Durham. Constance M.
Fraser. Durham Ph.D. 1951.
1253   The life and work of Anthony Bek, bishop of Durham. G.
Thomas. Wales M.A. 1915.
1254   The career of Robert Winchelsey, archbishop of Canterbury. J.H. Denton. Cambridge Ph.D. 1966.
1255   Archbishop Winchelsey: a sketch of a critical period in
the relations between church and state. F. Barton. London
M.A. 1912.
1256   A history of Walter Langton, bishop of Coventry and
Lichfield, 1296-1321. D. Whomsley. Wales M.A. 1959.
1257   Grievances of the English clergy in the late 13th and
early 14th centuries, with special reference to the gravamina
of 1309. Ursula R.Q. Henriques. Oxford B.Litt. 1940.
1258   The administration of a medieval diocese in the last
quarter of the 13th century and the first half of the 14th
century, illustrated from the Hereford registers. J.A.
Darbyshire. Manchester M.A. 1923.
1259   The administration of ecclesiastical courts in the province of Canterbury during the later middle ages. C.E.
Welch. Liverpool M.A. 1953.
1260   Pre-Reformation church courts in the diocese of Canterbury. B.L. Woodcock. Oxford B.Litt. 1950.
1261   York church courts. C.I.A. Ritchie. St. Andrews Ph.D.
1952.
1262   The clergy of the English secular cathedrals of the 14th
century with special reference to the clergy of Salisbury.
Kathleen Edwards. Manchester Ph.D. 1940.
1263   The episcopal administration of the diocese of Exeter in
the 14th century, with special reference to the registers of
Bishops Stapeldon, Grandisson and Brantingham. D.J. Cawthron.
London M.A. (Ext.) 1951.
1264   The administration of the diocese of Worcester in the
first half of the 14th century. R.M. Haines. Oxford D.Phil.
1959.
1265   The chapter of Ripon in the later middle ages. L.W.
Kitchen. Manchester M.A. 1939.
1266   The church in Chester, 1300-1540. D.H. Jones. Liverpool M.A. 1953.
1267   John de Dalderby, bishop of Lincoln 1300-20. C. Clubley.
Hull Ph.D. 1965.

The evolution of the theory and doctrine of the church 1268
in England as exemplified by Ockham, Wyclif and Cranmer. W.L.
Moser. Edinburgh Ph.D. 1927.

A survey of the origins and circulation of theological 1269
writings in English in the 14th, 15th and early 16th centuries,
with special consideration of the part of the clergy therein.
A.I. Doyle. Cambridge Ph.D. 1952/3.

Thomae de Chobham Summa confessorum: editio prioris 1270
partis. F. Broomfield. Cambridge Ph.D. 1960.

The administration of the diocese and province of York 1271
under Archbishop William Greenfield, 1306-15. Mrs. Katherine
Wood. Leeds M.A. 1962.

An edition, with introduction, of the Winchester 1272
cathedral custumal. Katharine A. Hanna. London M.A. (Ext.)
1954.

Adam de Orleton. G.A. Usher. Wales M.A. 1953. 1273

The chapter of Lichfield cathedral in the 14th century. 1274
Mrs. Hester T. Jenkins. Oxford B.Litt. 1956.

St. Peter Thomas, 1305-66. S.T. Manbré. Liverpool 1275
M.A. 1937.

The personnel and political activities of the English 1276
episcopate during the reign of Edward II. Kathleen Edwards.
London M.A. 1937.

Episcopal appointments and patronage in the reign of 1277
Edward II. W.E.L. Smith. Edinburgh Ph.D. 1930/1.

Patronage and the church: a study in the social 1278
structure of the secular clergy in the diocese of Durham,
1311-1540. R. Donaldson. Edinburgh Ph.D. 1955.

The episcopate of Richard de Kellawe, bishop of Durham 1279
1311-16. D.B. Foss. Durham M.A. 1966.

An edition of the archdeaconry of Cleveland section of 1280
the register of Archbishop Melton of York, 1317-40, with an
introduction studying aspects of the clergy in the diocese.
D.B. Robinson. Cambridge Ph.D. 1968.

Some aspects of church life in England during the reign 1281
of Edward III. Kathleen L. Wood-Legh. Cambridge Ph.D.
1932/3.

The history of the church in the reign of Edward III. 1282
Hilda M. Jones. Wales M.A. 1914.

John Grandisson, bishop of Exeter, 1327-69. R.A. Hors- 1283
field. Leeds M.A. 1966.

The life and register of Bishop Wolstan de Bransford. 1284
R.M. Haines. Durham M.Litt. 1954.

The central and local financial organisation and 1285
administrative machinery of the royal free chapel of St.
George within the castle of Windsor from its foundation (1348)
to the treasurership of William Gillot (1415-16). A.K.
Babette Roberts. London Ph.D. 1943.

The relations between the church and the English Crown 1286
from the death of Archbishop Stratford to the opening of the
Great Schism, 1349-78. J.R.L. Highfield. Oxford D.Phil.
1951.

Parish clergy in the diocese of Exeter in the century 1287
after the Black Death. G.R. Dunstan. Leeds M.A. 1939.

Parochial administration in the archdeaconry of 1288
Chester, 1350-1400. W. Mather. Manchester M.A. 1932.

The distribution of religious groups in England and 1289
Wales, 1350-1550: a study in social geography. F.H. Hansford
Miller. London M.Sc. 1965.

Medieval preaching in England, as illustrated by the 1290
period c.1350 to 1450. G.R. Owst. London Ph.D. 1924.

John Sheppey, bishop of Rochester, as preacher and 1291
collector of sermons. G. Mifsud. Oxford B.Litt. 1954.

Simon Sudbury, bishop of London and archbishop of 1292
Canterbury. W.L. Warren. Oxford D.Phil. 1956.

Wyclif and Lollardy in England. W.H. Leighton. Bir- 1293
mingham M.A. 1925.

1294   Lollard doctrine, with special reference to the controversy over image-worship and pilgrimages. J. Crompton. Oxford B.Litt. 1950.

1295   The Lollard movement in the dioceses of Bath and Wells, Worcester and Hereford. N.J. Davies. Wales M.A. 1966.

1296   An edition of the register of Henry Wakefield, bishop of Worcester 1375-95, with an introduction. W.M. Doody. London Ph.D. 1970.

1297   Ralph Erghum, with special reference to his tenure of the see of Salisbury 1375-88. Sylvia E. Overton. Oxford B.Litt. 1961.

1298   Clergy and laity in London 1376-1531. J.A.F. Thomson. Oxford D.Phil. 1960.

1299   The organisation of a college of secular priests as illustrated by the records of the college of Holy Trinity, Arundel, 1380-1544. R.B.K. Petch. London M.A. 1942.

1300   Robert Braybrooke, bishop of London (1381-1404), and his kinsmen. L.H. Butler. Oxford D.Phil. 1951.

1301   The life and writings of Adam Easton, O.S.B. L.J. Macfarlane. London Ph.D. 1955.

1302   Thomas of Chillenden's register: the earliest surviving register of testaments, 1396-1455, kept by the commissary-general of Canterbury. Brenda M. Duncombe (Mother Mary de Sales). London M.A. 1963.

1303   The English Church in the 15th century. F.R. Wortz. Leeds M.A. 1914.

1304   The episcopate in England and Wales in the reign of Henry IV. R.G. Davies. Manchester M.A. 1968.

1305   Some aspects of the religious history of Norfolk in the 15th century. C.B. Firth. London M.A. 1910.

1306   The place of the secular clergy in the society of 15th-century England. G. Templeman. London M.A. 1936.

1307   The church under the Lancastrians. P.H. Jones. Wales M.A. 1910.

1308   The cult of St. Bridget of Sweden in 15th-century England. F.R. Johnston. Manchester M.A. 1947.

1309   Reginald Pecock - a contribution to his biography. T. Kelly. Manchester M.A. 1945.

1310   Richard Ullerston, canon of Salisbury. A.H. Wood. Manchester M.A. 1936.

1311   The episcopal administration in the diocese of Hereford, 1400-c.1535. Enid L. Lonsdale. Liverpool M.A. 1957.

1312   The administration of the diocese of Bath and Wells, 1401-91. R.W. Dunning. Bristol Ph.D. 1963.

1313   The career of Henry Bowet, bishop of Bath and Wells, later archbishop of York. J.J.N. Palmer. Oxford B.Litt. 1964.

1314   Parliament and Convocation, with special reference to the pontificate of Henry Chichele, 1413-43. M. Oldfield. Manchester M.A. 1938.

1315   The Constitutions of Archbishop Chichele. Bridgett G. Carroll. Manchester M.A. 1932.

1316   New liturgical observances in later medieval England. R.W. Pfaff. Oxford D.Phil. 1965.

1317   Report on the chapter acts of Lincoln cathedral, 1402-27. Margaret Archer. Liverpool M.A. 1936.

1318   The diocese of Lincoln under Bishops Repingdon and Fleming. Margaret Archer. Oxford B.Litt. 1936.

1319   The administration of the see of London under Bishops Roger Walden (1405-6) and Nicholas Bubwith (1406-7), with a transcript of their registers. Una C. Hannam. London M.A. 1951.

1320   Thomas Langley, statesman and bishop. R.L. Storey. Durham Ph.D. 1954.

1321   Bishop Hallum of Salisbury and the reforming activities of his time. F.D. Hodgkiss. Manchester M.A. 1931.

An edition of the register of Robert Hallum, bishop of 1322
Salisbury 1408-17, with an introduction.   Joyce M. Wilkinson.
Oxford B.Litt. 1960.
     Studies in the Lollard heresy, being an examination of 1323
the evidence from the dioceses of Norwich, Lincoln, Coventry
and Lichfield and Ely, during the period 1430-1530.   J.D.
Fines.   Sheffield Ph.D. 1964.
     The ecclesiastical career of George Neville, 1432-76.   1324
Mrs. Gillian I. Keir, née Stannard.   Oxford B.Litt. 1970.
     John Carpenter, bishop of Worcester, 1444-76.   M.J.   1325
Morgan.   Birmingham M.A. 1960.
     Parish clergy in England, 1450-1530.   P. Heath.   London 1326
M.A. 1961.
     Thomas Rotherham, archbishop of York and chancellor of 1327
England: his life and times.   Mary F.H. Robinson.   Sheffield
M.A. 1940.
     Edward Storey, bishop of Chichester (1422-1503): a   1328
study in 15th-century ecclesiastical administration.   F.C.
Walden-Aspy.   London M.A. 1951.

Monasticism and Religious Orders

     English monasticism before 735.   R.T. Timson.   London   1329
M.A. 1957.
     The history of Winchcombe abbey.   G.T. Haigh.   Durham   1330
M.Litt. 1944.
     The history of the abbey of St. Albans.   L.F.R.   1331
Williams.   Oxford B.Litt. 1913.
     The anti-monastic reaction in England in the 10th cent- 1332
ury.   J. Matthews.   Manchester M.A. 1970.
     The pre-Conquest charters of Christchurch, Canterbury. 1333
N.P. Brooks.   Oxford D.Phil. 1969.
     The relations of the Norman monasteries with their   1334
English properties during the middle ages.   D.J.A. Matthew.
Oxford D.Phil. 1958.
     The English priories and manors of the abbey of Bec-   1335
Hellouin.   Marjorie M. Morgan.   Oxford D.Phil. 1942.
     Barking abbey: a study in its external and internal   1336
administration from the Conquest to the Dissolution.   Wini-
frid M. Sturman.   London Ph.D. 1961.
     Canterbury cathedral priory: a study in monastic   1337
administration.   R.A.L. Smith.   Cambridge Ph.D. 1941.
     Two obedientiary rolls of Selby abbey.   Mrs. Beryl   1338
Smith, née Holt.   Leeds M.A. 1949.
     Prior Dominic of Evesham and the survival of the   1339
English tradition after the Norman Conquest.   J.C. Jennings.
Oxford B.Litt. 1958.
     The history of the Cluniacs in England and Wales.   1340
Ethel M. Fussell.   Wales M.A. 1917.
     The greater English monasteries and their knights,   1341
1066-1215.   J.D. Anderson.   Oxford B.Litt. 1948.
     Odo of Ostia's history of the translation of St.   1342
Milburga and its connection with the early history of Wenlock abbey.   Angela J.M. Edwards.   London M.A. 1960.
     Historia Eliensis, Book III.   E.O. Blake.   Cambridge 1343
Ph.D. 1953.
     The derivation of the English monastic office-books as 1344
seen in the core of the Liber Responsalis.   J.D. Brady.   Cambridge M.Litt. 1963.
     A historical and archaeological account of Much Wen-   1345
lock priory and its dependent churches from the earliest
times to 1307.   E.A. Gee.   Birmingham M.A. 1937.
     The history of the Augustinian canons in England before 1346
1215, with special reference to the spread of their foundations and their relations with the secular clergy.   J.C.
Dickinson.   Oxford B.Litt. 1937.

1347   A study of the <u>Narratio de Fundatione</u> of Fountains abbey. L.G.D. Baker. Oxford B.Litt. 1967.

1348   The ecclesiastical relations of the reign of Stephen, with special reference to St. Bernard and the Cistercian reforming party, 1135-54. Margaret I. Megaw. Belfast M.A. 1939.

1349   The geographical significance of Cistercian foundations in England. R.A. Donkin. Durham Ph.D. 1953.

1350   The Cistercian movement in the north of England, with special reference to the early history of Byland abbey. Phyllis Auty. Oxford B.Litt. 1934.

1351   The monasteries and the medieval development of north-east Yorkshire. B.F. Waites. London M.A. 1957.

1352   The cartulary of the priory of Tocwith in the West Riding of Yorkshire. Gwenllian C. Ransome. Manchester M.A. 1930.

1353   An edition of the cartulary of Breedon priory, with introduction and critical apparatus. R.A. McKinley. Manchester M.A. 1950.

1354   Edition of the Kenilworth cartulary. C. Watson. London Ph.D. 1966.

1355   The foundation of Reading abbey and the growth of its possessions and privileges in England in the 12th century. B.R. Kemp. Reading Ph.D. 1966.

1356   Faversham abbey. C.R. Broughton. Durham M.A. 1952.

1357   The cartulary of Meaux: a critical edition. G.V. Orange. Hull Ph.D. 1964.

1358   An edition of the cartulary of Canonsleigh abbey (Harl. MS. 3660). Vera C.M. London. Liverpool M.A. 1962.

1359   Religious life for women in 12th-century canon law, with special reference to English houses. Zela M. Procter. London M.Phil. 1967.

1360   The history of the nunnery of St. Mary and St. Michael outside Stamford. Winifred M. Sturman. London M.A. 1944.

1361   An edition of the cartulary of Burscough priory. A.N. Webb. Liverpool M.A. 1966.

1362   Dieulacres abbey. M.J.C. Fisher. Keele M.A. 1967.

1363   St. Francis and England. G.R. Whitaker. Leeds M.A. 1919.

1364   The Franciscans in medieval English life. V. Green. Oxford B.Litt. 1936.

1365   Some later followers of St. Francis. Constance Mawson. Leeds M.A. 1918.

1366   The friars in England. Elizabeth E. Smith. Birmingham M.A. 1909.

1367   The work and influence of the friars in England for the first fifty years. Eulalie M. Davies. Birmingham M.A. 1915.

1368   Some aspects of the history of the English friars in the 13th century. W.J. Whitehouse. Birmingham M.A. 1923.

1369   Some political activities of the Franciscans in England in the 13th century. I.J. Sanders. Wales M.A. 1935.

1370   The Franciscans and Dominicans in Yorkshire. L.M. Goldthorp. Leeds M.A. 1932.

1371   Aelred of Rievaulx: a study of his works and of their place in Cistercian literature. K.A.J. Squire. Oxford B.Litt. 1958.

1372   An examination of the charges brought against the friars by Matthew Paris. Winifred Alty. Wales M.A. 1911.

1373   Critical edition of the cartulary of St. Gregory's priory, Canterbury. Audrey M. Murray. Oxford B.Litt. 1951.

1374   Edition of Blyth cartulary. R.T. Timson. London Ph.D. 1965.

1375   The organisation and financing of monastic building in England in the later middle ages. R.A. Smith. London M.A. 1952.

1376   Relations between English monasteries and their patrons in the 13th century. Susan M. Chenevix Trench. Oxford B.Litt. 1950.

The importance of Halesowen abbey in the life of the 1377
English people. A.G. Pound. Birmingham M.A. 1926.

The establishment and early development of the Carmel- 1378
ite order in England. K.J. Egan. Cambridge Ph.D. 1965.

A study of the nunnery of St. Mary Clerkenwell and its 1379
property with an edition of its cartulary. W.O. Hassall.
Oxford D.Phil. 1941.

Some chapters in the history of English nunneries in 1380
the later middle ages, c.1250-1535. Eileen E. Power. London
M.A. 1916.

Studies in 13th-century English Dominican history. 1381
W.A. Hinnebusch. Oxford D.Phil. 1939.

Some secular activities of the English Dominicans 1382
during the reigns of Edward I, Edward II and Edward III
(1272-1377). R.D. Clarke. London M.A. 1930.

Monasticism in Cheshire, 1285-1377. H.J. Hewitt. 1383
Liverpool M.A. 1917.

The development of the constitution of the Order of 1384
Preachers in the 13th and 14th centuries. Mrs. Georgina R.
Galbraith. Manchester Ph.D. 1922.

The memorandum book of Henry of Eastry, prior of Christ 1385
Church, Canterbury. T.L. Hogan. London Ph.D. 1966.

The Order of Minoresses in England. A.F. Claudine 1386
Bourdillon. Manchester M.A. 1925.

The relations between the mendicant friars and the 1387
secular clergy in England during the century after the issue
of the bull super cathedram (1300). Jean L. Copeland. London
M.A. 1937.

The Templars in England. Agnes M. Sandys. Manchester 1388
M.A. 1917.

The fate of the Knights Templar in England, with 1389
special reference to their lands. H.I. Millard. Wales M.A.
1918.

The organisation, personnel and functions of the medi- 1390
eval hospital in the later middle ages. Margaret A. Seymour.
London M.A. 1946.

Some aspects of the English Carmelites in the 15th 1391
century. Margaret E. Turner. Manchester M.A. 1933.

The English province of the Franciscans Conventual in 1392
the 15th century. D.W. Whitfield. Bristol M.A. 1953.

The priory of Durham in the time of John Wessington, 1393
prior 1416-46. R.B. Dobson. Oxford D.Phil. 1963.

Henry V and the monastic orders. K.M. Keeley. Man- 1394
chester M.A. 1936.

The abbey of St. Albans under John of Whethamstede. C. 1395
Esther Hodge. Manchester Ph.D. 1933.

Relations with Papacy

The jurisdiction of the papacy in cases of appeal and 1396
of first instance in England, with particular reference to
the southern province, 1198-1254. Jane E. Sayers. Oxford
B.Litt. 1960.

Twelfth-century decretal collections and their import- 1397
ance in English history. C. Duggan. Cambridge Ph.D. 1955.

Anglo-papal relations during the later years of the 1398
reign of King John, 1213-16. Stella M. Whileblood. Manchester M.A. 1947.

The enforcement of the Lateran decrees in England in 1399
the reign of Henry III. Eleanor M. Lang. Oxford B.Litt.
1931.

The legation of Cardinal Otto, 1237-41. Dorothy 1400
Williamson. Manchester M.A. 1947.

The English activities of the Cardinal Ottobuono, 1401
legate of the Holy See. A. Lewis. Manchester M.A. 1937.

The decretals of Gregory IX in relation to English 1402
history. P.G. Ward. Cambridge M.Litt. 1924.

1403   The concordats between the Holy See and England in the
14th and 15th centuries. Mary J. George. Liverpool M.A.
1915.

1404   The relations between the church and the English Crown
during the pontificates of Clement V and John XXII, 1305-34.
J.R. Wright. Oxford D.Phil. 1967.

1405   England and the Great Schism of the West. Catherine M.
Saum. Liverpool M.A. 1916.

1406   English views on reforms to be undertaken in the general
councils (1400-18), with special reference to the proposals
made by Richard Ullerston. Margaret M. Harvey. Oxford
D.Phil. 1964.

1407   Some aspects of the work of the English 'nation' at the
Council of Constance till the election of Martin V. C.M.D.
Crowder. Oxford D.Phil. 1953.

1408   England and the Council of Basel. A.N.E.D. Schofield.
London Ph.D. 1957.

1409   The English notaries at the papal curia in the early
15th century, with special reference to William Swan. Mrs.
Dorothy Newell. Manchester Ph.D. 1934.

INTELLECTUAL LIFE AND SCHOLARSHIP

1410   A study of the history of optics from ancient times to
the end of the 13th century. N.E. Woodcock. Exeter M.A.
1969.

1411   A history of the teaching of physics in England up to
1650. G.D. Bishop. London M.A. 1956.

1412   A study of mathematical methods in England to the 13th
century. Florence A. Yeldham. London Ph.D. 1931.

1413   History of the Vulgate in England from Alcuin to Roger
Bacon. H.H. Glunz. Cambridge Ph.D. 1931/2.

1414   Greek quotations in Anglo-Saxon writings. Annie Anderson. Oxford B.Litt. 1921.

1415   The authenticity of Asser's Life of Alfred. Mrs. Rosalind M. Lavington. Manchester M.A. 1969.

1416   Aelfric's 'Catholic Homilies', first series: the text
and manuscript tradition. P.A.M. Clemoes. Cambridge Ph.D.
1956.

1417   A critical edition of the Handboc or Enchiridion of
Byrhtferth. S.J. Crawford. Oxford D.Phil. 1929/30.

1418   Guthlac: an edition of the Old English prose life,
together with the poems in the Exeter Book. Jane A. Crawford.
Oxford D.Phil. 1967.

1419   The influence of bishops and of members of cathedral
bodies in the intellectual life of England, 1066-1216.
Eleanor Rathbone. London Ph.D. 1936.

1420   The place of Archbishop Lanfranc in 11th-century
scholastic development. Margaret T. Gibson. Oxford D.Phil.
1967.

1421   Anglo-Norman political songs. Isabel S.T. Aspin.
Oxford B.Litt. 1950.

1422   The Vita Wulfstani of William of Malmesbury. R.R.
Darlington. Reading Ph.D. 1929/30.

1423   A study of the Tractatus Eboracenses. Ruth C. Nineham.
Oxford B.Litt. 1951.

1424   Literary activity in the old English Benedictine houses
during the 12th century. Mother Norah Lester. Newcastle
M.Litt. 1967.

1425   Biblical commentators of the 12th and 13th centuries,
viewed as historical material and with special reference to
Stephen Langton. Beryl Smalley. Manchester Ph.D. 1929.

1426   Manuscripts and commentaries on Boethius De Consolatione
Philosophiae in England in the middle ages. Diane K. Bolton.
Oxford B.Litt. 1966.

A critical edition of the text of the letters of John   1427
of Salisbury. W.J. Millor. London Ph.D. 1939.
Early medieval humanism, as exemplified in the life and 1428
writings of John of Salisbury. H. Liebeschuetz. London M.A.
(Ext.) 1947.
John of Salisbury's Entheticus de dogmate philo-   1429
sophorum: the light it throws on the educational background
of the 12th century. C.R. Elrington. London M.A. 1954.
John of Salisbury and the Becket conference. Sybil V.   1430
Lumb. Leeds M.A. 1920.
Learning and literature of English Cistercians, 1167-   1431
1214, with special reference to John of Ford. C.J. Holds-
worth. Cambridge Ph.D. 1960.
A study of private book collections in England between 1432
c.1200 and the early years of the 16th century, with special
reference to books belonging to ecclesiastical dignitaries.
R.H. Bartle. Oxford B.Litt. 1957.
A contribution to the study of French as taught in   1433
England, 13th to 15th centuries. Jennifer Nicholson. London
Ph.D. 1936.
The value of the romance of Fulk and Fitzwarren as a   1434
source for 13th-century English history. G.G. Stephenson.
Oxford B.Litt. 1953.
An edition of some later letters of Peter of Blois   1435
(written while he was archdeacon of London) from MS. Erfurt
Amplonianus F. 71. Margaret E. Revell. Oxford B.Litt. 1958.
The teaching of grammar in England in the later middle 1436
ages. J.N.T. Miner. London Ph.D. 1959.
The Mendicants and English education in the 13th cent- 1437
ury. Ivy H. Tolley. London M.A. 1924.
The problem of the plurality of forms at the University 1438
of Oxford in the 13th century. D.A.P. Callus. Oxford D.Phil.
1938.
English canonists in the later middle ages: a histor-   1439
ical, biographical and literary study. K.R.N.St.J. Wykeham-
George. Oxford B.Litt. 1937.
William de Montibus. H. Mackinnon. Oxford D.Phil.   1440
1959.
Robert of Orford and his place in the scholastic   1441
controversies at Oxford in the late 13th century, with an
edition of his Reprobationes of Giles of Rome. A.P. Vella.
Oxford B.Litt. 1946.
Robert Winchelsea and his place in the intellectual   1442
movement of 13th-century Oxford, with an edition of his
Quaestiones in MS. Magdalen College, Oxford 217. A.J.C.
Smith. Oxford B.Litt. 1953.
Thomas Sutton's place in the development of Aristotel- 1443
ianism and Thomism at Oxford in the last quarter of the 13th
century. F.M.E. Kelley. Oxford B.Litt. 1966.
Studies in the life and philosophy of Robert Kilwardby. 1444
Eleonore Sommer. Cambridge Ph.D. 1935/6.
A study of the writings of William Rothwell, a 13th-   1445
century Dominican. J.J.H. Martin. Oxford B.Litt. 1960.
Schools and education in Gloucestershire and the neigh- 1446
bouring counties from 1280 until the Reformation. N.I. Orme.
Oxford D.Phil. 1969.
The use of Anglo-Norman in private and public documents 1447
of the 14th and 15th centuries. Helen Richardson. Oxford
B.Litt. 1939.
A study of certain kinds of scripts used in England in 1448
the late 14th and 15th centuries, and the origins of the
'Tudor Secretary' hand. M.B. Parkes. Oxford B.Litt. 1959.
An Anglo-Norman metrical 'Brut' of the 14th century.   1449
V.P. Underwood. London Ph.D. 1937.
A study of the English mystics of the 14th century,   1450
with special reference to the writings of Richard Rolle of
Hampole. W.B. Brash. Oxford B.Litt. 1918.

1451   The _Incendium Amoris_ of Richard Rolle of Hampole. Margaret Deanesly. Manchester M.A. 1915.

1452   The philosophic character of English 14th-century mysticism. J. Short. Edinburgh Ph.D. 1929.

1453   Early 14th-century physics of the Merton School with special reference to Dumbleton and Heytesbury. J.A. Weisheipl. Oxford D.Phil. 1957.

1454   Alexander Neckam. R.W. Hunt. Oxford D.Phil. 1936.

1455   Life and works of Odo of Cheriton. A.C. Friend. Oxford D.Phil. 1936.

1456   Roger Bacon. W.H. Johnson. Birmingham M.A. 1913.

1457   The life and writings of Adam of Buckfield, with special reference to his commentary on the _De Anima_ of Aristotle. Helen Powell. Oxford B.Litt. 1964.

1458   A study of Thomas Bradwardine's _De Causa Dei_ and its relation to contemporary Oxford thought. G. Leff. Cambridge Ph.D. 1955.

1459   A study of some Oxford schoolmen of the middle of the 14th century, with special reference to Worcester Cathedral MS. F. 65. S.L. Forte. Oxford B.Litt. 1947.

1460   The influence of the religious literature of Germany and the Low Countries on English spirituality c.1350-1475. R.W. Lovatt. Oxford D.Phil. 1965.

1461   _Piers Plowman_ as a work of moral theology. Grethe Hjort. Cambridge Ph.D. 1931/2.

1462   A study of John Wyclif's _Summa de Ente_ and its relation to contemporary Oxford philosophy. J.A. Robson. Cambridge Ph.D. 1958.

1463   A study of John Wyclif's treatise _De Mandatis Divinis_. J.F. McCristal. Oxford B.Litt. 1958.

1464   William Woodford, O.F.M., c.1330-c.1397. R.J.A.I. Catto. Oxford D.Phil. 1969.

1465   English Benedictines in the century preceding the Dissolution, with special reference to their connexion with the universities and with learning. Winifred D. Coates. Oxford B.Litt. 1931.

1466   John of Bromyard. Catherine Houlihan. Birmingham M.A. 1959.

1467   The teaching and study of arts in the University of Oxford c.1400-c.1520. J.M. Fletcher. Oxford D.Phil. 1961.

1468   The constitutions for the promotion of university graduates, 1417-38. J. Flitcroft. Manchester M.A. 1937.

1469   Humanism in England during the 15th century up to 1485. R. Weiss. Oxford D.Phil. 1938.

1470   Studies in intellectual life in England from the middle of the 15th century till the time of Colet. Naomi D. Hurnard. Oxford D.Phil. 1935.

1471   The life and works of Thomas Gascoigne. Winifred A. Pronger. Oxford B.Litt. 1932.

1472   The early history and organisation of the King's Hall, Cambridge. A.B. Cobban. Cambridge Ph.D. 1965.

1473   'The Equatorie of the Planetis', edited from Peterhouse MS. 75. 1. D.J. Price. Cambridge Ph.D. 1954.

1474   Thomas Chaundler. Shirley F. Bridges. Oxford B.Litt. 1949.

1476   William Caxton and Burgundy: a study of political and cultural relations in the late 15th century. Margaret L. Kekewich. London M.A. 1963.

1477   A biographical study of William Caxton, with special reference to his life and work in the Low Countries. W.J.B. Crotch. London M.A. 1927.

The survival and rediscovery of Egyptian antiquities in   1478
western Europe from late antiquity until the close of the 16th
century. Anne H.M. Roullet. Oxford D.Phil. 1969.

Celtic art in north Britain before A.D. 400. Mrs.   1479
Morna Simpson. Edinburgh Ph.D. 1965/6.

The historical significance of Dark Age Celtic metal-   1480
work in the British Isles. Mrs. Elizabeth Fowler. Oxford
B.Litt. 1962.

Some aspects of Old English vocabulary in the light of   1481
recent archaeological evidence. Rosemary J. Cramp. Oxford
B.Litt. 1958.

The site of Ad Gefrin: an investigation of its archaeo- 1482
logical and historical significance. B.K. Hope-Taylor. Cambridge Ph.D. 1961.

The Anglo-Saxon cemetery at Loveden hill, Hough-on-the- 1483
Hill, Lincolnshire, and its significance in relation to Dark
Age settlement of the eastern Midlands. K.R. Fennell.
Nottingham Ph.D. 1964.

The cemeteries at Barrington and Haslingfield in rel-   1484
ation to the Anglo-Saxon settlement of England. Patricia
Hilton. Leeds Ph.D. 1961/2.

The Saxon and medieval palaces at Cheddar. P.A. Rahtz. 1485
Bristol M.A. 1964.

Anglo-Saxon churches of Durham and Northumberland.   1486
E.C. Gilbert. London Ph.D. (Ext.) 1954.

The saucer brooch and its significance in Anglo-Saxon   1487
England. Mrs. Margaret Saunders. Oxford B.Litt. 1958.

The spear in Anglo-Saxon times. M.J. Swanton. Durham 1488
Ph.D. 1966.

The inscriptions on Anglo-Saxon rune stones. R.I.   1489
Page. Nottingham Ph.D. 1959.

Some leading types of the Anglian province of culture, 1490
5th to 7th century A.D., with their overseas connexions.
H.E.-F. Vierck. Oxford B.Litt. 1967.

Anglo-Saxon non-runic inscriptions. Elisabeth Barty. 1491
Cambridge Ph.D. 1967.

The sculpture of Cumberland in the Anglo-Saxon period: 1492
a survey and historical introduction. R.N. Bailey. Durham
M.A. 1959.

Anglo-Saxon decorative metalwork from Baginton,   1493
Warwickshire. J.B. Hicks. Birmingham M.A. 1957.

An architectural and documentary study of town defences 1494
in England and Wales, 1087-1520. Hilary L. Turner. Oxford
D.Phil. 1968.

The excavation of the old church of Perranzabuloe.   1495
T.F.G. Dexter. St. Andrews Ph.D. 1922.

Minor medieval monumental sculpture of the east Mid-   1496
lands. L.A.S. Butler. Nottingham Ph.D. 1961.

Norman domestic architecture in England. Margaret E.   1497
Wood. London M.A. 1934.

The Canterbury school of illumination (1066-1200).   1498
C.R. Dodwell. Cambridge Ph.D. 1951.

Medieval painted glass in England, 1170-1501. P. Nel- 1499
son. Liverpool Ph.D. 1930.

Schools of glass-painting in the Midlands, 1275-1430.   1500
P.A. Newton. London Ph.D. 1962.

Regional schools in English sculpture in the 12th   1501
century. G. Zarnecki. London Ph.D. 1951.

The decoration of Norman baptismal fonts in relation   1502
to English 12th-century sculpture. Renée Marcousé. London
Ph.D. 1940.

The scriptorium of Bury St. Edmunds in the 12th cent-   1503
ury. Elizabeth Parker. London Ph.D. 1965.

The king's master masons, 1245-1515. B.G. Morgan.   1504
Liverpool Ph.D. 1957/8.

1505   Contributions to the development of English medieval architecture based largely on a first-hand study of various monuments in Oxford. G.P. Brookfield. Oxford B.Litt. 1925.

1506   A study of medieval timber-framed construction based on Worcestershire. F.W.B. Charles. Liverpool M.A. 1962/3.

1507   The fabric rolls of Exeter cathedral. D.F. Findlay. Leeds Ph.D. 1939.

1508   MS. K. 26 in the library of St. John's College, Cambridge: a study of the style and iconography of its 13th-century illustrations. G.D.S. Henderson. Cambridge Ph.D. 1960.

1509   The development of armour and costume from the 14th century to the 17th century as illustrated in the memorial brasses of Essex. A.C. Edwards. Bristol M.A. 1937.

1510   The collegiate architecture of Oxford, from the late 14th century to the early 16th century. E.A. Gee. Oxford D.Phil. 1950.

1511   Figure paintings on rood screens in the churches of Norfolk and south Devonshire. Audrey M. Baker. London Ph.D. 1938.

1512   East Anglian church architecture of the 14th and 15th centuries, with special reference to the churches of the Stour valley. Cora J. Ough. London M.A. 1939.

1513   English medieval alabaster carvings. P. Nelson. Liverpool M.A. 1924.

1514   The use of plant-motives in marginalia of English illuminated manuscripts of the 14th and 15th centuries. Alice M. Houghton. Manchester M.A. 1942.

1515   St. Stephen's Chapel and the architecture of the 14th century in London. J.M. Hastings. Cambridge Ph.D. 1946/7.

1516   Exeter houses, 1400-1700. D. Portman. Exeter Ph.D. 1962.

1517   Some late medieval fortified manor-houses: a study of the building works of Sir John Fastolf, Ralph, Lord Cromwell, and Edward Stafford, 3rd duke of Buckingham. A.D.K. Hawkyard. Keele M.A. 1969.

LOCAL HISTORY

1518   The occupation of the counties Northumberland, Durham, Cumberland and Westmorland from the 4th to the 8th centuries, as revealed by the archaeological and historical evidence. G.S. Keeney. Oxford B.Litt. 1935.

1519   An analysis of the dwelling sites established in Cornwall and Devon between the 5th and the 11th centuries, and their contribution to the modern settlement pattern. W.L.D. Ravenhill. London Ph.D. 1957.

1520   Britain in the 5th century: a survey of the archaeological and literary evidence. Alison Birch. London M.A. 1954.

1521   The early Saxon occupation of Essex, with particular reference to the settlement at Mucking. Mrs. Barbara J. Kinnes, née Thomas. Leeds M.Phil. 1969.

1522   The Anglo-Saxon settlement of Warwickshire. Helen A. Maynard. Birmingham M.A. 1970.

1523   A study of the place-names of the pre-Conquest Kentish charters. T.E.A. Acum. London M.A. 1923.

1524   Somersetshire charters to A.D. 900. E.E. Barker. London M.A. (Ext.) 1961.

1525   Pre-Domesday geography in northern Berkshire. M. Staveley. Reading M.A. 1965.

1526   The development of rural settlement in the Isle of Wight before 1086. Christine Sibbit. Leicester M.A. 1967.

1527   The growth of self-government in the borough of Southampton as illustrated by its charters and letters patent. H.W. Gidden. London Ph.D. 1923.

The importance of Winchester as the capital of England 1528
from the 10th to the 12th century. P. Meadows. London M.A.
1911.

The medieval history of St. James's, Bristol. F.W.P. 1529
Hicks. Bristol M.A. 1932.

A short history of the growth of Redcliffe. G. Hol- 1530
gate. Bristol M.A. 1934.

The manor of Writtle, Essex, c.1086-c.1500. K.C. New- 1531
ton. Leicester M.A. 1967.

Medieval Newcastle-under-Lyme. T. Pape. Manchester 1532
M.A. 1926.

The social structure of the English shires on the Welsh 1533
border between the Norman Conquest and the 14th century.
Margaret U. Apps. Leeds Ph.D. 1944.

Shrewsbury - topography and domestic architecture to 1534
the middle of the 17th century. J.T. Smith. Birmingham
M.A. 1953.

The medieval borough of Shrewsbury. J.G. Speake. 1535
Wales M.A. 1939.

Some aspects of the history of the lordship of Oswes- 1536
try to 1300 A.D. D.C. Roberts. Wales M.A. 1939.

Kenilworth castle and priory. Edith N. Wells. Bir- 1537
mingham M.A. 1923.

A study of Plymouth. Margaret I. Lattimore. Exeter 1538
M.A. 1958.

The hundred of Leyland after the Conquest. F. Jackson. 1539
Liverpool M.A. 1913.

The history of Bromsgrove in the medieval and early 1540
Tudor period, 1066-1533. R.M. Haines. Durham M.A. 1948.

The manor of Spofforth. E.J. Fisher. Leeds M.A. 1933. 1541

Bradford dale: the history and descent of some manors 1542
in the neighbourhood of Bradford. W. Robertshaw. Leeds
M.A. 1935.

The early history of the manor and parish of Bradford, 1543
W. Riding, Yorks. H.I. Judson. London M.A. 1933.

The history of the parish of Phillack. J.H. Rowe. 1544
Leeds M.A. 1931.

A survey of the history of Bosley. R.W. Lloyd-Jones. 1545
Liverpool M.A. 1943.

The history of the manor of Islip from 1066 until the 1546
Dissolution. Barbara F. Harvey. Oxford B.Litt. 1953.

The manor of Headington. Evangeline Evans. Oxford 1547
B.Litt. 1927.

The honor of Leicester: a study in descent and admin- 1548
istration, with special reference to the Leicestershire fees
of the honor. L. Fox. Manchester M.A. 1938.

The economic organisation of the medieval borough, with 1549
special reference to Leicester and its guild merchants. E.H.
Smith. Wales M.A. 1912.

Early rentals and charters relating to the borough of 1550
Canterbury. W.G. Urry. London Ph.D. 1956.

A history of the manors of Witney and Adderbury from 1551
the 13th to the 16th century. Mrs. Patricia G.M. Hyde.
Oxford B.Litt. 1955.

The history of Cuxham (co. Oxon.) with special refer- 1552
ence to social and economic conditions during the middle ages.
P.D.A. Harvey. Oxford D.Phil. 1960.

The medieval borough of Henley. (1) Its history. (2) 1553
Its constitution. Phyllis M. Briers. Oxford B.Litt. 1935.

The economic and social structure of the parishes of 1554
Bromley, Hackney, Stepney and Whitechapel from the 13th to
the 16th century. K.G.T. McDonnell. London Ph.D. 1958.

An edition of the Lincolnshire final concords for the 1555
reign of John, 1199-1216. Margaret S. Rogers. Reading M.A.
1951.

Feet of fines of Warwickshire and Leicestershire for 1556
the reign of King John, 1199-1214. Margaret O. Harris.
Reading M.A. 1956.

1557   An edition of the feet of fines of the reign of John. G.M.D. Croton. Reading M.A. 1955.

1558   Alciston manor, Sussex, in the later middle ages. Judith Wooldridge. Bristol M.A. 1965.

1559   The manors of Great and Little Wymondley in the later middle ages. F.B. Stitt. Oxford B.Litt. 1951.

1560   The earls and earldom of Chester to 1254. A.B. Targett. Wales M.A. 1913.

1561   The chancery of the Anglo-Norman earls of Chester. A.P. Duggan. Liverpool M.A. 1951.

1562   A study of the earldom of Hereford in the 12th century, with an appendix of illustrative documents. D.G. Walker. Oxford D.Phil. 1954.

1563   A study of the administration of the Channel Islands in the 13th and early 14th centuries based mainly upon the assize rolls and other unprinted documents. J.H. Le Patourel. Oxford D.Phil. 1934.

1564   North Lancashire, its economic condition in the 13th and 14th centuries. H. Horton. Manchester M.A. 1949.

1565   Social and constitutional developments in 13th-century London: a study in social tendency. G.A. Williams. Wales M.A. 1952.

1566   London, 1216-1337: a study of the main factors in the social and constitutional development of the city. G.A. Williams. London Ph.D. 1960.

1567   The correspondence of the City of London, 1298-1370. G.F. Chapple. London Ph.D. 1938.

1568   Burgage tenure in medieval Bristol. E.W.W. Veale. London LL.D. 1931.

1569   The administration of Cheshire in the 13th and early 14th century. Margaret Tout. Manchester M.A. 1919.

1570   Contributions to the history of the earldom and county of Chester, 1237-1399, historical, topographical and administrative, with a study of the household of Edward the Black Prince and its relations with Cheshire. Mrs. Margaret Sharp, née Tout. Manchester Ph.D. 1925.

1571   The economic and social history of Cheshire in the reign of the three Edwards. H.J. Hewitt. London Ph.D. 1926.

1572   The administration of the counties of Norfolk and Suffolk in the reign of Henry IV. G.E. Morey. London M.A. 1941.

1573   The honour of Tutbury in the 14th and 15th centuries. Jean R. Birrell. Birmingham M.A. 1962.

1574   The court rolls of Alrewas in the 14th century. Mrs. Christine Kelly. Durham M.A. 1970.

1575   Some aspects of the economy of York in the later middle ages, 1300-1550. J.N. Bartlett. London Ph.D. 1958.

1576   Beverley Minster, government and society, 1381-1540. N. Heard. Hull Ph.D. 1962.

1577   The history of the borough of Great Yarmouth in the 14th century. Iris M. Nunn. Leeds M.A. 1931.

1578   Colchester and the countryside in the 14th century: a search for interdependence between urban and rural economy. R.H. Britnell. Cambridge Ph.D. 1970.

1579   The economic geography of Sussex during the 14th century, with special reference to the county's relations with lands across the sea. R.A. Pelham. Wales M.A. 1930.

1580   The social and economic history of Flixton in South Elmham, Suffolk, 1300-1600. J.M. Ridgard. Leicester M.A. 1970.

1581   A history of Clare, Suffolk, with special reference to its development as a borough during the middle ages, and to its importance as a centre of the woollen industry in the 15th, 16th and 17th centuries. Gladys A. Thornton. London Ph.D. 1927.

The decay of the manorial system during the first half   1582
of the 15th century, with special reference to manorial jurisdiction and to the decline of villeinage as exemplified in the
records of twenty-six manors in the counties of Berks., Hants
and Wilts. Lucy C. Latham. London M.A. 1928.
     King's Lynn, 1400-1600: developments in civic govern-   1583
ment. E.C. Glover. London M.Phil. 1970.
     The government of London and its relations with the   1584
Crown, 1400-50. Mrs. Caroline M. Barron. London Ph.D. 1970.
     Some aspects of parish life in the City of London from   1585
1429 to 1529. E.G. Ashby. London M.A. 1950.
     Personnel for the administration of Cambridgeshire in   1586
the reign of Henry VI. A.F. Bottomley. London M.A. 1952.
     The lordship of Middleham, especially in Yorkish and   1587
early Tudor times. Mrs. Gladys M. Coles. Liverpool M.A.
1961.
     The topography of medieval Oxford. D.A.M. Sturdy. Ox- 1588
ford B.Litt. 1965.
     The assessionable manors of the duchy of Cornwall in   1589
the later middle ages. M.J.J.R. Hatcher. London Ph.D. 1967.

                 M E D I E V A L   W A L E S

     The archaeology of east central Wales. H.N. Jerman.   1590
Wales M.A. 1934.
     The Anglo-Celtic frontier in the lowlands and uplands   1591
of the Dee basin of north-east Wales. J.I. Thomas. Liver-
pool M.A. 1964.
     Beliefs and practices of the Celtic Church in Britain. 1592
L. Hardinge. London Ph.D. 1964.
     Ritual background of Celtic heroes and saints - a study 1593
of some of the survivals of pagan elements in early Celtic
Christianity. A.D. Rees. Wales M.A. 1937.
     Norse relations with Wales. B.G. Charles. Wales M.A.   1594
1932.
     The characteristics of the early Christian church in   1595
Wales considered especially in relation to the churches in
Ireland and in Gaul. E. Davies. Oxford B.Litt. 1934.
     The older churches of North Wales. J.G. Hetherington. 1596
Leeds M.A. 1929.
     The history of the Eisteddfod. Elizabeth J. Lloyd.   1597
Wales M.A. 1913.
     Transport and communication in medieval Wales. W.H.   1598
Waters. Wales M.A. 1923.
     A contribution to the study of early invasions of   1599
Wales. H. Higgins. Liverpool M.A. 1921.
     The Norman conquests in Wales up to 1100 A.D.   J.W.   1600
Wilkinson. Wales M.A. 1901.
     Monasticism in South Wales after the Norman Conquest.   1601
F.G. Cowley. Wales Ph.D. 1965.
     The medieval pottery of the central Welsh border from   1602
the Conquest to 1400. P.A. Barker. Leicester M.A. 1966.
     Social classes in the Welsh border region in the early 1603
Norman period. T.A. Gwynne. Nottingham M.A. 1969.
     The family of Mortimer. B.P. Evans. Wales Ph.D. 1934. 1604
     The history of the Nannau family (Merionethshire) to   1605
1623. B.R. Parry. Wales M.A. 1958.
     Studies in the social and agrarian history of medieval 1606
and early modern Pembrokeshire. B.E. Howells. Wales M.A.
1956.
     The medieval boroughs of Pembrokeshire. P.G. Sudbury. 1607
Wales M.A. 1947.
     The history of the town and castle of Pembroke to 1603. 1608
E.P. Jones. Wales M.A. 1905.

1609 The castle and borough of Pembroke during the middle ages. H. Rees. Wales M.A. 1927.

1610 The lordship of Brecon, 1066-1325. W. Rees. Wales M.A. 1914.

1611 The history of the town, lordship and castle of Builth, from the 11th to the 16th centuries. G. Wozencroft. Wales M.A. 1919.

1612 History of the town and castle of Cardigan. G. Owen. Wales M.A. 1907.

1613 The Norman lordship of Glamorgan, its settlement and early organisation to the death of Gilbert de Clare, 1314. G. Nesta Jones. Wales M.A. 1921.

1614 The lordship of Glamorgan: a study in Marcher government. J.B. Smith. Wales M.A. 1957.

1615 The ecclesiastical history of Glamorgan during the middle ages, up to 1188, with special reference to the period A.D. 1056 to 1188. L.C. Simons. Wales M.A. 1914.

1616 The history of the borough of Kenfig, to 1485. J.H. Lewis. Wales M.A. 1922.

1617 The medieval lordship of Montgomery. Dora Ward. Wales M.A. 1924.

1618 The castle and town of Welshpool during the 12th and 13th centuries. Alicia G. Jones. Wales M.A. 1911.

1619 The boroughs of Radnor to the Act of Union and beyond. R.M. Morgan. Wales M.A. 1911.

1620 The early charter memoranda of the Book of Llandaff. Wendy E. Davies. London Ph.D. 1970.

1621 Llyfr Coch Asaph: a textual and historical study. O.E. Jones. Wales M.A. 1968.

1622 A critical study of the Latin texts of the Welsh laws. H.D. Emanuel. Wales Ph.D. 1960.

1623 Hywel Dda, together with an outline of the origins, affinities and history of the laws called after his name. W.H. Harris. Oxford B.Litt. 1912.

1624 A critical edition of the text of the Gwynedd (or Venedotian) code of medieval Welsh law. A.I.R. Wiliam. Oxford D.Phil. 1952.

1625 The policy of Powys in the 12th and 13th centuries. F.L. Rees. Wales M.A. 1911.

1626 The early history of Flintshire, with special reference to the foundation of the diocese of St. Asaph. J.F. Sharp. Liverpool M.A. 1924.

1627 The history of Valle Crucis abbey, Denbighshire. E.J. Fisher. Liverpool M.A. 1929.

1628 Pre-Edwardian castles in North Wales. H. Owen. Liverpool M.A. 1914.

1629 The influence of topographical conditions on the English campaigns in Wales in the 12th and 13th centuries. D.W. Rees. Wales M.A. 1923.

1630 The military geography of Gwynedd in the 13th century. G.R.J. Jones. Wales M.A. 1949.

1631 The cymwds of Gwynedd, prior to the Edwardian conquest of Wales. G.L. Jones. Wales M.A. 1919.

1632 The early history of Newcastle Emlyn, to include a study of the data relating to castle, town and lordship down to the Act of Union, 1536. T.J. James. Wales M.A. 1913.

1633 The medieval borough of Beaumaris and the commote of Dindaethwy, 1200-1600. C.M. Evans. Wales M.A. 1949.

1634 The history of the town and castle of Carmarthen to 1603. D.M. Roberts. Wales M.A. 1908.

1635 The development of the Penrhyn estate up to 1431. J.R. Jones. Wales M.A. 1955.

1636 Giraldus Cambrensis, De Invectionibus, transcribed from the Vatican manuscript and edited with an historical introduction. W.S. Davies. Wales M.A. 1921.

1637 Types of social life illustrated by the writings of Gerald of Wales. Dorothy Humphreys. Oxford B.Litt. 1936.

The life of St. David by Giraldus Cambrensis. T.B.   1638
Jones. Wales M.A. 1934.

The Friars in Wales. Ruth C. Easterling. Wales M.A.   1639
1913.

A study of Anglo-Welsh political relations, with   1640
special reference to constitutional matters, 1218-82. A.J.
Roderick. Wales M.A. 1935.

The Book of Aneirin. I. Williams. Wales M.A. 1907.   1641

The Welsh Church under Edward I. Elizabeth Thomas.   1642
Wales M.A. 1912.

The bishops and chapter of St. David's, c.1280-1407.   1643
W. Greenway. Cambridge M.Litt. 1959.

The growth and development of the municipal element in   1644
the principality of North Wales up to the close of the 14th
century. E.A. Lewis. Wales M.A. 1902.

The lordship and castle of Chirk, 1282-1660. Mary   1645
Jones. Wales M.A. 1920.

The barons of Edeyrnion, 1282-1485: a study of tenure   1646
by Welsh barony, with special reference to Edeyrnion. A.D.
Carr. Wales M.A. 1963.

The lordship of Denbigh, 1282-1425. D.H. Owen. Wales   1647
Ph.D. 1967.

Flint: the castle and town in the 13th and 14th cent-   1648
uries. E.O. Parry. Wales M.A. 1927.

The castle, town, and lordship of Kidwelly to 1300 A.D.   1649
A.J. Richard. Wales M.A. 1912.

The Edwardian settlement of Wales, 1284-1307. J.G.   1650
Edwards. Manchester M.A. 1915.

The Edwardian settlement of North Wales. W.H. Waters.   1651
Cambridge M.Litt. 1925/6.

Wales and the Marches in the reign of Edward II, with   1652
special reference to Glamorgan and the revolt of Llewelyn
Bren. T.A. Dyke. Wales M.A. 1912.

The history of Wales during the reign of Edward II,   1653
1307-27. J. Conway Davies. Wales M.A. 1914.

The principality of Wales under Edward the Black   1654
Prince. D.L. Evans. Oxford B.Litt. 1930.

The Lancaster and Bohun lordships in Wales in the 14th   1655
and early 15th centuries. R.R. Davies. Oxford D.Phil. 1965.

The available data for the Black Death in Wales. Wini-   1656
fred S. Williams. Wales M.A. 1920.

The religious and social condition of Wales at the   1657
outbreak of the Glyndwr movement, with special reference to
the attitude of the clergy, both regular and secular, to the
movement. J.R. Gabriel. Wales M.A. 1906.

The Welsh Church and Welsh politics in the war of Owen   1658
Glyndwr. J.T. Davies. Liverpool M.A. 1920.

Royal government in the southern counties of the   1659
principality of Wales, 1422-85. R.A. Griffiths. Bristol
Ph.D. 1962.

The rise and fall of the house of Dinefwr (the Rhys   1660
family), 1430-1530. J.M. Lloyd. Wales M.A. 1963.

Welsh politics from Mortimer's Cross to Bosworth Field.   1661
W.G. Jones. Liverpool M.A. 1908.

The bardic order in the 15th century. T.W.L. Davies.   1662
Wales M.A. 1910.

MEDIEVAL SCOTLAND

A new survey of contacts between Celtic Scotland and   1663
pre-Viking Northumbria (c.500-c.850). D.P. Kirby. Durham
Ph.D. 1962.

A critical examination of some of the sources for the   1664
history of the Picts from A.D. 550 to A.D. 850. Mrs. Isabel
B. Henderson. Cambridge Ph.D. 1962.

1665   Scoto-Celtic architecture - its place among the styles.
C. Sinclair. Glasgow Ph.D. 1932.

1666   A critical edition of the Senchus Fer nAlban, with an
assessment of its historical value. J.W.M. Bannerman. Cambridge Ph.D. 1964.

1667   The burgh of the Canongate and its court. A.H. Anderson. Edinburgh Ph.D. 1949.

1668   Scottish burghs: some aspects of their origins, development and plan. K. Alauddin. Glasgow B.Litt. 1969.

1669   The office of sheriff in Scotland; its origin and early
development. C.A. Malcolm. Edinburgh Ph.D. 1922.

1670   Queen Margaret and the influence she exerted on the
Celtic Church in Scotland. T.R. Barnett. Edinburgh Ph.D.
1925.

1671   Scottish monasticism: its relations with the Crown and
the church to the year 1378. D.E. Easson. St. Andrews Ph.D.
1928.

1672   The historical geography of Strathmore and its highland
boundary zone from A.D. 1100 to A.D. 1603. J. Gilbert.
Edinburgh Ph.D. 1954.

1673   Scottish royal ecclesiastical policy, 1107-1214, with
special reference to foreign influence in the spread of the
monastic orders and the personnel of the episcopate in England. G.W.S. Barrow. Oxford B.Litt. 1950.

1674   The De Tribus Processionibus of Richard St. Victor: a
critical text with introduction. W.J. Tulloch. Liverpool
M.A. 1945.

1675   Adam of Dryburgh. J.B.P. Bulloch. Edinburgh Ph.D. 1955.

1676   The sources of the Aberdeen breviary. J.D. Galbraith.
Aberdeen M.Litt. 1970.

1677   History of the clan Macrae. A. Macrae. London M.A.
1905.

1678   Strategy and tactics in medieval Scotland. J.D. Forbes.
Edinburgh Ph.D. 1927.

1679   The expansion of the English language in Scotland. L.W.
Sharp. Cambridge Ph.D. 1926/7.

1680   Feudal tenures in Scotland in the 12th and 13th centuries. Mrs. Isabel A. Durack. Edinburgh Ph.D. 1953.

1681   An examination of the grants of land made to the Scottish
Church in the 12th and 13th centuries, with special reference
to secular services. T. Davidson. Edinburgh Ph.D. 1930.

1682   The diocese of Glasgow in the 12th and 13th centuries.
With an edition of the bishops' acta (c.1140-1258). F.N.
Shead. Glasgow B.Litt. 1966.

1683   Ecclesiastical patronage in the medieval period, with
special reference to parochial benefices in Scotland. G.P.
Innes. Glasgow Ph.D. 1960.

1684   Appropriation of parish churches in medieval Scotland.
I.B. Cowan. Edinburgh Ph.D. 1961.

1685   An Anglo-Scottish baron of the 13th century: the acts
of Roger de Quincy, earl of Winchester and constable of Scotland. G.G. Simpson. Edinburgh Ph.D. 1966.

1686   The relations between England and Scotland during the
minority of Alexander III and during the Barons' Wars. W.A.
Cane. Manchester M.A. 1923.

1687   The organisation of the English occupation in Scotland,
1296-1461. D.W.H. Marshall. Oxford B.Litt. 1926.

1688   Death practices and burial rites in Scotland from the
later medieval period to 1780, with particular reference to
the influence of theology. R.S. Fredericks. Edinburgh Ph.D.
1967.

1689   The defence of the north-western border against the
Scots during the first half of the 14th century. T. Wood.
Manchester M.A. 1937.

1690   The Scottish wars of Edward III, 1327-35. R.G. Nicholson. Oxford D.Phil. 1961.

Scotsmen at universities between 1340 and 1410 and   1691
their subsequent careers: a study of the contribution of
graduates to the public life of their country. D.E.R. Watt.
Oxford D.Phil. 1957.
        The medieval universities of Scotland, 1410-1560. J.   1692
Durkan. Edinburgh Ph.D. 1959.
        Scotland and the Wars of the Roses, 1435-85. C. Mac-   1693
rae. Oxford D.Phil. 1939.
        The exchequer and Crown revenue of Scotland, 1437-1542. 1694
A.L. Murray. Edinburgh Ph.D. 1961.
        The economic administration of Coupar Angus abbey,   1695
1440-1560. J.L. Morgan. Glasgow Ph.D. 1929.
        James Kennedy, bishop of St. Andrews. Anne I. Cameron. 1696
Edinburgh Ph.D. 1924.
        The office of parish clerk in the Scottish Church be-   1697
tween 1450 and 1560. D.A. McKay. London Ph.D. (Ext.) 1960.
        The rise of a Scottish navy, 1460-1513. F.W. Robert-   1698
son. Edinburgh Ph.D. 1933/4.
        James III: a political study (1466-88). N.A.T. Mac-   1699
Dougall. Glasgow Ph.D. 1968.

                M E D I E V A L   I R E L A N D

        Ships and shipping in ancient and medieval Ireland.   1700
J.E. O'Neill. Belfast M.A. 1934.
        A descriptive and bibliographical list of Irish figure   1701
sculptures of the early Christian period, with a critical
assessment of their significance. E.H.L. Sexton. Oxford
B.Litt. 1940.
        S. Finnian of Clonard. Kathleen W. Hughes. London   1702
Ph.D. 1951.
        St. Columban. G.S.M. Walker. St. Andrews Ph.D.   1703
1952/3.
        The Fís Adamnám: a comparative study. J.J. Colwell.   1704
Edinburgh Ph.D. 1952.
        The Saxon element in early Irish history. Anne M.   1705
Scarre. Liverpool M.A. 1908.
        The decline of the native Irish monasticism from the   1706
9th to the 12th centuries. R.B. Knox. Belfast M.A. 1944.
        The Irish druids. Christine Standing. Leeds M.A.   1707
1916.
        The contacts between Britain and Ireland in the century 1708
preceding the Anglo-Norman invasion of Ireland. Brigid A.
Fitzgerald. Keele M.A. 1966.
        The Cistercians in Ireland and their economy, 1142-   1709
1541. S.A. Geraldine Carville. Belfast M.A. 1969.
        A history of Waterford: its life and government from   1710
1150 to 1800. F.C. Morris. Wales M.A. 1915.
        A study of the English dialects of Ireland, 1172-1800.   1711
P.J. Irwin. London Ph.D. 1935.
        An investigation into the history of the use of English 1712
in Ireland in medieval times, with special reference to the
nature of the dialects and the influence of standard English.
J.J. Hogan. Oxford B.Litt. 1926.
        The medieval Irish parliament. Helen Scott. London   1713
M.A. 1914.
        The De Burgh earls of Ulster. Olga F. Lamont. Belfast 1714
M.A. 1947.
        English law and its administration in Ireland c.1290 to 1715
c.1324, with special reference to the court of the justiciar.
G.J. Hand. Oxford D.Phil. 1960.
        An essay introductory to the De Pauperie Salvatoris of   1716
Richard Fitzralph, archbishop of Armagh, with transcript of
books V, VI, VII of the De Pauperie Salvatoris. Helen C.
Hughes. Manchester Ph.D. 1929.

1717   The council in Ireland, 1399-1452. Margaret C. Griffith. Oxford B.Litt. 1935.

1718   A study in the structure and history of the registers of Archbishops Prene and Mey, together with an edition of the register of Mey and a calendar of the register of Prene. W.G.H. Quigley and E.F.D. Roberts. Belfast Ph.D. 1955.

W O R L D

1719   The Calvinist tradition in education in France, Scotland and New England during the 16th and 17th centuries. I. Cassidy. Belfast Ph.D. 1966.

1720   A study in the history of the theory of value, production and distribution from 1650 to 1776. P.D. Groenewegen. London Ph.D. 1965.

1721   Studies in the theory of money, 1690-1776. D.W. Vickers. London Ph.D. 1956.

1722   History of the theory of international gold movements. F.I. Shaffner. Oxford B.Litt. 1928.

1723   Systems of limitation of currency. G.R. Elvey. Oxford B.Litt. 1926.

1724   Studies in the history of dyeing. C. Ross. London Ph.D. 1946.

1725   Dyeing and dyestuffs, 1750-1914. C.M. Mellor. Leeds M.A. 1963.

1726   The doctrine of continuous voyage, 1756-1815. O.H. Mootham. London M.Sc. 1926.

1727   An historical survey of mohair manufacture. Mrs. Milda Villers. Leeds M.A. 1960.

1728   Some studies in the history of soap manufacture. F.W. Gibbs. London M.Sc. 1937.

1729   Population theories and the interpretation of 19th- and 20th-century population movements. S.H. Coontz. London Ph.D. 1954.

1730   The development of world Methodism in the 19th and 20th centuries. J.W. Harris. Manchester M.A. 1961.

1731   The import of capital. R. Wilson. Oxford D.Phil. 1929/30.

1732   Wool prices, 1870-1950. B.P. Philpott. Leeds M.A. 1954.

1733   International trade in apparel wools, 1914-48. Helena V. Klein. London M.Sc. 1950.

1734   The part the press played: the influence of the press upon international relationships during the years 1896-1914. Mary Lewis. Birmingham M.A. 1930.

1735   Plans and protocols to end war. R.D. Roden. Edinburgh Ph.D. 1929.

1736   Effects of technological change on labour in selected sections of the iron and steel industries of Great Britain, the United States and Germany, 1901-39. Helen Gintz. London Ph.D. 1954.

1737   The developments of the grain trade in the 20th century, and their influence on the world wheat situation. A. Hayes. Oxford B.Litt. 1932.

1738   Pattern of world trade in coal, 1913-38. P. Chomchai. Oxford B.Litt. 1956.

1739   The origin and evolution of the Assembly of the League of Nations. P. Samuel. Wales M.A. 1935.

1740   The principles and policies of the Nine Power Treaty of 1922 in the light of subsequent developments. Yui Ming. Oxford D.Phil. 1941.

1741   The United States, the League and the Manchurian crisis. C. Chowdhury. London Ph.D. 1960.

1742   The Geneva treatment of the Manchurian and Abyssinian crises. Mong Ping Lee. London Ph.D. 1946.

The Dominions and the Italo-Abyssinian conflict. R.A. 1743
Williams. Wales M.A. 1951.

The attitude of the Dominions to organisation for 1744
international security and welfare, 1939-45. A.J. de B.
Forbes. Oxford D.Phil. 1954.

The historic-geographical significance of the Elbe- 1745
Saale frontier. M.F.C. Ward. London M.Phil. 1970.

Germany, the Soviet Union and world disarmament, 1926- 1746
33. Mrs. Pauline E. Helliar-Symons, née Lawrence. Wales
M.A. 1970.

The function of the permanent representative assembly 1747
in the pacific settlement of disputes; with special reference
to the development of the Assembly of the United Nations as
an organ of last resort. A. Bargman. London Ph.D. 1952.

M O D E R N   E U R O P E

GENERAL

The place of the olive in the economy of the Medi- 1748
terranean region. Kathleen de la Mare. Oxford B.Litt. 1930.

A geographical study of wheat and the wheat trade in 1749
Europe. Agatha Booker. Oxford B.Litt. 1929.

Climatic fluctuations in Europe in the late historical 1750
period. D.J. Schove. London M.Sc. (Ext.) 1953.

The development of the sundial between A.D. 1400 and 1751
1800. Kathleen Higgins. Oxford B.Sc. 1951.

Studies in the reputation and influence of the Abbot 1752
Joachim of Fiore, chiefly in the 15th and 16th centuries.
Marjorie E. Reeves. London Ph.D. 1932.

From analogy to experiment: the role of the analogy 1753
between the whole and the parts of nature in the development
of early modern thought (15th to 17th centuries). Mrs.
Dorothy M. Koenigsberger. Nottingham Ph.D. 1969.

The history of theories of painting in Italy and 1754
France, 1400-1700, with special reference to Poussin. A.F.
Blunt. Cambridge Ph.D. 1934/5.

The relation of the Eastern Church to the Western 1755
Churches from the 16th to the 18th century. T.P. Themelis.
Oxford B.Litt. 1907.

Issues dividing western Christendom on the doctrine of 1756
the church in the 16th and 17th centuries. R.H. Wilmer.
Oxford D.Phil. 1948.

Methods of political reasoning in the 16th and 17th 1757
centuries: the argument by correspondence and historical and
scientific empiricism. W.H. Greenleaf. London Ph.D. 1954.

The political theories of Martin Luther and Ulrich 1758
Zwingli: a study in contrasts. E.B. Moore. St. Andrews
Ph.D. 1965.

Religious controversies in the 16th century, their in- 1759
fluence in France and England. I. Georgević. Oxford B.Litt.
1918.

The problem of war to the religious thinker of the 16th 1760
century. R.F. Wright. London Ph.D. 1937.

The development of the 'just war' conception, 1761
especially since Grotius. G.D. Roos. Oxford B.Litt. 1936.

Public worship in 16th-century Calvinism. F.O. Reed. 1762
Oxford B.Litt. 1934.

The Anabaptist movement. R.J. Smithson. Glasgow Ph.D. 1763
1933.

Studies in the emergence and dissemination of the 1764
modern Jewish stereotype in western Europe. I. Shachar.
London Ph.D. 1967.

1765   Jewish medical ethics: a comparative and historical study of the Jewish religious attitude to medicine and its practice, with special reference to the 16th century. I. Jakobovits. London Ph.D. (Ext.) 1955.

1766   Cardinal Contarini at Regensburg: a study in Ecumenism, Catholicism and Curialism. P.C. Matheson. Edinburgh Ph.D. 1968.

1767   The Jesuits and the Council of Trent. G. Duckworth. Oxford B.Litt. 1939.

1768   The preliminary reduction of wind and pressure observations in north-west Europe, A.D. 1648-1955. D.J. Schove. London Ph.D. (Ext.) 1958.

1769   An historical and critical study of the Christian Unity movements since the peace of Westphalia. G.J. Slosser. London Ph.D. 1928.

1770   The Triple Alliance and the War of Devolution. Margaret O. Noël-Paton. London Ph.D. 1931.

1771   The history of enthusiasm as a factor in the religious and social problems of the 18th century. E.C. Walker. London Ph.D. 1930.

1772   The conception of history and progress in some writers of the European Enlightenment. R.V. Sampson. Oxford D.Phil. 1951.

1773   The maritime powers and the evolution of the war aims of the Grand Alliance, 1701-4. P.J. Welch. London M.A. 1940.

1774   The Great Peace: negotiations for the treaty of Utrecht, 1710-13. A.D. Maclachlan. Cambridge Ph.D. 1965.

1775   Privateering in the Seven Years War. D.N. Topley. Durham M.A. 1963.

1776   The peace of Paris of 1763. Zenab E. Rashed. Liverpool Ph.D. 1949.

1777   The relations between Great Britain and the papal states, 1792-1817. S.T. Leonard. Oxford D.Phil. 1968.

1778   The German policy of the pre-Fructidorian Directory. S.S. Biro. Oxford D.Phil. 1928/9.

1779   The economic history of the brush-making industry in England, France, Holland and the German-speaking countries up to the end of the 19th century. R.H. Kirby. London Ph.D. 1953.

1780   Municipal tribunals and international law: the development of international law by English and French courts in the 19th century. Dorothy B. McCown. London Ph.D. 1938.

1781   The politics of violence in the 19th century. G.L. Hearn. London Ph.D. 1954.

1782   Nationalist currents in 19th-century socialist doctrines. V.T.C.E.F. Egger. London Ph.D. 1949.

1783   Density of population in Europe, including special treatment of two countries about 1801 and 1861. J.P. Ryder. Manchester M.A. 1935.

1784   The social and economic background of attempts at a Concert of Europe from 1804 to 1825. H.G.A.V. Schenk. Oxford D.Phil. 1943.

1785   The Concert of Europe in German and British international theory, 1851-1914. C. Holbraad. Sussex D.Phil. 1967.

1786   The European Concert, June 1854 - July 1855. G.B. Henderson. Cambridge Ph.D. 1933/4.

1787   The Belgian and Polish revolutions of 1830 in international relations. J.A. Betley. Bristol M.A. 1954.

1788   Religion and the city, with reference to Bristol and Marseilles, 1830-80: a study in the comparative sociology of religion. R.M. Goodridge. London M.Phil. 1969.

1789   The educational work of the Congregation of the Assumption in Europe, 1839-1951. E.H. Whitaker. London M.A. 1952.

1790   A comparative study of secondary education in England and France in the 19th century. G.W.H. Cobby. London M.A. 1956.

The influence of 1848 on education. Olive W. Sinclair. 1791
London M.A. 1916.

Political economy and laissez faire, 1848-93. Joan E. 1792
Slater. London M.Sc. 1951.

The policy of Great Britain with reference to the con- 1793
tinental revolutions of 1848-9. C.F. Strong. London M.A.
1921.

The European Powers and the question of the Hungarian 1794
refugees of 1849. Y.T. Kurat. London Ph.D. 1958.

The Black Sea question during the Crimean War. I.F.D. 1795
Morrow. Cambridge Ph.D. 1926/7.

The genesis of the Crimean War. H.E. Howard. London 1796
M.A. 1932.

Napoleon III and Russia. A.S. Walker. Birmingham M.A. 1797
1917.

England and the First International 1864-72. H.J. 1798
Collins. Oxford D.Phil. 1959.

The German Social Democrats and the First Inter- 1799
national, 1864-72. R.P. Morgan. Cambridge Ph.D. 1958.

Anti-Semitism in Germany and Austria, 1867-1918. 1800
P.G.J. Pulzer. Cambridge Ph.D. 1960.

Aspects of a political theory of mass behaviour in the 1801
works of H. Taine, G. Le Bon and S. Freud, 1870-1930. J.S.
McClelland. Cambridge Ph.D. 1969.

Coal production and the growth of industry in the coal- 1802
fields of north-west Europe in the later 19th century. E.A.
Wrigley. Cambridge Ph.D. 1956/7.

Technical change, the labour force and education in the 1803
British and German iron and steel industries from 1860.
P.W. Musgrave. London Ph.D. 1964.

A study of the relationship between the diplomatic and 1804
commercial policies of France, Germany, Italy, Russia and
Austria-Hungary, 1871-1914. W. Koren. Oxford B.Litt. 1934.

European alliances and ententes, 1879-85: a study of 1805
contemporary British information. Agatha Ramm. London M.A.
1937.

The Russo-German Re-insurance Treaty, 1887-90. G. 1806
Lewinson. London Ph.D. 1953.

The financial aspect of the Franco-Russian alliance, 1807
1894-1914. Mrs. Olga Crisp. London Ph.D. 1954.

The Franco-Russian alliance, 1894-1904, with special 1808
reference to Great Britain. H.S. Robinson. London Ph.D.
1966.

The Franco-Italian rapprochement, 1898-1902. E.R. 1809
Lewis. Wales M.A. 1937.

British and continental labour policy: the political 1810
labour movement and labour legislation in England, France and
the Scandinavian countries, 1900-20. B.G. de Montgomery.
Oxford D.Phil. 1922.

The Anglo-French and Anglo-Belgian military and naval 1811
conversations, from the 'Entente' to the Great War. D.C.
Wadman. Wales M.A. 1939.

The British attitude to the Second Hague Conference - 1812
a study of newspaper opinion in England, 1906-7. R.J. Parry.
Wales M.A. 1937.

British policy and opinion and the Second Hague Con- 1813
ference. H.S.W. Corrigan. London M.A. 1934.

The Second International, 1914-23. Mrs. Hildamarie 1814
Meynell. Oxford B.Litt. 1956.

French policy and the Russian Revolution, 1917-24. 1815
A.C.E. Quainton. Oxford B.Litt. 1958.

Britain, Italy and the Versailles settlement, 1917-22. 1816
J.A. Stern. Cambridge Ph.D. 1970.

The organisation and procedure of the Paris Peace Con- 1817
ference of 1919. F.S. Marston. London Ph.D. 1943.

1818   Parliaments and the peace treaty: a comparative study of the reactions of the British and French parliaments to the treaty of peace of 1919. Bio Ling. London Ph.D. 1938.

1819   The new constitutions of Europe, a comparative study of post-war constitutions, with special reference to Germany, Poland, Czecho-Slovakia, Jugoslavia and the Baltic states. Agnes Headlam Morley. Oxford B.Litt. 1925/6.

1820   German relations with Italy, 1920-32, with special reference to the Danubian region. F.G. Stambrook. London Ph.D. 1960.

1821   Germany's political and military relations with Soviet Russia, 1918-26. G. Freund. Oxford D.Phil. 1955.

1822   German-Russian relations, 1921-34. L.E. Kochan. London Ph.D. 1951.

1823   The search for security (Autumn 1924 - Spring 1926): a study in English and French public opinion. S.R. Cottereau. Oxford B.Litt. 1952.

1824   Franco-Italian relations, 1935-40. P.C. Kent. London M.Sc. 1961.

1825   Franco-Polish relations, 1935-8: a study in policy and opinion. G. Sakwa. London M.Phil. 1968.

1826   The influence of Britain on French and Czechoslovakian policies in the Sudeten crisis, October 1937 to September 30, 1938. Françoise Domergue. London M.Sc. 1967.

1827   The planning of the bombing offensive in the Second World War and its contribution to German collapse. A.N. Frankland. Oxford D.Phil. 1951.

CENTRAL AND SOUTH-EAST EUROPE

1828   The Danube as an international waterway: an historical, political and economic survey. A. Puscariu. Birmingham Ph.D. 1928.

1829   Dubrovnik, 1358-1806: the vicissitudes of an east Adriatic port. F.W. Carter. London M.A. 1967.

1830   The history of the Serbian Church under Turkish rule. P. Yevtić. Oxford B.Litt. 1919.

1831   Stanislaw Orzechowski (1513-66). Halina-Maria Swiderska. Oxford D.Phil. 1960.

1832   A history of commercial relations between Scotland and Poland from 1550 to 1750. E.G. Macdonald. Strathclyde M.Litt. 1970.

1833   The origin, history and character of the pacta conventa of Henri de Valois, king of Poland. P. Skwarczynski. London Ph.D. 1953.

1834   The court of Rudolf II and the culture of Bohemia, 1576-1612. R.J.W. Evans. Cambridge Ph.D. 1968.

1835   The history of Jewish education in Central Europe from the beginning of the 17th century to 1782 (the edict of toleration issued by Joseph II of Austria). I. Fishman. London Ph.D. (Ext.) 1941.

1836   The Czech exiles and the Thirty Years War. W.V. Wallace. London M.A. 1953.

1837   The breakdown of the Anglo-Austrian alliance, 1748-56. Margaret B.B. Cobb. London M.A. 1935.

1838   The career of Prince Kaunitz, Austrian chancellor, 1753-92. M.G. Tucker. Bristol M.A. 1937.

1839   Anglo-Austrian relations during the reign of the Emperor Joseph II. H.F. Schwarz. Oxford B.Litt. 1931.

1840   The role of men of science in the Czech national revival movement, 1790-1848. J.G.F. Druce. London M.A. 1942.

1841   Fear of Jacobinism and the Jacobin trials in Austria. E. Wangermann. Oxford D.Phil. 1953.

1842   Anglo-Montenegrin relations, 1803-14. I. Avakumović. London M.A. 1954.

Metternich and the English government from the peace of 1843
Schönnbrün (14 October 1809) to Austria's final adherence to
the allies (10 August 1813). C.S.B. Buckland. Oxford B.Litt.
1930.
The origins of Anglo-Rumanian relations and the problem 1844
of the Russian protectorate in the principalities, 1821-59.
R.R.N.A.R. Florescu. Oxford B.Litt. 1951.
The colonisation of the Baragan (S.E. Romania), 1829- 1845
1964. T.R. McGlynn. London M.A. 1965.
Eduard von Bauernfeld and Austrian politics, 1830-50. 1846
J.D.A. Warren. Bristol M.Litt. 1970.
Polish society and the rebellion of November 1830. 1847
R.F. Leslie. London Ph.D. 1951.
Pro-Polish agitation in Great Britain, 1832-67. Mrs. 1848
Maria J.E. Copson-Niečko. London Ph.D. 1968.
Count Beust: a study in lost causes. J.F. Embling. 1849
Bristol M.A. 1934.
British opinion in regard to Austria (1848-67). Baron 1850
D.K.J. von Hirsch. Cambridge Ph.D. 1945.
British policy towards Serbia, 1837-9. S. Pavlowitch. 1851
London M.A. 1959.
The international relations of Serbia from 1848 to 1852
1860. Elizabeth F. Malcolm-Smith. Cambridge Ph.D. 1925/6.
The diplomatic relations between England and Serbia 1853
from the return of Milos to the death of Michael, 1859-67.
E. Frances Robinson. London M.A. 1925.
The antecedents of the 19th-century Hungarian state 1854
concept: an historical analysis. L.F. Péter. Oxford D.Phil.
1966.
Wielopolski's reforms and the January uprising. Irena 1855
M. Roseveare. London M.Phil. 1967.
British public opinion and the Polish insurrection of 1856
1863. K.S. Pasieka. Nottingham M.A. 1956.
Great Britain and the Polish question. W.F.F. Grace. 1857
Cambridge Ph.D. 1925.
Anglo-Hungarian economic relations, 1867-1914. Y. Don. 1858
London Ph.D. 1961.
Some political parties and party leaders among the 1859
German Austrians, 1867-1914. J.C.P. Warren. Sheffield M.A.
1958.
The relations between Great Britain and Austria-Hungary 1860
from the rising of Herzegovina to the conference of Constanti-
nople. C.L. Wayper. Cambridge Ph.D. 1949.
Serbia in international politics from the insurrection 1861
of Herzegovina (1875) to the Congress of Berlin (1878). M.D.
Stojanović. London Ph.D. 1930.
The Bulgarian atrocities agitation: a study in the 1862
politics of 'Virtuous Passion', 1876. R.T. Shannon. Cam-
bridge Ph.D. 1960.
British policy in south-east Europe, with particular 1863
reference to the European Danube Commission, 1878-1904. L.A.
Maher. Oxford D.Phil. 1968.
The German-Czech national conflict in Bohemia, 1879-93. 1864
H.G. Skilling. London Ph.D. 1940.
An analysis of Czech nationalism, 1880-1914, with 1865
special reference to T.G. Masaryk. J. Bradley. Cambridge
M.Litt. 1960.
The oil industry in Roumania, 1895-1948: a study in the 1866
relationship between the Roumanian state and private capital.
M.G. Pearton. London Ph.D. 1966.
The emergence of the Macedonian problem and relations 1867
between the Balkan states and the Great Powers, 1897-1903.
Mrs. Dorothy B. Goodman. London Ph.D. 1955.
Great Britain and the Macedonian question, 1903-8. 1868
Mrs. May A. Harben. London M.Sc. 1963.
The diplomatic relations between Great Britain and 1869
Austria-Hungary, 1906-12. F.R. Bridge. London Ph.D. 1966.

1870   Count Aehrenthal: a study in the foreign policy of Austria-Hungary, 1906-12. C. Petherick. Bristol M.A. 1936.

1871   Parliamentary government in Habsburg Austria with particular reference to the electoral reform of 1907 and to the parliamentary history of the years 1907-14. J. Clompus. Cambridge Ph.D. 1963.

1872   The Friedjung and Vasic trials in the light of the Austrian diplomatic documents, 1909-11. T.V. Gjurgjevic. Oxford D.Phil. 1956.

1873   The economic, military and political background to the entry of Greece into the Balkan Wars. G.S. Georghallides. Cambridge Ph.D. 1968.

1874   The policy of the Habsburg monarchy towards the Bohemian question, 1913-18. F.B.M. Fowkes. London Ph.D. 1967.

1875   British attitudes towards the Czechoslovak problem, 1914-38, with particular reference to the years 1914-29. M. Le Guillou. Hull M.A. 1963.

1876   The Habsburg monarchy in British policy, 1914-18. W.B. Fest. Oxford D.Phil. 1970.

1877   British opinion about the dissolution of the Habsburg monarchy and independence for the Czechs and Slovaks, 1914-18. H.H. Hanak. London M.A. 1958.

1878   The Czechs and the Habsburg monarchy, 1914-18. Z.A.B. Zeman. Oxford D.Phil. 1956.

1879   Monetary reconstruction in Czechoslovakia. S. Konovaloff. Oxford B.Litt. 1927.

1880   The origin and development of the Communist party of Czechoslovakia (until 1938). M.P. Mabey. Oxford D.Phil. 1955.

1881   A history of the Communist party of Bulgaria to 1935. J.A. Rothschild. Oxford D.Phil. 1955.

1882   History of the Communist party of Yugoslavia - an interim study. I. Avakumović. Oxford D.Phil. 1958.

1883   Political aspects of the agrarian problem in Roumania, 1918-45. H.L. Roberts. Oxford D.Phil. 1948.

1884   Relations between Yugoslavia and Bulgaria, 1918-41. D. Shepherd. Durham M.A. 1969.

1885   The struggle between Bolshevism and social democracy in Austria, 1918-20. R.A. Hine. Sussex M.Phil. 1969.

1886   Foreign trade of Poland between 1918 and 1939, with special reference to the trade with Britain. S. Florecki. Edinburgh Ph.D. 1944.

1887   Polish-Ukrainian relations, 1919-39. Z. Sliwowski. Oxford B.Litt. 1947.

1888   The problem of Austria at the Peace Conference, 1919. K.R. Stadler. London M.A. (Ext.) 1952.

1889   Britain and the Polish settlement 1919. F.R. Bryant. Oxford D.Phil. 1969.

1890   British policy and the Polish question at the Paris Peace Conference. P. Schofield. Kent M.A. 1969.

1891   Pilsudski and parliament: the crisis of constitutional government in Poland, 1922-31. A.B. Polonsky. Oxford D.Phil. 1968.

1892   Germany, Austria, and the Anschluss question, 1929 to 1938. J.D.W. Gehl. Oxford D.Phil. 1960.

1893   The assassination of King Alexander of Yugoslavia in 1934, and the political background of the crime. G. Cserenyey. London Ph.D. 1954.

1894   Austrian resistance to German rule and the development of Austrian national aspirations, 1938-45. K.R. Stadler. Nottingham Ph.D. 1970.

1895   The Balkans, the Great Powers and the European War, 1939-40. F.O. Marzari. London Ph.D. 1966.

The French invasions of England from the 12th century 1896
to the 19th (1101-1860). A.R. Rhys-Pryce. Belfast M.A.
1928.

Histoire générale de la ville de Chauny (Aisne) de sa 1897
fondation au commencement de la Troisième République. R.S.
Clegg. Leeds M.A. 1939.

The passing of the middle age and the advent of the 1898
Renaissance in French art. G.N. Kates. Oxford D.Phil. 1930.

The constitutional history of the French Church, 1438- 1899
1682, with special reference to the relations of church and
state. F. Streatfeild. Oxford D.Phil. 1921.

The movements of gold and silver money in the economic 1900
life of France, 1493-1660. F.C. Spooner. Cambridge Ph.D.
1953.

Francis Lambert of Avignon (1487-1530): a study in 1901
Reformation origins. R.L. Winters. Edinburgh Ph.D. 1935/6.

The Constable de Bourbon. F.J. Weaver. London M.A. 1902
1906.

The press of Robert Estienne, 1526-50: a historical 1903
study. A. Elizabeth Tyler. Oxford D.Phil. 1949.

André Thévet: his work as a geographer. Rachel E. 1904
Fowler. Oxford B.Litt. 1930.

Sixteenth-century ideas on the education of women in 1905
France. Margaret L.T. Enthoven. Oxford B.Litt. 1959.

Guillaume Rondelet and his circle. Mrs. Ruth G. Lewis, 1906
née Morton. Oxford D.Phil. 1968.

Some Cambridge contacts with France during Tudor and 1907
early Stuart times. T.S. Wyatt. Cambridge M.Litt. 1937/8.

The writings of Florens Wilson in relation to evangel- 1908
ical humanism. M.P.D. Baker-Smith. Cambridge Ph.D. 1970.

Some 16th-century French artists having connections 1909
with Scotland: the Quesnel family and Jehan Decourt. Sheila
M. Percival. Edinburgh Ph.D. 1962.

The diplomatic relations between England and France 1910
during the years 1558 to 1564. Millicent Booth. London M.A.
1933.

The secretaries of state in the age of Catherine de 1911
Medici. Nicola M. Sutherland. London Ph.D. 1958.

The political theory of the Huguenots from the massacre 1912
of St. Bartholomew to the publication of the Vindiciae contra
Tyrannos (1579). R.N.C. Hunt. Oxford B.Litt. 1925.

The duc de Mercoeur and the structure of the League in 1913
Brittany. B. Taylor. Oxford B.Litt. 1968.

Relations between England and France, 1589-1603. Elsie 1914
M. Griffiths. Birmingham M.A. 1921.

The fall of La Rochelle and the revival of the French 1915
monarchy. D. Parker. Liverpool Ph.D. 1968.

Sully and the development of a national administration 1916
in France, 1598-1610. D.J. Buisseret. Cambridge Ph.D. 1961.

Sully - l'homme et son oeuvre d'après Les économies 1917
royales. Elsie Westall. Liverpool M.A. 1947.

Religious toleration in the conflict of ideas in 17th- 1918
century France. W.J. Stankiewicz. London Ph.D. 1952.

The contribution to 17th-century French culture of the 1919
members of the Order of Minims. P.J.S. Whitmore. London
Ph.D. 1964.

Edmond Richer and the revival of Gallicanism, 1600-30. 1920
D.O. Soper. London Ph.D. 1929.

The embassy of Sir Thomas Edmondes in Paris, 1610-17. 1921
Ann Le Vin. Oxford B.Litt. 1965.

The assistance of the poor in Paris and in the north- 1922
eastern French provinces, 1614-60, with special reference to
the letters of S. Vincent de Paul. Elizabeth Archer. London
Ph.D. 1936.

1923 Buckingham's influence on England's policy with regard to France (from October 1623). Ella S. Goitein. London M.A. 1926.

1924 The English Republic and the Fronde: diplomacy, sea-war and intervention in Anglo-French relations, 1648-53. H.J. Smith. Oxford B.Litt. 1958.

1925 The financial administration of the French monarchy, 1653-61. J. Dent. London Ph.D. 1965.

1926 Cromwell and Mazarin, 1656 to 1658: an account of the Anglo-French alliance leading to the conquest of Dunkirk. J.A. Williamson. London M.A. 1909.

1927 The influence of Hobbes and Locke in the shaping of the concept of sovereignty in French political thought. I.M. Wilson. Oxford D.Phil. 1969.

1928 The relations between England and France during the Great Rebellion: the Civil War. Dorothy A. Bigby. London M.A. 1912.

1929 The problem of Anglo-French commercial rivalry in the reign of Charles II. Margaret A. Priestley. Oxford B.Litt. 1949.

1930 The commercial relations between England and France from 1660 to 1714. Ann Hambrook. London M.Sc. 1928.

1931 The aristocratic opposition to monarchical absolutism in French political thought during the reigns of Louis XIV and Louis XV. V.J. Buranelli. Cambridge Ph.D. 1951.

1932 The political theory of Louis XIV. P.W. Fox. London Ph.D. 1959.

1933 The machinery of repression under Louis XIV and its limitations, with special reference to the repression of the revolt of the Camisards. Esther J. Heap. London Ph.D. (Ext.) 1962.

1934 The French Church and the monarchy in the reign of Louis XIV: an administrative study. Mrs. Cynthia A. Dent, née Goulden. London Ph.D. 1967.

1935 The role of the higher aristocracy in France under Louis XIV, with special reference to the 'Faction of the Duke of Burgundy' and the provincial governors. R.C. Mettam. Cambridge Ph.D. 1967.

1936 Jean-Baptiste Colbert, marquis de Torcy. Ethel Allerton. Leeds M.A. 1932.

1937 The Oratory in France under Abel Louis de Sainte-Marthe, 1672-96. H.G. Judge. London Ph.D. 1959.

1938 Deistic thought in France, 1675-1745. C.J. Betts. Oxford D.Phil. 1966.

1939 A critical examination of Bossuet's attitude on the question of the Gallican Church. V.A.A. Barry. Oxford B.Litt. 1920.

1940 Leclerc et la république des lettres. Annie M. Barnes. Oxford D.Phil. 1935.

1941 Madame de Maintenon. Adeline Crutchley. Birmingham M.A. 1912.

1942 Madame de Maintenon. R.H.D.G. Byrne. Leeds M.A. 1915.

1943 Madame de Maintenon and St. Cyr. H.C. Barnard. London M.A. 1928.

1944 The history of free trade in France during the 18th and 19th century, with special reference to the individual thinkers. Marjorie M. Collinson. Birmingham M.Com. 1944.

1945 The movement for internal free trade in France during the 18th century. J.F. Bosher. London Ph.D. 1957.

1946 Development and evolution of the educational theory and practice of John Baptist de la Salle in the Congregation of the Brothers of the Christian Schools, in France, in the 18th and 19th centuries. W. Moran. London Ph.D. (Ext.) 1966.

1947 A social and economic study of the town of Vannes and its region during the 18th century. T.J.A. Le Goff. London Ph.D. 1970.

History of trade relations between Bordeaux and Britain 1948
in the 18th century, with special reference to the wine and
spirit trade. Annie E. Roberts. Wales M.A. 1926.

Town administration in France in the 18th century, with 1949
special reference to a group of towns in the <u>département de
l'Yonne</u>. Nora C. Temple. London Ph.D. 1959.

The administrative <u>noblesse</u> of France during the 18th 1950
century, with special reference to the <u>intendants</u> of the
<u>Généralités</u>. G.J. de C. Mead. London Ph.D. 1954.

Studies in the history and influence of the education 1951
of boys at Port Royal and in the older Oratorian colleges of
France. W.N. Littlejohns. London M.A. 1948.

Some aspects of the history of Jansenism in the 18th 1952
century. H.A.V. Moreton. Durham M.Litt. 1962.

The political academies of France in the early 18th 1953
century; with special reference to the Club de l'Entresol,
and to its founder the Abbé Pierre-Joseph Alary. E.R. Briggs.
Cambridge Ph.D. 1931/2.

The intellectual relations of Lord Bolingbroke with 1954
France. D.J. Fletcher. Wales M.A. 1953.

The political role of the Parlement of Paris, 1715-48. 1955
J.H. Shennan. Cambridge Ph.D. 1963.

Critical and historical edition of B.L. de Muralt's 1956
<u>Letters describing the Character and Customs of the English
and French Nations</u>, 1726, with an introduction and notes.
S.C. Gould. Oxford B.Litt. 1931.

Montesquieu's interpretation of religion. J.K. 1957
McDonald. Oxford B.Litt. 1961.

The life and ministry of Chauvelin, with particular 1958
reference to French foreign policy between 1731 and 1737.
A.M. Wilson. Oxford B.Litt. 1927.

A study of the policy of Mahé de la Bourdonnais, 1735- 1959
47. P.D. Hollingworth. Durham M.A. 1957.

The factions at the court of Louis XV and the succes- 1960
sion to Cardinal Fleury, 1737-45. (With a critical catalogue
of 18th-century memoirs.). Evelyn G. Cruickshanks. London
Ph.D. 1956.

Luc de Clapiers, marquis de Vauvenargues (1715-47). 1961
May G. Wallas. London Ph.D. 1926.

Edmé Bouchardon. Mrs. Nadia Zaki. Oxford D.Phil. 1962
1969.

Jean Nicholas Grou (1731-1803): the man and his work. 1963
R.C. Pitts. Edinburgh Ph.D. 1947.

The influence of England on the French 'Agronomes', 1964
1750-89. A.J.M.A. Bourde. Cambridge Ph.D. 1948.

The attack on 'feudalism' in 18th-century French 1965
thought. J.Q.C. Mackrell. London Ph.D. 1963.

The educational ideas of the Encyclopaedists. T.J. 1966
James. London Ph.D. (Ext.) 1946.

L'Abbé Guillaume Francis Raynal: his life and his 1967
political influence on the French Revolution. Marguerite C.
Flockhart. Oxford B.Litt. 1923.

Atheism and materialism in the French Enlightenment, 1968
1746-78. J.P. Reid. Oxford B.Litt. 1970.

The pays de Bray: a study in land use change, 1750- 1969
1965. H.D. Clout. London M.Phil. 1968.

Jean-Jacques Rousseau and the Jacobins. D. Higgins. 1970
Sheffield Ph.D. 1952.

The influence and interpretation of the political 1971
ideas of Rousseau in France up to 1791. Joan E. Bedale.
London Ph.D. 1956.

The study of the thermal properties of gases in rel- 1972
ation to physical theory, from Montgolfier to Regnault. R.
Fox. Oxford D.Phil. 1967.

Choiseul's foreign policy relative to England. Mrs. 1973
Mary J. Clark. Liverpool M.A. 1911.

1974   Turgot, social and economic reformer. Eliza A. Gearing. Liverpool M.A. 1911.

1975   Turgot: intendant of Limoges, 1761-74. D. Dakin. London Ph.D. 1936.

1976   Condorcet and the concept of social science in 18th-century France. K.M. Baker. London Ph.D. 1964.

1977   The social relations of England and France, 1763-93, in connection with their effect on the Revolutionary era. C.H. Lockitt. London M.A. 1911.

1978   The evidence of English visitors on the social and economic conditions of France, 1763-89 (May). J.A.R. Pimlott. Oxford B.Litt. 1934.

1979   The social and economic causes of the decline in the French birth-rate at the end of the 18th century. J.G.C. Blacker. London Ph.D. 1957.

1980   Revolution and evolution: the role of direct action in history, exemplified by the theories of F.N. Babeuf (1760-97), Henri, comte de Saint-Simon (1760-1825) and F.C.M. Fourier (1772-1837). P.E.J. Seltman. Cambridge Ph.D. 1956.

1981   Henri de Saint-Simon and the idea of organism. Mrs. Barbara A. Haines. Wales Ph.D. 1969.

1982   The Parlementaires of Bordeaux at the end of the 18th century, 1775-90. W. Doyle. Oxford D.Phil. 1968.

1983   Trends in radical propaganda on the eve of the French Revolution (1782-8). R.C. Darnton. Oxford D.Phil. 1964.

1984   Anglo-French colonial rivalry, 1783-1815. J.R.W. Gwynne-Timothy. Oxford D.Phil. 1953.

1985   The comte de Mirabeau in England, 1784-5. W.R. Fryer. Oxford B.Litt. 1940.

1986   Calonne and the Counter-Revolution, 1787-92. J.A. Johnson. London Ph.D. 1955.

1987   The role of the French bishops in the aristocratic revolt, 1787-8. Barbara A. Luckner. Manchester M.A. 1969.

1988   A social study of the town of Bayeux on the eve of the French Revolution. Olwen H. Hufton. London Ph.D. 1962.

1989   National sentiment in French socialism, 1789-1871. L.S. Edwards. London Ph.D. 1966.

1990   The clerical order on the eve of the French Revolution and its role in the Estates-General, May-June 1789. M.G. Hutt. Oxford B.Litt. 1955.

1991   Administrative study of the implementation of the civil constitution of the clergy in the diocese of Lisieux. Winifred Edington. London Ph.D. 1958.

1992   The noblesse in France in 1789: a study of opinion. B. Thomas. Wales M.A. 1950.

1993   The rural third estate in France in 1789: a study in opinion. A. Davies. Wales M.A. 1939.

1994   The control of education in France during the period 1789 to 1880. A.A.F. Timms. London M.A. 1952.

1995   Education in France during the Revolutionary and Napoleonic era, 1789-1815. E.W. Bishop. London M.A. 1927.

1996   A critical study of the educational activity of the French Revolution. J.G. Worth. Oxford B.Litt. 1921.

1997   'Bourgeois' and 'Bourgeoisie' from 1789 to 1844: a study in the evolution of French political theory. Mrs. Shirley M. Gruner. Durham M.A. 1967.

1998   The reception and reputation of some thinkers of the French Enlightenment in England between 1789 and 1824. S.F. Deane. Cambridge Ph.D. 1968.

1999   British policy and the problem of monarchy in France, 1789-1802. N.F. Richards. London Ph.D. 1955.

2000   Marie Antoinette and the French Revolution. Ruth E.A. Jones. Wales M.A. 1947.

2001   Popular thought in the French Revolution, 1789-94. R. Miliband. London Ph.D. 1957.

2002   An inquiry into the nature, extent and implications of the socialism of the French Revolution, during the period of the revolutionary government. Joan C. Searle. London Ph.D. 1935.

The concept of fraternity and its place in the French   2003
Revolution, 1789-94. P.B. Harris. London Ph.D. 1962.

The annexation policy of the French Revolution, 1789-   2004
93. J.P. McLaughlin. London Ph.D. 1951.

The Parisian wage-earning population and the insur-   2005
rectionary movements of 1789-91. G.F.E. Rudé. London Ph.D.
(Ext.) 1950.

The clubs and the press: a survey of their role in the   2006
development of the French Revolution, October 1789 - September
1791. I.J.G. Macgregor. St. Andrews Ph.D. 1970.

Great debates of the French Revolution: a study and   2007
evaluation of the oratory of the Constituent Assembly (May
1789 - September 1791), with special regard to those speeches
commonly attributed to Mirabeau. Rosemary Carter. London
M.A. 1966.

The idea of the sovereignty of the people, and the   2008
constitutional legislation of the French National Assembly,
1789-91. E. Thompson. London Ph.D. (Ext.) 1948.

Les Enragés and the French Revolution: an early attempt 2009
at practical socialism. R.B. Rose. Manchester M.A. 1953.

A study of Bertrand Barère and the French Revolution.   2010
Anne E. Shipley. St. Andrews M.Litt. 1969.

The commune of Paris, 1790-2. J.R. Firth. Leeds M.A.   2011
1913.

Political élites and social conflicts in the Sections   2012
of Revolutionary Paris, 1792 - Year III. R.M. Andrews.
Oxford D.Phil. 1970.

The composition and characteristics of the Girondin   2013
party in the Convention. M.J. Sydenham. London Ph.D. 1953.

The structure of terrorism in the French provinces in   2014
the year II: a case study. C.R. Lucas. Oxford D.Phil. 1969.

The administration of the transport service during the   2015
war against Revolutionary France, 1793-1802. Mary E.A.
Condon. London Ph.D. 1968.

The dechristianisation movement in the French Revol-   2016
ution, 1793-5. R.T.B. Lamb. Wales M.A. 1952.

The relations of the British government with the   2017
émigrés and Royalists of western France, 1793-5. Agnes King.
London Ph.D. 1931.

Great Britain and the French Royalists from 1794 to   2018
1797. H. Mitchell. London Ph.D. 1954.

The background and outbreak of the Anglo-French War of 2019
1793. J.T. Murley. Oxford D.Phil. 1959.

William Windham and the Counter-Revolution in the north 2020
and west of France, 1793-1801. J.R. Taylor. Manchester M.A.
1967.

The revolutionary tribunal at Marseilles and the re-   2021
pression of the Federalist revolt, 1793-4. W. Scott. Oxford
D.Phil. 1968.

The conflict of ideas between the Gironde and the Mon-   2022
tagne as reflected in the press, with particular references
to the period February to June 1793. Muriel J. Harrison.
Manchester M.A. 1960.

The first Committee of Public Safety, April to July   2023
1793. F.H. Brittenden. Oxford B.Litt. 1952.

The political ideas of Saint-Just, with special refer-   2024
ence to the work of the Committee of Public Safety. J.-P.
Yang. Oxford B.Litt. 1937.

St. Just: his place in the French Revolution. Lilian   2025
P. McCarthy. Oxford B.Litt. 1927.

The life and political career of Couthon. D.S. Bain.   2026
Manchester M.A. 1954.

Jean-Baptiste Carrier and the Terror in the Vendée.   2027
Elsé H. Carrier. Liverpool M.A. 1915.

Robespierre: the last phase. J.L. Tomlinson. Leeds   2028
M.A. 1913.

2029   The organisation and personnel of French central government under the Directory, 1795-9. C.H. Church. London Ph.D.
1963.

2030   British relations with France from the establishment of
the Directory to the coup d'état of Fructidor. J.R. Bracken.
Oxford B.Litt. 1939.

2031   The French diplomatic service, 1799-1814. E.A.L. Whitcomb. London Ph.D. 1970.

2032   The changing land use of the Sologne in the 19th century.
K. Sutton. London M.A. 1967.

2033   The prefecture of Jeanbon Saint-André in the department
of Mont-Tonnerre, 1802-13. G.D. Clack. Oxford D.Phil. 1970.

2034   The contemporary English view of Napoleon. F.J. MacCunn.
Oxford B.Litt. 1913.

2035   The changes effected in the character of secondary education in France under Napoleon. H. Armstrong. London M.A.
1939.

2036   Napoleon Bonaparte and the sale of Louisiana to the
United States. E.W. Lyon. Oxford B.Litt. 1928.

2037   Madame de Genlis, educationist. Phyllis J. Ward. Cambridge Ph.D. 1933/4.

2038   Charles Fourier's conception of a social science. I.D.
Lloyd-Jones. Cambridge Ph.D. 1964.

2039   The personnel of French public education, 1809 to 1830:
a study of Angers and Paris during the Empire and Restoration.
P.M. Pressly. Oxford D.Phil. 1970.

2040   The personnel of the French Prefectoral Corps under the
Restoration, 1814-30. N.J.M. Richardson. Cambridge Ph.D.
1964.

2040A   Liberal political thought in France, 1814-48. P.W.E.
Curtin. London Ph.D. 1939.

2041   The political importance of the newspaper press in the
French Restoration period, 1814-30. Irene Fozzard. Oxford
B.Litt. 1949.

2042   A study of the French banking system, with special
reference to the financing of industry and to the French
investment policy during the period 1815-1914. C. Fodrio.
London Ph.D. 1941.

2043   French political parties and their influence on the
foreign policy of France, 1815-30. Katharine E.C. Cox.
London M.A. 1956.

2044   The White Terror in the department of the Gard, 1814-21.
G. Lewis. Oxford D.Phil. 1966.

2045   Anti-Protestant riots and massacres in the department
of the Gard and British Nonconformist reactions, 1815-20.
G. Lewis. Manchester M.A. 1961.

2046   The ultra-royalist movement at Toulouse under the
second Restoration, 1815-30. D.C. Higgs. London Ph.D. 1964.

2047   Conspiracy to overthrow the Bourbon monarch in France,
1815-30. P.W.H. Savigear. Exeter Ph.D. 1969.

2048   The influence of Wellington on the internal politics of
France, 1815-18. Alwen I. Jones. Oxford B.Litt. 1935.

2049   The final settlement of French reparations and the
evacuation of France in 1818: a study of finance in diplomacy.
R.C. Kent. London Ph.D. 1970.

2050   The Revue Britannique, its origins in 1825 and its early
history to 1840. Kathleen M. Jones. Wales M.A. 1938.

2051   England and the Bourbon Restoration. Doris Higgins.
Liverpool M.A. 1922.

2052   The Revolution of 1830 and the establishment of the
Orleanist monarchy in the departments of the Haute-Marne,
Côte d'Or, Doubs and Vosges. Pamela M. Cartlidge. London
Ph.D. 1966.

2053   Louis Philippe, king of the French. Catherine I. Gavin.
Aberdeen M.A. 1931.

2054   Socialism and Romanticism in France, 1830-48. H.J.
Hunt. Oxford D.Phil. 1930/1.

The political philosophy of de Tocqueville. Mary   2055
Lumby. Leeds M.A. 1921.
The social and political thought of Count Gobineau.   2056
M.D. Biddiss. Cambridge Ph.D. 1968.
Aberdeen and Anglo-French diplomatic relations, 1841-6. 2057
J.R. Baldwin. Oxford B.Litt. 1936.
The relations between England and France during the   2058
Aberdeen-Guizot ministries, 1841-6. G. Wozencroft. London
Ph.D. 1932.
The relations between Louis Napoleon and Great Britain 2059
from 1848 to the outbreak of the Crimean War. F.W. Wright.
Birmingham M.A. 1925.
British diplomacy and the recognition of Louis   2060
Napoleon. Millicent E. Clark. London M.A. 1922.
The Basses-Pyrénées from 1848 to 1870: a study in   2061
departmental politics. V. Wright. London Ph.D. (Ext.) 1965.
French legitimism and Catholicism from the coup d'état 2062
of 1851 until 1865. A.G. Gough. Oxford D.Phil. 1967.
Art and society in mid 19th-century France. J.R.   2063
Gilling. Cambridge M.Litt. 1954.
The life and work of Stanislas Lépine. J.G. Couper.   2064
Oxford B.Litt. 1963.
The Parliamentarians of the Second Empire in France.   2065
T. Zeldin. Oxford D.Phil. 1957.
Some developments in French secondary education during 2066
the Second Empire. R.D. Anderson. Oxford D.Phil. 1967.
The Congress policy of Napoleon III. W.F.F. Grace.   2067
Liverpool M.A. 1925.
The duc de Persigny, 1808-72. S.B. Barnwell. Oxford   2068
B.Litt. 1952.
The character of British relations with France, 1859- 2069
65. Mary A. Anderson. London M.A. 1949.
Napoleon III and the panic of 1859. H.G. Fox. Bir-   2070
mingham M.A. 1930.
The annexation of Savoy and Nice by Napoleon III.   2071
F.R. Scott. Oxford B.Litt. 1923.
Anglo-French commercial relations, 1860-82. K.B. Clay- 2072
ton. Manchester M.A. 1954.
The isolation of France, 1868-70. J.R. Lester. Bir-   2073
mingham M.A. 1937.
Catholic opinion and the ecclesiastical policy of the 2074
government in France (1869-70). J.W. Pickersgill. Oxford
B.Litt. 1933.
The political activities of Paul Brousse, 1870-81.   2075
D.A.T. Stafford. London Ph.D. 1968.
Anglo-French relations, 1871-1904, with special refer- 2076
ence to the problem of Franco-German rivalry. M.H. Jones.
Wales M.A. 1938.
The 'École unique' in France: an historical survey of 2077
the movement, an appreciation of its aims, with some refer-
ence to political and social implications, and an account of
the objects hitherto achieved. W.H. Porter. London M.A.
1938.
The Committees (Commissions) in the Chambers of the   2078
French parliament (1875 to present time) and their influence
on ministerial responsibility. R.K. Gooch. Oxford D.Phil.
1924.
The British attitude towards French colonisation, 1875 2079
to 1887. Mrs. Joan P. Schwitzer. London Ph.D. 1954.
General Boulanger. S.S. Gee. Bristol M.A. 1938.   2080
Agricultural syndicats and interest groups in French   2081
politics, 1880-1910. G.R.I. Neave. London Ph.D. 1967.
Education for industry and commerce in French public   2082
elementary and secondary schools during the 19th century:
some historical and comparative aspects. N.J. Graves. London Ph.D. (Ext.) 1964.

2083   Some historical and comparative aspects of the teaching of geography in French public secondary schools during the 19th and 20th centuries. N.J. Graves. London M.A. 1957.

2084   Workers' education in France, 1890 to 1914. T.B. Caldwell. Leeds Ph.D. 1962.

2085   The political career of René Viviani. S.V. Gallup. Oxford B.Litt. 1966.

2086   The foreign policy of Théophile Delcassé to 1905. C.M. Andrew. Cambridge Ph.D. 1965.

2087   The diplomatic relations between England and France from 1898 to June 1905: the policy of M. Delcassé and the making of the Anglo-French Entente. E.J. Parry. Wales M.A. 1932.

2088   The development of variety chain-stores in France, 1900-60. Susan P. Thomas. Manchester M.A. 1964.

2089   French Catholics and the question of the separation of church and state, 1902-6. M.J.M. Larkin. Cambridge Ph.D. 1958.

2090   Anglo-French relations, 1904-6. J.D. Hargreaves. Manchester M.A. 1948.

2091   Background to the Newfoundland clauses of the Anglo-French agreement of 1904. F.F. Thompson. Oxford D.Phil. 1954.

2092   The parliamentary Right in France, 1905-19. M. Anderson. Oxford D.Phil. 1961.

2093   The nationalist revival in France, 1905-14. E.J. Weber. Cambridge M.Litt. 1956.

2094   The relationship of intellectuals to the Communist party in France, 1914-58. J.D. Caute. Oxford D.Phil. 1963.

2095   The political record of Maurice Paléologue. R.P. Ground. Oxford B.Litt. 1962.

2096   A study of the technical education of the French industrial worker since 1918 considered with reference to parallel developments in England and Wales. Phyllis J. Lamb. London M.A. 1965.

2097   The problems of French security, 1918-20, with special reference to the military terms of the western frontier of Germany. W.M. Jordan. London Ph.D. 1940.

2098   The nature and methods of parliamentary control over foreign policy in France since the signature of the treaty of Versailles, 28 June 1919. J. Howard. Oxford B.Litt. 1938.

2099   From Versailles to London: a study of public opinion and Anglo-French relations from the treaty of Versailles to the treaty of London, 1919-24. V.T. Owen. Wales M.A. 1964.

2100   The disintegration of the Cartel des Gauches and the politics of French government finance 1924-8. D.B. Goldey. Oxford D.Phil. 1961.

2101   Recent critiques of the doctrine of the sovereignty, with special reference to the writings of Professor Léon Duguit. W.D. Handcock. Oxford B.Litt. 1930.

2102   The politics of 'moral revolution' in France, 1926-51: a study of Liberal Catholicism. D.L. Lewis. London Ph.D. 1962.

2103   Strategy and diplomacy in France: some aspects of the military factor in the formulation of French foreign policy, 1934-9. R.J. Young. London Ph.D. 1969.

2104   French foreign policy, April 1938 - September 1939, with special reference to the policy of M. Georges Bonnet. A.P. Adamthwaite. Leeds Ph.D. 1966.

2105   Anglo-French relations, May to December 1940. P.M.H. Bell. Oxford B.Litt. 1958.

2106   The debate over defence policy in France, with special reference to nuclear armament, 1945-60. W.M.L. Mendl. London Ph.D. 1966.

Matthias Grünewald. C. Mitchell. Oxford B.Litt. 1938. 2107

The theology of Wolfgang Musculus, 1497-1563. R.B. 2108
Ives. Manchester Ph.D. 1965.

John Sturm: a pioneer of secondary education. J. 2109
Harvey. Glasgow Ph.D. 1926.

The Liturgia Sacra and Professio Fidei Catholicae of 2110
Valerandus Pollanus (Valérand Poullain), first minister of
the Reformed Church at Frankfort, 1554: transcribed and
translated, with a historical introduction and notes. J.
Gordon. Edinburgh Ph.D. 1928.

Humanism in the universities of Freiburg im Breisgau, 2111
Ingolstadt and Tübingen, 1485-1520. T.G. Heath. Oxford
D.Phil. 1966.

The Scottish abbey in Würzburg, 1595-1696. G.M. Dil- 2112
worth. Edinburgh Ph.D. 1968.

The political relations between England and Germany 2113
during the Thirty Years War, with an introductory chapter on
their relations between 1603 and 1618. E.A. Beller. Oxford
D.Phil. 1923.

Anglo-Palatine relations, 1612-32. J.M. Dennis. 2114
Liverpool Ph.D. 1967.

North-west Germany, Lippe and the Empire in early 2115
modern times. G. Benecke. St. Andrews Ph.D. 1970.

The imperial supreme judicial authority under the 2116
Emperor Charles VI and the crises in Mecklenburg and East
Frisia. M. Hughes. London Ph.D. 1969.

Field-Marshal Maximilian von Browne, 1705-57. C.J. 2117
Duffy. Oxford D.Phil. 1961.

The Dunkers: their origins, migrations, doctrines and 2118
development. J.T. Peters. Edinburgh Ph.D. 1942.

The international legal relations between Great 2119
Britain and Hanover, 1714-1837. I.B. Campbell. Cambridge
Ph.D. 1966.

Enlightened absolutism and revolution in the electorate 2120
of Mainz, 1743-93. T.C.W. Blanning. Cambridge Ph.D. 1967.

Hans David Ludwig von York and the development of 2121
Prussian light infantry, 1786-1812. P. Paret. London Ph.D.
1960.

The intellectual development of Wilhelm von Humboldt 2122
to 1809. R.E. Goldsmith. Oxford B.Litt. 1968.

Wilhelm von Humbold's ideas on education and his prac- 2123
tice of them in the service of the Prussian state. E. Ashmore. Sheffield M.A. 1958.

Heinrich von Kleist's participation in the political 2124
movements of the years 1805-9. R. Samuel. Cambridge Ph.D.
1937/8.

Aspects of the changing patterns of population in 2125
Bavaria. L. James. London Ph.D. 1967.

Humanism in German secondary education: an attempt to 2126
trace its influence in the 19th and 20th centuries. L.P.
de la Perrelle. London Ph.D. 1940.

The grain trade between England and Germany, 1815-70. 2127
H.G. Arnold. Manchester M.A. 1930.

Anglo-German trade, 1815-53. Hilda E. Fitter. London 2128
M.A. 1962.

Heinrich Luden and the origins of the German national- 2129
ist movement. W.E. Brown. Birmingham M.A. 1929.

Johann Gottlieb Fichte and the genesis of the national- 2130
ist movement in Germany. C.J. Child. Birmingham M.A. 1934.

The development of the consciousness of German 2131
nationality in Schleswig-Holstein, 1815-48. W. Carr. Sheffield Ph.D. 1955.

British attitudes to the Schleswig-Holstein question, 2132
1848-50. S.H. Short. Edinburgh Ph.D. 1969.

2133   Wilhelm Roscher: his life and works. W.D.D. Brewer. Birmingham M.Com. 1924.

2134   The Ruhr: an economic survey from the eighteen-forties up to present times. J.S. Dugdale. Liverpool M.A. 1955.

2135   British policy towards German unification 1848-51: from the March Revolution to the Dresden Conferences. G.G.M. Gillessen. Oxford D.Phil. 1958.

2136   The influence of American ideas at Frankfurt-am-Main, 1848-9. J.A. Hawgood. London M.A. 1928.

2137   Working-class associations in the German revolutions of 1848-9. P.H. Noyes. Oxford D.Phil. 1960.

2138   Policy of Baron von Holstein. M.P. Hornik. Oxford D.Phil. 1942.

2139   Bavaria and modern Germany. A.M. Brown. Durham Ph.D. 1935.

2140   Austro-British relations, 1863-6, with special reference to the German question. Nancy E.V. Smith. London M.A. 1935.

2141   Tirpitz and the birth of the German battle fleet. J. Steinberg. Cambridge Ph.D. 1965.

2142   The political career and influence of Georg, Ritter von Schönerer. J.C.P. Warren. London Ph.D. 1963.

2143   British Germanophiles, 1870-1914. G. Hollenberg. Oxford B.Litt. 1970.

2144   The theory of sovereignty in Germany from 1871 to 1921. R. Emerson. London Ph.D. 1927.

2145   The role of military and naval attachés in the British and German service, with particular reference to those in Berlin and London and their effect on Anglo-German relations, 1871-1914. L.W. Hilbert. Cambridge Ph.D. 1954.

2146   Real wages in Germany, 1871-1913. A.V. Desai. Cambridge Ph.D. 1963.

2147   Bismarck and the press: the example of the National Liberals, 1871-84. R.H. Keyserlingk. London Ph.D. 1965.

2148   Anglo-German relations, 1871-8. Maria D. Zier. London M.Sc. 1966.

2149   Lord Odo Russell as British ambassador in Berlin, 1872-8. Winifred A. Taffs. London Ph.D. 1932.

2150   The rise and decline of the German Social Democratic party. N. Herman. Sheffield M.A. 1949.

2151   The social policy of Bismarck. Annie Ashley. Birmingham M.A. 1912.

2152   The foreign policy of Bismarck from the Congress of Berlin until the initiation of the negotiations for the <u>Dreikaiserbund</u>, 1878-80. B. Waller. London Ph.D. 1963.

2153   Arnim and Bismarck. G.O. Kent. Oxford D.Phil. 1958.

2154   The British attitude to German colonial development, 1880-5. Margaret Adams. London M.A. 1935.

2155   The Anglo-German 'colonial marriage', 1885-94. R.J.P. Bünemann. Oxford B.Litt. 1955.

2156   Political attitudes in German universities during the reign of Wilhelm II. G.M. Schwarz. Oxford D.Phil. 1961.

2157   Lord Salisbury's foreign policy, 1888-92, with special reference to Anglo-German relations. D.R. Gillard. London Ph.D. (Ext.) 1952.

2158   The cultural, commercial and political relations between the State of Hamburg and Great Britain from 1890 to 1914. O.J.M. Jolles. Wales M.A. 1938.

2159   The German officer corps, 1890-1914. J.M. Kitchen. London Ph.D. 1966.

2160   The Kolonialrat, its significance and influence on German politics, 1890-1906. H.J.O. Pogge von Strandmann. Oxford D.Phil. 1970.

2161   The search for new forms of government in Germany after Bismarck's fall, 1890-6. J.C.G. Röhl. Cambridge Ph.D. 1965.

2162   The evolution of British public opinion with regard to Germany, as reflected in the press and journals of opinion between 1895 and 1903. R.E. Houseman. London M.A. 1934.

Germany and Zionism, 1897-1917. I. Friedman. London 2163
Ph.D. 1964.
The Anglo-German conventions of 1898 and their position 2164
in Anglo-German relations. P.M. Ridd. Bristol M.A. 1932.
Anglo-German diplomatic relations between 1898 and 2165
1904. A.S. Trickett. Manchester Ph.D. 1935.
The diplomatic relations between England and Germany, 2166
1898-1902. S.E. Lewis. London M.A. 1930.
Left-wing Liberalism in Germany, 1900-19. S.T. Robson. 2167
Oxford D.Phil. 1966.
The development of British military planning for a war 2168
against Germany, 1904-14. N.W. Summerton. London Ph.D.
1970.
Some aspects of the Anglo-German naval rivalry to 1914. 2169
M. Lewis. Wales M.A. 1968.
Clausewitz and Schlieffen: a study of the impact of 2170
their theories on the German conduct of the 1914-18 and 1939-
45 Wars. J.L. Wallach. Oxford D.Phil. 1965.
German diplomacy and peace negotiations: August 1914 - 2171
November 1917. L.L. Farrar. Oxford D.Phil. 1961.
The Independent Social Democratic party and the German 2172
Revolution, 1917-20. A.J. Ryder. London Ph.D. 1958.
The German Independent Social Democratic party, 1918- 2173
22. D.W. Morgan. Oxford D.Phil. 1969.
The German democratic press and the collapse of Weimar 2174
democracy. M. Eksteins. Oxford D.Phil. 1970.
'Der Stahlhelm, Bund der Frontsoldaten', 1918-35. V.R. 2175
Berghahn. London Ph.D. 1964.
The political attitudes of the German Protestant 2176
Church leadership, November 1918 to July 1933. J.R.C. Wright.
Oxford D.Phil. 1969.
America and the Weimar Republic: a study of the causes 2177
and effects of American policy and action in respect to
Germany, 1918-25. J.M. Hester. Oxford D.Phil. 1955.
The German Communist movement, 1918-23. N.B. Blumberg. 2178
Oxford D.Phil. 1950.
Patterns of intra-Western European trade, 1919-39, with 2179
special reference to Britain and Germany. H.C. Smith. Edin-
burgh M.Sc. 1970.
Official German attitudes and policies towards Danzig, 2180
1919-34. C.M. Kimmich. Oxford D.Phil. 1964.
The influence of the multi-party system on represent- 2181
ative government in Germany under the Weimar constitution
(1919-30). C.H. Jepsen. Oxford D.Phil. 1953.
Central and local government in Germany, with reference 2182
to the Weimar constitution of 1919. D.A. Worgan. Wales M.A.
1932.
The influence of Swiss theory and practice on the Wei- 2183
mar constitution, 1919. R.D. Milne. London M.A. 1934.
The foreign policy of Poincaré - France and Great 2184
Britain in relation with the German problem (1919-24).
J.E.L. Loyrette. Oxford B.Litt. 1955.
Britain's relations with France, with special reference 2185
to the German problem, 1919-21. J. Onek. London M.A. 1964.
German policy towards the Baltic states of Estonia and 2186
Latvia, 1920-6. J.W. Hiden. London Ph.D. 1970.
German foreign policy between East and West, 1921-6. 2187
Eleonore C.M. Breuning. Oxford D.Phil. 1966.
The N.S.D.A.P. in lower Saxony, 1921-33: a study of 2188
National Socialist organisation and propaganda. J.D. Noakes.
Oxford D.Phil. 1968.
Combination in German industries, 1924-8. Doreen 2189
Warriner. London Ph.D. 1930.
The National Socialist party in southern Bavaria, 1925- 2190
33: a study of its development in a predominantly Roman
Catholic area. G.F.M. Pridham. London Ph.D. 1969.

2191   A critical examination of the German delegation's policy at the World Disarmament Conference, 1932. P.S. Bagwell. London Ph.D. 1950.

2192   Ernst Jünger and the National Bolshevists. D.C.K. Jones. Cambridge Ph.D. 1969.

2193   The political journalism of Carl von Ossietzky. Mrs. Jean F. Pritchard, formerly Thomas. Cambridge M.Litt. 1970.

2194   Class and status in the Third Reich. D.L. Schoenbaum. Oxford D.Phil. 1965.

2195   The impact of the United States on German foreign policy, 1933-41. J.V. Compton. London Ph.D. 1964.

2196   The relationship between the German army and the Nazi party 1933-9. R.J. O'Neill. Oxford D.Phil. 1965.

2197   British government policies towards refugees from the Third Reich, 1933-9. A.J. Sherman. Oxford D.Phil. 1970.

2198   German public opinion and Hitler's policies, 1933-9. A.R. Wells. Durham M.A. 1968.

2199   England and the nature of the Nazi regime: a critical assessment of British opinion, 1933-9. H.B. Gotlieb. Oxford D.Phil. 1953.

2200   The British press and Germany, 1936-9. F.R. Gannon. Oxford D.Phil. 1968.

2201   German foreign policy, 1937-9. J.S. Conway. Cambridge Ph.D. 1955.

2202   The German settlement of the 'incorporated territories' of the Wartheland and Danzig-West Prussia, 1939-45. W.C. Wiseley. London Ph.D. 1955.

2203   German planning for an invasion of Great Britain, 1939-42. R.R.A. Wheatley. Oxford B.Litt. 1954.

2204   The armaments industry in the German economy in the Second World War. A.S. Milward. London Ph.D. 1960.

GREECE AND GREEK ISLANDS

2205   Cyril Lucaris, his life and work. G.A. Hadjiantoniou. Edinburgh Ph.D. 1948.

2206   The light thrown by the Klephtic ballads on the history of Greece in the period (1715 to 1821) before the War of Independence. J.W. Baggally. Oxford B.Litt. 1935.

2207   British occupation of the Ionian Islands, 1815-64. S.F. Markham. Oxford B.Litt. 1926.

2208   The Ionian Islands under British administration, 1815-64. J.J. Tumelty. Cambridge Ph.D. 1953.

2209   The Ionian Islands under the administration of Sir Thomas Maitland, 1816-24. B.R. Pearn. London M.A. 1924.

2210   The administration of Colonel Charles James Napier in the island of Cefalonia, 1822-30. Audrey H. Heron. London M.A. 1952.

2211   The campaign of the Roumeliot chieftains in western Greece under General Church, 1827-9. Mrs. Domna Dontas. London M.A. 1957.

2212   The relations of Count Capodistrias, president of Greece, with the Conference of London, 1828-31. D.C. Fleming. London M.A. 1958.

2213   British policy in Greece, 1832-43. L.J. Agourides. Oxford D.Phil. 1954.

2214   British policy towards the change of dynasty in Greece in the years 1862-3. E. Prevelakis. Oxford B.Litt. 1949.

2215   The policy of the European powers towards Greece, 1863-75. Mrs. Domna Dontas. London Ph.D. 1964.

2216   A study of the official and unofficial relations between Greece and Turkey from the armistice of Mudros to the present day. E.L.B. Curtis. London M.Sc. 1933.

Politics and propaganda under Giovanni II Bentivoglio. 2217
R.D.H. Gardner. Oxford B.Litt. 1963.

Biblical humanism and Catholic reform: a study of 2218
Renaissance philology and New Testament criticism from Lau-
rentius Valla to Pietro Martire Vermigli. M.W. Anderson.
Aberdeen Ph.D. 1964.

The Lodi dynasty, 1451-1526. S.A. Shere. London M.A. 2219
1934.

Egidio da Viterbo, 1469-1518: a study in Renaissance 2220
and reform history. F.X. Martin. Cambridge Ph.D. 1959.

Francesco Vettori: his place in Florentine diplomacy 2221
and politics. Rosemary J.F. Hughes. London Ph.D. 1958.

The development of the institutions of public finance 2222
at Florence during the last sixty years of the Republic, c.
1470-1530. L.F. Marks. Oxford D.Phil. 1955.

The financial policy of the Florentine Republic, 1494- 2223
1512. L.F. Marks. Oxford B.Litt. 1952.

The commercial development of Ancona, 1479-1551. P. 2224
Earle. London Ph.D. 1969.

The last period of the Sienese Republic (1487-1552), 2225
with particular reference to the ascendancy of the Petrucci
family. D.F. Corcos. Oxford B.Litt. 1955.

Politics and society in Perugia, 1488-1540. C.F. 2226
Black. Oxford B.Litt. 1967.

Filippo de' Nerli, 1485-1556: politician, adminis- 2227
trator and historian. Mrs. Kathryn V. Brown, née Underhill.
London Ph.D. 1968.

The diplomatic career of Machiavelli. G.A. Brucker. 2228
Oxford B.Litt. 1950.

The grand tour in Italy in the 16th, 17th and 18th 2229
centuries. Elizabeth M. Hutton. Cambridge Ph.D. 1936/7.

Studies in the religious life of Venice in the 16th 2230
and early 17th centuries: the Venetian clergy and religious
orders, 1520-1630. O.M.T. Logan. Cambridge Ph.D. 1967.

The service of the Scuole Grandi to the state and 2231
people of Venice in the 16th and early 17th centuries. B.S.
Pullan. Cambridge Ph.D. 1962.

The effect of the religious Reformation in Italy be- 2232
tween 1520 and 1550. G.K. Brown. Edinburgh Ph.D. 1930/1.

Reginald Pole and the evangelical religion: some pro- 2233
blems of Italian Christian humanism in the early Counter-
Reformation. D.B. Fenlon. Cambridge Ph.D. 1969.

The sack of Rome, 1527. Mrs. Judith A. Hook. Edin- 2234
burgh Ph.D. 1970.

The last Florentine Republic: 1527 to the fall of 2235
Niccoló Capponi. C. Roth. Oxford B.Litt. 1923.

The last Florentine Republic, 1527-30. C. Roth. Ox- 2236
ford D.Phil. 1924.

Anglo-Italian trade from the reign of Elizabeth to the 2237
French Revolution, with special reference to the port of
Leghorn. Elizabeth R. Poyser. Cambridge M.Litt. 1951.

Piero Soderini, gonfaloniere a vita of Florence, 1502- 2238
12. Roslyn L. Cooper. London Ph.D. 1965.

Daniele Barbaro, patriarch elect of Aquileia, with 2239
special reference to his circle of scholars and to his literary achievement. P.J. Laven. London Ph.D. 1957.

The family and early life of Sextus V. W.T. Selley. 2240
Bristol M.A. 1934.

The Pallavicini and Spinole in their relations to the 2241
Elizabethan government. G.W. Stafford. Manchester M.A.
1924.

Italian financiers of the 15th and 16th centuries, with 2242
special reference to Pallavicino and Spinola and their share
in Elizabethan finance. Bertha Hall. London M.Sc. 1928.

2243　　　The intellectual status of women in Italy in the later 16th century, with special reference to treatises on women and the position of women in literary academies. C.F. Fahy. Manchester Ph.D. 1954.

2244　　　The relations between James VI and I and Carlo Emanuele I, duke of Savoy. J. Thompson. St. Andrews Ph.D. 1941.

2245　　　The economy of certain Piedmontese noble families in the reign of Victor Amadeus II. S.J. Woolf. Oxford D.Phil. 1960.

2246　　　Anglo-Florentine cultural relations in the second half of the 18th century. B. Moloney. Cambridge Ph.D. 1962.

2247　　　Bishop Scipio dei Ricci and the synod of Pistoia: a critical survey. C.A. Bolton. Oxford B.Litt. 1938.

2248　　　Francesco Melzi d'Eril: an Italian statesman, 1796-1805. J.M. Roberts. Oxford D.Phil. 1953.

2249　　　The educational work and thought of Antonio Rosmini-Serbati (1797-1855), with special reference to his minor works. P.K. O'Leary. Belfast M.A. 1959.

2250　　　The educational work of John Bosco (1815-88). J. Kilcullen. Belfast M.A. 1959.

2251　　　Palmerston and the dawn of Italian independence, 1830-51. C.F. Strong. London Ph.D. 1925.

2252　　　Carlo Cattaneo and his interpretation of the Milanese insurrection of 1848. R.G. Murray. Cambridge Ph.D. 1963.

2253　　　The influence of the Italian question on Anglo-French relations, 1856-60, from the treaty of Paris to the annexation of Savoy and Nice. H.M. Vincent. Oxford B.Litt. 1948.

2254　　　British public opinion and the Italian Risorgimento, with special reference to the period 1859-61. D.F. Mackay. Oxford D.Phil. 1959.

2255　　　The Italian question and English politics, 1859-60. D.E.D. Beales. Cambridge Ph.D. 1957.

2256　　　The influence of English diplomacy on Italy. V. Eleanor L. Doorly. London M.A. 1912.

2257　　　Tuscany and the Italian Risorgimento, 1859-60. F.J. Skinner. London M.A. 1921.

2258　　　Anglo-Italian economic relations, 1861-83. P. Bolchini. London Ph.D. 1967.

2259　　　Great Britain and the Roman question. Elizabeth M. Wiskemann. Cambridge M.Litt. 1927/8.

2260　　　The foreign policy of Baron Ricasoli, 1861-2. J.R. Whittam. London Ph.D. 1968.

2261　　　British policy in the Italian question, 1866-71. H.E. Priestley. London Ph.D. 1931.

2262　　　The distribution of industry and settlement in the Milan area, with special reference to population changes since 1880. J.P. Cole. Nottingham Ph.D. 1961.

2263　　　Anglo-Italian relations, 1887-96. C.J. Lowe. London Ph.D. (Ext.) 1959.

2264　　　The traditional friendship: a study of British foreign policy towards Italy, 1902-15. R.J.B. Bosworth. Cambridge Ph.D. 1970.

2265　　　Italy 1914-15: from neutrality to intervention. R. Pryce. Cambridge Ph.D. 1955.

2266　　　Fiume as a problem in Anglo-Italian relations, 1915-20. S.G. Doree. London Ph.D. 1969.

2267　　　Factory councils and the Italian labour movement, 1916-21. M.N. Clark. London Ph.D. 1966.

2268　　　Italy's Austrian heritage, 1918-46. D.I. Rusinow. Oxford D.Phil. 1963.

2269　　　Pre-Fascist Italy: the rise and fall of the parliamentary régime. Margot Hentze. London Ph.D. 1938.

2270　　　The problem of regionalism in Italy: its historical background and present constitutional importance. B. Chapman. Oxford D.Phil. 1951.

Historical development of towns in the Netherlands. 2271
G.L. Burke. London M.Sc. (Ext.) 1951.

Nicolai Clenardi epistolae. L.J.F. Welton. Liverpool 2272
Ph.D. 1935.

The administration of the earl of Leicester in the 2273
United Provinces. Lilian A. Hodgkinson. Liverpool M.A.
1925.

The earl of Leicester's governorship of the Nether- 2274
lands, 1586-7. Frederika G. Oosterhoff. London Ph.D. 1967.

The rise of the Dutch East India Company. F.J. Tick- 2275
ner. Oxford B.Litt. 1952.

The royal palace at Amsterdam: an introduction to the 2276
city's 17th-century town hall and the sources of information
concerning it. Katherine D.H. Fremantle. London Ph.D. 1956.

Relations between England and Flanders, 1603-18. Nancy 2277
Applegate. Leeds M.A. 1948.

The Rotterdam patriciate, 1650-72. J.L. Price. London 2278
Ph.D. (Ext.) 1969.

The First Dutch Wars, 1652-4. A.C. Dewar. Oxford 2279
B.Litt. 1916.

The British attitude, public and official, to the Dutch 2280
alliance during the War of the Spanish Succession. D.S.
Coombs. London Ph.D. 1953.

The Dutch barrier, 1709-19. Isabel A. Morison. London 2281
Ph.D. 1929.

Diplomatic relations between Great Britain and the 2282
Dutch Republic, 1714-21. Ragnhild M.R.H. Hatton. London
Ph.D. 1947.

The study of _Politica_ in the Netherlands in the early 2283
18th century. C.R. Emery. London Ph.D. 1967.

The Anglo-French struggle for the control of Dutch 2284
foreign policy, 1755-63. Mrs. Alice M.C. Carter, née Le
Mesurier. London M.A. 1933.

England and the establishment of the kingdom of the 2285
Netherlands, 1813-16. G. Renier. London Ph.D. 1929.

Great Britain and the Scheldt, 1814-39. S.T. Bindoff. 2286
London M.A. 1933.

Free trade and protection in the Netherlands, 1819-25. 2287
H.R.C. Wright. Cambridge Ph.D. 1948.

Technological education in Belgium, 1830-1914. R.S. 2288
Betts. London M.Phil. 1968.

Anglo-Belgian relations, and their influence on British 2289
foreign policy in general, 1833-9. Norah P. Righton. London
M.A. 1927.

The development of the Dutch political party system, 2290
1848-1901. H.H. Ginsburg. Oxford B.Litt. 1948.

Population movements in Luxembourg between 1861 and 2291
1964. Kathleen M. Griffin. Nottingham M.A. 1966.

The policies of Stanley, Granville and Gladstone to- 2292
wards Luxemburg, Belgium and Alsace-Lorraine, 1867-71. M.R.D.
Foot. Oxford B.Litt. 1950.

The Luxemburg crisis of 1867, with special reference to 2293
British policy. G.A. Craig. Oxford B.Litt. 1938.

British policy towards Belgium from the Armistice to 2294
the fall of Lloyd George. Sally J. Marks. London Ph.D.
1968.

MEDITERRANEAN AND ISLANDS

The changing landscape of Malta during the rule of the 2295
order of St. John of Jerusalem, 1530-1798. B.W. Blouet. Hull
Ph.D. 1964.

The fortification of Malta by the knights of St. John, 2296
1530-1798. Mrs. Alison M. Hoppen, née Buchan. St. Andrews
Ph.D. 1970.

2297   The architecture of Malta during the period of the knights of St. John of Jerusalem, 1530-1798. J.Q. Hughes. Leeds Ph.D. 1952.

2298   Factors, historical and geographical, which have affected the location and development of the town of Leucosia (Nicosia), Cyprus. F.S. Maratheftis. Bristol M.A. 1958.

2299   The origins and development of the Royal University of Malta. E.W.N. Roe. London M.A. (Ext.) 1958.

2300   Cyprus under the Turks, 1571-8. H.C. Luke. Oxford B.Litt. 1919.

2301   British diplomatic relations with the Mediterranean, 1763-78. M.S. Anderson. Edinburgh Ph.D. 1952.

2302   Trends in the economic geography of Malta since 1800. W.H. Charlton. Durham Ph.D. 1960.

2303   Education in the Maltese Islands, 1800-1966. E.L. Galea. Southampton M.Phil. 1969.

2304   British strategy in the Mediterranean, 1803-10. P.G. Mackesy. Oxford D.Phil. 1953.

2305   Minorca under British rule. Ella Murdie. London M.A. 1931.

2306   Lord William Bentinck and the British occupation of Sicily, 1811-14. G.A. Rosselli. Cambridge Ph.D. 1952.

2307   The colonial administrations of Sir Thomas Maitland. C.W. Dixon. Oxford B.Litt. 1938.

2308   Malta as a British colony, 1824-51. Hilda I. Lee. London M.A. 1949.

2309   Maltese emigration 1826-85: an analysis and a survey. C.A. Price. Oxford D.Phil. 1952.

2310   The foreign policy of Charles Albert (1848-9), with special reference to England. J.P.H. Myres. Oxford B.Litt. 1932.

2311   Anglo-Sardinian relations, January 1859 - March 1860. Mildred Whibley. London M.A. 1923.

2312   The economic geography of Cyprus, 1878-1960. F.S. Walmsley. Liverpool M.A. 1963/4.

2313   The contribution of the Christian Orthodox Church of Cyprus to Cyprus education from 1878 to 1959. P.K. Persianis. London M.A. 1961.

2314   Education in Cyprus under the British administration, 1878-1958. A.K. Kouros. London Ph.D. (Ext.) 1959.

RUSSIA AND THE U.S.S.R.

2315   The history of the conflict between the 'Possessors' and the 'Non-Possessors' in Russia and its reflexion in the literature of the period - the end of the 15th century and the first half of the 16th century. J.L.I. Fennell. Cambridge Ph.D. 1951.

2316   Old Russian diplomatic vocabulary: a study based on the documents of the Posol'skiy Prikaz relating to the Holy Roman Empire, 1488-1699. Sunray C. Gardiner. London Ph.D. (Ext.) 1965.

2317   Economic relations between England and Russia in the 16th century. Mildred W. Smith. Wales M.A. 1918.

2318   The fall of Shaikh Ahmed Khan and the fate of the people of the Great Horde, 1500-4. L.J.D. Collins. London Ph.D. (Ext.) 1970.

2319   Maxim the Greek and the intellectual movements of Muscovy. J.V. Haney. Oxford D.Phil. 1970.

2320   The historical geography of Western Belorussia, 1550-1600. R.A. French. London Ph.D. 1968.

2321   The Russia Company. Gwen M. Posnette. Birmingham M.A. 1919.

2322   The policy and activities of the Muscovy Company in the late 16th and early 17th centuries. Mildred Wretts-Smith. London M.Sc. 1920.

The archpriest Avvakum and his Scottish contemporaries. 2323
Catherine B.H. Cant. London M.A. 1959.

The patriarch Nicon and the Russian Church. C.L. 2324
Graves. Oxford B.Litt. 1966.

The origin and early history of the theatre in Russia, 2325
1672-1756. Bertha Malnick. London Ph.D. 1936.

A survey of the stage in Russia from 1741 to 1783, with 2326
special reference to the development of the Russian theatre.
M.A.S. Burgess. Cambridge Ph.D. 1953.

The church reform of Peter the Great, with special 2327
reference to the Ecclesiastical Regulation of 1721. J.E.
Cracraft. Oxford D.Phil. 1968.

The place of Russia in British foreign policy, 1748- 2328
56. J.R.J. Gwyn. Oxford B.Litt. 1961.

St. Tikhon of Voronezh. Mrs. Nadejda Gorodetzky. Ox- 2329
ford D.Phil. 1944.

The Russian nobility and the legislative commission of 2330
1767. P. Dukes. London Ph.D. 1964.

Anglo-Russian relations during the War of American 2331
Independence, 1778-83. Isabel M. de Madariaga. London Ph.D.
1959.

Development of Pan-Slavist thought in Russia (from 2332
Karamzin to Danilevski, 1800-70). F.L. Fadner. London Ph.D.
1949.

History of Russian educational policy, 1801-1917. N. 2333
Hans. London Ph.D. 1926.

The secret committee and reforms of 1801-3 in Russia. 2334
Olga A. Narkiewicz. Manchester M.A. 1964.

Alexander Herzen: a study of his years in Russia, 2335
1812-47. Monica A. Partridge. London Ph.D. (Ext.) 1953.

The Romantic movement in Russia. L. Segal. Birming- 2336
ham M.A. 1919.

Russia and the West in the teaching of the Slavophiles: 2337
a study of a Romantic ideology. N.V. Riasanovsky. Oxford
D.Phil. 1949.

The Anglo-Russian grain trade, 1815-61. Mrs. Susan E. 2338
Fairlie. London Ph.D. 1959.

The Third Department: an examination of the establish- 2339
ment and practices of the political police in the Russia of
Nicholas I. P.S. Squire. Cambridge Ph.D. 1958.

Great Britain, Russia, and the Eastern question, 1832- 2340
41. G.H. Bolsover. London Ph.D. 1933.

British conceptions of Russia and Russian policy, 2341
1837-41. J.H. Gleason. Oxford B.Litt. 1932.

The relations between Great Britain and Russia from 2342
1848 to 1856. A.R. Cooke. Birmingham M.A. 1920.

The industrial geography of St. Petersburg, 1850-1914. 2343
J.H. Bater. London Ph.D. 1969.

A study of the Russian 'reactionary' writers in the 2344
second half of the 19th century. K.R.S. Tidmarsh. Oxford
D.Phil. 1956.

British views of Russia during the period of reform, 2345
1856-66. Mrs. Catherine K. Marshall. London M.A. 1963.

A critical survey of the Narodnik movement, 1861-81. 2346
Anne I.S. Branfoot. London Ph.D. 1926.

Social thought in the writings of Konstantin D. 2347
Ushinski. S. Ziring. London Ph.D. 1965.

N.K. Mikhailovsky and Russian radical thought in the 2348
final third of the 19th century. J.H. Billington. Oxford
D.Phil. 1953.

The relations between Great Britain and Russia, 1870- 2349
99. A.E. Jones. Birmingham M.A. 1917.

The reactions of England and the Great Powers to the 2350
remilitarisation of the Black Sea by Russia, 1870-1. J.H.
Laws. Wales M.A. 1962.

The Jewish question in the district of Wilno in 1880- 2351
1914. H.M. Winawer. Oxford B.Litt. 1948.

2352   Anglo-Russian relations, 1880-1907. D.W. Anthony. Wales M.A. 1952.

2353   Russian economic development, 1881-1914, with special reference to the railways and the role of government. B.E. Hurt. London Ph.D. 1963.

2354   Peasant colonisation of Siberia: a study of the growth of Russian rural society in Siberia, with particular emphasis on the years 1890 to 1918. H.J. Ellison. London Ph.D. 1955.

2355   Movements for Anglo-Russian reconciliation and alliance from March 1890 to December 1903. H.H. Page. Birmingham M.A. 1933.

2356   Socialism and Jewish nationalism in Russia, 1892-1907. J. Frankel. Cambridge Ph.D. 1961.

2357   'Legal Marxism' in Russia. R.K. Kindersley. Cambridge Ph.D. 1956/7.

2358   Lord Salisbury's attempts to reach an understanding with Russia, June 1895 - November 1900. A.W. Palmer. Oxford B.Litt. 1954.

2359   The Jewish Bund and the Russian Social-Democratic party 1897-1903/5. H. Shukman. Oxford D.Phil. 1961.

2360   The development of social-democracy in Russia, 1898-1907. J.L.H. Keep. London Ph.D. 1954.

2361   The social composition, structure and activity of Russian Social Democratic groups, 1898-1907. D.S. Lane. Oxford D.Phil. 1966.

2362   Julius Martov: his role and place in Russian social democracy. I. Getzler. London Ph.D. 1965.

2363   The growth and interrelations of political groups and parties in Russia, 1898 - May 1906. D.W. Treadgold. Oxford D.Phil. 1949.

2364   The legal trade union movement in Russia - the police socialism (1898-1903). D. Pospielovsky. London M.Phil. 1967.

2365   The economics of Russian farming, with particular reference to the years 1900-16. G.A. Pavlovsky. London Ph.D. 1929.

2366   Anglo-Russian relations and the formation of the Anglo-Russian agreement, 1903-7. A.W. Hopkins. Wales M.A. 1937.

2367   The British labour movement and its policy towards Russia from the first Russian Revolution until the treaty of Locarno. G.A. Ritter. Oxford B.Litt. 1959.

2368   The Liberation movement and its role in the first Russian Revolution. S. Galai. London Ph.D. 1967.

2369   The rise of the Constitutional-Democratic party in Russia, 1904-6. P.W. Enticott. London M.Phil. 1968.

2370   The Right radical movement in Russia, 1905-17. E.R. Zimmermann. London Ph.D. 1968.

2371   The Octobrists in Russian politics, 1905-17. J.F. Hutchinson. London Ph.D. 1966.

2372   The economic development of Russia from 1905 to 1914, with special reference to trade, industry and finance. Margaret S. Miller. London Ph.D. 1925.

2373   A political evaluation of P.A. Stolypin, 1906-11. G.B. Tokmakoff. London Ph.D. 1963.

2374   The Russian peasant movement, 1906-17. L.A. Owen. London Ph.D. 1933.

2375   The socio-economic mobility of the Russian peasantry, 1910-25, and the political sociology of rural society. T. Shanin. Birmingham Ph.D. 1969.

2376   Government and Duma in Russia (1907-14). G.A. Hosking. Cambridge Ph.D. 1970.

2377   British intervention in Russia, November 1917 to February 1920: a study in the making of foreign policy. R.H. Ullman. Oxford D.Phil. 1960.

2378   The United States and the Russian provisional government: the special diplomatic mission to Russia in the summer of 1917. J.G.K. Tengey. Aberdeen M.Litt. 1969.

The development of the Soviet budgetary system, 1917– 2379
41. R.W. Davies. Birmingham Ph.D. 1955.
The foreign policy of Soviet Russia in Europe, 1917–39. 2380
E. Bogomas. London M.Sc. 1945.
Soviet Russia's policy towards India and its effect on 2381
Anglo-Soviet relations, 1917–28. Z. Imam. London Ph.D.
1964.
Lenin's foreign policy, 1917–22: ideology or national 2382
interest? R. Gregor. London Ph.D. 1966.
L.D. Trotsky and the economics of Soviet isolation. 2383
R.B. Day. London Ph.D. 1970.
The East Karelian autonomy question in Finnish–Soviet 2384
relations, 1917–22. S. Churchill. London Ph.D. 1967.
The commissariat of education under Lunacharsky (1917– 2385
21). Mrs. Sheila M. Bruce, née Fitzpatrick. Oxford D.Phil.
1969.
Paul Milyukov and the Constitutional Democratic party. 2386
F.J. Piotrow. Oxford D.Phil. 1962.
The Russian peasant and the failure of rural govern- 2387
ment, March–October 1917. R.P. Bonine. London Ph.D. 1960.
The formation of the ruling class in Soviet society. 2388
S. Utechin. Oxford B.Litt. 1955.
The organisation of Soviet youth: a history of the 2389
All-Union Leninist Communist League of Youth (Komsomol).
S.I. Ploss. London Ph.D. 1957.
The hetmanate of P.P. Skoropadsky in the Ukraine in 2390
1918. Valentina Woropay. London M.A. 1959.
Nationality policy and nationalism in the Soviet 2391
Ukraine, 1920–9. W. Mykula. Oxford B.Litt. 1960.
Anglo-Soviet trade relations, 1920–3. A.M. Martin. 2392
Manchester M.A. 1969/70.
Problems of rural and industrial administration in the 2393
Soviet Union, 1923–7. Olga A. Narkiewicz. Manchester Ph.D.
1968.
The Russian village community, 1925–30. D.J. Male. 2394
Birmingham M.Com. 1967.
British policy towards the U.S.S.R. and the onset of 2395
the Second World War: March 1938 – August 1939. S. Aster.
London Ph.D. 1969.

For Russia in Asia see under CENTRAL ASIA

SCANDINAVIA AND FINLAND

Dr. Johannes Macchabaeus – John MacAlpin: Scotland's 2396
contribution to the Reformation in Denmark. M.A.F. Bredahl
Petersen. Edinburgh Ph.D. 1937.
The Counter-Reformation in Sweden. C.J.A. Oppermann. 2397
London M.A. 1922.
The overseas trade of Scotland, with particular refer- 2398
ence to the Baltic and Scandinavian trades, 1660–1707. T.C.
Smout. Cambridge Ph.D. 1960.
The position of England towards the Baltic Powers – 2399
i.e. Denmark and Sweden, including the Hanse towns – 1689–97.
Margery Lane. London M.A. 1911.
Marriage and population growth in Norway, 1735–1865. 2400
K.M. Drake. Cambridge Ph.D. 1964.
Anglo-Scandinavian economic and diplomatic relations, 2401
1755–63. H.S.K. Kent. Cambridge Ph.D. 1955.
Agricultural ideas and practice and social conditions 2402
in Denmark, 1756–86. Mrs. Norma Heigham. Oxford D.Phil.
1964.
Plans for agrarian reform in Denmark (1767–72). Mrs. 2403
Norma Heigham. Oxford B.Litt. 1958.

2404   Changes in Icelandic social structure since the end of the 18th century, with particular reference to trends in social mobility. J. Nordal. London Ph.D. 1954.

2405   Finland and Britain, 1854-1914. G.E. Maude. London Ph.D. (Ext.) 1970.

2406   The economic geography of the Norrbotten iron ore mining industry. E.A. Smith. Aberdeen Ph.D. 1967.

2407   A commercial geography of the port of Piteå from 1860 to the present day. I.G. Layton. London M.A. 1968.

2408   Sweden: parliamentary development, 1866-1921. D.V. Verney. Liverpool Ph.D. 1953/4.

2409   Norway's relations with belligerent powers in the First World War. O. Riste. Oxford D.Phil. 1963.

SPAIN AND PORTUGAL

2410   New evidence for the study of the historical geography of Galatia. I.W. MacPherson. Cambridge Ph.D. 1959.

2411   The revival of the Roman triumphal procession in Europe, and the history of the royal entry in Spain prior to 1600. C.A. Marsden. Cambridge Ph.D. 1964.

2412   Castles of Castilian seigneurial type built in the 15th and 16th centuries. A.E.W. Cooper. Cambridge Ph.D. 1969.

2413   The revolt of the comuneros in Castile, 1520-1. P. Byrne. Newcastle M.Litt. 1967.

2414   Education and the state in Habsburg Spain. R.L. Kagan. Cambridge Ph.D. 1968.

2415   Anglo-Spanish trade in the early Tudor period. G.E. Connell-Smith. London Ph.D. 1950.

2416   The government of Sicily under Philip II of Spain: a study in the practice of empire. H.G. Königsberger. Cambridge Ph.D. 1949.

2417   War and administrative devolution: the military government of Spain in the reign of Philip II. I.A.A. Thompson. Cambridge Ph.D. 1965.

2418   Spanish sea power in the Mediterranean during the reign of Philip II. C.A.H. Hartmann. Oxford B.Litt. 1922.

2419   English trade with peninsular Spain, 1558-1625. J. Pauline Croft. Oxford D.Phil. 1970.

2420   The trading relations and rivalry between England and Spain, 1558-88. W.E. Kaye. Manchester M.A. 1921.

2421   Anglo-Spanish relations, 1558-63. J.E. Straukamp. London Ph.D. 1966.

2422   The Spanish Road and the army of Flanders: a study of the formation and disintegration of a European army, 1567-1647. N.G. Parker. Cambridge Ph.D. 1968.

2423   The causes of the second rebellion of the Alpujarras, 1568-71. K. Garrad. Cambridge Ph.D. 1956.

2424   The embassy of Bernardino de Mendoza to England, 1578-84. G. Tejón. Oxford B.Litt. 1957.

2425   The Irish College at Salamanca, its early history and the influence of its work on Irish education. Mary B. Blake. Liverpool M.A. 1956/7.

2426   Spain and the English Catholic exiles, 1580-1604. A.J. Loomie. London Ph.D. 1957.

2427   The relations between the disaffected Irish with Spain during the reign of Elizabeth Tudor. Thomasina Huston. Belfast M.A. 1937.

2428   A commentary on certain aspects of the Spanish Armada drawn from contemporary sources. J.P.R. Lyell. Oxford B.Litt. 1932.

2429   Some aspects of the life and works of Don Carlos Coloma. Olga Turner. London Ph.D. 1950.

2430   Castile and Catalonia during the ministry of the Conde Duque de Olivares. J.H. Elliott. Cambridge Ph.D. 1955.

Philip II, Don Luis de Requesens, and the Netherlands: 2431
a Spanish problem in government, 1573-6. A.W. Lovett. Cambridge Ph.D. 1969.

Spain and the origins of the Thirty Years War. P. 2432
Brightwell. Cambridge Ph.D. 1967.

The economic decline of Spain in the 17th century: con- 2433
temporary Spanish views. H.G. Hambleton. London Ph.D. 1964.

Anglo-Spanish relations, 1603-25. A. MacFadyen. 2434
Liverpool M.A. 1960.

The Spanish province of Valencia, 1609-50. J.G. Casey. 2435
Cambridge Ph.D. 1968.

Aristocracy, war and finance in Castile, 1621-65: the 2436
titled nobility and the house of Béjar during the reign of
Philip IV. C.J. Jago. Cambridge Ph.D. 1969.

Anglo-Spanish relations 1625-60. A. MacFadyen. 2437
Liverpool Ph.D. 1967.

Anglo-Spanish relations from the Restoration to the 2438
peace of Aix-la-Chapelle, 1660-8. R.A. Stradling. Wales
Ph.D. 1968.

Spanish economic policy and its relation to trade with 2439
England culminating in the treaty of 1667. J.C. Salyer.
Oxford B.Litt. 1948.

Don Pedro Ronquillo and Spanish-British relations 2440
(1674-91). C.F. Scott. St. Andrews Ph.D. 1955.

Portuguese society in the reigns of D. Pedro II and D. 2441
Joao V, 1680-1750. J.F.H. Villiers. Cambridge Ph.D. 1963.

Anglo-Portuguese trade, 1700-70. H.E.S. Fisher. 2442
London Ph.D. 1961.

Administrative reform and economic recovery in Spain 2443
during the reign of Philip V, with particular attention to
the years 1700-24. B.J. Roud. Cambridge M.Litt. 1959.

Anglo-Portuguese relations during the War of the 2444
Spanish Succession. Mary E. Turner. Oxford D.Phil. 1952.

Spain during the War of the Succession, with special 2445
reference to French policy, 1700-15. H.A.F. Kamen. Oxford
D.Phil. 1963.

Diplomatic relations between Great Britain and Spain, 2446
1711-14. M.A. Martin. London Ph.D. 1962.

Gibraltar as a British possession to 1783. C.P.R. 2447
Clarke. Oxford B.Litt. 1934.

Anglo-Spanish diplomatic and commercial relations, 2448
1731-59. Jean O. McLachlan. Cambridge Ph.D. 1936/7.

Reaction in Spain to the Lisbon earthquake of 1755. 2449
N. Graveson. London M.Phil. 1967.

England, Spain and the family compact, 1763-83. J.A. 2450
Lalaguna Lasala. London Ph.D. 1968.

Jaime Balmes and the Roman Catholic revival of the 2451
19th century. A.L. Schutmaat. Edinburgh Ph.D. 1957.

The French administration in Spain, 1808-13. W. Top- 2452
ham. London Ph.D. (Ext.) 1950.

The attitude of the British government to the Portu- 2453
guese revolution of 1826-34. Phyllis M. Cowell. London M.A.
1927.

The place of the army in Spanish politics, 1830-54. 2454
E. Christiansen. Oxford D.Phil. 1964.

George Villiers, British ambassador at Madrid, 1835-8, 2455
with special reference to Anglo-French relations and the
British Auxiliary Legion. J.S. Leeming. London Ph.D. 1963.

British policy and the Spanish marriages, 1841-6. E. 2456
Jones Parry. London Ph.D. 1934.

Anglo-Portuguese relations, 1851-61. W.H.C. Smith. 2457
London Ph.D. 1965.

The significance of British policy towards Spain, 2458
1859-68. Suzanne Doyle. London M.A. 1949.

The diplomatic relations of England and Spain, 1868- 2459
80. C.J. Bartlett. London Ph.D. 1956.

2460   Francisco Pi y Margall and the Spanish Federal Republican party, 1868-74. C.A.M.S. Hennessy. Oxford D.Phil. 1958.

2461   The influence of Emilio Castelar on the formation and fortunes of the Spanish Republic of 1873. J.A. Brandt. Oxford B.Litt. 1924/5.

2462   The development of education in Spain since 1900. J.C. Develin. Oxford D.Phil. 1935.

2463   Revolution and social revolution: a contribution to the history of the anarcho-syndicalist movement in Spain, 1930-7. S.J. Brademas. Oxford D.Phil. 1954.

2464   The Carlist movement in Spain, 1931-7. R.M. Blinkhorn. Oxford D.Phil. 1970.

2465   The Right under the second Spanish Republic, 1931-6, with special reference to the C.E.D.A. R.A.H. Robinson. Oxford D.Phil. 1968.

2466   The relations of General Franco and the Spanish Nationalists with the Axis Powers, 1936-45. Elizabeth J. Parr. Wales Ph.D. 1956.

2467   International repercussions of the Spanish Civil War. Patricia A.M. Van der Esch. London Ph.D. 1950.

2468   The course of United States government policy towards the Spanish Civil War, 1936-9. G.W.C. Fee. Oxford B.Litt. 1959.

SWITZERLAND

2469   The life and thought of Balthasar Hübmaier (1485-1528). R.A. Mackoskey. Edinburgh Ph.D. 1956.

2470   The conception of the mission of the church in early reformed theology, with special reference to Calvin's theology and practice in Geneva. W.H. Clark. Edinburgh Ph.D. 1928.

2471   Geneva and the first refuge: a study of the social and economic effects of French and Italian refugees in Geneva in the 16th and early 17th centuries. J.C. Troust. Oxford D.Phil. 1968.

2472   The first and second editions (English and Latin) of the service book used by the English congregation of Marian exiles in Geneva, 1556-9. W.D. Maxwell. Edinburgh Ph.D. 1929.

2473   English foreign policy during the reign of William III: in particular the relations of England with the Swiss Protestants. L.A. Robertson. Oxford B.Litt. 1926.

2474   British travellers in Switzerland, with special reference to some women travellers between 1750 and 1850. Jean A. Mains. Edinburgh Ph.D. 1966.

2475   Educational work of Philipp Emanuel von Fellenberg. Ethel W. Gray. Belfast M.A. 1952.

2476   Anglo-Swiss relations, 1845-60. Ann G. Imlah. London Ph.D. 1963.

2477   Anglo-Swiss relations, 1914-18, with special reference to the allied blockade of the Central Powers. D.D. Driscoll. London Ph.D. 1969.

B R I T A I N :   L O N G   P E R I O D S

F R O M   T H E   1 5 T H   C E N T U R Y

POLITICAL HISTORY

2478   The history and place of public policy in English private law. C.L. Emrich. Oxford D.Phil. 1938.

2479   The history of mens rea in the law of homicide. A.W.G. Kean. Cambridge M.Litt. 1938/9.

Researches in the history of the rights of the subject 2480
in England. L.E.D. Horanszky de Hora. Aberdeen Ph.D. 1927.

Punishment as applied by the ordinary criminal courts 2481
from 1400 to 1747. R.A. MacTaggart. Glasgow Ph.D. 1969.

The history and development of the charitable trust 2482
from the 15th century onwards. G.H. Jones. London Ph.D.
1961.

The historical background of the English land law from 2483
1535. S.H. Brookfield. Liverpool M.A. 1935.

A history of English assizes from 1558 to 1714. J.S. 2484
Cockburn. Leeds Ph.D. 1970.

The action on the case: the development of the action 2485
as reflected on the plea rolls of the 16th and 17th centuries.
A.K. Kiralfy. London Ph.D. 1949.

The parliamentary representation of Grampound. R.C.D. 2486
Jasper. Leeds M.A. 1940.

The parliamentary representation of Glamorgan, 1536– 2487
1832. L.B. John. Wales M.A. 1934.

The parliamentary representation of Pembrokeshire, the 2488
Pembroke boroughs and Haverfordwest, 1536-1761. Mary E.
Jones. Wales M.A. 1958.

The parliamentary representation of Radnorshire, 1536– 2489
1832. D.R.L. Adams. Wales M.A. 1970.

The parliamentary representation of Monmouthshire and 2490
the Monmouth boroughs, 1536-1832. Ethel E. Havill. Wales
M.A. 1949.

The boroughs of North Wales: their parliamentary 2491
history from the Act of Union to the First Reform Act, 1536-
1832. G. Roberts. Wales M.A. 1928/9.

The evolution of radical theory after the Reformation. 2492
A.J. Clark. London M.A. 1910.

Political journalism, 1572-1714. R. Britton. Kent 2493
Ph.D. 1969.

The history of the Petitions of Right from the 17th 2494
century. M.F. Spungin. Oxford B.Litt. 1959.

The origins of the Petition of Right. L. Ehrlich. 2495
Oxford B.Litt. 1915.

ECONOMIC AND SOCIAL HISTORY

The changing landscape of rural Middlesex, 1500-1850. 2496
G.B.G. Bull. London Ph.D. 1958.

Changing agricultural landscapes in Cumberland. G.G. 2497
Elliott. Liverpool M.A. 1956.

Rural Cambridgeshire, 1520-1680. Mrs. H. Margaret 2498
Spufford. Leicester M.A. 1962.

Pauperism and vagrancy in Cambridgeshire to 1834. 2499
Ethel M. Hampson. Cambridge Ph.D. 1930/1.

Some aspects of the historical geography of central 2500
Surrey: a study in economic change. G.J. Ashworth. Reading
M.Phil. 1967/8.

Settlement and agriculture in North Wales, 1536-1670. 2501
B.M. Evans. Cambridge Ph.D. 1966.

The Petre lands in the Wid basin and adjacent areas 2502
from 1539 to 1939. Joyce G. Minton. London Ph.D. 1959.

A contribution to the historical geography of Needwood 2503
Forest, Staffordshire, from Elizabeth I to enclosure in the
early 19th century. P.H. Nicholls. London M.A. 1965.

West Cleveland land use, c.1550-1850. P.K. Mitchell. 2504
Durham Ph.D. 1965.

The economy of the Northamptonshire royal forests, 2505
1558-1714. P.A.J. Pettit. Oxford D.Phil. 1959.

Pre-inclosure agricultural systems in the East Riding 2506
of Yorkshire. A. Harris. London M.A. (Ext.) 1951.

Enclosure and the agricultural landscape of Lindsey 2507
from the 16th to the 19th century. S.A. Johnson. Liverpool
M.A. 1957.

2508   Lincolnshire glebe terriers of the deaneries of Calcewaith and Hill, 1577-1706. Olga Beaumont. Reading M.A.
1952.

2509   The rural economy of Oxfordshire, 1580-1730. M.A. Havinden. Oxford B.Litt. 1961.

2510   Economic changes in the manor of Cranborne (Dorset) in
the 16th and 17th centuries. Elizabeth B. Clarke. Oxford
B.Litt. 1939.

2511   Open field, enclosure and farm production in east
Worcestershire. J.A. Yelling. Birmingham Ph.D. 1966.

2512   The south-western peninsulas of England and Wales:
studies in agricultural geography, 1550-1900. T.R.B. Dicks.
Wales Ph.D. 1964.

2513   Development of the port of Harwich. Mrs. Frances N.
Mellen. London M.A. 1965.

2514   The contribution of Wales to the British empire in the
16th and 17th centuries. W.A. Bebb. Wales M.A. 1920.

2515   The historical geography of the paper-making industry
in England. A.H. Shorter. London Ph.D. 1954.

2516   The history of the Yorkshire woollen and worsted industries from the earliest times up to the Industrial Revolution.
H. Heaton. Birmingham M.Com. 1914.

2517   The historical geography of the Norfolk and Suffolk
woollen industry. J.S. Bishop. London M.A. 1929.

2518   The wool supply and the worsted cloth industry in Norfolk in the 16th and 17th centuries. K.J. Allison. Leeds
Ph.D. 1956.

2519   Aspects of the development of the Gloucestershire woollen
industry. Mrs. Jennifer Tann. Leicester Ph.D. 1964.

2520   Woollen trade and industry in the rural areas of
Gloucestershire. F.C. Raggatt. Bristol M.A. 1933.

2521   The internal wool trade in England during the 16th and
17th centuries: a study in economic history. P.J. Bowden.
Leeds Ph.D. 1952.

2522   The history of English coal mining, 1500-1750. Asta
W.R. Moller. Oxford D.Phil. 1932/3.

2523   The Willoughbys of Wollaton, 1500-1643, with special
reference to early mining in Nottinghamshire. R.S. Smith.
Nottingham Ph.D. 1964.

2524   The economic and social development of the Leicestershire and south Derbyshire coalfield, 1550-1914. C.P.
Griffin. Nottingham Ph.D. 1969.

2525   The development of the coal industry in the Radstock
area of Somerset from earliest times to 1830. J.A. Bulley.
London M.A. (Ext.) 1952.

2526   The geography of the south-west Lancashire mining industry, 1590-1799. J. Langton. Wales Ph.D. 1970.

2527   Studies in the history of mining and metallurgy to the
middle of the 17th century considered in relation to the progress of scientific knowledge and with some reference to
mining in Cornwall. P.C. Davey. London Ph.D. 1954.

2528   Changes of population in west Cornwall with the rise and
decline of mining. T.W. McGuinness. London M.Sc. 1938.

2529   The lead-mining industry of Swaledale. B. Jennings.
Leeds M.A. 1959.

2530   The lead industry in Cardiganshire. L. Jones. Wales
M.A. 1915.

2531   The lead and silver mining industry in Wales, 1558-1765.
L. Jones. Oxford B.Litt. 1923.

2532   Birmingham: an analysis of geographical influences on
the metal industries. Jean Rushton. London M.Sc. 1936.

2533   The history of the Midland glass industry, with special
reference to the flint glass section. D.N. Sandilands. Birmingham M.Com. 1927.

2534   The economic history of the modern English glass industry.
J.N. Reedman. Sheffield Ph.D. 1930.

2535   History of the alum trade. J. Rudsdale. Leeds M.A.
1932.

The Walsall and Midlands leather trades: a study in   2536
their history and organisation from the earliest times to the
present day. E. Tonkinson. Birmingham M.Com. 1948.
The English leather industry in the 16th and 17th cent- 2537
uries, 1563-1700. L.A. Clarkson. Nottingham Ph.D. 1960.
English leather glove trade. Muriel K. Fudge. Bristol 2538
M.A. 1930.
The location of footwear manufacture in England and   2539
Wales. P.R. Mounfield. Nottingham Ph.D. 1962.

ECCLESIASTICAL HISTORY

An historical and anthropological study of magic and   2540
religion amongst the gypsies of Britain. E.B. Trigg. Oxford
D.Phil. 1968.
A history of the attempts towards reunion between the   2541
Anglican and the Eastern-Orthodox churches, especially since
the 16th century. W.W. Price. Birmingham M.A. 1929.
Religious societies (ecclesiolae in ecclesia) from 1500 2542
to 1800, excluding those of the church of Rome. F.W.B.
Bullock. Cambridge Ph.D. 1937/8.
A history and source book on training for the ministry 2543
in the Church of England, 1511-1717. F. Bussby. Durham
M.Litt. 1952.
The controversy between Roman Catholics and Anglicans   2544
from Elizabeth to the Revolution. G. Windsor. Cambridge
Ph.D. 1967.
(1) The archdeacon's court: liber actorum; (2) epis-   2545
copal visitation book for the archdeaconry of Buckingham,
1662; (3) the study and use of archdeacon's court records,
illustrated from the Oxford records, 1566-1759. E.R.C.
Brinkworth. Birmingham M.A. 1951.
Puritan devotion, 1570-1700, and its place in the   2546
development of Christian piety. G.S. Wakefield. Oxford
B.Litt. 1954.
The worship of the English Puritans during the 16th,   2547
17th and early 18th centuries. D.H.M. Davies. Oxford D.Phil.
1943.
The indissolubility of marriage in Reformation and   2548
post-Reformation Anglican teaching and practice. A.R.
Winnett. London Ph.D. 1953.
The history of marriage and divorce in England since   2549
the Reformation. D.T.I. Jenkins. Birmingham M.A. 1963/4.
The organisation and development of cathedral worship   2550
in England since the Reformation. P.C. Moore. Oxford D.Phil.
1954.
Lay-preaching in England from the Reformation to the   2551
rise of Methodism: a study in its development, nature and
significance. J.H. Blackmore. Edinburgh Ph.D. 1951/2.
A study of the causes, administration and results of   2552
Lancashire church briefs, and studies of collections for
Lancashire and non-Lancashire briefs, with reference to col-
lections elsewhere in England. Joan Beck. London M.A. (Ext.)
1954.
The history of the doctrine of the Priesthood of All   2553
Believers. J.R. Crawford. Aberdeen Ph.D. 1958.
An investigation of the doctrine of the Priesthood of 2554
All Believers from the Reformation to the present day. C.C.
Eastwood. London Ph.D. 1957.
The inter-relation of civil and ecclesiastical author- 2555
ity in dealing with trials of bishops, 1558-1725. R.E. Head.
Oxford B.Litt. 1959.
Llenyddiaeth Gatholig y Cymry (1559-1829) rhyddiaith a 2556
barddoniaeth. (Catholic literature of the Welsh (1559-1829),
prose and poetry.) G. Bowen. Liverpool M.A. 1952/3.

2557   The parish registers of the churches of SS. Philip and Jacob and of St. Thomas in Bristol to 1812. D.K. Gosling. Bristol M.A. 1934.

2558   The theory and practice of the Lord's Supper among the early Separatists, Baptists and Independents, from 1580 to 1700. E.P. Winter. Oxford B.Litt. 1954.

2559   Our Lady of Batersey. The story of Battersea church and parish told from original sources. J.G. Taylor. London Ph.D. 1925.

CULTURAL HISTORY

   General

2560   English biography before 1700. D.A. Stauffer. Oxford B.Litt. 1931.

2561   Studies in the history of the song school at Durham from the early 15th century to the early 18th century. G.B. Crosby. Durham M.A. 1966.

2562   Efforts of patrons to establish endowed schools in Jersey and to provide scholarships at the English universities for Jersey scholars from 1477 to 1679. W. Moran. London M.A. (Ext.) 1964.

2563   The origin and development of academic costume and its bearing on the choir office robes of the Anglican clergy. F.R.S. Rogers. Bristol M.A. 1962.

2564   The education of English Catholics, 1559-1800. W.F. Hastings. London M.A. 1923.

2565   The provision for the vocational training of children in the East Riding, 1563-1811. K.J.R. Robson. Sheffield M.A. 1952.

2566   An investigation into the Lettice Dykes Educational Charity at East Bergholt in the county of Suffolk. M.H. Hyndman. Reading M.A. 1965/6.

2567   An outline of development in education in Wallasey, 1595-1962. B.E. Baylis. Wales M.A. 1964.

2568   The growth of educational institutions in Loughborough, with special reference to the history of Loughborough grammar school and the Burton charity. A. White. Nottingham Ph.D. 1962.

2569   The history of Nottingham High School, 1513-1903. A.W. Thomas. Nottingham Ph.D. 1956.

2570   A history of Whitchurch grammar school, Shropshire, 1550-1950. E. Clarke. Sheffield M.A. 1953.

2571   The history of Marlborough grammar school, 1550-1944, with some account of the mediaeval hospital of St. John Baptist, Marlborough. A.R. Stedman. London M.A. 1945.

2572   The history of St. Clement Danes Holborn Estate grammar school, 1552-1952. R.J.B. Pooley. London M.A. 1955.

2573   History of St. Peter's School, York. A. Raine. Durham M.A. 1946.

2574   Attitudes towards exercise and physical education in England: 1560-1714. D.W. Brailsford. Southampton Ph.D. 1966.

2575   History of Hampton-upon-Thames in the 16th and 17th centuries, with special reference to educational foundations. B. Garside. London M.A. 1930.

2576   The history of the grammar schools in Monmouthshire. M. Stephens. Wales M.A. 1957.

2577   The history of the Welsh language in Radnorshire since 1536. L.H. Owen. Liverpool M.A. 1953/4.

2578   The vicissitudes of the Welsh language in the Marches of Wales, with special reference to its territorial distribution in modern times. W.H. Rees. Wales Ph.D. 1947.

Transition from timber to brick in buildings of rural   2579
Leicestershire. V.R. Webster. Nottingham M.A. 1965.

The development of smaller domestic architecture in the 2580
Oxford region from the late 15th to the early 18th century.
D. Portman. Oxford B.Litt. 1960.

Country house building in Warwickshire, 1500-1914.   2581
G.C. Tyack. Oxford B.Litt. 1970.

Minor domestic architecture in the lower Trent valley,   2582
1550-1850. T.L. Marsden. Manchester M.A. 1952.

Minor domestic architecture in the county of Rutland   2583
and vicinity: an investigation of stages in the historical
development of the smaller rural house. T.L. Marsden. Manchester Ph.D. 1958.

Post-medieval timber-framed houses in England. K.H.   2584
Allmark. Manchester M.A. 1955.

The development of timber-framed buildings in Tewkes-   2585
bury. D.R. Franklin. Birmingham M.A. 1965.

Rural domestic architecture in south Lancashire, prior   2586
to the early 19th century. R.S. Partington. Manchester M.A.
1952.

Treasures of the Surrey churches in the diocese of   2587
Guildford. C.K.F. Brown. Leeds M.A. 1942.

The history of Welsh domestic art from the 16th cent-   2588
ury, as exhibited in the native furniture, with illustrations
together with a study of its relation to the furniture of
other parts of the British Isles and the continent of Europe.
D.R. Jones. Wales M.A. 1925.

The Oxford school of sculptors from 1550 to 1800.   2589
J.E.K. Esdaile. Oxford B.Litt. 1935.

LOCAL HISTORY

A study of the economic development of the commote of   2590
Carnwyllion from 1500. J.H. Morgan. Wales M.A. 1933.

The early history of Hunslet. G.G. Gamble. Leeds M.A.   2591
1948.

Local administration (excluding borough administration) 2592
as exemplified in Monmouthshire, 1536-1835. B. Howell. Wales
M.A. 1951.

The origins and early history of the Melton Mowbray town 2593
estate: a study in the government of an unincorporated town.
Dorothy Pockley. Leicester Ph.D. 1964.

The Scilly Islands during Tudor and Stuart times   2594
(approx. 1547-1700). T.F.G. Matthews. Oxford B.Litt. 1943.

A Kentish Wealden parish (Tonbridge), 1550-1750. C.W.   2595
Chalklin. Oxford B.Litt. 1960.

Sussex market towns, 1550-1750. G.O. Cowley. London   2596
M.A. 1965.

Evolution of local government authorities and areas in   2597
Suffolk, 1555 to 1894. J.H. Whitfield. Kent M.A. 1970.

Local government in Wales from the 16th to the 18th cent- 2598
ury, as exemplified by the work of the quarter sessions of
the county. T.H. Lewis. London Ph.D. (Ext.) 1941.

The history of South Shields in the 16th and 17th cent- 2599
uries. Dorothy W. McCallum. Durham M.A. 1936.

Borough courts of quarter sessions from the beginning   2600
until the end of the 17th century. M.A. Reed. Birmingham
M.A. 1958.

The court of Taunton in the 16th and 17th centuries.   2601
R.G.H. Whitty. London M.A. (Ext.) 1932.

Local government in the principality of Wales during   2602
the 16th and 17th centuries, as illustrated mainly by the
extant data relating to the county of Merioneth. I. Ab Owen
Edwards. Wales M.A. 1925.

2603   The borough of Tewkesbury, 1575-1714. Mary F. Redmond.
Birmingham M.A. 1950.
2604   The map of Kent, 1575 to 1807. B.T. Westmarland. London M.A. 1955.
2605   Maps of the Isle of Wight, from Boazio to Milne, 1591-
1791. A.J. Jubb. London M.A. 1959.
2606   Marine cartography in Britain from the 16th to the 19th
centuries. A.H.W. Robinson. London Ph.D. 1960.

SCOTLAND

2607   Origins and background of the law of succession to arms
and dignities in Scotland. Sir Rupert I.K. Moncreiffe, Bt.
Edinburgh Ph.D. 1958.
2608   The origin and nature of the legal rights of spouses and
children in the Scottish law of succession. J.C. Gardner.
Edinburgh Ph.D. 1927.
2609   The jurisdiction of the Scottish privy council, 1532-
1708. P.G.B. McNeill. Glasgow Ph.D. 1961.
2610   Scots burgh finances prior to 1707. G.S. Pryde. St.
Andrews Ph.D. 1926.
2611   The survival of a Celtic society in the Mackay country
formerly called Strathnaver in northern Scotland from the
16th century. I. Grimble. Aberdeen Ph.D. 1964.
2612   Witchcraft and the church in Scotland subsequent to the
Reformation. J. Gilmore. Glasgow Ph.D. 1948.
2613   History of church discipline in Scotland. I.M. Clark.
Aberdeen Ph.D. 1926.
2614   An historical survey of education in Angus to the year
1872 from original and contemporary sources, embracing early
education and the beginnings of systematic education; the
parish school system; burgh schools; schools of industry; and
the origin and establishment of infant schools. J.C. Jessop.
St. Andrews Ph.D. 1930.
2615   Education in Fife, from the Reformation to 1872. J.M.
Beale. Edinburgh Ph.D. 1953.
2616   Church and state in Scottish school education during the
Reformation period (1560-1700). B.M. Wyllie. London M.A.
1952.
2617   An enquiry into the history of registration for publication in Scotland. L. Ockrent. Edinburgh Ph.D. 1938.
2618   The influence of geographical factors on the economic
evolution of Scotland to the beginning of the 18th century,
mainly as revealed in the development of overseas trade,
especially that of the Clyde ports. J. Walker. Edinburgh
Ph.D. 1928.

IRELAND

2619   The composition and distribution of woods in Ireland
from the 16th century to the establishment of the first
Ordnance Survey. Eileen M. McCracken. Belfast M.Sc. 1944.
2620   The history of penal laws against Irish Catholics from
1534 to the treaty of Limerick (1691). R.W.D. Edwards.
London Ph.D. 1933.
2621   The financial administration of Ireland to 1817. T.J.
Kiernan. London Ph.D. 1929.

POLITICAL HISTORY

The Tudor privy council. D.N. Gladish. London M.A. 2622
1915.
The jurisdiction of the privy council under the Tudors. 2623
Edna F. White. London M.A. 1918.
The privy council under the Tudors, 1540-72. G.E. 2624
Taylor. Birmingham M.A. 1928.
Parliamentary representation in the 16th century. 2625
W.S. Dann. London M.A. 1911.
The relations between Henry VII and Wales. W.T. 2626
Williams. Wales M.A. 1914.
The relations of Henry VII with Scotland and Ireland 2627
(1485-97), illustrated from episodes in the life of Sir Henry
Wyatt (1460?-1537). Agnes E. Conway. London M.A. 1926.
The government of Calais, 1485 to 1558. P.T.J. Morgan. 2628
Oxford D.Phil. 1967.
The history of Calais under the deputyship of Arthur 2629
Plantagenet, Lord Lisle, 1533-40. J. Leese. Manchester M.A.
1929.
Life and works of Edmund Dudley. Dorothy M. Brodie. 2630
Cambridge Ph.D. 1935.
William Warham as statesman, scholar, and patron. 2631
Kathleen E. Hardy. Oxford B.Litt. 1943.
The career of John Tayler, Master of the Rolls (d. 2632
1534), as an illustration of early Tudor administrative
history. R.E. Brock. London M.A. 1950.
The early Tudor peerage, 1485-1547. Helen J. Miller. 2633
London M.A. 1950.
The judiciary in relation to legislation and constit- 2634
utional development during the reigns of Henry VII and
Henry VIII. J.J. MacGinley. London M.A. 1915.
Some aspects of the legal profession in the late 15th 2635
and early 16th centuries. E.W. Ives. London Ph.D. 1955.
Lawyers and law reporting in England in the 16th cent- 2636
ury. L.W. Abbott. London Ph.D. 1969.
The common law in the 16th century. J.F. Myers. 2637
Liverpool M.A. 1950.
The treason legislation of the reign of Henry VIII. 2638
Isobel D. Thornley. London M.A. 1917.
Sir Robert and Sir Richard Wingfield. Mrs. Patricia 2639
Buckland. Birmingham M.A. 1968.
English borough representation, 1509-58. M.G. Price. 2640
Oxford D.Phil. 1960.
The influence of the Renaissance on the English con- 2641
ception of the state. F.W.E.C. Caspari. Oxford B.Litt. 1936.
Sir Thomas Elyot: his life and his work. S.E. Lehm- 2642
berg. Cambridge Ph.D. 1956.
Sir Thomas Elyot's The Image of Governaunce: its 2643
sources and political significance. Mrs. Margaret N. Woolger.
Oxford B.Litt. 1970.
The two regiments: a study of the development of the 2644
theory of the relations of church and state during the
Reformation, with particular reference to England. W.D.J.
Cargill Thompson. Cambridge Ph.D. 1960.
The administration and parliamentary representation of 2645
Nottinghamshire and Derbyshire, 1529-58. Christine J. Black.
London Ph.D. 1966.
Local politics and the parliamentary representation of 2646
Sussex, 1529-58. R.J.W. Swales. Bristol Ph.D. 1964.
Some Spanish biographies of Sir Thomas More. R.O. 2647
Jones. London M.A. 1949.
Sir Thomas More and the divorce. Enid Edkins. Liver- 2648
pool M.A. 1916.

2649 Thomas Cromwell: aspects of his administrative work. G.R. Elton. London Ph.D. 1949.

2650 The life and times of John Dudley, earl of Warwick and duke of Northumberland, 1504(?)-1553. C. Sturge. London Ph.D. 1927.

2651 The rise to power of Edward Seymour, Protector Somerset, 1500-47. M.L. Bush. Cambridge Ph.D. 1965.

2652 The 'Acts of Union' and the Tudor settlement of Wales. P.R. Roberts. Cambridge Ph.D. 1966.

2653 The life and writings of William Thomas, d. 1554. P.J. Laven. London M.A. 1954.

2654 Sir John Forster: a study of Tudor politics. J. Howe. Newcastle M.Litt. 1970.

2655 Some aspects of the life and political career of Sir Richard Rich. Elizabeth P. McIntyre. Aberdeen M.Litt. 1968.

2656 The parliamentary representation of Wales and Monmouth-shire, 1542-58. P.S. Edwards. Cambridge Ph.D. 1970.

2657 The Commons in the parliament of 1545. Anne D. Tucker. Oxford D.Phil. 1966.

2658 The career and writings of Sir Thomas Smith, 1513-77. Mrs. Mary C. Dewar. London Ph.D. 1956.

2659 An enquiry into the state of public opinion from the establishment of King Henry VIII's supremacy over the church to the close of the Lincolnshire rebellion, drawn principally from the Letters and Papers of the reign of Henry VIII, volumes VII-XII, edited Gairdner. W.E. Milward. Liverpool M.A. 1907.

2660 Treason legislation in England, 1547-1603. W.J. Fitz-gerald. London M.A. 1963.

2661 On the causes and course of the rebellion of 1549 in Devon and Cornwall. W.J. Blake. London M.A. 1909.

2662 The Norfolk rising under Robert Kett, 1549. W.H.T. Walker. Wales M.A. 1921.

2663 The social and economic circumstances of Ket's rebellion, 1549. R.J. Hammond. London M.A. 1933.

2664 Popular subversion and government security in England during the reign of Queen Mary I. D.M. Loades. Cambridge Ph.D. 1962.

2665 The office of principal secretary to the Crown under Elizabeth and the early Stewarts. Florence M.G. Evans. Manchester M.A. 1919.

2666 The proclamations of Elizabeth I. F.A. Youngs. Cam-bridge Ph.D. 1969.

2667 The Elizabethan chancery: some legal and other aspects. W.J. Jones. London Ph.D. 1958.

2668 The house of lords under Elizabeth. J.E. Neale. Liver-pool M.A. 1915.

2669 The court of requests in the reign of Elizabeth. W.B.J. Allsebrook. London M.A. 1936.

2670 The court of star chamber in the reign of Queen Eliza-beth. Elfreda Skelton. London M.A. 1931.

2671 The problem of the North in the early years of Queen Elizabeth's reign. S. Charlesworth. Sheffield Ph.D. 1931.

2672 The Council in the Marches of Wales during the reign of Queen Elizabeth. P.H. Williams. Oxford D.Phil. 1955.

2673 The early career of Sir James Croft, 1518-70. Christina A. Mackwell. Oxford B.Litt. 1970.

2674 The career of Henry Hastings, 3rd earl of Huntingdon, 1536-95. M. Claire Cross. Cambridge Ph.D. 1959.

2675 Some aspects of the work of the Elizabethan intelligence service. L.E. Morris. Wales M.A. 1968.

2676 The parliamentary representation of Devon and Dorset, 1559-1601. J.C. Roberts. London M.A. 1958.

2677 The French religious wars in English politics and polit-ical theory. J.H.McM. Salmon. Cambridge M.Litt. 1957.

2678 Richard Hooker: a study in the history of political philosophy. A.P. d'Entrèves. Oxford D.Phil. 1932/3.

The place of Hooker in the history of thought. P.   2679
Munz. Cambridge Ph.D. 1948.
     The politics of Hooker. F.J.J. Shirley. London Ph.D.   2680
(Ext.) 1931.
     The personnel of the house of commons, 1563-7. Norah   2681
M. Fuidge. London M.A. 1950.
     The personnel of parliament, 1571. Helen Brady. Man-   2682
chester M.A. 1927.
     Sir Michael Hickes and the secretariat of the Cecils,   2683
c.1580-1612. A.G.R. Smith. London Ph.D. 1962.
     The political career of Sir Robert Naunton, 1563-1635.   2684
R.E. Schreiber. London Ph.D. 1967.
     The public career of Sir Julius Caesar, 1584-1614.   2685
L.M. Hill. London Ph.D. 1968.
     Personnel of the parliament of 1584-5. Hazel Matthews. 2686
London M.A. 1948.
     Members of the house of commons, 1586-7. R.C. Gabriel. 2687
London M.A. 1954.
     Some aspects of the Inns of Court, 1590-1640. W.R.   2688
Prest. Oxford D.Phil. 1965.
     Personnel of the parliament of 1593. Evelyn E. Traf-   2689
ford. London M.A. 1948.
     The personnel of parliament, 1597. Constance M. Davey. 2690
Manchester M.A. 1927.
     The personnel of the house of commons in 1601.   2691
Margaret K. Mort. London M.A. 1952.
     Treason and treason trials during the 17th century.   2692
Mrs. Norah W. Irvine. Durham M.A. 1936.
     The administrative work of the lord chancellor in the   2693
early 17th century. Jean S. Wilson. London Ph.D. 1927.
     The function and influence of privy councillors in   2694
parliament in the early 17th century. Dorothy Keane.
London M.A. 1930.
     Sir Robert Heath (1575-1649): some consideration of   2695
his work and life. I.H.C. Fraser. Bristol M.A. 1954.
     The king's principal secretaries of state under the   2696
early Stuarts. Florence M.G. Evans. Manchester Ph.D. 1921.
     Promotion and politics amongst the common law judges   2697
of the reigns of James I and Charles I. H.H.A. Cooper.
Liverpool M.A. 1964.
     Patronage and officers in the reign of James I. P.R.   2698
Seddon. Manchester Ph.D. 1967.
     The parliamentary franchise in the English boroughs in   2699
the Stuart period. E.C. Whitworth. London M.A. 1926.
     The borough franchise in the first half of the 17th   2700
century. Winifred A. Taffs. London M.A. 1926.
     The political activity and influence of the house of   2701
lords, 1603-29. D. Jean Dawson. Oxford B.Litt. 1950.
     Freedom of speech in the house of commons in the reign   2702
of James I. Sir Michael B.G. Oppenheimer, Bt. Oxford B.Litt.
1955.
     The development of English parliamentary judicature,   2703
1604-26. C.G.C. Tite. London Ph.D. 1970.
     The life and work of Sir Francis Kynaston. H.G.   2704
Seccombe. Oxford B.Litt. 1933.
     The life and works of Sir Francis Kynaston. C.F.   2705
Williamson. Oxford B.Litt. 1957.
     The parish of St. Stephen's, Coleman Street, London: a   2706
study in radicalism, c.1624-1664. D.A. Kirby. Oxford B.Litt.
1968.
     The parliamentary career of Sir John Eliot, 1624-9.   2707
J.N. Ball. Cambridge Ph.D. 1953.
     Studies in the institutions and personnel of English   2708
central administration, 1625-42. G.E. Aylmer. Oxford D.Phil.
1955.
     The court of star chamber, 1603-41, with special refer- 2709
ence to the period 1625-41. H.E.I. Phillips. London M.A.
1939.

2710   The political career of Francis Cottington, 1605-52. A.J. Cooper. Oxford B.Litt. 1966.

2711   A survey of the parliamentary elections of 1625, 1626 and 1628. J.D. Thomas. London M.A. 1952.

2712   John Pym. Ethel M. Beebee. Birmingham M.A. 1915.

2713   The power of the sword: a study in 17th-century political ideology. G.W.S.V. Rumble. Kent M.A. 1970.

2714   The judges of Westminster Hall during the Great Rebellion, 1640-60. S.F. Black. Oxford B.Litt. 1970.

2715   An introduction to the life and works of Francis Rous, puritan divine and parliamentarian (1581-1659). K.J. Harper. Wales M.A. 1960.

2716   John Berkenhead in literature and politics, 1640-63. P.W. Thomas. Oxford D.Phil. 1962.

2717   A study of the life and works of Sir John Berkenhead. S.P. Whitaker. London M.A. 1915.

2718   Controversial portraiture in the Thomason tracts (1640-61), with special reference to King Charles I. Lois M.G. Spencer. London Ph.D. 1959.

2719   The political thought of Sir Robert Filmer and his royalist contemporaries. Stella M.E. Trood. London M.A. 1922.

2720   The idea of government during the puritan rebellion. Winifred O'Brien. Liverpool M.A. 1929.

2721   The moderate Royalists and Puritans, and the conception of sovereignty in England prior to the Civil War. A.S.H. Hill. London Ph.D. 1933.

2722   The life of Christopher Love and his relation to contemporary movements. Clara G. Criddle. Wales M.A. 1933.

2723   The life and letters of Christopher Love, 1618-51. M.H. Jones. Wales M.A. 1932.

2724   The character, composition and organisation of the Long Parliament, 1640-53. R.N. Kershaw. Oxford B.Litt. 1923.

2725   The political career of Henry Marten, with special reference to the origins of republicanism in the Long Parliament. C.M. Williams. Oxford D.Phil. 1954.

2726   The Long Parliament and the fear of popular pressure, 1640-6. R. Yarlott. Leeds M.A. 1963.

2727   Sir Henry Vane the elder. Evelyn B. Wells. Manchester M.A. 1923.

2728   The political and administrative career of Sir Henry Vane the younger, 1640 to April 1653. Violet A. Rowe. London Ph.D. 1965.

2729   The careers and opinions of Hugh Peters and Sir Henry Vane the younger. J.M. Patrick. Oxford B.Litt. 1936.

2730   A report on the sources available for an account of the life of Sir Henry Vane, junior, during the period 1649-62. Edith M. Emlyn. Liverpool M.A. 1928.

2731   The political history of the parliamentary boroughs of Kent, 1642-62. Madeline V. Jones. London Ph.D. 1967.

2732   Political ideas in the royalist pamphlets of the period, 1642-9. I.D. Brice. Oxford B.Litt. 1970.

2733   Studies in royalism in the English Civil War, 1642-6, with special reference to Staffordshire. J.T. Pickles. Manchester M.A. 1968.

2734   The Great Civil War in Shropshire, 1642-9. W.J. Farrow. Manchester M.A. 1925.

2735   The Great Civil War in Shrewsbury. H. Beaumont. Sheffield M.A. 1934.

2736   Governor Gell, 1642-6: a study of the Civil War in Derbyshire. J.T. Brighton. Hull M.A. 1969/70.

2737   An edition of the memoirs of Sir Hugh Cholmley, with a contribution on his life and on the Civil War in Yorkshire. T.H. Brooke. Oxford B.Litt. 1937.

2738   The history of the counties of Glamorgan and Monmouth during the Great Civil War, 1642-8. Laetitia J. Thomas. Wales M.A. 1914.

The first Civil War in Glamorgan, 1642-6. C.M. Thomas. 2739
Wales M.A. 1963.

Royalist organisation in Wiltshire, 1642-6. G.A. 2740
Harrison. London Ph.D. 1963.

Royalist organisation in Gloucestershire and Bristol, 2741
1642-5. G.A. Harrison. Manchester M.A. 1961.

Henry Somerset, 5th earl and 1st marquis of Worcester, 2742
1577-1646; a biographical study. I.D. Thomas. Wales M.A.
1959.

Sir Thomas Myddelton II: 1586-1666. G.R. Thomas. 2743
Wales M.A. 1968.

The Eastern Association. C.A. Holmes. Cambridge Ph.D. 2744
1969.

The mixed-monarchy debate, 1642-4. S.J. Cumella. 2745
Strathclyde M.Sc. 1969/70.

The king's armies in the west of England, 1642-6. 2746
M.D.G. Wanklyn. Manchester M.A. 1966.

The life of Sir William Waller, 1598-1668. J.E. Adair. 2747
London Ph.D. 1966.

The Civil War in Warwickshire, 1642-6, with an intro- 2748
duction on the representation of Warwickshire in the Long
Parliament. P.H. Billingham. Oxford B.Litt. 1927.

The part played by the Catholics in the Civil War in 2749
Lancashire and Monmouthshire. K.J. Lindley. Manchester
M.A. 1965.

The Civil War in Somerset, 1642-6. C.W. Terry. 2750
London M.A. 1913.

Wolverhampton and the Great Civil War, 1642-5. T.J. 2751
Larkin. Birmingham M.A. 1928.

The proclamations issued by Charles I during the years 2752
1642-6, both during his progress to Oxford and his residence
there until the surrender of the city in 1646, relating
especially to Oxford and neighbouring counties. E.J.S.
Parsons. Oxford B.Litt. 1935.

Neutrals and neutralism in the English Civil War, 2753
1642-6. B.S. Manning. Oxford D.Phil. 1959.

The sequestration of estates, 1643-60. H.E. Chesney. 2754
Sheffield Ph.D. 1928.

The second Civil War, 1648. J.B. Crummett. Manchester 2755
M.A. 1957.

The part played by Walwyn and Overton in the Leveller 2756
movement. Joan E. Speak. Leeds M.A. 1949.

The life and works of William Walwyn the Leveller. 2757
Sheila H. Knapton. London M.A. 1949.

The Levellers and the origin of the theory of natural 2758
rights. L.H. Poe. Oxford D.Phil. 1957.

John Lilburne and his relation to the first phase of 2759
the Leveller movement, 1638-49. Pauline E. Gregg. London
Ph.D. 1939.

The Digger movement in the English Revolution. D.W. 2760
Petegorsky. London Ph.D. 1940.

The Ranters, 1649-60. J.F. McGregor. Oxford B.Litt. 2761
1969.

The Fifth Monarchy men: an analysis of their origins, 2762
activities, ideas and composition. B.S. Capp. Oxford D.Phil.
1970.

Oliver Cromwell's view of his political mission in the 2763
light of his theological and ecclesiastical presuppositions.
R.S. Paul. Oxford D.Phil. 1949.

The preservation of public order in Cromwellian London. 2764
M.W. Towse. Cambridge M.Litt. 1965.

The Upper House during the protectorates of Oliver and 2765
Richard Cromwell. Mercy C. Hart. London M.A. 1929.

The royalist party in England, October 1651 - September 2766
1658. D.E. Underdown. Oxford B.Litt. 1953.

2767   An analysis of the opposition to the major-generals, with special reference to Yorkshire and the North. H. Green-leaves. Oxford B.Litt. 1927.

2768   The correspondence of Henry Cromwell, 1655-9, and other papers, from the British Museum Lansdowne MSS. 821-3. C. Jones. Lancaster M.Litt. 1969.

2769   Politics and political theory in England, 1658-60. A.H. Woolrych. Oxford B.Litt. 1952.

2770   The members from the northern counties in Richard Crom-well's parliament. G.V. Chivers. Manchester M.A. 1954.

2771   Richard Cromwell's parliament, January 27th 1658/9 - April 22nd, 1659. Joan D. McKay. Liverpool M.A. 1951.

2772   The place of Sir Arthur Hesilrige in English politics, 1659-60. G.H. Brown. Oxford B.Litt. 1948.

MILITARY AND MARITIME HISTORY

2773   Wales and piracy: a study in Tudor administration, 1500-1640. Carys E. Hughes. Wales M.A. 1937.

2774   Welsh seamen, navigators, and colonisers, Elizabethan and Jacobean, together with some history of Welsh maritime and colonising activity during the period. E.R. Williams. Wales M.A. 1915.

2775   The military obligations of York citizens in Tudor times. N.J. Longbone. Leeds M.A. 1953.

2776   The military obligations of the English people, 1511-58. J.J. Goring. London Ph.D. 1955.

2777   Maritime activity under Henry VII. W.E.C. Harrison. London M.A. 1931.

2778   Supply services of English armed forces, 1509-50. C.S.L. Davies. Oxford D.Phil. 1963.

2779   The history of the Trinity House at Deptford, 1514-1660. G.G. Harris. London M.A. 1962.

2780   Piracy and privateering from Dartmouth and Kingswear, 1540-58. Ruth M.S. Tugwood. London M.A. 1953.

2781   English military organisation, c.1558-1638. L.O.J. Boynton. Oxford D.Phil. 1962.

2782   The economic aspects of Elizabethan privateering. K.R. Andrews. London Ph.D. 1951.

2783   Privateering in north-west European waters, 1568 to 1572. B. Dietz. London Ph.D. 1959.

2784   English sea-chaplains in the Royal Navy, 1577-1684. J. Curry. Bristol M.A. 1956.

2785   The naval chaplain in Stuart times. W.F. Scott. Oxford D.Phil. 1935.

2786   The beacons of north England, with special reference to the geographical plan of those provided in Elizabethan times. R.J. Wood. London M.Sc. 1937.

2787   Some aspects of the attempts of the government to suppress piracy during the reign of Elizabeth I. D.G.E. Hurd. London M.A. 1961.

2788   Sir Francis Drake: explorer. Kathleen M. Keegan. Bir-mingham M.A. 1924.

2789   The organisation and administration of the Elizabethan foreign military expeditions, 1585-1603. C.G. Cruickshank. Oxford D.Phil. 1940.

2790   Supplies for the army and navy under Elizabeth, 1595-1603. F. Mitchell. Manchester M.A. 1923.

2791   The navy under the early Stuarts and its influence on English history. C.D. Penn. London M.A. 1913.

2792   Naval administration, 1603-28. N. Clayton. Leeds Ph.D. 1936.

2793   Naval construction in the reign of James I. Mrs. Mar-garet Exley. Leeds M.A. 1949.

2794   The Royal Navy under the 1st duke of Buckingham, Lord High Admiral 1618-28. A.P. McGowan. London Ph.D. 1967.

Sea power and Welsh history, 1625-60. A. Eames. Wales 2795
M.A. 1954.

The adhesion of the Royal Navy to parliament at the   2796
outbreak of the Civil War. Isabel G. Powell. London M.A.
1919.

The navy during the Civil Wars and the Commonwealth,   2797
1642-51. M.L. Baumber. Manchester M.A. 1967.

Parliament and the navy, 1642-8: a political history of 2798
the navy during the Civil War. D.E. Kennedy. Cambridge
Ph.D. 1959.

The royalist army in the first Civil War, 1642-6. I.   2799
Roy. Oxford D.Phil. 1963.

Sir Thomas Morgan, Bt., 1604-79, 'soldier of fortune'.   2800
D.G. Lewis. Wales M.A. 1930.

ECONOMIC AND SOCIAL HISTORY

  Economic Theory and Finance

Parliamentary lay taxation, 1485-1547. R.S. Schofield. 2801
Cambridge Ph.D. 1963.

The causes and the progress of the growth of economic   2802
individualism in England in the 16th and at the beginning of
the 17th century. H.M. Robertson. Cambridge Ph.D. 1929/30.

The Tudor coinage, 1544-71. C.E. Challis. Bristol   2803
Ph.D. 1968.

Sir Thomas Gresham as financial agent of the Crown,   2804
with special reference to Antwerp loans, 1551-65. H. Buckley.
Manchester M.A. 1923.

Studies in Elizabethan government finance: royal   2805
borrowing and the sales of Crown lands, 1572-1603. R.B.
Outhwaite. Nottingham Ph.D. 1964.

William Cecil, Lord Burleigh, and the English patents   2806
of monopoly. A.J. Cooke. Manchester M.A. 1966.

Bodleian manuscripts relating to the later Tudors, with 2807
special reference to the currency literature of the period.
F.J. Routledge. Oxford B.Litt. 1920.

Economic thought in England, 1600-30, with reference to 2808
its evolution in the light of economic history. J.D. Gould.
Bristol M.A. 1951.

Government borrowing under the first two Stuarts   2809
(1603-42). R. Ashton. London Ph.D. 1953.

The career of Sir Arthur Ingram: a study in the   2810
finance and politics of the reign of James I. C.W. Sellars.
Leeds M.A. 1952.

The gold and silver thread monopolies granted by   2811
James I, 1611-21. M.A. Abrams. London Ph.D. 1929.

Public borrowing 1640-60, with special reference to   2812
government borrowing in the City of London between 1640 and
1650. W.P. Harper. London M.Sc. 1927.

Records of tax assessments, 1642-51. Muriel M. Colyer. 2813
London M.A. 1922.

The shipmoney levies under Charles I and their influ-   2814
ence on local feeling. Sarah E. Foster. London M.A. 1914.

Royalist composition fines and land sales in Yorkshire, 2815
1645-65. P.G. Holiday. Leeds Ph.D. 1966.

Financial and commercial policy under the Protectorate. 2816
M.P. Ashley. Oxford D.Phil. 1932/3.

The commercial factor in English policy, 1649-67. P.T. 2817
Hammond. Cambridge M.Litt. 1966.

The debentures market and military purchases of Crown   2818
land, 1649-60. I.J. Gentles. London Ph.D. 1969.

  Industry and Agriculture

The enclosure of Stamford open fields. S. Elliott.   2819
Nottingham M.A. 1965.

2820   Enclosure in Leicestershire, 1485-1607. L.A. Parker.
London M.A. (Ext.) 1948.
2821   The enclosure movement in South Wales during the Tudor
and early Stuart periods. T.I.J. Jones. Wales M.A. 1936.
2822   The estates of the earls of Devon, 1485-1538. Margaret
R. Westcott. Exeter M.A. 1959.
2823   The economic aspects of book production and distribution
between 1500 and 1650. Marjorie Plant. London M.Sc. 1934.
2824   The Bristol craft gilds during the 16th and 17th centuries. F.H. Rogers. Bristol M.A. 1949.
2825   The influence and development of the industrial guilds
in the larger provincial towns under James I and Charles I,
with special reference to the formation of new corporations
for the control of industry. F.J. Fisher. London M.A. 1931.
2826   Mining in the Lake counties in the 16th century. J.D.S.
Paul. London Ph.D. 1926.
2827   The status of journeymen in the 16th century. Florence
Roscoe. Manchester M.A. 1926.
2828   The enforcement of a seven years' apprenticeship under
the Statute of Artificers. T.K. Derry. Oxford D.Phil.
1930/1.
2829   The regulation of wages in England under the Statute of
Artificers. Nora M. Hindmarsh. London Ph.D. (Ext.) 1932.
2830   Some contributions to a study of work, wages and prices
in Wales in the 16th century. Annie B. Jones. Wales M.A.
1933.
2831   Agrarian conditions and changes in west Wales during the
16th century, with special reference to monastic and chantry
lands. G.D. Owen. Wales Ph.D. 1935.
2832   The earls of Worcester and their estates, 1526-1642.
W.R.B. Robinson. Oxford B.Litt. 1959.
2833   The economic development of the estates of the Petre
family in Essex in the 16th and 17th centuries. W.R. Emerson.
Oxford D.Phil. 1951.
2834   The changing composition of the class of larger landowners in Bedfordshire, Buckinghamshire and Northamptonshire
between the Reformation and the Civil War, illustrated by a
special study of the manorial holdings of the Verney, Spencer
and Dormer families. T. Hallinan. Oxford D.Phil. 1955.
2835   The land market in Devon, 1536-58. J.E. Kew. Exeter
Ph.D. 1967.
2836   The estates of William Farington of Worden, 1537-1610.
A.J. Atherton. Manchester M.A. 1953.
2837   The agrarian development of Wiltshire, 1540-1640. E.W.J.
Kerridge. London Ph.D. 1951.
2838   The Wiltshire woollen industry, chiefly in the 16th and
early 17th centuries. G.D. Ramsay. Oxford D.Phil. 1939.
2839   The development of the west of England woollen industry,
from 1550 to 1640. Kate E. Barford. London M.A. 1923.
2840   The cloth industry in Essex and Suffolk, 1558-1640. J.E.
Pilgrim. London M.A. 1938.
2841   The Lancashire textile industry in the 16th century. N.
Lowe. Manchester M.A. 1966.
2842   Agrarian conditions in east Berkshire, 1560-1660. Kathleen A. Brewin. London M.A. 1918.
2843   The agrarian history of Sussex, 1560-1640. J.C.K. Cornwall. London M.A. 1953.
2844   Essex rural settlement: some aspects of its evolution,
with particular reference to the 16th century. E. Grace
Farrell. Wales M.A. 1969.
2845   Agriculture and rural society in Essex, 1560-1640. F.
Hull. London Ph.D. 1950.
2846   Agrarian discontent under the early Stuarts and during
the last decades of Elizabeth. D.G.C. Allan. London M.Sc.
1950.
2847   Agrarian conditions in Norfolk and Suffolk during the
first half of the 17th century. J. Spratt. London M.A. 1935.

The Wealden landscape in the early 17th century and   2848
its antecedents. J.L.M. Gulley. London Ph.D. 1960.
    The Bridgewater estates in north Shropshire in the   2849
first half of the 17th century. E. Hopkins. London M.A.
1956.
    The industrial history of London, 1630-40, with   2850
special reference to the suburbs and those areas claiming
exemption from the authority of the lord mayor. J.L. Archer.
London M.A. 1934.
    Government and industry during the Protectorate. G.D.   2851
Ramsay. Oxford B.Litt. 1933.
    The early history of the iron industry in the Dudley   2852
area, with special reference to the claims of Dud Dudley.
W.J. Jenkins. Wales M.A. 1929.

Trade

    The trading communities of Totnes and Dartmouth in the   2853
late 15th and early 16th centuries. Laura M. Nicholls.
Exeter M.A. 1960.
    The trade and market in fish in the London area during   2854
the early 16th century, 1485-1563. J.P. McManus. London M.A.
1952.
    The Vintners' Company of London in the earlier 16th   2855
century. Mrs. Josephine P. Collins. Leeds M.Phil. 1968.
    The Merchant Adventurers in the first half of the 16th   2856
century. P.H. Ramsey. Oxford D.Phil. 1958.
    The relations of England and the Hanseatic League   2857
during the first half of the 16th century. W. Judson. Manchester M.A. 1924.
    The correspondence of Thomas Sexton, merchant of   2858
London, and his factors in Danzig, 1550-60. W. Sharpe.
London M.A. 1952.
    Henry Tooley, merchant of early Tudor Ipswich. J.G.   2859
Webb. London M.A. 1953.
    The maritime trade of the East Anglian ports, 1550-90.   2860
N.J. Williams. Oxford D.Phil. 1952.
    The seaborne trade of Southampton in the second half   2861
of the 16th century. Joan L. Thomas. Southampton M.A. 1954.
    The salt trade and monopolies in Great Britain, 1558-   2862
1603. E. Hughes. Manchester M.A. 1923.
    The foreign trade of Chester in the reign of Eliza-   2863
beth I. D.M. Woodward. Manchester M.A. 1965.
    The import trade of early Elizabethan London as shown   2864
by port book E 190/3/2 of 1565. J.E.G. Bennell. Oxford
B.Litt. 1970.
    A calendar and analysis, with introduction, of two   2865
Elizabethan port books (E 190/5/1 and E 190/5/6). F.E.
Leese. Oxford B.Litt. 1950.
    Mr. Customer Smythe, Customer of the port of London,   2866
1570-89. L.L.S. Lowe. Oxford B.Litt. 1950.
    Merchant adventurer - the story of Sir Thomas Smith.   2867
S.G. Evans. Leeds M.A. 1949.
    A comparative study of commercial fluctuations, 1600-   2868
40. B.E. Supple. Cambridge Ph.D. 1955.
    The trade of Newcastle-upon-Tyne and the north-east   2869
coast, 1600-40. Bertha Hall. London Ph.D. 1933.
    The import trade of London, 1600-40. Mrs. Annie M.   2870
Millard. London Ph.D. 1956.
    The greater merchants of London in the early 17th   2871
century. R.G. Lang. Oxford D.Phil. 1963.
    Shrewsbury, Oswestry and the Welsh wool trade in the   2872
17th century (especially in connexion with the crisis and
parliament of 1621). T.C. Mendenhall. Oxford B.Litt. 1936.
    A history of the Shrewsbury Drapers' Company during   2873
the 17th century, with particular reference to the Welsh
woollen trade. D.J. Evans. Wales M.A. 1950.

2874   The Eyres of Hassop: a Derbyshire gentry family, their rise and recusancy, 1470-1640. Rosamond Meredith. Sheffield M.A. 1963.

2875   The Mansells of Oxwich and Margam, 1487-1631. D.M. Cole. Birmingham M.A. 1966.

2876   The behaviour of the population of Poulton-le-Fylde in the 16th and first half of the 17th century, with some reference to economic and social conditions. Muriel Humphries. Liverpool M.A. 1969/70.

2877   Attitudes to usury in England in the 16th and 17th centuries. M.A.R. Lunn. Birmingham M.A. 1969.

2878   The London apothecaries and medical practice in Tudor and Stuart England. R.S. Roberts. London Ph.D. 1964.

2879   The courtier in early Tudor society, illustrated from select examples. R.E. Brock. London Ph.D. 1964.

2880   Knights and knighthood in Tudor England. H.H. Leonard. London Ph.D. 1970.

2881   People, land and literacy in 16th- and 17th-century Cambridgeshire. Mrs. H. Margaret Spufford. Leicester Ph.D. 1970.

2882   The alien contribution to the social and economic development of England and Wales in the 16th century. L.H. Williams. Wales M.A. 1953.

2883   The part played by aliens in the social and economic life of England during the reign of Henry VIII. T.G. Wyatt. London M.A. 1952.

2884   The regional distribution of wealth in England as indicated in the 1524/5 lay subsidy returns. J.D.S. Sheail. London Ph.D. 1968.

2885   Contemporary opinion upon the economic and social aspects of the Commonwealth, 1529-59. W.R.D. Jones. Wales M.A. 1963.

2886   The treatment of vagrancy and the relief of the poor and destitute in the Tudor period, based upon the local records of London to 1552 and Hull to 1576. Kitty Anderson. London Ph.D. 1933.

2887   Social conditions in Wales under the Tudors. J.C. Morrice. Oxford D.Phil. 1923.

2888   Social problems and social theories during the 16th century (1520-70) with special reference to the writings of More, Starkey, Crowley, Ascham, Latimer and Elyott. R.T. Davies. Wales M.A. 1921.

2889   A history of the Ralegh family of Fardel and Budleigh in the early Tudor period. M.J.G. Stanford. London M.A. 1955.

2890   The Lancashire gentry, 1529 to 1558, with special reference to their public services. J.B. Watson. London M.A. 1959.

2891   The Glamorgan gentry, 1536-1603. G.E. Jones. Wales M.A. 1963.

2892   A study of landed income and social structure in the West Riding of Yorkshire in the period 1535-46. R.B. Smith. Leeds Ph.D. 1963.

2893   The effects of the Reformation on the social conditions of England, 1535-70. Irene V. Harriss. Birmingham M.A. 1915.

2894   The influence of reformed doctrine on English charity in the 16th century. F.H. Barber. Bristol M.A. 1964.

2895   The gentry of south-west Wales, 1540-1640. H.A. Lloyd. Oxford D.Phil. 1964.

2896   The wealth of some Northamptonshire families, 1540-1640. Mary E. Finch. Cambridge Ph.D. 1954.

2897   The wealth of the magisterial class in Lancashire, c. 1590-1640. P.R. Long. Manchester M.A. 1968.

2898   Life and conditions in London prisons, 1553-1643, with special reference to contemporary literature. C. Dobb. Oxford B.Litt. 1953.

The Johnson letters, 1542-52. Barbara Winchester.   2899
London Ph.D. 1953.

Household accounts of Henry, earl of Derby. Mary G.   2900
McLoughlin. Liverpool M.A. 1954.

Alien immigration into and alien communities in Lon-   2901
don, 1558-1640. Irene Scouloudi. London M.Sc. 1936.

The Caernarvonshire squires, 1558-1625. E.G. Jones.   2902
Wales M.A. 1936.

The Elizabethan gentry of Norfolk: office-holding and   2903
faction. A.H. Smith. London Ph.D. 1959.

A memory of honour: a study of the house of Cobham in   2904
Kent in the reign of Elizabeth I. D.B. McKeen. Birmingham
Ph.D. 1964/5.

Witchcraft prosecutions in Essex, 1560-1680: a socio-   2905
logical analysis. A.D.J. Macfarlane. Oxford D.Phil. 1967.

The position of the recusant gentry in the social   2906
setting of Lancashire, 1570-1642. J. Cosgrove. Manchester
M.A. 1964.

The Gages of Firle, 1580-1640: an economic history of   2907
a recusant family in Sussex. S.W. Pearson. Sussex M.A.
1967/8.

Sussex country gentry in the reign of Elizabeth. Joyce 2908
E. Mousley. London Ph.D. 1956.

The Cliffords, earls of Cumberland, 1579-1646: a study 2909
of their fortunes based on their household and estate accounts.
R.T. Spence. London Ph.D. 1959.

The household accounts of Henry Percy, 9th earl of   2910
Northumberland (1564-1632). G.R. Batho. London M.A. 1953.

The Chatham Chest. E.G. Mawson. Liverpool M.A. 1931.   2911

The Yorkshire gentry on the eve of the Civil War. J.T. 2912
Cliffe. London Ph.D. 1960.

Social and economic policy and projects during the   2913
Interregnum, 1640-60. Margaret James. London Ph.D. 1927.

The social and economic condition of the Holland   2914
Division of Lincolnshire from 1642 to 1660. Gladys M. Hipkin.
Oxford B.Litt. 1930.

ECCLESIASTICAL HISTORY

English representation at the court of Rome in the   2915
early Tudor period. D.S. Chambers. Oxford D.Phil. 1962.

The political and intellectual activities of Cardinal   2916
John Morton and his episcopal colleagues. R.J. Knecht.
London M.A. 1953.

Canterbury jurisdiction and influence during the epis-   2917
copate of William Warham, 1503-32. M.J. Kelly. Cambridge
Ph.D. 1963.

The secular clergy in the diocese of Lincoln, 1514-21.   2918
Margaret Roper. Oxford B.Litt. 1962.

Church courts and people in the diocese of Norwich,   2919
1519-70. R.A. Houlbrooke. Oxford D.Phil. 1970.

The diocese of Exeter under Bishop Veysey. D.H. Pill.   2920
Exeter M.A. 1963.

Heresy and Reformation in the south-east of England,   2921
1520-59. J.F. Davis. Oxford D.Phil. 1968.

Heresies of William Tyndale. H.W. Callow. Liverpool   2922
M.A. 1911.

A study of the writings of the English protestant   2923
exiles, 1525-35, excluding their biblical translations.
Anthea M.A. Hume. London Ph.D. 1961.

The life and career of Edmund Bonner, bishop of London, 2924
until his deprivation in 1549. Mrs. Gina M.V. Alexander.
London Ph.D. 1960.

The conservative episcopate in England, 1529-35. J.J.   2925
Scarisbrick. Cambridge Ph.D. 1955.

2926   A calendar of the register of Cuthbert Tunstall, bishop of Durham. Gladys Hinde. London Ph.D. (Ext.) 1933.

2927   The sede vacante administration of Archbishop Thomas Cranmer, 1533-53. A.J. Edwards. London M.Phil. 1968.

2928   The extent and value of the property in London and Southwark occupied by the religious houses (including the prebends of St. Paul's and St. Martin's le Grand), the parish churches and churchyards, and the inns of the abbots and bishops, before the dissolution of the monasteries. Marjorie B. Honeybourne. London M.A. 1930.

2929   Lollardy in London on the eve of the Reformation. Eliza J. Davis. London M.A. 1913.

2930   Peter Martyr and the English Reformation. G. Huelin. London Ph.D. (Ext.) 1955.

2931   The bishops of Bath and Wells, 1535-1647: a social and economic study. Mrs. Phyllis M. Hembry. London Ph.D. 1956.

2932   The condition of the English parish clergy from the Reformation to 1660, with special reference to the dioceses of Oxford, Gloucester and Worcester. Dorothy M. Barratt. Oxford D.Phil. 1949.

2933   The condition of the clergy at the time of the Reformation in England. Myra K.R. Cotton. London M.A. 1916.

2934   A comparison of the influence of Wycliffe and Luther upon the Reformation in England. W.H. Leighton. Birmingham M.A. 1927.

2935   John a Lasco and the English Reformation. M.W. Slade. Bristol M.A. 1952.

2936   Martin Bucer and the English Reformation. C.L.R.A. Hopf. Oxford D.Phil. 1943.

2937   The contribution of Robert Barnes to the English Reformation. N.H. Fisher. Birmingham M.A. 1950.

2938   The attitude of Wales towards the Reformation. A. Davies. Wales M.A. 1911.

2939   The Reformation in the diocese of Llandaff. L. Thomas. Oxford B.Litt. 1926.

2940   A history of the Reformation in the archdeaconries of Lincoln and Stow, 1534-94. R.B. Walker. Liverpool Ph.D. 1959.

2941   The Reformation in Lancashire to 1558. C.A. Haigh. Manchester Ph.D. 1969.

2942   John Frith and his relation to the origin of the Reformation in England. R.E. Fulop. Edinburgh Ph.D. 1956.

2943   Changes of the Reformation period in Durham and Northumberland. Barbara N. Wilson. Durham Ph.D. 1939.

2944   The diocese of Coventry and Lichfield during the Reformation, with special reference to parochial life. Dorothy E. Lindop. Oxford B.Litt. 1937.

2945   The dissolution of the monasteries in Hampshire and the Isle of Wight. J. Kennedy. London M.A. (Ext.) 1953.

2946   The disposal of monastic property in land in the county of Devon following the Dissolution. Joyce A. Youings. London Ph.D. 1950.

2947   The suppression of the religious foundations of Devon and Cornwall. L.S. Snell. Leicester M.A. 1964.

2948   The disposal of the property of London monastic houses, with a special study of Holy Trinity, Aldgate. M.C. Rosenfield. London Ph.D. 1961.

2949   The income, administration and disposal of the monastic lands in Lancashire from the Dissolution to c.1558. R.J. Mason. London M.A. 1962.

2950   The monastic lands in Leicestershire after the dissolution of the monasteries. Mrs. Sybil M. Jack. Oxford B.Litt. 1961.

2951   The dissolution of the monasteries in Lincolnshire. G.A.J. Hodgett. London M.A. (Ext.) 1947.

2952   The disposal of the monastic property in the diocese of Llandaff at the time of the Reformation. T.J. Edwards. Wales M.A. 1928.

The dissolution of the English nunneries. Hilda T.   2953
Jacka. London M.A. 1917.

The sequestration of religious property in Norfolk at   2954
the Reformation. T.H. Swales. Sheffield Ph.D. 1965.

The suppression of chantries in England. S.E. Hodgson. 2955
Leeds M.A. 1931.

Studies in the redistribution of collegiate and chantry 2956
property in the diocese and county of York at the Dissolution. C.J. Kitching. Durham Ph.D. 1970.

The Reformation in the diocese of Lincoln, as illus-   2957
trated by the life and work of Bishop Longland (1521-47).
Gwendolen E. Wharhirst. Oxford B.Litt. 1938.

The English Reformation as reflected in the life and   2958
work of Thomas Becon. D.S. Bailey. Edinburgh Ph.D. 1947.

Some aspects of the life and work of a Reformation   2959
bishop as revealed in the writings of Richard Sampson, bishop
of Chichester. D.G. Lerpinière. London M.A. 1954.

Anglicanism: its progress until 1626. G.E. Hart.   2960
Bristol M.A. 1922.

Tithe disputes in the diocese of York, 1540-1639. D.M. 2961
Gransby. York M.Phil. 1968.

A first generation reformer: the career of Archbishop   2962
Robert Holgate. J.L. Secret. Hull M.A. 1969/70.

Thomas Cartwright and Cambridge, 1547-71. W.B.   2963
Whitaker. Bristol M.A. 1924.

The Reformation in the diocese of Salisbury (1547-62).   2964
I.T. Shield. Oxford B.Litt. 1960.

The career and influence of Bishop Richard Cox, 1547-   2965
81. G.L. Blackman. Cambridge Ph.D. 1953.

The administration of the diocese of Gloucester, 1547-   2966
79. F.D. Price. Oxford B.Litt. 1940.

Thomas Cranmer's doctrine of the sacraments. P.N.   2967
Brooks. Cambridge Ph.D. 1960.

John Bale, Protestant. E.E. Jones. Wales M.A. 1910. 2968

The early life of Christopher Goodman. S.J. Knox.   2969
Manchester M.A. 1951.

The effect of the Marian and Elizabethan religious   2970
settlements upon the clergy of the City of London, 1553-64.
E.L.C. Mullins. London M.A. 1948.

An account of the returned exiles of 1553-8 in England 2971
and Scotland. A.P. Kup. St. Andrews Ph.D. 1952.

The life of Thomas Stapleton, 1535-98. E.J. McDermott. 2972
London M.A. 1950.

The concept of the church in the writings of John Foxe. 2973
V.H. Olsen. London Ph.D. 1966.

The life of John Bradford, the Manchester martyr, c.   2974
1510-1555. P.F. Johnston. Oxford B.Litt. 1964.

The lower clergy in Lancashire, 1558-1642. D. Lambert. 2975
Liverpool M.A. 1964.

The doctrine of the church in the Church of England,   2976
from the accession of Elizabeth I to the outbreak of the
Civil War, 1558-1642. D.O. Platt. Cambridge Ph.D. 1955.

The introduction of the Elizabethan settlement into   2977
the universities of Oxford and Cambridge, with particular
reference to the Roman Catholics, 1558-1603. C.M.J.F. Swan.
Cambridge Ph.D. 1955.

Religious conflicts in Elizabethan Cambridge. H.C.   2978
Porter. Cambridge Ph.D. 1956.

Edwin Sandys and the settlement of religion in   2979
England, 1558-88. I.P. Ellis. Oxford B.Litt. 1962.

The Elizabethan religious settlement and Richard   2980
Hooker. J.C. Greider. Liverpool Ph.D. 1966/7.

Archbishop Parker and the Anglican settlement, 1558-63. 2981
Edith M. Herne. Birmingham M.A. 1928.

The early life of Archbishop Parker. A.E. Warren.   2982
Leeds M.A. 1912.

2983   The episcopal administration of Matthew Parker, archbishop
of Canterbury 1559-75. J.I. Daeley. London Ph.D. 1967.
2984   Archbishop Parker. S.A. Eley. Leeds M.A. 1935.
2985   Henry Bullinger of Zurich, his place in the Reformation,
with special reference to England. T.S. Taylor. Oxford
B.Litt. 1912.
2986   The action of the privy council in ecclesiastical matters
in the reign of Queen Elizabeth. P.P.W. Gendall. Leeds M.A.
1911.
2987   The ecclesiastical and religious position in the diocese
of Llandaff in the reign of Queen Elizabeth. Hilda M. Isaacs.
Wales M.A. 1928.
2988   Some Elizabethan controversies about the church and the
ministry. J.M. Corley. Durham M.Litt. 1959.
2989   The London parish clergy in the reign of Elizabeth I.
H.G. Owen. London Ph.D. 1957.
2990   Puritanism in the diocese of Chester to 1642. R.C.
Richardson. Manchester Ph.D. 1969.
2991   Puritanism in Leicestershire, 1558-1633. C.D. Chalmers.
Leeds M.A. 1963.
2992   The puritan classical movement in Elizabeth's reign.
Edna Bibby. Manchester M.A. 1929.
2993   The puritan classical movement in the reign of Elizabeth I. P. Collinson. London Ph.D. 1957.
2994   The kingdom at the threshold - a study of the apocalyptic
element in English puritanism in the 16th and 17th centuries.
P.B. Hawkridge. London Ph.D. 1943.
2995   Ecclesiastical discipline in the county of York, 1559-
1714, with special reference to the archdeacon's court. J.
Addy. Leeds M.A. 1961.
2996   Puritanism and the church courts in the diocese of York,
1560-1642. R.A. Marchant. Cambridge Ph.D. 1956.
2997   The court of High Commission in the province of York,
1561-1603. P. Tyler. Oxford B.Litt. 1961.
2998   The Ecclesiastical Commission within the province of
York, 1562-1640. P. Tyler. Oxford D.Phil. 1965.
2999   Puritanism in its Presbyterian development in the time
of Elizabeth. A. Peel. Oxford B.Litt. 1911.
3000   The relations between the English and Scottish Presbyterian movements to 1604. G. Donaldson. London Ph.D. 1938.
3001   The place of Edmund Grindal in the Elizabethan Church.
Y.C. Greer. Cambridge M.Litt. 1963.
3002   The origin of the Independents in the reign of Elizabeth,
Annie M.M. Wallbank. Birmingham M.A. 1927.
3003   The political thought of the Elizabethan Separatists.
S.H. Mayor. Manchester M.A. 1951.
3004   The development of the doctrine of the church among the
English Separatists, with especial reference to Robert Browne
and John Smyth. B.R. White. Oxford D.Phil. 1961.
3005   Robert Browne (1550-1633) as churchman and theologian.
D.C. Smith. Edinburgh Ph.D. 1936.
3006   The prose writings of some English recusants of the
reigns of Elizabeth and James I. G.H. Russell. Cambridge
Ph.D. 1950/1.
3007   English Catholicism and the printing-press, at home and
abroad, 1558-1640. D.M. Rogers. Oxford D.Phil. 1952.
3008   Elizabethan recusant literature, 1559-82. A.C. Southern
London Ph.D. 1946.
3009   John Jewel, bishop and theologian, 1522-71. P.W. Read.
Durham M.A. 1950.
3010   An examination of the Anglican definition of the church
as expounded by Bishop John Jewel. E.B. Jones. St. Andrews
Ph.D. 1964.
3011   The life and work of Bishop Richard Davies. G. Williams
Wales M.A. 1947.
3012   The life and times of Thomas Cooper, bishop of Lincoln
and Winchester, 1517-94. A.J.E. Lello. Sheffield M.A. 1959.

Puritanism in Hampshire and the Isle of Wight from the   3013
reign of Elizabeth to the Restoration. W.H. Mildon. London
Ph.D. (Ext.) 1934.

Puritanism in the county of Devon between 1570 and   3014
1641. I.W. Gowers. Exeter M.A. 1970.

Catholic doctrine and practice in the English Church   3015
during the period 1570-1625. R.C. Wylie. Oxford B.Litt.
1929.

Elizabethan Catholicism: the link with France. J.A.   3016
Bossy. Cambridge Ph.D. 1961.

Political thought of the Counter-Reformation in Eng-   3017
land, 1572-1615: a study of the Allen-Parsons party. T.H.
Clancy. London Ph.D. 1960.

'The political theories of Robert Persons'. A study of   3018
an English Jesuit's contribution to the political thought of
the Counter-Reformation. P.L. Wright. Oxford B.Litt. 1951.

A study of the Jesuit mission of 1580, with particular   3019
reference to its effects on Catholicism in England. Margaret
E. Whelan. Liverpool M.A. 1927.

The laws against Roman Catholic recusants, illustrated   3020
from the history of the North Riding of Yorkshire. Jennie
M. Price. Wales M.A. 1922.

Roman Catholicism in Oxfordshire from the late Eliza-   3021
bethan period to the Civil War (1580-1640). A. Davidson.
Bristol Ph.D. 1970.

Catholic recusants in Essex, c.1580 to c.1600. M.   3022
O'Dwyer. London M.A. 1960.

The implementation of the Elizabethan statutes against   3023
recusants, 1581-1603. F.X. Walker. London Ph.D. 1961.

Lancashire Elizabethan recusants. J.S. Leatherbarrow.   3024
Manchester M.A. 1940.

The Hampshire recusants in the reign of Elizabeth I,   3025
with some reference to the problem of the Church-Papists.
J.E. Paul. Southampton Ph.D. 1958.

Elizabethan recusancy in Cheshire. K.R. Wark. Man-   3026
chester M.A. 1966.

The history of the Counter-Reformation in Wales. T.C.   3027
Jones. Oxford B.Litt. 1923.

Welsh recusant clergy: a documentary study of the work   3028
of Welshmen connected with the seminaries of Douay and Rome
in the reign of Elizabeth I. J.M. Cleary. Liverpool M.A.
1965/6.

Recusancy in the diocese of Llandaff during the late   3029
16th and early 17th centuries. F.H. Pugh. Wales M.A. 1953.

The Welsh Elizabethan martyrs: the trial documents of   3030
Blessed Richard Gwyn, and Venerable William Davies. D.A.
Thomas. Liverpool M.A. 1965/6.

The theology and policy of John Whitgift, archbishop of 3031
Canterbury, 1583-1604. E.C. Brooks. Leeds M.A. 1957.

The life and work of John Whitgift, 1532-1604. P.M.   3032
Dawley. Cambridge Ph.D. 1937/8.

Whitgift. W.C. Thomas. Leeds M.A. 1915.   3033

The rise and decline of Calvinism in England during the 3034
archiepiscopate of Whitgift. Beatrice M.H. Thompson. Oxford
B.Litt. 1933.

John Whitgift: his character and work. E.J. Balley.   3035
Belfast M.A. 1927.

The ecclesiastical control of parochial life in the   3036
Nottingham archdeaconry, 1590-1610 as illustrated by the
Causes of Office. R.G. Riley. Nottingham M.A. 1954.

The life and theology of William Perkins. I. Breward.   3037
Manchester Ph.D. 1963.

John Penry and the Marprelate controversy in the light   3038
of recent research. D.D. Phillips. Wales M.A. 1914.

The Wisbech Stirs, 1595-8: a critical edition of docu-   3039
ments illustrating the conflicts among English Catholics in
the years preceding the appointment of George Blackwell, first
archpriest. Penelope Renold. London M.A. 1959.

3040   Benedict Canfield (William Fitch), Capuchin: the man
and his writings. C.J. Reel. Oxford B.Litt. 1948.
3041   The origins and early development of the revived English
Benedictine congregation, 1588-1647. D.C.J. Lunn. Cambridge
Ph.D. 1970.
3042   Methods of propaganda and transmission among the Baptists,
Congregationalists and Presbyterians in England in the years
1600-60. A.C. Piggott. Bristol M.A. 1954.
3043   A study of the accommodation movements between presbytery and episcopacy in the 17th century in Scotland, England
and Ireland. D.S. Hopkirk. Edinburgh Ph.D. 1947.
3044   Religion and society in east Yorkshire, 1600-60. H.I.B.
Dunton. Hull M.A. 1957.
3045   The history of religion in Wales from 1600 to 1640. Mary
D.A. Hughes. Oxford B.Litt. 1930.
3046   Pregethau Cymraeg William Griffith (? 1566-1612) ac Evan
Morgan (c.1574-1643). (The Welsh sermons of William Griffith
and of Evan Morgan.) G. Morgan. Wales M.A. 1969.
3047   The episcopate of William Cotton, bishop of Exeter
(1589-1621), with special reference to the state of the clergy
and the administration of the ecclesiastical courts. Irene
Cassidy. Oxford B.Litt. 1963.
3048   Studies in the finances of Durham priory in the early
17th century. R.A. Lomas. Durham M.A. 1964.
3049   Puritanism in the diocese of York, excluding Nottinghamshire, 1603-40. J.A. Newton. London Ph.D. (Ext.) 1956.
3050   Religious separatism and moral authority: some aspects
of religious intolerance in England, 1603-60. Irene C. Coltman. London M.A. 1949.
3051   The Lancashire recusants in the reigns of James I and
Charles I, with special reference to the part they played in
the Civil War. G.R. Allen. Durham M.A. 1958.
3052   The relation of church and state, with special reference
to the growth of the idea of religious toleration in England
under James I, 1603-16. Phyllis Doyle. London M.A. 1928.
3053   The ecclesiastical policy of James I: two aspects: the
Puritans (1603-5) - the Arminians (1611-25). F.H. Shriver.
Cambridge Ph.D. 1967.
3054   Arminianism in England, in religion and politics, from
1604 to 1640. N.R.N. Tyacke. Oxford D.Phil. 1969.
3055   Some aspects of the sufferings of Catholics under the
penal laws in the reign of James I. T.W. Lennon. Liverpool
M.A. 1939.
3056   The Hampton Court Conference. H.F. Humbert. Edinburgh
Ph.D. 1940.
3057   The Church of England and puritanism during the primacy
of Bancroft, 1604-10. S.B. Babbage. London Ph.D. 1942.
3058   Archbishop Richard Bancroft, 1544-1610. S.R. Day. Oxford D.Phil. 1956.
3059   The life and work of Bishop Lancelot Andrewes (1555-
1626). P.A. Welsby. Sheffield Ph.D. 1957.
3060   Lancelot Andrewes, churchman and theologian. A.W. Craig.
Edinburgh Ph.D. 1938/9.
3061   The political and ecclesiastical activities of Bishop
Williams in relation to the history of his times. Mildred E.
Hudson. London M.A. 1926.
3062   The doctrine of the church in the Caroline divines.
A.McK. Watts. Edinburgh Ph.D. 1960.
3063   The Anglican doctrine of the church in the 17th century.
M.C. Brown. Durham M.A. 1957.
3064   Richard Sibbes: a study in early 17th-century English
puritanism. F.E. Farrell. Edinburgh Ph.D. 1954/5.
3065   The practice of the cure of souls in 17th-century
English puritanism. L.T. Grant. Edinburgh Ph.D. 1960/1.
3066   Puritan ideas on colonisation, 1620-60. Joan E.M.
Bellord. London M.A. 1950.

John Cotton (1584-1652): churchman and theologian.   3067
Judith B. Welles. Edinburgh Ph.D. 1947.
     Alexander Ross (1590-1654): a biographical and critical 3068
study. C.P. Corney. Oxford B.Litt. 1954.
     A survey of the diocese of York during the arch-   3069
bishoprics of Samuel Harsnett and Richard Neile, 1628-40.
I.W. Hogg. Nottingham M.A. 1961.
     The rise to power of William Laud, 1624-9. P.L. Thirl- 3070
by. Cambridge M.Litt. 1960.
     Life and work of William Laud 1628-39, with special   3071
reference to his social and political activities. Katharine
L. McElroy. Oxford D.Phil. 1943.
     The university of Oxford and the Church of England in   3072
the time of William Laud. A.D. Hewlett. Oxford B.Litt. 1934.
     The life, times and writings of Jeremy Taylor. C.J.   3073
Stranks. Durham M.Litt. 1938.
     A biographical study of Sir John Lambe (c.1566-1646).   3074
Mary D. Slatter. Oxford B.Litt. 1952.
     The life and work of William Erbery (1604-54). J.I.   3075
Morgans. Oxford B.Litt. 1968.
     The life of Archbishop Juxon. J.R.M. Etherington.   3076
Oxford B.Litt. 1940.
     A study of the visitation books of the archdeaconry of 3077
Buckingham, 1633-6. E.R.C. Brinkworth. Oxford B.Litt. 1948.
     Richard Montague: Caroline bishop, 1575-1641. J.S.   3078
Macauley. Cambridge Ph.D. 1964.
     The Great Tew circle. J.I. Tanner. Nottingham Ph.D.   3079
1964/5.
     William Chillingworth. J. Waller. Cambridge Ph.D.   3080
1953.
     Truth and authority: the development of William   3081
Chillingworth's ideas of religious toleration. R.R. Orr.
London Ph.D. 1958.
     Study of life and works of Henry King, bishop of   3082
Chichester, 1592-1667. J.V.C. Carey. London M.A. 1951.
     Caroline puritanism as exemplified in the life and work 3083
of William Prynne. T. Fitch. Edinburgh Ph.D. 1949.
     William Prynne's ideal state church and his views on   3084
the sectaries. E. Stephenson. Manchester M.A. 1929.
     An examination of the fear of Catholics and of Catholic 3085
plots in England, 1637-45, with principal reference to central
sources. R. Clifton. Oxford D.Phil. 1967.
     The part played by Catholics in the English Civil War. 3086
K.J. Lindley. Manchester Ph.D. 1968.
     The Presbyterian-Independent controversy, with special 3087
reference to Dr. Thomas Goodwin and the years 1640-60. R.B.
Carter. Edinburgh Ph.D. 1960/1.
     Antinomianism in the period of English history 1640-60. 3088
Gertrude Huehns. London Ph.D. 1947.
     The administrative and disciplinary problems of the   3089
church on the eve of the Civil War in the light of the extant
records of the dioceses of Norwich and Ely under Bishop Wren.
D.W. Boorman. Oxford B.Litt. 1959.
     Matthew Wren, bishop of Hereford, Norwich and Ely. P. 3090
King. Bristol M.Litt. 1969.
     Puritanism and moral legislation before the Civil War. 3091
J.B.H. Jones. Wales M.A. 1954.
     Anglicanism during the Civil War and the Commonwealth. 3092
R. Daunton-Fear. Bristol M.A. 1943.
     The Baptist Confessions of Faith of the Civil War-   3093
Commonwealth period: a study of their origins, contents and
significance. W.T. Lumpkin. Edinburgh Ph.D. 1948.
     Thomas Edwards (1599-1647) and theories against   3094
religious toleration. W.H. Pritchard. Oxford B.Litt. 1964.
     The Westminster Directory: its origin and significance. 3095
F.W. McNally. Edinburgh Ph.D. 1958.

3096   How far is the Westminster Assembly an expression of 17th-century Anglican theology? M.W. Dewar. Belfast Ph.D. 1960.

3097   Early editions of the Westminster Confession. S.W. Carruthers. Edinburgh Ph.D. 1929.

3098   The English Catholics, 1649-60. Ellen M.M. Hurst. Liverpool M.A. 1929.

3099   The Catholics in England, 1649-60, with special reference to their political significance. Ena M.B. Cottrell. Oxford B.Litt. 1932.

3100   The condition and role of the Catholic minority during the puritan revolution. W.W. Piepenburg. Cambridge Ph.D. 1951.

3101   The life and work of the Rev. John Owen, D.D., the puritan divine, with special reference to the Socinian controversies of the 17th century. R.G. Lloyd. Edinburgh Ph.D. 1941/2.

3102   Dr. John Owen and the religious settlement of the Commonwealth and Protectorate. J.C.W. Davis. Liverpool M.A. 1949.

3103   Wales under the Propagation Act, 1650-3. T. Richards. Wales M.A. 1914.

3104   Vavasor Powell (1617-70): an account of his life, with special reference to religious movements in Wales in his time. D.E. Walters. Liverpool M.A. 1933.

3105   The life, work and thought of Vavasor Powell (1617-70). R.T. Jones. Oxford D.Phil. 1947.

3106   The controversy between Puritans and Quakers, to 1660. R.P. Bohn. Edinburgh Ph.D. 1955.

3107   The Quakers and politics, 1652-60. W.A. Cole. Cambridge Ph.D. 1955.

3108   A study in the interaction of political and religious forces in the period between the fall of Richard Cromwell and the Restoration of Charles II. J.L. Nightingale. Durham M.Litt. 1936.

CULTURAL HISTORY

General

3109   The administration and finances of the King's Works, 1485-1558. D.R. Ransome. Oxford D.Phil. 1960.

3110   The struggle for the freedom of the press from Caxton to Cromwell. W.M. Clyde. St. Andrews Ph.D. 1929.

3111   The control of the press in England before the granting of the charter to the Stationers' Company. W.N. Chaplin. London M.A. 1925.

3112   Essex schools before 1600. H.G. Williams. London M.A. 1924.

3113   Welsh schools of the 15th and 16th centuries. L.S. Knight. Wales M.A. 1914.

3114   A history of King Edward VI Grammar School, East Retford. A.D. Grounds. Sheffield M.A. 1968.

3115   The study and teaching of history in Tudor and Stuart England. Mrs. Joan Lewin. London M.A. 1955.

3116   An account of the education of women and girls in England in the time of the Tudors. Dorothy M. Meads. London Ph.D. 1929.

3117   Religious uniformity and English education in the 16th century. N. Wood. London Ph.D. 1928.

3118   The aims and methods of the English humanist educators of the 16th century. J.S. Williams. Liverpool M.A. 1914.

3119   The continuity of humanist ideas during the English Reformation to 1553. J.K. McConica. Oxford D.Phil. 1962.

3120   Early printed books of machines, 1569-1629. A.G. Keller. Cambridge Ph.D. 1967.

Practical mathematics in Elizabethan England: a survey   3121
of the literature of science. D.P.J. Wood. Cambridge Ph.D.
1953.

The humanism of John Skelton, with special reference to 3122
his translation of Diodorus Siculus. H.L.R. Edwards. Cambridge Ph.D. 1937/8.

John Skelton and the early Renaissance. I.A. Gordon.   3123
Edinburgh Ph.D. 1936.

Linguistic activity at the court of Henry VIII. Audrey 3124
Le Lièvre. Cambridge Ph.D. 1949/50.

A study of the university Letter Book (FF) 1509-35.   3125
Katherine F. Lindsay-MacDougall. Oxford B.Litt. 1950.

Wolsey's colleges at Oxford and Ipswich. F. Bate.   3126
Liverpool M.A. 1905.

The first century of the library of Corpus Christi   3127
College, Oxford (1517-1617). J.R. Liddell. Oxford B.Litt.
1933.

Sir Thomas More and education. E. Marion Chesters.   3128
Liverpool M.A. 1923.

Sir Thomas More as a satirist in his epigrams and   3129
Utopia. C.A. Thompson. Oxford B.Litt. 1947.

Henry Howard, earl of Surrey. E.R. Casady. Oxford   3130
B.Litt. 1931.

John Day, the Elizabethan printer. C.L. Oastler. Ox-   3131
ford B.Litt. 1965.

The life and work of John Day. S.R. Golding. London   3132
Ph.D. 1930.

Llyfr Edward ap Roger. (The book of Edward ap Roger.)   3133
J.F. Griffith. Wales M.A. 1969.

Literary societies in England from Parker to Falkland,   3134
c.1572-1640. W.R. Gair. Cambridge Ph.D. 1969.

The life of Sir Edward Dyer, 1543-1607. C.J. Reynolds. 3135
Oxford B.Litt. 1930.

The effect of government censorship on Elizabethan and   3136
Jacobean non-dramatic satire. Betty F. Shapin. London M.A.
1940.

A biography of Barnabe Riche. E.M. Hinton. Oxford   3137
B.Litt. 1928.

University and collegiate planning in the later 16th   3138
and 17th centuries. Mrs. Marion A.V. Ball. London M.A. 1961.

The collection and dissemination of news during the   3139
time of Shakespeare, with particular reference to the news
pamphlets, 1590-1610. D.C. Collins. London Ph.D. (Ext.)
1938.

A study of the Stationers' Register for the years   3140
1591-4 in relation to the social life and literature of the
period. G.B. Harrison. London Ph.D. 1928.

An elucidation of the death of Christopher Marlowe,   3141
through an examination of the lives and interests of certain
of his associates. Eugenie W. de Kalb. Cambridge Ph.D.
1928/9.

Wales in the 17th century; its literature and men of   3142
letters and action. J.C. Morrice. Oxford B.Litt. 1920.

The lives and labours of John Jones and Robert Vaughan, 3143
scribes of the 16th and 17th centuries. S. Jones. Wales M.A.
1926.

Welsh scholarship in the 17th century, with special   3144
reference to the writings of John Jones, Gellilyfdy. Mrs.
Nesta Lloyd, née Jones. Oxford D.Phil. 1970.

The vernacular writings of King James VI and I. S.R.   3145
Dunlap. Oxford B.Litt. 1937.

Science and supernaturalism in the Jacobean age.   3146
Frances S. Bullough. Aberdeen Ph.D. 1967.

An analysis of the cartographical material in John   3147
Speed's 'Theatre of the Empire of Great Britain'. Margaret
B. John. Wales M.Sc. 1945.

3148   A biography of William Herbert, 3rd earl of Pembroke.
J.R. Briley. Birmingham Ph.D. 1961.
3149   Bywyd a gwaith Dr. John Davies, Mallwyd. (Life and work
of Dr. John Davies.) R.F. Roberts. Wales M.A. 1950.
3150   State intervention in education in England under the
early Stuarts. L.G. Young. London M.A. 1938.
3151   State intervention and school education in the West
Riding during the Interregnum, 1649-60. J.E. Stephens.
Leeds M.A. 1963.
3152   The state and school education 1640-60, in England and
Wales: a survey based on printed sources. W.A.L. Vincent.
Oxford B.Litt. 1944.
3153   Education in the Commonwealth, 1642-60. E.W. Bishop.
London Ph.D. 1942.
3154   The scientific attitude of Francis Bacon. Elizabeth R.
Ryman. Cambridge Ph.D. 1953.
3155   The library of Sir Simonds D'Ewes. A.G. Watson. Oxford
B.Litt. 1961.
3156   Civil philosophy: science and politics in the thought of
Thomas Hobbes. Mrs. Brenda M. Pegrum, née Davies. London
Ph.D. 1966.
3157   Humphrey Moseley, bookseller. J.C. Reed. Oxford B.Litt.
1928.

The Arts and Music

3158   English monumental brasses of the 15th and early 16th
centuries, with special reference (a) to the conditions of
their manufacture, (b) to their characteristic forms and
distribution. Margaret L. Gadd. Manchester M.A. 1936.
3159   London churches, their music and musicians, 1485-1560.
H.C. Baillie. Cambridge Ph.D. 1957/8.
3160   Public spectacle in early Tudor policy, 1485-1547. S.
Anglo. London Ph.D. 1959.
3161   The English portrait and patronage of art from c.1520
to 1590. Erna Auerbach. London Ph.D. 1950.
3162   The Emperor Maximilian's gift of armour to King Henry
VIII and the silvered and engraved armour at the Tower of
London. C. Blair. Manchester M.A. 1963.
3163   Elizabethan pageantry as progaganda. R.C. Strong. London Ph.D. 1962.
3164   Attitudes official and private towards the theatre in
England (1558-1603). M.A. Ross. Bristol M.A. 1965.
3165   Documents relating to the history of the theatre in the
declared accounts of the treasurer of the Chamber, 1585-1642,
with an introduction and commentary. D.J. Cook. London M.A.
1958.
3166   Studies in the theatrical companies and actors of Elizabethan [sic] times, with special reference to the period
1616-42. G.E. Bentley. London Ph.D. 1929.
3167   The building of Wollaton Hall (1580-8). P.E. Rossell.
Sheffield M.A. 1957.
3168   The Puritans and music, with special reference to the
Commonwealth period. W.M. Lewis. Wales M.A. 1917.

LOCAL HISTORY

3169   The history of Swansea from the accession of the Tudors
to the Restoration settlement. W.S.K. Thomas. Wales Ph.D.
1958.
3170   The history of Taunton under the Tudors and Stuarts.
R.G.H. Whitty. London Ph.D. (Ext.) 1938.
3171   Local government under the Tudors. Nina M. Brameld.
London M.A. 1916.
3172   Carmarthenshire under the Tudors. T.H. Lewis. Wales
M.A. 1919.

Arwystli and Cyfeiliog in the 16th and 17th centuries: 3173
an agrarian and social study. E. Evans. Wales M.A. 1939.
    The Flemish and Dutch community in Colchester in the 3174
16th and 17th centuries. L.F. Roker. London M.A. (Ext.)
1963.
    The borough organisation of Southampton in the 16th 3175
century. Caroline E. Boden. London M.A. 1920.
    Sixteenth-century Courts of Sewers in south Lincoln- 3176
shire. Agnes M. Kirkus. Reading Ph.D. 1957/8.
    Town sanitation in the 16th century based on the 3177
records of a group of provincial towns. J.H. Thomas. Oxford
B.Litt. 1929.
    The city of Worcester in the 16th century. A.D. Dyer. 3178
Birmingham Ph.D. 1966.
    Some aspects of the social and economic history of York 3179
in the 16th century. D.M. Palliser. Oxford D.Phil. 1968.
    A calendar of the Caernarvonshire quarter sessions 3180
records, 1541-58, with a critical and historical introduction.
W.O. Williams. Wales M.A. 1956.
    City of Winchester: the first book of ordinances, 1552- 3181
1609, transcribed and annotated. T. Atkinson. Bristol M.A.
1940.
    The history of Eye, 1066-1602, with special reference 3182
to the growth of the borough in the reign of Elizabeth.
Elfrida Leaf. Leeds M.A. 1935.
    The Elizabethan corporation of Norwich, 1558-1603. 3183
J.F. Pound. Birmingham M.A. 1962.
    The corporation of York, 1580-1660. Barbara M. Wilson. 3184
York M.Phil. 1967.
    Wakefield in the 17th century. S.H. Waters. Leeds 3185
M.A. 1932.
    The sheriffs of the county of Kent, c.1580-c.1625. 3186
T.E. Hartley. London Ph.D. 1970.
    The earl of Hertford's lieutenancy of Wiltshire and 3187
Somerset, 1601-21. W.P.D. Murphy. London M.A. 1963.
    Local government in England, 1603-49, with special 3188
reference to the parish. Katharine L. McElroy. Oxford B.Litt.
1924.
    Calendar of the council minutes of the city of Chester 3189
from 1603 to 1642, with introduction and notes. Margaret J.
Groombridge. Manchester M.A. 1952.
    The government of the county of Essex, 1603-42. B.W. 3190
Quintrell. London Ph.D. 1965.
    The Caernarvonshire justices of the peace and their 3191
duties during the 17th century. J.G. Jones. Wales M.A. 1967.
    The work of the justices of the peace in Hampshire, 3192
1603-40. B.J. Richmond. Southampton M.Phil. 1969.
    County government in Somerset, 1625-40. T.G. Barnes. 3193
Oxford B.Litt. 1955.
    The Ditchfield grant of 25th September, 1628. Estella 3194
M. Lewis. Leeds M.A. 1930.
    Critical edition of the Norwich mayor's court minute 3195
books (1630-3), with introduction describing functions of the
court at that time. W.L. Sachse. Oxford B.Litt. 1937.
    Social and religious aspects of the history of Lanca- 3196
shire, 1635-55. B.G. Blackwood. Oxford B.Litt. 1956.
    The history of the municipality of the city of York 3197
1638 to 1663 as illustrated mainly from House Books (vols.
36 & 37) containing the minutes of the proceedings of the
corporation. J.L. Brockbank. London M.A. 1910.
    Buckinghamshire, 1640-60: a study in county politics. 3198
A.M. Johnson. Wales M.A. 1963.
    Kent and its gentry, 1640-60: a political study. A.M. 3199
Everitt. London Ph.D. 1957.
    The government and constitution of the City of London 3200
in relation to the national crisis of 1640 to 1642. Mrs.
Valerie L. Pearl. Oxford D.Phil. 1954.

3201   Newcastle upon Tyne from the Civil War to the Restoration. R. Howell. Oxford D.Phil. 1964.

3202   The minute book of the Bedford Corporation, 1647-64. C.G. Parsloe. London M.A. 1949.

3203   The town charters granted under the Protectorate. B.L.K. Henderson. London M.A. 1909.

3204   Rural Middlesex under the Commonwealth: a study based principally upon the parliamentary surveys of the royal estates. S.J. Madge. London M.Sc. 1922.

3205   The Commonwealth surveys for the North Riding of Yorkshire. T.S. Willan. Oxford B.Litt. 1932.

3206   A study of local government in Wales under the Commonwealth, with special reference to its relations with the central authority. T.M. Bassett. Wales M.A. 1941.

3207   The City of London and the state, 1658 to 1664: a study in political and financial relations. G.V. Chivers. Manchester Ph.D. 1962.

3208   The position of London in national affairs, 1658-61, having special regard to political and economic aspects. Maureen Weinstock. London M.A. 1934.

SCOTLAND

3209   Sheriff and sheriff-court in Scotland prior to the union of the crowns in 1603, with special reference to the Fife records of the 16th century. W.C. Dickinson. St. Andrews Ph.D. 1924.

3210   John, duke of Albany, 1481 to 1536, servant of Scotland and France. R.F. Whisker. Liverpool M.A. 1939.

3211   Foreign correspondence with Marie de Lorraine, queen of Scotland, from the originals in the Balcarres papers, 1537-48 and 1548-57. Marguerite Wood. Edinburgh Ph.D. 1925.

3212   William Dunbar: a biographical study. J.W. Baxter. Edinburgh Ph.D. 1951/2.

3213   The church in Shetland during the 16th and 17th centuries. E.W. Wallis. Edinburgh Ph.D. 1940.

3214   Scottish demonology in the 16th and 17th centuries and its theological background. Mrs. Christina J. Larner. Edinburgh Ph.D. 1962.

3215   Scottish Lollardy and its contribution to the Reformation in Scotland, with special reference to the Lollards of the west. T.M.A. Macnab. Glasgow Ph.D. 1933.

3216   The religious relations of England and Scotland in the early Reformation period. D. Davidson. Oxford B.Litt. 1923.

3217   The influence of England on the Scottish Reformation. D. Davidson. Edinburgh Ph.D. 1926.

3218   The Anglican tendencies in the Scottish Reformation and their bearing on the significance of the Concordat of Leith. Louise B. Taylor. Oxford B.Litt. 1932.

3219   George Wishart. O.H. Walker. Edinburgh Ph.D. 1924.

3220   John Craig (1512-1600), with special reference to his contribution to the up-building of the Reformed Church in Scotland. T.A. Kerr. Edinburgh Ph.D. 1954.

3221   The origins of John Knox's doctrine of just rebellion. A. Main. Aberdeen Ph.D. 1963.

3222   John Knox's superintendents. J. Bodonhelyi. Aberdeen Ph.D. 1936.

3223   The theory and practice of discipline in the Scottish Reformation. J.W. Prugh. Edinburgh Ph.D. 1959.

3224   The Scottish clergy at the Reformation. C.H. Haws. Glasgow Ph.D. 1968.

3225   The trial of George Buchanan before the Lisbon Inquisition. J.M. Aitken. Edinburgh Ph.D. 1939.

3226   Worship in the Scottish Reformed Church, 1550-1638. W. McMillan. Edinburgh Ph.D. 1925.

Painting in Scotland from the 14th to the 17th cent-   3227
uries, with particular reference to painted domestic decoration, 1550-1650. M.R. Apted. Edinburgh Ph.D. 1964.

The French ascendancy in Scotland, 1554-60. G.H.C.   3228
Burley. Birmingham M.A. 1929.

The last years of a frontier: a history of the Borders   3229
during the reign of Elizabeth. D.L.W. Tough. Oxford B.Litt.
1921.

The administration of the Scottish Borders in the 16th   3230
century. T.I. Rae. St. Andrews Ph.D. 1961.

An inquiry into the origins of the Presbyterian church   3231
polity in Scotland as devised by the Reformers of the 16th
century. Janet G. MacGregor. Edinburgh Ph.D. 1923.

Ministerial stipends in the Church of Scotland from   3232
1560 to 1633. N.V. Hope. Edinburgh Ph.D. 1944.

The General Assembly of the Kirk as the rival of the   3233
Scottish parliament, 1560-1618. Edith E. Macqueen. St.
Andrews Ph.D. 1927.

The origin and development of the General Assembly of   3234
the Church of Scotland, 1560-1600. D. Shaw. Edinburgh Ph.D.
1962.

Sunday observance in Scotland, 1560-1606. J.K. Carter. 3235
Edinburgh Ph.D. 1957.

The Scots Confession of 1560, its sources and distinc-   3236
tive characteristics. T. Muir. Edinburgh Ph.D. 1926.

The service of the Scottish mercenary forces in Ireland 3237
from 1565 to 1603, with an account of the mercenary system in
Ireland and of its effect on Scottish history. G.A. Hayes-
M'Coy. Edinburgh Ph.D. 1933/4.

The finances of James VI, 1567-1603. R.S. Brydon.   3238
Edinburgh Ph.D. 1925.

Foreign influences on Scottish politics, 1578-82. Mrs. 3239
Helen M. Ross. London M.A. 1932.

An annotated edition of George Buchanan's account of   3240
the personal reign of Mary Stuart, with a critical introduction. W.A. Gatherer. Edinburgh Ph.D. 1955.

The political career of Francis Stewart, earl of Both-   3241
well, 1588-94. H.G.M. Gordon. Aberdeen Ph.D. 1952.

The theory of limited monarchy in 16th-century Scot-   3242
land. J.H. Burns. Aberdeen Ph.D. 1952.

John Davidson of Prestonpans (1549-1604). R.M. Gillon. 3243
Edinburgh Ph.D. 1935/6.

Ecclesiastical administration in Scotland, 1600-38.   3244
W.R. Foster. Edinburgh Ph.D. 1963.

The Scottish privy council, 1603-25. W. Taylor.   3245
Edinburgh Ph.D. 1950.

The General Assembly of 1610. G.C. Wadsworth. Edin-   3246
burgh Ph.D. 1930/1.

John Spottiswoode, archbishop and chancellor, as   3247
churchman, historian and theologian. J. Perry. Edinburgh
Ph.D. 1950.

The times, life and thought of Patrick Forbes, bishop   3248
of Aberdeen, 1618-35. W.G.G. Snow. Edinburgh Ph.D. 1940.

Donald Cargill, Covenanter (1627?-1681): a background   3249
study, with special reference to his family and other formative influences. R.B. Tweed. Edinburgh Ph.D. 1963/4.

The early Covenanting movement as reflected in the   3250
life, work and thought of James Guthrie of Stirling (1612-61).
W.I. Hoy. Edinburgh Ph.D. 1952.

The historical setting of the Scottish Covenants of   3251
the reign of Charles I. J.W. McEwan. Glasgow Ph.D. 1930.

The later Covenanting movement, with special reference 3252
to religion and ethics. H.C. Macpherson. Edinburgh Ph.D.
1923.

The life of James Sharp, archbishop of St. Andrews.   3253
A.T. Miller. Edinburgh Ph.D. 1945/6.

3254	Samuel Rutherfurd, propagandist and exponent of Scottish Presbyterianism: an exposition of his position and influence in the doctrine and politics of the Scottish Church. W.McM. Campbell. Edinburgh Ph.D. 1938.

3255	A history of Scottish bookbinding to 1650. W.S. Mitchell. Aberdeen Ph.D. 1951.

3256	A study of Anglo-Scottish relations, 1637-43. Elizabeth A. Menzies. St. Andrews Ph.D. 1954.

3257	The proceedings of the General Assembly held in Glasgow, 1638. N. Meldrum. Edinburgh Ph.D. 1924.

3258	The ecclesiastical politics of Archibald Johnston, Lord Wariston, 1611-63. D. Cameron. Edinburgh Ph.D. 1930/1.

3259	The biography of Sir Robert Moray, 1608-73. A. Robertson. Oxford B.Litt. 1912.

3260	Ecclesiastical polity and religious life in Scotland during the Commonwealth and Protectorate. M.B. MacGregor. Glasgow Ph.D. 1929.

3261	William Guthrie, 1620-65. H.O. Bowman. Edinburgh Ph.D. 1953/4.

IRELAND

3262	Tudor rule in Ireland in the reigns of Henry VII and Henry VIII, with special reference to the Anglo-Irish financial administration. D.B. Quinn. London Ph.D. 1934.

3263	Anglo-Irish trade in the 16th century. Ada K. Longfield. London M.A. 1926.

3264	The Reformation in Ireland in the reign of Henry VIII. J.C.P. Proby. Oxford B.Litt. 1924.

3265	The policy of Henry VIII regarding the religious houses in Ireland. P. Rogers. Belfast M.A. 1928.

3266	An historical study of the career of Hugh O'Neill, 2nd earl of Tyrone, c.1550-1616. J.K. Graham. Belfast M.A. 1938.

3267	Earl of Tyrone's rebellion. Betta Singleton. Liverpool M.A. 1915.

3268	Sir John Perrot. P.C.C. Evans. Wales M.A. 1940.

3269	The career of Richard Boyle, 1st earl of Cork, in Ireland, 1588-1643. T.O. Ranger. Oxford D.Phil. 1959.

3270	Irish financial administrative reform under James I: the customs and state regulation of Irish trade. V.W. Treadwell. Belfast Ph.D. 1961.

3271	The history of Coleraine from the Londoners' plantation to the Restoration. H. Boyd. Belfast M.A. 1933.

3272	The Londonderry plantation, with special reference to the resulting relations between the Crown and the City, 1609-41. T.W. Moody. London Ph.D. 1934.

3273	The foundation and early history of the Irish Society, 1609-25. Marjorie E. Perrott. London M.A. 1920.

3274	The doctrine of the church as exemplified in the life and works of James Ussher, archbishop of Armagh. R.B. Knox. Belfast Ph.D. 1948.

3275	The ecclesiastical policy of James Ussher, archbishop of Armagh. R.B. Knox. London Ph.D. (Ext.) 1956.

3276	Wentworth in Ireland. Marguerite Gillman. Leeds M.A. 1919.

3277	Irish trade in the time of Strafford. Hilda M. Davis. London M.A. 1911.

3278	Strafford's ecclesiastical policy in Ireland. F.J.G. Angus. Belfast Ph.D. 1959.

3279	A history of the English forces employed in Ireland, 1641-9. H. Hazlett. Belfast M.A. 1935.

3280	A history of the military forces operating in Ireland, 1641-9. H. Hazlett. Belfast Ph.D. 1938.

3281	The negotiations between Charles I and the Confederation of Kilkenny, 1642-9. J. Lowe. London Ph.D. 1960.

HISTORICAL GEOGRAPHY

The historical geography of the woodlands of the   3282
southern Chilterns, 1600-1947. A.J. Mansfield. London M.Sc.
1952.
　　Some aspects of the historical geography of the Humber 3283
warplands, c.1600-1940. G.G. Robinson. Hull M.A. 1968/9.
　　The changing landscape of south-west Essex from 1600   3284
to 1850. R. Allison. London Ph.D. 1966.
　　Changes in the pattern of rural settlement in northern 3285
Essex between 1650 and 1850. Susan E. Cunningham. Man-
chester M.A. 1968.
　　Regional geography in Britain, 1650-1750. F.V. Emery.   3286
Oxford B.Litt. 1955.
　　A contribution to the historical geography of north-   3287
east Hampshire, c.1600-1850. G.I.M. Jones. London M.Phil.
1969.
　　Bournemouth - a geographical study. D.L.W. Sherry.   3288
Manchester M.A. 1969.
　　An analysis of the town plan of Nottingham: a study in 3289
historical geography. F.I. Straw. Nottingham M.A. 1967.
　　Bromley, Beckenham and Penge, Kent, since 1750: a com- 3290
parative study of the changing geography of three towns on
the southern fringe of the metropolis. Bessie Taylor
(Mother Mary Baptist). London Ph.D. 1966.
　　The settlement pattern of the Yorkshire wolds, 1770 to 3291
1850. M.B. Gleave. Hull M.A. 1960.
　　The growth of the borough and the distribution and   3292
density of population in the Chesterfield region since the
Industrial Revolution. F.C. Couzens. London Ph.D. (Ext.)
1941.
　　Population changes and industrial growth in Leicester- 3293
shire since the late 18th century. T.J. Chandler. London
M.Sc. 1955.
　　Rural settlement in North Wales since the late 18th   3294
century. Muriel M. Rees. Oxford B.Litt. 1951.
　　Population and settlement in Kesteven, c.1775-c.1885.   3295
D.R. Mills. Nottingham M.A. 1957.
　　Comparative studies in the historical geography of   3296
woodlands in south-east England and Wales, 1790-1919. J.A.
Evans. London Ph.D. 1970.
　　A regional study of urban development in coastal   3297
Sussex since the 18th century. H.C. Brookfield. London Ph.D.
1950.

POLITICAL HISTORY

Stamford and the Cecils 1700-1885: a study in political 3298
control. J.M. Lee. Oxford B.Litt. 1957.
　　The parliamentary history of Reading, 1750-1850.   3299
R.C.J.F. Baily. Reading Ph.D. 1944.
　　The royal instructions to colonial governors, 1783-   3300
1854: a study in British colonial policy. J.C. Beaglehole.
London Ph.D. 1929.
　　Imperial land policy, 1783-1848. R.G. Riddell. Oxford 3301
B.Litt. 1934.

General

3302   The effect of economic progress on profits and interest: an essay in the history of British economic thought, 1650-1850. G.S.L. Tucker. Cambridge Ph.D. 1954.

3303   The creation and liquidation of public debt in the United Kingdom during the 18th and 19th centuries economically and financially regarded. C.P. Spruill. Oxford B.Litt. 1922.

3304   Some aspects of English country banking, 1750 to 1844. L.S. Pressnell. London Ph.D. (Ext.) 1953.

3305   Some aspects of Bank of England policy, 1780-1850. J.K. Horsefield. Bristol M.A. 1949.

3306   The development of industries in London south of the Thames, 1750-1850. R.J. Hartridge. London M.Sc. 1955.

3307   The development of industry in Burton-upon-Trent prior to 1900. C.C. Owen. Sheffield Ph.D. 1969.

3308   The east Midlands industrial area: a regional study of industrial location. D.M. Smith. Nottingham Ph.D. 1961.

3309   The economic development of Wolverhampton, 1750-1850. D.B.M. Huffer. London M.A. 1958.

3310   Greater Nottingham: a geographical study of industrial development. J.M. Hunter. Reading Ph.D. 1953.

3311   The economic development of the Erewash valley: a study in economic geography. E. Pearson. London M.Sc. (Ext.) 1936.

3312   Industrial change and settlement in north-east Worcestershire, c.1775-1875. B.C.G. Nokes. London Ph.D. (Ext.) 1968.

3313   A geographical analysis of the development of certain industries in north-east England. P. Pilbin. Durham M.Sc. 1935.

3314   Industrial settlement in the Colne and Holme valleys, 1750-1960. J.C.R. Camm. Hull M.Sc. 1963.

3315   The economic development of Tees-side, 1750-1850. A.J. Parkinson. Durham M.A. 1951.

3316   The development of the coal, iron and shipbuilding industries of west Cumberland, 1750-1914. O. Wood. London Ph.D. (Ext.) 1952.

3317   The problems of the economic and social geography of the south central Lancashire coal and cotton area. P.J. Rimmer. Manchester M.A. 1960.

3318   Aspects of the modern economic geography of the Calder-Darwen valley towns, Lancashire. K. Wallwork. Manchester M.A. 1955.

3319   The evolution of an industrial landscape: the Calder-Darwen valley, Lancashire, from c.1740 to 1914. K.L. Wallwork. Leicester Ph.D. 1966.

3320   Lead, land and coal as sources of landlords' income in Northumberland between 1700 and 1850. W.M. Hughes. Newcastle Ph.D. 1963.

3321   The industrial development of Ashton-under-Lyne, 1780-1850. F. Kenworthy. Manchester M.A. 1929.

3322   The Industrial Revolution in Cornwall, 1740-1870. W.J. Rowe. Oxford D.Phil. 1950.

3323   The evolution of industries and settlements between Merthyr Tydfil and Abergavenny from 1740 to 1840. C. Davies. Wales M.A. 1949.

3324   A study of the economic development of the lower Conway valley and Creuddyn peninsula, 1750-1914. D.G. Griffith. Wales M.A. 1954.

3325   Aberdare, 1750-1850: a study in the growth of an industrial community. A.C. Davies. Wales M.A. 1963.

3326   The industrial history of the parish of Aberdare from 1800 to 1900. G.I. Thomas. Wales M.A. 1943.

3327   Certain aspects of the Industrial Revolution in South Wales, 1760-1850. A.H. John. Cambridge Ph.D. 1940.

The growth of industrialism in the valley of Ebbw Vale. 3328
F.J. Ball. London M.A. (Ext.) 1959.

The Llwchwr and Amman valleys to 1939: a study in 3329
industrial development. D. Davies. Wales M.A. 1959.

The industrial development of the Rhondda valleys to 3330
1910. E.D. Lewis. Wales M.A. 1940.

A study of the course of change in the customary and in 3331
the specified or normal hours of work of manual workers in
certain British industries and of the factors affecting
changes in the specified or normal hours from the 18th
century to the present day. M.A. Bienefeld. London Ph.D.
1969.

Wages in the Leeds area, 1770-1850. J.H. Lenton. 3332
Leeds M.Phil. 1969.

The influence of technological change on the social 3333
attitudes and trade-union policies of workers in the British
engineering industry, 1780-1860. K.R. Burgess. Leeds Ph.D.
1970.

Development of productive techniques in Birmingham, 3334
1760 to 1851. J.R. Immer. Oxford B.Litt. 1954.

Women workers and the Industrial Revolution, 1750-1850. 3335
Ivy Pinchbeck. London Ph.D. 1930.

The responsibilities of employers and others for the 3336
maintenance and support of injured workmen and their families,
including the families of deceased workmen, during the half
century before 1840. H. Smith. London M.A. (Ext.) 1964.

Specific Industries

A geographical study of the Cumberland coalfield. T.H. 3337
Bainbridge. Durham M.Sc. 1934.

A detailed survey of the history and development of the 3338
South Wales coal industry, c.1750 to c.1850. L.B. Collier.
London Ph.D. (Ext.) 1941.

A study of the Daucleddau coalfield, Pembrokeshire. 3339
G. Edwards. Birmingham M.A. 1950.

An economic and historical survey of the development of 3340
the anthracite industry, with special reference to the Swansea valley. D.G. John. Wales M.A. 1923.

The development of lead mining and of the coal and iron 3341
industries in north Derbyshire and south Yorkshire, 1700-1850.
G.G. Hopkinson. Sheffield Ph.D. 1958.

The economic and social conditions of lead-miners in 3342
the northern Pennines in the 18th and 19th centuries. C.J.
Hunt. Durham M.Litt. 1968.

The social and economic conditions of the Lancashire 3343
miner, to 1870. Dorothy I. Moore. Manchester M.A. 1921.

The copper industry in Lancashire and North Wales. 3344
J.R. Harris. Manchester Ph.D. 1952.

The history of the growth and organisation of the 3345
copper industry of Swansea and district. W.R. John. Wales
M.A. 1912.

Iron and steel industry of south Staffordshire, 1760- 3346
1950. D.B. Evans. Birmingham M.A. 1951.

The Dowlais ironworks and its industrial community, 3347
1760-1850: a local study in economic and social history of
the late 18th and early 19th centuries. K.T. Weetch. London
M.Sc. 1963.

The Crawshay dynasty: a study in industrial organis- 3348
ation and development, 1765-1867. J.P. Addis. Wales M.A.
1954.

The economic history of the British iron and steel 3349
industry, 1784-1897. A. Birch. Manchester Ph.D. 1953.

The slate industry of North Wales: a study of the 3350
changes in economic organisation from 1780 to the present day.
D.D. Pritchard. Wales M.A. 1935.

127

3351   The social and historical geography of the Ffestiniog slate industry. J.G. Jones. Wales M.A. 1959.
3352   The slate industry in North Wales, with special reference to Merioneth. E.L. Lewis. Wales M.A. 1917.
3353   An introduction to the development of the mechanical engineering industry, 1750-1900. A.T. Kings. London M.Sc. 1923.
3354   The historical geography of the engineering industry in Leicester. G.T. Rimmington. Leicester M.A. 1958.
3355   Studies in the history of textile technology. R.L. Hills. Manchester Ph.D. 1968.
3356   The Gloucestershire woollen industry in the 18th and 19th centuries. R. Perry. London Ph.D. (Ext.) 1947.
3357   The west of England woollen industry, 1750-1840. J.H. Morris. London M.Sc. 1934.
3358   The Industrial Revolution and the textile industries of Somerset. H.C. Oram. Bristol M.A. 1930.
3359   Bolton and the development of the cotton industry from the Industrial Revolution to 1870. Constance V. Bradley. Manchester M.A. 1921.
3360   The contribution of water power development to the progress of the cotton spinning industry, with particular reference to the Bolton district (period 1770-1845). E.J. Foulkes. Wales M.A. 1943.
3361   M'Connel and Kennedy, fine cotton spinners: a study in business enterprise in the cotton industry, 1795-1840. C.H. Lee. Cambridge M.Litt. 1966.
3362   The economic development of Norwich, 1750-1850, with special reference to the worsted industry. J.K. Edwards. Leeds Ph.D. 1963.
3363   The British hosiery trade: its history and organisation. F.A. Wells. London Ph.D. 1931.
3364   The Coventry silk-ribbon industry from the introduction of the use of the Dutch engine loom (c.1770) to the Cobden Commercial Treaty (1860). H. Miles. Oxford B.Litt. 1930.
3365   History of the Birmingham gun trade. Dorothy W. Young. Birmingham M.Com. 1936.
3366   An account of the needle industry up to the beginning of the factory system. S.H. Hardy. Birmingham M.Com. 1940.
3367   The history, development and organisation of the Birmingham jewellery trade. J.C. Roche. Birmingham M.Com. 1926.
3368   The Sheffield cutlery and allied trades and their markets in the 18th and 19th centuries. P.C. Garlick. Sheffield M.A. 1951.
3369   The development and location of the soap-manufacturing industry in Great Britain, 1700-1950. L. Gittins. London Ph.D. 1962.
3370   The economic development of the north Staffordshire potteries since 1730, with special reference to the Industrial Revolution. J. Thomas. London Ph.D. 1934.
3371   The history of the straw-hat and straw-plaiting industries of Great Britain to 1914, with special reference to the social conditions of the workers engaged in them. J.G. Dony. London Ph.D. 1941.
3372   A history of the nut and bolt industry in the west Midlands. J.A.C. Baker. Birmingham M.Com. 1965.
3373   A history of the pharmaceutical industry, with particular reference to Allen and Hanbury, 1775-1843. S.S. Stander. London M.Sc. 1965.
3374   Howards, chemical manufacturers, 1797-1837, a study in business history. A.W. Slater. London M.Sc. 1956.
3375   A historico-geographical survey of the alkali industry of Great Britain from 1789 to the present day. H. Thomas. London Ph.D. 1935.

3376   The growth and decline of the port of Whitehaven, Cumberland, 1650 to 1900. J.E. Williams. Leeds M.A. 1951.

The Dee estuary - an historical geography of its use as   3377
a port. J.P. Bethell. Wales M.Sc. 1952.
    The estuarine ports of the Exe and the Teign, with   3378
special reference to the period 1660-1880: a study in historical geography. E.A.G. Clark. London Ph.D. (Ext.) 1957.
    The haven of Milford and its influence on the human   3379
geography of the adjacent area with particular reference to
the period after 1700. J.A. Evans. Birmingham M.A. 1961.
    The Devon fishing industry, 1760-1860. A.M. Northway.   3380
Exeter M.A. 1969.
    The British Fisheries Society, 1786-1893. Jean M.   3381
Dunlop. Edinburgh Ph.D. 1952.
    The historical geography of the seafaring industry off   3382
the coast of Cardigan Bay during the 18th and 19th centuries.
Margaret E. Hughes. Wales M.A. 1962.
    Dover: the historical geography of the town and port   3383
since 1750. D.R.E. Philpott. London M.A. 1964.
    The geography of the port of Great Yarmouth, 1750-1850. 3384
D.A. Lewis. Manchester M.A. 1955.

Transport and Communications

    The postal history of Kent, 1633-1840. B. Austen.   3385
Kent M.A. 1970.
    Transport in the west Midlands from 1660 to 1840. D.W. 3386
Blundell. Birmingham M.Com. 1933.
    A geographical study of the development of roads   3387
through the Surrey-Sussex Weald to the south coast, during
the period 1700-1900. G. Joan Fuller. London Ph.D. (Ext.)
1950.
    The road transport system in England, 1700-1839. W.I.   3388
Albert. London Ph.D. 1968.
    The navigation of the river Great Ouse, 1700-c.1860.   3389
D.E. Summers. London M.A. (Ext.) 1969.
    The development of the road system in Glamorgan up to   3390
1844, with special reference to turnpike roads, together with
a bibliography of maps and topographical works. D.E. Fraser.
Wales M.A. 1940.
    A history of the development of the means of communic-   3391
ation in the county of Monmouth, 1760-1914. Mary A. Swallow.
London Ph.D. 1932.
    The development of communications in Glamorgan, with   3392
special reference to the growth of industry, between 1760 and
1840. Enid Walker. Wales M.A. 1947.
    The development and administration of roads in   3393
Carmarthenshire, 1760-1860. A.H.T. Lewis. Wales M.A. 1968.
    The English canal system in its geographical and indus- 3394
trial relations. R.W.G. Bryant. London M.Sc. 1939.
    Road and railway investment in Britain, 1750-1850.   3395
J.E. Ginarlis. Sheffield Ph.D. 1970.
    The Thames Navigation Commission, 1771-1867. H.S.   3396
Davies. Reading M.A. 1967.
    A study of the origin and growth of the canal settle-   3397
ment at Barnton in Cheshire between 1775 and 1845. D.A.
Iredale. Leicester Ph.D. 1966.
    Urban genesis and development: the case of canal-   3398
created river ports of the English Industrial Revolution.
J.D. Porteous. Hull Ph.D. 1969.
    Transport in the urban development of Kentish Thames-   3399
side since the late 18th century. R.F. Baker. London M.A.
1968.

Agrarian History

    A geographical study of open field cultivation in   3400
Derbyshire. J.C. Jackson. Leicester M.A. 1959.

3401   The development and distribution of landscape parks in the East and West Ridings of Yorkshire. B.E. Coates. Leeds M.A. 1960.

3402   Landscape gardens in the Chilterns. H.C. Prince. London M.A. 1954.

3403   Historical geography of Breckland, 1600 to 1850. M.R. Postgate. London M.A. 1961.

3404   An historical geography of the Sandlings of Suffolk, 1600 to 1850. Elizabeth D.R. Burrell. London M.Sc. 1960.

3405   The drainage of the Fens and its effects upon the parishes of the South Division of the Bedford Level, 1600-1850. Lucy M. Warren. London M.A. 1927.

3406   The coastal marshland of east Essex between the 17th and mid 19th centuries. D.W. Gramolt. London M.A. 1961.

3407   The reclamation of the middle level of the Fens. Phyllis M. Crowther. Reading Ph.D. 1929.

3408   The reclamation and land use of the Thames marshes of north-west Kent. Eileen E.M. Bowler. London Ph.D. 1968.

3409   The alluvial marshlands of the lower Thames estuary: a study in changing use patterns. B.E. Cracknell. London Ph.D. 1953.

3410   Geographical aspects of the reclamation and development of Hatfield Chase. B. Metcalfe. Leeds M.A. 1961.

3411   The Giffards of Chillingham, a Catholic landed family, 1642-1861. P.J. Doyle. Durham M.A. 1968.

3412   The Crosswood estate: its growth and economic development, 1683-1899. J.M. Howells. Wales M.A. 1956.

3413   The Camer estate, 1716-1852. Margaret Roake. Kent M.A. 1969.

3414   Glamorgan and the Bute estate, 1766-1947. J. Davies. Wales Ph.D. 1969.

3415   The Dudley estate: its rise and decline between 1774 and 1947. T.J. Raybould. Kent Ph.D. 1970.

3416   The Kingswinford estate of Lord Dudley: its development and organisation between 1774 and 1833. T.J. Raybould. Birmingham M.A. 1967.

3417   The financial affairs and estate management of the Cokes of Holkham in the 18th and 19th centuries. R.A.C. Parker. Oxford D.Phil. 1956.

3418   Some geographical aspects of the agriculture of Durham. A.S. Gaught. London Ph.D. (Ext.) 1939.

3419   The agricultural geography of Norfolk, with special reference to changes in land utilisation and human occupancy. J.E.G. Mosby. London Ph.D. 1938.

3420   Parliamentary enclosure in Oxfordshire, 1696-1882. W.E. Tate. Oxford B.Litt. 1947.

3421   The progress of enclosures in the county of Dorset since 1700. G.B. Endacott. Oxford B.Litt. 1938.

3422   The distribution of parliamentary enclosures in the West Riding of Yorkshire, 1729-1850. W.S. Rodgers. Leeds M.Com. 1953.

3423   The parliamentary enclosure movement in Leicestershire, 1730-1842. H.G. Hunt. London Ph.D. (Ext.) 1956.

3424   Some geographical aspects of the enclosure of the vale of Pickering in the 18th and 19th centuries. B. Loughbrough. Hull M.A. 1960.

3425   Warwickshire and the parliamentary enclosure movement. J.M. Martin. Birmingham Ph.D. 1965.

3426   Parliamentary enclosure in Bulmer wapentake. M. Kirk. Leeds M.A. 1948.

3427   The effect of parliamentary enclosure on the landscape of Caernarvonshire and Merioneth. C. Morgan. Wales M.Sc. 1959.

3428   The enclosure movement in Caernarvonshire, with special reference to the Porth-yr-aur papers. Gertrude A. Plume. Wales M.A. 1935.

Enclosure and agricultural improvement in the vale of 3429
Clwyd, 1750-1875. J.W. Edwards. London M.A. 1963.

Parliamentary enclosures in Lindsey. T.H. Swales. 3430
Leeds M.A. 1936.

The enclosure movement in Anglesey, 1788-1866. E.J. 3431
Jones. Wales M.A. 1924.

Changes in the agricultural geography of the south 3432
Hertfordshire plateau, 1750-1888. Aileen M. Carpenter. London M.A. 1965.

Changing agriculture and the moorland edge in the north 3433
York moors, 1750-1960. J. Chapman. London M.A. 1961.

The changing land-use in the upper basin of the river 3434
Mole. M.J. Frost. London M.Sc. 1963.

Changes in land utilisation in Uwchgwyrfai, Caernarvon- 3435
shire, 1750 to 1956. P.E. Jones. Wales M.A. 1959.

Changes in land utilisation in the upper Severn valley, 3436
Montgomeryshire, during the period 1750-1936. L.S. Andrews.
Wales M.Sc. 1940.

Changes in land utilisation in the Towy valley, 3437
Carmarthenshire, since the end of the 18th century. B.L.
Davies. Wales M.A. 1938.

The agriculture of the west midland conurbation. I. 3438
Davies. Birmingham M.A. 1955.

The history of Hertfordshire agriculture, 1750-1860. 3439
E.J. Connell. London M.Sc. 1966.

The agricultural history of Cheshire, 1750-1850. 3440
Clarice S. Davies. Manchester Ph.D. 1953.

The agrarian revolution in Cambridgeshire, 1770-1850. 3441
P.H.P. Watson. London M.A. (Ext.) 1951.

The agricultural revolution in East Anglia. Nora 3442
Walsh. Liverpool M.A. 1934.

An historical study of the agriculture of part of 3443
south-eastern Sussex from 1780. H.B. Smith. London M.A.
1940.

The historical geography of a part of east Sussex from 3444
1780 (with special reference to agriculture). E.W.H. Briault.
London Ph.D. 1939.

Agricultural change in south Lincolnshire, 1790-1875. 3445
D.B. Grigg. Cambridge Ph.D. 1961.

Social History

The demography of the British peerage: an analysis of 3446
the levels and trends of marriage, fertility and mortality
of the peerage, dukes to barons inclusive, from the beginning
of the 17th to the beginning of the 20th centuries. T.H.
Hollingsworth. London Ph.D. 1963.

Marriage patterns in the British peerage in the 18th 3447
and 19th centuries. D.N. Thomas. London M.Phil. 1969.

The poor law of 1601, with some consideration of modern 3448
developments of the poor law problem. Gladys Boone. Birmingham M.A. 1917.

Poor law administration in Glamorganshire before the 3449
Poor Law Amendment Act of 1834. W.E. Allin. Wales M.A. 1936.

Administration of the old 'poor law' in the West Derby 3450
hundred of Lancashire, 1607-1837. G.W. Oxley. Liverpool
M.A. 1966.

The origins of public superannuation schemes in Eng- 3451
land, 1684-1859. M. Raphael. London Ph.D. 1957.

The reaction of English Pembrokeshire to the social 3452
and intellectual movements of modern Wales since 1689.
Elnith R. Griffiths. Wales M.A. 1927.

Popular recreations in English society, 1700-1850. 3453
R.W. Malcolmson. Warwick Ph.D. 1970.

The treatment of poverty in Norfolk, from 1700 to 1850. 3454
Mrs. Muriel F. Lloyd Prichard. Cambridge Ph.D. 1949.

3455   The development of the great affiliated Friendly societies from their humble and often obscure origins in the 18th century. W.T. Bushrod. Manchester M.A. 1924.

3456   West of England Friendly societies of the 18th and 19th centuries, with particular reference to their insignia. Margaret D. Fuller. Reading M.A. 1957/8.

3457   The economic and social development of the Jews in England, 1730-1860. J. Rumney. London Ph.D. 1933.

3458   Lunacy legislation and administration in England, 1744-1845. Kathleen Jones. London Ph.D. (Ext.) 1953.

3459   Poor law administration in selected London parishes between 1750 and 1850. Ann J. Froshaug. Nottingham M.A. 1969.

3460   Poor law administration in Glamorgan, 1750-1850. K.E. Skinner. Wales M.A. 1956.

3461   Poverty and its treatment in Cardiganshire, 1750-1850. A.M.E. Davies. Wales M.A. 1968.

3462   The history of the Honourable Society of Cymmrodorion. Helen M. Jones. Wales M.A. 1939.

3463   Some aspects of the history of the Society of Arts, London, 1754-1952. K.W. Luckhurst. London Ph.D. 1957.

3464   Medical education and the rise of the general practitioner, 1760-1860. Mrs. Rachel E. Waterhouse. Birmingham Ph.D. 1950.

3465   Public health and hospital administration in Swansea and west Glamorgan from the end of the 18th century to 1914. G.D. Fielder. Wales M.A. 1962.

ECCLESIASTICAL HISTORY

3466   The changes and development within Presbyterianism in the counties of Derby, Leicester and Nottingham from its organisation in the Commonwealth to the transformation to Independency and Unitarianism c.1780. C.G. Bolam. Nottingham M.A. 1957.

3467   Nonconformity in Exeter, 1650-1875. A.A. Brockett. Exeter M.A. 1960.

3468   The Quakers in Leicestershire, 1648-1780. E.K.L. Quine. Nottingham Ph.D. 1968.

3469   Bristol Quakerism. R.S. Mortimer. Bristol M.A. 1946.

3470   The Society of Friends in Glamorgan, 1654-1900. Margaret F. Williams. Wales M.A. 1950.

3471   The history of the Society of Friends in Plymouth and west Devon from 1654 to the early 19th century. A.D. Selleck. London M.A. (Ext.) 1959.

3472   The consistory courts of the diocese of St. Davids, 1660-1858: studies of the records of the courts illustrative of their work and practice. W.T. Morgan. Wales M.A. 1962.

3473   Protestant Nonconformity in the Black Country, 1662-1851. A.G. Cumberland. Birmingham M.A. 1951.

3474   Nonconformity in Shropshire, 1662-1815: a study in the rise and progress of Baptist, Congregational, Presbyterian, Quaker and Methodist societies. R.F. Skinner. London Ph.D. (Ext.) 1967.

3475   The Arian movement in England. J.H. Colligan. Manchester M.A. 1911.

3476   Dissent and democracy. F.M. Scully. Bristol M.A. 1937.

3477   The renewed church of the United Brethren, 1722-1930. W.G.C. Addison. London Ph.D. (Ext.) 1931.

3478   The rise and growth of Welsh Wesleyan Methodism to 1858. A.H. Williams. Wales M.A. 1932.

3479   The Evangelicals in Oxford, 1735-1871. J.S. Reynolds. Oxford B.Litt. 1950.

3480   The history of Unitarianism in Birmingham from the middle of the 18th century to 1893. Emily Bushrod. Birmingham M.A. 1954.

The development of the Anglican and Roman Catholic   3481
clergy as a profession since the middle of the 18th century.
M.J. Woolgar. Leicester Ph.D. 1960.

The Baptists of north-west England, 1750-1850. G.A.   3482
Weston. Sheffield Ph.D. 1969.

The history of Congregationalism in Derbyshire from the 3483
Methodist revival to 1850. R. Mansfield. Manchester Ph.D.
1958.

The economic and social history of the principal   3484
protestant denominations in Leeds, 1760-1844. C.M. Elliott.
Oxford D.Phil. 1962.

The parish clergy of rural Oxfordshire from the instit- 3485
ution of Bishop John Butler (1777) to the translation of
Bishop Samuel Wilberforce (1869) with particular reference to
their non-ecclesiastical activities. Mrs. Diana McClatchey.
Oxford D.Phil. 1949.

A study of the Church of England in the diocese of Bath 3486
and Wells, 1790-1840. W.St.J. Kemm. Birmingham M.A. 1965.

The old dissenting meeting-house: its structure,   3487
furniture and services. G.R. Jones. Manchester M.A. 1919.

The Methodist class meeting: a historical study. P.D. 3488
Mackenzie. St. Andrews M.Th. 1970.

The architectural expression of Methodism in England 3489
in the 18th and 19th centuries. G.W. Dolbey. Manchester
M.A. 1962.

Nonconformity in Liverpool, 1786-1914. I. Sellers. 3490
Keele Ph.D. 1969.

The divisions and reunion of British Methodism, 1791- 3491
1932, with special reference to social and organisational
factors. R. Currie. Oxford D.Phil. 1966.

The development of Wesleyan Methodist principles and   3492
ideas, 1791-1914. I.D. Cleland. Nottingham M.Phil. 1970.

Church and ministry in Wesleyan Methodism from the   3493
death of John Wesley to the death of Jabez Bunting (1791-
1858). J.C. Bowmer. Leeds Ph.D. 1967.

Methodism from the death of Wesley, 1791, to the   3494
Wesleyan centenary, 1839. R.F. Wearmouth. Birmingham M.A.
1928.

Methodism and Anglicanism, 1791-1850. J.M. Turner.   3495
Bristol M.A. 1956.

CULTURAL HISTORY

The history of science teaching in England. Dorothy 3496
M. Turner. London Ph.D. 1928.

A history of the teaching of physics in England from   3497
1650 to 1850. G.D. Bishop. London Ph.D. 1959.

The study and teaching of history in English education 3498
from the 17th century to the death of Thomas Arnold. R.A.
Lewin. London M.A. 1955.

School and community in Okehampton, 1600 to 1903.   3499
R.L. Taverner. Wales M.A. 1963.

The Jewish schooling systems of London, 1656-1956.   3500
P.L.S. Quinn. London Ph.D. 1958.

Witney grammar school, 1660-1960. Mary A. Fleming.   3501
Reading M.A. 1959/60.

A history of Hipperholme School from 1660 to 1914, with 3502
a biography of its founder Matthew Brodley (1586-1648). P.
Facer. London M.A. 1966.

The work of religious societies in English education, 3503
1660-1870. F.M. Osborne. London M.A. 1925.

Nonconformist academies in Wales, 1662-1862. H.P.   3504
Roberts. Liverpool M.A. 1922.

The activities of Catholics in the matter of education 3505
in England. A.P. Braddock. London M.A. 1917.

3506   Roman Catholic education from 1700 to 1870: a study of Roman Catholic educational endeavour from the early 18th century to the Elementary Education Act of 1870. J. Kitching. Leeds Ph.D. 1967.

3507   The history of Brigg grammar school. F. Henthorn. London Ph.D. (Ext.) 1961.

3508   Elementary education in the Forest of Dean between the years 1698 and 1870. D.R.A. Williams. Bristol M.A. 1962.

3509   The development of elementary education in Gloucester-shire, 1698-1846. G.H. Hainton. Bristol M.A. 1952.

3510   The rise and progress of the periodical press in Wales up to 1860. Catherine Evans. Wales M.A. 1926.

3511   A history of the South Wales newspapers to 1855. R.D. Rees. Reading M.A. 1955.

3512   Chapters in the history of the provincial newspaper press, 1700-1855. D.F. Gallop. Reading M.A. 1952.

3513   The Derbyshire newspaper press, 1720-1855. J.D. Andrew. Reading M.A. 1954.

3514   The early newspaper press in Berkshire (1723-1855). K.G. Burton. Reading M.A. 1950.

3515   The Oliver Whitby School, Chichester: a study of the repercussions of contemporary trends, social and educational, in the fortunes of the school, 1702-1904. G.L. Barnard. London Ph.D. 1961.

3516   The development of chemistry in Britain through medicine and pharmacy from 1700 to 1850. J.K. Crellin. London Ph.D. 1969.

3517   The educational aims of pioneers in elementary Welsh education, 1730-1870. F. Williams. Wales M.A. 1929.

3518   Wesleyan Methodism's contribution to national education (1739-1902). H. Cloke. London M.A. 1936.

3519   A short history and a statistical survey of charity school education. R.W. Hitchcock. London M.A. 1933.

3520   A history of charity school education and a statistical survey of some measures of educational growth. R.W. Hitch-cock. London Ph.D. 1938.

3521   Science education in Ireland and Scotland, 1750-1900. B.B. Kelham. Manchester Ph.D. 1968.

3522   Elementary education provided by the governors of the Free Grammar School of King Edward VI in Birmingham, 1751-1883. J.C. Tyson. Birmingham M.A. 1960.

3523   Education and the handicapped, 1760-1960. D.G. Prit-chard. Liverpool Ph.D. 1963/4.

3524   Congregationalism and the education of the people, 1760-1914: the quest for freedom. A. McLellan. Birmingham M.A. 1963.

3525   A comparative study of the Sunday School movement in England and Wales. Dorothi M. Griffith. Wales M.A. 1923.

3526   The origin and development of the Sunday School movement in England from 1780 to 1880, in relation to the state pro-vision of education. J.K. Meir. Edinburgh Ph.D. 1954.

3527   The history and development of the Sunday School in England. W.A. Christie. Liverpool M.A. 1937.

3528   A history of education in York, 1780-1902. E. Benson. London Ph.D. (Ext.) 1933.

3529   Press and people, 1790-1850: opinion in three English cities. D. Read. Sheffield Ph.D. 1961.

3530   The educational activities of Baptists in England during the 18th and 19th centuries, with particular reference to the north-west. J.E. Watson. Liverpool M.A. 1947.

3531   The development of education in Hitchin, Hertfordshire, 1780-1880. K.R.J. Aitken. Nottingham M.A. 1960.

3532   The basic education of labour in Lancashire, 1780-1839. J.M. Sanderson. Cambridge Ph.D. 1966.

3533   The development of education in Accrington, 1790-1903. E. Stones. Sheffield M.A. 1957.

Demands for the education of girls between 1790 and   3534
1865. Shirley C. Gordon. London M.A. 1950.
The dame schools in Great Britain. J.H. Higginson.   3535
Leeds M.A. 1939.

LOCAL HISTORY

The social and economic history of the East Fen village 3536
of Wrangle, 1603-1837. F. West. Leicester Ph.D. 1966.
The corporation and community of Okehampton, 1623-1885. 3537
R.L. Taverner. London Ph.D. (Ext.) 1969.
A study of parish government, 1660-1894, illustrated by 3538
documents from the parish chest of Eye, Northants. R.A.
Shannon. London M.A. (Ext.) 1949.
An administrative history of the borough of Newport, in 3539
the county of Monmouth, 1623-1850. B.P. Jones. Wales M.A.
1955.
The history of Bury, Lancashire, from 1660 to 1876.   3540
Margaret Gray. Oxford B.Litt. 1963.
The parish of Ecclesfield in an era of change, 1672-   3541
1851. D.G. Hey. Leicester M.A. 1967.
Local government in the borough of Neath: a study in   3542
urban administration, 1694-1884. R.D. Till. Wales M.A.
1970.
The economic and social history of the Furness area   3543
from 1711 to 1875. J.D. Marshall. London Ph.D. (Ext.) 1956.
A study in demography based on the ancient Lancashire   3544
parish of Warton. R. Speake. Lancaster M.Litt. 1968.
The urban geography of Leicester. Jennifer Pugh.   3545
Leicester M.A. 1965.
A study of some of the social and economic changes in   3546
the town and parish of Amlwch, 1750-1850. J. Rowlands.
Wales M.A. 1960.
Social and economic development of Styal, 1750-1850.   3547
W.C. Lazenby. Manchester M.A. 1949.
The government and growth of the parish of Halifax,   3548
1760-1848. J.W. Houseman. Liverpool M.A. 1928.
Aspects of the economic and social geography of the   3549
Mansfield area. C.M. Law. Nottingham M.Sc. 1961.
A comparative study of the urban development of York   3550
and Lincoln. Patricia A. Grimshaw. Nottingham M.A. 1960.
The north-eastern expansion of London since 1770. H.   3551
Rees. London M.Sc. 1946.
Contribution towards the study of the economic develop- 3552
ment of Bristol in the 18th and 19th centuries. A.J. Pugs-
ley. Bristol M.A. 1921.
The economic and social development of Gainsborough,   3553
with special reference to the 18th and 19th centuries. T.H.
Chafer. Sheffield M.A. 1956.

SCOTLAND

Servitudes in the law of Scotland: principles, sources 3554
and influences which have affected the law. T.A. Ross.
Edinburgh Ph.D. 1931/2.
The Scottish woollen industry, 1603-1914. C. Gulvin.   3555
Edinburgh Ph.D. 1969.
The rise, progress and decline of the Quaker movement   3556
in Scotland. G.B. Burnet. Glasgow Ph.D. 1936.
The history of the Episcopal Church in the diocese of   3557
Brechin, 1688-1875. W. Christie. Dundee Ph.D. 1967.
Sunday observance in Scotland, 1689-1900. R.D.   3558
Brackenridge. Glasgow Ph.D. 1962.
The distribution and structure of the population of   3559
north-east Scotland, 1696-1931. K. Walton. Aberdeen Ph.D.
1951.

3560   Settlement in Trotternish, Isle of Skye, 1700-1958. M.D. MacSween. Glasgow B.Litt. 1962.

3561   Settlement changes in the south-west Highlands of Scotland, 1700-1960. R.A. Gailey. Glasgow Ph.D. 1961.

3562   The industrial archaeology of Galloway: the regional economy of south-west Scotland, 1700-1900. I.L. Donnachie. Strathclyde M.Litt. 1969.

3563   Division of commonty in Scotland: the use of 18th- and 19th-century estate plans held by the Scottish Record Office in a study of historical geography. I.H. Adams. Edinburgh Ph.D. 1967.

3564   The paper industry in Scotland, 1700-1861. A.G. Thomson. Edinburgh Ph.D. 1965.

3565   Scottish bleachfields, 1718-1862. Mrs. Enid M. Gauldie. St. Andrews B.Phil. 1967.

3566   The operation of the poor law in the north-east of Scotland, 1745-1845. Jean Lindsay. Aberdeen Ph.D. 1962.

3567   The migration of Highlanders into lowland Scotland, c. 1750-1890, with particular reference to Greenock. R.D. Lobban. Edinburgh Ph.D. 1970.

3568   The geography of crofting in Scotland. J.R. Coull. Aberdeen Ph.D. 1962.

3569   The crofting areas of Sutherland since 1756. P.T. Wheeler. London Ph.D. 1961.

3570   Locational factors in the development of the Scottish iron and steel industry, 1760-1970. W.D. Campbell. Edinburgh M.Sc. 1969/70.

3571   The history of deaf education in Scotland from 1760 to 1939. T.J. Watson. Edinburgh Ph.D. 1949.

3572   Population movements in Scotland, 1770-1850. D.F. Macdonald. Oxford D.Phil. 1932/3.

3573   Monymusk, 1770-1850: a study of the economic development of a Scottish estate. T.P. Soper. Aberdeen Ph.D. 1954.

3574   The Dumbarton Glass Work Company, c.1777-c.1850. J.C. Logan. Strathclyde M.Litt. 1970.

3575   Some geographical aspects of the Blair Atholl papers. Thelma Blance. Aberdeen Ph.D. 1956.

3576   Scottish experiments in rural education from the 18th century to the present day, with special reference to rural arts and crafts. J. Mason. Edinburgh Ph.D. 1930/1.

3577   The history of roads in the Highlands of Scotland in the 18th and 19th centuries contrasting the military roads (i.e. those of Wade and Caulfield) with the parliamentary roads (i.e. those constructed by Telford). J.S. Stephen. Aberdeen Ph.D. 1936.

3578   The Baptists in Scotland: an historical survey. J. Scott. Glasgow Ph.D. 1927.

3579   Electoral law and procedure in the 18th and 19th century in Scotland. W. Ferguson. Glasgow Ph.D. 1957.

IRELAND

3580   Aspects of the population geography of Co. Cork. T. Burke. Birmingham Ph.D. 1967.

3581   The collieries of east Tyrone from the mid 17th century to the present day. W.A. McCutcheon. Belfast M.A. 1958.

3582   A survey of turf working in Co. Down. L.T. Brown. Belfast M.Sc. 1968.

3583   Scottish ecclesiastical influence upon Irish Presbyterianism from the non-subscription controversy to the union of the synods. R. Allen. Belfast M.A. 1940.

3584   The population of Ireland from 1750 to 1846, and the social and economic factors associated with its increase. K.H. Connell. London Ph.D. (Ext.) 1948.

3585   The Evangelicals in the Church of Ireland, 1784-1859. A.R. Acheson. Belfast Ph.D. 1967.

The development and distribution of Methodism in Ire-   3586
land: a demographic study. J.H. Cooke. Belfast M.A. 1964.
     A history of Methodism in Ireland from Wesley's death   3587
in 1791 to the reunion of Primitives and Wesleyans in 1878.
June R. Binns. Belfast M.A. 1960.
     A critical survey of the development of secondary educ- 3588
ation in Ireland, 1791-1880, with special reference to schools
in Ulster. G. Stevenson. Belfast M.A. 1957.
     The history of iron shipbuilding in the Queen's Island   3589
up till July 1874. D. Rebbeck. Belfast Ph.D. 1950.
     A history of inland transport in Ireland down to the   3590
period of the railways. P. O'Kelly. London M.Sc. 1922.
     The development and subsequent decline of the chief   3591
inland waterways and standard gauge railways of the north of
Ireland. W.A. McCutcheon. Belfast Ph.D. 1962.

B R I T A I N :   1 6 0 0 - 1 8 3 2

For items covering the period 1600-60 see above under 1485-1660

POLITICAL HISTORY

   General

     The parliamentary representation of Yorkshire boroughs, 3592
1640-85. P.A. Bolton. Leeds M.A. 1966.
     The political career of Philip, 4th Lord Wharton, 1613- 3593
96. G.F.T. Jones. Oxford D.Phil. 1957.
     Richard Vaughan, 2nd earl of Carbery, 1606-86. T.S.   3594
Williams. Wales M.A. 1936.
     Colonel Philip Jones, 1618-74. A.G. Veysey. Wales   3595
M.A. 1958.
     The evolution of the administration of the treasury in   3596
England during the years 1660-1714. Doris M. Gill. London
M.A. 1919.
     Members of parliament and elections in Derbyshire,   3597
Leicestershire and Staffordshire between 1660 and 1714.
Pamela W.U. Ward. Manchester M.A. 1959.
     Surrey politics in later Stuart England, 1660-1714.   3598
J.S.T. Turner. Newcastle M.Litt. 1969.
     The parliamentary history of the borough of Tamworth,   3599
Staffordshire, 1661-1837. D.G. Stuart. London M.A. (Ext.)
1958.
     The relations between Lords and Commons in the reign of 3600
Charles II. A.R. Leamy. Leeds M.A. 1966.
     The activities of Welsh members of parliament, 1660 to   3601
1688. D.M.E. Williams. Wales M.A. 1952.
     The republican party in England from the Restoration   3602
to the Revolution. J. Walker. Manchester Ph.D. 1931.
     Post-Restoration Nonconformity and plotting, 1660-75.   3603
W.G. Johnson. Manchester M.A. 1967.
     A critical study of the political activities of Andrew   3604
Marvell. Ivy C. Robbins. London Ph.D. 1926.
     The ministerial career of the 1st earl of Shaftesbury,   3605
1660-73. K.H.D. Haley. Oxford B.Litt. 1949.
     A biography of Thomas Clifford, 1st Lord Clifford of   3606
Chudleigh. J.J.S. Shaw. Glasgow Ph.D. 1935.
     Hyde and the Convention parliament of 1660. T.W.   3607
Evans. London M.A. 1964.
     Robert Harley: his early life and political con-   3608
nexions, 1661-1702. R.B. Ballinger. Cambridge M.Litt. 1955.
     The Cavalier house of commons: court and country man-   3609
oeuvres, 1663-74. L.T. Witcombe. Manchester Ph.D. 1963.

3610   England and the Orangist party from 1665 to 1672.   R.R.
Goodison. London M.A. 1934.
3611   The fall of Clarendon.   A. Dobson.   Leeds M.A. 1919.
3612   The political.career of Laurence Hyde, earl of Rochester,
as it illustrates government policy and party grouping under
Charles II and James II. Margaret F. Yates. London Ph.D.
1935.
3613   The political career of William, 3rd Lord Howard of
Escrick (1626?-1694). Phyllis H. Goodman. Oxford B.Litt.
1948.
3614   Sir John Vaughan, chief justice of common pleas, 1603-
74. J.G. Williams. Wales M.A. 1952.
3615   The circumstances of the treaty of Dover. Annie H.
Madan. Birmingham M.A. 1909.
3616   Sir William Coventry and the origin of the country party
under Charles II. A.H.G. Cox. Manchester M.A. 1926.
3617   The parliamentary career of Sir William Coventry and of
Mr. Henry Coventry. D.T. Witcombe. Oxford B.Litt. 1954.
3618   The development of parties during the ministry of Danby.
E.S. de Beer. London M.A. 1923.
3619   Danby. A. Mabel Evans. Leeds M.A. 1918.
3620   The history of parliamentary representation in the city and
county of Durham, 1675-1832. C.W. Daykin. Durham M.Litt. 1961.
3621   Politics and parties in the county of Buckinghamshire,
1678-1815. C.E.S. Drew. Oxford B.Litt. 1931.
3622   Titus Oates and the Popish Plot. R.C.F. Dolley. London
M.A. 1911.
3623   Wales and the Border counties in relation to the Popish
Plot. Ida M. O'Leary. Wales M.A. 1924.
3624   The Whigs, 1678-85. J.R. Jones. Cambridge Ph.D. 1952.
3625   The organisation of the Whig party during the Exclusion
crisis, 1678-81. V.H. Simms. London M.A. 1934.
3626   The Rye House plot; with special reference to its place
in the Exclusion contest and its consequences till 1685.
Doreen J. Milne. London Ph.D. 1949.
3627   The origins and early development of the Whig party,
with special reference to Shaftesbury and Locke. O.W. Furley.
Oxford B.Litt. 1953.
3628   Robert Spencer, earl of Sunderland, 1641-1702. J.P.
Kenyon. Cambridge Ph.D. 1954.
3629   The life of Robert Spencer, 2nd earl of Sunderland, 1640-
1702, with special reference to his work as secretary of
state. P.L. Norrish. Liverpool M.A. 1936.
3630   The office of secretary of state, 1681-1782. M.A.
Thomson. Oxford D.Phil. 1930/1.
3631   The administrative work of the English privy council,
1679-1714. Jennifer J. Carter. London Ph.D. 1958.
3632   The career and writings of Charles Davenant, 1656-1714.
D.A.G. Waddell. Oxford D.Phil. 1954.
3633   The Monmouth rebellion. C.D. Curtis. Bristol M.A. 1939.

3634   The elections to parliament in the county of Lancaster,
1688-1714. Janet M. Wahlstrand. Manchester M.A. 1956.
3635   The invitation to William of Orange in 1688. R.D.
Jones. Wales M.A. 1969.
3636   The Convention parliament, 1688-9. A. Simpson. Oxford
D.Phil. 1939.
3637   The country party in the reign of William III. D.A.
Rubini. Oxford D.Phil. 1966.
3638   The house of lords in the reign of William III, 1688-
1702. A.S. Turberville. Oxford B.Litt. 1912.
3639   Elections to the house of commons in the reign of
William III. J.H. Plumb. Cambridge Ph.D. 1935/6.
3640   The Whigs and their relations with William III in the
period from 1689 to 1698. A.K. Powis. London M.A. 1947.
3641   The representative history of the county, town and
university of Cambridge, 1689-1832. D. Cook. London Ph.D.
1935.

The treasury and the exchequer in the reign of William 3642
III. S.B. Baxter. Cambridge Ph.D. 1954.

The life and career of William Blathwayt. R.A. Pres- 3643
ton. Leeds M.A. 1932.

Mary II of England and her life during the years 1689- 3644
94: influence on politics, on the Anglican Church, and on
society. Nellie M. Waterson. Oxford B.Litt. 1925.

The development of Jacobite ideas and policy, 1689- 3645
1746. G.H. Jones. Oxford D.Phil. 1950.

The Jacobites in England and Wales, 1689-1723. Alma 3646
C. Turnbull. Liverpool M.A. 1949.

Jacobite activities in Great Britain, 1702-8. A. 3647
Davies. Wales M.A. 1951.

The history of the fourth parliament of William III. 3648
J.F.H. Beddow. Oxford B.Litt. 1912.

Northamptonshire county elections and electioneering 3649
(1695-1832), based mainly on the Isham and Cartwright muni-
ments. E.G. Forrester. Oxford B.Litt. 1939.

Parliamentary debates in 1701 from the reports of 3650
foreign observers. J.F.G. Lowe. Liverpool M.A. 1960.

Elections and electioneering in the constituencies of 3651
Nottinghamshire, 1702-1832. J.H. Moses. Nottingham Ph.D.
1965.

Parliament and the protestant Dissenters, 1702-19. 3652
Mrs. Patricia M. Ansell. London M.A. 1962.

The house of commons 1702-14: a study in political 3653
organisation. W.A. Speck. Oxford D.Phil. 1966.

The bishops in politics, 1702-14. N. Dodds. Newcastle 3654
M.Litt. 1968.

The influence of the peerage on English parliamentary 3655
elections, 1702-13. G.S. Holmes. Oxford B.Litt. 1952.

The Whig party, 1702-8. E.L. Ellis. Wales M.A. 1949. 3656

Henry St. John and the struggle for the leadership of 3657
the Tory party, 1702-14. H.T. Dickinson. Newcastle Ph.D.
1968.

The political career of Daniel Finch, 2nd earl of 3658
Nottingham, 1647-1730. H.G. Horwitz. Oxford D.Phil. 1963.

The administration of Daniel Finch, 2nd earl of 3659
Nottingham, as secretary of state under Queen Anne, 1702-4.
W.A. Aiken. Cambridge M.Litt. 1932/3.

The career of Robert Harley, earl of Oxford, from 1702 3660
to 1714. B.W. Hill. Cambridge Ph.D. 1961.

The political evolution of Robert Harley, 1702-12. 3661
K.C. Turpin. Oxford B.Litt. 1940.

Robert Harley, secretary of state. A.J.D.M. McInnes. 3662
Wales M.A. 1961.

A critical study of George Granville, Lord Lansdowne. 3663
Frances E. Handasyde. Oxford B.Litt. 1931.

The public career of John, 2nd earl of Stair, to 1720. 3664
J.R.T. Wood. Edinburgh Ph.D. 1970.

The Whig Junto in relation to the development of party 3665
politics and party organisation from its inception to 1714.
E.L. Ellis. Oxford D.Phil. 1962.

The general election of 1705. Elisabeth A. Cunnington. 3666
London M.A. 1938.

The political life and influence of Joseph Addison. 3667
P.H.B.O. Smithers. Oxford D.Phil. 1953.

The political career of Robert Harley, 1708-14. D.R.P. 3668
Pugh. Wales M.A. 1951.

The domestic policy of Robert Harley and the Tory 3669
ministry from 1710 to 1714. Winifred T.H. Bolton. London
M.A. 1930.

The Whig party, 1710-14. J.A. Johnston. Wales M.A. 3670
1953.

Mercantile interests in the house of commons, 1710-13. 3671
Marjorie D. McHattie. Manchester M.A. 1949.

3672   The general election of 1710. Mary E. Ransome. London M.A. 1938.

3673   The English court in the reign of George I. J.M. Beattie. Cambridge Ph.D. 1963.

3674   The Tory party in the reign of George I. L.W. Hanson. Oxford B.Litt. 1930.

3675   William Shippen as an opposition leader, 1714-43. C.T.R. Buckley. Oxford B.Litt. 1930.

3676   The parliamentary representation of North Wales, 1715-84. P.D.G. Thomas. Wales M.A. 1953.

3677   Elections in Kent and its parliamentary representation, 1715-54. A.N. Newman. Oxford D.Phil. 1957.

3678   Jacobitism and the English government, 1717-31. P.S. Fritz. Cambridge Ph.D. 1967.

3679   The English attorney in the 18th century. R. Robson. Cambridge Ph.D. 1956.

3680   The law of trusts in the 18th century up to the death of Lord Hardwicke. B.F. Brown. Oxford D.Phil. 1931/2.

3681   A consideration of the relationship between some religious and economic organisations and the government, especially from 1730 to 1742. N.C. Hunt. Cambridge Ph.D. 1951.

3682   The duke of Bedford and his friends. E. Davies. Liverpool M.A. 1908.

3683   John, 4th duke of Bedford, 1710-71. G.F. Thomas. Wales M.A. 1953.

3684   The public life of John, 4th duke of Bedford (1710-71). R.H. Owen. Wales M.A. 1923.

3685   The establishment of the Pelham régime. J.B. Owen. Oxford D.Phil. 1953.

3686   A biographical sketch of Sir George Savile, 1726-84, with an appendix of his letters. Teresa Lightbound. Liverpool M.A. 1916.

3687   The life and career of Henry Fiennes Pelham-Clinton, 1720-94, 9th earl of Lincoln (1730) and 2nd duke of Newcastle-under-Lyme (1768), based on MSS. and papers at present in the keeping of the University of Nottingham. C. Priestley. Nottingham M.A. 1958.

3688   Toryism from 1745 to 1761. T.E. Howard. Liverpool M.A. 1939.

3689   Government and the house of commons, 1747-54. Jean M. Spendlove. Oxford B.Litt. 1956.

3690   Politics in Norfolk, 1750-1832. B.D. Hayes. Cambridge Ph.D. 1958.

3691   The parliamentary history of the city of Bristol, 1750-90. P.T. Underdown. Bristol M.A. 1948.

3692   The parliamentary elections in York City, 1754-90. F.C. Price. Manchester M.A. 1958.

3693   The parliamentary representation of the boroughs of Chippenham, Cricklade, Downton, Hindon, Westbury and Wootton Bassett, in Wiltshire, from 1754 until 1790. J.A. Cannon. Bristol Ph.D. 1958.

3694   Cumberland and Westmorland elections, 1754-75. B. Bonsall. Manchester M.A. 1954.

3695   The parliamentary representation of the Sussex boroughs, Bramber, Midhurst, Lewes, Rye and Winchelsea, 1754-68. Margaret M. Cramp. Manchester M.A. 1953.

3696   The parliamentary representation of the boroughs of Pontefract, East Retford and Newark, 1754-68. C. Bradley. Manchester M.A. 1953.

3697   The Oxfordshire election of 1754. R.J. Robson. Oxford B.Litt. 1947.

3698   Under-secretaries of state, 1755-75. L. Scott. Manchester M.A. 1950.

3699   George III and the Whig opposition (1760-94): a study of the organisation, principles, policy and conduct of the Rockingham-Portland Whigs. D.J. Turner. Nottingham Ph.D. 1953.

The early history of Roman Catholic emancipation, 1760-93. Florence E. Round. Birmingham M.A. 1930. 3700

Public opinion in the west Midlands, 1760-93. J. Money. Cambridge Ph.D. 1967. 3701

Parliamentary elections in Essex (excluding Harwich), 1761-8. A. Pickersgill. Manchester M.A. 1953. 3702

The relations between the duke of Newcastle and the marquis of Rockingham and mercantile interests in London and the provinces, 1761-8. D.H. Watson. Sheffield Ph.D. 1968. 3703

The duke of Newcastle and his friends in opposition, 1762-5. A. Hardy. Manchester M.A. 1956. 3704

The administration of the system of transportation of British convicts, 1763-93. W. Oldham. London Ph.D. 1933. 3705

An appreciation of Walpole's <u>Memoirs of the reign of King George III</u>, with special reference to Walpole's political ideas. F. Spencer. Manchester M.A. 1946. 3706

Criticism of Horace Walpole's treatment of William Pitt (earl of Chatham), 1760-8. Gertrude M. Dalrymple. Liverpool M.A. 1909. 3707

Some political aspects of the career of Alexander Wedderburn, Lord Loughborough and earl of Rosslyn. Helen C. Sheridan. Liverpool M.A. 1919. 3708

The political papers of Charles Jenkinson, 1761-6. Ninetta Jucker. Manchester M.A. 1936. 3709

An edition of the selected papers of George Grenville, 1763-6. J.R.G. Tomlinson. Manchester M.A. 1956. 3710

The duke of Grafton. Gladys M. Imlach. Liverpool M.A. 1914. 3711

The political correspondence of Charles Lennox, 3rd duke of Richmond, from 1765 to 1784. Alison Gilbert. Oxford D.Phil. 1956. 3712

The relations of the Rockingham Whigs with William Pitt, earl of Chatham, 1765-78. R.B. Levick. Oxford B.Litt. 1961. 3713

The Rockingham Whigs, 1768-74. G. Sturgess. Manchester M.A. 1970. 3714

Charles Yorke, 1764-70: an analysis of his private and political correspondence as contained in the Hardwicke MSS. J.T. Park. Manchester M.A. 1949. 3715

A critical examination of the Chatham correspondence, 1765-8. N.G. Anderton. Manchester M.A. 1946. 3716

The political relations of the Chatham party. G.H. Grierson. Liverpool M.A. 1907. 3717

The political career of General Conway. Hilda I. Clark. Liverpool M.A. 1917. 3718

Constitutional aspects of the ministry of Lord North. A.B. Archer. Liverpool M.A. 1910. 3719

Lord North's relations with cabinet colleagues, 1767 to 1774. L.H. Brown. Oxford B.Litt. 1956. 3720

The unpublished letters of the Chatham correspondence, from the resignation of Chatham, October 1768, to the end of 1770. Violet Morewood. Manchester M.A. 1935. 3721

The debates of the house of commons, 1768-74. P.D.G. Thomas. London Ph.D. 1958. 3722

Edmund Burke as member of parliament for Bristol: a study of his relations both with his colleague Henry Cruger and with his constituents, and of the political situation in the city during the years 1774-80. P.T. Underdown. London Ph.D. (Ext.) 1955. 3723

The battle of the admirals, 1778-9. D. Williams. Wales M.A. 1969. 3724

Political opinion in the north of England, 1780-1837. F.B. Walker. Belfast M.A. 1913. 3725

The Bowood circle, 1780-93; its ideas and its influence. J.D. Jarrett. Oxford B.Litt. 1956. 3726

3727   Charles Jenkinson as secretary at war, with special
reference to the period from the general election of September
1780 to the fall of North's administration in March 1782.
Olive R. Gee. Oxford B.Litt. 1949.

3728   The Gordon Riots, 1780. Laura H. Thraves. Liverpool
M.A. 1910.

3729   The causes of anti-Romanist fanaticism in Great Britain
in the 18th century, with special reference to the Lord
George Gordon Riots. Katharine Morris. Wales M.A. 1926.

3730   George Tierney. H.K. Olphin. London M.A. 1933.

3731   The formation and character of the second Rockingham
administration. J.F. Brown. Manchester M.A. 1951.

3732   The second Rockingham ministry. D. Wall. Sheffield
M.A. 1956.

3733   The cabinet in the late 18th and early 19th centuries,
1782-1820. L.V. Sumner. Manchester M.A. 1931.

3734   Charles James Fox and the disintegration of the Whig
party, 1782-94. L.G. Mitchell. Oxford D.Phil. 1969.

3735   The evolution of the Tory party, 1783-1815. Margaret
M. Ashworth. Manchester M.A. 1925.

3736   The peerage under Pitt, 1784-1806. W.F. Quine. Liverpool M.A. 1931.

3737   The general election and members of the parliament of
1784-90. Evelyn J. Southall. Manchester M.A. 1952.

3738   The political ideas and activities of William Roscoe,
1787-1801. Mrs. Jenny E. Graham. Liverpool M.A. 1970.

3739   The Regency crisis of 1788, with particular reference
to its effects on the internal relations of the Whig party,
especially the relationship between Fox and Burke. J.W.
Derry. Cambridge Ph.D. 1961.

3740   The Irish influence on the liberal movement in England,
1789-1832, with special reference to the period 1815-32. R.
Cassirer. London Ph.D. 1940.

3741   Henry Addington, Speaker of the house of commons, 1789-
1801. D.A. Schofield. Southampton M.A. 1959.

3742   The life of Davies Gilbert (1767-1839): a study in
patronage and political responsibility. A.C. Todd. London
Ph.D. (Ext.) 1958.

3743   Richard Locke: a record of a strenuous life. F.M. Ward.
Bristol M.A. 1937.

3744   Charles Watkin Williams Wynn, 1775-1850. Gwyneth Evans.
Wales M.A. 1935.

3745   The Whig party, 1789-94. F. O'Gorman. Cambridge Ph.D.
1965.

3746   Parliamentary representation of South Wales, 1790-1830.
R.D. Rees. Reading Ph.D. 1962.

3747   Public order in England, 1790-1801. C. Emsley. Cambridge M.Litt. 1970.

3748   Defence and public order in Northumberland, 1793-1815.
J.A. Huitson. Newcastle M.Litt. 1967.

3748A   Lt. Gov. J.G. Simcoe and the Home Office, 1791-7. S.R.
Mealing. Oxford B.Litt. 1952.

3749   Church and state in English politics, 1800-33. G.F.A.
Best. Cambridge Ph.D. 1955.

3750   The political activities of the 'Saints' in parliament,
1800-24. F.U. Woods. Manchester M.A. 1924.

3751   Addington and the Addingtonian interest in parliament,
1801-12. J.G. Rogers. Oxford B.Litt. 1952.

3752   Sir Robert Peel the elder, and early factory legislation.
F.E. Manning. Bristol M.A. 1932.

3753   William Huskisson (1770-1830), imperial statesman and
economist. S.M. Hardy. London Ph.D. 1943.

3754   Lord Brougham and the Whig party up to 1834. A. Aspinall. Manchester Ph.D. 1924.

3755   The political career of Lord Brougham from 1805 to 1830.
Nellie Williams. Liverpool M.A. 1913.

The general elections of 1806 and 1807. M.G. Hinton. 3756
Reading Ph.D. 1959.

Spencer Perceval at the treasury, 1807-12. D.E. Gray. 3757
Manchester Ph.D. 1961.

The Whig party, 1807-12. M. Roberts. Oxford D.Phil. 3758
1935.

The movement for Catholic emancipation, 1807-29. Ana- 3759
stasia Quirk. Liverpool M.A. 1913.

Catholic emancipation as an issue in English politics, 3760
1820-30. G.I.T. Machin. Oxford D.Phil. 1961.

The political importance of the 'Westminster Committee' 3761
of the early 19th century, with special reference to the
years 1807-22. W.E. Saxton. Edinburgh Ph.D. 1957.

George Canning and the Tory schism, 1809-22. Janet 3762
Veitch. Liverpool Ph.D. 1932.

The domestic relations of George Canning. Janet 3763
Veitch. Liverpool M.A. 1927.

The conduct of public business in the house of commons, 3764
1812-27. P. Fraser. London Ph.D. 1957.

Lord Liverpool as prime minister (1812-27). Stella Y. 3765
Mathias. Liverpool M.A. 1913.

Lord Liverpool's administration, 1815-22. J.E. Cook- 3766
son. St. Andrews Ph.D. 1970.

Lord Liverpool and liberal toryism, 1820-7. W.R. 3767
Brock. Cambridge Ph.D. 1942.

The Whigs in opposition, 1815-30. A.V. Mitchell. Ox- 3768
ford D.Phil. 1964.

The general election of 1818. L.V. Sumner. Manchester 3769
Ph.D. 1969.

Sir R.J. Wilmot Horton, Bt., politician and pamphlet- 3770
eer. E.G. Johnes. Bristol M.A. 1936.

The work of Sir Robert Peel as secretary of state for 3771
the Home department, 1822-30. Elizabeth A.W. Kinsey. Manchester M.A. 1927.

Criminal law reform during Peel's tenure of office as 3772
Home Secretary, 1822-7. J.A. Gulland. London M.A. 1930.

John Wilson Croker's influence on Sir Robert Peel. 3773
C.N. Breiseth. Oxford B.Litt. 1962.

William Thompson, his life and writings. R.K.P. Pank- 3774
hurst. London Ph.D. 1952.

Glamorgan: a study of the concerns of the county and 3775
the work of its members in the house of commons from 1825 to
1835. Enid Ball. London Ph.D. (Ext.) 1965.

The political career of Michael Sadler. Dorothy Har- 3776
greaves. Manchester M.A. 1926.

The political and electioneering influence of the 4th 3777
duke of Newcastle. J.M. Golby. Nottingham M.A. 1961.

An edition of the correspondence of the 1st marquess of 3778
Anglesey relating to the general elections of 1830, 1831 and
1832 in Caernarvonshire and Anglesey. L. Jones. Liverpool
M.A. 1956.

Foreign and Colonial Relations

Colonial admiralty jurisdiction in the 17th century. 3779
Helen J. Crump. London Ph.D. 1930.

The Board of Trade in colonial administration, 1696- 3780
1720. I.K. Steele. London Ph.D. 1964.

The international legal relations between Great Britain 3781
and Hanover, 1714-1837. I.B. Campbell. Cambridge Ph.D.
1966.

Parliament and foreign policy, 1715-31. G.C. Gibbs. 3782
Liverpool M.A. 1953.

The problem of imperial communications during the 18th 3783
century, with special reference to the post office. J.T.
Dixon. Leeds M.A. 1964.

3784   The career of the earl of Shelburne, 1760-83. Evelyn M. Scrimiger. Liverpool M.A. 1909.

3785   Lord Shelburne and British imperialism, 1763-83. R.A. Humphreys. Cambridge Ph.D. 1932/3.

3786   The diplomatic correspondence of John, earl of Sandwich, 9 September 1763 - 10 July 1765. F. Spencer. Manchester Ph.D. 1953.

3787   Proceedings in parliament with regard to the Government of India, 1763-73. J.C. Airey. Liverpool M.A. 1911.

3788   Parliament and the affairs of the East India Company, 1765-84. Gwendoline F. Pecker. Liverpool M.A. 1910.

3789   Barlow Trecothick and other associates of Lord Rockingham during the Stamp Act crisis, 1765-6. D.H. Watson. Sheffield M.A. 1958.

3790   The Committee of the Whole House to consider the American Papers (January and February 1766). B.R. Smith. Sheffield M.A. 1956.

3791   The East India Company crisis, 1770-3. R. Beard. Birmingham M.A. 1928.

3792   The East India interest and the British government, 1784-1833. C.H. Philips. London Ph.D. 1938.

3793   The influence of the East India Company 'interest' on the English government, 1813-33. C.H. Philips. Liverpool M.A. 1937.

3794   Exploration and the economic development of the empire, 1782-98, with special reference to the activities of Sir Joseph Banks. D.L. Mackay. London Ph.D. 1970.

3795   British opinion and colonial policy, 1783-1839. A.J. Weir. Edinburgh Ph.D. 1924.

3796   The colonial policy of Charles Jenkinson, Baron Hawkesbury and 1st earl of Liverpool, as president of the Committee for Trade, 1784-1800. C.B. Fergusson. Oxford D.Phil. 1952.

3797   Impeachment of Warren Hastings. P.J. Marshall. Oxford D.Phil. 1962.

3798   The Colonial Office and the plantation colonies, 1801-34: a study of imperial government in evolution. D.J. Murray. Oxford D.Phil. 1963.

3799   The press and the colonies. H.F.G. Tucker. Bristol M.A. 1936.

3800   The foreign policy of Lord Minto, 1807-13. K.M. Sarkar. Cambridge M.Litt. 1937.

3801   The working of the British Colonial Office, 1812-30. D.McM. Young. London Ph.D. 1955.

3802   Castlereagh and the Holy Alliance. H.C. Hamilton. Birmingham M.A. 1926.

3803   Robert Wilmot Horton and colonial policy in the age of Tory reform. J.S. Sutton. Keele M.A. 1970.

3804   The governorships of Sir G. Lowry Cole in Mauritius (1823-8) and the Cape of Good Hope (1828-33): a study in colonial administration. K.S. Hunt. London Ph.D. 1970.

3805   The foreign policy of Wellington, 1828-30. A.C.F. Beales. London M.A. 1927.

Radicalism and Reform Movements

3806   Public order and popular disturbances in England, 1689-1714. M. Beloff. Oxford B.Litt. 1937.

3807   A study of popular disturbances in Britain, 1714-54. D.G.D. Isaac. Edinburgh Ph.D. 1953.

3808   The causes of the movement for radical parliamentary reform in England between 1763 and 1789, with special reference to the influence of the so-called Rational Protestants. Gwendolyn B.M. Whale. Oxford B.Litt. 1930.

3809   Major John Cartwright: his place in contemporary radical movements. A.A. Eaglestone. Oxford B.Litt. 1930.

3810   Thomas Spence and his connections. Olive D. Rudkin. London M.A. 1924.

The Yorkshire County Association and the reform move- 3811
ment, 1779-80. C.M. Wilcock. Manchester M.A. 1953.
Some aspects of Unitarianism and radicalism, 1760-1810. 3812
G.M. Ditchfield. Cambridge Ph.D. 1968.
Nottingham radicalism, 1785-1835. M.I. Thomis. 3813
Nottingham Ph.D. 1966.
The reform movement in England previous to the French 3814
Revolution. R.J. McAlpine. Liverpool M.A. 1907.
Reform movements in Derby and Derbyshire, 1790-1852. 3815
E. Fearn. Manchester M.A. 1964.
English democratic societies and popular radicalism, 3816
1791-1800. J. Walvin. York D.Phil. 1970.
British democratic societies in the period of the French 3817
Revolution. W.A.L. Seaman. London Ph.D. 1954.
The influence of the French Revolution on the political 3818
and social life of Wales. W.P. Williams. Wales M.A. 1925.
Popular disturbances in Wales, 1792-1832. D.J.V. 3819
Jones. Wales Ph.D. 1966.
Radicalism and political repression in the north of 3820
England, 1791-7. A.V. Mitchell. Manchester M.A. 1958.
Movements for political and social reform in Sheffield, 3821
1792-1832. H.N. Crawshaw. Sheffield M.A. 1954.
The Association of the Friends of the People, 1792-6. 3822
P.J. Brunsdon. Manchester M.A. 1961.
The north of England agitation for the abolition of the 3823
slave trade, 1780-1800. E.M. Hunt. Manchester M.A. 1959.
The campaign for the abolition of the British slave 3824
trade and its place in British politics, 1783-1807. A.M.
Rees. Oxford B.Litt. 1952.
Abolitionist societies, 1787-1838. E.C. Toye. London 3825
M.A. 1936.
William Smith, M.P., 1756-1835, and his importance in 3826
the movements for parliamentary reform, religious toleration,
and the abolition of the slave trade. B. Aspinwall. Man-
chester M.A. 1962.
William Smith and the politics of dissent, 1791-1828. 3827
R.W. Davis. Cambridge M.Litt. 1962.
The abolition and emancipation movements in England. 3828
Ida M. Garton. Leeds M.A. 1919.
The development of abolitionism, 1807-23. T.M. Birt- 3829
whistle. London M.A. 1948.
Great Britain and the abolition of the slave trade, 3830
1807-17. E. Smallpage. Liverpool M.A. 1922.
Great Britain and the abolition of the slave trade by 3831
the other Powers (1812-22) with special reference to the
efforts of Castlereagh. K. MacKenzie. Oxford B.Litt. 1953.
A critical edition of the correspondence of Sir Thomas 3832
Fowell Buxton, Bart., with an account of his career to 1823.
F.C. Stuart. London M.A. 1957.
Joseph Hume, M.P.: political activities, 1818-25. Con- 3833
stance G. Smith. Liverpool M.A. 1921.
The political influence of William Cobbett, 1794-1815. 3834
Eva Knox. Liverpool M.A. 1907.
The reform movement and county politics in Cornwall, 3835
1809-52. W.B. Elvins. Birmingham M.A. 1959.
The reform movement on Tyneside and Wearside, 1812-32. 3836
Mary B.G. Allan. Liverpool M.A. 1920.
The Tory attitude towards parliamentary reform, 1815- 3837
32. Elsie M. Atkins. London M.A. 1931.
Political movements in the West Riding, 1815-32. D.O. 3838
Parker. Manchester M.A. 1923.
Some aspects of Lancashire radicalism, 1816-21. W.W. 3839
Kinsey. Manchester M.A. 1927.
Peterloo: a study in Manchester political history. D. 3840
Read. Oxford B.Litt. 1955.
The movement for parliamentary reform in Manchester, 3841
1825-32. J.M. Main. Oxford B.Litt. 1951.

3842   Owenite socialism in the period 1817-40. Mrs. Florence
L.P. Knight. Manchester M.A. 1966.
3843   Organisations and ideas behind the efforts to achieve
a general union of the working classes in England in the
early eighteen-thirties. W.H. Oliver. Oxford D.Phil. 1954.

Political Thought

3844   The proper role of the state as seen by British economists in the period 1603-1834. D.E. Bland. Sheffield Ph.D.
1967.
3845   Machiavelli and secular political thought in England
during the 17th century. F. Raab. Oxford D.Phil. 1962.
3846   Some aspects of English Utopian thought in the 17th
century. J.C. Davis. Manchester M.A. 1963.
3847   The history of Utopianism in England in the 17th century. J.M. Patrick. Oxford D.Phil. 1952.
3848   Authority in church and state, with special reference
to the 17th century. P.S. Belasco. London Ph.D. 1928.
3849   The controversial writings of William Prynne. W.M.
Lamont. London Ph.D. 1960.
3850   The political writings of William Prynne. K.G.M. Ratcliffe. Durham M.A. 1961.
3851   Magna Carta: its influence on politics and political
thought since 1640. Anne Pallister. Nottingham Ph.D. 1966.
3852   Interests and the public interest in English political
and social thought, 1640-1700. J.A.W. Gunn. Oxford D.Phil.
1966.
3853   The political ideas of the English Radicals, particularly
in Nonconformist circles, from John Lilburne to John Wilkes.
Beryl H. Lewis. Wales M.A. 1925.
3854   The political ideas of the Quakers of the 17th century.
P.S. Belasco. London M.Sc. 1926.
3855   The origins of John Locke's theory of toleration.
E.I.R. de Marchi. Oxford B.Litt. 1961.
3856   A bibliography of John Locke. Mrs. Charlotte S. Johnston. Oxford D.Phil. 1956.
3857   John Locke as a conservative: an edition of Locke's
first writings on political obligation. P. Abrams. Cambridge Ph.D. 1962.
3858   The origins of the political opinions of John Locke.
A.H. Maclean. Cambridge Ph.D. 1947.
3859   The controversy over the origins of the Commons, 1675-
88: a chapter in the history of English historical and political thought. J.G.A. Pocock. Cambridge Ph.D. 1952.
3860   William Penn: a study in the Quaker doctrine of political
authority, as exemplified particularly in his colonial
experiment. R.J. Oman. Edinburgh Ph.D. 1958.
3861   The English Revolution and the doctrines of non-resistance and resistance: a study in sovereignty, 1688-1714. J.C.
Corson. Edinburgh Ph.D. 1934/5.
3862   Anthony Collins: the man and his works. J. O'Higgins.
Oxford D.Phil. 1966.
3863   The political ideas of Daniel Defoe. E. Illingworth.
Leeds M.A. 1961.
3864   The moral and political philosophy of Anthony Ashley
Cooper, 3rd earl of Shaftesbury (1671-1713). J.F. Harrison.
Durham Ph.D. 1970.
3865   A bibliography of Henry St. John, Viscount Bolingbroke.
G.G. Barber. Oxford B.Litt. 1963.
3866   The conception of political party in England in the
period 1740-83. D. Thomson. Cambridge Ph.D. 1938.
3867   The life and works of Josiah Tucker. H.G. Brown. Bristol M.A. 1925.
3868   The social and political thought of Joseph Priestley.
Margaret E. Leslie. Cambridge Ph.D. 1966.

The political thought of Edmund Burke. A.B.C. Cobban. 3869
Cambridge Ph.D. 1925/6.
The political thought of the English Romanticists. C. 3870
Brinton. Oxford D.Phil. 1923.
The aims and work of Richard Price, 1723-91. B. Jen- 3871
kins. Wales M.A. 1927.
The political importance of Dr. Price. Blodwen M. 3872
Parry. Liverpool M.A. 1934.
Society and social reform in English political thought, 3873
1789-97. W.E. Christian. London Ph.D. 1970.
The economic and political theory of William Godwin 3874
and his debt to French thinkers. H.K. Prescot. Oxford
D.Phil. 1930/1.
A life of William Godwin. F.K. Brown. Oxford D.Phil. 3875
1925.
Ideas of parliamentary representation in England, 3876
1815-32. J.F. Lively. Cambridge M.Litt. 1957.
The political economists and politicians from Waterloo 3877
to the Reform Bill. S.G. Checkland. Birmingham M.Com. 1947.
Political and social ideas in England, 1820-37. C.H. 3878
Driver. London M.A. 1926.

MILITARY AND NAVAL HISTORY

Ballistics in the 17th century. A.R. Hall. Cambridge 3879
Ph.D. 1950.
Plymouth Dock: a survey of the development of the royal 3880
dockyard in Hamoaze during the sailing ship era. A.E.
Stephens. London Ph.D. 1940.
The development of Portsmouth as a naval base as illus- 3881
trating the growth of British naval policy. H.J. Sparks.
London M.A. 1911.
Portsmouth and Gosport: a study in the historical geo- 3882
graphy of a naval port. F.N.G. Thomas. London M.Sc. 1961.
Administration of the navy under James II of England. 3883
E.C. Lowe. Liverpool M.A. 1934.
Parliament and the navy, 1688-1714. J.A. Johnston. 3884
Sheffield Ph.D. 1968.
The lords commissioners of the admiralty, 1689-1714. 3885
G.F. James. Birmingham M.A. 1937.
The English navy during the Revolution of 1688 and its 3886
condition at the commencement of the reign of William III.
E.B. Powley. Oxford B.Litt. 1924.
The naval side of 'King William's War' - opening phase 3887
16/26 November 1688 to 31 December 1689. E.B. Powley. Ox-
ford D.Phil. 1962.
Naval policy and public opinion in the War of the 3888
League of Augsburg, 1689-97. J.A. Lawson. Leeds M.A. 1952.
William III and the northern crowns during the Nine 3889
Years War, 1689-97. S.P. Oakley. London Ph.D. 1961.
English naval administration at the close of the 17th 3890
century. K.W. Wood. Leeds M.A. 1935.
The Commission for Victualling the Navy, the Commission 3891
for Sick and Wounded Seamen and Prisoners of War and the
Commission for Transport, 1702-14. Paula K. Watson. London
Ph.D. 1965.
The secretary at war and the administration of the army 3892
during the War of the Spanish Succession. I.F. Burton. Lon-
don Ph.D. 1960.
British military and naval operations: Catalonia and 3893
Valencia, 1705-11. H.T. Dickinson. Durham M.A. 1963.
The Malplaquet campaign and its aftermath: Flanders, 3894
1709-11. H.G. Bowen. Wales M.A. 1961.
The social and professional background of the officers 3895
of the British army, 1715-63. J.W. Hayes. London M.A. 1956.

3896   The British search by sea for the Northwest passage, 1719-94. G. Williams. London Ph.D. 1959.
3897   British naval administration in the war of 1739-48. D.A. Baugh. Cambridge Ph.D. 1961.
3898   Lord George Germain. Grace H. Gilcriest. Liverpool M.A. 1914.
3899   The administration of Newcastle and Pitt: the departments of state and the conduct of the war, 1754-60, with particular reference to the campaigns in North America. C.R. Middleton. Exeter Ph.D. 1969.
3900   British oceanic convoys in the Seven Years War, 1756-63. R.P. Crowhurst. London Ph.D. 1970.
3901   The naval administration of the 4th earl of Sandwich, 1771-82. M.J. Williams. Oxford D.Phil. 1962.
3902   Some letters of Sir James Murray between January 1773 and 16 April 1780. E. Robson. Manchester M.A. 1948.
3903   The Navy Board's administration of the maritime logistics of the British forces during the American War, 1775-83. D. Syrett. London Ph.D. 1966.
3904   The life and times of Admiral Rodney. H.C. Malkin. London M.A. (Ext.) 1957.
3905   An enquiry into faction among British naval officers during the War of the American Revolution. J.A. Davies. Liverpool M.A. 1964.
3906   The Royal Welch Fusiliers in the American War of Independence. G.O. Jones. Wales M.A. 1958.
3907   Charles Middleton, afterwards Lord Barham, and naval administration, 1778-1805. S. Riddick. Liverpool M.A. 1939.
3908   Admiralty administration, 1783-1806. Patricia K. Crimmin. London M.Phil. 1967.
3909   The early life and services of Sir John Jervis, Lord St. Vincent, and their influence on his later career and character. W.F. Scott. Oxford B.Litt. 1929.
3910   Life in the British army, 1793-1820, in relation to social conditions. T.H. McGuffie. London M.A. 1940.
3911   The recruitment of the land forces in Great Britain, 1793-9. J.R. Western. Edinburgh Ph.D. 1953.
3912   Schemes for the reform of naval recruitment, 1793-1815. C. Oprey. Liverpool M.A. 1961.
3913   French prisoners of war on parole in Britain, 1803-14. R. Bennett. London Ph.D. (Ext.) 1964.
3914   The career of Sir Robert Wilson (1777-1849), with special reference to his diplomatic and military activities during the years 1806-15. G.M.D.G. Costigan. Oxford B.Litt. 1930.
3915   The Copenhagen expedition, 1807. A.N. Ryan. Liverpool M.A. 1951.
3916   The Dardanelles expeditions of 1807. R.C. Gwilliam. Liverpool M.A. 1955.
3917   A geographical consideration of the Peninsular War. J.C. Hawtin. Wales M.A. 1967.
3918   Wellington's headquarters in the Peninsula, 1809-14: with especial reference to the quarter-master-general's department. S.G.P. Ward. Oxford B.Litt. 1955.
3919   The English navy and the Anglo-American War of 1812. K.S. Dent. Leeds M.A. 1949.
3919A   The Royal Navy in the War of 1812. F.C. Drake. Manchester M.A. 1961.

ECONOMIC AND SOCIAL HISTORY

    Finance

3920   A history of inheritance taxation in England. L. Dunn. London Ph.D. 1956.
3921   Commercial fluctuations and currency disturbances of the 17th century. W.J. Hinton. Wales M.A. 1915.

The English public revenue, 1660-88. C.D. Chandaman. 3922
London Ph.D. 1954.

The advancement of the king's credit, 1660-72. H.G. 3923
Roseveare. Cambridge Ph.D. 1962.

The last period of the great farm of the English 3924
customs, 1660-71. C.C. Crews. London M.A. 1935.

The genesis of English banking, with particular refer- 3925
ence to the private banking of the goldsmiths, the evolution
of English paper money and the early history of the Bank of
England. R.D. Richards. London Ph.D. 1928.

History of the land tax in England, 1692-1798. W.R. 3926
Ward. Oxford D.Phil. 1951.

The English national debt, 1693-1754. P.G.M. Dickson. 3927
Oxford D.Phil. 1958.

The operation of the English Navigation Acts during the 3928
18th century. E.H. Rideout. Liverpool M.A. 1931.

The economic policy of the Board of Trade, 1696-1714. 3929
R.G. Mathias. Oxford B.Litt. 1939.

The organisation of the English customs system, 1696- 3930
1786. Bessie E. Hoon. London Ph.D. 1934.

The great recoinage of 1696-9 (a particular study of 3931
the question of currency devaluation). Li Ming-hsun. London
Ph.D. 1940.

Godolphin and the organisation of public credit, 1702- 3932
10. J.G. Sperling. Cambridge Ph.D. 1955.

Aspects of capital and credit in Lancashire during the 3933
18th century. B.L. Anderson. Liverpool M.A. 1966.

The South Sea Company and the Assiento. Lilian E.M. 3934
Batcheler. London M.A. 1924.

The political aspect of the South Sea Bubble. E. Wag- 3935
staff. London M.A. 1934.

The public revenue and expenditure of Great Britain 3936
and its administration, 1774-92. J.E.D. Binney. Oxford
D.Phil. 1952.

The development of the London money market, 1780-1830. 3937
K.F. Dixon. London Ph.D. 1962.

A history of Boyd, Benfield & Co.: a study in merchant 3938
banking in the last decade of the 18th century. S.R. Cope.
London Ph.D. 1947.

The government and the wage-earner, 1789-1815. K. 3939
Hyman. London M.Sc. 1932.

Government revenue, 1793-1815: a study of fiscal and 3940
financial policy in the wars against France. P.K. O'Brien.
Oxford D.Phil. 1967.

Financial reconstruction in England, 1815-22. A.W. 3941
Acworth. Oxford B.Litt. 1925.

Foreign trade and economic growth: the balance of pay- 3942
ments as a factor limiting economic expansion in the British
economy during the years 1819-35. P.K. Chaudhuri. Cambridge
M.Sc. 1962/3.

The monetary reform of 1821. P.C. Kimball. Oxford 3943
B.Litt. 1930.

The crisis of 1825. E. Thomas. London M.Sc. 1938. 3944

Trade and Industry

English coasting trade and inland navigation from 1600 3945
to 1750. T.S. Willan. Oxford D.Phil. 1934.

The trade of Chester and the state of the Dee navig- 3946
ation, 1600-1800. C. Armour. London Ph.D. 1956.

The Welsh coal trade during the Stuart period, 1603- 3947
1709. B.M. Evans. Wales M.A. 1928.

The place of Whitehaven in the Irish coal trade, 1600- 3948
1750. W.H. Makey. London M.A. 1952.

A description of the trade and shipping of Hull during the 3948A
17th century, including a consideration of social and industrial
problems, together with a brief account of the trading organisations and kindred societies within the port. W.J. Davies.
Wales M.A. 1937.

3949   The direction and control of foreign trade by the state under the Stuarts, 1603-88. F. Adshead. London M.A. 1908.

3950   The English interest in the Eastland, 1620-80. R.W.K. Hinton. Cambridge Ph.D. 1950.

3951   The economic and commercial development of the city and port of Exeter, 1625-88. W.B. Stephens. London Ph.D. (Ext.) 1954.

3952   Geographical aspects of the maritime trade of Kent and Sussex, 1650-1750. J.H. Andrews. London Ph.D. 1954.

3953   The mercantile aspect of English foreign policy during the reign of Charles II. D.G.E. Hall. London M.A. 1917.

3954   The organisation and finance of the English shipping industry in the late 17th century. R. Davis. London Ph.D. 1955.

3955   English docks and harbours, 1660-1830. D. Swann. Leeds Ph.D. 1960.

3956   The marketing of food, fodder and livestock in the London area in the 17th century, with some reference to the sources of supply. P.V. McGrath. London M.A. 1947.

3957   The history of English agricultural imports and exports, 1660-1713. F.G. Carnell. Oxford B.Litt. 1945.

3958   The sugar trade of Bristol. I.V. Hall. Bristol M.A. 1925.

3959   The life and writings of John Cary. H.T. Lane. Bristol M.A. 1932.

3960   The history of the tobacco trade in England. A. Rive. Cambridge M.Litt. 1926/7.

3961   Leeds woollen merchants, 1700-1830. R.G. Wilson. Leeds Ph.D. 1964.

3962   Home demand as a factor in 18th-century English economic growth: the literary evidence. R.A. Kent. Cambridge M.Litt. 1969.

3963   The role of London in the Atlantic slave trade, 1680-1776. C.J. French. Exeter M.A. 1970.

3964   The role of Bristol in the Atlantic slave trade, 1710-69. D.G. Rees. Exeter M.A. 1970.

3965   The Bristol slave trade in the 18th century. P.D. Richardson. Manchester M.A. 1969.

3966   Liverpool's trade in the reign of Queen Anne. Brenda R. Poole. Liverpool M.A. 1961.

3967   Samuel Garbett, 1717-1803, a Birmingham pioneer. P.S. Bebbington. Birmingham M.Com. 1938.

3968   The development of the capitalist employer in industry during the Industrial Revolution. W. Bradburn. Manchester M.A. 1914.

3969   Wage-rates: 1750-1800. G.H.A. Stephens. Oxford B.Litt. 1931.

3970   The industrial development of Merioneth, 1750-1820: being an investigation into the economic organisation and history of certain distinctive industries in the county during this period. M.J. Jones. Wales M.A. 1937.

3971   The history of the Industrial Revolution in Monmouthshire. T.E. Jones. Wales M.A. 1929.

3972   The abolition of the slave trade and its effects on the commerce of Liverpool, 1770-1835. S.N. Syder. Liverpool M.A. 1954/5.

3973   The Liverpool slave trade from 1789 to 1791. J.E. Merritt. Nottingham M.A. 1959.

3974   Investment in Liverpool shipping, 1815 to 1835. F. Neal. Liverpool M.A. 1962.

3975   The history of an 18th-century combination in the copper-mining industry. G.C. Allen. Birmingham M.Com. 1922.

3976   The growth of free trade ideas, 1800-30. W.J. Rawle. Birmingham M.Com. 1939.

3977   The Luddite disturbances and the machinery of order. F.O. Darvall. London Ph.D. (Ext.) 1932.

3978   The Luddite disturbances throughout the cotton-manufacturing area, 1812. Dora Halstead. Liverpool M.A. 1917.

The British economy in the trade cycle, 1820-30. J.A. 3979
Cope. Oxford B.Litt. 1959.
    A north-east miners' union (Hepburn's Union) of 1831-2. 3980
W.H. Johnson. Durham M.A. 1959.

Specific Industries

    The history of English coal-mining in the 17th century. 3981
Asta W.R. Moller. Oxford B.Litt. 1923.
    The building trades in the Midlands in the 17th cent- 3982
ury. E.F.T. Richards. Birmingham M.A. 1939.
    Shipbuilding mainly for the Crown, in the Southampton 3983
area from 1650 to 1820. A.J. Holland. Southampton M.A.
1961.
    A history of shipbuilding in the north east of England. 3984
D.J. Dougan. Durham M.A. 1968.
    The pottery trade and north Staffordshire, 1660-1760. 3985
Lorna M. Weatherill. Keele M.Sc. 1969.
    The economic history of the Staffordshire pottery 3986
industry. E.S. Dane. Sheffield M.A. 1929.
    Geographical aspects of the development of transport 3987
and communications affecting the pottery industry of north
Staffordshire during the 18th century. Mrs. Annie L. Thomas.
Manchester M.A. 1933.
    Josiah Wedgwood, an 18th-century entrepreneur. B.E.S. 3988
Trueman. Nottingham M.A. 1960.
    Sixty years of coalmining enterprise on the north 3989
Warwickshire estate of the Newdigates of Arbury, 1680-1740.
A.W.A. White. Birmingham M.A. 1969.
    The charcoal iron trade in the Midlands, 1690-1720. 3990
B.L.C. Johnson. Birmingham M.A. 1950.
    Two partnerships of the Knights: a study of the mid- 3991
land iron industry in the 18th century. R.A. Lewis. Bir-
mingham M.A. 1949.
    John Wilkinson and the Bradley ironworks. W.A. Smith. 3992
London M.A. (Ext.) 1968.
    The London Lead Company in North Wales, 1693-1792. 3993
J.N. Rhodes. Leicester Ph.D. 1970.
    The lead-mining industry in Cardiganshire from 1700 to 3994
1830. O. Beynon. Wales M.A. 1938.
    An examination of Sir Humphrey Mackworth's industrial 3995
activities, with special reference to the governor and
Company of the Mine Adventurers of England. S. Evans. Wales
M.A. 1950.
    John Dunton (1659-1732) and the English book trade. 3996
S.R. Parks. Cambridge Ph.D. 1966.
    The decline of the common press. J.P.W. Gaskell. 3997
Cambridge Ph.D. 1956.
    Jacob Tonson: his life and work, and the enterprises 3998
of his publishing house from 1678 to his death in 1736 (and
a handlist of Jacob Tonson's publications). H.M. Geduld.
Sheffield M.A. 1954.
    The Cambridge University Press, 1696-1712: a biblio- 3999
graphical study. D.F. McKenzie. Cambridge Ph.D. 1960.
    The firm of Lintot. Marjorie W. Barnes. London M.A. 4000
1942.
    The ancestry, life and connections of William Caslon, 4001
the premier English type-founder. J. Ball. Sheffield M.A.
1968.
    The hand-made nail trade of Birmingham and district. 4002
E.I. Davies. Birmingham M.Com. 1933.
    The hand-made nail trade of Dudley and district. K. 4003
Henn. Birmingham M.Com. 1927.
    The silk industry in London, 1702-66. Natalie K.A. 4004
Rothstein. London M.A. 1961.
    The geographical basis of the natural silk industry of 4005
the west Pennines. C.L. Mellowes. London M.A. (Ext.) 1933.

4006   The silk industry in London, 1760-1830, with special reference to the condition of the wage-earners and the policy of the Spitalfields Acts. W.M. Jordan. London M.A. 1931.

4007   The rise and decline of the serge industry in the south-west of England, with special reference to the 18th century. W.G. Hoskins. London M.Sc. 1929.

4008   The growth of textile factories in Derbyshire during the 18th century. P.B. Sidey. Durham M.A. 1965.

4009   The Industrial Revolution in the textile industries of Wiltshire. H.R. Exelby. Bristol M.A. 1928.

4010   W.G. and J. Strutt, 1758-1830: a study in social and industrial organisation. R.S. Fitton. London Ph.D. (Ext.) 1953.

4011   The Midlands cotton and worsted spinning industry, 1769-1800. S.D. Chapman. London Ph.D. (Ext.) 1966.

4012   The early English cotton industry. G.W. Daniels. Manchester M.A. 1920.

4013   The development of the British cotton industry, 1780-1815. M.M. Edwards. London Ph.D. 1965.

4014   The concentration and localisation of the British cotton industry. A.J. Taylor. Manchester M.A. 1947.

4015   The handloom weavers in the English cotton industry during the Industrial Revolution. D. Bythell. Oxford D.Phil. 1968.

4016   Handloom weavers in the Stockport district, 1780-94. G. Taylor. Manchester M.A. 1922.

4017   Thomas Cheek Hewes (1768-1832) - millwright and machine maker of Manchester. S.B. Smith. Manchester M.Sc. 1969.

4018   The Darley Abbey cotton spinning and paper mills, 1783-1810: a study in industrial and social organisation. Jean Forrest. London M.Sc. (Ext.) 1957.

4019   The West Riding wool textile industry, 1780-1835: a study of fixed capital formation. D.T. Jenkins. York D.Phil. 1970.

4020   The development of the coal industry in south Yorkshire before 1830. R.M. Cox. Sheffield M.A. 1960.

4021   The history of coal during the Industrial Revolution. J.J. Jory. London Ph.D. (Ext.) 1931.

4022   The history of coalmining in Gower from 1770 to 1832. R.P. Roberts. Wales M.A. 1953.

4023   The papers of John Buddle, colliery viewer, in the Mining Institute, Newcastle-upon-Tyne: an annotated list and assessment of their value to the economic historian. F.S. Hewitt. Durham M.A. 1961.

4024   The financial history of Matthew Boulton, 1759-1800. J.E. Cule. Birmingham M.Com. 1935.

4025   Early industrial organisation: a history of the firm of Boulton and Watt. E. Roll. Birmingham Ph.D. 1930.

4026   The Albion Steam Flour Mill: a chapter in the Boulton and Watt Co-partnership. O.A. Westworth. Birmingham M.Com. 1930.

4027   Some aspects of the London furniture industry in the 18th century. E.T. Joy. London M.A. 1955.

Transport and Communications

4028   The evolution of the road-book and road-strip. E.J. Hopkins. Wales M.A. 1952.

4029   The Aire and Calder Navigation: a river navigation in 18th-century Yorkshire. W.N. Slatcher. Manchester M.Sc. 1967.

4030   The turnpike trusts of Islington and Marylebone from 1700 to 1825. C.A.A. Clarke. London M.A. 1955.

4031   The roads of Buckinghamshire, with special reference to turnpike roads. Joan Chibnall. London M.Sc. 1963.

4032   Turnpike trusts in Northumberland. W.G. Dodds. Durham M.A. 1965.

The turnpike trusts of Wales: a study in transport   4033
economics. E.W. Barton. Wales M.A. 1915.
The origin and planning of the military road from New-   4034
castle to Carlisle. W. Lawson. Durham M.A. 1966.
John Loudon McAdam - colossus of roads. R.H. Spiro.   4035
Edinburgh Ph.D. 1950.
Anthony Todd and the British post office, 1738-98.   4036
K.L. Ellis. Oxford D.Phil. 1954.
Investment in canals and house-building in England,   4037
1760-1815. J.R. Ward. Oxford D.Phil. 1970.
The impact of the construction of the Bridgewater Canal 4038
on land use in adjacent areas. A.J. Williams. Manchester
M.A. 1957.
The Birmingham canals, 1766-1800. S.R. Broadbridge.   4039
Manchester M.A. 1970.
Thames and Severn: birth and death of a canal. H.G.W.   4040
Household. Bristol M.A. 1958.

Agrarian History and Landownership

The development of leasehold tenure in south Lanca-   4041
shire, with particular reference to the 17th century. H.L.
Jones. Manchester M.A. 1924.
The historical geography of the Forest of Dean during   4042
the 17th century. J.C. Stuttard. Cambridge M.Sc. 1941.
The ownership and occupation of the land in Devonshire, 4043
1650-1800. W.G. Hoskins. London Ph.D. (Ext.) 1938.
The English yeomanry in the 17th century. I.D.A.   4044
Abbott. Oxford B.Litt. 1928.
Four Yorkshire landowning families, 1640-1760. P. Roe- 4045
buck. Hull Ph.D. 1969/70.
Two families and their estates: the Grimstons and the   4046
Cowpers from c.1650 to c.1815. C.G.A. Clay. Cambridge Ph.D.
1966.
The sale of delinquents' estates during the Interregnum 4047
and the land settlement at the Restoration - a study of land
sales in south-eastern England. I. Joan Thirsk. London
Ph.D. 1950.
Rural society in south-east Lindsey, 1660-1840. B.A.   4048
Holderness. Nottingham Ph.D. 1968.
The landed gentry in Merioneth, c.1660-1832, with   4049
special reference to the estates of Hengwrt, Nannau, Rug and
Ynysymaengwyn. P.R. Roberts. Wales M.A. 1963.
Agriculture and society in Glamorgan, 1660-1760. M.I.   4050
Williams. Leicester Ph.D. 1967.
A social and economic study of some west Cornwall   4051
landed families, 1690-1760. Mrs. Veronica M. Chesher. Ox-
ford B.Litt. 1956.
A great landed estate in the 18th century: aspects of   4052
management on the Leveson-Gower properties, 1691-1833. J.R.
Wordie. Reading Ph.D. 1967.
Demography and land use in the late 17th and 18th cent- 4053
uries in Middlesex. L. Martindale. London Ph.D. 1968.
Land use in Cornwall at the end of the 17th century.   4054
G.K. Whyatt. Wales M.A. 1959.
The agricultural landscape of the Hampshire chalklands, 4055
1700-1840. M.C. Naish. London M.A. 1961.
Influences of the improvements in agriculture during   4056
the reigns of George I and George II. M.J. Truscott. London
M.A. 1914.
Landownership and agrarian trends in the 18th century.   4057
G.E. Mingay. Nottingham Ph.D. 1958.
The landed gentry of Pembrokeshire in the 18th century. 4058
D.W. Howell. Wales M.A. 1965.
A history of the manors of Mapledurham Gurney and   4059
Mapledurham Chazey with special reference to the management
of the estate in the 18th century. Moira H. Long. Oxford
B.Litt. 1953.

4060   A study of some London estates in the 18th century.
Mrs. Brenda A.S. Swann. London Ph.D. 1964.
4061   East Sussex landownership: the structure of rural
society in an area of old enclosure, 1733-87. D.K. Worcester.
Cambridge Ph.D. 1950.
4062   English agriculture, 1760-1830. J. Cresswell. London
M.Sc. (Ext.) 1935.
4063   An agricultural geography of north-west Wiltshire, 1773-
1840. B.R. Dittmer. London M.A. 1963.
4064   The agricultural geography of the Welsh border in the
late 18th and early 19th centuries. D. Thomas. Wales M.A.
1957.
4065   The economic position of the tenantry in the north Cotswolds, 1775-1830. J.R. Stayt. Oxford B.Litt. 1955.
4066   A study of the small landowner and of the tenantry
during the years 1780-1832 on the basis of the land tax
assessments. E. Davies. Oxford D.Phil. 1926.
4067   Property in land in south Bedfordshire, with special
reference to the land tax assessments, 1750-1832. E.O.
Payne. London Ph.D. 1939.
4068   Arthur Young and the English landed interest, 1784-1813.
C. Veliz. London Ph.D. 1959.
4069   The landed society and the farming community of Essex in
the late 18th and early 19th centuries. C. Shrimpton. Cambridge Ph.D. 1965.
4070   The financial administration of the Bridgwater estates,
1780-1800. Edith Malley. Manchester M.A. 1929.
4071   The geography of the drainage areas of the Cynon and
Clydach rivers on the eve of the Industrial Revolution. D.S.
Prosser. Wales M.Sc. 1945.
4072   Agricultural change in east Cheshire, 1790-1820.
Clarice S. Davies. Manchester M.A. 1949.
4073   The Board of Agriculture, 1793-1822, with special reference to Sir John Sinclair. Winifred Harrison. London M.A.
1955.
4074   The work of women in agriculture in the late 18th and
early 19th centuries, and the influence of the agrarian
revolution thereon. Ivy Pinchbeck. London M.A. 1927.
4075   Oxfordshire about 1800 A.D.: a study in human geography.
Audrey M. Lambert. London Ph.D. 1953.
4076   Historical geography of Surrey about the year 1800.
Phyllis M. Wilkins. London M.Sc. 1943.
4077   The revolt of the Hampshire agricultural labourers and
its causes, 1812-31. Alice M. Colson. London M.A. 1937.
4078   The agricultural labourers' revolt of 1830 in Kent,
Surrey and Sussex. Monju Dutt. London Ph.D. 1967.
4079   The unrest in rural England in 1830, with special reference to Berkshire. N. Gash. Oxford B.Litt. 1934.

    Social History

4080   The social condition of England during the 17th century
as illustrated by the Southampton documents. F.W. Camfield.
London M.A. 1907.
4081   The regulation of marital and sexual relationships in
17th-century England, with special reference to the county
of Essex. A.D.J. Macfarlane. London M.Phil. 1968.
4082   The parish overseer in Essex, 1597-1834. E.G. Thomas.
London M.A. (Ext.) 1956.
4083   English travellers abroad, 1604-67, their influence on
English society and politics. J.W. Stoye. Oxford D.Phil.
1951.
4084   A history of the Waterhouse charity, Halifax. J. Clayton. Leeds M.A. 1943.
4085   The Gawdys of West Harling, Norfolk: a study of education
and social life in the 17th century. C.D. Price. Wales M.A.
1950.

Sir John Wynne's History of the Gwydir family as an   4086
historical document. Mrs. Gwladys Roberts. Liverpool M.A.
1912.

English personal letters and private diaries of 1640-   4087
80: a study of the general mental attitude of the period as
illustrated by individual types, together with a brief examination of the colloquial language of the time. Margaret T.
Williamson. London Ph.D. 1929.

The subscription books of the diocese of Worcester and   4088
class structure under the later Stuarts. P. Morgan. Birmingham M.A. 1952.

The Warwickshire gentry, 1660-1730. A.M. Mimardière.   4089
Birmingham M.A. 1963.

French refugees in England during the 17th century.   4090
A.W. Nicholls. Oxford B.Litt. 1923.

Five studies of the aristocracy, 1689-1714. H.D.   4091
Turner. Cambridge Ph.D. 1964.

The English poor laws and social conditions. Dorothy   4092
Marshall. Cambridge Ph.D. 1925/6.

Thomas Firmin, F.R.S. (1632-97). H.W. Stephenson.   4093
Oxford D.Phil. 1949.

Demographic change in Bedfordshire from 1670 to 1800.   4094
N. Tranter. Nottingham Ph.D. 1966.

Sunday in the 18th century (1677-1837). W.B. Whitaker. 4095
London Ph.D. 1937.

The foundation and early history of Aske's Hoxton   4096
Hospital, 1689-1755. J.R. Meredith. Birmingham M.A. 1964.

Bristol Corporation of the Poor, 1696-1834. Emily E.   4097
Butcher. Bristol M.A. 1930.

The development of medicine in the Sheffield region up   4098
to 1815. Monica C. Hamilton. Sheffield M.A. 1957.

A history of medicine in Wales in the 18th century.   4099
J.G.P. Jones. Liverpool M.A. 1956/7.

The role of smallpox inoculation in the growth of   4100
population in 18th-century Britain. P.E. Razzell. Oxford
D.Phil. 1969.

Some aspects of the rise of the medical profession in   4101
the 18th century as a factor in the growth of the professional
middle classes. Bernice M. Smith. London Ph.D. 1951.

Life and times of Thomas Dover, M.A., 1662-1742. K.E.   4102
Dewhurst. Oxford B.Litt. 1954.

Workhouses in the 18th century, with particular refer-   4103
ence to the industrial aspect. Elizabeth M.M. Zucker. Manchester M.A. 1925.

Poor law administration in Warwickshire - Butlers   4104
Marston, 1713-1822. Mrs. Joan Lane. Wales M.A. 1970.

A study of the methods of poor relief in the Winchester 4105
area, 1720-1845. L.F.C. Pack. Southampton M.A. 1967.

Some aspects of the history of the administration of   4106
the poor laws in Birmingham between 1730 and 1834. Mary
McNaulty. Birmingham M.A. 1942.

The old and the new poor law in east Yorkshire, c.1760- 4107
1850. N.D. Hopkin. Leeds M.Phil. 1968.

Phases of poor law policy and administration, 1760-   4108
1834. J.H. Howard. Liverpool M.A. 1921.

The administration of the poor laws in Dorset, 1760-   4109
1834, with special reference to agrarian distress. G.A. Body.
Southampton Ph.D. 1965.

Antiokh Kantemír: a study of his literary, political   4110
and social life in England, 1732-8. R.J.M. Evans. London
Ph.D. (Ext.) 1959.

Vincenzo Martinelli and his circle in London, 1748-74.   4111
Elizabeth H. Thorne. London Ph.D. 1946.

A study of the private and political life of General   4112
Paoli during his thirty years' exile in England. Mrs. D.W.
Frances St.C. Vivian. Cambridge M.Litt. 1948.

4113   Humanitarian and religious elements in early English prison reform, 1773-1835. R.S.E. Hinde. Oxford B.Litt. 1948.

4114   Ideas on social welfare, 1780-1834, with special reference to Friendly societies and allotment schemes. D.C. Barnett. Nottingham M.A. 1961.

4115   The bishops and the poor law, 1782-1832. W.A. Parker. Manchester M.A. 1939.

4116   Dr. Thomas Percival, a medical pioneer and social reformer, 1740-1804. R.B. Hope. Manchester M.A. 1947.

4117   The life of Samuel Roberts, a Sheffield philanthropist, 1763-1848. T. Clitheroe. Leeds M.A. 1940.

4118   The family economy of the working classes in the cotton districts, 1784-1833. Frances Collier. Manchester M.A. 1921.

4119   The effects of migration from the countryside to the towns on the social lives, conditions and habits of English workers during the Industrial Revolution, as revealed by specified autobiographical evidence. S.H. Kim. Manchester M.A. 1965.

4120   The development of the feminist idea in England, 1789-1833. Rub J.T. Saywell. London M.A. 1936.

4121   British women writers and the origin of the feminist movement in England in the latter part of the 18th century. A.F. Watson. Manchester M.A. 1963.

4122   The emigration policies and experiments of the British government after the Napoleonic Wars, 1815-30. H.J.M. Johnston. London Ph.D. 1970.

4123   French émigrés in England, 1789-1802: their reception and impact on English life. Ethel M. Wilkinson. Oxford B.Litt. 1953.

4124   French artists visiting England, 1815-30. Suzanne Lodge. London Ph.D. 1966.

4125   French travellers in England from 1820 to 1830. Ethel Jones. Wales M.A. 1925.

4126   Gabriele Rossetti in England. E.R.P. Vincent. Oxford D.Phil. 1932/3.

ECCLESIASTICAL HISTORY

General

4127   The Savoy Conference of 1661: its background, chronology, documents and results. J.E. Aydelotte. Cambridge M.Litt. 1968.

4128   A liturgical colloquy. An examination of the records of the Savoy Conference, 1661, with a judgement as to the abiding nature of the liturgical issues involved in the proceedings, proposals, disputations, declarations, and outcome of the conference. F.E. Ball. Oxford B.Litt. 1958.

4129   Persecution and toleration in the period 1660-90. Lucy M. Burtt. Birmingham M.A. 1922.

4130   The idea of toleration under the later Stuarts. G.S. Plant. London Ph.D. 1936.

4131   Religious toleration in England in the years immediately following the Restoration. E.L. Orme. Bristol M.A. 1918.

4132   Recusancy and Nonconformity in Devon and Somerset, 1660-1714. K.M. Beck. Bristol M.A. 1961.

4133   Growth of the idea of religious toleration in England, 1689-1727. A.B. Miller. Edinburgh Ph.D. 1938/9.

4134   The controversy concerning miracles in England during the 17th and 18th centuries, with special reference to the period 1700-50. E.K. Feaver. Edinburgh Ph.D. 1937.

4135   The history of the S.P.C.K. in Wales from its foundation to the early years of the Welsh Methodist movement and of the Welsh Circulating Charity Schools, 1699-1740. Correspondence and minutes of the S.P.C.K. relating to Wales, 1699-1740. Mary Clement. Wales Ph.D. 1952.

Hanes yr S.P.C.K. yn Sir Gaerfyrddin o 1700 hyd 1750,   4136
gyda chyfeiriad arbennig at John Vaughan, Cwrt Derllys, a'i
waith. (History of the S.P.C.K. in Carmarthenshire from 1700
to 1750, with special reference to John Vaughan, of Cwrt
Derllys, and his work.) Mary Clement. Wales M.A. 1940.

The work of Henry Newman, secretary of the Society for   4137
Promoting Christian Knowledge, 1708-43. L.W. Cowie. London
Ph.D. (Ext.) 1954.

Wesley and the Latitudinarians' controversy on grace.   4138
B.H. Smythe. Durham M.A. 1956.

The relation of Methodism and the Church of England   4139
between 1738 and 1830. W.R. Davies. Manchester M.A. 1959.

Methodism and the Church of England in Cornwall, 1738-   4140
1838: an historical survey of Cornish Methodism, its rise,
growth, and relation to the Church of England. H.M. Brown.
London Ph.D. (Ext.) 1947.

The humanitarian movement in England in the 18th cent-   4141
ury, with special reference to the relation between the
revival in religious life and industrial change: a study in
the sociology of religion. W.J. Warner. London Ph.D. 1929.

The Rev. William Grimshaw (1708-63) and the 18th-   4142
century revival of religion in England. F. Baker. Nottingham Ph.D. 1952.

The evangelical revival in 18th-century England as   4143
reflected in the life and work of William Romaine (1714-95).
D.G. Davis. Edinburgh Ph.D. 1949.

The evangelical revival as reflected in the life and   4144
works of John William de la Fléchère (1729-85). W.C. Lockhart. Edinburgh Ph.D. 1936.

John William Fletcher of Madeley as theologian. W.R.   4145
Davies. Manchester Ph.D. 1965.

The 18th-century Welsh awakening with its relationships 4146
to the contemporary English evangelical revival. R.W. Evans.
Edinburgh Ph.D. 1956.

John Berridge, an early Evangelical. D.V. Treanor.   4147
Durham M.A. 1959.

The life of the Rev. Rowland Hill (1744-1833) and his   4148
position in the evangelical revival. P.E. Sangster. Oxford
D.Phil. 1964.

The work of the Reverend Thomas Tregenna Biddulph, with 4149
special reference to his influence on the evangelical movement in the west of England. Leslie P. Fox. Cambridge Ph.D.
1954.

The attitude of Edmund Burke (1729-97) towards   4150
Christianity and the churches. J.E. McCabe. Edinburgh Ph.D.
1951.

Some aspects of the theory of religious toleration in   4151
England, 1787-1833. Ursula R.Q. Henriques. Manchester Ph.D.
1959.

Church and society in 18th-century Devon. A. Warne.   4152
Leeds Ph.D. 1964.

A survey of religious life in Birmingham, 1790 to 1830. 4153
C.F.B. Hubbard. Birmingham M.A. 1935.

Church of England

The rise and spread of Socinianism in England before   4154
1689. H.J. McLachlan. Oxford D.Phil. 1949.

The Laudian party, 1649-62, and its influence on the   4155
church settlement of the Restoration. R.S. Bosher. Cambridge Ph.D. 1949.

The revival of Anglicanism during the Restoration   4156
period, with special reference to the diocese of Durham.
C.H. Beaglehole. Durham M.Litt. 1947.

The treatment of social and economic questions by   4157
Anglican divines during the reign of Charles II. R.B.
Schlatter. Oxford B.Litt. 1935.

4158   The social and economic ideas in the writings of
religious leaders, 1660-88. R.B. Schlatter. Oxford D.Phil.
1938.

4159   Studies in the ecclesiastical court and archdeaconry of
Nottingham, 1660-89. W.A. Pemberton. Nottingham Ph.D. 1952.

4160   The events leading to Robert Sanderson's nomination to
the see of Lincoln and his administration of the diocese,
1660-3. C.E. Davies. Oxford B.Litt. 1969.

4161   The episcopate of Dr. Seth Ward, bishop of Exeter (1662-
7) and Salisbury (1667-1688/9) with special reference to the
ecclesiastical problems of his time. E. Anne O. Whiteman.
Oxford D.Phil. 1951.

4162   The Anglican 'Via media', with special reference to the
ecclesiastical conditions in Lancashire during the years
1662-89. F.F. Rigby. Manchester M.A. 1943.

4163   A study of the act books of the Court of Arches A6 and
A7, covering the period from Michaelmas term 1668 to Michaelmas term 1670, together with the relevant documents still
surviving. Mrs. Patricia M. Pugh. Oxford B.Litt. 1954.

4164   William Sancroft, as archbishop of Canterbury 1678-90.
R.A. Beddard. Oxford D.Phil. 1965.

4165   The life and times of Thomas Tenison, 1636-1715. E.F.
Carpenter. London Ph.D. 1943.

4166   A study of Francis Turner, bishop of Ely 1684-90, with
special reference to his political activity. C. Emmott.
Oxford B.Litt. 1930.

4167   The Huguenots and the Church of England. G.H. Sully.
Leeds M.A. 1954.

4168   The political faith of the English Nonjurors. Lucy M.
Hawkins. London Ph.D. 1927.

4169   The life and opinions of Henry Dodwell the elder, 1641-
1711. J.S. Hannon. Liverpool M.A. 1960.

4170   A history of the proprietary chapels of Bath. W.J.
Jenkins. Bristol M.A. 1947.

4171   The religious societies in the Church of England, 1678-
1743, and their influence on John Wesley and the Methodist
movement. D. Pike. Leeds M.A. 1960.

4172   The various societies in the Church of England in the
first half of the 18th century. G.V. Portus. Oxford B.Litt.
1911.

4173   Edmund Gibson, bishop of London, 1669-1748. N. Sykes.
Oxford D.Phil. 1923.

4174   Bishop Gibson and the Convocation controversy. N. Sykes.
Leeds M.A. 1921.

4175   The Anglican Church and political parties, 1701-37.
Sylvia L. Chandler. Birmingham M.A. 1930.

4176   Higher ecclesiastical administration in the diocese of
Carlisle, 1702-68. A. Armstrong. Birmingham M.A. 1951.

4177   The political and ecclesiastical activities of William
Nicolson, bishop of Carlisle, 1702-18. P.J. Dunn. London
M.A. 1931.

4178   The condition of the diocese of St. Davids during the
first half of the 18th century, including the study of the
relevant data in the 'Ottley Papers'. J.V. Davies. Wales
M.A. 1936.

4179   The foundation and early years of Queen Anne's Bounty.
A.W.J. Savidge. London M.A. 1953.

4180   The life and work of Bishop Zachary Pearce, 1690-1774.
W.S. Andrews. London Ph.D. 1953.

4181   White Kennett (1660-1728), bishop of Peterborough: a
study in the political and ecclesiastical history of the
early 18th century. G.V. Bennett. Cambridge Ph.D. 1954.

4182   Thomas Sherlock, bishop of Bangor, Salisbury and London:
his work for church and state. E.F. Carpenter. London M.A.
1934.

4183   Isaac Maddox and the dioceses of St. Asaph and Worcester,
1736-59. J.L. Salter. Birmingham M.A. 1962.

Religious and educational movements in the diocese of   4184
St. Asaph in the 18th century. J.A. Thomas. Liverpool M.A.
1951.

Anglican theological thought, 1750-1833, with special   4185
reference to the pre-Tractarians. J.K. Boulton-Jones. Leeds
Ph.D. 1968.

The Church of England in the county of Derbyshire,   4186
1772-1832. M.R. Austin. London Ph.D. (Ext.) 1969.

The life and interests of the Rev. Sir Richard Kaye,   4187
an 18th-century pluralist. J.T. Drinkall. Leicester Ph.D.
1965.

The life and thought of Alexander Knox, 1757-1831.   4188
J.T.A. Gunstone. Durham M.A. 1955.

The life and work of Alexander Knox, 1757-1831. G.W.   4189
Hughes. Edinburgh Ph.D. 1936/7.

The public work and influence of Shute Barrington,   4190
bishop of Durham, 1791-1826. G.G. Armstrong. Durham M.Litt.
1937.

The Clapham sect. E.M.F. Howse. Edinburgh Ph.D.   4191
1934/5.

The Clapham sect: its history and influence. M.G.   4192
James. Oxford D.Phil. 1950.

Bishop Reginald Heber (1783-1826), poet, preacher,   4193
churchman. R.E. Makepeace. Edinburgh Ph.D. 1951.

William Van Mildert, bishop. R.A. Cochrane. Durham   4194
M.Litt. 1950.

Protestant Nonconformity

The origins of the English Independents, with some   4195
consideration of their spiritual relations with the Anabaptists. D.H. Jones. Birmingham M.A. 1929.

The origins and early history of Independency in Suf-   4196
folk to 1688. H.D. Greenwood. Oxford B.Litt. 1949.

Presbyterians and Independents, 1603-85: their relation 4197
to the government, and its reactions on their relations with
one another. E. Ingham. Manchester M.A. 1935.

The development of Independency in Derbyshire from the   4198
Restoration to the Methodist revival. R. Mansfield. Manchester M.A. 1951.

Some contributions to the early history of Nonconform-   4199
ity in Rossendale. Kathleen Gray. Wales M.A. 1942.

Early Nonconformity, with local illustrations. C.E.   4200
Wright. Leeds M.A. 1916.

Early Nonconformity in Lincolnshire. Jessie Plumb.   4201
Sheffield M.A. 1940.

Protestant Nonconformity and some social and economic   4202
questions, 1660-1800. E.D. Bebb. Sheffield Ph.D. 1934.

English Presbyterian thought from 1662 to the found-   4203
ation of the Unitarian movement. Olive M. Griffiths.
Bristol Ph.D. 1933.

Thomas Hall, 1610-65. A. Grime. Manchester M.A. 1925. 4204
John Corbet, 1620-80. A. Grime. Edinburgh Ph.D.   4205
1932/3.

John Flavel of Dartmouth, 1630-91. K.S. Chang. Edin-   4206
burgh Ph.D. 1951/2.

Richard Baxter - Puritan and mystic. A.R. Ladell.   4207
Leeds M.A. 1922.

Richard Baxter's influence on English Nonconformity in   4208
the 17th and 18th centuries in organisation and theology.
J.E. Roberts. Leeds Ph.D. 1950.

The Rev. Richard Baxter and Margaret Charlton: being   4209
an examination of 'The breviate of a life of Margaret Charlton' by Richard Baxter (1681) together with kindred material.
J.T. Wilkinson. Birmingham M.A. 1930.

4210   The Baptist movement in England in the late 17th century
as reflected in the work and thought of Benjamin Keach, 1640-
1704. W.E. Spears. Edinburgh Ph.D. 1953.

4211   The 'discipline' of the Society of Friends as a regular
national body, with particular reference to church government,
based on a study of the epistles of the yearly meetings,
1669-1738. W.A. Lloyd. Cambridge Ph.D. 1947.

4212   The political importance of English protestant Nonconformity, 1673-88. R.R. Osborn. Oxford B.Litt. 1937.

4213   The Toleration Act of 1689 and freedom for protestant
Nonconformists, 1660-1830. A.G. Cumberland. London Ph.D.
(Ext.) 1957.

4214   The influence of Jonathan Edwards on the religious life
of Britain in the 18th century and the first half of the 19th
century. D.E. Edwards. Oxford B.Litt. 1954.

4215   The life and work of Philip Doddridge, as illustrating
the internal and external relationships of the English
Independent churches during the first half of the 18th century. F.W. Harris. Oxford B.Litt. 1951.

4216   The aims and practices of the English Dissenters from
the close of Anne's reign to the rise of the Wesleyan movement. D. Coomer. Liverpool M.A. 1944.

4217   The Quaker understanding of the ministerial vocation,
with special reference to the 18th century. Mrs. Lucia K.
Beamish. Oxford B.Litt. 1965.

4218   John Kelsall, a study in religious and economic history.
H.G. Jones. Wales M.A. 1938.

4219   The roots and development of John Wesley's organisation.
J.C.MacB. Miller. Edinburgh Ph.D. 1951.

4220   The relation of William Law to John Wesley and the
beginnings of Methodism. E.W. Baker. Edinburgh Ph.D. 1940/1.

4221   John Wesley's conflict with Antinomianism in relation
to the Moravians and Calvinists. E.P. Crow. Manchester Ph.D.
1964.

4222   An examination of the views of John Wesley in relation
to the protestant Reformation. R.G. Ashman. Wales Ph.D.
1949.

4223   The history of Methodism in Cornwall in the 18th century.
R.A.F. Mears. Oxford B.Litt. 1925.

4224   The contribution of John Wesley to the social and educational life of Bristol and neighbourhood. G.T. Brigg.
Bristol M.A. 1959.

4225   Early Methodism in Bristol, with special reference to
John Wesley's visits to the city, 1739-90, and their impres-
sion on the people. W.A. Goss. Bristol M.A. 1932.

4226   The origins and influence of Methodism in the north
Staffordshire potteries before 1820. R. Moss. London M.A.
1949.

4227   The influence of the Methodist movement on social life
in Wales. E.C. Lloyd. Oxford B.Litt. 1921.

4228   The development and organisation of the Methodist Society
in Wales, 1735-50. W.G. Hughes-Edwards. Wales M.A. 1966.

4229   Early Methodist associations and societies in Wales.
M. Gelly. Wales M.A. 1919.

4230   The origin and growth of the Methodist movement in Wales
in the 18th century, in the light of the unpublished MS.
correspondence of Howell Harris at Trevecka. M.H. Jones.
Wales Ph.D. 1929.

4231   A study of Howell Harris and the Trevecka 'family' (1752-
60). A.W. Owen. Wales M.A. 1957.

4232   An analysis of the spread of Methodism in Yorkshire
during the 18th and early 19th centuries (1740-1831), with
special reference to the environment of this movement. B.
Greaves. Leeds M.A. 1961.

4233   Aspects in the rise of the Methodist movement in the
industrial area of west Yorkshire, 1740-1830. J.F. Wilkinson. Birmingham M.A. 1964.

The Moravian Church in the north of England. G.C. 4234
Birch. Durham M.A. 1966.

Moravian and Methodist: relationships and influences in 4235
the 18th century. C.W. Towlson. London Ph.D. (Ext.) 1955.

The Yorkshire Evangelicals in the 18th century, with 4236
special reference to Methodism. J.D. Walsh. Cambridge Ph.D.
1956.

The evangelical work of the Baptists in Leicester- 4237
shire, 1740-1820. G. Jackson. London M.A. (Ext.) 1955.

Baptist laymen of the 18th century. T.R. Jones. Leeds 4238
M.A. 1938.

John Gill, Baptist theologian, 1697-1771. R.E. Sey- 4239
mour. Edinburgh Ph.D. 1954.

The Particular Baptists in England, 1760-1820. O.C. 4240
Robison. Oxford D.Phil. 1963.

Methodism and the working class, 1760-1821. E.P. 4241
Stigant. Keele M.A. 1968.

Abraham Booth, 1734-1806: a study of his thought and 4242
work. R.A. Coppenger. Edinburgh Ph.D. 1953/4.

The contribution of certain Methodists from the area 4243
of Llynan and Eifion (Caerns.) to religious education and
literature, with special reference to the work of Sion Lleyn
(John Roberts 1749-1817). R.L. Griffiths. Liverpool M.A.
1965/6.

The controversy between John Wesley and the countess 4244
of Huntingdon: its origin, development and consequences.
J.E. Hull. Edinburgh Ph.D. 1959.

Selina, countess of Huntingdon. M. Francis. Oxford 4245
B.Litt. 1958.

The life and work of Thomas Haweis (1734-1820). A.S. 4246
Wood. Edinburgh Ph.D. 1950/1.

The life of the Rev. Robert Dall, 1745 to 1828. P. 4247
Smallpage. Liverpool M.A. 1929.

David Bogue, D.D., 1750-1825, pioneer and missionary 4248
educator. C. Terpstra. Edinburgh Ph.D. 1958/9.

The life and thought of Dr. Edward Williams, with 4249
special reference to his influence on Welsh and English Nonconformity. W.T. Owen. London Ph.D. 1960.

Adam Clarke, LL.D. (1760?-1832) as church leader in 4250
early Methodism. R.J. Wells. Edinburgh Ph.D. 1957.

The Bristol dispute of 1794/5, a crucial period in 4251
English Methodism, with a clarification and an assessment of
the role of Joseph Benson. H.J. Downey. Edinburgh Ph.D.
1957.

The social and political influence of Methodism in the 4252
Napoleonic period, 1789-1815. M.L. Edwards. London Ph.D.
1934.

Rev. Richard Watson, 1781-1833, his work and religious 4253
thought. W.H. Littleton. Edinburgh Ph.D. 1955/6.

John Rippon, D.D. (1751-1836) and the Particular Bapt- 4254
ists. K.R. Manley. Oxford D.Phil. 1967.

The life and teaching of Robert Hall, 1764-1831. M.H. 4255
MacLeod. Durham M.Litt. 1957.

Robert Hall (1764-1831): a study of his thought and 4256
work. G.J. Griffin. Edinburgh Ph.D. 1948.

William Roby (1766-1830) and the revival of Independ- 4257
ency in Lancashire and the North. W.G. Robinson. Manchester
Ph.D. 1951.

The revival of Dissent, 1800-35. M.B. Whittaker. Cam- 4258
bridge M.Litt. 1959.

Roman Catholicism

Catholic recusancy in Wiltshire, 1661-1791. J.A. 4259
Williams. Bristol M.A. 1961.

The position of Roman Catholics in England from 1685 to 4260
1688. Louise S. Moore. Cambridge M.Litt. 1955.

4261   The toleration of the Roman Catholics in England under William III and Anne. C. Robinson. Leeds M.A. 1933.

4262   Catholics in Staffordshire from the Revolution to the Relief Acts, 1688-1791. Marie B. Rowlands. Birmingham M.A. 1965.

4263   The Catholic body in England from 1715 to 1829, with special reference to the Catholic laity. C.P. Purcell. Oxford B.Litt. 1927.

4264   The revival of Roman Catholicism in South Wales in the late 18th and early 19th centuries. G.J.J. Lynch. Wales M.A. 1941.

CULTURAL HISTORY

General

4265   The education of girls in England, 1600-1800. Elizabeth M.D. Morris. London M.A. 1926.

4266   The education of women in England, 1603-1715. Elizabeth S. Bier. Oxford B.Litt. 1928.

4267   The education of Englishwomen in the 17th century. Phyllis Woodham Smith. London M.A. 1921.

4268   The ideas and achievements of benefactors to English education in the 17th century, with particular reference to schools. Myrtle E.A. Boultwood. London M.A. 1952.

4269   Arabic studies in 17th-century England, with special reference to the life and work of Edward Pococke (1604-91). P.M. Holt. Oxford B.Litt. 1952.

4270   Hebraic studies in 17th-century England. A.D. Hallam. Leeds M.A. 1949.

4271   Conservative opinion and the New Science, 1630-80, with special reference to the life and work of Meric Casaubon. M.R.G. Spiller. Oxford B.Litt. 1968.

4272   The puritan contribution to scientific education in 17th-century England. C.E.A. Turner. London Ph.D. 1952.

4273   Early Quaker education. Dorothy G.B. Hubbard. London M.A. 1939.

4274   The history of Old English and Old Norse studies in England from the time of Francis Junius till the end of the 18th century. J.A.W. Bennett. Oxford D.Phil. 1938.

4275   Sprat's History of the Royal Society, edited from the original copies and MSS., together with the comments of Henry Stubbe and others, remarks on the life of the author, a list of his works, notes, appendices and bibliography. H.W. Jones. Leeds Ph.D. 1948.

4276   A consideration of problems concerning the origin and background of the Royal Society. Margery I.N. Purver. Oxford D.Phil. 1959.

4277   Joseph Glanvill and the 17th-century reaction against enthusiasm. Mrs. Marion J. Waller, née Swift. St. Andrews Ph.D. 1968.

4278   Education in Glamorgan, 1650-1800. U. Wiliam. Wales M.A. 1956.

4279   The conflict of social, political and religious ideals in English education, 1660-1714. L.W. Cowie. London M.A. 1947.

4280   French influence on English higher education, 1660-1730. J.W.A. Smith. Leeds Ph.D. 1956.

4281   The grammar schools in England and Wales, 1660-1714. W.A.L. Vincent. Oxford D.Phil. 1967.

4282   English grammar schools, 1660-1714. A.M.d'I. Oakeshott. London Ph.D. 1969.

4283   The English mathematical schools, 1670-1720. J.B.L. Allen. Reading Ph.D. 1970. -

4284   Patterns of mathematical thought in the later 17th century, with particular reference to developments in England. D.T. Whiteside. Cambridge Ph.D. 1960.

A study of the educational aspects of the Huguenot   4285
settlements in England. P.J.F. Luget. London M.A. 1952.
The educational writings of John Locke: a critical   4286
edition. J.L. Axtell. Cambridge Ph.D. 1966.
The antiquarian collections of Nathaniel Johnston   4287
(1627-1705). Mrs. Janet D. Martin. Oxford B.Litt. 1956.
Ralph Thoresby and his circle: with special reference   4288
to the state of historical scholarship in his time. J.J.
Saunders. London M.A. (Ext.) 1936.
The correspondence of Arthur Charlett (Master of Uni-   4289
versity College, 1692-1722) in its antiquarian and historical
aspects. S.G. Gillam. Oxford B.Litt. 1948.
The correspondence of Anthony Wood. With an edition of   4290
the Anthony Wood-Ralph Sheldon correspondence. E.G. McGehee.
London M.A. 1954.
Richard Rawlinson, collector, antiquary, and topo-   4291
grapher. B.J. Enright. Oxford D.Phil. 1957.
The historical and antiquarian interests of Thomas   4292
Tanner (1674-1735), bishop of St. Asaph. M.J. Sommerlad.
Oxford D.Phil. 1962.
The life and work of Dr. William Stukeley (1687-1765).   4293
S. Piggott. Oxford B.Litt. 1946.
Attacks on scholars and scholarship in the late 17th   4294
and early 18th century. D.K.C. Todd. London Ph.D. 1963.
The life and work of Griffith Jones, Llanddowron, 1683-   4295
1761. J.G.T. Thomas. Leeds M.A. 1940.
Nonconformist academies in Wales in the 18th century.   4296
W.P. Thomas. Wales M.A. 1928.
The curricula of dissenting academies in the reign of   4297
George III. H.J. McLachlan. Manchester M.A. 1930.
The circulating libraries of the 18th century. Hilda   4298
M. Hamlyn. London M.A. 1948.
Abraham Tucker of Merton College, 1705-74. A.W. Hook.   4299
Edinburgh Ph.D. 1960/1.
Simon Ockley: his contribution to Arabic studies and   4300
influence on western thought. Azza M.A.H. Kararah. Cam-
bridge Ph.D. 1955/6.
Dr. Isaac Watts - his pedagogic writings and their   4301
place in 18th-century education, together with introductory
biographical material. J.H.K. Rose. London M.A. (Ext.)
1965.
The Society for the Encouragement of Learning, and its   4302
place in the history of publishing. C.H. Atto. London Ph.D.
1938.
The development of the provincial newspaper, 1700-60.   4303
G.A. Cranfield. Cambridge Ph.D. 1952.
Paper wars in the reign of Anne: a study of political   4304
journalism. Mrs. Lee S. Horsley. Birmingham Ph.D. 1970.
The life and works of George, Lord Lyttelton, 1709-73.   4305
A.V. Rao. London Ph.D. 1929.
A study of the literary and philosophical societies of   4306
the latter half of the 18th century in England. E.W. Jones.
Wales M.A. 1956/7.
Thomas Tyrwhitt (1730-86) and his contribution to   4307
English scholarship. T.J.A. Monaghan. Oxford D.Phil. 1947.
The evangelical revival and the religious education of   4308
children, 1738-1800. P.E. Sangster. Oxford B.Litt. 1961.
Women writers on education, 1750-1800. N.M. Fletcher.   4309
London M.A. 1952.
St. John Baptist de la Salle: the work of the Brothers   4310
of the Christian Schools, and its significance in the history
of English education. W.J. Battersby. London Ph.D. 1947.
Brasenose College in the time of Principal Ralph Caw-   4311
ley (1770-7). W.T. Coxhill. Oxford B.Litt. 1946.
The growth and importance of the newspaper press in   4312
Manchester, Liverpool, Sheffield and Leeds between 1780 and
1800. D. Clare. Manchester M.A. 1960.

4313   The life, works, and letters of Hannah More, with
special reference to her influence in the social and educational movements of the 18th and early 19th centuries.
Winifred J.E. Moul. London M.A. 1933.

4314   The origins of elementary education in Somerset with
particular reference to the work of Hannah More in the Men-
dips. P. Belham. Bristol M.A. 1953.

4315   Elementary schools and school books in England at the
close of the 18th and beginning of the 19th centuries. P.H.
Sandall. London M.A. 1929.

4316   The guiding ideas in British 18th-century natural
history. P.C. Ritterbush. Oxford D.Phil. 1961.

4317   The life and work of Smithson Tennant, M.D., F.R.S.,
1761-1815, with an account of some aspects of 18th- and
early 19th-century science. A.E. Wales. Leeds M.Sc. 1940.

4318   William Hyde Wollaston and his influence on early 19th-
century science. D.C. Goodman. Oxford D.Phil. 1965.

4319   English political satire, 1800-30. J.E. Oxley. London
Ph.D. 1941.

4320   The contribution of Francis Place and the Radicals to
the growth of popular education, 1800-40. J.L. Dobson.
Durham Ph.D. 1959.

4321   The educational history of the National Society, 1811-
33. H.J. Burgess. London M.A. 1949.

4322   The works schools of the Industrial Revolution in Wales.
L.W. Evans. Wales Ph.D. 1953.

4323   The early development of industrial education in Manchester. Patricia A. Stern. Manchester M.Sc. 1966.

4324   The struggle for the freedom of the press, 1819-32.
W.H. Wickwar. London M.A. 1926.

4325   The London Magazine, 1820-9. T.R. Hughes. Oxford B.Litt.
1931.

Art and Architecture

4326   Documentary sources on the history of artists' colours
in England, c.1600-1835. Rosamund D. Harley. London Ph.D.
1967.

4327   The Smithson family, their work and drawings. M.
Girouard. London Ph.D. 1957.

4328   Craftsmen and their work in England, 1660-1720. G.W.
Beard. Leeds M.A. 1969.

4329   Sir Godfrey Kneller and the evolution of the English
baroque portrait. J.D. Stewart. London Ph.D. 1968.

4330   Sir Thomas Parkyns and his buildings. B.L. Twelvetrees.
Nottingham M.Phil. 1970.

4331   Joseph Smith, patron and collector. Mrs. Frances St.C.
Vivian. London Ph.D. 1966.

4332   Charles Bridgeman: royal gardener. P. Willis. Cambridge Ph.D. 1961/2.

4333   The building and furnishing of Harewood House, 1755-
1855. Anthea R. Mullins. Leeds M.A. 1967.

4334   The restoration of Audley End, 1762-97. J.D. Williams.
Wales M.A. 1964.

4335   James Wyatt, architect, 1746-1813. A. Dale. Oxford
B.Litt. 1935.

4336   English country houses, 1780-1815. Sandra Blutman.
London M.Phil. 1968.

4337   William Wilkins, R.A. G. Walkley. Cambridge M.Litt.
1939/40.

4338   Sir Jeffry Wyatville - architect to the king. D. Lin-
strum. Leeds Ph.D. 1970.

4339   The Italianate fashion in early 19th-century England.
C.P. Brand. Cambridge Ph.D. 1951/2.

A survey of the manor in 17th-century Gower. G.H.   4340
Eaton. Wales M.A. 1936.

The parish in the 17th century in the North Riding.   4341
Eleanor Trotter. London M.A. 1913.

Watercourses in the parish of St. Margaret's, West-   4342
minster, in the 17th century; a problem of local administration. A.C. Wood. Oxford B.Litt. 1938.

Transcript and translation, with introduction and notes, 4343
of a 17th-century cartulary relating to Middlewich. Joan
Varley. Liverpool M.A. 1938.

The corporation of the borough and foreign of Walsall. 4344
E.J. Homeshaw. Birmingham M.A. 1958.

The social and economic development of Wednesbury,   4345
1650-1750. A.J. Bartley. London M.A. (Ext.) 1967.

The economic and social history of Leicester, 1660-   4346
1835. W.A. Jenkins. London M.A. (Ext.) 1952.

A survey of the economic and administrative life of   4347
Kingston-upon-Thames, 1660-1720. J. Whitter. London M.Sc.
1933.

The causes and progress of the financial decline of   4348
the corporation of London, 1660-94. J.R. Kellett. London
Ph.D. 1952.

The rulers of London; the composition of the courts of 4349
aldermen and common council of the City of London, 1660 to
1689. J.R. Woodhead. London M.A. 1961.

The economic history of Cornwall in the 17th century. 4350
J.C.A. Whetter. London Ph.D. 1965.

The economy of Kent under the later Stuarts. D.C.   4351
Coleman. London Ph.D. 1951.

The economic development of Essex in the later 17th   4352
and early 18th centuries. K.H. Burley. London Ph.D. 1957.

The economic administration of Middlesex from the   4353
accession of Charles II to the death of George II, studied in
the records of quarter sessions. E.G. Dowdell. Oxford
D.Phil. 1928/9.

Minutes of proceedings in quarter sessions held for the 4354
parts of Kesteven in the county of Lincoln, 1674-95. S.A.
Peyton. Reading Ph.D. 1931/2.

Politics and government in St. Albans, 1685-1835.   4355
H.C.F. Lansberry. London Ph.D. 1964.

Local government in St. Marylebone, 1688-1835: a study 4356
of the vestry and the turnpike trust. F.H.W. Sheppard. London Ph.D. 1953.

The activities of the corporation of the borough of   4357
Leicester from 1688 to 1835. R.W. Greaves. Oxford D.Phil.
1936.

A survey of local government in Hertfordshire, 1700-   4358
1832. H. Adams. London Ph.D. (Ext.) 1931.

The provision and administration of bridges over the   4359
lower Thames, 1701-1801, with special reference to Westminster and Blackfriars. Patricia M. Carson. London M.A.
1954.

Nottinghamshire in the 18th century: a study of the   4360
movements leading to the industrial revolutions of the 19th
century. J.D. Chambers. London Ph.D. 1927.

The economic and social condition of England on the eve 4361
of the Industrial Revolution, with special reference to
Lancashire. L.W. Moffit. Edinburgh Ph.D. 1921.

The practice and functions of local government as   4362
illustrated in Lancashire towns in the century before the
Municipal Corporations Act (1835), with a consideration of
the more immediate effects of the reform. W. Scrivens.
Liverpool M.A. 1934.

The work of the North Riding quarter sessions in the   4363
early 18th century. J.S. Cockburn. Leeds LL.M. 1961.

4364   A calendar of the Merioneth quarter sessions rolls, 1733-65, with a critical and historical introduction. W.K. Williams-Jones. Wales M.A. 1967.

4365   The economic development of Hull in the 18th century. G. Jackson. Hull Ph.D. 1960.

4366   The social and economic development and organisation of the Lake District, 1750-1814. D. Berry. Manchester M.A. 1955.

4367   Economic history of Poole, 1756-1815. E.F.J. Mathews. London Ph.D. (Ext.) 1958.

4368   The economic and social development of the St. Helens area during the latter half of the 18th century. J.R. Harris. Manchester M.A. 1950.

4369   Studies in the history of Liverpool, 1756-83. Winifred M. Barrow. Liverpool M.A. 1925.

4370   Liverpool during the Seven Years War. Marjorie Buchan-Sydserff. Liverpool M.A. 1934.

4371   The making of modern Liverpool, 1760-1820. H.A. Turner. Birmingham M.A. 1939.

4372   A history of local government in Stockport between 1760 and 1820. J. Thorp. Manchester M.A. 1940.

4373   The economic and social development of Stockport from 1815 to 1836. Phyllis M. Giles. Manchester M.A. 1950.

4374   The history of Helston, 1768-91. H.S. Toy. Bristol M.A. 1931.

4375   The Middlesex magistrate, 1760-1820: some social and economic aspects of the work of J.P.s. Iris E.V. Forrester. London M.A. 1934.

4376   Local government in Gloucestershire, 1775-1800: a study of the justices of the peace and their work. Esther A.L. Moir. Cambridge Ph.D. 1955.

4377   Civic government of Durham, 1780-1835. Mary Todd. Liverpool M.A. 1924.

4378   Social and economic trends in the rural west Midlands, 1785-1825. J.M. Martin. Birmingham M.Com. 1960.

4379   The condition of England during the Revolutionary and Napoleonic periods, as illustrated by the history of Birmingham between the years 1789 and 1815. D.J. Davies. Wales M.A. 1924.

4380   The politics and administration of the borough of Morpeth in the late 18th century. J.M. Fewster. Durham Ph.D. 1960.

4381   The government of Lancashire, 1798-1838. A.F. Davie. Manchester M.A. 1966.

4382   Somerset, 1800-30: an inquiry into social and economic conditions. J.F. Lawrence. Durham M.Litt. 1939.

4383   The social structure and development of London, c.1800-1830. H.A. Shearring. Oxford D.Phil. 1955.

SCOTLAND

4384   The human geography of the Firth of Forth and its hinterland in the 17th century. J.M. Hunt. Oxford B.Litt. 1959.

4385   Dr. Edmund Castell, 1606-85. M. Zamick. St. Andrews Ph.D. 1934.

4386   John Brown of Wamphray: a study of his life, work and thought. I.B. Doyle. Edinburgh Ph.D. 1956.

4387   Pastoral care in the Church of Scotland in the 17th century. T.E. Weir. Edinburgh Ph.D. 1960/1.

4388   The career and significance of Sir James Montgomerie of Skelmorlie (c.1654-94). J. Halliday. Glasgow B.Litt. 1963.

4389   The house of Hamilton in its Anglo-Scottish setting in the 17th century: with a calendar of the correspondence in the Hamilton archives at Lennoxlove to 1712. Rosalind K. Marshall. Edinburgh Ph.D. 1970.

The law, custom and practice of the parliament of 4390
Scotland, with particular reference to the period 1660-1707.
G.W. Iredell. London Ph.D. (Ext.) 1966.

The administration of Scotland during the reigns of 4391
Charles II and James VII. W.B. Gray. Oxford B.Litt. 1920.

The military forces and the public revenue of Scotland, 4392
1660-88. W.B. Gray. Edinburgh Ph.D. 1922.

The political opposition to Lauderdale in Scotland, 4393
1660-79. A.J. Patrick. Birmingham M.A. 1957.

Scotland under Lauderdale. Edith E.B. Thomson. St. 4394
Andrews Ph.D. 1928.

Archbishop Leighton: his characteristic position as 4395
theologian and ecclesiastic. D.S. Hopkirk. Oxford B.Litt.
1926.

A critical evaluation of the Scottish Conventiclers 4396
from the Restoration to the Revolution (1662-88). E.W.
Etheridge. Edinburgh Ph.D. 1959.

James Fraser of Brea (1639-99): his life and writings, 4397
with special reference to his theory of universal redemption
and its influence on religious thought in Scotland. D. Fraser.
Edinburgh Ph.D. 1944.

The Presbyterian-Episcopalian controversy in Scotland 4398
from the Revolution settlement till the accession of George I:
a survey and critical review with a bibliography and bibliographical notes. T. Maxwell. Edinburgh Ph.D. 1954.

The rise and development of the evangelical movement 4399
in the Highlands of Scotland from 1688 to 1800. J. MacInnes.
Edinburgh Ph.D. 1941.

Reactions to Jacobitism in Scottish ecclesiastical life 4400
and thought, 1690-1760. D.H. Whiteford. Edinburgh Ph.D.
1966.

The Commission of the General Assembly of the Church of 4401
Scotland, 1690-1735. R.E. Green. Glasgow Ph.D. 1969.

Ecclesiastical discipline in the Church of Scotland, 4402
1690-1730. R.M. Graham. Glasgow Ph.D. 1964.

Aspects of Arminianism in Scotland. M.C. Kitshoff. 4403
St. Andrews M.Th. 1968.

A social and economic history of the Highlands of 4404
Scotland from the Revolution of 1689 to the '45'. H. Holdsworth. Leeds M.A. 1936.

The political relations of England and Scotland under 4405
William III and Anne, with particular reference to the
religious factors. A.C. Cheyne. Oxford B.Litt. 1954.

The Darien scheme and the Church of Scotland. J.C. 4406
Ramsay. Edinburgh Ph.D. 1949.

Ministers to the soldiers of Scotland. A.C. Dow. 4407
Aberdeen Ph.D. 1957.

The changing rural geography of Scottish lowlands, 4408
1700-1820, with estate plans and bibliography. Betty M.W.
Third. Edinburgh Ph.D. 1953.

Agricultural change in Roxburghshire and Berwickshire, 4409
1700-1815. R.A. Dodgshon. Liverpool Ph.D. 1970.

Scottish farming in the 18th century. J.E. Handley. 4410
London Ph.D. (Ext.) 1933.

The transformation of the Highlands of Scotland in the 4411
18th century. H.J. Ewart. Aberdeen Ph.D. 1935.

Some aspects of the social and economic development of 4412
a Highland parish (Kirkmichael, Banffshire) in the 18th
century. J.V. Gaffney. Edinburgh Ph.D. 1952.

Education in Edinburgh in the 18th century. A. Law. 4413
Edinburgh Ph.D. 1959.

The clubs and societies of 18th-century Scotland. D.D. 4414
McElroy. Edinburgh Ph.D. 1951/2.

Music and society in lowland Scotland in the 18th 4415
century. D.C. Johnson. Cambridge Ph.D. 1970.

Edinburgh magazines, 1739-1826. D.S.M. Imrie. St. 4416
Andrews Ph.D. 1936.

4417   A social and economic history of Leith in the 18th century. J.S. Marshall. Edinburgh Ph.D. 1969.

4418   The Union of England and Scotland considered with regard to the action of English statesmen and the development of opinion in England. P.W. Skirrow. Oxford B.Litt. 1927.

4419   Queen Anne's ministers and the administration of Scotland, 1707-14. P.W.J. Riley. London Ph.D. 1957.

4420   The Falls of Dunbar - an 18th-century mercantile family of Scotland. D.S. Alexander. Glasgow B.Litt. 1969.

4421   The pastoral ministry in the Church of Scotland in the 18th century, with special reference to Thomas Boston, John Willison and John Erskine. S.A. Woodruff. Edinburgh Ph.D. 1966.

4422   John Willison of Dundee, 1680-1750. W.D. Pomeroy. Edinburgh Ph.D. 1953.

4423   The life and writings of Thomas Boston of Ettrick. W. Addison. Edinburgh Ph.D. 1936/7.

4424   George Campbell (1719-96), his life and thought. A.R. McKay. Edinburgh Ph.D. 1950/1.

4425   James Hog of Carnock (1658-1734), leader in the evangelical party in early 18th-century Scotland. C.L. Moffat. Edinburgh Ph.D. 1961.

4426   The Scottish evangelical revival of 1742. A. Fawcett. Glasgow Ph.D. 1951/2.

4427   John Glas (1695-1773). J.T. Hornsby. Edinburgh Ph.D. 1936.

4428   The organisation of the Jacobite army, 1745-6. Jean E. McCann. Edinburgh Ph.D. 1963.

4429   The religious and ecclesiastical life of the north-west Highlands, 1750-1843: the background of the Presbyterian emigrants to Cape Breton, Nova Scotia. G.E. MacDermid. Aberdeen Ph.D. 1967.

4430   The estate of Marchmont in the mid 18th century. G.S. Maxton. Edinburgh Ph.D. 1934/5.

4431   Road development in Ayrshire, 1750-1835. A.K. Goodwin. Strathclyde M.Litt. 1970.

4432   Moderatism and the moderate party in the Church of Scotland 1752-1805. I.D.L. Clark. Cambridge Ph.D. 1964.

4433   The early development of Moderatism in the Church of Scotland. H.R. Sefton. Glasgow Ph.D. 1964.

4434   The introduction and development of Wesleyanism in Scotland. D.L. Macfarlane. Edinburgh Ph.D. 1931/2.

4435   The early Methodist lay preachers and their contribution to the 18th-century revival in Scotland. J.S. Wilder. Edinburgh Ph.D. 1948.

4436   Archibald McLean, 1733-1812, Baptist pioneer in Scotland. R.D. Mitchell. Edinburgh Ph.D. 1950.

4437   The early political careers of James 'Fingal' Macpherson (1736-96) and Sir John Macpherson (1744-1821). J.N.M. Maclean. Edinburgh Ph.D. 1967.

4438   The Scottish Whigs and the reform of the court of session, 1785-1830. N.T. Phillipson. Cambridge Ph.D. 1967.

4439   The Edinburgh professoriate, 1790-1826, and the university's contribution to 19th-century British society. A.C. Chitnis. Edinburgh Ph.D. 1968.

4440   Archibald Bruce of Whitburn (1746-1816), with special reference to his view of church and state. R.G. Hall. Edinburgh Ph.D. 1954/5.

4441   David Steuart Erskine, 11th earl of Buchan, a study of his life and correspondence. J.G. Lamb. St. Andrews Ph.D. 1964.

4442   The origins of Congregationalism in Scotland. G.L.S. Thompson. Edinburgh Ph.D. 1932/3.

4443   The life and work of James Alexander Haldane, 1768-1851. D.E. Wallace. Edinburgh Ph.D. 1955.

4444   Greville Ewing (1767-1841): architect of Scottish Congregationalism. W.R.N. Gray. Edinburgh Ph.D. 1961/2.

William Tytler, his son Alexander Fraser Tytler (Lord   4445
Woodhouselee), and the encouragement of literature in late
18th-century Edinburgh. Claire Lamont. Oxford B.Litt. 1969.

The first Statistical Account as a basis for studying   4446
the agrarian geography of late 18th-century Scotland. Mrs.
Valerie Morgan. Cambridge Ph.D. 1969.

The attitude of the clergy to the Industrial Revolution 4447
as reflected in the first and second Statistical Accounts.
C.F. Smith. Glasgow Ph.D. 1953.

Aspects of the Scottish economy during the American War 4448
of Independence. N.E. McClain. Strathclyde M.Litt. 1968.

The influence of the French Revolution on religious   4449
life and thought in Scotland, with special reference to
Thomas Chalmers, Robert Haldane and Neil Douglas. W.M. Kirkland. Edinburgh Ph.D. 1951.

Thomas Carlyle and Edinburgh, 1809-34. I.McD. Camp-   4450
bell. Edinburgh Ph.D. 1970.

Andrew Thomson, 1779-1831, leader of the evangelical   4451
revival in Scotland. J.W. Craven. Edinburgh Ph.D. 1956.

Thomas McCrie, D.D., churchman and historian. P.C.   4452
Wotherspoon. Edinburgh Ph.D. 1953.

The geography of the Nithsdale-Annandale region, Dum-   4453
friesshire, 1813-16. J.D. Wood. Edinburgh Ph.D. 1962.

Radical reform movements in Scotland from 1815 to 1822, 4454
with particular reference to events in the west of Scotland.
W.M. Roach. Glasgow Ph.D. 1970.

The life and work of John Galt. Jennie W. Aberdein.   4455
Aberdeen Ph.D. 1934.

IRELAND

Local administration in the Irish counties prior to   4456
1800, with particular reference to the period 1600-1800. J.
Rafferty. Belfast M.Com.Sc. 1932.

The barony of Lecale, Co. Down: a study of regional   4457
personality. R.H. Buchanan. Belfast Ph.D. 1958.

The rise and decline of three ports of North Down -   4458
Bangor, Groomsport and Donaghadee. Barbara A. McNeill. Belfast M.A. 1955.

Anglo-Irish trade, 1660-1800. L.M. Cullen. London   4459
Ph.D. 1959.

The history of the Irish newspaper, 1685-1750. R. La   4460
V. Munter. Cambridge Ph.D. 1961.

Social conditions in Ireland in the 17th and 18th cent- 4461
uries as illustrated by early Quaker records. Isabel Grubb.
London M.A. 1916.

English schools in Ireland in the 17th and 18th cent-   4462
uries. Catherine Murray. Belfast M.A. 1954.

The subscription controversy in Irish Presbyterianism   4463
from the plantation of Ulster to the present day, with reference to political implications in the late 18th century. W.
McMillan. Manchester M.A. 1959.

The principle of nonsubscription to creeds and con-   4464
fessions of faith as exemplified in Irish Presbyterian
history. R. Allen. Belfast Ph.D. 1944.

The relations between the Irish Presbyterians and the   4465
government from the Declaration of Indulgence (1687) to the
repeal of the Test Act (1780). J.C. Beckett. Belfast M.A.
1942.

Huguenots in the ministry of the churches in Ireland - 4466
their place and contribution. J.C. Combe. Belfast Ph.D.
1970.

The political significance of the career of the earl of 4467
Tyrconnell in Irish history, and its relation to the cause of
James II, 1685-91. Mary E. Brady. Cambridge M.Litt. 1943.

4468   Irish economic thought and the Irish economy in the 18th century. A. Collins. Belfast M.Sc. 1970.

4469   The Foster interest in Louth, 1700-1832. A.P.W. Malcomson. Belfast Ph.D. 1970.

4470   Ireland and the administration of James Butler, 2nd duke of Ormonde, lord lieutenant of Ireland 1703-7. G.E.I. Crosby. Liverpool M.A. 1935.

4471   The rise and decline of the Ballycastle coalfield and associated industries, 1720-1840. G.A. Wilson. Belfast M.A. 1951.

4472   The 'undertakers' in Ireland and their relations with the lord lieutenant, 1724-71. J.L. McCracken. Belfast M.A. 1942.

4473   Central and local administration in Ireland under George II. J.L. McCracken. Belfast Ph.D. 1948.

4474   The government of Ireland, 1767-85: a study in Anglo-Irish political administration. Edith M. Johnston. St. Andrews Ph.D. 1956.

4475   The more immediate effects of the American Revolution on Ireland, 1775-85. Theresa M. O'Connor. Belfast M.A. 1938.

4476   Anglo-Irish commercial relations, 1779-85, with special reference to the negotiations of 1785. J.A.G. Whitlaw. Belfast M.A. 1958.

4477   The impact of Wesley on Ireland. T.E. Warner. London Ph.D. (Ext.) 1954.

4478   The origin and nature of the Gracehill Moravian settlement (1764-1855), with special reference to the work of John Cennick in Ireland (1746-55). S.G. Hanna. Belfast M.A. 1964.

4479   A political and ecclesiastical biography of Thomas Hussey, D.D., F.R.S. (1741/6-1803). J.S.B. Cullen. Oxford D.Phil. 1965.

4480   The history and associations of the Belfast Charitable Society. R.W.M. Strain. Belfast Ph.D. 1955.

4481   The education of Irish Catholics, 1782-1831. J.J. Sullivan. Belfast Ph.D. 1959.

4482   The popular Catholic school in Ireland, 1782-1830. P.J. Dowling. London Ph.D. 1929.

4483   A social and economic history of Belfast, 1790-1800. J.J. Monaghan. Belfast M.A. 1936.

4484   The transformation of Presbyterian radicalism in the north of Ireland, 1792-1825. A.T.Q. Stewart. Belfast M.A. 1956.

4485   The parliamentary background of the Irish Act of Union of 1800. G.C. Bolton. Oxford D.Phil. 1960.

4486   The act of legislative union between Great Britain and Ireland, with particular reference to the political career of Castlereagh. H.M. Hyde. Belfast M.A. 1933.

4487   A social and economic history of Belfast, 1801-25. J.J. Monaghan. Belfast Ph.D. 1940.

4488   Irish parliamentary representation, 1801-20. P.J. Jupp. Reading Ph.D. 1967.

4489   The Clare election, 1828. Helena P. Carberry. Liverpool M.A. 1934.

For items covering the period 1800-32 see above under 1600-1832

POPULATION AND MIGRATION

The rural population of England and Wales, 1801-1951. 4490
S.W.E. Vince. London Ph.D. (Ext.) 1955.

Changes in the distribution of the population since 4491
1800. Winifred R. Luke. London M.A. (Ext.) 1939.

Cleveland and Teesside: a geographical study of popul- 4492
ation and occupational changes since 1800. Ida Bowes.
London M.A. 1948.

Some aspects of the population growth and structure in 4493
the Warwickshire coalfield since 1800. R.C. Bunker. Birmingham M.A. 1952.

Berkshire: some studies based on the census returns. 4494
G.R. Lucas. Reading M.A. 1954.

Population and urban growth in east Bristol, 1800-1914. 4495
F. Hewitt. Bristol Ph.D. 1966.

Some aspects of the growth and distribution of popul- 4496
ation in Hertfordshire since 1801. D.J.M. Hooson. London
Ph.D. 1955.

A study of planned urban and rural industrial settle- 4497
ments and communities in the United Kingdom during the 19th
century. P. Taylor. Durham Ph.D. 1960/1.

Population change and population structure 1801-61 in 4498
the Peak district of Derbyshire. Ray Gurney. Liverpool
Ph.D. 1970.

The population of Northamptonshire, 1801-1951. C.D. 4499
Morley. Birmingham M.A. 1957.

The changes in population distribution in the Tern 4500
'basin' of north-east Shropshire, with special reference to
the Wellington-Oakengates conurbation, 1801-1951. K.C. Riley.
London M.A. 1958.

The economic significance of the present population 4501
distribution in Gloucestershire and its relationship to economic developments during the past 150 years in the county.
H.C. Andrews. London M.Sc. (Ext.) 1956.

Urban change in East Anglia in the 19th century. Lucy 4502
Caroe. Cambridge Ph.D. 1966.

Stages in the growth of urban settlement in central 4503
Cornwall. M.E. Witherick. Birmingham Ph.D. 1963.

A study of the development of urban spheres of influ- 4504
ence in Leicestershire. P.R. Odell. Birmingham Ph.D. 1954.

Leicester's rural-urban fringe: a study of industry 4505
and settlement. Gladys Starmer. Nottingham M.A. 1959.

Population in the dales of north-east England. A.E. 4506
Smailes. London M.A. 1933.

Aspects of the social geography of Nidderdale, 4507
Wensleydale and the northern part of the vale of York. R.J.
Johnston. Manchester M.A. 1964.

The geographical significance of population changes in 4508
Carmarthenshire since 1802. F.G. Hannell. Bristol Ph.D.
1952.

A demographic study of central Snowdonia and its coast- 4509
lands in the 19th century. Kathleen M. O'Kelly. Manchester
M.A. 1961.

Population in central Wales: changes in number and 4510
distribution, 1801-1931. J.E.C. Jenkins. London M.A. 1939.

The geographical reasons for the growth of the popul- 4511
ation of south Staffordshire, east Warwickshire and Leicestershire from 1801 to 1931. Gladys M. Sarson. London Ph.D.
(Ext.) 1937.

4512   Nineteenth-century changes in the distribution of population in the south Staffordshire coalfield. R.D. Bramwell. Birmingham M.A. 1935.

4513   A sociological and statistical study of the population of the vale of Glamorgan during the first half of the 19th century. M.I. Williams. Wales M.A. 1939.

4514   The migration of the wage-earning classes in England in the early part of the 19th century. A. Redford. Manchester Ph.D. 1922.

4515   The geographical variation of rural population change in eastern Nottinghamshire, 1811-1911, with particular reference to the correlative effect on this variation of changes in agriculture, rural industry and transport. M.J. Croft. Leeds M.A. 1961.

4516   A study of emigration from Great Britain, 1802-60. Monica G. Page. London Ph.D. 1931.

4517   Emigration from the British Isles, 1815-1921. W.A. Carrothers. Edinburgh Ph.D. 1921.

4518   The role of the United Kingdom in the transatlantic emigrant trade, 1815-75. M.A. Jones. Oxford D.Phil. 1956.

4519   An inquiry into the changing distribution of population in the Chilterns since 1821. R.S.G. Brocklebank. London Ph.D. 1937.

4520   An investigation of changes in population density and distribution, together with changes in agricultural practice in Pembrokeshire during the period 1831-1931. G.I. Lewis. Birmingham M.A. 1937.

4521   Some geographical aspects of the depopulation of rural Wales since 1841. V.C. Davies. London Ph.D. (Ext.) 1955.

4522   A study of the changes in the distribution and density of population in Worcestershire during the period 1841-1931, and of the geographical factors involved. E.R.G. Wood. Birmingham M.A. 1950.

4523   Population changes in Worcestershire (south of the Birmingham conurbation) and Gloucestershire, 1851-1951. A.T. Allen. Wales M.Sc. 1961.

4524   Population migration into and from Staffordshire and Warwickshire, 1841-1901. R. Lawton. Liverpool M.A. 1950.

4525   The upper Calder basin, Yorkshire, in the mid 19th century: a study in historical geography. B. Barnes. Manchester M.A. 1961.

4526   Changes in industry, population and settlement on the exposed coalfield of south Yorkshire, 1840-1908. M. Jones. Nottingham M.A. 1967.

4527   Population and settlement growth in the south Yorkshire coalfield. R. Blackledge. Birmingham M.A. 1951.

4528   Aspects of the population and settlement geography of the South Wales coalfield, 1850-1926. P.N. Jones. Birmingham Ph.D. 1965.

4529   The urban geography of the north-eastern rim of the Glamorgan coalfield. L.H. Bolwell. Wales M.A. 1961.

4530   A study of socio-geographic change in the central Welsh marchland since the mid 19th century. G.J. Lewis. Leicester Ph.D. 1969.

4531   The distribution of population in England and Wales in 1851. T.E. Hilton. Manchester M.A. 1938.

4532   The internal migration of population in England and Wales, 1851-1911. J. Heads. Cambridge M.Sc. 1956.

4533   Rural depopulation in Wales, 1881-1901: an enquiry into its extent, nature, causes, and consequences, with a brief discussion of some of the more important remedies. R. Jones. Belfast M.A. 1911.

4534   The structure and classification of settlement in the Oxfordshire Cotswolds. J.M. Griffiths. Reading M.A. 1955.

4535   A study of the changes in the geographical distribution of industry and population in England and Wales during the 20th century. J.E.S. Orrin. Wales M.A. 1932.

A study of statistics of population and occupations in   4536
the counties, urban and rural districts of Wales, 1901-31.
Mary A. Richards. Wales M.Sc. 1942.

Migration from the United Kingdom to the Dominions   4537
in the inter-war period, with special reference to the
Empire Settlement Act of 1922. S. Wertimer. London Ph.D.
1952.

POLITICAL HISTORY

General

The geographic distribution of political opinion in   4538
the county of Glamorgan for the parliamentary elections
1820-1950. H.M. Williams. Wales M.A. 1951.

Political and electioneering activity in south-east   4539
Wales, 1820-52. I.W.R. David. Wales M.A. 1959.

Politics in Anglesey and Caernarvonshire 1826-52, with   4540
special reference to the Caernarvon boroughs. R.G. Thomas.
Wales M.A. 1970.

Politics in the borough of Colchester, 1812-47. M.E.   4541
Speight. London Ph.D. 1969.

Political issues in the county of Kent, 1820-46. Julia 4542
H. Andrews. London M.Phil. 1967.

Sir James Graham as politician and Home Secretary,   4543
1818-46. D.W.J. Johnson. Oxford B.Litt. 1948.

The political career of Sir John Bowring (1792-1872),   4544
between 1820 and 1849. G.F. Bartle. London M.A. 1959.

Sir Richard Vyvyan and Tory politics, with special   4545
reference to the period 1825-46. B.T. Bradfield. London
Ph.D. 1965.

The political career of Henry, 3rd Earl Grey, 1826-52.   4546
R. Job. Durham M.Litt. 1959.

The relief of the Jewish disabilities in England, 1829- 4547
58. I. Shapira. London M.A. 1934.

Daniel O'Connell and Catholic emancipation. N.E.L.   4548
Guest. Birmingham M.A. 1931.

Daniel O'Connell and the Irish parliamentary party,   4549
1830-47. A.D. Macintyre. Oxford D.Phil. 1963.

The development of a railway interest, and its relation 4550
to parliament, 1830-68. G.K. Roberts. London Ph.D. 1966.

Party politics in the county of Staffordshire during   455
the years 1830-47. G.B. Kent. Birmingham M.A. 1959.

Politics in Leeds, 1830-52. D. Fraser. Leeds Ph.D.   4553
1969.

Life and times of the Rt. Hon. Charles Buller. E.   4554
Sweetman. London Ph.D. 1952.

The early career and correspondence of Richard Wood,   4555
1830-41. A.B. Cunningham. London Ph.D. 1956.

The life and work of H.S. Tremenheere. C. Holmes.   4556
Nottingham M.A. 1964.

James Silk Buckingham (1786-1855) - social and polit-   4557
ical reformer. S.T. King. London M.A. 1933.

The political career of Henry Goulburn, 1784-1856.   4558
W.J. Stranz. Durham M.Litt. 1949.

A consideration of the use of non-ministerial organis- 4559
ation in the administrative and executive work of the central
government, with special reference to the period 1832-1919.
B.B. Schaffer. London Ph.D. 1956.

A consideration of the experience, in Britain, of   4560
administrative commissions represented in parliament by
non-ministerial commissioners, with special reference to
the Ecclesiastical Commission, the Charity Commission and
the Forestry Commission. F.M.G. Willson. Oxford D.Phil.
1953.

4561   An enquiry into the change in the character of the house of commons, 1832-1901. J.A. Thomas. London Ph.D. 1926.

4562   Public opinion and parliament since 1832. Dorothy C. Johnson. Oxford B.Litt. 1922.

4563   The elimination of corrupt practices at British elections. C. O'Leary. Oxford D.Phil. 1959.

4564   The comparative study of parliamentary representation in the new borough constituencies created in 1832. S.F. Woolley. London M.A. (Ext.) 1937.

4565   The effects of the Reform Bill of 1832 on the Lancashire constituencies, especially Liverpool. W.K. Hunt. Manchester M.A. 1924.

4566   Politics and party organisation in Oldham, 1832-1914. D. Bickerstaffe. Durham M.A. 1964.

4567   Lincolnshire politics, 1832-85. R.J. Olney. Oxford D.Phil. 1970.

4568   Politics and opinion in 19th-century Bradford, 1832-80, with special reference to parliamentary elections. D.G. Wright. Leeds Ph.D. 1966.

4569   Elections and political behaviour in Durham and Newcastle, 1832-74. T.J. Nossiter. Oxford D.Phil. 1968.

4570   The parliamentary representation of Wales and Monmouthshire during the 19th century - but mainly till 1870. O. Parry. Wales M.A. 1924.

4571   The party politics of the Black Country and neighbourhood, 1832-67. V. Tunsiri. Birmingham M.A. 1964.

4572   Parliamentary elections in Derby and Derbyshire, 1832-65. C.E. Hogarth. Manchester M.A. 1957.

4573   The private member of parliament, 1833-68. J.K. Glynn. London Ph.D. 1949.

4574   Financial aspects of a parliamentary career in aristocratic and democratic Britain: a study of the expense of membership in the house of commons, with special reference to the 19th century. W.B. Gwyn. London Ph.D. 1956.

4575   The transition from Whiggism to Liberalism. D.G. Southgate. Oxford D.Phil. 1949.

4576   Lord John Russell and the development of relations between parliament, cabinet and parties, 1832-52. Mildred E. Gibbs. Manchester Ph.D. 1928.

4577   Lord John Russell and the leadership of the house of commons, 1835-41. V.B.P. Jones. Wales M.A. 1970.

4578   The general elections of 1835 and 1837 in England and Wales. D.H. Close. Oxford D.Phil. 1967.

4579   The idea of political representation in the United States and Great Britain, 1836-56. J.L. Moore. Oxford B.Litt. 1953.

4580   Lord Melbourne's second administration and the opposition, 1837-41. R.H. Cameron. London Ph.D. 1970.

4581   The relations of Sir Robert Peel with the Crown, 1837-46. J.W. Horton. Oxford B.Litt. 1950.

4582   The opposition to Sir Robert Peel in the Conservative party, 1841-6. D.R. Fisher. Cambridge Ph.D. 1970.

4583   The Victorian house of lords. A.L. Sachar. Cambridge Ph.D. 1923.

4584   The Russell administration, 1846-52. F.A. Dreyer. St. Andrews Ph.D. 1962.

4585   John Bright and the representation of Manchester in the house of commons, 1847-57. J. Skinner. Wales M.A. 1965.

4586   The development of English socialism from 1848 to 1884. Muriel John. London M.A. 1934.

4587   Administrative legislation and adjudication in Great Britain and the United States. E.R. Baltzell. Oxford D.Phil. 1923.

4588   Public opinion and administrative reform in Britain between 1848 and 1854. A.D. Gidlow-Jackson. London M.A. 1958.

The concept of parliamentary representation in Great   4589
Britain, 1850-1918: a history of its development.   A.P. Dean.
Oxford B.Litt. 1951.
Francis Pulszky's political activities in England,   4590
1849-60.   T.G. Kabdebo.   London M.Phil. 1969.
The Liberal party and nationalism, 1850-1914.   G.E.H.   4591
Griffith.   Wales M.A. 1957.
Cardiff politics, 1850-75.   I. Humphreys.   Wales M.A.   4592
1970.
The political influence of the Prince Consort.   U.F.J.   4593
Eyck.   Oxford B.Litt. 1958.
Three Northumberland constituencies in the general   4594
election of 1852: North and South Northumberland and Tyne-
mouth.   Anne E. Carnick.   Durham M.A. 1966.
The relations of statutory and voluntary authorities in 4595
public administration in England and Wales.   Muriel McKie.
Oxford B.Litt. 1930.
The changing role of the administrative class of the   4596
British home civil service, 1853-1965.   G.K. Fry.   London
Ph.D. 1967.
Treasury control of civil establishments, 1856-74.   4597
M.W. Wright.   Oxford D.Phil. 1963.
Specialist policy in government growth: aspects of   4598
state activity, 1860-1900.   R.M. MacLeod.   Cambridge Ph.D.
1967.
The social and political ideas of Frederic Harrison in 4599
relation to English thought and politics, 1855-86.   P. Adel-
man.   London Ph.D. 1968.
Aspects of academic radicalism in mid-Victorian Eng-   4600
land: a study in the politics of thought and action, with
special reference to Frederic Harrison and John Morley.   C.A.
Kent.   Sussex D.Phil. 1968.
Some aspects of the radical and democratic career of   4601
the 1st marquess of Ripon (1827-1909).   A.F. Denholm.   Wales
M.A. 1966.
The life and career of Sir William Christopher Leng,   4602
1825-1902: a prominent Victorian journalist.   K.G. March.
Sheffield M.A. 1966.
The early life and political development of James Keir 4603
Hardie, 1856-92.   F. Reid.   Oxford D.Phil. 1969.
The formation of the Liberal party, 1857-68.   J.R.   4604
Vincent.   Cambridge Ph.D. 1962.
The Liberal party on Merseyside in the 19th century.   4605
C.D. Watkinson.   Liverpool Ph.D. 1968.
The growth of Liberal organisation in Manchester from the   4606
eighteen-sixties to 1903.   P. Whitaker.   Manchester Ph.D. 1956.
Disraeli.   Dorothy I. Hart.   Birmingham M.A. 1921.   4607
Sir James Fitzjames Stephen: a study of his thought and 4608
life.   J.P.C. Roach.   Cambridge Ph.D. 1953.
The political career of Sir Edward Baines, 1800-90.   4609
J.R. Lowerson.   Leeds M.A. 1965.
The career of Arthur Hamilton Gordon, 1st Lord Stan-   4610
more, to 1875.   J.K. Chapman.   London Ph.D. 1954.
Parliamentary elections in Blackburn and the Blackburn 4611
hundred, 1865-80.   J.C. Lowe.   Lancaster M.Litt. 1970.
The Reform Bill of 1867.   P. Carter.   Wales M.A. 1952.   4612
The making of the Second Reform Bill.   F.B. Smith.   4613
Cambridge Ph.D. 1962.
The debate on democracy at the time of the Second   4614
Reform Act, 1867.   M.W. Davies.   Wales M.A. 1969.
The evolution of the franchise in England, with special 4615
reference to the Reform Act of 1867 and to the political in-
fluence of organised Christianity.   W.G.H. Cook.   London
M.Sc. 1922.
Central organisation and leadership in the Conservative 4616
party under the conditions created by the Reform Bill of
1867.   E.J. Feuchtwanger.   Southampton Ph.D. 1958.

4617   British labour and parliament, 1867-93. W.K. Lamb.
London Ph.D. 1933.
4618   The cabinet in the late 19th century. S. Gale. Leeds
M.A. 1956.
4619   The English cabinet, 1868-1917. W. Yu. London Ph.D.
1937.
4620   A geographical study of the results of British parliamentary elections from 1868 to 1910. D.J. Morrish. London
M.Sc. (Ext.) 1955.
4621   The general election of 1868: a study in the bases of
mid-Victorian politics. H.J. Hanham. Cambridge Ph.D. 1954.
4622   Mr. Gladstone's leadership of the parliamentary Liberal
party, 1868-74. J.D. Clayton. Oxford D.Phil. 1961.
4623   The political significance of R.A. Cross. T.O. Hughes.
Wales M.A. 1954.
4624   The rise of Richard Assheton Cross and his work at the
Home Office, 1868-80. F.J. Dwyer. Oxford B.Litt. 1955.
4625   The career of A.J. Mundella, with special reference to
his Sheffield connections. Margaret Higginbotham. Sheffield M.A. 1941.
4626   The radical attitude towards the monarchy and the house
of lords, 1868-85. E.G. Collieu. Oxford B.Litt. 1936.
4627   Social and political aspects of the British monarchy,
1870-87. E.T. Galpin. Cambridge M.Litt. 1952.
4628   A study of the attitude and policies of the British
political parties towards Welsh affairs, disestablishment of
the church, education and governmental devolution, in the
period 1870-1920. K.O. Morgan. Oxford D.Phil. 1958.
4629   The history of the Co-operative party in Manchester and
Salford. Cynthia I. Arditti. Manchester M.A. 1953.
4630   John Morley: a political study, with special emphasis
on the relationship between his political thought and practice. D.A. Hamer. Oxford D.Phil. 1965.
4631   The political ideas of Sir Alfred Comyn Lyall, 1873-
1903. Mrs. Parveen Hassan. Durham M.Litt. 1962.
4632   The railway interest, 1873-1913. G. Alderman. Oxford
D.Phil. 1969.
4633   The history of civil procedure in the Supreme Court of
Judicature since 1873. J.A. Burnes. Oxford D.Phil. 1958.
4634   The influence of public opinion on the development of
English law, 1880-1914. S.D. Temkin. Liverpool M.A. 1938.
4635   The political career of Lord Randolph Churchill. Mary
Dempsey. Liverpool M.A. 1949.
4636   The origins of the revolt of the British labour movement
from Liberalism, 1875-1906. D.W. Crowley. London Ph.D.
1952.
4637   Henry George and British socialism, 1879-1924. P.d'A.
Jones. Manchester M.A. 1953.
4638   H.M. Hyndman and British socialism, 1881-1921. C.
Tsuzuki. Oxford D.Phil. 1959.
4639   The influence of socialist ideas on English prose
writing and political thinking, 1880-95. Mrs. Mira S.
Wilkins. Cambridge Ph.D. 1957.
4640   Origins and early history of the Independent Labour
Party, 1880-1900. H.M. Pelling. Cambridge Ph.D. 1951.
4641   The nature of propaganda and its function in democratic
government: an examination of the principal theories of propaganda since 1880. T.H. Qualter. London Ph.D. 1956.
4642   Liberalism in England, 1880-1914. W.G.K. Duncan. London Ph.D. 1930.
4643   The decline of the Liberal party, 1880-1900. B.D. Rubinstein. London Ph.D. 1956.
4644   The Liberal party and the house of lords, 1880-95. J.E.
Williams. Wales M.A. 1961.
4645   The general election of 1880 in England, Scotland and
Wales. T.O. Lloyd. Oxford D.Phil. 1959.

T.P. O'Connor and Liverpool politics, 1880-1929. L.W. 4646
Brady. Liverpool Ph.D. 1968.

Fabian doctrine and its influence in English politics. 4647
A.M. McBriar. Oxford D.Phil. 1949.

Fabianism and the Fabians, 1884-1914. E.J.E. Hobsbawm. 4648
Cambridge Ph.D. 1950.

Fabian thought and social change in England from 1884 4648A
to 1914. R.D. Howland. London Ph.D. 1942.

The Webbs: a study of the influence of intellectuals in 4649
politics (largely between 1889 and 1918). M. Warner. Cambridge Ph.D. 1966.

The origin and development of the standing committees 4650
of the house of commons, with special reference to their
procedure, 1882-1951. G.M. Higgins. Oxford B.Litt. 1953.

Geographical aspects of parliamentary constituencies 4651
in the United Kingdom, with special reference to the period
1885 to 1948. G.E. Daniels. London M.A. 1963.

Economic and political origins of the Labour party from 4652
1884 to 1906. Dorothy Good. London Ph.D. 1936.

London working-class politics and the formation of the 4653
London Labour party, 1885-1914. P.R. Thompson. Oxford
D.Phil. 1964.

The Reform Bills of 1884 and 1885. R.C. Reed. Wales 4654
M.A. 1949.

The Third Reform Bill, 1884-5. G.A. Jones. Cambridge 4655
Ph.D. 1970.

Joseph Chamberlain and the Unauthorised Programme. A. 4656
Simon. Oxford D.Phil. 1970.

A study of the social origins and character of British 4657
political leaders, 1886-1936. W.L. Guttsman. London M.Sc.
1950.

The Liberal party and collectivism, 1886-1906. L.A. 4658
Clark. Cambridge M.Litt. 1957.

The Irish nationalist movement in Great Britain, 1886- 4659
1908. E.P.M. Wollaston. London M.A. 1958.

The earlier history of the Home Rule movement. Dorothy 4660
Freeling. Birmingham M.A. 1927.

The Salisbury administration and Ireland 1885-92. L.P. 4661
Curtis. Oxford D.Phil. 1959.

An analysis and criticism of the rhetoric of the 4662
debates on the Irish Home Rule Bill of 1886. R.A. Hufford.
Durham M.Litt. 1959.

The genesis and significance of the 1886 'Home Rule' split 4663
in the Liberal party. D.G. Hoskin. Cambridge Ph.D. 1964.

The Liberal Unionist party until December 1887. J.K. 4664
Lindsay. Edinburgh Ph.D. 1955.

The general election of 1886 in Great Britain and 4665
Ireland. D.C. Savage. London Ph.D. 1958.

The great debate, 1893-4. J.F. Finn. Warwick M.A. 4666
1968/9.

The educational and political work of the countess of 4667
Warwick, 1861-1938. Mrs. Margaret A. Blunden, née Haigh.
Exeter M.A. 1966.

The Independent Labour Party, 1893-1918. C.T. Solberg. 4668
Oxford B.Litt. 1939.

An examination of the Labour party during its formative 4669
years, 1900-20. R.T. Spooner. Birmingham M.A. 1949.

Socialism in Gwynedd, 1900-20. C. Parry. Wales Ph.D. 4670
1967.

The history of the Socialist Labour Party of Great Britain 4671
from 1902 until 1921, with special reference to the development of its ideas. D.M. Chewter. Oxford B.Litt. 1965.

The Socialist Labour Party and the working-class move- 4672
ment on the Clyde, 1903-21. Helen R. Vernon. Leeds M.Phil.
1967.

The press and parliamentary privilege in Britain during 4673
the 20th century. C.K. Seymour-Ure. Oxford D.Phil. 1968.

4674 The development of the concept of 'national efficiency' and its relation to politics and government, 1900-10. G.R. Searle. Cambridge Ph.D. 1966.

4675 Elections and the electorate in north-west England: an enquiry into the course of political change, 1900-14. P.F. Clarke. Cambridge Ph.D. 1967.

4676 Parliamentary elections and party organisation in Walsall constituency, 1906-45. K.J. Dean. Birmingham M.A. 1969.

4677 The general election of 1906. A.K. Russell. Oxford D.Phil. 1962.

4678 Some aspects of the history of the Liberal party in Britain between 1906 and 1914. A.S. King. Oxford D.Phil. 1962.

4679 Liberal policies and nationalist politics in Ireland, 1905-10. A.C. Hepburn. Kent Ph.D. 1968.

4680 The development of parliamentary opposition in Britain, 1906-45, with special reference to the leader of the opposition. M.A. Mills. London Ph.D. 1970.

4681 The Conservative party 1906-11: a study of the internal difficulties of the party. R.B. Jones. Oxford B.Litt. 1960.

4682 Arthur Balfour and the leadership of the Unionist party in opposition, 1906-11: a study of the origins of Unionist policy towards the Third Home Rule Bill. J.R. Fanning. Cambridge Ph.D. 1968.

4683 National and local issues in politics: a study of east Sussex and the Lancashire spinning towns, 1906-10. Grace A. Jones. Sussex D.Phil. 1964/5.

4684 The political theory of the British Guild Socialists. S.T. Glass. Oxford B.Litt. 1963.

4685 The British general elections of 1910. N. Blewett. Oxford D.Phil. 1967.

4686 Evolution of a national party: Labour's political organisation, 1910-24. R.I. McKibbin. Oxford D.Phil. 1970.

4687 The Parliamentary Labour party and its relations with the Liberals, 1910-14. S.E. Hassam. Aberdeen M.Litt. 1967.

4688 The rise of the Labour party in Leicester. D. Cox. Leicester M.A. 1959.

4689 The outsider: aspects of the political career of Sir Alfred Mond, 1st Lord Melchett (1868-1930). G.M. Bayliss. Wales Ph.D. 1969.

4690 The deviations of the parliamentary system of the United Kingdom since 1911. P.H. Siriex. Oxford B.Litt. 1934.

4691 The development of British socialist thought, 1912-18. J.M. Winter. Cambridge Ph.D. 1970.

4692 The Unionists and Ireland. P.J. Buckland. Birmingham M.A. 1966.

4693 The Ulster crisis: opposition to the Third Home Rule Bill, 1912-14. A.T.Q. Stewart. Belfast Ph.D. 1966.

4694 Southern Unionism, 1885-1922, with special reference to the period after 1914. P.J. Buckland. Belfast Ph.D. 1969.

4695 Unionist and Conservative members of parliament, 1914-39. J.M. McEwen. London Ph.D. 1959.

4696 The decline of the Liberal party in the United Kingdom, 1914-26. J.M. McEwen. Manchester M.A. 1953.

4697 The Liberal party during the First World War, with special reference to the split of 1916. E.I. David. Cambridge M.Litt. 1968.

4698 The Liberal party: division and decline, 1916-29. N.C. Edsall. London M.A. 1960.

4699 The Parliamentary Liberal party in Britain 1918-24. T.G. Wilson. Oxford D.Phil. 1959.

4700 The political influence of organised ex-service men in England and Wales, 1917-57. J.G.G. Wotton. London Ph.D. 1960.

4701 The 1918 election, with particular reference to the elections in South Wales, Somerset and Bristol. S.E. Hughes. Wales M.A. 1969.

The Independent Labour Party, 1918-32. A.J.B. Marwick. 4702
Oxford B.Litt. 1960.

The Independent Labour Party, 1918-32, with special 4703
reference to its relationship with the Labour party. R.E.
Dowse. London Ph.D. (Ext.) 1962.

The Liverpool Labour party, 1918-63. R.J. Baxter. Ox- 4704
ford D.Phil. 1969.

The evolution and working of the British electoral 4705
system, 1918-50. D.H.E. Butler. Oxford D.Phil. 1951.

The political life of Viscount Swinton, 1918-38. A. 4706
Earl. Manchester M.A. 1961.

British public opinion and government policy in Ire- 4707
land, 1918-22. D.G. Boyce. Belfast Ph.D. 1969.

The economic and social policy of the Conservative 4708
party during the period 1919-39. S.G. Lees. Manchester M.A.
1953.

Unemployed labour as a pressure group in Great Britain, 4709
1919-39. R.J. Irvine. Oxford B.Litt. 1951.

The formation of the Communist party of Great Britain, 4710
1918-21. W.F.H. Kendall. Oxford B.Litt. 1966.

The origins of the Communist party of Great Britain and 4711
its early history, 1920-7. L.J. Macfarlane. London Ph.D.
(Ext.) 1962.

Some aspects of the politics of decontrol in Great 4712
Britain and the United States, 1919-21. Mrs. Susan M.H.
Armitage. London Ph.D. 1968.

The 'shadow cabinet' in British politics, with parti- 4713
cular reference to its development since 1922. D.R. Turner.
Wales M.A. 1966.

The general election of 1922. M.S.R. Kinnear. Oxford 4714
D.Phil. 1965.

The British general election of 1929. E.A. Rowe. Ox- 4715
ford B.Litt. 1959.

The Labour government and the unemployment question, 4716
1929-31. R.J.A. Skidelsky. Oxford D.Phil. 1967.

The British Fascist movement, 1932-40: its development 4717
and significance. R.J. Benewick. Manchester Ph.D. 1963.

The Commonwealth party, 1942-5. A.L.R. Calder. Sussex 4718
D.Phil. 1968.

Foreign and Colonial Relations

The origin and growth of the protectorate system, with 4719
special study of the system as developed in British colonial
history (1800-48). W.E. Philpott. London M.A. 1934.

Aspects of British colonial policy 1825-37, with parti- 4720
cular reference to the administrations of Major General Sir
Richard Bourke in Cape Colony and New South Wales. Alice H.K.
King. Oxford D.Phil. 1960.

Attitudes within the Colonial Office towards imperial 4721
control of colonial legislation, 1826-65, with particular
reference to the South Australian crisis, which led to the
passing of the Colonial Laws Validity Act. D.B. Swinfen.
Oxford D.Phil. 1965.

The influence of the Wakefield School on British 4722
colonial policy. K.L.P. Martin. Manchester M.A. 1920.

The house of commons and foreign policy between the 4723
First and Second Reform Acts. A.C. Turner. Oxford B.Litt.
1948.

The exercise of the judicial function of the privy 4724
council, 1833-1954. F.O. Akinrele. Hull LL.M. 1955.

The problem of the Indian immigrant in British 4725
colonial policy after 1834. I. Mary Cumpston. Oxford D.Phil.
1950.

India, Britain, Russia: a study in British opinion, 4726
1838-78. V.K. Chavda. Leeds Ph.D. 1961.

4727 James Stephen, the development of the Colonial Office and the administration of three Crown colonies, Trinidad, Sierra Leone and Ceylon. T.J. Barron. London Ph.D. 1969.

4728 Anti-slavery sentiment in Great Britain, 1841-54; its nature and its decline, with special reference to its influence upon British policy towards the former slave colonies. Elsie I. Pilgrim. Cambridge Ph.D. 1953.

4729 British colonial administration, 1841-52. W.P. Morrell. Oxford D.Phil. 1927.

4730 The character of the foreign policy of the earl of Aberdeen, 1841-6. Muriel E. Chamberlain. Oxford D.Phil. 1961.

4731 The life of Sir Edmund Walker Head, Bart. J.A. Gibson. Oxford D.Phil. 1938.

4732 Attitudes to peace and war in the eighteen-forties and the eighteen-nineties: a comparison of the two decades. Mrs. Mary A. McCollester. Cambridge M.Litt. 1965.

4733 The ideas and activities of John Bright in relation to the empire, 1843-89. J.L. Sturgis. London M.A. 1963.

4734 John Bright as a critic of foreign policy. Joyce E. Sanderson. Birmingham M.A. 1923.

4735 The administration of the British diplomatic service and Foreign Office, 1848-1906. R.A. Jones. London Ph.D. 1968.

4736 British foreign policy, 1850-71. J.C. Kite. Birmingham M.A. 1916.

4737 The role of the British parliament in colonial affairs, 1850-60. Margaret W. Kerr. Oxford B.Litt. 1952.

4738 Edmund Hammond, permanent under-secretary of state for foreign affairs, 1854-73. Mary A. Anderson. London Ph.D. 1956.

4739 The attitude of the Colonial Office towards the working of responsible government, 1854-68. Dorothy P. Clarke. London Ph.D. 1953.

4740 Great Britain and belligerent maritime rights from the Declaration of Paris, 1856, to the Declaration of London, 1909. M.R. Pitt. London Ph.D. 1964.

4741 English policy and the execution of the treaty of Paris. W.E.E. Mosse. Cambridge Ph.D. 1950.

4742 Sir Edward Hertslet and his work as librarian and keeper of the papers of the Foreign Office from 1857 to 1896. Shirley Hall. London M.A. 1958.

4743 The formation of policy in the India Office, 1858-66; with special reference to the Political, Judicial, Revenue, Public and Public Works Departments. D. Williams. Oxford D.Phil. 1962.

4744 The foreign policy of Lord Malmesbury, 1858-9. H. Hearder. London Ph.D. 1954.

4745 The role of free trade treaties in British foreign policy, 1859-71. A. Iliasu. London Ph.D. 1965.

4746 The colonial policy of the 5th duke of Newcastle, 1859-64. C.C. Eldridge. Nottingham Ph.D. 1966.

4747 Idealism and foreign policy: a study of the relations of Great Britain with Germany and France, 1860-78. Anna A.W. Ramsay. Edinburgh Ph.D. 1925.

4748 The select committee of 1861 on colonial military expenditure, and its antecedents. Marjorie G. Chappell. London M.A. 1933.

4749 From status to contract: a biographical study of Sir Henry Maine, 1822-88. G.A. Feaver. London Ph.D. 1962.

4750 Edward Cardwell at the Colonial Office, 1864-6 - some aspects of his policy and ideas. Gabrielle J. Sellers. Oxford B.Litt. 1958.

4751 The foreign secretaryship of Lord Stanley, July 1866 to December 1868. K. Bourne. London Ph.D. 1955.

4752 The Judicial Committee of the Privy Council and the distribution of legislative powers in the British North America Act, 1867. G.P. Browne. Oxford D.Phil. 1963.

The place of foreign affairs in British party politics   4753
during the period 1868-92. T.M. Moloney. London M.A. 1957.
    Imperial defence, 1868-87: a study in decisive impulses 4754
behind the change from 'colonial' to 'imperial' defence. D.M.
Schurman. Cambridge Ph.D. 1955.
    The discussion of imperial affairs in the British   4755
parliament, 1868-80. P.J. Durrans. Oxford D.Phil. 1970.
    The influence of the treasury on the making of British 4756
colonial policy, 1868-80. Ann M. Burton. Oxford D.Phil.
1960.
    The influence of parliament upon the foreign policy of 4757
the Gladstone government, 1868-74. Sheila Lambert. London
M.A. 1949.
    British policy in West Africa, the Malay peninsula and 4758
the South Pacific during the colonial secretaryships of Lord
Kimberley and Lord Carnarvon, 1870 to 1876. W.D. McIntyre.
London Ph.D. 1959.
    A.J. Balfour and the evolution and problems of the   4759
British empire, 1874-1906. D.O'N. Judd. London Ph.D. 1967.
    John Morley and the empire before 1886. D.J.B.   4760
Trotter. Manchester M.A. 1967.
    British imperial policy, 1874-80. R.L. Kirkpatrick.   4761
Oxford D.Phil. 1953.
    Evelyn Baring's liberal policies in Egypt and India,   4762
1877-85. L.P. Burns. Cambridge Ph.D. 1967.
    British public opinion and the rise of imperialist   4763
sentiment in relation to expansion in Africa, 1880-1900.
Patricia F. Knight. Warwick Ph.D. 1969.
    The views on imperial affairs of Henry Labouchere and   4764
his activities in this connexion, 1880-6. R.J. Hind. London
Ph.D. (Ext.) 1967.
    Liberal imperialism, 1885-1906. R.W. Edwards. Wales   4765
M.A. 1957.
    Factors and variations in Liberal and radical opinion   4766
on foreign policy, 1885-99. R.H. Gross. Oxford D.Phil. 1950.
    Public opinion and the movement for disarmament, 1888- 4767
98. Merze Tate. Oxford B.Litt. 1935.
    The colonial and imperial conferences, 1887-1911: a   4768
study in imperial organisation and politics. J.E. Kendle.
London Ph.D. 1965.
    The invasion of the United Kingdom: public controversy 4769
and official planning, 1888-1918. H.R. Moon. London Ph.D.
1968.
    The internationalism in the work and thought of William 4770
Ewart Gladstone, with reference to present-day theory and
practice of internationalism. J.D. Evans. Wales M.A. 1938.
    The foreign policy of the Gladstone and Rosebery   4771
administrations, 1892-5. T.B. Miller. London Ph.D. 1954.
    The imperial idea in English fiction: a study in the   4772
literary expression of the idea, with special reference to
the works of Kipling, Conrad and Buchan. A.G. Sandison.
Cambridge Ph.D. 1963.
    The role of empire in English letters after Kipling.   4773
C. Conybeare. London M.Phil. 1968.
    British opinion on the development of the Commonwealth 4774
of Nations, 1895-1926. F.S. Morley. Edinburgh Ph.D. 1931/2.
    The Liberal party and foreign affairs, 1895-1905. T.   4775
Boyle. London M.Phil. 1969.
    Liberal imperialists, 1895-1905. H.C.G. Matthew. Ox- 4776
ford D.Phil. 1970.
    The Liberal party and South Africa 1895-1902. J.E.   4777
Butler. Oxford D.Phil. 1963.
    Radical and Labour attitudes to empire, 1896-1914.   4778
B.J. Porter. Cambridge Ph.D. 1967.
    Sir Wilfrid Laurier and the imperial problem, 1896-   4779
1906. J.A. Colvin. London Ph.D. 1955.

4780   The attitude and policy of the main sections of the
British labour movement to imperial issues, 1899-1924. I.
Henderson. Oxford B.Litt. 1965.
4781   The Boer War and the British working class, 1899-1902:
a study in working-class attitudes and reactions to imperialism. R.N. Price. Sussex D.Phil. 1968.
4782   The effects of the Boer War on British diplomatic relations, 1899 - April 1904. R. Hughes. Wales M.A. 1941.
4783   British foreign policy, 1899-1902. J.A.S. Grenville.
London Ph.D. 1954.
4784   A history of the Pan-African movement in Britain, 1900-
48. P.O. Esedebe. London Ph.D. 1968.
4785   Aspects of defence policy, 1900-14, with particular
reference to naval-military co-operation. J. Bertie. Manchester M.A. 1967.
4786   The end of isolation: British foreign policy, 1900-5.
G.W. Monger. Cambridge Ph.D. 1962.
4787   Youth and empire: a study of the propagation of imperialism to the young in Edwardian Britain. J.O. Springhall.
Sussex D.Phil. 1968.
4788   British policy towards American-Japanese relations,
1901-7. R.W. Davies. London M.Sc. 1958.
4789   The idea of economic imperialism, with special reference
to the life and works of E.D. Morel. R. Wuliger. London
Ph.D. 1953.
4790   British pacifism, 1906-16: a study in the ideology and
activities of the British peace movement during the early
years of the 20th century. H.S. Weinroth. Cambridge Ph.D.
1968.
4791   The elimination of war: an examination of the work of
Sir Norman Angell. R.J. Feilding. Sussex M.Phil. 1966/7.
4792   The elimination of war: a study of the writings of Sir
Norman Angell on international affairs from 1903 to 1939.
R. Goldstein. Wales M.A. 1966.
4793   The Dominions Department of the Colonial Office: origins
and early years, 1905-14. J.A. Cross. London Ph.D. (Ext.)
1965.
4794   The African policy of the Liberal government, 1905-9.
R. Hyam. Cambridge Ph.D. 1963.
4795   Opposition to Grey's foreign policy and its connection
with the demand for open diplomacy. E.C. Sterne. Leeds
M.A. 1957.
4796   Radical Liberal criticism of British foreign policy,
1906-14. A.J. Dorey. Oxford D.Phil. 1965.
4797   The Colonial Office and political problems in Ceylon
and Mauritius, 1907-21. L.B.L. Crook. London Ph.D. 1969.
4798   British defence strategy, 1906-14. D.W. Dawson. Manchester M.A. 1966.
4799   The formulation of a continental foreign policy by
Great Britain, 1908-12. M.L. Dockrill. London Ph.D. 1969.
4800   The formation of British Labour's foreign policy, 1914-
20. C.D. Armistead. St. Andrews M.Litt. 1970.
4801   Attitudes to the war and to the conduct of the war on
the western front, 1914-18. A.E. Brown. Wales M.A. 1967.
4802   Politicians at war, July 1914 to May 1915: a study, with
special reference to the emergence of David Lloyd George as
a war leader. G.C.L. Hazlehurst. Oxford D.Phil. 1969.
4803   The shell crisis of 1915. T. Holder. Liverpool M.A.
1967.
4804   The development of British war aims, August 1914 -
March 1915. M.G. Ekstein-Frankl. London Ph.D. 1969.
4805   The abolition of war: a study in the ideology and
organisation of the peace movement, 1914-19. K.G. Robbins.
Oxford D.Phil. 1965.
4806   A study of the ideology of pacifism and its background,
with special reference to Britain, 1915-45. D.A. Martin.
London Ph.D. 1964.

War aims, peace moves and strategy in British policy, 4807
1916-18. V.H. Rothwell. Leeds Ph.D. 1970.
Lord Robert Cecil and the League of Nations. P.S. 4808
Raffo. Liverpool Ph.D. 1967.
The Dominions and British foreign policy, 1919-23: a 4809
study in intergovernmental co-operation. M.D. Henderson.
London Ph.D. 1970.
Labour's foreign policy, 1919-24. T.Z. Winnicki. Cam- 4810
bridge M.Litt. 1950.
The theory and practice of internationalism in the 4811
British Labour party, with special reference to the inter-
war period. G.W. Shepherd. London Ph.D. 1952.
British public opinion and British naval policy, 1919- 4812
22. J.W. Sears. Oxford B.Litt. 1957.
Great Britain and the Locarno treaties (December 1924 - 4813
October 1925). C.E. Moreton. London M.Phil. 1969.
The foreign policy of the second Labour administration, 4814
1929-31, with special reference to disarmament, foreign trade
and the German situation. D. Carlton. London Ph.D. 1966.
British attitudes towards disarmament and rearmament, 4815
1932-5. J.P. Kyba. London Ph.D. 1967.
The influence of the Dominions on British foreign 4816
policy, 1933-9. K.H. Boothroyd. Sheffield M.A. 1966.
The Spanish Civil War and British opinion. K.W. Wat- 4817
kins. London Ph.D. 1961.
British left-wing attitudes to the Spanish Civil War. 4818
D.P.F. Lancien. Oxford B.Litt. 1965.
British policy in Europe from the Munich Agreement to 4819
the Polish Guarantee, 29 September 1938 to 31 March 1939.
R.J. Richards. Durham M.A. 1967.

Reform Movements and Labour Movement

The economic ideas of the urban industrial working 4820
class of England during the years 1800-50. W.H. Warburton.
Birmingham M.Com. 1939.
Economic conditions and working-class movements in the 4821
city of Bath, 1800-50. R.S. Neale. Bristol M.A. 1962.
The working-class movement in the Black Country, 1815- 4822
67. G.J. Barnsby. Birmingham M.A. 1965.
History of the labour movement in England, 1825-52: the 4823
problem of leadership and the articulation of demands. D.C.
Morris. London Ph.D. 1952.
London working-class movements, 1825-48. I.J. 4824
Prothero. Cambridge Ph.D. 1967.
London radicalism, 1829-41, with special reference to 4825
the relationship of its middle- and working-class components.
D.J. Rowe. Southampton Ph.D. 1965.
A study in London radicalism: the Democratic Associ- 4826
ation, 1837-41. Jennifer A. Bennett. Sussex M.A. 1967/8.
Some aspects of Sheffield radicalism. Mrs. Betty 4827
Culcheth. Durham M.A. 1960.
Joseph Parkes of Birmingham and the part which he 4828
played in radical reform movements from 1825 to 1845. Jessie
K. Buckley. London M.A. 1924.
The reform movement in Birmingham, 1830-48. H.G. 4829
Smith. London Ph.D. (Ext.) 1929.
English radicalism, 1832-52. S. Maccoby. London Ph.D. 4830
1934.
Welsh anti-slavery sentiments, 1795-1865: a survey of 4831
public opinion. G.E. Owen. Wales M.A. 1964.
Relations between British and American abolitionists 4832
from British emancipation to the American Civil War. D.M.
Turley. Cambridge Ph.D. 1970.
Some connections between British and American reform 4833
movements, 1830-60, with special reference to the anti-
slavery movement. L. Billington. Bristol M.Litt. 1966.

4834   Some American reformers and their influence on reform movements in Great Britain from 1830 to 1860. Gloria C. Taylor. Edinburgh Ph.D. 1960.

4835   Social aspects of the Chartist movement. H.J.R. Bennett. Birmingham M.A. 1927.

4836   Chartism and the churches, with special reference to Lancashire. N.J. McLellan. Edinburgh Ph.D. 1947.

4837   Chartism in Suffolk. H. Fearn. Sheffield M.A. 1952.

4838   The Chartist movement in Wales. Myfanwy Williams. Wales M.A. 1919.

4839   Chartism in Brighton. T.M. Kemnitz. Sussex D.Phil. 1969.

4840   The life of James Bronterre O'Brien. A. Plummer. Oxford B.Litt. 1928.

4841   George Julian Harney. A. Schoyen. London Ph.D. 1951.

4842   Feargus O'Connor, Irishman and Chartist: a study of his life and work. E.L.H. Glasgow. Manchester Ph.D. 1951.

4843   The teachings of Karl Marx: their influence on English labour organisations, 1850-1900. H. Morgans. Wales M.A. 1936.

4844   The Northern Reform Union, 1858-62. C. Muris. Durham M.A. 1953.

4845   George Howell and working-class politics, 1859-95. R.G.G. Wheeler. London M.Phil. 1969.

4846   The Reform League, from its origins to the passing into law of the Reform Act of 1867. A.D. Bell. Oxford D.Phil. 1961.

4847   The working classes, the Reform League and the reform movement in Lancashire and Yorkshire. M.R. Dunsmore. Sheffield M.A. 1961.

4848   The reform movement in Northumberland. Florence M. Iddon. Liverpool M.A. 1923.

4849   The activity and influence of the English positivists on labour movements, 1859-85. R.J. Harrison. Oxford D.Phil. 1955.

4850   George Odger and the English working-class movement, 1860-77. D.R. Moberg. London Ph.D. 1954.

4851   The women's suffrage movement in Britain, 1866-1914. Mrs. Constance M. Rover. London Ph.D. (Ext.) 1966.

4852   The politics of women's suffrage in Britain and the United States of America, 1906-20. D.R. Morgan. Cambridge Ph.D. 1967.

4853   The British labour movement, 1868-1906. B.J. Atkinson. Oxford D.Phil. 1970.

4854   The labour movement in Wigan, 1874-1967. D. Brown. Liverpool M.A. 1968/9.

4855   The movement for direct labour representation in Wales, 1893-1906. K.O. Fox. Wales M.A. 1965.

4856   The miners and politics in England and Wales, 1906-14. R.G. Gregory. Oxford D.Phil. 1963.

4857   The impact of the labour unrest, 1910-14, on the British labour movement. J.D. Fraser. Leicester Ph.D. 1968.

4858   The new liberalism in Great Britain and the United States - a study in reform thought, with special reference to the problem of industrial concentration. M.R. Wilson. Manchester M.A. 1967.

4859   The labour movement in Birmingham, 1927-45. R.P. Hastings. Birmingham M.A. 1959.

4860   Left-wing pressure groups in the British labour movement, 1930-40: some aspects of the relations between the Labour Left and the official leadership, with special reference to the experience of the I.L.P. and the Socialist League. S. Hornby. Liverpool M.A. 1965/6.

4861   The Left in Britain, 1931-41. J. Jupp. London M.Sc. 1956.

ARMY, NAVY AND AIR FORCE

The development of English admiralty jurisdiction and 4862 practice since 1800. F.L. Wiswall. Cambridge Ph.D. 1967.

The army 1815-54 as an institution: to be considered as 4863 regards the administration, organisation, composition, and its relations to the political and social conditions of the country. M.F. Cunliffe. Oxford B.Litt. 1947.

Development of British naval gunnery, 1815-53. D.F. 4864 MacMillan. London Ph.D. 1967.

The introduction of the screw propellor into the navy, 4865 1830-60. W.M. Petty. London M.Phil. 1969.

A history of the royal dockyard schools, with parti- 4866 cular reference to the Portsmouth school. D.R. Jack. London M.A. (Ext.) 1969.

Manning the Royal Navy: the reform of the recruiting 4867 system, 1847-61. R. Taylor. London M.A. 1954.

The history of the introduction of the percussion 4868 breech-loading rifle into British military service, 1850-70. C.H. Roads. Cambridge Ph.D. 1961.

The army and public opinion from 1854 to the end of 4869 1873. H.S. Wilson. Oxford B.Litt. 1955.

The naval defence of British sea-borne trade, 1860- 4870 1905. B.McL. Ranft. Oxford D.Phil. 1967.

The emergence of the modern British capital ship, 4871 1863-70. S.L. Sandler. London Ph.D. 1965.

The introduction and operation of short service and 4872 localisation in the British army, 1868-92. B.J. Bond. London M.A. 1962.

The effect and impact of the administrative reform 4873 movement upon the army in the mid Victorian period. J. Wheaton. Manchester Ph.D. 1968.

Edward Cardwell's abolition of the purchase system in 4874 the British army, 1868-74: a study in the administrative and legislative processes. N.H. Moses. London Ph.D. 1969.

The origin and development of the British and Imperial 4875 General Staffs to 1916. J. Gooch. London Ph.D. 1970.

The origins and recruitment of the British army élite, 4876 1870-1959. C.B. Otley. Hull Ph.D. 1965.

The Barracks Act of 1890: its motives and consequences, 4877 with special reference to Shorncliffe camp. R. Brook. Wales M.A. 1962.

The development of the British army, 1899-1914. J.K. 4878 Dunlop. London Ph.D. 1936.

The military departments and the Committee of Imperial 4879 Defence, 1902-14: a study in the structural problems of defence organisation. N.J. d'Ombrain. Oxford D.Phil. 1969.

The labour movement in Great Britain and compulsory 4880 military service, 1914-16. M.I. Thomis. London M.A. 1959.

The development of official treatment of conscientious 4881 objectors to military service, 1916-45. J.M. Rae. London Ph.D. 1965.

History of the development of the doctrine of strategic 4882 bombing, 1914-26. R.A. Leonard. London M.Phil. 1969.

The theory of strategic air power in the Royal Air 4883 Force, 1918-39: concepts and capabilities. N.H. Jones. London M.A. (Ext.) 1968.

The R.F.C. and R.A.F. in Macedonia: 1916-18. T.S.D. 4884 Neilon. Glasgow B.Litt. 1969.

ECONOMIC AND SOCIAL HISTORY

Finance

Capital investment in north-eastern England, 1800- 4885 1913. A.G. Kenwood. London Ph.D. 1962.

4886   The growth of government expenditure in the United
Kingdom in the 19th century. J. Veverka. Edinburgh Ph.D.
1961/2.
4887   The origins and early history of savings banks in Great
Britain. S.M. Procter. Liverpool M.A. 1929.
4888   Fiscal policy and the silk industry, 1800-50. Z. Majid-
Hamid. Leicester M.A. 1967.
4889   The history of the public debts of the United Kingdom
from 1815 to 1939, and the economic doctrine relating there-
to. R.O. Roberts. Wales M.A. 1942.
4890   Wales and the corn laws, 1815-46. T.H. Williams. Wales
M.A. 1952.
4891   Opinion on the operation of the bank rate, 1822-60.
A.B. Cramp. London Ph.D. 1960.
4892   The rise and growth of English joint stock banking.
S.E. Thomas. London Ph.D. (Ext.) 1934.
4893   British sugar taxation since the Napoleonic Wars. J.L.
Mackie. London Ph.D. 1939.
4894   Some theoretical views on bank note circulation in England between 1827 and 1913. E.L.X. Coppieters. London
M.Sc. 1953.
4895   Ebenezer Elliott: a study, including an edition of his
works. E.R. Seary. Sheffield Ph.D. 1933.
4896   The history of slave compensation, 1833-45. R.E.P.
Wastell. London M.A. 1933.
4897   Manchester and the Manchester school, 1830-57. J.A.
Williams. Leeds M.A. 1966.
4898   The activities and organisation of the Anti-Corn-Law
League, 1838-46. N. McCord. Cambridge Ph.D. 1956.
4899   The free traders, 1840-6. Sarah J. Caldwell. Leeds
M.A. 1911.
4900   Sir Robert Peel and the free trade movement in the first
half of the 19th century, especially during the years 1842-7.
W.W. Rollinson. Birmingham M.A. 1930.
4901   The history of the Imperial Continental Gas Association,
1824-1900: a study in British economic enterprise on the
continent of Europe in the 19th century. N.K. Hill. London
Ph.D. 1951.
4902   The development of banking in the south-western counties
in the 19th century, with particular reference to Devon and
Cornwall in the period 1840-90. N.L. Armstrong. London
Ph.D. (Ext.) 1937.
4903   Mr. Gladstone's fiscal and financial policy, 1841-5.
F.E. Hyde. London Ph.D. 1931.
4904   Lord Derby and the Protectionist party, 1845-52. R.M.
Stewart. Oxford D.Phil. 1967.
4905   Trends in business organisation in Great Britain since
1856, with special reference to the financial structure of
companies, the mechanism of investment, and the relations
between the shareholder and the company. J.B. Jefferys.
London Ph.D. 1938.
4906   Auditors in Britain: patterns of role continuity and
change: a study in economic and accounting history. N.
Aranya. London Ph.D. 1970.
4907   A study of the British economy in the crisis of 1857.
J.R.T. Hughes. Oxford D.Phil. 1955.
4908   Joint stock company failures, 1862-1914. G.F. Todd.
Oxford B.Litt. 1932.
4909   Investment trusts and investment companies in the United
States and Great Britain since 1868. S.L. Baskin. London
Ph.D. 1966.
4910   Joint stock companies in Great Britain, 1890-1930. A.
Essex-Crosby. London M.Com. 1937.
4911   The role of the state in British economics from 1870 to
1914. D.E. Bland. Durham M.Litt. 1968.
4912   Home and foreign investment in Great Britain, 1870-1913.
A.K. Cairncross. Cambridge Ph.D. 1935/6.

Home and foreign investment: some aspects of capital   4913
formation, finance and income in the United Kingdom, 1870-
1913. C.H. Feinstein. Cambridge Ph.D. 1959.
British overseas investment in iron ore mining, 1870-   4914
1914. M.W. Flinn. Manchester M.A. 1952.
British investment in overseas mining, 1880-1914. J.W. 4915
McCarty. Cambridge Ph.D. 1961.
Sir Stafford Northcote's Sinking Fund and the re-   4916
demption of debt between 1874 and 1914. P.C. Gordon Walker.
Oxford B.Litt. 1930.
Aspects of taxation and expenditure in the United King- 4917
dom, 1890-1914, with special reference to the growth of the
social services. E.M. Bowen. Wales M.A. 1934.
Tariff reform and the Conservative party, 1895-1906.   4918
B.H.P. Turner. London Ph.D. 1967.
The origins of the tariff reform movement. B.H. Smith. 4919
Birmingham M.A. 1938.
The tariff reform movement, 1903-14. Mrs. Jean Wright. 4920
Oxford B.Litt. 1960.
The Unionist free traders, 1903-10. R.A. Rempel. Ox-   4921
ford D.Phil. 1967.
Fluctuations in new capital issues on the London money 4922
market, 1899 to 1913. G.L. Ayres. London M.Sc. 1934.
The British income tax since 1900. A.H.F. Dolley.   4923
Oxford B.Litt. 1929.
British overseas investment in the British empire,   4924
1900-39. H.W. Richardson. Manchester M.A. 1961.
British capital export, 1900-13. J.H.A.M. Lenfant.   4925
London Ph.D. 1949.
The technique of government borrowing - a study of the 4926
methods employed by the British treasury in its borrowing
operations, 1914-39. Y.-C. Ma. London Ph.D. 1942.
British financial policy and the trade cycle, 1918-39. 4927
G.D. Garton. Liverpool M.A. 1951/2.
British overseas investment, 1918-31. J.M. Atkin.   4928
London Ph.D. 1968.
Birmingham public opinion in relation to the economic 4929
development of the count y, and the achievement of the
policies of protection and imperial preference in the period
1919-32. J.R.S. Marsh. Birmingham M.A. 1961.
Some aspects of British international monetary policy, 4930
1924-31. D.E. Moggridge. Cambridge Ph.D. 1970.
Studies in the abolition of economic controls in Great 4931
Britain after the two world wars. D.H. Aldcroft. Manchester
Ph.D. 1962.

Industry and Employment

General

The development of the industrial landscape of western 4932
South Wales during the 19th and 20th centuries. H.W.E.
Davies. London M.Sc. 1955.
Economic development of Lonsdale in the 19th century.   4933
D.M. Clark. Liverpool M.A. 1968.
An economic geography of Montgomeryshire in the 19th   4934
century. J.M. Powell. Liverpool M.A. 1962.
The industrial history of Flintshire in the 19th cent- 4935
ury. P.T. Williams. Liverpool M.A. 1933.
The industrialisation of Flintshire in the 19th cent-   4936
ury, being an examination of the changes and developments in
the principal industries from 1815 to 1914. C.R. Williams.
Wales M.A. 1950.
Historical geography of manufacturing industry in the   4937
south-east of England in the 19th century. A.H. Shorter.
Manchester M.A. 1948.

187

4938   The organisation of industrial employment in England in the early 19th century. Marie Jones. Manchester M.A. 1933.

4939   The factory system and the Factory Acts, 1802-50. Gertrude Baylis. Birmingham M.A. 1930.

4940   Unemployment in British industries, 1815-50. A.D. Gayer. Oxford D.Phil. 1930/1.

4941   The life and times of Thomas Attwood. K.E. Richardson. Nottingham Ph.D. 1965.

4942   Co-operation and the Owenite-Socialist communities in Britain, 1825-45. R.G. Garnett. London Ph.D. (Ext.) 1970.

4943   The factory controversy, 1830-53. Mrs. Ann P.W. Robson. London Ph.D. 1958.

4944   The factory movement, c.1830-1850. J.T. Ward. Cambridge Ph.D. 1957.

4945   The development of factory legislation from 1833 to 1847: a study of legislative and administrative evolution. M.W. Thomas. London Ph.D. 1948.

4946   The attitude of the Tory party to labour questions, 1832-46. R.L. Hill. Oxford B.Litt. 1928.

4947   The movements for shorter hours, 1840 to 1875. J.S. Hodgson. Oxford D.Phil. 1940.

4948   Industrial organisation in Leicester, 1844-1914: a study in changing technology, innovation and conditions of employment. P. Head. Leicester Ph.D. 1960.

4949   The location of industry in metropolitan Essex. May Greenfield. London M.A. 1950.

4950   The location of industry in London, 1851-1939. P.G. Hall. Cambridge Ph.D. 1959.

4951   The location of industry in inner north-east London: a study in industrial geography. J.E. Martin. London Ph.D. 1961.

4952   Industry in south-east London (Bermondsey and Southwark). M.D. Avery. London M.A. 1963.

4953   A geographical analysis of the growth of industrial activity in the north-west London area. Mildred Gascoigne. Durham M.A. 1936.

4954   The employment of married women in England, 1850-1950. Mrs. Leonore Lockwood. London M.A. 1956.

4955   The employment of women in Great Britain, 1891-1921. Mrs. Sallie Hogg. Oxford D.Phil. 1968.

4956   The industrial development of Birmingham and the Black Country, 1860-1914. G.C. Allen. Birmingham Ph.D. 1928.

4957   The development of consumers' co-operation in the north-east coast area. N.S. Ross. Durham Ph.D. 1939.

4958   Some social consequences of the casual labour problem in London, 1860-90, with particular reference to the East End. G. Stedman Jones. Oxford D.Phil. 1970.

4959   The course of public opinion and legal decision, including legislation relating to economic combination and monopoly mainly in Great Britain, in the period 1880-1914. Leonora D.F. Peck. Wales M.A. 1929.

4960   Factory legislation and its administration, 1891-1924. H.A. Mess. London Ph.D. 1926.

4961   Trends in capital, employment and output in the British manufacturing industry, 1900-62. I. Aristidou. London Ph.D. 1966.

4962   Industrial change and its effects upon labour, 1900-14. A.L. Levine. London Ph.D. 1954.

4963   Labour and unemployment, 1900-14. K.D. Brown. Kent Ph.D. 1969.

4964   The growth of manufacturing in the Brighton conurbation, 1901-63. B. Thompson. Sussex M.Phil. 1966/7.

4965   Public ownership in Great Britain: a study in the origin and development of socialist ideas concerning the control and administration of publicly owned industries and services. G.N. Ostergaard. Oxford D.Phil. 1953.

New growth industries in an era of stagnation and de-   4966
pression, 1919-39. J. Harrop. Liverpool M.A. 1966.
The problem of unemployment in the United Kingdom,   4967
1919-29. K.J. Hancock. London Ph.D. 1959.
The social and economic effects of unemployment in   4968
Manchester, 1919-26. F.J. Rosamond. Manchester M.A. 1970.
The social and economic effects of unemployment in the 4969
coal and steel industries of Sheffield between 1925 and 1935.
B.J. Elliott. Sheffield M.A. 1969.
Changes in the economic geography of the vale of Glou-   4970
cester since the First World War. K.J. Noyes. Manchester
M.A. 1958.
Changes in the industrial geography of west Cumberland, 4971
1928-57. Mary R. Hall. Manchester M.A. 1962.

Industrial Relations

The history of trade unions in the Yorkshire woollen   4972
and worsted industries during the 19th and 20th centuries.
J.F. Weatherhead. Oxford B.Litt. 1924.
The progress of labour organisation in the pottery   4973
industry of Great Britain. W.H. Warburton. Oxford B.Litt.
1928.
A history of trade unionism in Leicester to the end of 4974
the 19th century. J. Walton. Sheffield M.A. 1952.
The history of the miner's bond in Northumberland and   4975
Durham: with special reference to its influence on industrial
disputes. H. Scott. Manchester M.A. 1946.
The general strike during 100 years. A. Plummer. Lon- 4976
don M.Sc. 1927.
English trade unions and the problem of emigration,   4977
1840-80. R.V. Clements. Oxford B.Litt. 1954.
Trade unions and public opinion, 1850-75. R.A.   4978
Buchanan. Cambridge Ph.D. 1957.
A history of trade unionism in the provincial printing 4979
industry during the 19th century. A.E. Musson. Manchester
M.A. 1950.
History of industrial relations in the British printing 4980
industry. J. Child. Oxford D.Phil. 1953.
A hundred years of progress: the record of the Scottish 4981
Typographical Association, 1853-1952. Sarah C. Gillespie.
Glasgow Ph.D. 1954.
Social and economic aspects of combination in the   4982
printing trade before 1875. J.H. Richards. Liverpool M.A.
1957.
The antecedents and beginnings of the Amalgamated   4983
Society of Engineers. T.H. Robinson. Oxford B.Litt. 1928.
Labour relationships in engineering and shipbuilding   4984
on the north-east coast in the second half of the 19th cent-
ury. J.F. Clarke. Newcastle M.A. 1966.
Labour in the merchant service, 1850-1920. A. McGeogh. 4985
Birmingham M.Com. 1921.
British commercial travellers and their organisations,   4986
1850-1914. B.J. Avari. Manchester M.A. 1970.
Trades councils in England and Scotland, 1858-97. W.H. 4987
Fraser. Sussex D.Phil. 1968.
Industrial conciliation and arbitration, 1860-1914.   4988
J.H. Porter. Leeds Ph.D. 1968.
Labour organisation of miners of south Yorkshire from 4989
1858 to 1914. F. Machin. Oxford B.Litt. 1930.
Industrial relations in Birmingham and the Black Coun- 4990
try, 1860-1914. A. Fox. Oxford B.Litt. 1952.
Wages and labour organisation in the brass trades of   4991
Birmingham and district. T.H. Kelly. Birmingham Ph.D. 1930.
Railway labour, 1830-70. P.W. Kingsford. London Ph.D. 4992
1951.

4993   Development of labour relations in the British railways since 1860. G.C. Halverson. London Ph.D. 1952.

4994   The history of the Amalgamated Society of Railway Servants, 1871-1913. P.S. Gupta. Oxford D.Phil. 1960.

4995   Labour relations in the baking industry in England and Wales since 1860, with special reference to the impact of technical and economic change on union administration and bargaining procedure. R.F. Banks. London Ph.D. 1965.

4996   Agricultural labourers' trade unionism in four midland counties, 1860-1900. P.L.R. Horn. Leicester Ph.D. 1968.

4997   Bradford women in organisation, 1867-1914. Mrs. J.C. Scott. Bradford M.A. 1970.

4998   The growth of trade unionism in England from 1867 to 1906 in its political aspects. A.E.P. Duffy. London Ph.D. (Ext.) 1956.

4999   Aspects of trade union interest in judicial reform, 1867-82. D.C. Stainton. Southampton M.Phil. 1968.

5000   The National Union of Teachers: a study of the political process within an association of professional workers. W. Roy. London Ph.D. 1963.

5001   The status, functions and policy of the trade union official, 1870-1930. P.J. Head. Cambridge M.Litt. 1956.

5002   Trade unionism in the Port of London, 1870-1914. J.C. Lovell. London Ph.D. 1966.

5003   The origins and development of new unionism, 1870-1910. E.L. Taplin. Liverpool M.A. 1966/7.

5004   The labour movement in Hull, 1870-1900, with special references to new unionism. R. Brown. Hull M.Sc. 1966.

5005   A history of the trade disputes and the formation and operation of the several sliding scale agreements in the South Wales coal trade, 1870-1903, with special reference to the work of Sir William Thomas Lewis, 1st Baron Merthyr of Senghenydd. B. Evans. Wales M.A. 1944.

5006   A study of industrial relations in the British tinplate industry, 1874-1939. E.H. Jones. Wales M.A. 1941.

5007   The life and work of William John Parry, Bethesda, with particular reference to his trade union activities among the slate quarrymen of North Wales. J.R. Williams. Wales M.A. 1953.

5008   The Liverpool Trades Council and politics, 1878-1918. S. Maddock. Liverpool M.A. 1958/9.

5009   The history of the Manchester and Salford Trades Council. L. Bather. Manchester Ph.D. 1956.

5010   The development of industrial relations in the Nottinghamshire coalfield. A.R. Griffin. Nottingham Ph.D. 1963.

5011   Trade unionism in the coal industry until 1900, with particular reference to Lancashire. R.C. Challinor. Lancaster Ph.D. 1970.

5012   A history of industrial relations in the South Wales coal industry to 1912. E.W. Evans. Wales Ph.D. 1955.

5013   The political, social and economic factors influencing the growth of trade unionism among the Derbyshire coal miners, 1880-1944. J.E. Williams. Sheffield Ph.D. 1959.

5014   Industrial relations and the social structure: a case study of the Bolton cotton-mule spinners, 1880-1910. E. Thorpe. Salford M.Sc. 1969/70.

5015   Unskilled labour unions in South Wales, 1889-1914. P.W. Donovan. London M.Phil. 1969.

5016   A study of the development of labour relations in the British furniture trade. N. Robertson. Oxford B.Litt. 1955.

5017   The National Union of Agricultural Workers. M. Madden. Oxford B.Litt. 1957.

5018   British newspaper journalism, 1900-56: a study in industrial relations. H.C. Strick. London Ph.D. 1957.

5019   The Electrical Trades Union and the growth of the electrical industry to 1926. D.R. Lewis. Oxford D.Phil. 1970.

The National Transport Workers' Federation, 1910-27.   5020
G.A. Phillips. Oxford D.Phil. 1969.
The Workers' Union, 1898-1929. R. Hyman. Oxford   5021
D.Phil. 1968.
Methodism and syndicalism in the Rhondda valley, 1906   5022
to 1926. C.E. Gwyther. Sheffield Ph.D. 1967.
Syndicalism and industrial unionism in England until   5023
1918. E.L. Burdick. Oxford D.Phil. 1950.
The demand for 'Workers' Control' in the coal mining,   5024
engineering and railway industries, 1910-22. B. Pribićević.
Oxford D.Phil. 1957.
Rank-and-file movements amongst the miners of South   5025
Wales, 1910-26. M.G. Woodhouse. Oxford D.Phil. 1970.
Rank and file militancy in the British engineering   5026
industry, 1914-18. J.S. Hinton. London Ph.D. 1969.
National consultation and co-operation between trade   5027
unionists and employers in Britain, 1911-39. R.F. Charles.
Oxford D.Phil. 1970.
The National Minority movement: a study in the organis- 5028
ation of trade union militancy in the inter-war period. R.
Martin. Oxford D.Phil. 1965.
The Durham Miners' Association, 1919-47. W.R. Garside. 5029
Leeds Ph.D. 1969.
A.J. Cook: miners' leader in the General Strike. W.G.   5030
Quine. Manchester M.A. 1964.
The miners' unions of Northumberland and Durham, 1918- 5031
31, with special reference to the General Strike of 1926. A.
Mason. Hull Ph.D. 1968.
The relations between government and the trade unions   5032
in the General Strike of May 1926. L.D. Thomson. London
Ph.D. 1952.
Labour relations in the South Wales coal mining indus-   5033
try, 1926-39. W.J. Anthony-Jones. Wales Ph.D. 1959.

Specific Industries

The Forest of Dean and Bristol-Somerset coalfields: a   5034
comparative study in industrial geography during the 19th and
20th centuries. J.F. Davis. London Ph.D. 1959.
Development and location of the clay brickmaking   5035
industry in the south-east Midlands of England since 1800.
L.J. Collier. London Ph.D. 1966.
The location and development of London's leather manu-   5036
facturing industry since the early 19th century. J. Statham.
London M.A. 1965.
The Northampton boot and shoe industry and its signi-   5037
ficance for social change in the borough from 1800 to 1914.
W.C. Griffin. Wales M.A. 1968.
Shoemakers of Somerset: a history of C. & J. Clark,   5038
1833-1903. G.B. Sutton. Nottingham M.A. 1959.
An historical geography of the Cotswold woollen indus-   5039
try in the 19th and early 20th centuries. Irene Ellis.
Wales M.A. 1946.
The credit structure of the West Riding wool textile   5040
industry in the 19th century. A.J. Topham. Leeds M.A. 1955.
Dewsbury Mills: a history of Messrs. Wormalds and   5041
Walker Ltd., blanket manufacturers of Dewsbury, with an econ-
omic survey of the Yorkshire woollen cloth industry in the
19th century. F.J. Glover. Leeds Ph.D. 1959.
A history of Messrs. John Foster & Son, Ltd., 1819-91. 5042
(With an outline history of the worsted industry during the
19th century.) E.M. Sigsworth. Leeds Ph.D. 1954.
The Yorkshire woollen and worsted industries, 1800-50. 5043
R.M. Hartwell. Oxford D.Phil. 1955.
Growth, decline and locational change in the English   5044
silk industry of the 19th century: a study in historical geography. P.D. Wilde. Keele Ph.D. 1970.

5045   A history of the slate quarrymen in Caernarvonshire in the 19th century. Gweirydd Ellis. Wales M.A. 1931.

5046   The historical geography of the copper mining industry in Devon and Cornwall from 1800 to 1900. J.C. Goodridge. London Ph.D. (Ext.) 1967.

5047   The silversmithing trade in London and the provinces in the first half of the 19th century. Shirley Bury. Reading M.A. 1959/60.

5048   Industrial and social conditions in the Wrexham coal-field (1800-60). D.T. Morgan. Liverpool M.A. 1927.

5049   The pitmen of Tyneside and Weardale: conditions of their life and work in the first half of the 19th century: with some reference to the keelmen and sailors engaged in the coal trade. Bessie B.F. Allan. Liverpool M.A. 1920.

5050   Hours of work in the coal-mining industry of Great Britain since the early part of the 19th century, with special reference to Northumberland and Durham and with an account of certain movements connected therewith. N.H. Booth. Oxford B.Litt. 1930.

5051   The history of the development of the steam engine to the year 1850, with special reference to the work of west-country engineers. W.R.M. Caff. London M.Sc. (Ext.) 1937.

5052   The development and organisation of the British iron industry, 1815-67. A. Birch. Manchester M.A. 1951.

5053   The career of Richard Smith (1783-1868), manager of Lord Dudley's mines and ironworks. R.P. Fereday. Keele M.A. 1966.

5054   The Birmingham steel pen trade. F.L. Timings. Birmingham M.Com. 1926.

5055   William Felkin, 1795-1874. S.D. Chapman. Nottingham M.A. 1960.

5056   The development of the London brewing industry, 1830-1914, with special reference to Whitbread and Company. Diana M. Knox. Oxford B.Litt. 1956.

5057   The rise of the British rubber industry. W. Woodruff. Nottingham Ph.D. 1953.

5058   Regional functions of the mineral transport system in the South Wales coalfield, 1830-1951. E. Brooks. Cambridge Ph.D. 1958.

5059   Changes in the location of the British glass industry since about 1833. C.M. Brown. London Ph.D. 1970.

5060   The telegraph industry, 1837-90. J.L. Kieve. London M.Phil. 1970.

5061   The Ashworth cotton factories and the life of Henry Ashworth, 1794-1880. R. Boyson. London Ph.D. 1967.

5062   The history of John Bowes and Partners up to 1914. O.E. Mountford. Durham M.A. 1967.

5063   Legislation relating to mining in the 19th century (1840-67). A.T. Flight. London Ph.D. 1937.

5064   An examination of education and training in the coal-mining industry from 1840 to 1947, with special reference to the work and influence of the mines inspectorate. R.H.B. Calvert. Nottingham M.Phil. 1970.

5065   Her Majesty's inspectors of mines, 1843-62. A.J. Cassell. Southampton M.Sc. 1962.

5066   History of tinplate manufacture in Llanelly. H. Hancocks. Wales M.A. 1965.

5067   The history of the catering industry, with special reference to the development of J. Lyons & Co. Ltd. to 1939. D.J. Richardson. Kent Ph.D. 1970.

5068   The metal-working machine tool industry in England, 1850-1914, with special reference to Greenwood and Batley Ltd. R.C. Floud. Oxford D.Phil. 1970.

5069   The London letterpress printing industry, 1850-1941. B.W.E. Alford. London Ph.D. 1962.

5070   The English cotton industry, 1850-96. D.A. Farnie. Manchester M.A. 1953.

The house of Spencer, 1853-91: a study in business   5071
history. P.L. Payne. Nottingham Ph.D. 1954.
The Sun Mill Co. Ltd.: a study in democratic invest-   5072
ment, 1858-1959. R.E. Tyson. Manchester M.A. 1962.
A geography of the paper-making industry in England and 5073
Wales from 1860. P.W. Lewis. Hull Ph.D. 1968.
The Lancashire cotton famine, 1861-4. W.O. Henderson.   5074
London Ph.D. 1932.
A study of the location and migration of the furniture   5075
industry in metropolitan England. J.L. Oliver. London Ph.D.
1963.
The development of the engineering industries, with   5076
special reference to machinery production since 1870. J.M.
Jackson. Manchester Ph.D. 1953.
The development and location of the specialist agri-   5077
cultural engineering industry, with special reference to East
Anglia. C.J. Lines. London M.Sc. 1961.
The economic history of British shipbuilding, 1870-   5078
1914. S. Pollard. London Ph.D. 1951.
The economic development of the inland coal-fields,   5079
1870-1914. B.R. Mitchell. Cambridge Ph.D. 1955.
The heavy iron and steel industry in South Wales and   5080
Monmouthshire, 1870-1950. J.P. Addis. Wales Ph.D. 1957.
The Monmouthshire and South Wales Coal Owners' Associ-   5081
ation, 1873-1914. L.J. Williams. Wales M.A. 1957.
The effect of the growth of an industrial concern   5082
(Brunner, Mond & Co.) on local politics and affairs in the
Weaver valley, 1873-98. Hilda M. Rooke. Manchester M.A. 1965.
A history of the Lancashire cotton industry between the   5083
years 1875 and 1896. R. Smith. Birmingham Ph.D. 1954.
The location of the British car industry, 1888-1940.   5084
D.R. Littlewood. Leicester M.A. 1962.
Rolls Royce: the growth of a firm. I.S. Lloyd. Cam-   5085
bridge M.Sc. 1951.
Some aspects of the British motor manufacturing indus-   5086
try during the years 1919-30. A. Holme. Sheffield M.A.
1964.
The economic geography of the development and present   5087
position of Lowestoft as a port and holiday resort. A.H.
Woolner. London M.Sc. (Ext.) 1956.
The development of settlement on the Isle of Thanet in   5088
its geographical setting, with special reference to the
growth of the holiday industry. W.T.W. Morgan. London M.Sc.
1950.
The seaside resort towns of England and Wales. J.A.   5089
Barrett. London Ph.D. 1958.
The Lincolnshire coast holiday region. R.E. Pearson.   5090
Nottingham M.A. 1965.
The history and development of the iron and steel   5091
welded tube trade, with particular reference to the rise and
eventual decline of the trade in the town of Wednesbury,
Staffordshire. S.J. Langley. Birmingham M.Com. 1948.
The British electrical industry, 1875-1914. I.C.R.   5092
Byatt. Oxford D.Phil. 1962.
'The technological challenge': some aspects of the   5093
early development of the electrical lighting industry, with
special reference to England and the U.S.A., 1882-1919. J.P.
Brown. Sheffield M.A. 1964.
The development of the electricity supply industry in   5094
Great Britain. S. Judek. Edinburgh Ph.D. 1946/7.
The growth and progress of electrical manufacturing   5095
industry in Great Britain. Elsie Yates. Manchester M.A.
1936.
The development and organisation of the artificial silk 5096
industry in Great Britain. E. Jones. Wales M.A. 1940.
Mechanisation in British and American bituminous coal   5097
mines, 1890-1939. C.A. Paull. London M.Phil. 1968.

5098   The cotton spinning industry in the Oldham district, 1896-1914. F. Jones. Manchester M.A. 1959.
5099   The tobacco manufacturing industry of Great Britain in the 20th century. W.C. Woolley. Wales M.A. 1953.
5100   The sugar beet and sugar refining industry in the United Kingdom, 1900-52. E.D. Altschuler. Manchester M.A. 1953.
5101   The development and location of the aluminium industry in the United Kingdom. T.G.L. Hopkins. Oxford B.Litt. 1958.
5102   An economic history of the British aircraft industry, 1908-48. R.F. Ryder. Southampton M.Sc. 1957/8.
5103   Developments in the British film industry before 1918. Rachel Low. London Ph.D. 1951.
5104   The positions of the skilled and less skilled workman in the engineering and building trades (1914-25). J.R. Hicks. Oxford B.Litt. 1927.
5105   The South Wales coalfield during government control, 1914-21. J. Thomas. Wales M.A. 1925.
5106   The development of the road (motor) haulage industry in Great Britain, with special reference to the years 1918-46. S.M.B. Green. Oxford B.Litt. 1948.
5107   The development of the South Wales tinplate industry, with special reference to 1919-39. E.E. Watkin. Wales M.A. 1949.
5108   The British shipbuilding industry, with special reference to the period 1919-39. L. Jones. Wales M.A. 1952.
5109   The British iron and steel trades since 1920. E. Davies. Wales M.A. 1937.
5110   The United Kingdom meat market, 1920-59. R.H. Tuckwell. Cambridge M.Sc. 1963/4.

    Trade

5111   English foreign trade in the first half of the 19th century, together with some observations on the war period of 1793-1814. J.S. Jones. London M.Sc. 1928.
5112   Retail trade in Great Britain, 1800-50. D.G. Alexander. London Ph.D. 1967.
5113   The function of the merchant in specific Liverpool import trades, 1820-50. D.M. Williams. Liverpool M.A. 1964.
5114   The policy of the Board of Trade in relation to British tariffs and foreign trade, 1830-42. Lucy M. Brown. London Ph.D. 1955.
5115   Business in two continents, 1845-73. [Rathbones of Liverpool in America and Asia.] Sheila Marriner. Liverpool Ph.D. 1957/8.
5116   The influence of the coal trade upon the development of the mercantile marine and the foreign trade of Great Britain during the second half of the 19th century. E. Pritchard. Oxford B.Litt. 1924.
5117   Changes in the pattern of the British export trade (with special reference to the continent) between 1851 and 1873. Jean Cheetham. Manchester M.A. 1955.
5118   British trade fluctuations, 1868-86: a chronicle and a commentary. W.W. Rostow. Oxford B.Litt. 1938.
5119   The development of the overseas trade of the British empire, with particular reference to the period 1870-1939. K. Evans. Manchester M.A. 1956.
5120   British overseas trade, 1870-1914. S.B. Saul. Birmingham Ph.D. 1953.
5121   The British economy and the trade cycle, 1886-96. W.A. Sinclair. Oxford D.Phil. 1958.
5122   The geographical basis, character and organisation of the import trade of London from the East Indies, with special reference to the 20th century. L. Brettle. Oxford B.Litt. 1930.

The dock companies in London, 1796-1864: a history of   5123
the agitation for, and provision of, wet docks in the Port of
London. R.A.H. Page. Sheffield M.A. 1959.

A study of the function of Ipswich as a centre in East   5124
Anglia and its development as a port since 1805. A.J. Starr.
London M.Sc. 1939.

The major provincial seaports of England, 1800-50, ex-   5125
cluding their coastwise trade. D.F. King. Manchester M.A.
1959.

History of the port of Cardiff in relation to its   5126
hinterland with special reference to the years 1830-1914.
T.M. Hodges. London M.Sc. (Ext.) 1946.

A geographical study of the trade of the Dorset ports,   5127
1815-1914. P.J. Perry. Cambridge Ph.D. 1963.

The Holyhead road, 1810-42: a study in highway admin-   5128
istration. M. Hughes. Wales M.A. 1963.

The development of road transport in Cumberland, West-   5129
morland and the Furness district of Lancashire, 1800-85.
L.A. Williams. Leicester Ph.D. 1967.

British railway management in the 19th century, with   5130
special reference to the career of Captain Mark Huish (1808-
67). T.R. Gourvish. London Ph.D. 1967.

The origins and development of four constituent lines   5131
of the North-Eastern Railway, 1824-54. D. Brooke. Hull M.A.
1961.

The history of the Barry Dock and Railways Company in   5132
relation to the development of the South Wales coalfield.
L.N.A. Davies. Wales M.A. 1938.

A railway geography of the east Midlands, 1830-1905.   5133
N. Cossons. Liverpool M.A. 1969.

The railway as a factor in the location of manufactur-   5134
ing industry in the east Midlands. G.E. Bell. Nottingham
Ph.D. 1958.

A study of the transport facilities of the Nottingham-   5135
shire-Derbyshire coalfield. S.R. Shaw. London M.A. (Ext.)
1956.

Port developments and commerce of Newport, Monmouth-   5136
shire, 1835-1935. Edith M.E. Davies. Wales M.A. 1938.

Geographical aspects of the railway industry. B.J.   5137
Turton. Nottingham Ph.D. 1960.

The evolution of the railway network of south-east   5138
England. E.A. Course. London Ph.D. 1958.

The growth of south-east London, 1836-1914, with   5139
special reference to the development of communications.
Mrs. Eileen M. Rolfe, née Pierce. London Ph.D. 1968.

A century's extension of passenger transport facilities 5140
(1830-1930), within the present London Transport Board's area
and its relation to population spread. Minnie L. Moore.
London Ph.D. 1948.

The historical geography of the Newcastle and Carlisle   5141
railway system up to 1914. G. Whittle. Belfast M.A. 1969.

The history of employment in the British Post Office.   5142
L.S. Martinuzzi. Oxford B.Litt. 1952.

The development of public passenger transport services   5143
in Wales. E. Roberts. Wales M.Sc. 1960.

The historical geography of railways in Yorkshire.   5144
J.H. Appleton. Durham M.Sc. 1958.

The finances of the Lancashire and Yorkshire Railway,   5145
1835-73. S.A. Broadbridge. London Ph.D. 1957.

Railways in the northern Pennines to 1880. H.W.   5146
Parris. Leeds M.A. 1954.

The regulation of railways by the government in Great   5147
Britain: the work of the Board of Trade and the Railway
Commissioners, 1840-67. H.W. Parris. Leicester Ph.D. 1959.

5148   Some geographical aspects of the construction of the London and Birmingham Railway and its influence on the growth of towns along the route. P.S. Richards. London M.A. 1957.

5149   Studies in the railway geography of the Birmingham region. P.L. Clark. Birmingham M.A. 1952.

5150   The East Anglian Railways Company: a study in railway and financial history. D.I. Gordon. Nottingham Ph.D. 1964.

5151   The effect of the railways on the growth of the economy of England and Wales, 1840-70. G.R. Hawke. Oxford D.Phil. 1968.

5152   History of the Eastern Counties railway in relation to contemporary economic development. Evelyn Doble. London Ph.D. 1939.

5153   Sir William Mackinnon, shipowner, 1823-93. I.K. Orchardson. London Ph.D. 1970.

5154   An examination of the factors which link Bristol dock policy with the development of the tramp shipping of the port, 1840-90. J.R. Stevens. Bristol M.A. 1940.

5155   The changing industrial geography of the port and city of Bristol since 1851: a study in port function. D.J. Webb. London M.Phil. 1967.

5156   A British ship-owning company in the late 19th and early 20th centuries: an analysis of the voyage accounts of William Thomson & Co. T.E. Milne. Glasgow B.Litt. 1966.

5157   The development and decline of public transport services in mid Wales, 1861-1966, and the effects thereof. G.W. Jones. London M.A. 1968.

5158   The tramways of Kingston-upon-Hull, 1871-1945. G.A. Lee. Sheffield Ph.D. 1967.

5159   The streets and street traffic of Manchester, 1890-1914: a case study of the traffic problem. B.W. Beacroft. Leicester M.A. 1963.

5160   An analysis of public passenger transport services in West Yorkshire, 1896-1963. D. Scrafton. London Ph.D. (Ext.) 1968.

5161   Government intervention in the British merchant service in the 19th century. R.G. Newey. Exeter M.A. 1970.

5162   State subsidies to the British merchant marine, 1900-50. L. Saletan. London M.Sc. 1952.

5163   The railway rates problem and combination amongst the railway companies of Great Britain, 1893-1913. P.J. Cain. Oxford B.Litt. 1968.

5164   The economic development of the port of Bristol, 1900-45. F.E. Cooke. London M.Sc. (Ext.) 1953.

5165   The beginnings of British civil air transport, 1919-24. E. Birkhead. Leicester M.A. 1959.

5166   A political and economic history of the development of internal civil aviation in Great Britain from 1919 to 1939. H.C.L. Leech. Manchester M.A. 1950.

5167   A geographical study of the evolution of civil air transport, 1918-57. A.F. Williams. Bristol Ph.D. 1960.

Agrarian History

5168   The history of the agricultural geography of Great Britain since 1800. J. McDermott. London M.Sc. (Ext.) 1943.

5169   A study of a rural and maritime community in the 19th century, with special reference to the relation between agriculture and shipping. D. Thomas. Liverpool M.A. 1928.

5170   The response of agriculture in Staffordshire to the price changes of the 19th century. R.W. Sturgess. Manchester Ph.D. 1965.

5171   Harvest technology and labour supply in Britain, 1790-1870. E.J.T. Collins. Nottingham Ph.D. 1970.

5172   Aspects of agricultural and rural change in Kent, 1800-1900. D.W. Harvey. Cambridge Ph.D. 1961.

Some aspects of the economic geography of the Sussex   5173
South Downs and contiguous land in the 19th century. Aileen
E. Swanwick. Cambridge M.Sc. 1952/3.

Economic and social aspects of landownership in the   5174
19th century. F.M. Reid. Oxford B.Litt. 1957.

The draining of the marshlands of east Yorkshire. June 5175
A. Sheppard. London Ph.D. 1956.

Welsh agriculture, 1815-1914. D.W. Howell. London   5176
Ph.D. 1970.

The evolution of high farming, 1815-65, with reference 5177
to Herefordshire. E.L. Jones. Oxford D.Phil. 1962.

The agricultural labourer in west Oxfordshire: an   5178
account of some aspects of the life of west Oxfordshire agricultural labourers and the economic background in the 19th
century. D.N. Bates. Birmingham M.A. 1955.

The Norfolk agricultural labourer, 1834-84. Lillie M. 5179
Springall. London Ph.D. 1935.

Changing attitudes to the employment of women and   5180
children on the land between the eighteen-thirties and the
eighteen-seventies, with particular reference to the county
of Sussex. Mrs. Ena M. Ainsworth. Sussex M.A. 1969/70.

Land use changes in West Gower, 1840-1950. J.C. Grove. 5181
Wales M.A. 1956.

Changes in land utilisation in the south-east of   5182
Denbighshire, 1840-1938. J.B. Jarvis. Wales M.A. 1940.

The land utilisation of the London basin: a study of   5183
the existing conditions and historical changes, 1840-1935.
E.C. Willatts. London Ph.D. (Ext.) 1937.

Changes in the agricultural geography of the parishes   5184
of Bockleton, Kyre Magna, Tenbury Township and Foreign
(Worcs.) and Hampton Charles (Herefs.) from 1841 to c.1958.
Mrs. Constance Pritchard. Birmingham M.A. 1965.

The changes in the numbers of agricultural labourers   5185
and in their wages and efficiency during the past fifty
years, and the causes of these changes, with special reference to Wales. E. Hughes. Wales M.A. 1909.

The treatment of 'land' in English social and political 5186
theory, 1840-85. Mrs. Joyce Macaskill. Oxford B.Litt. 1959.

The economic and social background of the English   5187
landed interest, 1840-70, with particular reference to the
estates of the dukes of Northumberland. F.M.L. Thompson.
Oxford D.Phil. 1956.

The rural landscape of the Blackmore vale, c.1840.   5188
R.F.J. Chiplen. Exeter M.A. 1969.

An agricultural geography of Essex, c.1840. E.A. Cox. 5189
London M.A. 1963.

The agricultural geography of the Chilterns, c.1840.   5190
F.D. Hartley. London M.A. 1953.

The development of market gardening in England, 1850-   5191
1914. R.J. Battersby. London Ph.D. 1960.

Market gardening in eastern and central Bedfordshire.   5192
F. Beavington. London Ph.D. 1961.

A historical and economic study of the development and 5193
organisation of the market gardening industry in the vale of
Evesham. H.J. Meredith. Oxford B.Litt. 1929.

Changes in land utilisation in the East Anglian Breck- 5194
land during the past 100 years. E.H. Griffith. Wales M.A.
1955.

The influence of legislation and economic conditions on 5195
the rent of agricultural land since 1850, with special reference to East Anglia and with a statistical analysis of some
East Anglian farm rents. Carleen O'Loughlin. Cambridge
M.Sc. 1953.

A study of capital and rental values of agricultural   5196
land in England and Wales between 1858 and 1958. J.T. Ward.
London Ph.D. 1960.

5197   Landownership and rural population, with special reference to Leicestershire in the mid 19th century. D.R. Mills. Leicester Ph.D. 1963.

5198   The history of the earl of Scarbrough's estate, 1860-1900. T.W. Beastall. Manchester M.A. 1954.

5199   An examination of some factors influencing population changes in rural communities in an area of the north-east Midlands of England, 1861-1911, with special reference to the impact of agricultural depression. M.F. Bunce. Sheffield Ph.D. 1970.

5200   The agricultural geography of the Chilterns, 1870-1951. J.T. Coppock. London Ph.D. 1960.

5201   Agricultural co-operation in Hampshire. H. Newman. Cambridge M.Litt. 1949.

5202   A portion of west Sussex: a study of agriculture and population. E. Cook. Liverpool M.A. 1939.

5203   The history of landownership since 1870, with special reference to conditions in Cambridgeshire. J.J. Macgregor. Oxford B.Litt. 1938.

5204   The economic development of agriculture in east Lancashire, 1870-1939. T.W. Fletcher. Leeds M.Sc. 1954.

5205   English agriculture and the labourer, 1840-85, with special reference to the depression of the 'seventies'. Norah Yates. Birmingham M.A. 1930.

5206   The effects of agricultural depression on the English estates of the dukes of Sutherland, 1870-1900. R. Perren. Nottingham Ph.D. 1967.

5207   The making of a landed élite: social mobility in Lancashire society. R.O. Knapp. Lancaster Ph.D. 1970.

5208   The draining of the Somerset Levels. M. Williams. Wales Ph.D. 1960.

5209   Land reform, 1880-1919: a study of the activities of the English Land Restoration League and the Land Nationalisation Society. A.J. Peacock. Southampton M.A. 1962.

5210   Jesse Collings and the back to the land movement. W.I. Wilks. Birmingham M.A. 1964.

5211   The migration of farmers in relation to the economic development of agriculture in Great Britain since 1880. E. Lorrain-Smith. Oxford B.Litt. 1931.

5212   A study of the changes that have taken place in farm size in Carmarthenshire since the end of the 19th century. J.W.G. Jasper. Wales M.Sc. 1959.

5213   The progress of land settlement in England since 1892, with a historical introduction. G.-L. von dem Knesebeck. Oxford B.Litt. 1935.

5214   An historical review of the development of British agricultural policies and programmes since 1900. A.V. Vickery. Oxford B.Litt. 1958.

5215   The derelict villages of Durham County. A. Temple. Durham M.Litt. 1940.

5216   British agricultural developments in the inter-war period 1919-39, with special reference to the contribution of interest groups. Priscilla J. Baines. Oxford B.Litt. 1969.

5217   Labour on the land since 1920. W.H. Pedley. Oxford B.Litt. 1940.

5218   A study of land-use changes in the period 1928-55 in part of south-west Yorkshire. R.M. Koerner. Sheffield M.A. 1961.

Social History

5219   The development of the law relating to children in the 19th and 20th centuries. T.E. James. London Ph.D. 1957.

5220   The reform of the law and administration of charities in the 19th century. B. Hargrove. London Ph.D. 1963.

Social conditions in the Black Country in the 19th   5221
century. G.J. Barnsby. Birmingham Ph.D. 1969.
The social history of British coalminers, 1800-45.   5222
P.E.H. Hair. Oxford D.Phil. 1955.
An historical study of the educational effects of the   5223
provision made for the social (as distinct from the scholastic) welfare of children and young persons in England since
1800. Christina L.H. Cowper. London M.A. 1930.
Magazines for women: a sociological study of their   5224
character and function in the period 1800 to the present day.
Cynthia L. White. London Ph.D. 1968.
The Liverpool Corporate Estate: a study of the develop- 5225
ment of housing in the Moss Lake Fields area of Liverpool,
1800-75. P. Mathias. Liverpool M.A. 1956/7.
The history of food adulteration in Great Britain in   5226
the 19th century, with special reference to bread, tea and
beer. J. Burnett. London Ph.D. 1958.
Aspects of the history of crime in England and Wales   5227
between 1805 and 1860. K.K. Macnab. Sussex D.Phil. 1965.
An account of the progress of penal reform in England   5228
from 1810 to 1930, together with some conclusions. H.H.
Ayscough. London Ph.D. 1933.
The influence of social, economic and administrative   5229
change on crime and criminals in selected areas of England,
1815-75. J.J. Tobias. London Ph.D. 1965.
Bywyd a gwaith Dr. Owen Owen Roberts, 1793-1866. (The   5230
life and work of Dr. O.O. Roberts.) E.H. Owen. Wales M.A.
1939.
The life and work of James Braid, surgeon, with special   5231
reference to his influence on the development of hypnotism
as an orthodox medical procedure. C.A.S. Wink. Oxford
B.Litt. 1969.
Recreations and amusements of the industrial working   5232
classes in the second quarter of the 19th century, with
special reference to Lancashire. K. Allan. Manchester M.A.
1947.
The growth and development of popular entertainment and   5233
pastimes in the Lancashire cotton towns, 1830-70. M.B.
Smith. Lancaster M.Litt. 1970.
Capitalism and class-consciousness in earlier 19th-   5234
century Oldham. J.O. Foster. Cambridge Ph.D. 1967.
The development of Friendly societies in England, 1815-   5235
75. P.H.J.H. Gosden. London Ph.D. 1959.
Some aspects of social and political life in England   5236
during the 19th century in relation to contemporary theory.
Nellie M. Waterson. Birmingham M.A. 1921.
Robert Owen and social legislation. E. Lloyd. Wales   5237
M.A. 1932.
The development of the poor laws in Caernarvonshire and   5238
Anglesey, 1815-1914. C.F. Hughes. Wales M.A. 1945.
The administration of the poor law in the West Riding   5239
of Yorkshire (1820-55). M.E. Rose. Oxford D.Phil. 1965.
The temperance question in England, 1828-69. B.H.   5240
Harrison. Oxford D.Phil. 1965.
Drink and sobriety in Wales, 1835-95. W.R. Lambert.   5241
Wales Ph.D. 1970.
Movements towards social reform in South Wales during   5242
the period 1832-50. Lillian Williams. Wales M.A. 1933.
The place of the Irish Catholics in the social life of   5243
the north of England, 1829-51. J.H. Treble. Leeds Ph.D.
1969.
The Irish in London - a study of migration and settle-   5244
ment in the past 100 years. J.A. Jackson. London M.A. 1958.
The origin and growth of the Irish community in Car-   5245
diff. J.V. Hickey. Wales M.A. 1959.
The influence of Christianity on social progress, as   5246
illustrated by the career of Lord Shaftesbury. J.W. Bready.
London Ph.D. 1927.

5247   The 7th earl of Shaftesbury as social reformer. Evelyn
M. Wightman. Birmingham M.A. 1923.
5248   Social administration in Lancashire, 1830-60: poor law,
public health and police. E. Midwinter. York D.Phil. 1967.
5249   Public opinion and the police in Lancashire, 1838-42.
D. Foster. Sheffield M.A. 1965.
5250   Machinery of public order in the Chartist period. F.C.
Mather. Manchester M.A. 1948.
5251   A study of local sanitary administration in certain
selected areas, 1830-75. A.J. Archer. Wales M.A. 1968.
5252   Edwin Chadwick and the public health movement, 1832-54.
R.A. Lewis. Birmingham Ph.D. 1949.
5253   Urban administration and health: a case study of Hanley
in the mid 19th century. W.E. Townley. Keele M.A. 1969.
5254   Public health in Leeds in the 19th century: a study in
the growth of local government responsibility. Jean Toft.
Manchester M.A. 1966.
5255   The administration of the poor law in the rural areas
of Surrey, 1830-50. W. Pike. London M.A. 1950.
5256   A history of the relieving officer in England and Wales
from 1834 to 1948. R.C. Mishra. London Ph.D. 1969.
5257   Poor law administration in west Glamorgan from 1834 to
1930. J.E. Thomas. Wales M.A. 1951.
5258   The education of pauper children in Monmouthshire, 1834-
1929. D.B. Hughes. Wales M.A. 1967.
5259   The care and education of pauper children in England and
Wales, 1834 to 1896. A.M. Ross. London Ph.D. 1955.
5260   The care and education of children in Union workhouses
of Somerset, 1834-70. G.F. Baker. London M.A. (Ext.) 1960.
5261   The education of pauper children: policy and administration, 1834-55. F. Duke. Manchester M.A. 1968.
5262   Poor law and public health administration in the area
of Merthyr Tydfil Union, 1834-94. T.D. Jones. Wales M.A.
1961.
5263   The medical services of the new poor law 1834-71.
Gladys R. Hodgkinson. London Ph.D. 1951.
5264   The history of poor law administration in north-east
Lancashire, 1834-71. R. Boyson. Manchester M.A. 1960.
5265   Local administration of the poor law in the Great
Broughton and Wirral Unions and the Chester Local Act Incorporation, 1834-71. M.D. Handley. Wales M.A. 1969.
5266   The English poor law of 1834, with special reference to
its working between 1834 and 1847: a study in social pathology. J.M. Mackinnon. London M.A. 1930.
5267   The working of the new poor law, 1834-42. H. Levy.
Manchester M.A. 1923.
5268   Town-country relations in England and Wales in the pre-
railway age, as revealed by the Poor Law Unions. Eileen M.
Pierce. London M.A. 1957.
5269   The administration of the poor law in the Unions of
Southwell and Basford, 1836-71. M. Caplan. Nottingham Ph.D.
1967.
5270   Poor law administration, 1840-3, with particular reference to the Cardiff Union. Valerie J. Russell. Wales M.A.
1967.
5271   Victoria Park, Manchester: a study of its administration
and its relations with local government, 1836-1954. M.
Spiers. Manchester M.A. 1961.
5272   Origins and achievements of Winchester College pupils,
1836 to 1934. T.J.H. Bishop. London Ph.D. 1962.
5273   Influences on the growth of literacy in Victorian working-
class children. A.C.O. Ellis. Liverpool M.A. 1970.
5274   The royal household since the accession of Queen
Victoria. Mrs. Angur B. Joshi. Oxford B.Litt. 1961.
5275   Personal injuries claims in Victorian Britain. H. Smith.
London Ph.D. (Ext.) 1970.

Some aspects of the historical development and present   5276
organisation of voluntary welfare societies for adult deaf
persons in England, 1840-1963. C.K. Lysons. Liverpool M.A.
1964/5.

The historical development, from the mid 19th century,   5277
of services for physically handicapped children, with special
reference to the development of social work and its place in
these services today. Margaret E. Paisley. London M.Sc.
1964.

The Rebecca riots in Wales. Mabel Williams. Wales   5278
M.A. 1913.

History of the Italian exiles in London, 1816-48.   5279
Margaret C.W. Wicks. Edinburgh Ph.D. 1930/1.

The European revolutionaries in London, 1848-70. H.P.   5280
Grosshans. Oxford B.Litt. 1950.

Housing in urban areas, 1840-1914. J.N. Tarn. Cam-   5281
bridge Ph.D. 1961/2.

The housing of the working classes in Britain, 1850-   5282
1914: a study of the development of standards and methods of
provision. Winifred V. Hole. London Ph.D. 1965.

Fluctuations in house-building in the South Wales coal-   5283
field, 1851-1954. J.H. Richards. Wales M.A. 1956.

Family structure in 19th-century Lancashire. M. Ander-   5284
son. Cambridge Ph.D. 1969.

The English middle-class concept of the standard of   5285
living and its relation to marriage and family size, 1850-
1900. J.A. Banks. London M.A. 1952.

The effect of married women's employment in the cotton   5286
textile districts on the organisation and structure of the
home in Lancashire, 1840-80. Margaret Hewitt. London Ph.D.
1953.

'The servant question': a study of the domestic labour   5287
market, 1851-1917. Sheila J. Richardson. London M.Phil.
1967.

Changes in the social status of women in England: an   5288
analysis of the married women's property and divorce controversies, 1854-7. P. Softley. Leicester M.A. 1962.

The Divorce Act of 1857: the genesis, and the arguments 5289
produced for and against it at the time. L. Bairstow. Durham M.A. 1951.

Women and poor law administration, 1857-1909. Mrs.   5290
Elizabeth M. Ross. London M.A. 1956.

The use of short-term building and repairing leases by   5291
Crown and corporate landowners on English urban estates in
the 19th century, with special reference to London. D.A.
Reeder. Leicester M.A. 1961.

Residential displacement by railway construction in   5292
north Lambeth, 1858-61. H.C. Binford. Sussex M.A. 1967/8.

The historical development and present-day significance 5293
of byelaw-housing morphology, with particular reference to
Hull, York and Middlesbrough. C.A. Forster. Hull Ph.D.
1969.

Housing legislation in England, 1851-67, with special   5294
reference to London. Vera Zoond. London M.A. 1932.

The recruitment, regulation and role of prostitutes in   5295
Britain from the middle of the 19th century to the present
day. Mrs. Helen R.E. Ware. London Ph.D. 1969.

The English prison officer, 1850-1968. J.E. Thomas.   5296
York D.Phil. 1970.

Geographical and historical aspects of the public water 5297
supply of London, 1852-1902. R.W. Morris. London Ph.D.
1941.

The history of the Caernarvonshire police force, 1856-   5298
1900. J.O. Jones. Wales M.A. 1956.

The rise and growth of the Liverpool police force in   5299
the 19th century. W.R. Cockcroft. Wales M.A. 1969.

5300   The National Association for the Promotion of Social Science (1857-86): some sociological aspects. R.J. Pemble. Nottingham M.A. 1968.

5301   The late Victorian revolt, 1859-95. P.T. Cominos. Oxford D.Phil. 1958.

5302   The utilisation of hospital in-patient services for the physically ill in England and Wales between 1861 and 1938. R.A. Pinker. London M.Sc. 1965.

5303   The origins and development of England's first state hospitals, with special reference to the services provided by the Metropolitan Asylums Board for patients with infectious diseases, 1867-1930. Gwendoline M. Ayers. London Ph.D. (Ext.) 1967.

5304   The genesis of modern British town planning: a study in economic and social history of the 19th and 20th centuries. W. Ashworth. London Ph.D. 1950.

5305   Thomas Coglan Horsfall, 1841-1932, pioneer of the town-planning movement in England. Josephine P. Reynolds. Liverpool M.A. 1952/3.

5306   The history of the Howard League for Penal Reform. A.G. Rose. Manchester Ph.D. 1960.

5307   John Ruskin as social reformer. F.U. Stribley. Birmingham M.A. 1925.

5308   The British anti-vaccination movement in the 19th century. D.L. Ross. Leicester M.Sc. 1968.

5309   Sanitary administration of Liverpool, 1847-1900. W. Bate. Liverpool M.A. 1954/5.

5310   The Ladies' Sanitary Association and the origins of the health visiting service. W.C. Dowling. London M.A. 1963.

5311   The role of Dr. Dyke in the public health administration of Merthyr Tydfil, 1865-1900. B.A. Frampton. Wales M.A. 1968.

5312   Some aspects of state activity in public health, 1858-71: with special reference to the Medical Department of the Privy Council and the Local Government Act Office. R.J. Lambert. Cambridge Ph.D. 1960.

5313   Sanitary administration under the Local Government Board, 1871-88. R.K.J.F. Young. Oxford B.Litt. 1964.

5314   The Charity Organisation Society and the rise of the Welfare State. C. Woodard. Cambridge Ph.D. 1961.

5315   The British Humanist movement, 1860-1966. Mrs. Susan Budd. Oxford D.Phil. 1969.

5316   George Jacob Holyoake and the secularist movement in Britain, 1841-61. E. Royle. Cambridge Ph.D. 1968.

5317   The social sources of the Salvation Army, 1865-90. Christine Ward. London M.Phil. 1970.

5318   The contribution of the Salvation Army to the religious and moral education of children and young people in Great Britain, 1865-1965. Marie K. Beard. London M.A. (Ext.) 1968.

5319   The Conservative party and some social problems primarily affecting the condition of the working classes, 1866-80. P. Smith. Oxford D.Phil. 1965.

5320   The organised provisions for cultural activities in urban centres and their impact on the community, 1870-1910, with special reference to the city of Bristol. Helen E. Meller. Bristol Ph.D. 1968.

5321   The development of physical recreation in Liverpool in the 19th century. R. Rees. Liverpool M.A. 1967/8.

5322   The development of physical recreation in the Birmingham district from 1871 to 1892. D.D. Molyneux. Birmingham M.A. 1957.

5323   The English elementary school considered as an agent of social transformation, 1870-1918. E.G. Pells. Oxford B.Litt. 1928.

The condition of the rural population of England and   5324
Wales, 1870-1928. A study of physical and mental conditions
of the rural population, (a) in relation to migration and its
effects in age and sex selection, (b) in relation to income
and standards of living, (c) in relation to changes in social
organisation. D.J. Davies. Wales Ph.D. 1931.

The British medical profession and state intervention   5325
in public health, 1870-1911. Jeanne L. Brand. London Ph.D.
1953.

The concept of evolution in social theory from Spencer   5326
to Hobhouse. J.W. Burrow. Cambridge Ph.D. 1961.

The development of old age pensions policy in Great   5327
Britain, 1878-1925. Patricia M. Williams. London Ph.D.
1970.

The development of 'The new biography': biographies of   5328
the Victorians, 1881-1915. S.J. Walker. Nottingham Ph.D.
1959.

A study of English uniformed youth movements, 1883-   5329
1935: their origins, development and social and political
influence. P. Wilkinson. Wales M.A. 1968.

Canon Barnett and the first thirty years of Toynbee   5330
Hall. Mrs. Emily K. Abel. London Ph.D. 1969.

The political left wing (the Liberals and emergent   5331
Labour party) and the issue of alien Jewish immigration,
1880-1910. J.A. Garrard. Manchester M.Sc. 1965.

The economic and social history of alien immigrants to   5332
Leeds, 1880-1914. J. Buckman. Strathclyde Ph.D. 1968.

The alien invasion: the origins of the Aliens Act. B.   5333
Gainer. Cambridge Ph.D. 1969.

The problem of unemployment in English social policy,   5334
1886-1914. José F. Chambers. Cambridge Ph.D. 1970.

The Liberal party and the social problem, 1892-1914.   5335
H.V. Emy. London Ph.D. 1969.

Ideas concerning social policy and their influence on   5336
legislation in Britain, 1902-11. J. Brown. London Ph.D.
1964.

Housing in Coventry: the development of municipal   5337
action, 1890-1908. A.T. Mallier. Birmingham M.Soc.Sc. 1970.

Government and housing: a study in the development of   5338
social policy, 1906-39. P.R. Wilding. Manchester Ph.D.
1969/70.

Fifty years of public health and social welfare in   5339
Bath, 1896-1945. J.F. Blackett. Bristol M.A. 1949.

A study of social change and educational opportunity in 5340
west Cumberland from 1900 to the present day. Mrs. Mary H.
Watkinson. London M.A. 1958.

The child in public care, 1900 to 1939: a historical   5341
study. N.G. Middleton. London M.Phil. 1968.

The Poor Law Commission, 1905-9: an investigation of   5342
its task and achievement. A. Maltby. Liverpool M.A. 1969.

Social legislation and theory in Great Britain from   5343
1906 to 1914. T.W. Price. Oxford B.Litt. 1930.

Housing policy in four Lincolnshire towns, 1919-59.   5344
O.A. Hartley. Oxford D.Phil. 1969.

Fluctuations in investment in housing in Britain and   5345
America, 1919-39. G.P. Braae. Oxford D.Phil. 1960.

The approach of the Conservative party to social policy 5346
during World War II. H. Kopsch. London Ph.D. 1970.

Air raid shelters in Britain in the Second World War.   5347
Mary M.M. Harrison. Birmingham M.A. 1949.

The politics of race under the impact of migration: the 5348
United States (1900-30) and the United Kingdom (1948-68).
I. Katznelson. Cambridge Ph.D. 1969.

General

5349   The influence of the Church of England and dissent upon Methodism in the 19th century. F. Hunter. Manchester M.A. 1939.

5350   Evangelicalism in England in the first half of the 19th century as exemplified in the life and works of William Jay (1769-1853). H.E. Pressly. Edinburgh Ph.D. 1950.

5351   The attitude of the Evangelicals to the empire and imperial problems (1820-50). A.F. Madden. Oxford D.Phil. 1950.

5352   Ebenezer Henderson (1784-1858), missionary, traveller, teacher, biblical scholar: his life and work in the north of Europe, with special reference to the great missionary awakening. J.H. Glassman. Edinburgh Ph.D. 1958.

5353   William Palmer and the Orthodox Church. F.J. Thomson. Cambridge Ph.D. 1963/4.

5354   The early Tractarians and the Eastern Church. P.E.O. Shaw. Oxford B.Litt. 1924.

5355   The attitude of the Tractarians to the Roman Catholic Church, 1833-50. R.H. Greenfield. Oxford D.Phil. 1956.

5356   The influence of North American evangelism in Great Britain between 1830 and 1914 on the origin and development of the ecumenical movement. J.W. White. Oxford D.Phil. 1963.

5357   The part played in British social and political life by the protestant Nonconformists between the years 1832 and 1859, with special reference to the disestablishment of the Church of England. B.J. Mason. Southampton M.A. 1958.

5358   The agitation for disestablishment of the Church of England in the 19th century (excluding Wales), with special reference to the minutes and papers of the Liberation Society. W.H. Macintosh. Oxford D.Phil. 1956.

5359   Christian Socialism, its rise and development, its economic and social results, and its relation to other working-class movements. I. Evans. Wales M.A. 1912.

5360   Robert Owen and Christian Socialism. F. Fraser. Edinburgh Ph.D. 1927.

5361   The social and religious thought of Charles Kingsley, and his place in the Christian Socialist school of 1848-54. H.W. West. Edinburgh Ph.D. 1947.

5362   Religious organisations in Wales considered in relation to economic conditions, 1850-1930. E.T. Lewis. Wales M.A. 1965.

5363   The relations between organised religion and English working-class movements, 1850-1914. S.H. Mayor. Manchester Ph.D. 1960.

5364   Religion and the working classes in mid 19th-century England. Hilary A. Evans. London M.Phil. 1970.

5365   The churches and society in Leicestershire, 1851-81. D.M. Thompson. Cambridge Ph.D. 1969.

5366   A factual and analytical account of the religious awakening in the United Kingdom in the years 1855-65. J.E. Orr. Oxford D.Phil. 1948.

5367   The religious awakening of 1858-60 in Great Britain and Ireland. O. Bussey. Edinburgh Ph.D. 1947.

5368   The influence of the Evangelicals upon the origin and development of voluntary charitable institutions in the second half of the 19th century. Kathleen J. Heasman. London Ph.D. 1960.

5369   A study of the work of revivalist movements in Great Britain and Ireland from 1870 to 1914 and of their effect upon organised Christianity there. P.B. Morgan. Oxford B.Litt. 1961.

English churches and the working classes, 1880-1900,   5370
with an introductory survey of tendencies earlier in the
century. K.S. Inglis. Oxford D.Phil. 1956.
     The Labour Church and allied movements of the late 19th 5371
and early 20th centuries. D.F. Summers. Edinburgh Ph.D.
1958/9.
     The relation of theology to social theory and action in 5372
the Christian Social movement in England from 1877 to 1914.
E.V. Newman. Oxford B.Litt. 1936.
     Christian Socialism in Britain and the U.S.A., 1880-   5373
1914. P.d'A. Jones. London Ph.D. 1964.
     Frederick Lewis Donaldson and the Christian Socialist   5374
movement. Mrs. Barbara J. Butler. Leeds M.Phil. 1970.
     Baron Friedrich von Hügel and the Modernist crisis in   5375
England. L.F. Barmann. Cambridge Ph.D. 1970.
     Religion and politics in Liverpool since 1900. D.A.   5376
Roberts. London M.Sc. (Ext.) 1965.
     Principles and characteristics of missionary policy   5377
during the last fifty years, as illustrated by the history
of the London Missionary Society. N. Goodall. London Ph.D.
1950.
     Authority in church and state: aspects of the thought   5378
of J.N. Figgis and his contemporaries. D.G. Nicholls. Cambridge Ph.D. 1962.

  Church of England

     The history of the English clergy, 1800-1900. C.K.F.   5379
Brown. Oxford D.Phil. 1949.
     A sociological analysis of the clergyman's role, with   5380
special reference to its development in the early 19th century. A.J. Russell. Oxford D.Phil. 1970.
     The intellectual development of E.B. Pusey, 1800-50.   5381
D.W.F. Forrester. Oxford D.Phil. 1967.
     The attitudes of English churchmen, 1800-50, toward   5382
the Reformation. W.J. Baker. Cambridge Ph.D. 1966.
     The diocese of Exeter, 1800-40. J.H. Bettey. Birming- 5383
ham M.A. 1956.
     Anglican church extension and related movements, c.   5384
1800-1860, with special reference to London. B.I. Coleman.
Cambridge Ph.D. 1968.
     The Church Building Commission, 1818-56. M.H. Port.   5385
Oxford B.Litt. 1956.
     Ecclesiastical reorganisation and church extension in   5386
the diocese of Llandaff, 1830-90. W.D. Wills. Wales M.A.
1965.
     Bishop Blomfield. P.J. Welch. London Ph.D. (Ext.)   5387
1952.
     The Church of England in its relations with parliament   5388
and Crown, 1825-45. L.O. Henderson. London Ph.D. (Ext.)
1961.
     Relations between church and state in England between   5389
1829 and 1839. F.M. Scully. Oxford B.Litt. 1935.
     The Anglican establishment, 1830-1930. G. Youell.   5390
Keele M.A. 1969.
     The relations between the Church of England and the   5391
state from 1838 to 1870. H.K. Smith. Sheffield M.A. 1946.
     The Church of England and society, 1830-50. C. Brack- 5392
well. Birmingham M.A. 1949.
     The Church of England in the town of Derby, 1824-85.   5393
M.R. Austin. Birmingham M.A. 1967.
     The Church of England and society in Birmingham, c.   5394
1830-1866. D.E.H. Mole. Cambridge Ph.D. 1961.
     John Kaye and the diocese of Lincoln. R. Foskett.   5395
Nottingham Ph.D. 1957.
     Edward Copleston, bishop of Llandaff. W.J. Cratchley. 5396
Oxford B.Litt. 1938.

5397   Frederick Denison Maurice. A.C. Smith. Sheffield M.A. 1950.
5398   Hugh James Rose, rector of Hadleigh, Suffolk. Dorothy M.B. Snow. Oxford B.Litt. 1960.
5399   The Oxford Movement and church unity. F.S. Downs. St. Andrews Ph.D. 1960.
5400   Richard Bagot, bishop of Oxford, and the Oxford Movement, 1833-45. A.H. Mead. Oxford B.Litt. 1966.
5401   The Oxford Movement in a Manchester parish: the Miles Platting case. H.E. Sheen. Manchester M.A. 1941.
5402   New Anglican bishoprics, 1836-1919, their creation and endowment in England, with special reference to Truro and Birmingham. P.S. Morrish. London M.A. 1965.
5403   The formation of the see of Ripon and the episcopate of its first bishop, Charles Thomas Longley. A.M.G. Stephenson. Oxford B.Litt. 1960.
5404   A history of the Church Pastoral-Aid Society, 1836-61. P.B. Coombs. Bristol M.A. 1960.
5405   The episcopate of Samuel Wilberforce, bishop of Oxford 1845-69, and of Winchester 1869-73, with special reference to the administration of the diocese of Oxford. R.K. Pugh. Oxford D.Phil. 1957.
5406   The evangelical party in the Church of England, 1855-65. B.E. Hardman. Cambridge Ph.D. 1964.
5407   John Charles Ryle and the evangelical party in the 19th century. J.S. Casson. Nottingham M.Phil. 1969.
5408   The revival of the 'religious life' in the Church of England during the 19th century. A.M. Allchin. Oxford B.Litt. 1956.
5409   The development of church life in the rural deanery of Cleveland, c.1850-1880. C.H.N. Smith. Nottingham M.A. 1965.
5410   The life of J.B. Lightfoot (1828-89), with special reference to the training of the ministry. D.J. Wilson. Edinburgh Ph.D. 1955/6.
5411   Conflicts over religious inquiry among the Anglican clergy in the eighteen-sixties. Margaret A. Worden. Oxford D.Phil. 1968.
5412   Social and educational backgrounds of English diocesan bishops, 1860-1960. D.H.J. Morgan. Hull M.A. 1964.
5413   Some aspects of the career of William Thomson as archbishop of York, 1863-90. H.K. Smith. Sheffield Ph.D. 1953.
5414   Dean Farrar: a study in 19th-century Anglicanism. J.R. Jackson. Edinburgh Ph.D. 1957.
5415   The first Lambeth Conference of 1867. A.M.G. Stephenson. Oxford D.Phil. 1964.
5416   Gladstone and the Anglican Church in Ireland and England, 1868-74. J.F.M.D. Stephen. Cambridge M.Litt. 1955.
5417   Anglican attitudes to church, state and society during Mr. Gladstone's first ministry, 1868-74. P.T. Marsh. Cambridge Ph.D. 1962.
5418   Social concern in the Church of England, as revealed in its pronouncements on social and economic matters, especially during the years 1880-1940. F.W. Jones. London Ph.D. (Ext.) 1968.
5419   George Body, D.D., 'Canon Missioner' of Durham. St.J.A. Turner. Durham M.A. 1961.
5420   Henry Scott Holland, 1847-1918. J.H. Foster. Wales Ph.D. 1970.
5421   The development of constitutional autonomy in the established church in later Victorian England. R.S.M. Withycombe. Cambridge Ph.D. 1970.
5422   Social thought in the Church of England from 1918 to 1933. J.K. Oliver. Cambridge M.Litt. 1964.

The development of Methodism in Yorkshire in the 19th   5423
century. B. Greaves. Liverpool Ph.D. 1968.

A study of the theological developments among Noncon-   5424
formists in Wales during the 19th century. G. Richards. Oxford B.Litt. 1956.

A survey of Baptist expansion in England from 1795 to   5425
1850, with special reference to the emergence of permanent
structures of organisation. S.M. Stone. Bristol M.A. 1959.

John Foster (1770-1843): and his contribution to   5426
religious thought. S.T. Habel. Edinburgh Ph.D. 1945.

The Baptists in the borough of Leeds during the 19th   5427
century: a study of local church history. R.J. Owen. Leeds
M.Phil. 1970.

Baptism in Nonconformist theology, 1820-1920, with   5428
special reference to the Baptists. J.R.C. Perkin. Oxford
D.Phil. 1955.

Political and social attitudes of representative Eng-   5429
lish Unitarians (1795-1850). I. Sellers. Oxford B.Litt.
1956.

The origin and early development of Primitive Methodism 5430
in Derbyshire, 1810-70. G.M. Morris. Nottingham M.A. 1960.

Primitive Methodism in Nottinghamshire, 1815-1932.   5431
G.M. Morris. Nottingham Ph.D. 1967.

Cornish Methodism: a study in division, 1814-57. M.S.   5432
Edwards. Birmingham M.A. 1962.

The attitude of the Welsh Independents towards working- 5433
class movements, including public education, from 1815 to
1870. R.I. Parry. Wales M.A. 1931.

The political activities of Dissenters in the East and   5434
West Ridings of Yorkshire, 1815-50. R.W. Ram. Hull M.A.
1964.

Methodism and the working classes of England, 1800-50.   5435
R.F. Wearmouth. London Ph.D. 1935.

The clash between radicalism and conservatism in   5436
Methodism, 1815-48. J.H.S. Kent. Cambridge Ph.D. 1951.

The origins and early development of the Plymouth   5437
Brethren. P.L. Embley. Cambridge Ph.D. 1967.

The origins of the Plymouth Brethren, c.1825-1850.   5438
H.H. Rowdon. London Ph.D. 1965.

The Catholic Apostolic Church, sometimes called   5439
'Irvingite': a historical study. P.E.O. Shaw. Edinburgh
Ph.D. 1935.

The contribution of Quakers to some aspects of local   5440
government in Birmingham, 1828-1902. M.H. Bailey. Birmingham M.A. 1952.

Quakerism and public service, chiefly between 1832 and   5441
1867. Erica I.J. Martineau. Oxford B.Litt. 1938.

Quakers and society in Victorian England. Mrs. Eliza-   5442
beth M. Isichei, née Allo. Oxford D.Phil. 1967.

The constitutional authority of Dr. Jabez Bunting over   5443
Wesleyan Methodism as seen through his correspondence. W.B.
Maynard. Durham M.A. 1970.

Methodist secessions and social conflict in south   5444
Lancashire, 1830-57. D.A. Gowland. Manchester Ph.D. 1966.

Baptists in Lancashire, 1837-87: a study of mid-   5445
Victorian dissent. J.H. Lea. Liverpool Ph.D. 1970.

Nonconformity in the eastern counties, 1840-85, with   5446
reference to its social background. J.C.G. Binfield. Cambridge Ph.D. 1965.

Bywyd a gwaith Dr. Lewis Edwards. (The life and work of 5447
Lewis Edwards of Bala.) T.L. Evans. Wales M.A. 1949.

Bywyd a gwaith John Evans (I.D. Ffraid). (The life and   5448
work of John Evans.) W.L. Roberts. Wales M.A. 1950.

Life and teaching of John Pulsford, 1815-97. N.H. Kew. 5449
Oxford B.Litt. 1955.

5450   History of the British 'Churches of Christ'. A.C. Watters. Edinburgh Ph.D. 1940.

5451   Wesleyan Methodism from 1850 to 1900 in relation to the life and thought of the Victorian age. P.C. Pearson. Manchester M.A. 1965.

5452   A statistical study of the development of Nonconformity in North Wales in the 19th century, with special reference to the period 1850-1901. W.A. Evans. Liverpool M.A. 1928.

5453   The life, work and thought of John Angell James (1785-1859). J.R. Kennedy. Edinburgh Ph.D. 1956/7.

5454   A history of Congregationalism in Suffolk from 1870 to 1940. J.H. Bennett. Oxford B.Litt. 1953.

5455   The dissenting reformed churches of England with respect to the doctrine of the church from 1870 to 1940, with special reference to the Congregational churches. J.W. Grant. Oxford D.Phil. 1948.

5456   John Clifford and radical Nonconformity. M.R. Watts. Oxford D.Phil. 1966.

5457   The history of the Free Church Council, 1892-1939. E.K.H. Jordan. Oxford D.Phil. 1953.

Roman Catholicism

5458   A survey of liberal Catholic theories of biblical inspiration, 1810-1910. J.T. Burtchaell. Cambridge Ph.D. 1966.

5459   William George Ward and 19th-century Catholicism. K.T. Hoppen. Cambridge Ph.D. 1966.

5460   The organisation and administration of Roman Catholic dioceses in England and Wales in the mid 19th century. R.J. Schiefen. London Ph.D. 1970.

5461   Newman and the use of history. J.D. Holmes. Cambridge Ph.D. 1970.

5462   The Acton-Newman relations. H.A. Macdougall. Cambridge Ph.D. 1960.

5463   Cardinal Newman. Helen M. Herrick. Liverpool M.A. 1932.

5464   The public life and influence of Henry Edward Manning, 1865-92, excluding his attitude towards the temporal power. V.A. McClelland. Birmingham M.A. 1958.

CULTURAL HISTORY

General

5465   The development of the architectural profession in Great Britain, 1800-1945. B.L.B. Kaye. London Ph.D. 1951.

5466   The career of Sir Robert Smirke, R.A. J.M. Crook. Oxford D.Phil. 1962.

5467   Joseph Hanson. D. Evinson. London M.A. 1966.

5468   The design of English domestic architecture from about 1850 to 1914. J.A.M. Bell. Manchester Ph.D. 1963.

5469   The origin and development of the idea of prehistory and related concepts in archaeology. Mrs. Judith M. Rodden. Cambridge M.Litt. 1964.

5470   Antiquarian and archaeological scholarship in Warwickshire, 1800-60. Barbara J. Ronchetti. Birmingham M.A. 1952.

5471   The early history of the Yorkshire Philosophical Society: a chapter in the history of provincial science. A.D. Orange. London Ph.D. (Ext.) 1970.

5472   The history of the Society for the Diffusion of Useful Knowledge. T.L. Jarman. Oxford B.Litt. 1933.

5473   The Society for the Diffusion of Useful Knowledge, 1826-46. Monica C. Grobel. London M.A. 1933.

5474   Newspapers and opinion in three midland cities, 1800-50. D. Fraser. Leeds M.A. 1962.

The history of the agitation against the stamp duty on   5475
newspapers, 1830-55. Marjorie G. Moore. London M.A. 1935.
The unstamped press in London and the taxes on know-   5476
ledge, 1830-6. Mrs. Patricia L. Hollis. Oxford D.Phil.
1968.
The press in Northumberland and Durham, 1855-1906.   5477
J.M. Milne. Newcastle M.Litt. 1969.
George Potter and the Bee-Hive newspaper. S.W. Colt-   5478
ham. Oxford D.Phil. 1956.
Aspects of chemical affinity in the 19th century. T.H.   5479
Levere. Oxford D.Phil. 1969.
The problem of the chemical elements, from Humphrey   5480
Davy to Benjamin Brodie the younger. D.M. Knight. Oxford
D.Phil. 1964.
Walter Bagehot: a study in Victorian ideas. M.A.-M.   5481
Nasr. London Ph.D. 1949.
The life and work of Henry Clifton Sorby, LL.D., F.R.S.   5482
(1826-1908). N. Higham. Leeds M.A. 1962.
The life and letters of Griffith Evans, pioneer in   5483
protozoon pathology, 1835-1935. Mrs. Jean E. Ware. Wales
M.A. 1966.
The development of Darwin's evolutionary thought after   5484
1859. P.J. Vorzimer. Cambridge Ph.D. 1964.
Edward Edwards, 1812-86, and the early history of muni-   5485
cipal public libraries in England. W.A. Munford. London
Ph.D. (Ext.) 1963.
Valentine Cameron Prinsep, in relation to the practice   5486
and theory of academic painting in late 19th-century England.
P.V. Saville. Oxford B.Litt. 1970.
M.H. Baillie Scott. J.D. Kornwolf. London Ph.D. 1968.   5487
A natural law criticism of Bernard Bosanquet's polit-   5488
ical theory. Elizabeth A. McClure. Cambridge M.Litt. 1951.
The history of freedom of speech and of the press in   5489
England since 1900. A.F. Dawn. London M.Sc. 1933.
The history of The Observer, 1905-10. A.M. Gollin.   5490
Oxford D.Phil. 1957.

Education

General

The theology of church and state in relation to the   5491
concern for popular education in England, 1800-70. B.R.
Marshall. Oxford D.Phil. 1956.
Scottish influence on English education between 1800   5492
and 1840. E. Kerr-Waller. London M.A. 1952.
Education with a tradition: an account of the educ-   5493
ational work of the Society of the Sacred Heart, 1800-1935.
Mary F.M. O'Leary. London Ph.D. (Ext.) 1935.
The educational experience of the Sisters of Notre Dame 5494
de Namur, 1804-1964. Margaret P. Linscott. Liverpool Ph.D.
1964/5.
A life of Charles Knight (1791-1873), with special   5495
reference to his political and educational activities. Althea
C. Cherry. London M.A. 1942.
The influence of industry and commerce on the develop-   5496
ment of educational facilities in England and Wales, 1830 to
1870. J.A. Purton. London M.Sc. 1958.
Education and the political parties, 1830-70. R.E.   5497
Aldrich. London M.Phil. 1970.
The development of parliamentary opinion in respect to   5498
education, 1832-70. Mary K. Wilkinson. Wales M.A. 1925.
Steps towards a national system of education in England 5499
1833-70, with special reference to the report of the Newcastle Commission 1861. F.P. Burns. Oxford B.Litt. 1965.

5500   The influence of the Massachusetts system of education on the movement for a national system in England and Wales in the 19th century. P.N. Farrar. Liverpool M.A. 1963/4.

5501   The passing of the Education Act of 1870; a study of the formation of public opinion, 1843-70. E.E. Rich. London Ph.D. 1932.

5502   An investigation into public opinion and the passing of the Education Act of 1870. R.B. Grove. London M.A. 1949.

5503   Birmingham and the movement for national education, 1867-77: an account of the work and influence of the National Education League. A.F. Taylor. Leicester Ph.D. 1960.

5504   The Endowed Schools Acts and the education of 'poor' children, 1869-1900. P. Gordon. London M.Sc. 1965.

5505   The origins of the Endowed Schools Act, 1869, and its operation in England from 1869 to 1895. F.E. Balls. Cambridge Ph.D. 1964.

5506   The work and influence of Dorothea Beale in the light of developments in the education of girls and women since 1850. M.P.G. Kerr. London M.A. 1952.

5507   An investigation into the educational ideas and contribution of the British political parties, 1870-1918. L.O. Ward. London Ph.D. 1970.

5508   A history of the origin and development of the Dual System in England and Wales with special reference to the period 1870 to 1944. Marjorie A. Cruickshank. Leeds Ph.D. 1955.

5509   Trade unionist, Co-operative and Socialist organisations in relation to popular education, 1870-1902. W.P. McCann. Manchester Ph.D. 1960.

5510   Nonconformity and education in England and Wales, 1870-1902. H. Foreman. London M.A. (Ext.) 1967.

5511   John Scott Lidgett, 1854-1953, and the education of the people. D.H. Thomas. London Ph.D. 1960.

5512   The influence of Sidney and Beatrice Webb on English education, 1892-1903. E.J.T. Brennan. Sheffield M.A. 1959.

5513   The growth of the public system of education in England and Wales, 1895-1935. G.A.N. Lowndes. Oxford B.Litt. 1937.

5514   The educational policies of the Labour party, 1900-61. R.S. Barker. London Ph.D. 1968.

5515   The reaction of the established church to educational legislation, 1918-59. A. Pomfret. London M.A. 1969.

5516   The political parties and the development of their attitude to educational problems, 1918-42. D.W. Dean. London M.Phil. 1968.

Administration

5517   State intervention in English education as illustrated by the relations between the state and the teacher in the early half of the 19th century. J. Gross. Liverpool M.A. 1932.

5518   The development of the central authority for education in England, 1833-99. A.S. Bishop. Liverpool Ph.D. 1967/8.

5519   The Education Department, 1839-64: a study of social policy and the growth of government. J.R.B. Johnson. Cambridge Ph.D. 1968.

5520   The Department of Science and Art: policies and administration to 1864. C. Duke. London Ph.D. 1966.

5521   The Science and Art Department, 1853-1900. H. Butterworth. Sheffield Ph.D. 1968.

5522   The emergence and development of inspectorates of schools in the 19th century, with special reference to Yorkshire. E.L. Edmonds. Sheffield M.A. 1955.

5523   The work of Her Majesty's inspectors of schools, 1839-49. Nancy Ball. Birmingham M.A. 1961.

5524   The life and work of Sir James Kay-Shuttleworth. F. Smith. Wales Ph.D. 1923.

The educational work and thought of Robert Lowe. J.P.   5525
Sullivan. London M.A. 1952.

Educational administration in England and Wales, 1870-   5526
1950: a case study in central-local government relations.
W.B. Rust. London Ph.D. 1955.

A study of the Private Schools Association (latterly   5527
Independent Schools) in relation to changing policies in the
administration of education by national and local government
agencies, 1880-1944. G.B. Robinson. London M.A. 1966.

A critical and historical study of the relations   5528
between state and education from 1886 to 1926. E. Whitehead.
Oxford B.Litt. 1934.

The administration of education, 1902-14. L.F.W.   5529
White. London Ph.D. 1934.

The Education Act of 1902: a study of its background,   5530
scope and legislative problems. P.L.P. Clarke. London Ph.D.
1964.

A study of the Education (Provision of Meals) Act,   5531
1906, against its social, political and economic background.
L.I. Andrews. London M.A. 1966.

The historical antecedents, 1834-1906, of the Educ-   5532
ation (Provision of Meals) Act, 1906. D.F. Adams. London
Ph.D. 1954.

The Education Act 1918: an assessment of its place in   5533
the development of educational administration in England.
L.I. Andrews. London Ph.D. 1970.

Regional Education

Some aspects of the development of education in Newbury 5534
in the 19th century. T.V.B. Morrison. Reading M.Phil.
1966/7.

A history of the education of children in the Blackburn 5535
hundred to 1870. C. Birtwistle. London M.Sc. (Ext.) 1952.

The development of education in Chorley and district   5536
from 1800 to 1902. K.P.C. Thorne. Lancaster M.Litt. 1970.

The development of education in Barnsley in the 19th   5537
century, prior to direct state intervention. H.C. Hillary.
Sheffield M.A. 1941.

The development of the educational facilities of South- 5538
port, 1825-1944. W.E. Marsden. Sheffield M.A. 1959.

The development of public education in Nelson, Lanca-   5539
shire, 1832-1902. G.I. Hawkes. Wales M.A. 1964.

St. Helens, 1845 and afterwards: an illustration of   5540
educational development. W.A. Fawcett. Liverpool M.A. 1936.

The educational work of the Sisters of Notre Dame in   5541
Lancashire since 1850. Margaret P. Linscott. Liverpool M.A.
1959/60.

The history of education and educational institutions   5542
in Nottinghamshire, excluding the city of Nottingham, from
1800 to 1930. Edith M. Becket. London Ph.D. (Ext.) 1936.

The history of education in Nottingham, with special refer- 5542A
ence to the 19th century. D. Wardle. Nottingham Ph.D. 1965.

Rural education in Shropshire in the 19th century.   5543
J.P. Dodd. Birmingham M.A. 1958.

The progress of education in Bristol. H.J. Larcombe.   5544
Bristol M.A. 1924.

Educational development in the city of Bath, 1830-1902, 5545
with special reference to its interrelations with social and
economic change. R.B. Hope. Bristol Ph.D. 1970.

A history of education in Rotherham and district up to   5546
1902. R. Harrison. Bristol M.A. 1951.

Isaac Ironside and education in the Sheffield region in the 5547
first half of the 19th century. J. Salt. Sheffield M.A. 1960.

Thomas Asline Ward: his life and achievements and their 5548
effect upon the development of Sheffield. G.D. Jennett.
Sheffield M.A. 1954.

5549   The history of education in the town of Brecon to 1902.
T.P. Jones. London M.A. (Ext.) 1965.
5550   The development of education in Swansea, 1846-1902.
Jean A. Weaver. Wales M.A. 1957.
5551   Church and chapel as sources and centres of education
in Wales during the second half of the 19th century. L.S.
Jones. Liverpool M.A. 1940.
5552   A history of education in the towns of Barry and Penarth
together with the neighbouring parishes of Leckwith, Llandough
juxta Penarth, Lavernock, Sully, St. Andrews, Wenvoe, High-
light, Porthkerry and Penmark during the period 1860-1930.
J. Thomas. Wales M.A. 1933.
5553   The life and work of Sir Isambard Owen (1850-1927), with
particular reference to his contribution to education in
Wales. G.A. Jones. Wales M.A. 1967.
5554   Educational policy and administration change: a study
of evolving concepts and practices in educational administration in a Welsh rural county (Montgomeryshire, 1870-1967).
J.A. Davies. London Ph.D. (Ext.) 1968.
5555   The development of educational provision in the rural
county of Shropshire between 1870 and 1914, with particular
reference to the policy of the county council. T.D.M. Jones.
Keele M.A. 1968/9.
5556   A historical investigation of the development of a local
system of education in the city of Birmingham from 1870 to
1924. M.E.J. Shewell. London M.A. 1952.
5557   Education in West Hartlepool before the Act of 1902.
A.C. Klottrup. Sheffield M.A. 1969.
5558   Public education in late Victorian Lancashire. E.C.
Midwinter. Liverpool M.A. 1969/70.
5559   Elementary and secondary education in Hampshire between
1890 and 1914. D.C. Savage. Southampton M.Phil. 1970.
5560   Some researches into education in Dartford, Kent, with
reference to Kentish educational development as a whole, from
1902 until the middle of the 20th century. J.W. Butler.
London Ph.D. 1959.
5561   The organisation, development and administration of
public education in the area of the London County Council,
1903-22. P.H. Andrews. London Ph.D. 1963.
5562   The development of education in Chesterfield, 1919-44.
R.M. Lewis. Sheffield M.A. 1961.

Elementary Education

5563   The contribution of Methodism to popular education,
1800-50. H.F. Mathews. Liverpool M.A. 1946.
5564   The development of elementary education in the 19th
century: the role of the Committee of the Privy Council on
Education and the Hertfordshire gentry. J.S. Hurt. London
Ph.D. 1968.
5565   The elementary school manager and the management of
education, 1800-1902. P. Gordon. London Ph.D. 1970.
5566   English elementary schools, 1801-40. A. Birtles. Leeds
M.A. 1911.
5567   The development of Catholic elementary education in the
19th century in the five counties of the diocese of Nottingham. J. Bastow. Nottingham M.Phil. 1970.
5568   The history and development of boys' preparatory schools
in England. F.C. Pritchard. London M.A. 1938.
5569   A study of rewards and punishments in the elementary
schools of England and Wales, 1800-93. P.J. Rooke. London
M.A. (Ext.) 1962.
5570   A study of the education of the working class in Stockport during the 19th century. I.J.D. Steele. Sheffield M.A.
1968.
5571   Manchester and the movement for national elementary
education, 1800-70. S.E. Maltby. Manchester M.A. 1916.

The changing social content of elementary education as 5572
reflected in school books in use in England, 1808-70. M.
Goldstrom. Birmingham Ph.D. 1968.

The origin, development and organisation of certain 5573
Lancastrian schools in London, Middlesex and Surrey: a comparative study. J.R. Carr. London M.A. 1963.

The educational influence of Robert Owen in England, 5574
with particular reference to the infant schools directly
developed from the New Lanark pattern between 1819 and 1839.
D.A. Turner. London M.Phil. 1969.

The contribution of Henry Brougham to the movement for 5575
the extension of elementary education in England between 1815
and 1839. Monica Molloy. Liverpool M.A. 1956/7.

The Liverpool Corporation schools and the movement for 5576
national elementary education: an account of an experiment.
J. Murphy. Liverpool Ph.D. 1955/6.

The work of the established church in the education of 5577
the people, 1833-70. H.J. Burgess. London Ph.D. 1954.

The Church of England's contribution to popular educ- 5578
ation in England after 1833. C.K.F. Brown. Oxford B.Litt.
1941.

The education of children engaged in industry in Eng- 5579
land, 1833-76. A.H. Robson. London Ph.D. 1930.

Sir Thomas Wyse and the Central Society of Education. 5580
I.D. Harry. Wales M.A. 1932.

The Ragged School Union and the education of the London 5581
poor in the 19th century. E.A.G. Clark. London M.A. 1967.

Voluntary effort in English elementary schools, 1846 5582
to 1870: a study of the contribution of school managers to
educational developments. Nancy Ball. Keele Ph.D. 1970.

Methodism and the education of the people (since 1851). 5583
H.F. Mathews. London Ph.D. (Ext.) 1954.

A historical survey of legislation bearing on the educ- 5584
ation of mentally deficient children in England and Wales,
1850-1955. R.P. Singh. London M.A. 1960.

The dissemination of Froebelian doctrines and methods 5585
in the English system of elementary education, 1854 to 1914.
Irene M. Lilley. London M.A. 1963.

Some researches into public elementary education in 5586
Dartford, Kent, in the second half of the 19th century. J.W.
Butler. London M.A. 1956.

The development of elementary education in Walsall, 5587
1862-1902. P. Liddle. London M.A. (Ext.) 1967.

The elementary schools of Bath, 1862-1902. P.F. Speed. 5588
Bristol M.A. 1958.

The contribution of the National Society to Welsh educ- 5589
ation (1811-70). T.P. Jones. London Ph.D. (Ext.) 1968.

A contribution to the history of elementary education 5590
in North Wales (up to 1870), with special reference to
National schools. T.R. Hughes. Liverpool M.A. 1935.

The history of church schools in Swansea during the 5591
19th century to 1870. A.L. Trott. Wales M.A. 1941.

A history of elementary education in Wales, 1847-70. 5592
A.L. Trott. Wales Ph.D. 1966.

The struggle for the Elementary Education Act and its 5593
implementation - 1870 to 1873. D. Roland. Oxford B.Litt.
1958.

Some aspects of the making of policy in elementary 5594
education in England and Wales, 1870-95. Mrs. Gillian R.
Sutherland, née Thomas. Oxford D.Phil. 1970.

The problems of English elementary education since 5595
1870: the evolution of opinion and the development of the
system. H.A. Grimshaw. London M.Sc. 1918.

A history of the English village school in the light of 5596
changing educational policy and organisation between the
Forster Act of 1870 and the Balfour Act of 1902. H.B.A.
Wise. Oxford B.Litt. 1960.

5597   Provision for schooling in an English village, Wraysbury - 1870-1944. J.L. Robson. London M.A. (Ext.) 1965.

5598   Elementary school work, 1875-1925. R.D. Bramwell. Durham Ph.D. 1958.

5599   The history of the Birmingham School Board, 1870-1903. A.F. Taylor. Birmingham M.A. 1955.

5600   A history of education in Bradford during the period of the Bradford School Board, 1870-1904. A.J. Evans. Leeds M.A. 1947.

5601   The work of the school board in rural Essex, 1870 to 1903. Barbara J. Smith. London M.A. 1968.

5602   Elementary education in the Lewisham district at the time of the School Board for London, 1870-1903. D.H.B. Andrews. London M.A. 1965.

5603   The school boards of Stoke-upon-Trent and Burslem, 1870-1903. S. Clews. Sheffield M.A. 1962.

5604   A history of elementary education in the Fylde area of Lancashire during the period 1870-1903. W. Bentley. Liverpool M.A. 1960/1.

5605   The organisation and administration of elementary education by the school board of three selected districts of Surrey, Mitcham, Woking and Betchworth, between 1870 and 1903. J.A. Dewey. London M.A. 1964.

5606   Truant schools of the School Board for London. T.D. Morgan. London M.A. 1956.

5607   The early years of the Tynemouth School Board. B.G. Everett. Durham M.A. 1964.

5608   A general survey of the school board movement as it affected Monmouthshire, with special reference to the town of Newport. D.E. Davies. Wales M.A. 1927.

5609   The work of the Llanwonno School Board following the 1870 Education Act to 1902. Anita Jordan. Wales M.A. 1968.

5610   The history of the Chesterfield School Board, from 1870 to 1912. W.R. Covell. Sheffield M.A. 1952.

5611   A survey of the administrative problems facing the voluntary public elementary day schools during the period 1890-7. D. Tunstall. London M.A. 1959.

5612   The voluntary schools in four Lancashire county boroughs, 1903-63: a study of policies and provision. S.E. Kelly. Keele M.A. 1968/9.

5613   An examination of the political and legislative background to the development of Catholic elementary education in England in the early 20th century. R. Pattison. Leeds Ph.D. 1969.

5614   The development of senior elementary schools in three administrative areas of Worcestershire, 1918-44. W.D. Robinson. Keele M.A. 1969/70.

Secondary Education

5615   The Methodist contribution to 19th-century secondary education. F.C. Pritchard. London Ph.D. (Ext.) 1947.

5616   The place of secondary education in Welsh society, 1800-1918. J.R. Webster. Wales Ph.D. 1959.

5617   The content and quality of secondary education at an English Catholic seminary in the 19th century - Ushaw, 1808-63. J.S. Malone. London M.A. (Ext.) 1969.

5618   A history of Harrow School and its relationship to its neighbourhood throughout the 19th century. T.F. May. London M.Phil. 1969.

5619   The educational work of the Very Reverend Charles John Vaughan. M.D.W. Poole. Sheffield M.A. 1966.

5620   The Victorian public school, 1828-1902: the school as a community. J.R. de S. Honey. Oxford D.Phil. 1970.

5621   The history of Hazelwood School, Birmingham, and its influence on educational developments in the 19th century. C.G. Hey. Wales M.A. 1954.

John Ford, 1801-75: the life, work and influence of a   5622
Quaker schoolmaster. L.J. Stroud. London Ph.D. (Ext.) 1947.

The internal organisation of boys' secondary schools in 5623
England during the middle decades of the 19th century. R.H.
Sturman. London M.A. 1932.

The established church and the education of the Victor- 5624
ian middle classes: a study of the Woodard schools, 1847-91.
W.B.D. Heeney. Oxford D.Phil. 1962.

The life and work of Nathaniel Woodard, with special   5625
reference to the influence of the Oxford Movement on English
education in the 19th century. R. Perry. Bristol M.A. 1932.

The Lancashire Public School Association, later the   5626
National Public School Association, in its role as a pressure
group, with an account of the Manchester Model Secular School,
later the Manchester Free School. D.K. Jones. Sheffield
M.A. 1965.

The origin and subsequent development of St. Mary's   5627
College, Hammersmith, 1847-99. J.A. Britton. London M.A.
1964.

A short history of secondary grammar education in   5628
Jersey, as exemplified in the story of Victoria College,
Jersey. P. Ahier. London M.A. (Ext.) 1963.

The life and influence of Edward Thring. C.J. Rigby.   5629
Oxford D.Phil. 1969.

The development of the theory and practice of further   5630
education in England since the Act of 1870. T.D. Buxton.
London M.A. 1955.

The history of education in Wales from 1870, with   5631
special reference to secondary education to 1920. T.I. Ellis.
Wales M.A. 1930.

A comparative study of the curriculum and organisation   5632
of secondary education in England and the United States
between 1870 and 1900. B.S. Cane. London M.A. 1957.

Public opinion and reform of secondary education, 1888- 5633
1902, as reflected in parliament and the national press. D.R.
Felsenstein. London M.A. 1965.

The development of secondary education in Radnorshire,   5634
1889-1963. R.S. Griffiths. Wales M.A. 1965.

The development of secondary education in Montgomery-   5635
shire since 1889. L.H. Williams. Wales M.A. 1962.

A study in the growth of state secondary education in   5636
Breconshire, 1889-1939. J. Llewellyn. Wales M.A. 1968/9.

The development of secondary education in south   5637
Pembrokeshire, 1889-1939. K.D. Evans. Wales M.A. 1970.

The changing environment of the London grammar school, 5638
1900-50. F.C. Campbell. London Ph.D. 1953.

The development in London of elementary education of a   5639
higher type, 1900-10. R. Morley. London M.A. 1961.

The concept and nature of the grammar school in rel-   5640
ation to the development of secondary education since 1902.
Olive L. Banks. London Ph.D. 1953.

The development of the bilateral system of secondary   5641
education in Caernarvonshire, 1903 to date. P.E. Owen. London Ph.D. 1961.

A critical survey of Board of Education policy in rel-   5642
ation to resulting reforms in post-primary and secondary
education since 1904. J.T.R. Graves. Oxford B.Litt. 1939.

The Labour party and the organisation of secondary   5643
education, 1918-65. M.H. Parkinson. Manchester M.A. 1968.

Higher Education

Higher education in Lancashire in the 19th century. E. 5644
Smith. Oxford B.Litt. 1922.

The origins and development of the university movement   5645
in Wales, with particular reference to the period 1800-89.
I.J. Morgan. Wales M.A. 1929.

5646   Henry Robinson Hartley: his family, his life and the establishment of the Hartley Institution. A. Anderson. Southampton M.A. 1962.

5647   The University of London, 1820-60, with special reference to its influence on the development of higher education. F.G. Brook. London Ph.D. 1958.

5648   Roman Catholics and higher education in England, 1830-1903. V.A. McClelland. Sheffield Ph.D. 1968.

5649   A history of the Royal Academy Schools, 1837-78. H.C. Morgan. Leeds Ph.D. 1968.

5650   The social and economic aspects of higher education for women between 1844 and 1870, with special reference to the North of England Council. Stella R. Wills. London M.A. 1952.

5651   Higher education for women: the opposition in England during the 19th century. Joan N. Burstyn. London Ph.D. (Ext.) 1968.

5652   Susanna and Catherine Winkworth, 1830-60. B.H. Jackson. Manchester M.A. 1969.

5653   The early development of the university extension movement under the influence of James Stuart. H. Gordon. Sheffield M.A. 1941.

5654   The development of education in theological colleges in the Church of England and in the Protestant Episcopal Church of America, 1900-50. S.F.D. Walters. Oxford D.Phil. 1957.

Adult Education

5655   The development of adult education in Warrington during the 19th century. W.B. Stephens. Exeter M.A. 1958.

5656   George Birkbeck, pioneer of adult education. T. Kelly. Liverpool Ph.D. 1957.

5657   The origin and development of the Yorkshire Union of Mechanics' Institutes. J. Popple. Sheffield M.A. 1960.

5658   The Mechanics' Institute movement in Lancashire and Yorkshire, 1824-60, with particular reference to the institutions in Manchester, Ashton-under-Lyne and Huddersfield. Mrs. Mabel Tylecote, née Phythian. Manchester Ph.D. 1930.

5659   Social and religious influences in adult education in Yorkshire between 1830 and 1870. J.F.C. Harrison. Leeds Ph.D. 1955.

5660   The Mechanics' Institutes of South Wales. T. Evans. Sheffield Ph.D. 1966.

5661   The miner's search for self-improvement: the history of evening classes in the Rhondda valley from 1862 to 1914. Margaret Turner. Wales M.A. 1967.

5662   The development of state-aided evening schools for adults between 1870 and 1902. K.A. Percy. Nottingham M.A. 1969.

5663   The London School Board and the development of evening education, 1870-93. S. Somper. London M.A. 1954.

Technical and Other Subjects

5664   The teaching of geography in 19th-century Britain. P.J. Hart. London M.A. 1957.

5665   The historical development of the history syllabus in boys' secondary schools in England, 1800-1900. M.A.F. Cooper. London M.A. 1950.

5666   The place of history in English secondary education from c.1830 to 1890. G.M.D. Henderson-Howat. Oxford B.Litt. 1963.

5667   The sciences and humanities in English grammar schools in relation to the climate of opinion, 1805-1904. N.W. Saffin. London M.A. 1957.

5668   The place of the Royal Institution of South Wales in the history of scientific and general education in the 19th century. H.M. Davies. Wales M.A. 1940.

The development of scientific education during the 5669
second half of the 19th century, with special reference to
the influence of John Tyndall. D. Thompson. Sheffield M.A.
1955.

The teaching of science in England during the latter 5670
half of the 19th century, and Huxley's influence on its
development. W. Hall. Sheffield M.A. 1931.

The scientific and educational influence of Sir Henry 5671
Enfield Roscoe (1833-1915), with particular reference to his
work in Manchester. N. Limgard. Liverpool M.A. 1969/70.

The development of the teaching of chemistry in Eng- 5672
land, 1799-1853. M.S. Byrne. Durham M.A. 1968.

The evolution of technical education in 19th-century 5673
England. P. Keane. Bath Ph.D. 1970.

The development of technical education in Essex. 5674
Marjorie M. Collison. London M.A. 1955.

The effect of national developments on technical educ- 5675
ation in Bury, Oldham and Preston before 1889. T.A. Smith.
Liverpool M.A. 1966/7.

The history of Gloucester Technical College. P.G. 5676
Rossington. Bristol M.A. 1963.

The development of education in Swindon, with particular 5677
reference to the influence and requirements of the railway works
and other local industries. B. Lloyd. Bristol M.A. 1954.

Origins and development of the administration of tech- 5678
nical education in England, c.1850-1904. P.E. Hannon. London M.A. 1960.

The historical development of technical and vocational 5679
education within the area of the county borough of West Ham
since 1850. J.R. Soar. London M.A. 1966.

The history of technical education in Rotherham with 5680
particular reference to the period 1850-1918. H.P. Reilly.
Sheffield M.A. 1952.

The development of technical education in England from 5681
1851 to 1889, with special reference to economic factors.
D.H. Thomas. London Ph.D. 1940.

The history of technical education in Nottinghamshire, 5682
1851-1902. H.K. Briscoe. Sheffield M.A. 1952.

Commercial education in England during 1851 to 1902: an 5683
institutional study. M.A. Dalvi. London Ph.D. 1957.

Public opinion and technical education in England, 5684
1867-1906. (A study of the awakening of English opinion to
the importance of scientific research and technical education
as factors of economic and military power.) J. Blanchet.
Oxford D.Phil. 1953.

An enquiry into the policy of the Free Churches with 5685
reference to religious education in the schools, 1870-1944.
D.H. Thomas. Wales M.A. 1955.

Developments since 1870 in the teaching of religion in 5686
the public elementary schools of England, with special reference to senior schools. O. White. Oxford B.Litt. 1939.

The evolution of special education, 1893-1939. P.H. 5687
Butterfield. London Ph.D. 1970.

The London Polytechnic movement, with special reference 5688
to Quintin Hogg. F. Johnson. London M.A. 1929.

Post-elementary education in the area of the London 5689
Technical Education Board, 1893-1904. P.H. Andrews. London
M.A. 1959.

Teaching Profession

The training of teachers in England and Wales during 5690
the 19th century. R.W. Rich. London Ph.D. (Ext.) 1934.

Sir James Kay-Shuttleworth: an examination of the in- 5691
fluence of his work and ideas in the field of elementary
teacher training from 1840 to 1899. G.H.W. Peach. London
M.A. 1970.

5692   A history of the College of Sarum St. Michael (Salisbury Training College) from its foundation in 1841 until 1902. B.D. Bevan. London M.A. (Ext.) 1970.

5693   The history of the training of teachers for secondary schools in England, c.1846-1930. Miriam G. Fitch. London M.A. 1931.

5694   A critical examination of teacher training in Wales, 1846-98. L.M. Rees. Wales Ph.D. 1968/9.

5695   The registration of teachers in England and Wales from 1846 to 1899, with special reference to the development of common interest and professional independence. F.L. Massey. London M.A. 1957.

5696   Individual, local and national bargaining for teachers' salaries in England and Wales: a study of the period 1858-1944. S.E. Barnes. London Ph.D. 1959.

5697   The development of professional status among the elementary teachers under the School Board for London, 1870-1904. R.A. Williams. London M.A. 1953.

5698   The determination of teachers' salaries, with particular reference to secondary schools, 1870-1919. H.D. Papworth. London M.A. 1964.

5699   The secondary schoolmaster, 1895-1914: a study of the qualifications, conditions of employment and professional associations of masters in English secondary schools. G. Baron. London Ph.D. 1952.

5700   The training of teachers in England and Wales, 1900-39. A. Shakoor. Leicester Ph.D. 1964.

5701   The history of Bangor Normal College from its inception to 1908. L.M. Rees. Wales M.A. 1955.

LOCAL HISTORY

5702   The economic and social development of extra-metropolitan Middlesex during the 19th century (1800-1914). M. Rees. London M.Sc. 1955.

5703   The economic and social development of Dewsbury in the 19th century. D.A. Dean. Sheffield M.A. 1963.

5704   Some aspects of the economy of Hull in the 19th century, with special reference to business history. Joyce M. Bellamy. Hull Ph.D. 1965.

5705   The evolution of Preston townscapes. K.M. Spencer. Liverpool M.A. 1968.

5706   London, 1801-51: a geographical study. O.H.K. Spate. Cambridge Ph.D. 1937.

5707   Urban growth in Bradford and environs, 1800-1960. M.J. Mortimore. Leeds M.A. 1963.

5708   The growth, development and modern functions of the county borough of Bradford. H.B. Hodgson. Leeds M.A. 1939.

5709   Studies in the development of the parish of Bradford, 1800-47. Lucy Flanagan. Liverpool M.A. 1931.

5710   The functions and growth of the city of Exeter, 1800-41. N.M. Simmonds. Exeter M.A. 1959.

5711   Victorian Exeter, 1837-1914. R. Newton. Exeter Ph.D. 1966.

5712   The development of municipal government in Swansea in the 19th century. T. Ridd. Wales M.A. 1955.

5713   The development of quarter sessions government in Devonshire in the 19th century and the transition to county council government. D.R. Tucker. London M.A. (Ext.) 1949.

5714   The transition from quarter sessions to county councils in the 19th century. B.J.V. Scott. Exeter M.A. 1962.

5715   The social and economic development of Crewe, 1800-1923. W.H. Chaloner. Manchester Ph.D. 1939.

5716   The social and economic development of Crewe, 1830-80. W.H. Chaloner. Manchester M.A. 1937.

Nuneaton: a study in urban growth. D. Milburn. London 5717
M.Sc. 1959.

Geographical aspects of the development of Wirksworth   5718
from the beginning of the 19th century to the present. F.S.
Ottrey. Nottingham M.A. 1966.

Lincoln: a study in urban morphology. R. Knowles.   5719
Nottingham M.A. 1962.

An urban study of Loughborough. Gladys H. Wedlock.   5720
Nottingham M.A. 1952.

Wolverton: a study in urban geography. Moira Courtman. 5721
London M.Phil. 1968.

The development of Buxton and Matlock since 1800. T.   5722
Marchington. London M.A. 1961.

The public accounts of the county of Lancaster from   5723
1820 to 1889. D. Gregory. Leeds M.A. 1966.

The administration of the county of Lancashire, 1838-   5724
88. A.F. Davie. Manchester Ph.D. 1968.

The old and the new: the corporation of Bristol, 1820-   5725
51. G.W.A. Bush. Bristol Ph.D. 1965.

The work of the Halifax town trustees from the passing   5726
of the Improvement Act of 1823 to the incorporation of the
borough in 1848. G.R. Dalby. Leeds M.A. 1953.

The economic development of York, 1830-1914. B.F.   5727
Duckham. Manchester M.A. 1956.

The social structure of York, 1841-51. W.A. Armstrong. 5728
Birmingham Ph.D. 1967.

The social and economic history of St. Helens, 1830-   5729
1900. T.C. Barker. Manchester Ph.D. 1951.

The social and economic development of Middlesbrough,   5730
1830-88. W.S. Martin. Manchester M.A. 1945.

Local government in Penzance, 1830-75. R.J. Sadler.   5731
Wales M.A. 1951/2.

Southampton in the early dock and railway age, 1830-60. 5732
Patricia H. Morris. Southampton M.A. 1957.

The development of local government in Salford, 1830-   5733
53. R.L. Greenall. Leicester M.A. 1970.

Urban development and redevelopment in Croydon, 1835-   5734
1940. R.C.W. Cox. Leicester Ph.D. 1970.

Some aspects of the urban development of Croydon, 1870- 5735
1940. R.C.W. Cox. Leicester M.A. 1966.

Reading, 1835-1930: a community power study. A.F.   5736
Cook. Reading Ph.D. 1970.

The social, economic and political development of   5737
Derby, 1835-88. J.D. Standen. Leeds M.A. 1959.

Early Fleetwood, 1835-47. J.H. Sutton. Lancaster   5738
M.Litt. 1968.

The Municipal Reform Act, 1835. G.B.A.M. Finlayson.   5739
Oxford B.Litt. 1959.

Coventry and the Municipal Corporations Act, 1835: an   5740
investigation of the workings of Coventry Corporation mainly
between 1750 and 1835, and a critical examination of the
Commissioners' Report of 1833. S.E. Kerrison. Birmingham
M.A. 1939.

The suburban development of Greater London, south of   5741
the Thames, 1836-1914. H.J. Dyos. London Ph.D. 1952.

Local government and some aspects of social change in   5742
the parishes of Lambeth, Battersea, and Wandsworth, 1838-88.
Janet Roebuck. London Ph.D. 1968.

Capital investment in the western suburbs of Victorian   5743
London. D.A. Reeder. Leicester Ph.D. 1965.

The Potteries of Kensington: a study of slum develop-   5744
ment in Victorian London. Mrs. Patricia E. Malcolmson.
Leicester M.Phil. 1970.

The social and economic development of Nottingham in   5745
the 19th century. R.A. Church. Nottingham Ph.D. 1960.

The social structure of Nottingham and adjacent dis-   5746
tricts in the mid 19th century. R.J. Smith. Nottingham Ph.D.
1968.

5747   Township boundaries in Furness and Cartmel in the first edition of the Ordnance Survey (1846-7). C.J. Hogg. Liverpool M.A. 1951.

5748   Social and economic conditions in the industrial towns of the West Riding of Yorkshire in the hungry forties. Joyce Hargrave. Leeds M.A. 1940.

5749   Social and administrative development of Chadderton, 1847-1914. Elsie Beech. Manchester M.A. 1949.

5750   The city of Wakefield: a study of the growth and functions of an urban settlement. Rosie Bentham. London M.A. 1939.

5751   Some geographical aspects of urban development in the lower Lea valley since 1850. Alison D. Grady. London M.A. 1958.

5752   The economic development of Kettering, 1850-1914. B.J. Loasby. Cambridge M.Litt. 1957.

5753   The social and economic development of Whitstable, with particular reference to local government administration. R.A.R. Gray. Kent M.A. 1970.

5754   A history of the development of Walthamstow, 1851-1901. R. Wall. London M.Phil. 1969.

5755   Suburban growth in north-west Kent, 1861-1961. Mary Waugh. London Ph.D. 1968.

5756   Mansfield: the evolution of an urban landscape, 1863-1963. J.R.G. Jennings. Nottingham Ph.D. 1966.

5757   The role of religious dissent in the reform of municipal government in Birmingham, 1865-76. E.P. Hennock. Cambridge Ph.D. 1956.

5758   The development of city government in the United States and the United Kingdom, with special reference to the period since 1870. E.S. Griffith. Oxford D.Phil. 1925.

5759   Changes in land use in the borough of Northampton during the past 100 years. M.F. Collins. Oxford B.Litt. 1970.

5760   The economic and social development of South Kirkby and South Elmsall, 1873-1921. W.G. Branford. Leeds M.A. 1957.

5761   The growth of Aylesbury and the development of its urban morphology, 1878-1957. C.J. Cheshire. Birmingham M.A. 1958.

5762   The social structure and economy of south-west Wales in the late 19th century. J.H. Davies. Wales M.A. 1967.

5763   Barry: an urban and social geography, 1885-1966. J.A. Giggs. Wales Ph.D. 1967.

5764   A history of local government in the West Riding of Yorkshire since 1888. H. Roberts. Leeds M.Comm. 1943.

5765   A study of the change in social origins, political affiliations and length of service of members of the Leeds City Council, 1888-1953. Brenda M. Powell. Leeds M.A. 1958.

5766   The political structure of the Wolverhampton Borough Council since 1900. G.W. Jones. Oxford D.Phil. 1965.

5767   Eccles: a study in town development. Audrey E. Lumb. Manchester M.A. 1958.

5768   Geographical aspects of the evolution of Boston, Lincolnshire, in the 20th century. F.H. Molyneux. Nottingham M.A. 1968.

5769   An economic geography of Alfreton, Heanor and Ripley with special reference to changes in the 20th century. G.A. Measures. Nottingham M.A. 1969.

5770   A comparative study of the contemporary and pre-war urban geography of the East End of London. Gillian M.L. Simpson. London M.A. 1959.

SCOTLAND

5771   The history of the teaching of classics in Scotland until 1872. G.M. Sutton. St. Andrews Ph.D. 1956.

5772   Education in Aberdeenshire before 1872. I.J. Simpson. Aberdeen Ph.D. 1942.

Scottish teachers and educational policy, 1803-72:   5773
attitudes and influence. J.D. Myers. Edinburgh Ph.D. 1970.
    A history of education in Stirlingshire up to the Act   5774
of 1872. A. Bain. St. Andrews Ph.D. 1960.
    A survey of church influence on education in Scotland,   5775
with special reference to the extent and content of religious
teaching in the day schools before 1872. D.M. McFarlan.
Glasgow Ph.D. 1956/7.
    The Scottish tradition in education: an intimate study   5776
of the early 19th century. I.D.B. Finlayson. Glasgow Ph.D.
1956/7.
    An enquiry into the reading habits of the working   5777
classes in Scotland from 1830 to 1840. A.R. Thompson. Glasgow B.Litt. 1961.
    A history of the public library movement in Scotland.   5778
W.R. Aitken. Edinburgh Ph.D. 1956.
    The development of public libraries in Scotland. W.E.   5779
Tyler. Strathclyde M.A. 1967.
    A history of the Scottish farm worker, 1800-50. G.F.B.   5780
Houston. Oxford B.Litt. 1954.
    James Loch and the house of Sutherland, 1812-55. E.S.   5781
Richards. Nottingham Ph.D. 1967.
    The development of the port and trade of Dundee, 1815-   5782
1967. N.I. Beckles. Dundee Ph.D. 1968.
    The decline of the handloom weaving industry in Scot-   5783
land during the years 1815-45. Mrs. Brenda P.R. Gaskin.
Edinburgh Ph.D. 1955.
    James Young, Scottish industrialist and philanthropist.   5784
J. Butt. Glasgow Ph.D. 1964.
    William Lindsay Alexander (1808-84), the man and his   5785
work. C.C. Wallick. Edinburgh Ph.D. 1950/1.
    William Arnot: his life, work and thought. S.H.   5786
Merriam. Edinburgh Ph.D. 1956.
    The influence, direct and indirect, of the writings of   5787
Erskine of Linlathen on religious thought in Scotland. R.A.
Reid. Edinburgh Ph.D. 1930.
    The contribution of Thomas Erskine of Linlathen and his   5788
writings to Scottish theology. J.C. Conn. St. Andrews Ph.D.
1935.
    John Brown of Edinburgh, 1784-1858, churchman and theo-   5789
logian. W.L. McCoy. Edinburgh Ph.D. 1956.
    William Symington, churchman and theologian, 1795-1862.   5790
R. Blackwood. Edinburgh Ph.D. 1962/3.
    Robert Murray McCheyne (1813-43): a study of an early   5791
19th-century Scottish Evangelical. D.V. Yeaworth. Edinburgh Ph.D. 1957.
    Coal mining in the west of Scotland in the 19th cent-   5792
ury: the Dixon enterprises. A. Slaven. Glasgow B.Litt. 1967.
    The growth and fluctuations of the Scottish pig iron   5793
trade, 1828-73. R.H. Campbell. Aberdeen Ph.D. 1956.
    The economic history of the Scottish iron and steel   5794
industry, with particular reference to the period 1830-80.
I.F. Gibson. London Ph.D. 1955.
    Religion and society in the early 19th century: a com-   5795
parative study of church parties within the established
churches of Massachusetts and Scotland. Wendy S. Wilson.
Aberdeen M.Litt. 1969.
    The voluntary controversy in the Church of Scotland,   5796
1829-43. A.B. Montgomery. Edinburgh Ph.D. 1953.
    The failure and recovery of social criticism in the   5797
Scottish Church, 1830-1950. D.C. Smith. Edinburgh Ph.D.
1964.
    Middle-class housing and the growth of suburban com-   5798
munities in the West End of Glasgow, 1830-1914. M.A. Simpson. Glasgow B.Litt. 1970.
    The American Negro in Scotland in the 19th century.   5799
E.S.H. Dixon. Edinburgh M.Litt. 1968/9.

5800   Glasgow parliamentary constituency, 1832-46. D.A. Teviotdale. Glasgow B.Litt. 1963.

5801   Scottish Chartism and its economic background. L.C. Wright. Edinburgh Ph.D. 1951.

5801A   The Chartist movement in Scotland. A. Wilson. Oxford D.Phil. 1951.

5802   Andrew A. Bonar, 1810-92: a study of his life, work and religious thought. R.E. Palmer. Edinburgh Ph.D. 1955.

5803   Railways and the transformation of the Scottish economy. W. Vamplew. Edinburgh Ph.D. 1969.

5804   School inspection in Scotland, 1840-1966. T.R. Bone. Glasgow Ph.D. 1967.

5805   The life and work of William Bell Scott, 1811-90. Mrs. Vera Smith. Durham Ph.D. 1953.

5806   Note issue in Scottish banking, 1844-1953. M. Gaskin. Liverpool M.A. 1954/5.

5807   Aspects of the population geography of the eastern border counties of Scotland, 1850-1967. Joan MacC. Galt. Edinburgh Ph.D. 1968.

5808   The rural-urban fringe of Edinburgh, 1850-1967. A.J. Strachan. Edinburgh Ph.D. 1969.

5809   The renascence of churchmanship in the Church of Scotland, 1850-1920. W. Horsburgh. St. Andrews Ph.D. 1958.

5810   The Scots coal industry, 1854-66. A.T. Youngson. Aberdeen Ph.D. 1953.

5811   An economic history of shipbuilding and engineering, with special reference to the west of Scotland. W.S. Cormack. Glasgow Ph.D. 1930.

5812   Changing forms of church life: a study of the churches and town of St. Andrews, 1865-1965. W.F. Hobbs. St. Andrews Ph.D. 1968.

5813   The origin and development of the Old Catholic group of churches, etc. W.H. de Voil. Edinburgh Ph.D. 1937.

5814   Education in Lanarkshire: a historical survey on the Act of 1872 from original and contemporary sources. Mary M. Mackintosh. Glasgow Ph.D. 1969.

5815   The ad hoc administration of education in Scotland, 1872-1929. J.H. Walker. Glasgow Ph.D. 1970.

5816   The School Board of Glasgow, 1873-1919. J.M. Roxburgh. Glasgow B.Litt. 1969.

5817   The Scottish economy during the 'Great Depression', 1873-96, with special reference to the heavy industries of the south-west. T.J. Byres. Glasgow B.Litt. 1963.

5818   The Liberal party in Scotland, 1885-95. J.G. Kellas. London Ph.D. 1962.

5819   The industrial geography of Ayrshire and its development since 1900. D.F. Hagger. London M.Sc. 1955.

5820   Local authority housing in Dundee, 1919-39. W.D. Carroll. Dundee B.Phil. 1969.

5821   A survey of Scottish internal transport since 1920. R.T. Foster. Wales M.A. 1965.

IRELAND

5822   The application in Ireland of English and British legislation made before 1801. A.G. Donaldson. Belfast Ph.D. 1952.

5823   Urban settlements of Co. Antrim. D.A. Clerk. Belfast M.A. 1949.

5824   The development of education in the county of Londonderry from 1800 to 1922. W.D. Hamilton. Belfast M.A. 1963.

5825   A history of the Londonderry shirt industry. E.H. Slade. Belfast M.A. 1937.

5826   The historical geography of Londonderry in the 19th century. J.H. Johnson. London Ph.D. 1962.

The economic significance of the London companies as 5827
landlords in Ireland during the period 1800-70. Olive Robinson. Belfast Ph.D. 1957.

The Downshire estates in Ireland under the 3rd marquis 5828
of Downshire, 1801-45: a study of Irish estate management in
the first half of the 19th century. W.A. Maguire. Belfast
Ph.D. 1968.

Irish immigration into Great Britain, 1798-1838. 5829
Barbara M. Kerr. Oxford B.Litt. 1939.

Irish immigration in Great Britain during the first half 5830
of the 19th century. F.L. Wilson. Manchester M.A. 1946.

The civil administration of Ireland, 1801-48. S.M. 5831
Houghton. Manchester M.A. 1924.

An assessment of the social, religious and political 5832
aspects of Congregationalism in Ireland in the 19th century.
J.M. Henry. Belfast Ph.D. 1965.

Presbyterian missionary activity among Irish Roman 5833
Catholics in the 19th century. R.J. Rodgers. Belfast M.A.
1969.

History of the ruling eldership in Irish Presbyterian- 5834
ism. J.M. Barkley. Belfast M.A. 1952.

The training of teachers in Ireland from 1811 to the 5835
present day. J.W. Musson. Belfast Ph.D. 1955.

The influence of the Rev. Henry Cooke on the political 5836
life of Ulster. J. Jamieson. Belfast M.A. 1950.

Robert Sullivan - an Irish educationalist and bene- 5837
factor: a study of his life and times. J. Robinson. Belfast
M.A. 1962.

The emergence of the Irish banking system, 1820-45. 5838
G.L. Barrow. London Ph.D. (Ext.) 1970.

The struggle for tenant-right in Ulster, 1829-50. B.A. 5839
Kennedy. Belfast M.A. 1943.

Geographical factors in the growth and decline of the 5840
ports of north-east Ireland. Sybil Ward. Belfast M.A.
1940.

The chief factors determining the developments in 5841
primary education, Ireland 1831-1947. W. Jacques. Belfast
Ph.D. 1952.

Catholic reaction to mixed elementary education in Ire- 5842
land between 1831 and 1870. M. McKeown. Belfast M.A. 1962.

The development of National schools in Belfast, 1831- 5843
51. A. Jordan. Belfast M.A. 1970.

The development of educational facilities for handi- 5844
capped children in Ireland, with particular reference to the
deaf in Ulster. J.G. McClelland. Belfast M.A. 1965/6.

The Irish Board of Works, 1831-78, with particular 5845
reference to the Famine years. A.R.G. Griffiths. Cambridge
Ph.D. 1968.

An investigation into the effects of the 1832 Reform 5846
Act on the general elections of 1832, 1835 and 1837 in Ireland. R.C. Brewer. London M.Sc. (Ext.) 1965.

The condition of the Irish peasantry, 1840-50. P. 5847
Hinckley. Leeds M.A. 1917.

The internal migration of labour in Ireland, 1841-1911. 5848
M.E.M. El Rayah. Belfast M.A. 1961.

The development of the urban pattern of Ireland, 1841- 5849
81. H.L. Mason. Wales Ph.D. 1970.

The relations between Great Britain and Ireland: 1841- 5850
8. K.B. Nowlan. Cambridge Ph.D. 1955.

The political and social teachings of the Young Ire- 5851
landers, 1842-8. G.R. Clarke. Belfast M.A. 1936.

An economic history of livestock in Ireland since the 5852
Famine. J. O'Donovan. Oxford B.Litt. 1931.

Irish overseas emigration and the state during the 5853
great Famine. O.O.G.M. MacDonagh. Cambridge Ph.D. 1952.

5854　　　The regional variations in the fall of population in Ireland, 1846-61, following the great Irish Famine. S.H. Cousens. Cambridge Ph.D. 1958.

5855　　　The administration of the poor laws in Ireland till 30 November 1921 and in Northern Ireland from 1 December 1921 till present date, 1942. H. Miller. Belfast M.Com.Sc. 1942.

5856　　　The economic history of the engineering industry in the north of Ireland to 1914. W.E. Coe. Belfast Ph.D. 1964.

5857　　　Institutional factors in the development of Irish agriculture, 1850-1915. J.P. Huttman. London Ph.D. 1970.

5858　　　An economic history of agriculture in Northern Ireland, 1850-1900. D.L. Armstrong. Belfast Ph.D. 1952.

5859　　　The general election of 1852 in Ireland. J.H. Whyte. Oxford B.Litt. 1951.

5860　　　Newman's work for university education in Ireland. J.S.F. McGrath. Oxford D.Phil. 1948.

5861　　　The Irish university question and party politics, 1865-79. P. Ramsden. Durham M.A. 1965.

5862　　　The Catholic movement for the disestablishment of the Irish Church, 1864-9. E.R. Norman. Cambridge Ph.D. 1964.

5863　　　Irish land reform and English Liberal politics, 1865-70. E.D. Steele. Cambridge Ph.D. 1963.

5864　　　The economic objects and results of land legislation in Ireland in the Gladstonian era. E.R. Nuttall. Wales M.A. 1936.

5865　　　The Irish Protestant churches and social and political issues, 1870-1914. A.J. Megahey. Belfast Ph.D. 1969.

5866　　　The Catholic Church and Irish politics, 1879-92. C.J. Woods. Nottingham Ph.D. 1968.

5867　　　William Abraham, 1842-1922. E.W. Evans. Wales M.A. 1953.

5868　　　The Ulster issue against its social and economic background, c.1880-93: the evolution and interaction of society and politics in Ulster from about 1880 to the defeat of the Second Home Rule Bill. B.P. Lenman. Cambridge M.Litt. 1965.

5869　　　Trade union beginnings in Belfast and district, with special reference to the period 1881-1900 and to the work of the Belfast and District United Trades Council during that period. D.W. Bleakley. Belfast M.A. 1955.

5870　　　A study of devolution, with special reference to the government of Northern Ireland. P.N.S. Mansergh. Oxford D.Phil. 1936.

5871　　　Public opinion and educational reform in the north of Ireland, 1900-54. J.E. Holmes. Belfast M.A. 1968/9.

5872　　　Joseph Devlin: Ulsterman and Irishman. F.J. Whitford. London M.A. (Ext.) 1959.

5873　　　The educational work of Sir Bertram Windle, F.R.S. (1858-1929), with particular reference to his contributions to higher education in Ireland. H. Neeson. Belfast M.A. 1962.

5874　　　Wages and prices in Belfast, 1914-23. W. Semple. Belfast M.Com.Sc. 1923.

5875　　　The economic life of Ireland since 1918. E.G. Thomas. Manchester Ph.D. 1934.

5876　　　An outline political geography of Northern Ireland since Partition. J.R.V. Prescott. Durham M.A. 1958.

5877　　　The Irish Free State and Commonwealth development, 1919-32. G.H. Byrne. Belfast M.A. 1969.

5878　　　Church and state in the Republic of Ireland. J.H. Whyte. Belfast Ph.D. 1970.

5879　　　The career of Michael Collins, with special reference to the treaty of 1921. Mrs. Patricia A. Freeman. Bristol M.A. 1963.

5880　　　The senate in Northern Ireland, 1921-62. P.F. McGill. Belfast Ph.D. 1965.

5881　　　The development of industry in the Republic of Ireland since 1922: a geographical investigation. D.J. Dwyer. London Ph.D. 1960.

The development of post-primary education in Eire   5882
since 1922, with special reference to vocational education.
P.K. O'Leary. Belfast Ph.D. 1962.

MIDDLE AND NEAR EAST

Royal directives in respect of land tenure in the first 5883
Babylonian dynasty. Sulamith Hönigsberg. Manchester M.A.
1951.
    A study of land tenure in the Old Babylonian period,   5884
with special reference to the Diyala region, based on published and unpublished texts. A. Suleiman. London Ph.D.
1966.
    The occupation of Palestine during the 3rd and 2nd   5885
millenia B.C. in the light of place-name evidence. B.S.J.
Isserlin. Oxford D.Phil. 1954.
    Tudhaliyaš IV and his successors. T. Kryska-Karski.   5886
Birmingham Ph.D. 1957.
    The settlement of the Hebrews in Canaan. M.J.C. Din-   5887
woodie. Edinburgh Ph.D. 1936.
    The metallurgical industry of Israel under Solomon in   5888
its historical, political and economic context. D. Gerrish.
Durham M.A. 1964.
    A study of the Aramaeans down to the fall of Nineveh,   5889
612 B.C. F. Tomkinson. Wales M.A. 1932.
    Elementary education in the Babylonian Talmud. N.   5890
Morris. London M.A. 1932.
    Jew and Gentile - the attitude of Jew to Gentile, 586   5891
B.C. - 67 B.C. J.C. Whitney. Leeds M.A. 1948.
    Historical geography of Palestine from the Persian to   5892
the Arab conquests, 536 B.C. to A.D. 640. M. Avi-Yonah.
London Ph.D. (Ext.) 1958.
    The Persian period of Israel's history. C.C. Keet.   5893
London M.A. 1953.
    The position of the Jewish community in Palestine in   5894
the first two centuries after the Exile. G.L. Jones. Wales
M.A. 1930.
    The movement towards 'Scribism' in the history of   5895
Israel. J.W. Lightley. Belfast M.A. 1912.
    Urban settlement and water utilisation in south-   5896
western Khuzistan and south-eastern Iraq from Alexander the
Great to the Mongol conquest of 1258. J.F. Hansman. London
Ph.D. 1970.
    Hellenism in Palestine, 323-129 B.C., with special   5897
reference to the causes of the Maccabean rebellion. F.A.
Gordon-Kerr. Durham M.A. 1967.
    The documents in the first book of the Maccabees and   5898
the foreign policy of the Maccabees. Anita Mittwoch. London
M.A. 1954.
    The Arabian East and the Far East, their commercial and 5899
cultural relations during the Graeco-Roman and the Perso-
Arabian periods. S.A.S. Hozayyen. Liverpool M.A. 1933.
    A history of Smyrna from the earliest times to 180 A.D. 5900
C.J. Cadoux. London M.A. 1911.
    The expansion of Christianity in Asia Minor during the   5901
first four centuries, with particular reference to Phrygia,
Lycaonia and Isauria. H.W. Callow. Manchester M.A. 1924.
    The design and decoration of neo-Assyrian public   5902
buildings. J.E. Reade. Cambridge Ph.D. 1970.
    A dissertation on the trade routes of the province of   5903
Asia Minor within the first three centuries of the Christian
era. A.H. Watts. London Ph.D. 1926.
    Historico-geographical aspects of the trade routes of   5904
the Syrian desert. Dawlat A. Sadek. Durham Ph.D. 1951.

5905   The church of Jerusalem, A.D. 30-100: an investigation of the growth of internal factions and the extension of its influence in the larger church. J.J. Scott. Manchester Ph.D. 1969.

5906   The Kushano-Sassanian episode: cultural cross-currents in Bactria, A.D. 225-375. A.D.H. Bivar. Oxford D.Phil. 1956.

5907   The business life of the Jews in Babylon from the 3rd to the 6th century. L. Jacobs. London Ph.D. (Ext.) 1952.

5908   Origen and the Jews: aspects of Jewish-Christian relations in 3rd-century Palestine. N.R.M. De Lange. Oxford D.Phil. 1970.

5909   South Arabia in the 5th and 6th centuries C.E., with reference to relations with central Arabia. K.S. Al-Asali. St. Andrews Ph.D. 1968.

5910   The missionary activity of the ancient Nestorian Church. J. Stewart. Edinburgh Ph.D. 1925.

5911   The Council of Chalcedon and the Armenian Church. N.K. Sarkissian. Oxford B.Litt. 1960.

5912   The mobility of the Arab armies in the early conquests. D.R. Hill. Durham M.Litt. 1963.

5913   A history of Islamic textiles up to the Mongol conquest. R.B. Serjeant. Cambridge Ph.D. 1939/40.

5914   Contributions to the history of the Islamic mint in the middle ages. A.S. Ehrenkreutz. London Ph.D. 1952.

5915   A musical history of the Arabs of the middle ages. H.G. Farmer. Glasgow Ph.D. 1926.

5916   Caliphate and kingship in medieval Persia. A.H. Siddiqi. London Ph.D. 1934.

5917   Land administration in Iraq, from the Muhammadan period to present times: based on original Arabic sources and official administration reports. A. Platts. London Ph.D. 1927.

5918   The early history of Basra: a study of the organisation of an Islamic misr. S.A. El Ali. Oxford D.Phil. 1949.

5919   The role of the Arab provincial governors in early Islam. A.M. Al-Adhami. St. Andrews Ph.D. 1964.

5920   Muslim sea-power in the eastern Mediterranean from the 7th to the 10th century. A.M. Fahmy. London Ph.D. 1948.

5921   The tribal policy of the Prophet Muhammad. I. Goldfeld. Cambridge Ph.D. 1970.

5922   The termination of hostilities in the early Arab conquests, A.D. 634-56. D.R. Hill. London Ph.D. (Ext.) 1970.

5923   Studies in the social history of the Umayyad period, as revealed in the Kitāb al-Aghānī. N. Akel. London Ph.D. 1960.

5924   'Alī b. Abī Tālib in Ithna-'Asharī Shī'ī belief. J. Eliash. London Ph.D. 1966.

5925   The Umayyad caliphate, 65-86/684-705: a political study. A.A.A. Dixon. London Ph.D. 1969.

5926   The early history of Islamic schism in Iraq. G.M. Hinds. London Ph.D. (Ext.) 1969.

5927   Studies on the history of the Qarmati and Ismaili movements from the 8th to the 11th centuries. B. Lewis. London Ph.D. (Ext.) 1939.

5928   The background and early life of An Lu-Shan. E.G. Pulleyblank. London Ph.D. 1951.

5929   The Arab conquest of Transoxiana. H.A.R. Gibb. London M.A. 1922.

5930   The scholars of Nishapur, 700-1250. M.M. Nouri. Edinburgh Ph.D. 1967.

5931   Early Shi'ism in Iraq. W.W. Rajkowski. London Ph.D. 1955.

5932   The 'Abbasid caliphate, 132/750-170/786. F. Omar. London Ph.D. 1967.

5933   The northern Hijaz in the writings of the Arab geographers, 800-1150. A. Al-Wohaibi. London Ph.D. 1969.

The civil war between Amin and Ma'mūm. S.A. Hamdi. 5934
London M.A. 1948.
The Yu'firid dynasty of San'ā. C.L. Geddes. London 5935
Ph.D. 1959.
The reign of Mu'tasim, 218-27/833-42. O.S.A. Ismail. 5936
London Ph.D. 1963.
The role of the Turks in Iraq during the caliphate of 5937
Mu'tasim, 218-27/833-42. L.I. Ahmad. Manchester Ph.D. 1965.
The caliphate of Al-Mutawakkil: religious, political 5938
and social aspects. A. Muhammad. Edinburgh M.Litt. 1970.
The reign of al-Mutawakkil, with special reference to 5939
religion, culture and government in the Islamic empire. M.S.
Miah. London Ph.D. 1963.
The Saffārid dynasty of Sīstān (247/861-399/1009). 5940
M.M. Hossain. Cambridge M.Litt. 1967.
Studies on the economic life of Mesopotamia in the 10th 5941
century. A.A.A.K. Duri. London Ph.D. 1942.
The 'Ubaid period in Mesopotamia and its Persian 5942
affinities. Joan L. Lines. Cambridge Ph.D. 1953.
Basra 295-447/907-1055. A.J. Naji. London Ph.D. 1970. 5943
Abbāsid and Fātimid political relations during the 5944
Buwaihid period. H.C. Abou Saïd. Cambridge Ph.D. 1966.
The Buwayhid dynasty of Baghdad, from the accession of 5945
'Izz al-Dawla to its extinction, A.H. 356-447/A.D. 967-1055.
M. Kabir. London Ph.D. 1953.
The Fatimid caliphate, 386/996-487/1094. B.I. Beshir. 5946
London Ph.D. 1970.
The emirate of Aleppo, 392/1002-487/1094. S. Zakkar. 5947
London Ph.D. 1969.
The transition from Ghaznavid to Seljuq rule in the 5948
Islamic East. C.E. Bosworth. Edinburgh Ph.D. 1961.
A critical study of the sources for the history of the 5949
Saljūqs of Persia and Syria. V.A. Hamdani. Oxford D.Phil.
1938.
Contributions to the study of Seljūq institutions. Ann 5950
K.S. Lambton. London Ph.D. 1939.
An edition of charters of privileges granted by 5951
Fātimids and the Mamlūks (c.500 to 900 A.H.) to S. Catherine's
monastery, Mt. Sinai. E. Khedoori. Manchester M.A. 1958.
Studies in the traditional historiography of the 5952
Maronites in the period 1100-1516. K.S. Salibi. London
Ph.D. 1953.
The 'Abbasid caliphate (575/1179-656/1258). A.M. 5953
Rashad Mohamad. London Ph.D. 1963.
A study of the urban life in Syria between A.D. 1200 5954
and 1400, aiming mainly at finding the extent to which such
life was continued. Nicola A. Ziadeh. London Ph.D. (Ext.)
1950.
The society and institutions of the empire of Trebi- 5955
zond. A.A.M. Bryer. Oxford D.Phil. 1967.
Relations between Persia and China under Mongol domin- 5956
ation. M. Honda. Cambridge Ph.D. 1957.
The historical geography of Iraq between the Mongolian 5957
and Ottoman conquests (1258-1534 A.D.). M.R. Al-Feel.
Reading Ph.D. 1959.
Ibn Taimiya and his projects of reform. S. Haque. 5958
London Ph.D. 1937.
An historical geography of the Ottoman empire from the 5959
earliest times to the end of the 16th century, with detailed
maps to illustrate the expansion of the sultanate. D.E.
Pitcher. London M.A. 1958.
The influence of spiritual forces on society and pol- 5960
itics in Tīmūrid Iran, 1335-1502. A.S. Hussaini. Cambridge
Ph.D. 1967.

5961   The <u>Responsa</u> of Rabbi Joseph ibn Leb: a study in the religious, social and economic conditions of the Jewish communities within the Ottoman empire during the 16th to 17th centuries. H. Cooper. London Ph.D. (Ext.) 1964.

5962   The development of the early Safawid state under Isma'īl and Tahmāsp, as studied in the 16th-century Persian sources. R.M. Savory. London Ph.D. 1958.

5963   The Iranian caravanserai during the Safavid period. M.-Y. Kiani. London Ph.D. 1970.

5964   The relations between the Mughul emperors of India and the Safavid Shahs of Iran. R. Islam. Cambridge Ph.D. 1957.

5965   The Ottoman Turks and the Portuguese in the Persian Gulf, 1534-81. S. Özbaran. London Ph.D. 1969.

5966   The relations between the Crimean Tatars and the Ottoman empire, 1578-1608, with special reference to the role of Gāzī Girāy Khan. C.M. Kortepeter. London Ph.D. 1962.

5967   The Turkish documents relating to Edward Barton's embassy to the Porte, 1588-98. Susan A. Skilliter. Manchester Ph.D. 1965.

5968   The letter-book of William Clarke, merchant in Aleppo, 1598-1602. P.R. Harris. London M.A. 1953.

5969   A history of the Levant Company. A.C. Wood. Oxford D.Phil. 1934.

5970   The Levant Company, 1603-81. W. Roby. Manchester M.A. 1927.

5971   The Levant Company, mainly from 1640 to 1753. G.P. Ambrose. Oxford B.Litt. 1933.

5972   The activities of the English East India Company in Persia and the Persian Gulf, 1616-57. W.C. Palmer. London Ph.D. 1933.

5973   Jews in Yemen in 17th-19th century according to Hebrew sources with comparison with Arabic Yamani sources. N.El-H.H.M.A.El-A. Mawi. St. Andrews Ph.D. 1970.

5974   The Ya'rubi dynasty of Oman. R.D. Bathurst. Oxford D.Phil. 1967.

5975   Arab settlement in Oman: the origins and development of the tribal pattern and its relationship to the Imamate. J.C. Wilkinson. Oxford D.Phil. 1970.

5976   Paul Rycaut as consul and man of letters at Smyrna (1667-78). Sonia P. Anderson. Oxford B.Litt. 1970.

5977   The commercial and diplomatic relations of England and Turkey, 1680-99. A.C. Wood. Oxford B.Litt. 1923.

5978   English diplomacy between Austria and the Ottoman empire in the war of the Sacra Liga, 1684-99, with special reference to the period 1688-99. C.J. Heywood. London Ph.D. 1970.

5979   The province of Damascus from 1723 to 1783, with special reference to the 'Azm Pashas. A.K. Rafeq. London Ph.D. 1963.

5980   Nādir Shāh. L. Lockhart. London Ph.D. 1935.

5981   Karīm Khān Zand: a critical history based on contemporary sources. J.R. Perry. Cambridge Ph.D. 1970.

5982   The first Sa'udi state in Arabia (with special reference to its administrative, military and economic features) in the light of unpublished materials from Arabic and European sources. M.S.M. El-Shaafy. Leeds Ph.D. 1967.

5983   The Utbī states in eastern Arabia in the second half of the 18th century. A.M. Abu Hakima. London Ph.D. 1960.

5984   English traders in Syria, 1744-91. A.K.M. Gharaybeh. London Ph.D. 1951.

5985   English travellers in Syria. Eva J.S. Saigh. Leeds M.A. 1942.

5986   The later history of the Levant Company, 1753-1835. Ina S. Russell. Manchester Ph.D. 1935.

5987   British trade with Turkey and the decline of the Levant Company, 1790-1825. Ina S. Russell. Manchester M.A. 1932.

5988   A critical edition of the Persian correspondence of Col. Sir John Murray, 1788-96. I.M. Khan. London M.A. 1925.

Ottoman diplomacy and the Great European Powers, 1797– 5989
1802. T. Naff. London Ph.D. 1960.

A history of Russian activities in Syria in the 19th 5990
century. D. Hopwood. Oxford D.Phil. 1964.

British policy towards Persia and the defence of 5991
British India, 1798-1807. E.R. Ingram Ellis. London Ph.D.
1968.

The relations of Britain and Persia, 1800-15. S.F. 5992
Shadman. London Ph.D. 1939.

Turkish and Egyptian rule in Arabia, 1810-41. A.H.M. 5993
El Batrik. London Ph.D. 1947.

British policy in the Persian Gulf, 1813-43. J.B. 5994
Kelly. London Ph.D. 1956.

The diplomatic relations of Persia with Britain, Russia 5995
and Turkey, 1815-30. F. Adamiyat. London Ph.D. 1949.

British policy in Iraq, 1828-43, with special reference 5996
to the Euphrates expedition. M.G.I. Khan. London Ph.D. 1967.

A comparative study of Anglo-Turkish relations: c.1830- 5997
70 and 1919-39. Oya Köymen. Strathclyde Ph.D. 1967.

The policy of Lord Palmerston in the Near Eastern 5998
question from the date of his accession to office in November
1830 to the date of his retirement in August 1841. Margaret
H. Mackenzie. Oxford B.Litt. 1928.

The activities and influence of David Urquhart, 1833- 5999
56, with special reference to the affairs of the Near East.
Margaret H. Jenks. London Ph.D. 1964.

British policy in Lebanon, 1839-46. R. Alam. London 6000
M.Phil. 1969.

Britain and the pacification of the Lebanon, 1841-5. 6001
A.B. Cunningham. London M.A. 1950.

The Tanzimat in Syria and Palestine, 1840-61: the 6002
impact of the Ottoman reforms on some aspects of life. M.M.
Maoz. Oxford D.Phil. 1966.

British railway investment in Turkey, with special 6003
reference to the Imperial Ottoman Railway from Smyrna to
Aidin, 1856 to 1935. J.F. Woods. London M.Phil. 1969.

Anglo-Persian relations, 1856-1907. K.C. Cleak. 6004
Bristol M.A. 1938.

Ecclesiastical opinion in England on the Eastern 6005
question, from the treaty of Paris to the treaty of Berlin.
S.B.R. Poole. London M.A. 1934.

British interests in the Tigris-Euphrates valley, 1856- 6006
88. Winifred Bamforth. London M.A. 1948.

The Constantinople embassy of Sir Henry Bulwer, 1858- 6007
65. K. Bell. London Ph.D. 1961.

The participation of the Armenian community in Ottoman 6008
public life in eastern Anatolia and Syria, 1860-1908. M.K.
Krikorian. Durham Ph.D. 1963.

French influence in the Mutaoarrifiya of the Lebanon, 6009
1860-85. J.P. Spagnolo. Oxford D.Phil. 1965.

Sir Henry Elliott, British ambassador at Constanti- 6010
nople, 1867-77, with particular reference to the period 1867-
74. D.T. Rees. Wales M.A. 1940.

Foreign trade in the economic development of Iraq, 6011
1869-1939. M.S. Hasan. Oxford D.Phil. 1958.

Municipal government in Baghdad and Basra, 1869-1914. 6012
Albertine Jwaideh. Oxford B.Litt. 1954.

Land and tribal administration of Lower Iraq under the 6013
Ottomans from 1869 to 1914. Albertine Jwaideh. Oxford
D.Phil. 1958.

British policy in the Middle East, 1874-80. L.E. 6014
Frechtling. Oxford D.Phil. 1939.

The Eastern question and European diplomacy in the 6015
period 1876-8: with special reference to British policy.
W.A. Gauld. Liverpool M.A. 1923.

British public opinion and the Eastern question, 1877- 6016
8. H.St.C. Cunningham. Sussex D.Phil. 1969.

6017   The last embassy of Sir Austen Henry Layard (March 1877
- August 1878). Beryl Williams. Wales M.A. 1939.
6018   British foreign policy in the Near East from the Congress of Berlin to the accession of Ferdinand of Coburg.
W.N. Medlicott. London M.A. 1926.
6019   Great Britain and Turkey, 1878-85. R.A. Spencer. Oxford D.Phil. 1950.
6020   British, French and German interests in Asiatic Turkey,
1881-1914. H.S.W. Corrigan. London Ph.D. 1954.
6021   Turks, Arabs, and Jewish immigration into Palestine,
1882-1914. N.J. Mandel. Oxford D.Phil. 1965.
6022   British policy in Persia, 1885-92. Rose L. Coughlin.
London Ph.D. 1954.
6023   The embassy of Sir William White at Constantinople,
1886-91. C.L. Smith. Oxford D.Phil. 1954.
6024   The political aspects of foreign oil interests in Iran
down to 1947. G.R. Nikpay. London Ph.D. 1956.
6025   British political relations with Kuwait, 1890-1921.
F.M. Al-Khatrash. Durham M.A. 1970.
6026   British relations with the Persian Gulf, 1890-1902.
M.A. Daud. London Ph.D. 1957.
6027   The place of Constantinople and the Straits in British
foreign policy, 1890-1902. Margaret M. Jefferson. London
M.A. 1959.
6028   British policy and diplomacy in the Near East during
the Liberal administrations August 1892 to June 1895.
K.H.W. Hilborn. Oxford D.Phil. 1960.
6029   The Armenian question and British policy in Turkey,
1894-6. D.C. Weeks. London M.A. 1950.
6030   Britain and the Eastern question, 1894-6. E.
Khavessian. Oxford B.Litt. 1961.
6031   The problem of the Straits, 1896-1936. E.W. Griffiths.
Wales M.A. 1952.
6032   England and the Near East, 1896-8. G.S. Papadopoulos.
London Ph.D. (Ext.) 1950.
6033   The Palestine problem, 1900-50; some geographical con-
siderations. H.F. Frischwasser. Oxford B.Litt. 1950.
6034   British government interest in Middle East oil concessions, 1900-25. Mrs. Marian R. Kent, formerly Jack.
London Ph.D. 1968.
6035   British foreign policy in the Near East, 1903-9, with
special reference to projects for the internal reform of the
Ottoman empire. W.E. Walters. Wales M.A. 1937.
6036   Iraq: a study in political consciousness, 1908-21.
G.R. Atiyyah. Edinburgh Ph.D. 1968.
6037   Great Britain, Russia and the Turkish Straits, 1908-23.
R.R.J. Mulligan. London M.A. 1953.
6038   British policy and public opinion on the Turkish
question, 1908-14. M. Heymann. Cambridge Ph.D. 1957.
6039   Turkish-Syrian relations in the Ottoman constitutional
period, 1908-14. T.E.A.M. Harran. London Ph.D. 1969.
6040   The Committee of Union and Progress in Turkish politics,
1908-13. F.-U. Ahmad. London Ph.D. 1966.
6041   Anglo-Russian relations in Persia, 1909-15. D.W.
Spring. London Ph.D. 1968.
6042   Anglo-Russian relations in Persia, 1912-14. Eva F.
Roskies. London M.Sc. 1965.
6043   The development of British policy in Iraq from 1914 to
1926. D.E.B. Fuleihan. London Ph.D. 1970.
6044   The birth of the mandate idea and its fulfilment in
Iraq up to 1926. H.J.F. Mejcher. Oxford D.Phil. 1970.
6045   Aspects of Anglo-French rivalry over the question of
Middle East mandates, 1915-20. S.K. Garrett. Keele M.A.
1970.
6046   Mark Sykes and the formation of British policy towards
the Middle East, 1915-19. R.D. Adelson. Oxford B.Litt.
1970.

The Palestinian Arab reactions to Zionism and the　6047
British mandate, 1917-39.　A.-W.S. Kayyali.　London Ph.D.
1970.
A study of the official and unofficial relations be-　6048
tween Greece and Turkey from the armistice of Mudros to the
present day.　E.L.B. Curtis.　London M.Sc. 1933.
Allied policies in Turkey from the armistice of Mudros,　6049
30 October 1918, to the treaty of Lausanne, 24 July 1923.
A.E. Montgomery.　London Ph.D. 1969.
Syria and the Lebanon in international politics, from　6050
Mudros to Maisalûn, 1918-20.　Z.N.-U.-D. Zeine.　London Ph.D.
1956.
The growth of the opposition in Turkish politics, 1919-　6051
46.　A.A. Cruickshank.　Oxford D.Phil. 1964.
British relations with France in 1919-20, with special　6052
emphasis on the Arab Middle East.　J.T. Nevakivi.　London
Ph.D. 1963.
The 1924 constitution of Turkey: a critical survey.　S.　6053
Ramadan.　Belfast M.A. 1963.
Gentile Zionism and Anglo-Zionist diplomacy, 1929-39:　6054
some aspects of the role played by Gentile Zionists in rel-
ations between the British government and the Jewish Agency.
N.A. Rose.　London Ph.D. 1968.
Nazism and the German Christian communities in Pales-　6055
tine, 1932-9.　Mrs. Ann N. Ussishkin.　London M.A. 1965.

A F R I C A

GENERAL

The effect of geographical factors on the spread of　6056
Islam, with special reference to Africa.　H.M. Gohar.　Bris-
tol M.A. 1930.
International relations on the south-east coast of　6057
Africa, 1796-1856.　Mabel V. Jackson.　London Ph.D. 1938.
Missionaries as transmitters of western civilisation　6058
in 19th-century Africa.　R.W. Goodloe.　St. Andrews Ph.D.
1956.
African education in British Africa, 1800-1966.　W.　6059
Liu.　Reading M.Phil. 1966/7.
Blackwood's and Africa.　C.A. Marin.　Edinburgh M.Litt. 6060
1970.
Palmerston's policy towards East and West Africa, 1830-　6061
65.　R.J. Gavin.　Cambridge Ph.D. 1959.
Liberated Africans and British policies, 1840-1920.　6062
J.U.J. Asiegbu.　Cambridge Ph.D. 1966.
The Aborigines Protection Society and British Southern　6063
and West Africa.　H.C. Swaisland.　Oxford D.Phil. 1968.
Glasgow and Africa: connexions and attitudes, 1880-　6064
1900.　W. Thompson.　Strathclyde Ph.D. 1970.
The foreign policy of the Gladstone administration of　6065
1880-5, with special reference to German policy in South-West
Africa.　Dorothy E. Searle.　Wales M.A. 1933.
Bismarck and British colonial policy: the problem in　6066
South-West Africa, 1883-5.　W.O. Aydelotte.　Cambridge Ph.D.
1934/5.
Great Britain and the Brussels Anti-Slave Trade Act of　6067
1890.　Mrs. Suzanne Miers.　London Ph.D. 1969.
The Indian problem in eastern and southern Africa.　L.　6068
James.　Liverpool M.A. 1940.
Problems of international co-operation considered with　6069
reference to the boundaries of the Gambia, Ghana, Liberia
and Nigeria.　M.R. Ofoegbu.　London M.Sc. 1966.

231

6070   A geographical study of nomadic migrations in Tunisia.
J.I. Clarke.   Aberdeen Ph.D. 1956.

6071   The social and economic background of Christianity in
North Africa down to 430, with special reference to the
Donatist schism. W.H.C. Frend. Oxford D.Phil. 1940.

6072   The Christian inscriptions of North Africa: a study in
the popular religion of the early (western) church. I.T.
Gillan.   Edinburgh Ph.D. 1943.

6073   The life of the Christians in North Africa in the time
of Tertullian. C.B. Daly. Belfast M.A. 1938.

6074   Life in northern Africa during the Vandal occupation.
J.J. Campbell.   Belfast M.A. 1934.

6075   The rise of the 'Alawi dynasty in Morocco, 1631-72.
B.A. Mojuetan. London Ph.D. 1969.

6076   The occupation of Tangier and its relation to English
naval strategy in the Mediterranean, 1661-84. A. Jamieson.
Durham M.A. 1961.

6077   The influence of the Barbary states in international
relations, with special reference to the United States.
R.K. Irons. Oxford D.Phil. 1934.

6078   Britain and Barbary, 1815-40. R.G. Wallace. Birmingham M.A. 1968.

6079   Tripoli during the reign of Yusuf Pasha Qaramanli. K.
Folayan. London Ph.D. 1970.

6080   British policy towards Tunis (1830-81). A. Raymond.
Oxford D.Phil. 1954.

6081   Tunis from 1855 to 1879: primarily based on the des-
patches of Consul-General Richard Wood. M.M. Safwat. Liverpool M.A. 1937.

6082   British policy towards Tunis, 1875-99. A. Marsden.
London Ph.D. 1963.

6083   The establishment of the French protectorate over Tunis:
its diplomatic history from the Congress of Berlin to the
formation of the Triple Alliance, July 1878 to May 1882.
T. Lewis. Wales M.A. 1950.

6084   The Great Powers and Tunis, 1878-81. M.M. Safwat.
London Ph.D. 1940.

6085   The Morocco question, 1880-92. F.V. Parsons. London
Ph.D. 1954.

6086   Europe and Morocco, particularly from 1900 to 1911.
E.T. Glendon.   Birmingham M.A. 1923.

6087   British policy in relation to Morocco, 1902-6. E.W.
Edwards. Wales M.A. 1939.

6088   Economic development of Morocco under French protection.
T.H. Jupp. Bristol M.A. 1935.

6089   Britain, France and Germany and the Moroccan question
(March 1905 - January 1906). J.M.R. Le Breton. Oxford
D.Phil. 1953.

6090   The Moroccan question, April 1906 - February 1909.
H.M.H. Sobhy. London Ph.D. 1962.

6091   The English press and the Moroccan crisis of 1911. H.G.
Riddell. Liverpool M.A. 1949.

6092   The French administration of tribal areas of Morocco.
R.L. Bidwell. Cambridge Ph.D. 1969.

6093   A study of Lyautey's administration of Morocco in relation to indigenous and Islamic institutions. A.M. Schram.
Durham Ph.D. 1967.

EGYPT AND NORTH-EAST AFRICA

6094   The place of Egypt in the prehistory of the Old World.
S.A.S. Hozayyen. Manchester Ph.D. 1935.

6095   Slavery in Pharaonic Egypt. A.M. Bakir. Oxford D.Phil.
1946.

The Amarna period: a study of the internal politics 6096
and external relations of the late XVIIIth dynasty of Egypt.
F.J. Giles. London Ph.D. 1960.

A study of the social and economic factors operating 6097
in ancient Egypt from the death of Rameses III to the commencement of the XXVth dynasty. B.G. Haycock. Durham Ph.D.
1962.

The foreign relations of the Napatan-Meroitic kingdom 6098
in the Sudan, from the 8th century B.C. to the 4th century
A.D. B.J. Haycock. Durham M.Litt. 1966.

Epilydes and autochthones: a survey of the relations 6099
between the immigrants and the Libyans of North Africa, 631-
111 B.C. A.O.A. Kwapong. Cambridge Ph.D. 1959.

The Alexandrians: from the foundation of the city to 6100
the Arab conquest. A study of their political organisation
and their economic and administrative role in Egypt. M.A.H.
el Abbadi. Cambridge Ph.D. 1960.

The origins of Alexandrian Christianity. J.M. Fen- 6101
nelly. Manchester Ph.D. 1967.

Contributions to the classical archaeology of the 6102
Eastern Desert of Egypt. D. Meredith. Wales M.A. 1952.

The political geography of Eritrea. J.S. Dugdale. 6103
London M.Phil. 1967.

Aspects of migration in the Anglo-Egyptian Sudan. 6104
D.B. Mather. London Ph.D. (Ext.) 1954.

The advance of Islam in the western and central Sudan. 6105
G. Lighton. Manchester M.A. 1935.

Lower Nubia in the early Byzantine period. L.P. Kir- 6106
wan. Oxford B.Litt. 1935.

The history of Muslim education, with special reference 6107
to Egypt. A.M.G. Shalaby. Cambridge Ph.D. 1950/1.

The Arabs and the eastern Sudan from the 7th to the 6108
early 16th century. Y.F. Hasan. London Ph.D. 1964.

Egyptian maritime power in the early middle ages, 640- 6109
1171. I.A. El Adawi. Liverpool Ph.D. 1948.

The agriculture of Egypt during the Arab period, 642- 6110
1517 A.D. A.F.M.M. Weheba. London M.A. 1952.

Some aspects of Shī'īte propaganda under the Fatimids 6111
in Egypt. H.I. Hassan. London Ph.D. 1927.

The financial system of Egypt, 564-741 A.H./1169-1341 6112
A.D. H.M. Rabie. London Ph.D. 1969.

The organisation and role of the pilgrimage during the 6113
Mamlūk period. A.A. Ankawi. Cambridge Ph.D. 1969.

Church and state in Ethiopia, 1270-1527. Tadesse Tam- 6114
rat. London Ph.D. 1968.

The geography of Egypt in the Mamluk times. Y.A.A. 6115
Ismail. Reading Ph.D. 1953.

Some unpublished Arabic texts relating to the reign of 6116
Baybars I. Syedah F. Sadeque. London Ph.D. 1949.

A critical edition of an unknown source for the life of 6117
al-Malik al-Zāhir Baibars, with introduction, translation
and notes. A.A. Al-Khowayter. London Ph.D. 1960.

The administrative and social conditions of Ethiopia 6118
under the first Salomonid kings (1268-1520). W.E.R. Barnett.
Oxford B.Litt. 1951.

Foreign relations of Egypt in the 15th century (1422- 6119
1517). M.M. Ziada. Liverpool Ph.D. 1930.

George Baldwin and British interests in Egypt, 1775-98. 6120
Rosemarie J. Said. London Ph.D. 1968.

Anglo-Egyptian relations: some aspects of British 6121
interest in Egypt in the late 18th century, 1775-98. M.A.
Anis. Birmingham Ph.D. 1950.

British penetration of the Sahara and western Sudan, 6122
1788-1861. A.A. Boahen. London Ph.D. 1959.

The origin of scientific excavation in Egypt and its 6123
development during the 19th century. Mary D.F. Cheever.
London M.A. 1938.

6124   Urban studies in the Nile delta from the beginning of the 19th century onwards: a study in historical geography. Y.A.R. El Gowhary. Reading Ph.D. 1964/5.

6125   Changing values in Egyptian agriculture from 1800 to the present time. G.H. Thomas. London M.A. 1939.

6126   The Sudan in Anglo-Egyptian relations: a case study in power politics (1800-1956). L.A. Fabunmi. London Ph.D. 1958.

6127   Caravan trade and routes in the northern Sudan in the 19th century. H.A. Ahmed. Durham M.A. 1967.

6128   The beginnings of the Egyptian question and the rise of Mehemet Ali, 1800-12. S. Ghorbal. London M.A. 1924.

6129   The rise of the kingdom of Shoa, 1813-89. R.H.K. Darkwah. London Ph.D. 1966.

6130   British attitudes towards the Sudan, 1820-96. A.I. Mohamed. Edinburgh Ph.D. 1966.

6131   Cotton production and the development of the economy in 19th-century Egypt, 1821-1914. E.R.J. Owen. Oxford D.Phil. 1965.

6132   'Al-Hājj 'Umar b. Sa'īd al-Fūtī al-Turi (c.1794-1864) and the doctrinal basis of his Islamic reformist movement in the western Sudan. J.R. Willis. London Ph.D. 1970.

6133   The beginnings of British and French missionary educational activity in Egypt, 1825-63. J. Sislian. London M.A. 1956.

6134   European religious missions in Ethiopia, 1830-68. D.E. Crummey. London Ph.D. 1967.

6135   Trade and politics in the Ethiopian region, 1830-55. M. Abir. London Ph.D. 1964.

6136   The growth of British influence in Abyssinia and on the African coast of the Red Sea, 1840-85. Margaret M. Law. London M.A. 1931.

6137   Anglo-Egyptian relations and the construction of the Alexandria-Cairo-Suez railway, 1833-58. O.A.-A. Omar. London Ph.D. 1966.

6138   Palmerston's attitude towards Mehemet Ali, 1834-8 (with an introduction on the development of the Near Eastern question, 1788-1834). R.L. Baker. Oxford B.Litt. 1928.

6139   The agricultural policy of Mahomet Ali in Egypt. Helen A. Rivlin. Oxford D.Phil. 1953.

6140   British policy in reference to Mehemet Ali, 1839-41. W.G. Turner. London M.A. 1928.

6141   The southern Sudan, 1839-89. J.R. Gray. London Ph.D. 1957.

6142   'Rifā 'ah Rāfi 'al-Tahṭāwī (1801-73) and the cultural impact of France. S.A.S. Galadanci. Cambridge M.Litt. 1970.

6143   The history of the Suez Canal concession, 1854-66. M. Kassim. London M.A. 1924.

6144   Commercial cotton growing in the Sudan between 1860 and 1925. H.A.A. Ahmed. Durham Ph.D. 1970.

6145   The Khedive Ismaïl and slavery in the Sudan. M.F. Shukry. Liverpool Ph.D. 1935.

6146   The origins and development of the foreign policy of Menelik II, 1865-96. R.A. Caulk. London Ph.D. 1966.

6147   The financial question and the reorganisation of the Egyptian administration, 1865-85. H.K. El-S. Abulleef. Bristol M.A. 1948.

6148   Parliamentary institutions and political parties in Egypt, 1866-1924. J. Landau. London Ph.D. 1949.

6149   Egypt in British political thought, 1875-1900. A.A.H. Knightbridge. Oxford D.Phil. 1963.

6150   Economic development of Egypt since 1876. A.R. Fikry. London M.Sc. 1918.

6151   The public finances of modern Egypt, with special reference to the period 1876-1942. A.M.K. El Bey. London Ph.D. 1946.

      Al-Musqtataf, 1876-1900: a study of the influence of   6152
Victorian thought on modern Arabic thought. Mrs. Nadia R.
Farag. Oxford D.Phil. 1969.
      The domestic and foreign affairs of Egypt from 1876 to   6153
1882. A.A.-R. Mustafa. London Ph.D. 1955.
      A critical edition of the memoirs of Yūsif Mikhaīl,   6154
with an introduction, translation, notes and commentary.
S.M. Nur. London Ph.D. 1963.
      The role of the military in the formulation of French   6155
policy towards the Western Sudan, 1879-99. A.S. Kanya-
Forstner. Cambridge Ph.D. 1965.
      The nationalist movement in Egypt, 1879-82. M.S.   6156
Ashur. Birmingham M.A. 1925.
      The Sudan and the Mahdist revolution of 1881-5. M. El 6157
Shibeika. London Ph.D. 1949.
      The rebellion of Urabi Pasha in Egypt, 1881-2. Y.   6158
Cohen. Oxford B.Litt. 1958.
      British military policy and the defence of Egypt, 1882- 6159
1914. D.R. Facey-Crowther. London Ph.D. 1969.
      A historical survey of education in Egypt, 1882-1922.   6160
J. Williams. London M.A. 1956.
      Higher education in the Sudan from its origins to 1966, 6161
with special reference to university education. E.S.M. El-
Gizouli. Durham Ph.D. 1968.
      The Copts under British rule, 1882-1914. S.M. Seikaly. 6162
London Ph.D. 1967.
      Lord Rosebery, Egypt and the Sudan, 1882-98. Mahassin 6163
A.G.H. El-Safi. Edinburgh M.Litt. 1969.
      Gladstone and the invasion of Egypt in 1882. A.A.H.   6164
Knightbridge. Oxford B.Litt. 1960.
      Lord Cromer and his successors in Egypt. R.C. Mowat. 6165
Oxford D.Phil. 1970.
      Cromer and the Egyptian nationalists, 1882-1907. Afaf 6166
Loutfi el Sayed. Oxford D.Phil. 1963.
      The relations between 'Abbās Hilmī and Lord Cromer.   6167
M.G.E.D. El-Mesaddy. London Ph.D. 1966.
      The re-organisation of the Egyptian army and its con-   6168
tribution to the reconquest of the Egyptian Sudan, 1882-99.
J. Clementson. Durham M.A. 1970.
      The European Powers and the British occupation of   6169
Egypt, 1882-5. Marian Phillips. Wales M.A. 1937.
      Anglo-Italian relations, 1884-5, and the Italian   6170
occupation of Massawah. F.T. Fries. Cambridge Ph.D. 1939.
      The Egyptian question in British foreign policy, with   6171
special reference to 1885-7. D.C. Weeks. London Ph.D.
1952.
      The Emin Pasha Relief Expedition, 1886-90. I.R. Smith. 6172
Oxford D.Phil. 1969.
      The Egyptian question in British diplomacy, 1887-97.   6173
M. Clarke. Manchester M.A. 1954.
      The personal rule of the Khalifa 'Abdallahi al-   6174
Ta'aishi'. P.M. Holt. Oxford D.Phil. 1954.
      Shayk Ali Yusuf, political journalist and Islamic   6175
nationalist: a study in Egyptian politics, 1889-1913. A.R.
Kelidar. London Ph.D. 1967.
      The Egyptian policy of Lord Salisbury, 1895-9. Muriel 6176
J. Grieve. Oxford B.Litt. 1966.
      Anglo-French competition for the control of the upper 6177
basin of the Nile, 1890-9: its development, and resolution
in the Fashoda crisis. G.N. Sanderson. London Ph.D. 1959.
      The Anglo-Egyptian dispute over the Sudan and its   6178
effect on political and constitutional development in that
country. M. Abbas. Oxford B.Litt. 1950.
      An economic history of the Gezira scheme, 1898-1956. 6179
A.W. Abdel Rahim. Manchester Ph.D. 1968.
      An economic history of the Sudan, 1899-1956. A.W.   6180
Abdel-Rahim. Manchester M.A. 1963.

6181 The constitutional development of the Sudan, 1899-1956. M. Abdel-Rahim. Manchester Ph.D. 1964.
6182 The development of transport and economic growth in the Sudan, 1899-1957. O.M. Osman Abdou. London Ph.D. 1960.
6183 The Islamic policies of the Sudan government, 1899-1924. M.M. Rahman. Durham M.A. 1967.
6184 Administration in the Anglo-Egyptian Sudan, 1899-1916. G. Warburg. London Ph.D. 1968.
6185 Modern education in the Sudan, 1898-1965. N.E. Mohamed. Edinburgh Ph.D. 1969.
6186 Educational development in the Sudan, 1899-1956. M.O. Beshir. Oxford B.Litt. 1966.
6187 Education in the southern Sudan, 1898-1948. Lilian M. Sanderson. London Ph.D. (Ext.) 1966.
6189 An historical study of Ismā'īl b. 'Abd Al-Qādir: <u>Kitāb Sa'ādat Al-Mustahdī Bi-Sīrat Al-Imām Al-Mahdī</u>. H. Shaked. London Ph.D. 1969.
6190 Migration as a factor in the geography of western Libya, 1900-64. R.S. Harrison. Cambridge Ph.D. 1966.
6191 Urbanisation in Egypt and its implications for education, 1900-60. A.-F.A.K. Galal. London M.A. 1963.
6192 A history of education in the Sudan, with special reference to the development of girls' schools. Lilian M. Sanderson. London M.A. (Ext.) 1962.
6193 Education and social change in the Sudan, 1900-58. M.K. Osman. London M.A. 1965.
6194 Social and political thought in Egypt, 1900-14. J.M. Ahmed. Oxford B.Litt. 1954.
6195 Secondary education in the Sudan, 1905-55 (an historical review with special reference to political and social influences). E.-F. Mahgoub. London M.Phil. 1967.
6196 The evolution of the Egyptian political élite, 1907-21: a case study of the role of the large landowners in politics. W. Kazziha. London Ph.D. 1970.
6197 Sir Reginald Wingate as high commissioner in Egypt, 1917-19. Janice J. Terry. London Ph.D. 1968.
6198 National policy and popular education in Egypt, 1919-58. A.H. Ebeid. Oxford D.Phil. 1964.
6199 British administration and Sudanese nationalism, 1919-39. G.M.A. Bakhiet. Cambridge Ph.D. 1965.
6200 Agrarian reform in Egypt since independence, 1922-65. A.M.O. Atta. Oxford D.Phil. 1970.
6201 The working of parliamentary institutions in Egypt, 1924-52. M.F. El-Khatib. Edinburgh Ph.D. 1953/4.
6202 The Anglo-Egyptian treaty of 1936, with special reference to the contemporary situation in Egypt and the Sudan. H.A. Ibrahim. London Ph.D. 1970.

EAST AND CENTRAL AFRICA

6203 The medieval history of the coast of Tanganyika, with special reference to recent archaeological discoveries. G.S.P. Freeman-Grenville. Oxford D.Phil. 1957.
6204 The historical tradition of Busoga, Uganda. D.W. Cohen. London Ph.D. 1970.
6205 Migration and settlement among the southern Luo peoples, 1500-1900: a case study of oral traditions as a historical source. B.A. Ogot. London Ph.D. 1965.
6206 The emergence and growth of the kingdom of Nkore in Western Uganda, c.1500-1896. S.R. Karugire. London Ph.D. 1969.
6207 The Abaluyia of western Kenya and their neighbours; their history down to 1930. G.S. Were. Wales Ph.D. 1966.
6208 A history of the Kikuyu to 1904. G. Muriuki. London Ph.D. 1970.

The role of the Yao in the development of trade in east-central Africa, 1698-c.1850. E.A. Alpers. London Ph.D. 1966. 6209

Government and politics in the Akuapem state, 1730-1850. M.A. Kwamena-Poh. London M.A. (Ext.) 1968. 6210

The British exploration of East Africa, 1788-1885, with special reference to the activities of the Royal Geographical Society. R.C. Bridges. London Ph.D. 1963. 6211

The Zambesi Prazos in the 18th century. M.D.D. Newitt. London Ph.D. 1967. 6212

European and Arab activities on the East African coast, 1798-1856, and the local reaction to them. Mrs. Christine S. Nicholls, née Metcalfe. Oxford D.Phil. 1968. 6213

The pastoral tribes of northern Kenya, 1800-1916. E.R. Turton. London Ph.D. 1970. 6214

History of British relations with Zanzibar, 1800-86. O.T. Lewis. Wales M.A. 1936. 6215

British imperial policy in relation to Madagascar, 1810-96. R.E.P. Wastell. London Ph.D. 1944. 6216

The history of the Temne in the 19th century. E.A. Ijagbemi. Edinburgh Ph.D. 1968. 6217

Race and cultural attitudes of the British precursors of imperialism in Central Africa, 1840-90. H.A.C. Cairns. Oxford D.Phil. 1963. 6218

The missionary factor in East Africa. R.A. Oliver. Cambridge Ph.D. 1951. 6219

The Malagasy and Europeans: a study of Madagascar's foreign policy, 1861-95. P.M. Mutibwa. Sussex D.Phil. 1970. 6220

The British and Uganda, 1862-1900. D.A. Low. Oxford D.Phil. 1957. 6221

The Holy Ghost Fathers in East Africa, 1863 to 1914. J.A.P. Kieran. London Ph.D. 1966. 6222

Britain and the end of slavery in East Africa. Eleanor M. Glyn-Jones. Oxford B.Litt. 1957. 6223

Friends' mission work in Madagascar up to 1927 and its doctrinal implications. E.A.O. Peetz. Oxford B.Litt. 1961. 6224

Geographic aspects of the development of white settlement patterns in British Tropical East Africa since 1870. D.R. Petterson. London Ph.D. 1952. 6225

A history of African education in Nyasaland, 1875-1945. R.J. MacDonald. Edinburgh Ph.D. 1969. 6226

The history of Nyasaland and north-eastern Rhodesia, 1875-95. A.J. Hanna. London Ph.D. 1948. 6227

Livingstonia Mission and the evolution of Malawi, 1875-1939. K.J. McCracken. Cambridge Ph.D. 1967. 6228

The origins and development of the Church of Scotland Mission, Blantyre, Nyasaland. A.C. Ross. Edinburgh Ph.D. 1968. 6229

History of the Imperial British East Africa Company, 1876-95. Marie J. de Kiewiet. London Ph.D. 1955. 6230

The origins and development of the African Lakes Company, 1878-1908. H.W. Macmillan. Edinburgh Ph.D. 1970. 6231

The influence of Madagascar on international relations, 1878-1904. J.S. Swinburne. London M.Phil. 1969. 6232

A political history of Nyanza, 1883-1945. J.M. Lonsdale. Cambridge Ph.D. 1964. 6233

The role of the Foreign Office in the affairs of East Africa, 1883-95. Jennifer S. Hines. London M.A. 1955. 6234

The British Somaliland Protectorate to 1905. A.M. Brockett. Oxford D.Phil. 1970. 6235

Indian settlement in East Africa, c.1886 to 1945. J.S. Mangat. London Ph.D. 1967. 6236

Nyasaland migrant labour in British Central Africa, 1890-1939. F.E. Sanderson. Manchester M.A. 1960. 6237

Customary law and administration of justice in Malawi, 1890-1933. Emily N. Maliwa. London M.Phil. 1967. 6238

6239   Legal status of women in Malawi - pre-colonial period to 1964. Emily N. Maliwa. London Ph.D. (Ext.) 1970.

6240   The development of modern African politics and the emergence of a nationalist movement in colonial Malawi, 1891-1958. R.K. Tangri. Edinburgh Ph.D. 1970.

6241   The King's African Rifles: a study in the military history of East and Central Africa, 1890-1914. H. Moyse-Bartlett. London Ph.D. 1954.

6242   History of the Zanzibar Protectorate, 1890-1913. L.W. Hollingsworth. London Ph.D. 1951.

6243   German evangelical missions in Tanganyika, 1891-1939, with special reference to the Southern Highlands. Marcia Wright. London Ph.D. 1966.

6244   The Scottish Mission in Kenya, 1891-1923. B.G. McIntosh. Edinburgh Ph.D. 1969.

6245   Land and labour in Nyasaland, 1891-1914. B.S. Krishna-murthy. London Ph.D. 1964.

6246   Anglo-Portuguese relations in south-central Africa, 1890-1900. P.R. Warhurst. Oxford B.Litt. 1960.

6247   The trust in imperial central African policy. R.E. Robinson. Cambridge Ph.D. 1951.

6248   Sir Gerald Portal's mission to Uganda, 1893. A.S. Baxendale. Birmingham M.A. 1954.

6249   The establishment of administration in the East Africa Protectorate to 1912. G.H. Mungeam. Oxford D.Phil. 1965.

6250   Education in Uganda, 1894-1945. Felice V. Carter. London Ph.D. 1967.

6251   The Swahili-speaking communities of the Kenya coast, 1895-1965. A.I. Salim. London Ph.D. 1968.

6252   Studies in district administration in the East Africa Protectorate, 1895-1918. T.H.R. Cashmore. Cambridge Ph.D. 1966.

6253   Labour in the East African Protectorate, 1895-1918. A.H.L. Clayton. St. Andrews Ph.D. 1970.

6254   Land policy, legislation and settlement in the East Africa Protectorate, 1895-1915. M.P.K. Sorrenson. Oxford D.Phil. 1963.

6255   The work of the Mill-Hill Fathers in relation to the spread of Roman Catholicism from Nsambya throughout the vicariate of the Upper Nile, Uganda, from 1895 to 1914. H.P. Gale. London Ph.D. 1955.

6256   The development of African local government in Kenya between 1900 and 1962. D.M. Lyon. Nottingham Ph.D. 1966.

6257   The marketing of cotton in Uganda, 1900-50. C. Ehrlich. London Ph.D. 1958.

6258   Politics in Bukedi, 1900-39: an historical study of administrative change among the segmentary peoples of eastern Uganda under the impact of British colonial rule. M.J. Twaddle. London Ph.D. 1967.

6259   Immigrant influences upon the development of policy in the protectorate of Uganda, 1900-25, with particular reference to the role of the Legislative Council. G.F. Engholm. London Ph.D. 1968.

6260   A study of selected aspects of the political geography of British East Africa with special reference to the boundaries of Kenya. E.D. Morgan. Wales M.A. 1953.

6261   The economic development of the Nyanza province of Kenya Colony, 1903-53: a study of an African economy. H. Fearn. London Ph.D. 1957.

6262   The African education policy of the Kenya government, 1909-39. Sally P. Abbott. London M.Phil. 1970.

6263   The German administration in Tanganyika, 1906-11: the governorship of Freiherr von Rechenberg. J. Iliffe. Cambridge Ph.D. 1965.

6264   British policy in Central Africa, 1908-26. M.L. Chanock. Cambridge Ph.D. 1968.

Kikuyu 1913: an ecumenical controversy. G.D. White. 6265
London Ph.D. 1970.

The contribution of the missions to educational 6266
structure and administrative policy in Tanganyika, 1918-61.
A. Smith. Sheffield M.A. 1963.

Development policy in East Africa between the wars: a 6267
study of the political influences involved in the making of
British policy, 1919-39. E.A. Brett. London Ph.D. 1966.

Tanganyika under British administration, 1920-55. 6268
Margaret L. Bates. Oxford D.Phil. 1958.

The East African tea industry, 1920-56: a case study 6269
in the development of a plantation industry. M.D. McWilliam.
Oxford B.Litt. 1957.

The American background of the Phelps-Stokes commis- 6270
sions and their influences in education in East Africa,
especially in Kenya. K.J. King. Edinburgh Ph.D. 1968.

The traditional history of the Buganda kingdom, with 6271
special reference to the historical writings of Sir Apolo
Kaggwa. M.S. Kiwanuka. London Ph.D. 1965.

The Alliance High School and the origins of the Kenya 6272
African élite, 1926-62. B.E. Kipkorir. Cambridge Ph.D.
1970.

THE CONGO

British policy towards West Central Africa, 1816-87, 6273
and the development of British influence and commerce there-
in, with special reference to the activities of Sir William
Mackinnon and to British connexions with the Association
Internationale Africaine and the Comité d'Études du Haut-
Congo. R.T. Anstey. London Ph.D. 1957.

The formation of the Congo Free State, with special 6274
reference to the work of Sir Henry Morton Stanley. Gwladys
P. Jones. Wales M.A. 1935.

English-speaking missions in the Congo Independent 6275
State, 1878-1908. Ruth M. Slade. London Ph.D. 1957.

Germany, Belgium, Britain and Ruanda-Urundi, 1884-1919. 6276
W.R. Louis. Oxford D.Phil. 1962.

Great Britain and the Congo question, 1892-1913. 6277
S.J.S. Cookey. London Ph.D. 1964.

British diplomacy and the Anglo-Congo treaty of 1894. 6278
Y.-S. Wei. Cambridge Ph.D. 1948/9.

SOUTHERN AFRICA

South African travel literature in English to the end 6279
of the 17th century. N.H. Mackenzie. London Ph.D. 1940.

Constitutional development at the Cape of Good Hope, 6280
1795-1854. G. von W. Eybers. London M.A. 1916.

The beginnings of missionary enterprise in South 6281
Africa, 1795-1812. Kathleen M. Reynolds. London M.A. 1927.

The London Missionary Society in South Africa during 6282
the years 1798-1836. D.K. Clinton. Oxford B.Litt. 1935.

The origin and growth of Presbyterian ordinances of 6283
worship among English-speaking European South Africans prior
to the formation of the Presbyterian Church of South Africa
in 1897. J. Dalziel. Edinburgh Ph.D. 1957.

The influence of the Church of Scotland on the Dutch 6284
Reformed Church of South Africa. F.W. Sass. Edinburgh Ph.D.
1956.

The growth and distribution of white population in 6285
South Africa from the second British occupation (1806) until
1951. Eileen M. McCracken. Belfast Ph.D. 1962.

The unification of South Africa, 1806-1909. J.H. 6286
Washington. London M.Sc. 1921.

6287   Colonial policy and slavery in South Africa, 1806-26.
Isobel E. Edwards. Oxford B.Litt. 1937.
6288   The colonial policy of the Liverpool administration,
with special reference to British settlement in South Africa.
Isobel E. Edwards. Wales M.A. 1931.
6289   Missionary imperialism in Bechuanaland, 1813-96. A.J.
Dachs. Cambridge Ph.D. 1968.
6290   Lord Charles Somerset (governor of the Cape, 1815-27):
a reassessment. Mary C. Hughes. Liverpool Ph.D. 1964.
6291   Life and work of Robert Moffat, with particular reference to the expansion of missions and white settlement north
of the Orange River, 1817-70. W.C. Northcott. London Ph.D.
1961.
6292   Emigration from Great Britain to South Africa, 1820 to
1840. J.D. Whitcomb. Birmingham M.A. 1953.
6293   Wesleyan missions on the eastern frontier of Cape Colony,
1820-40, with special reference to the Kaffir War of 1834-5.
N.K. Hurt. London M.A. 1958.
6294   The relations of the Amampondo and the colonial authorities 1830-86, with special reference to the role of the
Wesleyan missionaries. D.G.L. Cragg. Oxford D.Phil. 1959.
6295   The church in Basutoland, 1833-84. Mrs. Pauline E.
Beavan. Southampton M.A. 1966.
6296   Colonial policy on the northern and eastern frontiers
of the Cape of Good Hope, 1834-46. J. Roxborough. Oxford
B.Litt. 1953.
6297   Life of Moshoeshoe I. P.B. Sanders. Oxford D.Phil.
1970.
6298   The economic development of Natal, 1843-85. Maybelle
F. Bitensky. London M.A. 1955.
6299   The development of the white community in Natal, 1845-
72. W.P. Bromiley. London Ph.D. 1937.
6300   The career of Sir Harry Smith in South Africa. Eliza
B. Hawkins. Oxford B.Litt. 1922.
6301   The policy of the British government towards the South
African Dutch republics, 1848-72. C.W. de Kiewiet. London
Ph.D. 1927.
6302   Taxation of Africans in South Africa, 1849-1939. S.B.
Ngcobo. London Ph.D. 1964.
6303   White conflict and non-white participation in the
politics of the Cape of Good Hope, 1853-1910. S. Trapido.
London Ph.D. 1970.
6304   Public opinion and the acquisition of Bechuanaland and
Rhodesia, 1868-96. Daphne Trevor. London Ph.D. 1936.
6305   Basutoland and the High Commission, with particular
reference to the years 1868-84: the changing nature of the
imperial government's 'special responsibility' for the territory. J.A. Benyon. Oxford D.Phil. 1968.
6306   The economic and social geography of Basutoland. N.C.
Pollock. Oxford B.Litt. 1956.
6307   The policy of South African confederation, 1870-81.
C.F. Goodfellow. Cambridge Ph.D. 1961.
6308   British relations with the Transvaal from 1874 to 1881.
W.G. Murray. Oxford D.Phil. 1937.
6309   The history of Nyasaland and north-eastern Rhodesia,
1875-95. A.J. Hanna. London Ph.D. 1948.
6310   The ultimatum of Sir Bartle Frere to the Zulu King
Cetshwayo in December 1878. G.B. Regan. Kent M.A. 1970.
6311   A history of the Lozi people. Mutumba Mainga. London
Ph.D. (Ext.) 1969.
6312   A political history of Barotseland, 1878-1965. G.L.
Caplan. London Ph.D. 1968.
6313   The second Gladstone administration and the Transvaal,
1880-5: an analysis of policy. D.M. Schreuder. Oxford
D.Phil. 1968.

Christian missions in Northern Rhodesia, 1882-1924   6314
(with special reference to the history of the London Missionary Society, the Primitive Methodist Missionary Society, the
South African General Mission, the Plymouth Brethren, and the
Universities Mission to Central Africa). R.I. Rotberg. Oxford D.Phil. 1960.
     The railway and customs policy of the South African   6315
states and colonies, 1885-1910. J. van der Poel. London
Ph.D. 1929.
     The Bechuanaland Protectorate, 1885-95. A. Sillery.   6316
Oxford D.Phil. 1962.
     The constitutional history and law of Southern Rhode-   6317
sia, 1888 to 1964, with special reference to imperial control.
Mrs. Claire Palley. London Ph.D. 1965.
     The growth of a plural society: social, economic and   6318
political aspects of Northern Rhodesian development 1890-
1953, with special reference to the problem of racial relations. L.H. Gann. Oxford D.Phil. 1964.
     The making and implementation of land policy in Rhode-   6319
sia, 1890-1936. R.H. Palmer. London Ph.D. (Ext.) 1968.
     Native segregation in Southern Rhodesia: a study of   6320
social policy. R. McGregor. London Ph.D. (Ext.) 1940.
     The development of Rhodesia under the British South   6321
Africa Company (1890-1914), with some indication of subsequent developments. J.W. Fisher. Wales M.A. 1924.
     The growth of the public system of education in   6322
Southern Rhodesia, 1892-1910. J.M. Williams. Wales M.A.
1959.
     The challenge of Rhodesia to European liberal thought.   6323
M.C. Steele. Edinburgh M.Litt. 1968.
     The development of Northern Rhodesia under the British   6324
South Africa Company, 1894-1914: a study in white penetration,
growth of administration, and racial relations. L.H. Gann.
Oxford B.Litt. 1955.
     African reaction to European rule in the Northern Pro-   6325
vince of Northern Rhodesia, 1895-1939: a study of the genesis
and development of political awareness among a colonial
people. H.S. Meebelo. London Ph.D. (Ext.) 1969.
     Earl Grey's native policy in South Africa, with special 6326
reference to Natal. Phyllis Lee. Sheffield M.A. 1930.
     The achievement of self-government in Southern Rhode-   6327
sia, 1898-1923. J.D. Fage. Cambridge Ph.D. 1949.
     The technological development and growth of the   6328
Northern Rhodesian copperbelt, 1899-1960, with particular
reference to the Nchanga Mine. F.L. Coleman. Edinburgh
Ph.D. 1965.
     Labour policies on the Northern Rhodesian copperbelt,   6329
1924-64. Mrs. Elena L. Berger, née Plotnikoff. Oxford
D.Phil. 1969.
     The building of the Benguela Railway and the related   6330
railway and economic development of Northern Rhodesia and
Katanga, 1900-31. S.E. Katzenellenbogen. Oxford D.Phil.
1969.
     The imperial government and British Indians in the   6331
Transvaal. P.D. Pillay. London Ph.D. 1967.
     Reconstruction in the Transvaal, 1900-5. D.J.N.   6332
Denoon. Cambridge Ph.D. 1965.
     The imperial policy of the Liberal party: the settle-   6333
ment of South Africa, 1902-10. G.B. Pyrah. Leeds Ph.D.
1952.
     Black and white in self-governing Natal: an assessment 6334
of the 1906-8 disturbances. Mrs. Shula E. Marks. London
Ph.D. 1967.
     The Orange Free State: a study in the interrelation of   6335
geography and history. M. Dawson. London M.A. 1926.

6336 The African National Congress of South Africa: aspects of ideology and organisation between 1912 and 1951. A.P. Walshe. Oxford D.Phil. 1968.

6337 Britain and Southern Rhodesia, 1923-39: British opinion and the politics of 'African Affairs'. N.L. Chaduka. Liverpool M.A. 1970.

WEST AFRICA

6338 The mapping of West Africa in the 14th and 15th centuries, as illustrative of the development of geographical ideas. G.H. Kimble. London M.A. 1931.

6339 International rivalry in West Africa (1454-1559). J.W. Blake. London M.A. 1935.

6340 The Mbundu and neighbouring peoples of central Angola under the influence of Portuguese trade and conquest, 1482-1790. D.B. Birmingham. London Ph.D. 1964.

6341 The Dutch West India Company on the west coast of Africa up to 1660. Alice M. Cousins. Belfast M.A. 1953.

6342 The rise and development of legitimate trade in palm oil with West Africa. N.H. Stilliard. Birmingham M.A. 1938.

6343 Trade and politics on the Gold Coast: 1640-1720. K.Y. Daaku. London Ph.D. 1964.

6344 A history of the upper Guinea coast, 1545-1800. W.A. Rodney. London Ph.D. 1966.

6345 The external trade of the Loanga coast and its effects on the Vili, 1576-1870. Phyllis M. Martin. London Ph.D. 1970.

6346 Old Calabar, 1600-1891. A.J.H. Latham. Birmingham Ph.D. 1970.

6347 Akwamu, 1650-1750: a study of the rise and fall of a West African empire. I.G. Wilks. Wales M.A. 1959.

6348 The role of Shaikh Sidiyya and the Qadiriyya in Southern Mauritania: an historical interpretation. C.C. Stewart. Oxford D.Phil. 1970.

6349 The spread and development of Islam in the middle Volta basin in the pre-colonial period. N. Levtzion. London Ph.D. 1965.

6350 The struggle for power on the Senegal and Gambia, 1660-1713. Thora G. Stone. London M.A. 1921.

6351 Ashanti and her neighbours, c.1700-1807. J.K. Fynn. London Ph.D. 1964.

6352 British slave-trading activities on the Gold and Slave Coasts in the 18th century and their effects on African society. S. Tenkorang. London M.A. 1964.

6353 The connection of Bristol with the African slave trade. A. Mary Richards. Bristol M.A. 1923.

6354 Factors in Ashanti political expansion (1700-1830). P.K. Arhin. Oxford B.Litt. 1966.

6355 The English establishments on the Gold Coast in the second half of the 18th century. Eveline C. Martin. London M.A. 1921.

6356 Dahomey and its neighbours, 1708-1818. I.A. Akinjogbin. London Ph.D. 1963.

6357 The British West African settlements, 1751-1821: a study in local administration. Eveline C. Martin. London Ph.D. 1926.

6358 The provision and administration of education in the Gold Coast from 1765 to 1865. F.L. Bartels. London M.A. 1949.

6359 Education in Sierra Leone, 1787-1914. Nathalia I.K. Eleady-Cole. London M.Phil. 1967.

6360 The traditional courts and their successors in Ghana's legal history (1800-1914). A.K. Mensah-Brown. London Ph.D. 1970.

The Nupe kingdom in the 19th century: a political   6361
history. M.D. Mason. Birmingham Ph.D. 1970.
West Africa and the Muslim pilgrimage: an historical   6362
study, with special reference to the 19th century. O.A.R.
El-Nagar. London Ph.D. 1969.
British measures for the suppression of the slave trade 6363
from the west coast of Africa, 1807-33. Elsie I. Herrington.
London M.A. 1923.
The rise and fall of Fulani rule in Adamawa, 1809-1901. 6364
M.Z. Njeuma. London Ph.D. 1969.
The autonomous kingdom of Dahomey, 1818-94. D.A. Ross. 6365
London Ph.D. 1967.
A history of the settlements of liberated Africans in   6366
the colony of Sierra Leone in the first half of the 19th
century. D.A.V. Stephen. Durham M.A. 1962.
Liberated Africans and the history of Lagos Colony to   6367
1886. Jean F. Herskovits. Oxford D.Phil. 1960.
The economic history of Liberia. G.W. Brown. London   6368
Ph.D. 1938.
Senior African civil servants in British West Africa,   6369
1808-95. L.A. Mbye. Birmingham Ph.D. 1969.
British policy in relation to Sierra Leone, 1808-52.   6370
G.R. Mellor. London M.A. 1935.
International rivalry in the Bights of Benin and   6371
Biafra, 1815-85. W.H. Scotter. London Ph.D. 1933.
British policy in relation to the Gold Coast, 1815-50.   6372
P.G. James. London M.A. 1935.
Government and opinion in the Gambia, 1816-1901. Mrs.   6373
Florence K.O. Mahoney. London Ph.D. 1963.
The role of the missionaries in the political, economic 6374
and social development of Ghana, c.1820-c.1880. S.K. Odamtten.
Birmingham M.A. 1963.
Military and naval factors in British West African   6375
history, 1823-74: being an examination of the organisation of
British naval and military forces in West Africa, and their
role in the struggle for the coast and the principal rivers.
P.M. Mbaeyi. Oxford D.Phil. 1966.
Trade and politics in the Niger delta, 1830-79. K.O.   6376
Diké. London Ph.D. 1950.
British enterprise on the Niger, 1830-69. C.C. Ife-   6377
mesia. London Ph.D. 1959.
The Presbyterian Church of Ghana, 1835-1960: a younger   6378
church in changing society. J.N. Smith. Edinburgh Ph.D.
1963.
The study of the recruitment, training and placing of   6379
teachers in the primary and secondary school levels in western
Nigeria, 1842-1927. B.O. Rotimi. London M.A. 1955.
The provision of education in Nigeria with reference to 6380
the work of the Church Missionary Society, Catholic Mission
and the Methodist Missionary Society. P.E.B. Inyang. London
M.A. 1958.
Christian missions and the making of Nigeria, 1841-91.   6381
J.F.A. Ajayi. London Ph.D. 1958.
The Egba state and its neighbours (1842-72). S.O.   6382
Biobaku. London Ph.D. (Ext.) 1951.
The history of the training of African Christian   6383
ministers in Ghana, 1842-1965. J.K. Agbeti. London Ph.D.
1969.
British relations with the Gold Coast, 1843-80. Freda   6384
Wolfson. London Ph.D. 1951.
The education of the West African peoples, with   6385
especial reference to the Yoruba tribes of Southern Nigeria.
H. Dallimore. Oxford B.Litt. 1929.
A history of the Yoruba mission, 1843-80. W.O. Ajayi.   6386
Bristol M.A. 1959.
The Ewe people and the coming of European rule, 1850-   6387
1914. D.E.K. Amenumey. London M.A. 1964.

6388   Ijebu and its neighbours, 1851-1914. O.O. Ayantuga.
London Ph.D. 1965.
6389   The rise of Ibadan as a Yoruba power, 1851-93. Mrs.
Bolanle A. Awe. Oxford D.Phil. 1964.
6390   A history of the Niger and northern Nigerian missions,
1857-1914. W.O. Ajayi. Bristol Ph.D. 1963.
6391   Imperial policy towards the British settlements in West
Africa, 1860-75. Cherry J. Gertzel. Oxford B.Litt. 1953.
6392   The Catholic contribution to education in western
Nigeria from 1861 to 1926. M.J. Walsh. London M.A. 1951.
6393   British policy in Liberia, 1862-1912. D.M. Foley.
London Ph.D. 1965.
6394   The development of the legal system in the colony of
Lagos, 1862-1905. J. Gordon. London Ph.D. 1967.
6395   Christianity in the Niger delta, 1864-1918. G.O. Tasie.
Aberdeen Ph.D. 1969.
6396   Edward W. Blyden, 1832-1912, and Pan-Negro nationalism.
H.R. Lynch. London Ph.D. 1964.
6397   Expansion of the Lagos Protectorate, 1863-1900. A.A.B.
Aderibigbe. London Ph.D. 1959.
6398   Britain's role in the regulation of the arms traffic in
West Africa, 1873-1919. P.F. Teba. Cambridge M.Litt. 1967.
6399   British official attitudes in relation to economic
development in the Gold Coast, 1874-1905. R.E. Dumett.
London Ph.D. 1966.
6400   The development of the Gold Coast under British administration, 1874-1904. Heather Dalton. London M.A. (Ext.)
1957.
6401   The political and social implications of missionary
enterprise in the evolution of modern Nigeria, 1875-1914.
E.A. Ayandele. London Ph.D. 1964.
6402   British policy in relation to Portuguese claims in West
Africa, 1876 to 1884. Irene Bains. London M.A. 1940.
6403   The railways of West Africa - a geographical and historical analysis. R.J. Church. London Ph.D. (Ext.) 1943.
6404   British policy and chartered company administration in
Nigeria, 1879-1900. J.E. Flint. London Ph.D. 1957.
6405   An economic history of Lagos, 1880-1914. A.G. Hopkins.
London Ph.D. 1964.
6406   Origins of British methods of tropical development in
West African Dependencies, 1880-1906. O. Omosini. Cambridge
Ph.D. 1969.
6407   Traditional and modern élites in the politics of Lagos,
1884-1938. P.D. Cole. Cambridge Ph.D. 1970.
6408   The Berlin West African Conference, 1884-5. Sibyl E.
Crowe. Cambridge Ph.D. 1939.
6409   The boundary arrangements for Nigeria, 1884-1906: an
objective study in colonial boundary-making. J.C.O. Anene.
London Ph.D. 1960.
6410   The external trade of the Gold Coast (Ghana) and Nigeria,
1885-1945. S.I. Edokpayi. London M.Sc. 1958.
6411   Britain, France and the Dahomey-Niger hinterland, 1885-
98. B.I. Obichere. Oxford D.Phil. 1967.
6412   The political history of Ashanti, 1888-1935. W. Tordoff.
London Ph.D. 1961.
6413   The African churches of Yorubaland, 1888-1922. J.B.
Webster. London Ph.D. 1963.
6414   The constitutional development of the Gold Coast. B.E.
Kwaw-Swanzy. Cambridge M.Litt. 1955.
6415   The rise of nationalism in the Gold Coast. D.B. Kimble.
London Ph.D. 1960.
6416   The establishment and development of British administration in the Niger delta, with special reference to the
work and letters of C.M. Macdonald, 1889-95. A.W. Webb.
London Ph.D. 1970.

The establishment and consolidation of imperial govern- 6417
ment in Southern Nigeria, 1891-1904. (Theory and practice in
a colonial protectorate.) J.C.O. Anene. London M.A. 1952.

Humanitarian pressure-groups and British attitudes to 6418
West Africa, 1895-1915. K.K.D. Nworah. London Ph.D. 1966.

Lord Salisbury and tropical Africa, 1895-1900: a study 6419
in attitudes to imperial expansion. (Selected areas.) G.N.
Uzoigwe. Oxford D.Phil. 1967.

The British occupation and development of Northern 6420
Nigeria, 1897-1914. A.O. Anjorin. London Ph.D. 1966.

The Sierra Leone Frontier Police: a study in the 6421
functions and employment of a colonial force. N.H.R. Etheridge. Aberdeen M.Litt. 1967.

Sir Alfred Jones and the development of West African 6422
trade. P.N. Davies. Liverpool M.A. 1963.

John Holt, a British merchant in West Africa in the 6423
era of 'Imperialism'. Cherry J. Gertzel. Oxford D.Phil.
1959.

The West African Frontier Force, an instrument of 6424
imperial policy, 1897-1914. S.C. Ukpabi. Birmingham M.A.
1964.

Anglo-French relations, with special reference to West 6425
Africa, 1898-1904. M.O.E. Nwafor. London M.A. 1959.

Nigerian administrative law: the first fifty years, 6426
1900-50. I.M. Okonjo. London Ph.D. (Ext.) 1970.

West African aspects of the Pan-African movements, 6427
1900-45. J.A. Langley. Edinburgh Ph.D. 1968.

The introduction and establishment of western education 6428
in Northern Nigeria by the British colonial administration
during the period 1900-21. Vivian Jones. Wales M.A. 1967.

A history of education in relation to the development 6429
of the protectorate of Northern Nigeria, 1900-19, with
special reference to the work of Hanns Vischer. Sonia F.
Graham. London Ph.D. 1955.

The development of British administrative control of 6430
Southern Nigeria, 1900-12: a study in the administrations of
Sir Ralph Moor, Sir William MacGregor and Sir Walter Egerton.
S.M. Tamuno. London Ph.D. 1962.

The development of adult literacy and adult education 6431
and their influence on social change in Ghana, 1901-57. K.O.
Hagan. Oxford B.Litt. 1968.

The development of welfare policy and practices in 6432
Ghana, 1901-57. P. Hodge. Nottingham M.A. 1965.

A history of local government and voluntary associ- 6433
ations in the rural areas of the colony of Sierra Leone from
1905 to the present. C.R.A. Cole. Durham M.A. 1963.

The development of secondary education in western 6434
Nigeria, 1909-60. J.T. Horgan. Belfast M.A. 1970.

British shipping and the growth of the West African 6435
economy, 1910-50. P.N. Davies. Liverpool Ph.D. 1967.

The prophet Harris and his work in Ivory Coast and 6436
western Ghana. G.M. Haliburton. London Ph.D. 1966.

The newspaper press in British West Africa, 1918-39. 6437
W.D. Edmonds. Bristol M.A. 1951.

Aspects of nationalist thought among French-speaking 6438
West Africans, 1921-39. J.S. Spiegler. Oxford D.Phil. 1968.

The development of the teaching profession in Nigeria, 6439
1926-64. U. Onwuka. Oxford B.Litt. 1966.

The civil service of Nigeria: problems and progress of 6440
its Nigerianisation, 1940 to the present day. O. Nwanwene.
London Ph.D. (Ext.) 1967.

Constitutional developments in Nigeria, 1944-56. K. 6441
Ezera. Oxford D.Phil. 1957.

The transfer of power in Ghana, 1945-57. R.J.A.R. 6442
Rathbone. London Ph.D. 1968.

A S I A

GENERAL

6443   The Portuguese in India and the East Indies, 1497-1548.
T.H. Jenkins. Birmingham M.A. 1924.
6444   The development and organisation of English trade to
Asia, 1553-1605. D. Fischer. London Ph.D. 1970.
6444A   The history of St. Helena and the route to the Indies,
1659-1702. W.C. Palmer. London M.A. 1924.
6445   The Suez Canal and the trends of British trade to and
from the Middle and the Far East during the period 1854-1966.
A.R. Yousri. St. Andrews Ph.D. 1968.
6446   The strategy of Christian mission to the Muslims:
Anglican and Reformed contributions in India and the Near
East from Henry Martyn to Samuel Zwemer, 1800-1938. L.L.
Vander Werff. Edinburgh Ph.D. 1968.
6447   The Burma-China boundary since 1886. K.M. Nyunt. London Ph.D. 1960.
6448   A comparative study of British and American colonial
educational policy in Ceylon and the Philippines from 1900
to 1948. Swarna Jayaweera. London Ph.D. (Ext.) 1966.
6449   Economic and political relations of India with Iran and
Afghanistan since 1900. T. Basu. Cambridge M.Litt. 1942.
6450   British policy and the defence of Asia, 1903-5, with
special reference to China and India. B.G. Willcock.
Nottingham M.A. 1964.
6451   Britain and the termination of the India-China opium
trade, 1905-13. Mrs. Margaret J.B.C. Markey, née Lim.
London Ph.D. 1969.
6452   Local government in India and Burma, 1908 to 1937: a
comparative study of the evolution and working of local
authorities in Bombay, the United Provinces and Burma. H.R.
Tinker. London Ph.D. 1951.

INDIA AND PAKISTAN

Ancient and Medieval

6453   The agricultural geography of the United Provinces.
B.N. Mukherji. Edinburgh Ph.D. 1939.
6454   Position of the S'ūdras in ancient India to A.D. 500.
R.S. Sharma. London Ph.D. 1956.
6455   The evolution of Hindu marriage, with special reference
to rituals (c.1000 B.C. - A.D. 500). Nilakshi Sengupta.
London Ph.D. 1958.
6456   The development of marriage in ancient India. B.C.
Paul. London Ph.D. 1949.
6457   Some aspects of the earliest social history of India
(especially the pre-Buddhistic ages). S.C. Sarkar. Oxford
D.Phil. 1922.
6458   The historical geography and topography of Bihar from
the Vedic period to the Muslim invasion. M.S. Pandey. London Ph.D. 1958.
6459   Ancient Indian warfare, with special reference to the
Vedic period. S.D. Singh. London Ph.D. 1962.
6460   Peace and war in ancient India. W.S. Armour. Oxford
B.Litt. 1921.
6461   The art of war in ancient India. P.C. Chakravarti.
London Ph.D. 1938.
6462   History of Indian asceticism in pre-Buddhistic times.
J.P. Singh. London Ph.D. 1960.
6463   The early history of the cult of the goddess Manasā.
P.K. Maity. London Ph.D. 1963.
6464   The early history of the cult of the Mother Goddess in
northern Indian Hinduism, with special reference to iconography. M. Rahman. London Ph.D. 1965.

History and doctrines of the Ajivikas: a study of 6465
ancient Indian heterodoxy. A.L. Basham. London Ph.D. 1950.
Some aspects of Indian society as depicted in the Pāli 6466
canon. N.K. Wagle. London Ph.D. 1963.
Republican and quasi-republican institutions in ancient 6467
India, with special reference to the time of the Buddha. J.P.
Sharma. London Ph.D. 1962.
Ancient Indian education: an enquiry into its origin, 6468
development and ideals. F.E. Keay. London M.A. 1917.
The political history of Bengal to the rise of the 6469
Pāla dynasty (c.326 B.C. to A.D. 750). B. Das. London Ph.D.
1965.
The history and development of the Mauryan Brāhmī 6470
script. C.S. Upasak. London Ph.D. 1959.
Asoka and the decline of the Mauryas. Romila Thapar. 6471
London Ph.D. 1958.
The early history of south-east Bengal in the light 6472
of recent archaeological material. M.H. Rashid. Cambridge
Ph.D. 1969.
Studies in the economic life of northern and western 6473
India, c.200 B.C. - A.D. 300. G. Adhya. London Ph.D. 1962.
India in the time of Patañjali. B.N. Puri. Oxford 6474
B.Litt. 1951.
The lower Indus country, c. A.D. 1 to 150. B.N. 6475
Mukherjee. London Ph.D. 1963.
Cultural history of the Satavahana dynasty. C.K. 6476
Gairola. London Ph.D. 1949.
The history of the Andhra region, c. A.D. 75-350. 6477
Ranjana Mukherjee. London Ph.D. 1965.
The socio-economic organisation of northern India (c. 6478
200 A.D. - c.600 A.D.). R. Sarker. London Ph.D. 1947.
Coins and currency systems in early south India, c.225 6479
A.D. - 1300 A.D. B.D. Chattopadhyaya. Cambridge Ph.D. 1969.
Court life in ancient India, A.D. 300-700. R.V. Desh- 6480
mukh. Oxford B.Litt. 1929.
The economic life of northern India in the Gupta period 6481
(c. A.D. 300 - A.D. 550). S.K. Maity. London Ph.D. 1956.
The dynasties of the Gupta period. Jatis Chandra De. 6482
London M.A. 1922.
The structure and composition of the Kautilīya Arthaś- 6483
āstra. T.R. Trautmann. London Ph.D. 1968.
The Hūnas in India. Atreyi Ray. London Ph.D. 1965. 6484
The evolution of script in north-eastern India, from 6485
c. A.D. 400 to 1200, with special reference to Bengal. S.
Bhattacharyya. London Ph.D. 1969.
Some historical aspects of the inscriptions of Bengal 6486
from the 5th to the 12th century A.D. B. Sen. London Ph.D.
1933.
Economic history of Bengal, c.400-1200 A.D. Mrs. 6487
Kamrunnesa Islam. London Ph.D. 1966.
Decline of the kingdom of Magadha from c.455 A.D. to 6488
c.1000 A.D. B.P. Sinha. London Ph.D. 1948.
History of the western Chalukyas (political and admin- 6489
istrative). G. Raychaudhuri. London Ph.D. 1948.
The Guhila dynasties of Mewar, c. A.D. 550-1303. J.P. 6490
Singh. London Ph.D. 1965.
The political history of Maharashtra from the earliest 6491
times to c.1000 A.D. V.R. Deoras. London Ph.D. 1940.
The political history of northern India, before and 6492
during the reign of Harsa, c. A.D. 550-650. Mrs. Devahuti
Singhal. London Ph.D. 1956.
The theory of government in ancient India. Beni 6493
Prasad. London Ph.D. 1926.
Sovereignty in ancient Indian polity - a study in the 6494
evolution of the early Indian state. H. Sinha. London Ph.D.
1935.

6495   The role and limits of state authority in northern India in the early historical period: an empirical examination of the administration of government. I.W. Mabbett. Oxford D.Phil. 1963.

6496   Aspects of kingship in ancient India to c. 300 A.D. J.W. Spellman. London Ph.D. 1960.

6497   The political and cultural history of the Punjab, including the North-West Frontier Province in its earliest period. L. Chandra. London Ph.D. 1940.

6498   Kingship in northern India, c. A.D. 600 - A.D. 1200. R.C.P. Singh. London Ph.D. 1957.

6499   The history of Kanauj to the Moslem conquest. R.S. Tripathi. London Ph.D. 1929.

6500   Caste and class in pre-Muslim Bengal: studies in social history of Bengal. N. Kundu. London Ph.D. (Ext.) 1963.

6501   The social life of women in early medieval Bengal. Mrs. Shahanara Husain. London Ph.D. (Ext.) 1965.

6502   The economic life of northern India, c. A.D. 700-1200. L. Gopal. London Ph.D. 1962.

6503   Feudalism in northern India, c. A.D. 700-1200. Mrs. Krishna K. Gopal. London Ph.D. 1962.

6504   Everyday life in the Pāla empire, with special reference to material remains. Mrs. Shahanara Husain. London M.A. 1960.

6505   Mithila and Magadha, 700 A.D. - 1100 A.D. L. Jha. London Ph.D. 1949.

6506   Some geographical factors in the history of the Punjab and Sind from 712 A.D. to 1605 A.D., with special reference to river control of settlement. M.I.R. Khan. London Ph.D. 1929.

6507   The knowledge of India possessed by Arab geographers down to the 14th century A.D., with special reference to southern India. S.M.H. Nainar. London Ph.D. 1938.

6508   Muslim rule in Sind in the 8th, 9th and 10th centuries. A.A. Puri. London Ph.D. 1936.

6509   Evolution of Bengal: an outline of its historical geography from the earliest times to the end of the Moslem period. N.N. Ghose. Liverpool M.A. 1933.

6510   Dynastic history of Bengal (c.750-1200 A.D.). A.M. Chowdhury. London Ph.D. 1965.

6511   History of the Gurjara-Pratihāras. B.N. Puri. Oxford D.Phil. 1954.

6512   Political history of Gujarat, c. A.D. 750-950. Shobhana K. Mehta. London Ph.D. 1961.

6513   Inter-state relations in northern India, c. A.D. 800-1200. S.G. Bajpai. London Ph.D. 1967.

6514   The land system in south India between c.800 and 1200 A.D. K.M. Gupta. London Ph.D. 1926.

6515   The history of the Paramara dynasty in Malwa, Arthuna, and Chandravati, 808-1310 A.D. D. Ganguli. London Ph.D. 1930.

6516   The Paramara dynasty of Malwa. Sailendranath Dasgupta. London M.A. 1922.

6517   Social conditions in ancient Kashmir, c. A.D. 855-1150. S. Kumar. London Ph.D. 1969.

6518   The dynastic history of northern India from c.916 to 1196 A.D. Hemchandra Ray. London Ph.D. 1929.

6519   The early history of the Buwaihid dynasty, 320-356 A.H. S. Hasan. London Ph.D. 1928.

6520   A political history of Rohana from c.991 to 1255 A.D. G.S. Ranawella. London Ph.D. 1966.

6521   Sultán Mahmúd of Ghazna and his times. M. Nazim. Cambridge Ph.D. 1927/8.

6522   The political history of the Telugu country, from c. A.D. 1000 to A.D. 1565. P. Sreenivasachar. London Ph.D. 1933.

History of the Candellas of Jejākabhukti. N.S. Bose. 6523
London Ph.D. 1954.

Kashmir under the Loharas, A.D. 1003-1171. Krishna 6524
Mohan. London Ph.D. 1958.

The dynastic history of the Hoysala kings. J.D.M. 6525
Derrett. London Ph.D. 1949.

The Hoysala style of temple architecture and sculpture, 6526
11th to 14th centuries. S. Settar. Cambridge Ph.D. 1970.

The Chisti and Suhrawardi movements in India to the 6527
middle of the 16th century. S.N. Hasan. Oxford D.Phil.
1948.

The history of Darfur from A.D. 1200 to 1700. A.J. 6528
Arkell. Oxford B.Litt. 1939.

Life and conditions of the people of Hindustan, A.D. 6529
1200-1550. K.M. Ashraf. London Ph.D. 1932.

An outline of the system of the administration of 6530
justice under the Muslims in India, based mainly upon cases
decided by Muslim courts between 1206 and 1720. M.B. Ahmad.
Cambridge M.Litt. 1938/9.

The role of the nobility during early Turkish rule in 6531
India, 1210-66. K.G. Asghar. Edinburgh Ph.D. 1969.

The administration of the sultanate of Delhi. I.H. 6532
Qureshi. Cambridge Ph.D. 1939.

The sultans of Delhi and their attitude towards 6533
religion, 1206-1320. S.M. Husain. Manchester M.A. 1964.

The sultans of Delhi and their non-Muslim subjects, 6534
1206-1320. A.D. Muztar. Manchester M.A. 1965.

The sultanate of Delhi, 1206-90 A.D. A.B.M. Habib- 6535
ullah. London Ph.D. 1936.

The army under the sultans of Delhi (A.D. 1210-1526). 6536
Y.M. Khan. London M.A. 1956.

European attitudes to Indian art from the middle of the 6537
13th to the end of the 19th century. P. Mitter. London
Ph.D. 1970.

The social and economic development of Islamic society 6538
in north India, 1290-1320. M. Aleem. London Ph.D. 1952.

The rise and fall of Muhammad bin Tughluq (1325-51). 6539
M. Husain. London Ph.D. 1935.

Some aspects of Indian Islam in the 14th century. 6540
S.M. Husain. Manchester Ph.D. 1967.

Social and political life in the Vijayanagara empire, 6541
1346-1646 A.D. B.A. Saletore. London Ph.D. 1931.

The sultanate of Jaunpur. M.M. Saeed. London Ph.D. 6542
1965.

Early Indian bhakti, with special reference to Kabīr: 6543
a historical analysis and re-interpretation. Krishna Sharma.
London Ph.D. 1965.

The kingdom of Bijãpur. P.M. Joshi. London Ph.D. 6544
1935.

The life and doctrine of Gurū Nānak. W.H. McLeod. 6545
London Ph.D. 1965.

From 16th Century

Portuguese society in India in the 16th and 17th cent- 6546
uries. K.J. Crowther. Oxford D.Phil. 1960.

The life and times of Srikṛṣṇa-Chaitanya. D. Acharyya. 6547
London Ph.D. 1967.

The political institutions of Bijapur, 1536-1686, and 6548
Golconda, 1518-1636. I.A. Ghauri. London Ph.D. 1961.

Early English travellers in India: a study in the 6549
travel literature of the Elizabethan and Jacobean periods
with particular reference to India. R.C. Prasad. Edinburgh
Ph.D. 1959.

The history of Humayun from 1530 to 1540 A.D. S. 6550
Banerji. London Ph.D. 1925.

6551   The history of the Arghuns and Tarkhans of Sind. M.H. Siddiqi. Manchester Ph.D. 1958.

6552   History of the Afghans in India, 1545-1631 A.D., with especial reference to their relations with the Mughals. M.A. Rahim. London Ph.D. 1954.

6553   The relations between the Mughul emperors of India and the Safavid shahs of Iran. R. Islam. Cambridge Ph.D. 1957.

6554   A study of urban centres and industries in the central provinces of the Mughal empire between 1556 and 1803. H.K. Naqvi. London Ph.D. 1965.

6555   The agrarian system of Mughal India (1556-1707). I.M.H. Habib. Oxford D.Phil. 1958.

6556   The provincial government of the Mughals, 1556-1659 A.D. P. Saran. London Ph.D. 1936.

6557   The Mogul diplomacy from Akbar to Aurangzeb. Abdur Rahim. London Ph.D. 1932.

6558   The Mughal nobility in India to 1658, with special reference to its political significance. M. Ali. London M.A. 1955.

6559   The political structure of the Mughal empire in northern India, and its practical working up to the year 1657. I. Hasan. London Ph.D. 1932.

6560   The north-west frontier policy of the Mughals, 1556-1658. M.J. Khan. Cambridge Ph.D. 1937.

6561   The political relations of the Mughals with the Deccan states, 1556-1658 A.D. Y.M. Khan. London Ph.D. 1958.

6562   The Mughal empire beyond the Indus: a study in imperial ambitions in the north-west during the reigns of Akbar, Jahangir and Shah Jahan. M.A.A. Ansari. London M.A. 1955.

6563   The religious policy of Akbar, 1556-1605. A. Bashir. London Ph.D. 1953.

6564   Mirza 'Abdu'r-Rahīm Khan-i-khanan: soldier, statesman, and patron of letters. A. Ali. Cambridge Ph.D. 1931/2.

6565   The role of Shaikh Ahmad of Sarhind in Islam in India. M.Q. Baig. London Ph.D. 1964.

6566   Commercial relations between India and England, 1600-1757. B. Krishna. London Ph.D. 1922.

6567   The first Islamic movement in India in the 17th century. M. Aslam. Manchester M.A. 1962.

6568   An administrative study of the development of civil service in India during the Company's régime. A.K. Ghosal. London Ph.D. 1940.

6569   Revenue administration of the sirkars under the East India Company down to 1802. Lanka Sundaram. London Ph.D. 1930.

6570   The development of the English East India Company, with special reference to its trade and organisation, 1600-40. K.N. Chaudhuri. London Ph.D. 1962.

6571   Some aspects of the historical geography of East Pakistan, 1608-1857. Bilquis Jahan. London Ph.D. 1969.

6572   The growth and development of the Indian tea industry and trade. S.M. Akhtar. London Ph.D. 1932.

6573   The Dutch in Coromandel, 1605-90. T. Raychaudhuri. Oxford D.Phil. 1957.

6574   The reign of the Emperor Shah Jehan. N.L. Ahmed. Oxford B.Litt. 1927.

6575   The history of the Shahjahan of Delhi. B.P. Saksena. London Ph.D. 1931.

6576   The provinces of Bihar and Bengal under Shāhjahān. K.M. Karim. London Ph.D. 1965.

6577   Trade and commercial organisation in Bengal, with special reference to the English East India Company, 1650-1720. S. Chaudhuri. London Ph.D. 1969.

6578   War of succession between the sons of Shah Jahan, 1657-8, with special reference to the part of nobility. I.A. Ghauri. London M.A. 1959.

The court of Aurangzib as a centre of literature and 6579
learning. R.A. Muhammadi. London Ph.D. 1949.
Bengal in the reign of Aurangzib, 1658-1707. Mrs. 6580
Anjali Basu. London Ph.D. 1965.
Sir William Norris, Bt., and his embassy to Aurangzeb 6581
(1657-1702). H. Das. Oxford B.Litt. 1923.
Sir Josiah Child and the East India Company. A.L. 6582
Crowe. London Ph.D. 1956.
Anglo-Mughal relations in western India and the 6583
development of Bombay, 1662-90. G.Z. Refai. Cambridge Ph.D.
1968.
The military system of the Mahrattas: its origin and 6584
development from the time of the Shivaji to the fall of the
Mahratta empire. S. Sen. Oxford B.Litt. 1927.
The history and literature of the Gaulyad Vaisnavas 6585
and their relation to other Vaisnava schools. S. Das. Lon-
don Ph.D. 1935.
The Indian calico trade and its influence on English 6586
history. P.J. Thomas. Oxford B.Litt. 1922.
The cotton industry in the Madras Presidency, with 6587
special reference to the domestic and factory systems. G.
Ranganayakula. Oxford B.Litt. 1926.
The cotton industry in India to 1757. J.N. Varma. 6588
London M.Sc. 1922.
English social life in India in the 18th century. 6589
T.G.P. Spear. Cambridge Ph.D. 1931/2.
The early history of female education in India. R.B. 6590
Mathur. London Ph.D. 1947.
The East India Company's land policy and management in 6591
Bengal from 1698 to 1784. M. Huq. London Ph.D. 1952.
The East India Company and the economy of Bengal from 6592
1704 to 1740. S. Bhattacharyya. London Ph.D. 1953.
The commercial progress and administrative development 6593
of the East India Company on the Coromandel coast during the
first half of the 18th century. R.N. Banerji. London Ph.D.
(Ext.) 1965.
Trade and politics in Banjarmasin, 1700-47. Goh Yoon 6594
Fong. London Ph.D. 1969.
Murshid Quli Khan and his times. A. Karim. London 6595
Ph.D. 1962.
Rise and fall of the Rohilla power in Hindustan, 1707- 6596
74 A.D. A.F.M.K. Rahman. London Ph.D. 1936.
The East India Company in Madras, 1707-44. R.N. 6597
Banerji. London M.A. 1955.
The reign of Shahu Chhatrapati, 1708-49. A.G. Powar. 6598
London Ph.D. 1934.
The life and career of Mir Qamaruddin Nizam ul Mulk 6599
Asaf Jah I. Y. Prasad. London Ph.D. 1927.

From mid 18th Century

Malabar in Asian trade, 1740-1800. A.R. das Gupta. 6600
Cambridge Ph.D. 1961.
British relations with Tanjore, 1748-99. C.S. Rama- 6601
nujam. London Ph.D. (Ext.) 1968.
The Indian salt industry, trade, and taxation, 1756- 6602
1932. B. Ghosh. London Ph.D. 1933.
The life and career of Jonathan Duncan, 1756-95. V.A. 6603
Narain. London Ph.D. 1958.
Muhammad Reza Khan, Naib Nazim and Naib Diwan of 6604
Bengal, 1756-75. A.M. Khan. London Ph.D. 1966.
Some aspects of Indian foreign trade, 1757-1893. I.D. 6605
Parshad. London Ph.D. 1928.
The British impact on the Indian cotton textile 6606
industry, 1757-1865. J.G. Borpujari. Cambridge Ph.D. 1970.
Alexander Dalrymple, cosmographer and servant of the 6607
East India Company. H.T. Fry. Cambridge Ph.D. 1967.

6608 The history of the occupation and rural administration of Bengal by the English Company from the time of Clive to the permanent settlement under Cornwallis. W.K. Firminger. Oxford B.Litt. 1917.

6609 The social condition of the British community in Bengal, 1757-1800. S. Ghosh. London Ph.D. 1966.

6610 The movement of opinion in England as regards Indian affairs, 1757-73. E. Emmett. Manchester M.A. 1921.

6611 The career of Mir Jafar Khan, 1757-65. A.C. Ray. London Ph.D. 1952.

6612 English relations with Haidar Ali, 1760-82. B. Sheik Ali. London Ph.D. 1960.

6613 The interaction of England and India during the early years of George III. Dorothy Dudley. Liverpool M.A. 1909.

6614 The revenue administration of Chittagong from 1761 to 1785. A.M. Serajuddin. London Ph.D. 1964.

6615 The Dutch East India Company and Mysore, 1762-90. J. van Lohuizen. Cambridge Ph.D. 1958.

6616 The debts of the Nawab of Arcot, 1763-76. J.D. Gurney. Oxford D.Phil. 1968.

6617 The settlement of the Madras Presidency, 1765-1827. Annie Bradley. Manchester M.A. 1920.

6618 The land revenue history of the Rajshahi Zamindari, 1765-93. A.B.M.U. Mahmood. London Ph.D. 1966.

6619 A study of Murshidabad district, 1765-93. K.M. Mohsin. London Ph.D. 1966.

6620 Life and conditions of the people of Bengal (1765-85). Z. Ahmad. Oxford D.Phil. 1965.

6621 The judicial administration of the East India Company in Bengal, 1765-82. B.B. Misra. London Ph.D. 1947.

6622 The Bengali Muslims and English education (1765-1835). M.F. Rahman. London M.A. 1948.

6623 The relations of the Mahrattas with the British power. I. Kathleen Walker. Manchester M.A. 1920.

6624 Slavery in the Bengal Presidency under East India Company rule, 1772-1843. A.K. Chattopadhyay. London Ph.D. 1963.

6625 The social policy of the East India Company with regard to sati, slavery, thagi and infanticide, 1772-1858. Benedicte Hjejle. Oxford D.Phil. 1958.

6626 An inquiry into the collections of the land revenue in Bengal, 1772-4. R.B. Ramsbotham. Oxford B.Litt. 1924.

6627 A study of the legal and administrative records of Dacca as illustrating the policy of Warren Hastings in east Bengal. Freda M. Sachse. Oxford B.Litt. 1934.

6628 Hastings' experiments in the judicial administration. N.J.M. Yusuf. London Ph.D. 1930.

6629 The administration of Bengal under Warren Hastings. Sophia Weitzman. Manchester Ph.D. 1921.

6630 The residency of Oudh during the administration of Warren Hastings. C.C. Bracewell. Manchester M.A. 1923.

6631 The evolution of civil procedure in Bengal from 1772 to 1806. Z. Rahman. London Ph.D. 1967.

6632 The administration of criminal justice in Bengal from 1773 to 1861. T. Banerjee. London Ph.D. 1955.

6633 Henry Dundas and the government of India, 1773-1801. B. Dé. Oxford D.Phil. 1961.

6634 Henry Dundas and the government of India, 1784-1800. Dorothy Thornton. Liverpool M.A. 1925.

6635 Lauchlin Macleane and his connexion with East India Company politics, 1773-8. J.N.M. Maclean. Oxford B.Litt. 1965.

6636 Relations of the governor-general and council with the governor and council of Madras under the Regulating Act of 1773. A. Dasgupta. London Ph.D. 1929.

6637 British Indian administration: a historical study. K.R. Ramaswami Aiyangar. London M.Sc. 1936.

Rohilkhand from conquest to revolt, 1774-1858: a study 6638
in the origins of the Indian Mutiny uprising. E.I. Brodkin.
Cambridge Ph.D. 1968.

The development up to 1818 of the relations of the 6639
British power in India with the native states. Phyllis J.
Mudie. Manchester M.A. 1920.

Sir Elijah Impey in India, 1774-83. B.N. Pandey. Lon- 6640
don Ph.D. 1958.

British relations with the Peshwa and Sindhia, 1782- 6641
1802. C.S. Ramanujam. London M.A. 1957.

Sir William Jones and the beginnings of Indology. S. 6642
Mukherjee. London Ph.D. 1963.

The life and works of Sir William Jones. R. Hassan. 6643
Durham M.Litt. 1966.

A comparative study of the early Wahhabi doctrines and 6644
contemporary reform movements in Indian Islam. M.A. Bari.
Oxford D.Phil. 1954.

The relations between the board of commissioners for 6645
the affairs of India and the court of directors, 1784-1816.
P. Chandra. London Ph.D. 1932.

British commercial interests and the expansion of the 6646
Bombay Presidency, 1784-1806. Mrs. Pamela Nightingale.
Cambridge Ph.D. 1964.

The relations between Oudh and the East India Company 6647
from 1785 to 1801. P. Basu. London Ph.D. 1938.

The administrative and judicial reforms of Lord Corn- 6648
wallis in Bengal, 1786-93 (excluding the Permanent Settlement). A. Aspinall. Manchester M.A. 1922.

The downfall of Tipu Sultan, 1793-9. Susilkumar Datta. 6649
London Ph.D. 1924.

Thomas Munro and the development of administrative 6650
policy in Madras, 1792-1818: the origins of 'the Munro
system'. T.H. Beaglehole. Cambridge Ph.D. 1960.

A historical survey and assessment of the ecclesiast- 6651
ical and missionary policy of the East India Company. I.J.
Gash. Oxford B.Litt. 1968.

A study of missionary policy and methods in Bengal from 6652
1793 to 1905. W.B.S. Davis. Edinburgh Ph.D. 1942.

Christian schools in Bengal prior to 1857. D.H. 6653
Emmott. Bristol M.A. 1960.

The contribution of Christian missionaries to education 6654
in Bengal, 1793-1837. M.A. Laird. London Ph.D. 1968.

The Christian missionaries in Bengal, 1793-1833. K. 6655
Sengupta. London Ph.D. 1966.

British Baptist missions and missionaries in India, 6656
1793-1837. E.D. Potts. Oxford D.Phil. 1963.

The achievements of Christian missionaries in India, 6657
1794-1833. K. Ingham. Oxford D.Phil. 1949.

Education in Kerala and the missionary contribution to 6658
it during the first half of the 19th century. J. Thaikoodan.
London M.Phil. 1967.

Trade and finance in the Bengal Presidency, 1793-1833. 6659
A. Tripathi. London Ph.D. 1954.

The governor-generalship of Sir John Shore, 1793-8. 6660
A.W. Mahmood. Oxford B.Litt. 1939.

The structure and organisation of the Bengal native 6661
infantry, with special reference to problems of discipline,
1796-1852. Amiya Sen. London Ph.D. 1961.

Baji Rao II. P. Gupta. London Ph.D. 1936. 6662

The constitutional relations of the Marquess Wellesley 6663
with the home authorities. Beatrice L. Frazer. Liverpool
M.A. 1917.

Southern India under Wellesley, 1798-1805. A.S. 6664
Bennell. Oxford B.Litt. 1951.

The growth of agricultural labour in the Madras Presid- 6665
ency in the 19th century. Mrs. Dharma Kumar. Cambridge
Ph.D. 1962.

6666   The commercial and diplomatic relations between India and Tibet in the 19th century. H.A. Lamb. Cambridge Ph.D. 1958.

6667   Anglo-Sikh relations, 1799-1849. B.J. Hasrat. Oxford D.Phil. 1957.

6668   The Panjab as a sovereign state, 1799-1839. G. Lall. London Ph.D. 1923.

6669   The financial history of the Mysore state, 1799-1831. M.H. Gopal. London Ph.D. 1930.

6670   The development of the cotton industry in India, from the early 19th century. S. Deshpande. Oxford B.Litt. 1924.

6671   The history of the cotton-mill industry in western India. K.B. Bharucha. London Ph.D. 1927.

6672   Education of girls and women in Bengal (1800-99), with special reference to the founding and development of the Bethune College. A. Sen. London M.A. 1958.

6673   Patronage and education in the East India Company civil service, 1800-57. J.T. Beyer. Edinburgh M.Litt. 1966/7.

6674   The formation of British land-revenue policy in the ceded and conquered provinces of northern India, 1801-33. M.I. Husain. London Ph.D. 1964.

6675   David Scott on the north-east frontier of India and in Assam. N.K. Barooah. London Ph.D. 1964.

6676   Evolution of the structure of civil judiciary in Bengal, 1800-31. C. Sinha. London Ph.D. 1967.

6677   The administration of the Delhi Territory, 1803-32. Jessie Holmes. London Ph.D. 1955.

6678   Development of education in Orissa under the British (1803-1946). B.N. Rath. London M.A. 1948.

6679   The British conquest and administration of Orissa, 1803-19. B.C. Ray. London Ph.D. 1957.

6680   Lord William Bentinck in Madras, 1803-7. Mrs. Maya Gupta. London Ph.D. 1969.

6681   British policy towards the Pathans and the Pindaris in central India, 1805-18. B. Ghosh. London Ph.D. 1964.

6682   Philip Francis and the problem of British government in Bengal. Sophia Weitzman. Manchester M.A. 1919.

6683   Sir Charles Metcalfe's administration and administrative ideas in India, 1806-35. D.N. Panigrahi. London Ph.D. 1965.

6684   The influence of the home government on land revenue and judicial administration in the presidency of Fort William in Bengal, from 1807 to 1822. B.S. Baliga. London Ph.D. 1933.

6685   Richard Jenkins and the Residency at Nagpur, 1807-18. F.A. Hagar. Cambridge M.Litt. 1958.

6686   Lord Minto's administration in India (1807-13), with especial reference to his foreign policy. Amita Majumdar. Oxford D.Phil. 1963.

6687   Henry Russell's activities in Hyderabad, 1811-20. Zubaida Yazdani. Oxford B.Litt. 1967.

6688   A historical survey to 1958 of the struggle to achieve compulsory education in India, with special reference to Bombay State. C.K. Kazi. London M.A. 1962.

6689   The development of the Muslims of Bengal and Bihar, 1813-56, with special reference to their education. A.R. Mallick. London Ph.D. 1953.

6690   The governor-generalship of the marquess of Hastings, 1813-23, with special reference to the Supreme Council and Secretariat, the Residents with native states, military policy, and the transactions of the Palmer Company. R.J. Bingle. Oxford D.Phil. 1965.

6691   The relations of the British government in India with the Indian states, 1813-23. M.S. Mehta. London Ph.D. 1928.

6692   Control and administration of education in Bengal - an historical study. S.C. Dutt. London M.A. 1950.

6693   The development of mountain warfare in India in the 19th century. S. Chandra. London M.Phil. 1968.

254

The invasion of Nepal: John Company at war, 1814-16. 6694
J.C. Pemble. London Ph.D. 1968.

Social policy and social change in western India, 1817- 6695
30. K. Ballhatchet. London Ph.D. 1954.

The influence of western thought on the social, educ- 6696
ational, political and cultural development of India, 1818-40.
V. Datta. Cambridge M.Litt. 1954.

The development of public opinion in Bengal, 1818-35. 6697
A.F.S. Ahmed. London Ph.D. 1961.

Land resumption in Bengal, 1819-46. A.M. Waheeduz- 6698
zaman. London Ph.D. 1969.

Land revenue administration in the ceded and conquered 6699
provinces and its economic background 1819-33. Mrs. Asiya
Siddiqi. Oxford D.Phil. 1963.

Utilitarian influence and the formation of Indian 6700
policy, 1820-40. E.T. Stokes. Cambridge Ph.D. 1952.

The diplomatic career of Sir Claude Wade: a study of 6701
British relations with the Sikhs and Afghans, July 1823 to
March 1840. E.R. Kapadia. London M.A. 1938.

The influence of the home government on the development 6702
of the land revenue and judicial administration in the presidency of Fort William in Bengal from 1823 to 1840. B. Mitra.
London M.A. 1936.

British policy on the north-east frontier of India 6703
(1826-86). S. Gupta. Oxford D.Phil. 1948.

The social and administrative reforms of Lord William 6704
Bentinck. G. Seed. St. Andrews Ph.D. 1949.

Lord William Bentinck and the Indian states, 1828-35. 6705
K.N. Pandey. London Ph.D. 1957.

Lord William Bentinck in Bengal, 1828-35. Cynthia E. 6706
Barrett. Oxford D.Phil. 1954.

Sati and its abolition. M. Sharadamma. Oxford B.Litt. 6707
1953.

Tribal unrest on the south-west frontier of the Bengal 6708
Presidency, 1831-3. J.C. Jha. London Ph.D. 1961.

An historical survey of the development of primary 6709
education in Mysore, India. K. Basaviah. London M.A. 1953.

Islamic religious instruction in the schools of the 6710
Punjab and Bengal in the British period. M. Ishaq. London
M.A. 1956.

A historical survey of the training of teachers in 6711
Bengal in the 19th and 20th centuries. S. Bhattacharya.
London M.A. 1954.

An enquiry into the development of training of teachers 6712
in the Punjab during the British period. Aquila B. Berlas.
London M.A. 1949.

The training of teachers in the Bombay Presidency 6713
during the British period: a historical survey. N.L. Vaidya.
London M.A. 1955.

Female education in Bengal. Violet I. Alphonso. Lon- 6714
don M.A. 1931.

Problems of educational finance in India, 1833-82. 6715
S.C. Majumdar. London M.A. 1957.

The growth and present status of Catholic secondary 6716
education in the province of Bombay. E.A. Pires. London
M.A. 1942.

Working of the Supreme Government of India and its 6717
constitutional relations with the home authorities, 1833-53.
A.C. Banerjee. Cambridge M.Litt. 1967.

The Bengali reaction to Christian missionary activ- 6718
ities, 1833-57. M.M. Ali. London Ph.D. 1963.

British educational policy in Bengal, 1833-54. J.F. 6719
Hilliker. London Ph.D. 1968.

The abolition of the East India Company's monopoly, 6720
1833. D. Eyles. Edinburgh Ph.D. 1955.

6721   Migration of Indian labour to British plantations in Mauritius, Natal and Fiji, 1834-1914. K. Sircar. London M.Sc. 1964.

6722   Labour emigration from India to the British colonies of Ceylon, Malaya and Fiji during the years 1850 to 1921. Lucy Colaco (Sister Lucile). London M.Sc. 1957.

6723   The development and significance of transport in India (1834-82). K.E. Verghese. Oxford D.Phil. 1963.

6724   The administration of Mysore under Sir Mark Cubbon, 1834-61. K.N.V. Sastri. London Ph.D. 1930.

6725   Lord Macaulay and the Indian legislative council, 1834-8. C.D. Dharkar. London M. . 1931.

6726   The internal policy of Lord Auckland in British India, from 1836 to 1842, with special reference to education. D.P. Sinha. London Ph.D. 1953.

6727   The administration of Guntur district, with special reference to local influences on revenue policy, 1837-48. R.E. Frykenberg. London Ph.D. 1961.

6728   The first Agha Khan and the British, 1838-68: a study in British Indian diplomacy and legal history. Zawahir Noorally. London M.A. 1964.

6729   Eldred Pottinger and the north-west frontier, 1838-42. D.W.F. Gourlay. St. Andrews B.Phil. 1954.

6730   Anglo-Sikh relations, 1839-49. Kahan C. Khanna. London Ph.D. 1932.

6731   The history and development of rural education in the United Provinces of Agra and Oudh, 1840-1926. S.N. Chaturvedi. London M.A. 1931.

6732   The contribution of Scottish missions to the rise of responsible churches in India. J.M. Orr. Edinburgh Ph.D. 1967.

6733   The Rev. James Long and protestant missionary policy in Bengal, 1840-72. G.A. Oddie. London Ph.D. 1964.

6734   The first contribution of the Wesleyan Methodist missionaries to southern India. P.W. de Silva. London M.Phil. 1968.

6735   The growth of urban leadership in western India, with special reference to Bombay City, 1840-85. Christine E. Dobbin. Oxford D.Phil. 1967.

6736   Lord Ellenborough's ideas on Indian policy. Kathleen I. Garrett. London M.A. 1935.

6737   The British conquest of Sind. K.A. Chishti. London M.A. 1938.

6738   The British administration of Sind between 1843 and 1865: a study in social and economic development. Hamida Khuhro. London Ph.D. 1965.

6739   Biography of Maharaja Dalip Singh. K.S. Thaper. Oxford B.Litt. 1934.

6740   British policy towards the Panjab, 1844-9. S.S. Bal. London Ph.D. 1963.

From mid 19th Century

6741   Development of Indian railways, 1842-1928. N. Sanyal. London Ph.D. 1929.

6742   The early history of the East Indian Railway, 1845-79. Mrs. Hena Mukherjee. London Ph.D. 1966.

6743   British investment in Indian Guaranteed Railways, 1845-75. W.J. Macpherson. Cambridge Ph.D. 1955.

6744   Reorganisation of the Punjab government, 1847-57. R.C. Lai. London Ph.D. 1937.

6745   A critical survey of the history of primary education in the state of Jammu and Kashmir, India, with special reference to developments since 1846. Champa Tickoo. London M.A. 1966.

A critical survey of the growth of primary education   6746
in the Punjab since the annexation (1847-1947) British period.
M.Q.H. Khan. London M.A. 1949.

An enquiry into the purpose and development of Catholic 6747
education in Madras (1850-1950). Mary A. Dunne. London
M.Phil. 1967.

A critique of British educational policies in India,   6748
1854-1921. Mary J. Quinn. London M.Phil. 1968.

The marquis of Dalhousie and education in India, 1848-   6749
56. Kamala Ghosh. Sheffield Ph.D. 1963.

Studies in the economic and social development of   6750
India, 1848-56. M.N. Das. London Ph.D. 1957.

The development and organisation of the inspectorate   6751
in the Punjab, with special reference to West Pakistan, 1849-
1957. I.Z.-un-N. Malik. London M.A. 1961.

Land systems in the Punjab (including North Western   6752
Frontier Province) as affected by British rule between 1849
and 1901. R. Ahmad. Oxford D.Phil. 1963.

Some aspects of the administration of the Punjab, 1849- 6753
58. S.K. Soni. Durham Ph.D. 1965.

Local self-government in the Madras Presidency, 1850-   6754
1919. K.K. Pillay. Oxford D.Phil. 1948.

Muslim politics in India, 1857-1922, with special   6755
reference to the influence of Sir Syed Ahmed Khan. Saleem
Naz. St. Andrews B.Phil. 1969.

Local government services in India: a case study of   6756
Punjab, 1860-1960. D.R. Sachdeva. London Ph.D. 1967.

Agrarian conditions in the North-Western Provinces and   6757
Oudh, 1860-1900: an enquiry into the extent of their transformation under British rule. Elizabeth M. Whitcombe. London Ph.D. 1968.

The practice of female infanticide in India and its   6758
suppression in the North-Western Provinces. Mrs. Lalita N.
Panigrahi. London Ph.D. 1965.

The missionary activities of the C.M.S. and the   6759
C.E.Z.M.S. in Kashmir during the second half of the 19th
century. S.Z. Ahmed Shah. London M.A. 1958.

The rise of business corporations in India and their   6760
development during 1851-1900. R.S. Rungta. London Ph.D.
1965.

History of the development of Rangoon, 1852-1900. Thet 6761
Tun. London M.A. 1958.

The recruitment of Indians into the covenanted civil   6762
service of India, 1853-92. M.R. Anwar. Manchester M.A.
1960.

The relations of the Court of Directors, the India   6763
Board, the India Office and the Government of India, 1853-65.
P.K. Chattarji. Cambridge Ph.D. 1967.

Sir Charles Wood and the evolution of modern   6764
university education in India during the 19th century.
Kamala Sen. Sheffield M.A. 1961.

Sir Charles Wood's Indian policy, 1853-66. R.J.   6765
Moore. London Ph.D. 1964.

The origin and development in Bengal of the principles   6766
involved in Sir Charles Wood's despatch on education of 19
July 1854. D.P. Sinha. London M.A. 1939.

The development and reconstruction of university educ-   6767
ation in Pakistan since 1854. S.M.A. Aziz. London M.A.
1957.

Some aspects of the social history of Bengal, with   6768
special reference to the Muslims, 1854-84. Mrs. Latifa
Khatoon. London M.A. 1956.

British policy and Baluchistan, 1854-76. T.A. Heath-   6769
cote. London Ph.D. 1970.

British land policy in Oudh, 1856-68. J. Raj. London 6770
Ph.D. 1957.

6771   A historical survey of the financial policy of the
Government of India from 1857 to 1900 and of its economic and
other consequences. H.S. Bhai. Leeds Ph.D. 1934.
6772   Some aspects of English protestant missionary activities
in Bengal, 1857-85. Mrs. Tripti Chaudhuri. Oxford B.Litt.
1968.
6773   British public opinion regarding Indian policy at the
time of the Mutiny. Jessie Holmes. London M.A. 1936.
6774   The rise of the Muslim middle class as a political
factor in India and Pakistan, 1858-1947. A.H.M. Nooruzzaman.
London Ph.D. 1964.
6775   Influence of European political doctrines upon the evolution of the Indian governmental institutions and practice,
1858-1938. G. Prashad. London Ph.D. 1941.
6776   The image of India: some literary expressions of the
British experience in India. Mrs. Benita Parry. Birmingham
M.A. 1966.
6777   The Council of India, 1858-1919. S. Singh. London
Ph.D. 1955.
6778   Muslim politics in the Indo-Pakistan sub-continent,
1858-1916. M. Chughtai. Oxford D.Phil. 1961.
6779   The development of the Indian administrative and financial system, 1858-1905, with special reference to the relations
between the central government and the provinces. P.J.
Thomas. Oxford D.Phil. 1935.
6780   The educational movement of Sir Syed Ahmed Khan, 1858-
98. Mrs. Rahmani B.M.R. Hassaan. London Ph.D. 1960.
6781   Development of social and political ideas in Bengal,
1858-84. B.C. Bhattacharya. London Ph.D. 1934.
6782   The relations between the Indian central and provincial
governments, with special reference to the presidencies of
Madras and Bombay, 1858-82. D.N. Singh. London M.A. 1956.
6783   The reorganisation of the Indian armies, 1858-79. A.H.
Shibly. London Ph.D. 1969.
6784   The relations between the home and Indian governments,
1858-70. Z.H. Zoberi. London Ph.D. 1950.
6785   The agrarian economy and agrarian relations in Bengal,
1859-85. B.B. Chaudhuri. Oxford D.Phil. 1968.
6786   The evolution of the Indian income tax, 1860-1922: a
historical, critical and comparative study. J.P. Niyogi.
London Ph.D. 1929.
6787   Capital development of India, 1860-1913. A. Krishnasawmi. London Ph.D. 1941.
6788   Indian finance, 1860-98, from the Mutiny to the stabil-
isation of exchange. C.N. Vakil. London M.Sc. 1921.
6789   The origin and early history of public debt in India.
P. Datta. London Ph.D. 1931.
6790   The Bombay political service, 1863-1924. I.F.S. Copland. Oxford D.Phil. 1969.
6791   British policy on the north-east frontier of India,
1865-1914. D.P. Choudhury. London Ph.D. 1970.
6792   A study of the Anglo-Indian official mind. E.C.T. Chew.
Cambridge Ph.D. 1970.
6793   Sir Richard Temple and the Government of India, 1868-
80; some trends in Indian administrative policy. G.R.G.
Hambly. Cambridge Ph.D. 1961.
6794   British government and society in the presidency of
Bengal, c.1868-c.1880: an examination of certain aspects of
British attitudes, behaviour and policy. J.M. Compton.
Oxford D.Phil. 1969.
6795   Lord Mayo's viceroyalty, 1869-72, with special reference
to problems of external security and internal stability.
M.A. Hossain. London M.Phil. 1968.
6796   Development of Indian foreign trade, 1870-1930. Parimal
Ray. London Ph.D. 1931.
6797   Agricultural problems and conditions in the Bombay
Presidency, 1870-1914. M.A. Tata. London M.Sc. 1922.

Sir Alexander Cunningham and the beginnings of Indian   6798
archaeology. A. Imam. London Ph.D. 1963.
Population changes in west Bengal, 1872-1951. Mrs.   6799
Anima Bhattacharyya. London M.A. 1963.
Public opinion and the India policy, 1872-80. Mrs.   6800
Uma Das Gupta. Oxford D.Phil. 1969.
Lord Northbrook's Indian administration, 1872-6. E.C.   6801
Moulton. London Ph.D. 1964.
Some aspects of the history of British investments in   6802
the private sector of the Indian economy, 1875-1914. N.Z.
Ahmed. London M.Sc. 1955.
Indian external policy, with special reference to the   6803
north-western and eastern frontiers, 1876-98. D.P. Singhal.
London Ph.D. 1955.
British military policy and the defence of India: a   6804
study of British military policy, plans and preparations
during the Russian crisis, 1876-80. A.W. Preston. London
Ph.D. 1966.
The internal administration of Lord Lytton, with   6805
special reference to social and economic policy, 1876-80.
L.M. Gujral. London Ph.D. 1958.
Political relations between India and Nepal, 1877-1923. 6806
K. Mojumdar. London Ph.D. 1968.
Social and administrative policy of the government of   6807
Bengal, 1877-90. Mrs. Rokeya Kabeer. London M.A. 1959.
Some aspects of the Hindu-Muslim relationship in India, 6808
1876-92. Mrs. Shamsun Nahar. London M.Phil. 1967.
A critical review of the work of Scottish Presbyterian   6809
missions in India, 1878-1914. T.G. Gehani. Strathclyde
Ph.D. 1966/7.
The state and the co-operative movement in the Bombay   6810
Presidency, 1880-1930. I.J. Catanach. London Ph.D. 1960.
The growth of political organisation in the Allahabad   6811
locality, 1880-1925. C.A. Bayly. Oxford D.Phil. 1970.
The policy of Sir James Fergusson as governor of   6812
Bombay Presidency, 1880-5. A.K. Gupta. London Ph.D. 1967.
The viceroyalty of Lord Ripon, 1880-4. S. Gopal. Ox-   6813
ford D.Phil. 1951.
The reform of local self-government in India under Lord 6814
Ripon, 1880-4: a study in the formation of policy. Mrs.
Qamrun Rahman. London M.Phil. 1968.
State policy and economic development in Mysore state   6815
since 1881. Udayam Abhayambal. London Ph.D. 1931.
Some aspects of the history of the Muslim community in   6816
Bengal, 1884-1912. Mrs. Sufia Ahmed. London Ph.D. 1960.
The ideological differences between moderates and ex-   6817
tremists in the Indian national movement, with special
reference to Surendranath Banerjea and Lajpat Rai, 1883-1919.
D. Argov. London Ph.D. 1964.
The evolution of representative government in India,   6818
1884-1909, with reference to central and provincial legislative councils. S. Chakravarty. London Ph.D. 1954.
Politics and change in the Madras Presidency, 1884-94:   6819
a regional study of Indian nationalism. R. Suntharalingam.
London Ph.D. 1966.
The development of political institutions in the state   6820
of Travancore, A.D. 1885-1924. V.M. Ittyerah. Oxford B.Litt.
1930.
The influence of western, particularly English, polit-   6821
ical ideas on Indian political thought, with special reference to the political ideas of the Indian National Congress,
1885-1919. S. Ghosh. London Ph.D. 1950.
The origins and development to 1892 of the Indian   6822
National Congress. Iris M. Jones. London M.A. 1946.
The development of Muslim political philosophy in the   6823
Indo-Pakistan sub-continent. S.J. Iqbal. Cambridge Ph.D.
1955.

6824   Muslim politics and government policy: studies in the development of Muslim organisation and its social background in North India and Bengal, 1885-1917. Mrs. Janet M. Rizvi, née Clarke. Cambridge Ph.D. 1969.

6825   Muslims in India: a political analysis (from 1885 to 1906). R.A. Zakaria. London Ph.D. 1948.

6826   The internal policy of the Indian government, 1885-98. H.L. Singh. London Ph.D. 1953.

6827   British relations with Kashmir, 1885-93. D.K. Ghose. London Ph.D. 1963.

6828   Oil prices and the Indian market, 1886-1964. B. Dasgupta. London Ph.D. 1966.

6829   Indian politics, 1888-1908. G. Johnson. Cambridge Ph.D. 1967.

6830   Jury and police reform during the Indian viceroyalty of Lord Lansdowne, 1888-94. Mrs. Razia Rahman. London Ph.D. 1969.

6831   British policy on the north-west frontier of India, 1889-1901. L. Harris. London Ph.D. 1960.

6832   The north-west frontier of India, 1890 to 1908, with a survey of policy since 1849. C.C. Davies. Cambridge Ph.D. 1925/6.

6833   The development of the Indian National Congress, 1892 to 1909. Pansy C. Ghosh. London Ph.D. 1958.

6834   The internal administration of Lord Elgin in India, 1894-8. P.L. Malhotra. London Ph.D. 1966.

6835   British famine and agricultural policies in India, with special reference to the administration of Lord George Hamilton, 1895-1903. P. Bandyopadhyay. London Ph.D. 1969.

6836   The emergence of Indian nationalism. A. Seal. Cambridge Ph.D. 1962.

6837   The development of nationalist ideas and tactics and the policies of the Government of India, 1897-1905. J.R. McLane. London Ph.D. 1961.

6838   Indian education and politics, 1898-1920. Mrs. Aparna Basu. Cambridge Ph.D. 1967.

6839   The reign of 'Alī Dīnār, last sultan of Darfūr, 1898-1916. A.B. Theobald. London Ph.D. (Ext.) 1962.

6840   The economic policy of the Government of India, 1898-1905. Edna R. Bonner. London M.A. 1955.

6841   Curzon, Kitchener and the problem of Indian army administration, 1899-1909. J.E. Lydgate. London Ph.D. 1965.

6842   Lord Curzon and the Indian states, 1899-1905. I.A. Butt. London Ph.D. 1963.

6843   Development of education in India under Lord Curzon, 1899-1905. Mrs. Hamida I. Butt. London M.Phil. 1968.

6844   Development and organisation of primary education in East Pakistan since 1900. A.F.M.A. Bari. London M.A. 1958.

6845   A critical analysis of factors influencing the growth of female education in Bengal during the early 20th century (1900-37). Arumima Pal. London M.Phil. 1967.

6846   The growth of the idea of Commonwealth in India, 1900-29. S.R. Mehrotra. London Ph.D. 1960.

6847   Agricultural co-operation in British India. J. Matthai. Oxford B.Litt. 1917.

6848   A study of the population of East Pakistan from 1901 to the present day. M.A.S. Patwari. Leeds M.A. 1965.

6849   The administration of the North-West Frontier Province, 1901-19. Lal Baha. London Ph.D. 1968.

6850   A study of India's balance of payments during 1901-13 and 1924-36. B.S. Rao. Cambridge Ph.D. 1956.

6851   The partition of Bengal and its annulment: a survey of the schemes of territorial redistribution of Bengal, 1902-11. S.Z.H. Zaidi. London Ph.D. 1964.

6852   The new province of Eastern Bengal and Assam, 1905-11. M.K.U. Molla. London Ph.D. 1966.

Britain and Muslim India: a study of British public 6853
opinion vis-à-vis the development of Muslim nationalism in
India, 1905-47. K.K. Aziz. Manchester Ph.D. 1960.
Bengali political unrest, 1905-18, with special refer- 6854
ence to terrorism. H. Chakrabarti. Oxford D.Phil. 1968.
Imperial policy in India, 1905-10. Mrs. Vina Mazumdar. 6855
Oxford D.Phil. 1963.
Lord Minto and the Indian nationalist movement, with 6856
special reference to the political activities of the Indian
Muslims, 1905-10. S.R. Wasti. London Ph.D. 1962.
The politics of U.P. Muslims, 1906-22. F.C.R. Robin- 6857
son. Cambridge Ph.D. 1970.
The All-India Muslim League in Indian politics, 1906- 6858
12. M. Rahman. London Ph.D. 1968.
The military in politics in India and Pakistan since 6859
1907. H.A. Rizvi. Leeds M.Phil. 1970.
Indian politics and the British Right, 1914-22. M.R. 6860
Hassaan. London Ph.D. 1963.
British reform policy and Indian politics on the eve 6861
of the rise of Gandhi. R.J. Danzig. Oxford D.Phil. 1968.
Gandhi in India, 1915-20: his emergence as a leader 6862
and the transformation of politics. Judith M. Brown. Cam-
bridge Ph.D. 1968.
Soviet Russia's policy towards India and its effect on 6863
Anglo-Soviet relations, 1917-28. Z. Imam. London Ph.D.
1964.
Labour organisation in the Bombay cotton mills, 1918- 6864
29. R.K. Newman. Sussex D.Phil. 1970.
The Indian National Congress, 1918-23. G. Krishna. 6865
Oxford D.Phil. 1960.
The minorities in southern Asia and public policy, with 6866
special reference to India, mainly since 1919. J.H. Beagle-
hole. London Ph.D. 1965.
The origin and development of left-wing movements and 6867
ideas in India, 1919-47. L.P. Sinha. London Ph.D. 1955.
The effects of diarchy upon the educational develop- 6868
ments in Bengal, 1919-35. S.K. Dutta Gupta. London M.A.
1963.
The working of the Bengal legislative council under the 6869
Government of India Act, 1919. J.G. Drummond. Cambridge
Ph.D. 1939.
Aspects in the history of the Indian National Congress, 6870
with special reference to the Swarajya party, 1919-27. R.A.
Gordon. Oxford D.Phil. 1970.
Political parties in the Bombay Presidency, 1920-9. 6871
D.S. Chavda. London M.Sc. 1967.
The Central Legislative in British India, 1921-47. 6872
M.D. Rashiduzzaman. Durham Ph.D. 1964.
Origins of Indian foreign policy: a study of Indian 6873
nationalist attitudes to foreign affairs, 1927-39. T.A.
Keenleyside. London Ph.D. 1966.
The British Conservative party and Indian problems, 6874
1927-35. S.C. Ghosh. Manchester Ph.D. 1963.
Indian constitutional development, 1927-35. Mrs. 6875
Maqbul B. Hassen. Cambridge M.Litt. 1957.
The rise and growth of the Praja Socialist party of 6876
India (1934-55). H.K. Singh. Oxford B.Litt. 1958.
The formation of the Government of India Act, 1935. W. 6877
Ahmad. Cambridge Ph.D. 1969.
The impact of planning upon federalism in India, 1951- 6878
64. Mrs. Amiya Chatterji. Cambridge Ph.D. 1966.

6879   A geographical analysis of the historical development
of towns in Ceylon. Mrs. Lakshmi K. Ratnayake. Edinburgh
Ph.D. 1968.
6880   Tiruvālīśvaram: a study of its history and inscriptions.
K.D. Swaminathan. London Ph.D. 1964.
6881   The historical geography of Ceylon before A.D. 1500.
P.P. Udagama. London M.A. 1958.
6882   Social institutions in Ceylon from the 5th century B.C.
to the 4th century A.D. H. Ellawala. London Ph.D. 1962.
6883   Early history of Buddhist education in Ceylon (3rd
century B.C. to 16th century A.D.). D.D. Samaraweera. London M.A. 1949.
6884   The evolution and history of the Buddhist monastic order,
with special reference to the sangha in Ceylon. G. Panabokke.
Lancaster Ph.D. 1969.
6885   The history of the Buddhist sangha in Ceylon from the
reign of Sena I to the invasion of Māgha. R.A.L.H. Gunawar-
dana. London Ph.D. 1965.
6886   A historical criticism of the Mahāvamsa. G.C. Mendis.
London Ph.D. 1930.
6887   History of kingship in Ceylon up to the 4th century A.D.
T. Hettiarachchy. London Ph.D. 1970.
6888   The rise and decline of Chola power in Ceylon. W.M.K.
Wijetunga. London Ph.D. 1962.
6889   Economic conditions of Ceylon, c. A.D. 1070-1344. W.I.
Siriweera. London Ph.D. 1970.
6890   The age of Parākramabāhu I. Sirima Wickramasinghe.
London Ph.D. 1958.
6891   The decline of Poḷonnaruva and the rise of Dambedeniya,
c.1180-1270 A.D. A. Liyanagamage. London Ph.D. 1963.
6892   The Buddhist sangha in Ceylon, c.1200-1400 A.D. Y.
Dhammavisuddhi. London Ph.D. 1970.
6893   Dravidian settlements in Ceylon and the beginnings of
the kingdom of Jaffna. K. Indrapala. London Ph.D. 1966.
6894   The kingdom of Jaffna, c.1250-1450. S. Pathmanathan.
London Ph.D. 1969.
6895   Political history of the kingdom of Koṭṭe, c. A.D. 1400-
1521. G.P.V. Somaratna. London Ph.D. 1969.
6896   Portuguese rule over the kingdom of Kotte during the
captain-generalcy of Dom Jeronimo de Azevedo, 1594-1612.
T.B.H. Abeysingha. London Ph.D. 1963.
6897   The educational work of Jesuits in Ceylon in the 17th
century, 1602-58. W.L.A. Don Peter. London M.A. (Ext.)
1955.
6898   The Portuguese in Ceylon, 1617-38. C.R. de Silva. London Ph.D. 1968.
6899   The establishment of Dutch power in Ceylon, 1638-58.
K.W. Goonewardena. London Ph.D. 1953.
6900   Dutch power in Ceylon, 1658-87. S. Arasaratnam. London Ph.D. 1956.
6901   The internal politics of the Kandyan kingdom, 1707-60.
Mrs. Lorna S. Dewaraja. London Ph.D. 1970.
6902   Customs and institutions connected with the domestic
life of the Sinhalese in the Kandyan period. M.P. Tillakaratne. London Ph.D. 1967.
6903   The Dutch in Ceylon, 1743-66. D.A. Kotelawele. London
Ph.D. 1968.
6904   The advent of the British to Ceylon, 1762-1803. V.L.B.
Mendis. London M.Phil. 1967.
6905   Dutch rule in maritime Ceylon, 1766-96. V. Kanapathypillai. London Ph.D. 1969.
6906   Ceylon under the British occupation: its political and
economic development, 1795-1833. C.R. de Silva. London
Ph.D. 1932.

A study of the history of Christianity in Ceylon in the 6907
British period from 1796 to 1903 with special reference to
the protestant missions. C.N.V. Fernando. Oxford B.Litt.
1942.

The history and the problems of Christian education in 6908
the protestant mission schools of Ceylon. D.K. Wilson. Oxford B.Litt. 1954.

The British administration of the Maritime Provinces of 6909
Ceylon, 1796-1802. U.C. Wickremeratne. London Ph.D. 1964.

Education in Ceylon since the British occupation. A. 6910
Cumaraswamy. London M.A. 1932.

Educational developments under the British in Ceylon 6911
during the period 1796 to 1834. T.R.A. Ruberu. London Ph.D.
1961.

A study of educational policy in Ceylon during the 19th 6912
century. K.L.V. Alagiyawanna. London Ph.D. (Ext.) 1968.

A historical and analytical account of export taxation 6913
in Ceylon, 1802-1958. S.T.G. Fernando. Manchester M.A. 1961.

The development of the Ceylon civil service, 1802-33. 6914
P.D. Kannangara. London Ph.D. 1965.

Methodism in north Ceylon: its history and influence, 6915
1814-90. D.K. Wilson. London Ph.D. (Ext.) 1969.

A critical survey of Pirivena education in Ceylon from 6916
1815, with special reference to Vidyodaya and Vidyalankara
Pirivena. H. Ratanasara. London Ph.D. 1965.

An analysis of the monetary experience of Ceylon, 1825- 6917
1954. H.A. de S. Gunasekera. London Ph.D. 1956.

Some aspects of the history of the coffee industry in 6918
Ceylon, with special reference to the period 1823-85. I.M.
van den Driesen. London Ph.D. 1954.

The Commission of Eastern Enquiry in Ceylon, 1829-37: 6919
a study of a royal commission of colonial inquiry. V.K.
Samaraweera. Oxford D.Phil. 1969.

The supply of Sinhalese labour to Ceylon plantations, 6920
1830-1930: a study of imperial policy in a peasant society.
L.R.U. Jayawardena. Cambridge Ph.D. 1963.

Peasant agriculture in Ceylon, 1833-93. A.C.L. 6921
Ameerali. London M.Phil. 1970.

The development of public education in Ceylon, 1832-69. 6922
C. Godagé. London M.A. 1962.

Some aspects of British economic and social policy in 6923
Ceylon, 1840-71. M.W. Roberts. Oxford D.Phil. 1965.

Some aspects of the development of social policy in 6924
Ceylon, 1840-55, with special reference to the influence of
missionary organisations. K.M. de Silva. London Ph.D.
1961.

Education in the Roman Catholic missions in Ceylon in 6925
the second half of the 19th century, 1842-1905. C. Fernando.
London M.A. 1963.

The administration of Sir Henry Ward, governor of 6926
Ceylon, 1855-60. S.V. Balasingham. London M.A. 1954.

The policies of the government of Ceylon concerning 6927
education and religion, 1865-85. L.A. Wickremeratne. Oxford D.Phil. 1967.

English-educated Ceylonese in the official life of 6928
Ceylon from 1865 to 1883. W.M.D.D. Andradi. London Ph.D.
1967.

Some issues between church and state in Ceylon in the 6929
education of the people from 1870 to 1901. A. Rajaindran.
London Ph.D. 1964.

The governorship of Sir William Henry Gregory in 6930
Ceylon. B.E.St.J. Bastiampillai. London M.A. 1963.

History of plantation agriculture of Ceylon, 1886-1931, 6931
with special reference to tea and rubber. S. Rajaratnam.
London M.Sc. 1961.

The urban labour movement in Ceylon, with reference to 6932
political factors, 1893-1947. V.K. Jayawardena. London Ph.D.
1964.

6933   The control of education in Ceylon: the last fifty years of British rule and after (1900-62). C.S.V. Jayaweera. London M.A. (Ext.) 1966.
6934   The analysis of external trade and economic structure of Ceylon, 1900-55. Mrs. Olga E.B. Gunewardena. Oxford B.Litt. 1959.
6935   Social and political change in Ceylon, 1900-19, with special reference to the disturbances of 1915. P.V.J. Jayasekera. London Ph.D. 1970.
6936   The nationalist movement in Ceylon between 1910 and 1931, with special reference to communal and elective problems. D.K. Greenstreet. London Ph.D. 1959.
6937   The development of a new élite in Ceylon, with special reference to educational and occupational background, 1910-31. P.T.M. Fernando. Oxford D.Phil. 1968.
6938   The Manning constitution of Ceylon, 1924-31. A.J. Wilson. London Ph.D. 1956.
6939   Constitutional developments in Ceylon during the period 1928-48. S. Namasivayam. Oxford B.Litt. 1948.
6940   The working of the Donoughmore constitution of Ceylon, 1931-47 (a study of a colonial central government by executive committees). I.D.S. Weerawardana. London Ph.D. 1951.
6941   The role of the Ceylon civil service before and after independence. W.A. Wiswa Warnapala. Leeds Ph.D. 1970.

INDIAN OCEAN AND MAURITIUS

6942   The western shores of the Indian Ocean before Vasco da Gama. H.E. Edwards. London M.A. 1930.
6943   Surveying and charting the Indian Ocean: the British contribution, 1750-1838. W.A. Spray. London Ph.D. 1966.
6944   Printing in the Mascarene Islands (Ile de France and Bourbon) from 1767 to 1810. Marie M.A. Toussaint. London Ph.D. (Ext.) 1947.
6945   Constitutional development of Mauritius, 1810-1948. D. Napal. London M.A. (Ext.) 1962.
6946   The expedition to Mauritius in 1810 and the establishment of British control. A.G. Field. London M.A. 1931.
6947   The slave trade at Mauritius, 1811-29. Mary K. Jones. Oxford B.Litt. 1936.
6948   The trade of the eastern Indian Ocean, 1830 to 1845, with special reference to the internal maritime trade of the region. A.C. Staples. London M.A. 1965.
6949   Mauritius, 1832-49: a study of a sugar colony. Brenda M. Howell. London Ph.D. 1951.
6950   The economic development of the Mauritius sugar industry. M.J.R. Lamusse. Oxford B.Litt. 1958.
6951   Mauritius as a problem in Crown Colony administration, 1849-57. J.R. Fowler. London M.Phil. 1970.
6952   Politics in Mauritius since 1934. Mrs. Adele D. Simmons. Oxford D.Phil. 1969.
6953   History of Indian indentured immigration into Mauritius. Pravina Dhanda. London M.Phil. 1970.
6954   British defence policy in the Indian Ocean region between the Indian Independence Act 1947 and the British defence review 1966. P.G.C. Darby. Oxford D.Phil. 1969.

CENTRAL ASIA

6955   A study of early Turanian history based upon original Chinese sources. H.W. Thomasson. Manchester M.A. 1925.
6956   A cultural history of Assam of the early period, c.400 A.D. - 1200 A.D. B. Barua. London Ph.D. 1947.
6957   The history of civilisation of the people of Assam to the 12th century A.D. P.C. Choudhury. London Ph.D. 1953.

The rise of the Turkish empire in central Asia (A.D.   6958
552-615). Y.-F. Chu. Oxford B.Litt. 1937.

Some aspects of the Uighur empire, 744-840. C.P.   6959
Mackerras. Cambridge M.Litt. 1964.

Nat pat and ordos (camps and tents): a study of the   6960
way of life and military organisation of the Khitan emperors
and their people. Lo-Huan Fu. London Ph.D. 1950.

The history of medieval Assam (A.D. 1228-1603). N.N.   6961
Acharyya. London Ph.D. 1957.

The East India Company's relation with Assam, 1771-   6962
1826. S.K. Bhuyan. London Ph.D. 1938.

Anglo-Afghan relations from 1809 till 1839. M.A. Naim. 6963
Oxford B.Litt. 1965.

The diplomatic career of Sir Claude Wade: a study of   6963A
British relations with the Sikhs and Afghans, July 1823 to
March 1840. E.R. Kapadia. London M.A. 1938.

British administration in Assam, 1824-45, with special 6964
reference to the hill tribes on the frontier. H. Barpujari.
London Ph.D. 1949.

British policy in central Asia, 1830-43. M.E. Yapp.   6965
London Ph.D. 1959.

British rule in Assam, 1845-58. B. Chaudhuri. London   6966
Ph.D. 1956.

The history of education in Assam, 1854 to 1912.   6967
Shanti Chaliha. London M.A. 1955.

The expansion of Russia in east Asia, 1857-60. Mrs.   6968
Rosemary K.I. Quested. London Ph.D. (Ext.) 1963.

The economic background of the Russian conquest of   6969
central Asia in the second half of the 19th century. Audrey
J. Lunger. London Ph.D. 1953.

Aspects of the economic development of the Assam   6970
valley, 1858-84. A.C. Barua. London M.A. 1960.

The Afghan policy of Lord Lawrence, 1864-9. N. Kundu. 6971
London M.A. 1959.

British policy on the 'roof of the world', 1865-95,   6972
with special reference to the Anglo-Russian agreement of
1895. G.J. Alder. Bristol Ph.D. 1959.

Anglo-Afghan relations, 1869-80. S. Chakravarty.   6973
Cambridge Ph.D. 1967.

Anglo-Russian relations in central Asia, 1873-87. L.P. 6974
Morris. London Ph.D. 1969.

Anglo-Russian relations from 1878 to 1885, with particular 6975
reference to Central Asia. Edith Jones. Wales M.A. 1934.

Anglo-Russian relations concerning Afghanistan, 1882-6; 6976
the delimitation of the north-west frontier of Afghanistan.
M.J. Jennings. London M.A. (Ext.) 1953.

The growth of local self-government in Assam, 1874-   6977
1919. A.K. Barkakoty. London Ph.D. 1949.

Afghanistan: its place in the Middle Eastern diplomatic 6978
system, 1878-1919. M. Khan. Durham Ph.D. 1950.

The consolidation of the central authority in Afghan-   6979
istan under Amīr 'Abd Al-Rahmān, 1880-96. M.H. Kakar. London M.Phil. 1968.

Russian policy in central Asia in the light of the   6980
Pahlen Report of 1908-9. D.S.M. Williams. London Ph.D. 1969.

The development of secondary education in Assam with   6981
special reference to the period from 1919 to 1947. B.
Pathak. London M.A. 1959.

SOUTH-EAST ASIA

Early Indonesian commerce and the origins of Śrīvijaya. 6982
O.W. Wolters. London Ph.D. 1962.

The historical geography of the Malay peninsula before 6983
A.D. 1500. P. Wheatley. London Ph.D. (Ext.) 1958.

Indian political and cultural influence in Cambodia   6984
(Kambiya) from the 6th to the 14th centuries. B.R. Chatterji.
London Ph.D. 1926.

6985   The history of Burma to 1824. G.E. Harvey. Oxford
B.Litt. 1922.

6986   The Buddhist Church in Burma during the pagan period,
1044-1287. Than Thun. London Ph.D. 1956.

6987   The beginnings of English trade with Guinea and the
East Indies, 1550-99. Kate M. Eliot. London M.A. 1915.

6988   The organisation of the English factories in the East
Indies, 1600-42. Mary W. Thomas. London M.A. 1920.

6989   The factory of the English East India Company at Bantam,
1602-82. D.K. Bassett. London Ph.D. 1955.

6990   English trade and policy in Borneo and the adjacent
islands, 1667-1786. T.C.P. Edgell. London M.A. 1935.

6991   English trade in the South China Sea, 1670-1715. Ma Yi
Yi. London Ph.D. 1958.

6992   Trincomalee and the East Indies squadron, 1746 to 1844.
H.A. Colgate. London M.A. 1959.

6993   Admiral Sir Samuel Cornish and the conquest of Manila
in the latter part of the Seven Years War. J.N. Tracy.
Southampton M.Phil. 1967.

6994   Burma's relations with her eastern neighbours in the
Konbaung period, 1752-1819. M.K. Thet. London Ph.D. 1950.

6995   British projects and activities in the Philippines,
1759-1805. Elisa A. Julian. London Ph.D. 1963.

6996   British West Sumatra during the Presidency period, 1760-
85. Jeyamalar Kathirithamby. London Ph.D. 1965.

6997   Settlement in British Borneo, with special reference to
North Borneo. Y.-L. Lee. Oxford B.Litt. 1960.

6998   Indians in Malaya: some aspects of their arrival and
settlement, with special reference to the period of British
rule, 1786-1957. K.S. Sandhu. London Ph.D. 1965.

6999   English expeditions to the Dutch East Indies during the
Revolutionary and Napoleonic Wars. S.G. Rainbow. London
M.A. 1933.

7000   The Chinese in south-eastern Asia and the East Indies.
G.J. Miles. London M.A. 1932.

7001   The Chinese in Indochina. A.G. Marsot. Oxford B.Litt.
1970.

7002   A history of educational policy of the Straits Settlements from 1800 to c.1925. D.D. Chelliah. London Ph.D.
(Ext.) 1940.

7003   British and Dutch policy in Borneo, 1809-88. G.W.
Irwin. Cambridge Ph.D. 1953.

7004   The native policy of Sir Stamford Raffles. J.S. Bastin.
Oxford D.Phil. 1955.

7005   Estates and plantations in Java, 1812-34. G.R. Knight.
London Ph.D. 1968.

7006   An investigation into the history of education in
Malaysia, 1816-1963. F.H.K. Wong. London Ph.D. (Ext.) 1965.

7007   A history of education in Negri Sembilan. G. Sutcliffe.
London M.A. (Ext.) 1956.

7008   Some aspects of the history of the mission schools of
Malaya, with special reference to the development of the
grants-in-aid system. D.F. Cooke. London M.A. (Ext.) 1963.

7009   British policy towards the Dutch and the native princes
in the Malay archipelago, 1824-71. P.N. Tarling. Cambridge
Ph.D. 1956.

7010   The growth of British power in the 19th and 20th centuries in Malaya and the East Indies, with special attention
to the Straits Settlements and the protected Malay States.
L.A. Mills. Oxford D.Phil. 1924.

7011   The plantation rubber industry in Malaya: its origin
and development to 1922. J.H. Drabble. London Ph.D. 1968.

7012   The Malayan tin industry to 1914, with special reference
to the states of Perak, Selangor, Negri Sembilan and Pahang.
Wong Lin Ken. London Ph.D. 1959.

7013   A survey of the history of education in Burma before the
British conquest and after. Kaung Maung. London M.A. 1929.

Administrative beginnings in British Burma, 1826-43. 7014
Barbara J. Stewart. London Ph.D. 1930.

The origins of the Siamese Forward Movement in western 7015
Laos, 1850-92. N.J. Brailey. London Ph.D. 1969.

The development of Siamese relations with Britain and 7016
France in the reign of Maha Mongkut, 1851-68. Neon Snidvongs.
London Ph.D. 1961.

The rice industry of Burma, 1852-1940. Mrs. Saw Siok 7017
Hwa. London Ph.D. 1963.

The administration of British Burma, 1852-85. Mrs. 7018
Janell A. Mills, née Nilsson. London Ph.D. 1970.

The Straits Settlements and the contest for North 7019
Sumatra, 1858-96. A.J.S. Reid. Cambridge Ph.D. 1965.

The attitudes and policies of Great Britain and China 7020
toward French expansion in Cochin China, Cambodia, Annam and
Tongking, 1858-83. B.L. Evans. London Ph.D. 1961.

British policy in the South China Sea area, with 7021
special reference to Sarawak, Brunei and North Borneo, 1860-
88. L.R. Wright. London Ph.D. 1963.

The movement to remove the Straits Settlements from the 7022
control of India, culminating in the transfer to the Colonial
Office in 1867. Constance M. Turnbull. London Ph.D. (Ext.)
1962.

Indian labour migration to Malaya, 1867-1910. D.A. 7023
Calman. Oxford B.Litt. 1955.

The origins of British political control in Malaya, 7024
1867-78. C.D. Cowan. London Ph.D. 1956.

English, German, Spanish relations in the Sulu 7025
question, 1871-7. S.C. Hunter. London M.Sc. 1963.

The constitutional history of Malaya, with special 7026
reference to the Malay states of Perak, Selangor, Negri
Sembilan and Pahang, 1874-1914. P.L. Burns. London Ph.D.
1966.

Anglo-French relations with Siam, 1876-1904. B.S.N. 7027
Murti. London Ph.D. 1952.

Tradition and change in a Malay state: the economic 7028
and political development of Kedah, 1879-1923. Sharom bin
Ahmat. London Ph.D. 1969.

British policy in the Malay peninsula, 1880-1909. 7029
Eunice Thio. London Ph.D. 1956.

The political geography of Malaya. E.H.G. Dobby. 7030
London Ph.D. 1945.

The administration and development of North Borneo by 7031
the British North Borneo Chartered Company, 1881-1902. K.G.P.
Tregonning. Oxford B.Litt. 1952.

Anglo-Chinese diplomacy regarding Burma, 1885-97. Mrs. 7032
Nancy Iu. London Ph.D. 1960.

The role of transport and foreign trade in the economic 7033
development of Burma under British rule (1885-1914). Maung
Shein. Cambridge Ph.D. 1960.

British administration in Upper Burma, 1885-97. J.S. 7034
Sidhu. London M.A. 1963.

Britain, France and Siam, 1885-96. P.J.N. Tuck. Ox- 7035
ford D.Phil. 1970.

Sir Charles Crosthwaite and the consolidation of Burma. 7036
Mya S. May-Oung. Oxford B.Litt. 1930.

British foreign policy towards Siam, 1890-1900. S. 7037
Xuto. London Ph.D. 1958.

The provincial administration of Siam from 1892 to 7038
1915: a study of the creation, the growth, the achievements,
and the implications for modern Siam, of the Ministry of the
Interior under Prince Damrong Rachanuphap. T. Bunnag. Oxford D.Phil. 1969.

Anglo-French tensions on the upper Mekong river, 1892- 7039
1902. M.J. Chandran. London Ph.D. 1967.

The political and economic conditions of Indians in 7040
Burma, 1900-41. N.R. Chakravarti. London Ph.D. 1969.

7041   Control of the opium trade in Malaya, 1900-12. Margaret J.B.C. Lim. London M.Sc. 1965.

7042   The Anglo-Siamese negotiations, 1900-9. Mrs. Thamsook Numnonda, née Ratanapun. London Ph.D. 1966.

7043   The political development of Burma during the period 1918-35. Tin Ohn. London M.A. 1950.

7044   The origins of the Communist party of the Philippines and the Comintern of 1919 to 1930. A.S. Araneta. Oxford D.Phil. 1966.

7045   The political and constitutional evolution of Burma from 1923 to 1936. A. Ram. London Ph.D. 1962.

7046   The political career of Pridi Banomyong: a chapter in the history of modern Thailand. Elizabeth G. Rokkan. Wales M.A. 1957.

FAR EAST

7047   Feudal society in ancient China. Tai Hua Lee. London Ph.D. 1939.

7048   The Chiu Chang Suan Shu and the history of Chinese mathematics during the Han period. Wang Ling. Cambridge Ph.D. 1956.

7049   A study of the life of Ts'ai Tu Yung'jztu. T.-L. Chen. Oxford B.Litt. 1955.

7050   The rise and development of the Korean kingdom of Koguryŏ from the earliest times to A.D. 313. K.H.J. Gardiner. London Ph.D. 1964.

7051   A study of the Ch'iang, with special reference to their settlements in China from the 2nd to the 5th century A.D. Margaret I. Scott. Cambridge Ph.D. 1953.

7052   The Christian Church of the T'ang dynasty. J. Foster. Birmingham M.A. 1938.

7053   Financial administration under the T'ang dynasty: an historical commentary to Chiu T'ang Shu, chapters 48 and 49. D.C. Twitchett. Cambridge Ph.D. 1955.

7054   The Tang government between two rebels: from An Lu-Shan to Chu Tz'u. Kwan Lai-Hung. London M.A. (Ext.) 1968.

7055   The Shen-Ts'e armies and the palace commissions in China, 755-875 A.D. Y.-W. Liu. London Ph.D. 1970.

7056   The structure of power in North China during the Five Dynasties. Wang Gung Wu. London Ph.D. 1957.

7057   European travellers in Mongol Asia, 1206-1368. G.T. Severin. Oxford B.Litt. 1967.

7058   Relations between Persia and China under Mongol domination. M. Honda. Cambridge Ph.D. 1957.

7059   João Rodrigues and his description of Japan: translation and editing of an early 17th-century manuscript describing social life in contemporary Japan, with an assessment of its accuracy and value. M.J. Cooper. Oxford D.Phil. 1969.

7060   Sino-Tibetan relations in the 17th century. Z. Ahmad. Oxford B.Litt. 1966.

7061   The life of Ch'i Piao-chia: a translation of the nien-p'u in Ch'i Chung-min Kung jih-chi. A.D.S. Roberts. Oxford B.Litt. 1970.

7062   Ku Yen-Wu, 1613-82: a short biography. W.J. Peterson. London M.A. 1964.

7063   Kumazawa Banzan: the life and thought of a 17th-century Japanese Confucian. I.J. McMullen. Cambridge Ph.D. 1969.

7064   A study of the 'Peking Altan Tobci'. C.R. Bawden. Cambridge Ph.D. 1955.

7065   The concept of the mandate of heaven in the political thought of Wang Fu-chih, 1619-92, including an annotated translation of part of his Sung lun. Alison H. Black. Glasgow M.Litt. 1970.

A sociological analysis of Chinese legal institutions, 7066
with special reference to those of the Ch'ing period, 1644-
1911. Mrs. Sybille M. van der Sprenkel. London M.Sc. 1956.

The Han-Lin Academy: a biographical approach to career 7067
patterns in the early Ch'ing, 1644-1795. A. Lui Yuen Chung.
London Ph.D. 1968.

Ogyū Sorai. J.R. McEwan. Cambridge Ph.D. 1951/2. 7068

Arai Hakuseki - being a study of his political career 7069
and some of his writings, with special reference to the
Hankampu. Joyce I. Ackroyd. Cambridge Ph.D. 1951/2.

China as treated by English and French writers in the 7070
first half of the 18th century. S.-P. Yu. Oxford B.Litt.
1932.

Britain and China, 1757-1839, with special reference 7071
to the attempts to open diplomatic relations. Ellie L. Wong.
Oxford B.Litt. 1953.

Anglo-Chinese relations and the Macartney embassy 7072
(1775-1800). E.H. Pritchard. Oxford D.Phil. 1932/3.

Some aspects of British trade and finance in Canton, 7073
with special reference to the role of Anglo-Spanish trade in
the eastern seas, 1784-1834. Cheong Weng Eang. London Ph.D.
1963.

The growth of the Chinese diplomatic service as illus- 7074
trated by Anglo-Chinese relations, 1793-1877. T.-T. Wang.
Cambridge Ph.D. 1969.

An English translation of the 'Hikayat Abdullah' and a 7075
critical examination of the subject-matter for the light it
may throw on the history of the Far East, 1800-50. A.H.
Hill. Oxford D.Phil. 1955.

Ezo under the Tokugawa Bakufu, 1799-1821: an aspect of 7076
Japan's frontier history. J.J. Stephan. London Ph.D. 1969.

British trade and the opening of China, 1800-42. M.M. 7077
Greenberg. Cambridge Ph.D. 1949.

The Hakka-Punti war. J.A.G. Roberts. Oxford D.Phil. 7078
1969.

Trade and war in the eastern seas, 1803-10. C.N. 7079
Parkinson. London Ph.D. 1935.

Christian missions and foreign relations in China - an 7080
historical study. C.M. Drury. Edinburgh Ph.D. 1932/3.

An investigation into the work of the De La Salle 7081
Brothers in the Far East. F. Wong Hoy Kee. London M.A.
1961.

Education in modern China, with special reference to 7082
the influence upon it of western civilisation. V.W.W.S.
Purcell. Cambridge Ph.D. 1935/6.

British interest in trans-Burma trade routes to China, 7083
1826-76. Ma Thaung. London Ph.D. 1955.

The development of the English-language press on the 7084
China coast, 1827-81. P. Clarke. London M.A. 1961.

A hundred years of economic relations between China 7085
and Great Britain, 1834-1934. P.-G. Chow. Edinburgh Ph.D.
1938.

Hong Kong as a factor in British relations with China, 7086
1834-60. E.S. Taylor. London M.Phil. 1967.

Anglo-Chinese relations, 1834-60. Sarah D. Wool- 7087
dridge. Birmingham M.A. 1930.

Great Britain and the opening of Japan, 1834-58. W.G. 7088
Beasley. London Ph.D. 1950.

Modernisation and politics in China, as seen in the 7089
career of Shen Pao-Chen (1820-79). D.B.P. Pong. London
Ph.D. 1969.

The state economic policies of the Ch'ing government, 7090
1840-95. C.-J. Ch'en. London Ph.D. 1956.

The geographical growth and development of Hong Kong, 7091
1841-1941. S.G. Davis. London Ph.D. (Ext.) 1946.

Treaty obligations between China and Great Britain. 7092
Ching Lin Hsia. Edinburgh Ph.D. 1922.

7093   Western enterprise in China, 1842-95. E.T. Le Fevour. Cambridge Ph.D. 1961.

7094   British opinions and policy on China between the first and second Anglo-Chinese Wars (1842-57). S.-C. Koay. Leeds M.Phil. 1967.

7095   China's monetary system 1845-95, and its role in economic development. F.H.H. King. Oxford D.Phil. 1959.

7096   Horatio Nelson Lay: his role in British relations with China, 1849-65. J.J. Gerson. London Ph.D. 1967.

7097   The development of the church in the diocese of Fukien, South China, 1850-1950. D.K. Akehurst. Durham M.A. 1958.

7098   Some aspects of the Taiping rebellion in China, 1850-64. J.C. Cheng. Cambridge Ph.D. 1950.

7099   British attitudes and policy towards the Taiping rebellion in China, 1850-64. J.S. Gregory. London Ph.D. 1957.

7100   The origin of the Chinese maritime customs. J.K. Fairbank. Oxford D.Phil. 1936.

7101   British policy in relation to the origin of the Chinese Imperial Maritime Customs Service, 1850-4 inclusive. J.K. Fairbank. Oxford B.Litt. 1931.

7102   The writings on Japan and the Japanese of English and American visitors, 1852-1910. P.M. Barr. London M.A. 1964.

7103   French policy towards Japan, 1854-94. R.L. Sims. London Ph.D. 1968.

7104   British diplomatic relations with China, 1854-69. W. Davies. Wales M.A. 1938.

7105   The system of extra-territoriality in Japan, 1855-99. F.C. Jones. Bristol M.A. 1930.

7106   Yoshida Shōin, the forerunner of the Meiji Restoration. H.J.J.M. van Straelen. Cambridge Ph.D. 1949.

7107   Anglo-Chinese diplomatic relations, 1856-60. Pei-Huan Chiang. London Ph.D. 1939.

7108   British enterprise in south-western China, 1858-90. W.T.K.-K. Chan. Oxford B.Litt. 1965.

7109   Anglo-Chinese diplomatic relations, with special reference to the revision of the treaty of Tientsin, 1858-70. Tang-Li Chao. London Ph.D. 1952.

7110   British trade and traders in Japan, 1859-69. J. McMaster. London Ph.D. 1962.

7111   British loans to China from 1860 to 1913, with special reference to the period 1894-1913. C.S. Chen. London Ph.D. 1940.

7112   The International Settlement, Shanghai. Y.S. Ch'en. London Ph.D. 1940.

7113   Sir Harry Parkes: British representative in Japan, 1865-82. G. Daniels. Oxford D.Phil. 1967.

7114   The deposition of Li Hsiu-ch'eng. C.A. Curwen. London Ph.D. 1968.

7115   Economic growth in Japan, 1867-1913, with special reference to demographic factors. D.W. Anthony. Wales M.Sc. 1964/5.

7116   Labour and the trade union movement in the Japanese coal-mining industry. R.M.V. Collick. Oxford D.Phil. 1970.

7117   The Margary affair and the Convention of Chefoo. S.-T. Wang. Oxford B.Litt. 1938.

7118   Kuo Sung-tao's mission to Great Britain. O.H.-L. Wong. Cambridge Ph.D. 1970.

7119   British policy towards treaty revision with Japan, 1882-94. E.E.G. Zau. Bristol M.Litt. 1967.

7120   Anglo-Chinese relations in the provinces of the West river and the Yangtze river basins, 1889-1900. L.R. Marchant. London M.A. 1965.

7121   British foreign policy in relation to Japan, 1890 to 1902. W.A. Silk. Wales M.A. 1944.

7122   British foreign policy towards Japan, 1892-5. C.W. Tooley. London M.A. 1953.

China's political fin-de-siècle, 1894-1900: a study in   7123
the diplomatic relations of the Powers with China.   P. Joseph.
London Ph.D. 1926.
     British policy in the Chinese question, 1894-8. Eliza- 7124
beth S. Parkin. London M.A. 1953.
     The Russian sphere of influence in China, 1895-1917   7125
(including Manchuria but excluding Inner and Outer Mongolia,
Chinese Turkestan and Tibet). Mrs. Rosemary K.I. Quested.
London M.A. 1957.
     British policy and the Chinese revolutionary movement, 7126
1895-1912. Mary Man Yue Sun. London Ph.D. 1968.
     Anglo-Chinese diplomacy, 1895-1911. T.T.G. Mar. Lon- 7127
don Ph.D. 1929.
     The battle of concessions in China, 1895-1900. H.M.   7128
Lo. Cambridge Ph.D. 1957.
     Anglo-Russian-American relations in the Far East, 1897- 7129
1904. A.P. Simkin. London Ph.D. 1967.
     The Great Powers and the Far East, from the seizure of 7130
Kiao-chau to the Boxer settlement, 1897-1901. Mabel I. Grimshaw. Birmingham M.A. 1929.
     British policy towards China and the Boxer movement,   7131
1898-1902. L.K. Young. Oxford D.Phil. 1960.
     The United States and old world diplomacy, 1898-1914,   7132
with special reference to China. R.J. Shiman. London Ph.D.
1929.
     United States policy in the Pacific area, 1898-1922,   7133
with special reference to China and the Open Door. Daphne
J. Treais-Smart. Birmingham M.A. 1956.
     British diplomacy in China and the Open Door policy.   7134
T.-T. Wang. Cambridge M.Litt. 1964.
     The Anglo-Japanese alliance and the Dominions, 1902-11. 7135
N.R. Bennett. London Ph.D. 1966.
     The Anglo-Japanese alliance, 1902-11, with particular   7136
reference to British naval and military opinion. T.A.
Chivers. Wales M.A. 1962.
     The Anglo-Japanese alliances, 1902-23. J. Wright.   7137
Newcastle M.Litt. 1968.
     The origins and negotiation of the Anglo-Japanese   7138
agreement of 1902. I.H. Nish. London M.A. 1958.
     The diplomacy of the Anglo-Japanese alliance, 1902-7.   7139
I.H. Nish. London Ph.D. (Ext.) 1962.
     British foreign policy in relation to the Russo-   7140
Japanese War. R.W. Barnett. Oxford B.Litt. 1937.
     The gentry democracy in Shanghai, 1905-14. J.M.D.   7141
Elvin. Cambridge Ph.D. 1968.
     Japanese policy in Korea and Manchuria and its effect   7142
on the Anglo-Japanese alliance, 1905-10. T. Iwanami. Oxford B.Litt. 1965.
     Chinese socialism to 1913. M.G. Bernal. Cambridge   7143
Ph.D. 1966.
     Sir John Jordan and the affairs of China, 1906-16,   7144
with special reference to the 1911 revolution and Yüan Shih-
K'ai. Lau Kit-Ching. London Ph.D. 1968.
     British policy towards China during the Hsuang-Tung   7145
regency and the revolution, 1909-12. L.E. Kelly. Nottingham
M.A. 1965.
     British policy in the Far East, 1911-15, with special   7146
reference to relations with Japan. P.C. Lowe. Wales Ph.D.
1967.
     British policy towards China, with special reference to 7147
the Shantung question, 1918-22. P. Richards. London Ph.D.
1970.
     Anglo-Japanese relations, 1917-19: some problems facing 7148
the Alliance. K. Yamashita. Oxford B.Litt. 1966.
     Anglo-Japanese relations 1918-22, with special refer-   7149
ence to the Siberian intervention. S.G. McClure. London
M.Sc. 1960.

7150   The functioning of parliamentary government in Japan, 1918-32, with special reference to the control of foreign policy. S. Rose. Oxford D.Phil. 1951.
7151   The Kwangsi clique in Kuomintang politics, 1921-36. Diana C.M. Lary. London Ph.D. 1969.
7152   The rise of the Chinese Nationalist party and the foundation of the Nanking regime, 1924-9. P.D. Cavendish. Cambridge Ph.D. 1968.
7153   Baron Shidehara's China policy, with special reference to the period between 1924 and 1927. H. Oka. Oxford B.Litt. 1962.
7154   The silver standard in China, 1926-35. C.-C. Ho. Liverpool M.A. 1950.
7155   American diplomatic policy in China, 1928-33. J.W. Christopher. Oxford D.Phil. 1948.
7156   Japanese foreign policy since 1915, with special reference to the events in 1931 and 1932. W.J.A. Harris. London M.Sc. 1940.
7157   The origins of the Shantung question at the Paris Peace Conference. J.-C. Kuo. Oxford B.Litt. 1964.
7158   The first and second national congress of the Chinese Soviet Republic, 1931 and 1934. D.K. Waller. London Ph.D. 1968.
7159   The British foreign policy on the Manchurian incident in the League of Nations. C. Nomura. Oxford B.Litt. 1959.
7160   The presentation of the Manchurian question in the English press, 1931-3. K.C. Cheng. London Ph.D. 1938.
7161   Japan's political failure in China 1935-40: a study of the establishment of Japanese-sponsored government in China. R.F. Nottage. Oxford B.Litt. 1965.
7162   British opinion of the Sino-Japanese War, 1937-41. E.C. Tai. London Ph.D. 1952.
7163   The embassy of Sir Robert Craigie to Tokio, 1937-41. Vivian J. Soule. London Ph.D. 1966.
7164   Anglo-Japanese relations, 1937-41. H. Kawai. Oxford B.Litt. 1965.
7165   British policy in the Far East, 1937-9. P.A. Herriman. Durham M.A. 1965.
7166   The Chinese Communist bases (Ken-Chü-Ti) in North China, 1938-43: a study of their growth and anti-Japanese activities, with special reference to administration and mass mobilisation programmes at the village level. Lee Ngok. London Ph.D. 1968.
7167   The economic background of the modern diplomacy of the Great Powers in the Far East since the World War. T.-K. Chow. London M.Sc. 1934.
7168   Anglo-American-Canadian relations, with special reference to Far Eastern and naval issues, 1918-22. M.G. Fry. London Ph.D. 1964.

A M E R I C A

GENERAL

7169   The effects of irrigation on movements of population, and on the food supply of the world, with special reference to America. J.N.L. Baker. Oxford B.Litt. 1923.
7170   English voyages to America, 1496-1603, and the idea of primitive society. T.N. Marsh. Oxford B.Litt. 1956.
7171   Bristol voyages to the New World between 1576 and 1612. E.R. Gath. Bristol M.A. 1914.
7172   Anglo-native relations in North America in early Stuart times up to 1644. G.S.B. Haslop. Leeds M.A. 1932.

Iroquois and Europeans: a study of a 17th-century con-   7173
tact situation. Marian R. Nicholson. London M.A. 1955.
England's colonial policy and administration in North   7174
America and the West Indies, 1681-8. P.S. Haffenden. London
Ph.D. 1955.
Anglican spiritual aid to foreign settlers and native   7175
peoples in 18th-century America. J.A. Thomas. Sheffield
Ph.D. 1955.
The origin of protestant churches in relation to   7176
settlement, from the founding of Halifax to the American
Revolution. I.F. MacKinnon. Edinburgh Ph.D. 1930.
A comparison of the British system of local government   7177
in the American colonies in the half century preceding the
Revolution with that in British Canada before the Rebellion
of 1837. W.J. Mulholland. Oxford B.Litt. 1920.
The treasury administration of contracts for the supply 7178
of the British armies in North America and the West Indies,
1775-83. N. Baker. London Ph.D. 1967.
British policy in the North American cod fisheries,   7179
with special reference to foreign competition, 1776-1819.
G.O. Rothney. London Ph.D. 1939.
The attitude of British travellers to North America   7180
between 1790 and 1850. P. Mitcham. Edinburgh Ph.D. 1958.
A comparison of the currency and banking systems of   7181
Canada and the United States, with some reference to that of
Great Britain. C.E. Johnston. Oxford B.Litt. 1920.
The Royal Navy on the north-west coast of North   7182
America, 1810-1910. B.M. Gough. London Ph.D. 1969.
Vice-Admiral Sir Alexander Milne, K.C.B., and the North 7183
American and West Indian station, 1860-4. R.A. Courtemanche.
London Ph.D. 1967.

CANADA

The history of Nova Scotia prior to 1763. J.B. Breb-   7184
ner. Oxford B.Litt. 1925.
The English in Newfoundland, 1577-1660. Mrs. Gillian   7185
M. Cell. Liverpool Ph.D. 1964.
The West Country - Newfoundland fisheries (chiefly in   7186
the 17th and 18th centuries). K. Matthews. Oxford D.Phil.
1968.
The development of government in Newfoundland, 1638-   7187
1713. A. Mary Field. London M.A. 1924.
The historical geography and cartography of the   7188
Canadian West, 1670-1795: the discovery, exploration, geo-
graphic description and cartographic delineation of Western
Canada to 1795. R.I. Ruggles. London Ph.D. 1958.
British rule in Nova Scotia, 1713-84. W.S. MacNutt.   7189
London M.A. 1932.
The history of Newfoundland, 1713-63. Janet Paterson. 7190
London M.A. 1931.
The early history of the Presbyterian Church in Western 7191
Canada from the earliest times to the year 1881. J.C. Walker.
Edinburgh Ph.D. 1928.
Historical geography: the disposition of farm lands in   7192
western Manitoba. J.L. Tyman. Oxford D.Phil. 1970.
The contribution of the Scottish Church to New Bruns-   7193
wick Presbyterianism. F.E. Archibald. Edinburgh Ph.D.
1932/3.
Historical geography of the Mackenzie river valley,   7194
1750-1850. J.K. Stager. Edinburgh Ph.D. 1962.
The history of Newfoundland and Labrador, 1754-83.   7195
G.O. Rothney. London M.A. 1934.
The Acadian deportation: causes and development. Naomi 7196
E.S. Griffiths. London Ph.D. (Ext.) 1969.

273

7197 The establishment of British government in Isle St. John (Prince Edward Island), 1758-84. Helen J. Champion. London M.A. 1934.

7198 The Imperial Land Regulations as applied to Canada, 1763-1841. N. Macdonald. Edinburgh Ph.D. 1931/2.

7199 Canada in British politics, from 1763 to 1783. Marjorie G. Reid. Oxford B.Litt. 1922.

7200 British policy and Canada, 1774-91: a study in 18th-century mercantilism. G.S. Graham. Cambridge Ph.D. 1928/9.

7201 Newfoundland in colonial policy, 1775-93. W.L. Morton. Oxford B.Litt. 1935.

7202 The establishment of constitutional government in New-foundland, 1783-1832. A.H. McLintock. London Ph.D. 1938.

7203 Aspects of the mapping of southern Ontario, 1783-1867. Mrs. Marilyn B. MacK. Olsen. London M.Phil. 1968.

7204 The Church of England in Nova Scotia, 1783-1816. Judith J. Fingard. London M.Phil. 1967.

7205 The Church of England in British North America, 1787-1825. Judith J. Fingard. London Ph.D. (Ext.) 1970.

7206 The purpose and immediate operation of the Canada Act of 1791. F.H. Soward. Oxford B.Litt. 1922.

7207 Education and society in Upper Canada, 1791-1850. R.D. Gidney. London M.Phil. 1969.

7208 Lord Selkirk's work in Canada. C.B. Martin. Oxford B.Litt. 1912.

7209 Emigration to British North America under the early passenger acts, 1803-42. Kathleen A. Walpole. London M.A. 1929.

7210 The working of the 1791 constitutional experiment in Lower Canada, 1805-11. L.A.H. Smith. Oxford B.Litt. 1955.

7211 The Canadian Northwest in 1811: a study in the histor-ical geography of the Old Northwest of the fur trade on the eve of the first agricultural settlement. E.DeW. Ross. Edinburgh Ph.D. 1962.

7212 British policy towards Canada, from the War of 1812 to the Rebellion of 1837. K.L.P. Martin. Oxford B.Litt. 1921.

7213 Political unrest in Upper Canada, 1815-36. Aileen Dun-ham. London Ph.D. 1924.

7214 Origins of self government in Nova Scotia, 1815-36. J.S. Martell. London Ph.D. 1935.

7215 The constitutional and financial aspects of the admin-istration of Lord Dalhousie in Canada. C.G. Gilmore. Durham Ph.D. 1930.

7216 The expansion of the Church of England in Rupert's Land from 1820 to 1839 under the Hudson's Bay Company and the Church Missionary Society. A.N. Thompson. Cambridge Ph.D. 1962.

7216A Ungava venture of the Hudson Bay Company, 1830-43. A.G.R. Cooke. Cambridge Ph.D. 1970.

7217 The Union Bill of 1822 and the subsequent union schemes in their relation to British policy in Canada prior to 1937. E.J. Hutchins. Oxford B.Litt. 1929.

7218 Colonial Office government in British North America, 1828-47. P.A. Buckner. London Ph.D. 1969.

7219 The political history of Newfoundland, 1832-64. Ger-trude E. Gunn. London Ph.D. 1959.

7220 A history of the 'Real Old Timers' of Fort Edmonton (Canada) and its hinterland. Irene M. Harper. Cambridge M.Litt. 1931/2.

7221 The geography of the province of Lower Canada in 1837. W.H. Parker. Oxford D.Phil. 1958.

7222 The economic history of the province of Canada, 1845-51. G.N. Tucker. Cambridge Ph.D. 1929/30.

7223 Elections and politics in Canada West under responsible government, 1847-63. J. Wearing. Oxford D.Phil. 1965.

7224 Responsible government in Canada. Rosa W. Langstone. Birmingham M.A. 1930.

7225 The work of Sir Edmund Head in British North America, 1848-61. D.G.G. Kerr. London Ph.D. 1937.

Life of Lord Mount Stephen, 1829-1921. Heather M. 7226
Donald. London Ph.D. 1952.

The Ontario grammar schools, 1853-71. G. Milburn. 7227
Durham M.A. 1960.

The Reciprocity treaty of 1854: its history, its rel- 7228
ation to British colonial and foreign policy and to the
development of Canadian fiscal autonomy. D.C. Masters. Oxford D.Phil. 1935.

The history of the Canadian constitution. R. Johnston. 7229
Belfast M.A. 1912.

Studies in the evolution of dominion status: (a) the 7230
governor-generalship of Canada; and (b) the development of
Canadian nationalism. Gwendoline Neuendorff. London Ph.D.
1941.

Agriculture and politics in Ontario since 1867. Marion 7231
J. MacLeod. London Ph.D. 1962.

The determinants and behaviour of the Canadian money 7232
stock, 1867-1961. H.G. Walsh. Cambridge M.Sc. 1967.

The development of Canadian financial institutions, 7233
1867-1929. R. Bertrand. London M.Sc. 1961.

The history of the Canadian civil service. R.MacG. 7234
Dawson. London M.Sc. 1920.

British opinion on the federation of Canada. J.A. 7235
Gibson. Oxford B.Litt. 1934.

The Colonial Office and Canada, 1867-87. D.M.L. Farr. 7236
Oxford D.Phil. 1952.

The terms of trade with Canada, 1869-1952. J. Pari- 7237
zeau. London Ph.D. 1955.

Political unrest in the Canadian North-West, with 7238
special reference to the first Riel rebellion, 1869-70.
G.F.G. Stanley. Oxford B.Litt. 1932.

The second Riel rebellion, 1870-86. G.F.G. Stanley. 7239
Oxford D.Phil. 1935.

Aspects of the Canadian economy, 1871-1914. J. 7240
Pickett. Glasgow B.Litt. 1966.

A study of certain powers of the Canadian governor- 7241
generalship under Lord Dufferin, 1872-8. R.G. Irving. Oxford B.Litt. 1964.

Authority and policy in the Canadian militia, 1874- 7242
1904. D.D.P. Morton. London Ph.D. 1968.

The Canadian Northwest: a study in sub-Arctic economic 7243
development, 1898-1958. K.J. Rea. London Ph.D. 1959.

The economics of the settlement of the prairie pro- 7244
vinces of Canada, 1900-31. Sarah Common. London Ph.D. 1933.

Mergers in Canadian industry, 1900 to 1963. C.J. 7245
Maule. London Ph.D. 1966.

Real investment in Canada, 1900 to 1930. K.A.H. Buck- 7246
ley. London Ph.D. 1950.

Government and politics in Newfoundland, 1904-34: pre- 7247
lude to the surrender of dominion status. S.J.R. Noel. Oxford D.Phil. 1965.

The 4th Earl Grey as governor-general of Canada, 1904- 7248
11. Mary E. Hallett. London Ph.D. 1970.

Canada's relations with Britain, 1911-19: problems of 7249
imperial defence and foreign policy. G.L. Cook. Oxford
D.Phil. 1969.

Politics and the party system in the three prairie 7250
provinces, 1917-58. S.G.D. Smith. Oxford B.Litt. 1959.

The British Columbia labour movement in the inter-war 7251
period: a study of its social and political aspects. P.A.
Phillips. London Ph.D. 1967.

A history of the Communist party of Canada, 1919-29. 7252
W. Rodney. London Ph.D. 1961.

A history of the Social Credit movement. E.E. 7253
McCarthy. Leeds M.A. 1947.

The settlement of labour disputes in Canada. N.McL. 7254
Rogers. Oxford B.Litt. 1921.

7255   Canadian policy towards international institutions, 1939-50. D.G. Anglin. Oxford D.Phil. 1956.

7256   The development of Canadian naval bases. A.L. Pidgeon. Oxford B.Litt. 1948.

COLONIAL AMERICA

7257   The role of British capital in the development of the United States, c.1600-1914. T.C. Coram. Southampton M.Sc. 1967.

7258   The English background of the Dorchester group and its impact on American culture in the 17th and 18th centuries. Ann N. Hansen. Oxford B.Litt. 1963.

7259   Bristol and Virginia in the 17th century. N.C.P. Tyack. Bristol M.A. 1930.

7260   Emigration from Taunton to New England, 1625-45. H.J. Wickenden. Bristol M.A. 1929.

7261   Migration from East Anglia to New England before 1660. N.C.P. Tyack. London Ph.D. 1951.

7262   The relations of the English Baptists with New England in the 17th century. J. Brewer. Leeds B.D. 1953.

7263   The effect of the discovery of the American frontier on English shipping, 1650-88. J.L. Dawson. Edinburgh Ph.D. 1956.

7264   The origin and early history of Presbyterianism in Virginia. D.L. Beard. Edinburgh Ph.D. 1932/3.

7265   The Congregationalism of New England and its repercussions in England and Scotland, 1641-62. D.F. Chatfield. Edinburgh Ph.D. 1964.

7266   The Church of England in the American colonies, 1675-1775. J.B. Bell. Oxford D.Phil. 1964.

7267   British administration of the American colonies, 1689-1783. J.D. Doty. Oxford B.Litt. 1923.

7268   The House of Hancock. W.T. Baxter. Edinburgh Ph.D. 1945/6.

7269   A study of sound and unsound currency in Massachusetts from 1690 to 1763. A.V. Barber. Oxford B.Litt. 1929.

7270   The British naval stores and forests policy in New England, 1690-1775. J.J. Malone. London Ph.D. 1956.

7271   The presbytery as organ of church life and government in American Presbyterianism from 1706 to 1788. B.S. Schlenther. Edinburgh Ph.D. 1964/5.

7272   An investigation into the causes, extent and character of emigration from the northern ports of Ireland to colonial America. R.J. Dickson. Belfast Ph.D. 1949.

7273   The influence of the Ulster Scots upon the achievement of religious liberty in the North American colonies of Virginia, North and South Carolina, 1720-75. R.L. Jones. St. Andrews Ph.D. 1961.

7274   The economic development of the American colonies, with special reference to the relations with the mother country. Constance A. Joseph. Birmingham M.Com. 1928.

7275   Governor William Franklin. Felicitas M. Doherty. Oxford B.Litt. 1931.

7276   Oglethorpe and social and religious movements in England and Georgia. L.F. Church. London Ph.D. 1928.

7277   Colonial Georgia in British policy, 1732-65. T.R. Reese. London Ph.D. 1955.

7278   The social and evangelistic work of George Whitefield in America. J.F. Alexander. Edinburgh Ph.D. 1955.

7279   Anglo-Virginian relations, 1748-64. Gwenda Morgan. Southampton M.Phil. 1970.

7280   British intervention in defence of the American colonies, 1748-56. D.S. Graham. London Ph.D. 1969.

7281   The political and economic relations of English and American Quakers, 1750-85. Anne T. Gary. Oxford D.Phil. 1935.

The impact of the American problem on British politics, 7282
1760-80. C.R. Ritcheson. Oxford D.Phil. 1951.
The evolution of the Southern Indian boundary line in   7283
the British American colonies, 1763-75. L. de Vorsey. Lon-
don Ph.D. 1965.
Sir John Wentworth and his times. Kathleen E. Stokes.   7284
London Ph.D. 1938.
The political theory of Thomas Jefferson. O. Rockey.   7285
Oxford B.Litt. 1925.
The development of the idea of American independence,   7286
with particular reference to the leading colonials of revol-
utionary America. J.L. Cuthbert. Sheffield M.A. 1964.
Maryland and the American Revolution. Mary J. Broad-   7287
bent. Sheffield M.A. 1949.
The Loyalists of the American Revolution, 1775-83.   7288
J.R. Hutchinson. Sheffield M.A. 1955.
William Smith, American Loyalist, 1728-83. Marjory S.   7289
Sinclair. Oxford B.Litt. 1928.
The Howes and the American Revolution. T.S. Anderson.   7290
Oxford D.Phil. 1929/30.
The West Country and the American colonies, 1763-83,   7291
with special reference to the merchants of Bristol. W.R.
Savadge. Oxford B.Litt. 1951.
The American Revolutionary movement in Scottish   7292
opinion, 1763 to 1783. D.I. Fagerstrom. Edinburgh Ph.D.
1951.
English opinion on the American War of Independence,   7293
as reflected in contemporary pamphlet literature. T.P. Brock-
way. Oxford B.Litt. 1925.
The movement of opinion in England concerning America   7294
prior to the Declaration of American Independence. D.G.
Martin. Liverpool M.A. 1911.
English politics and the American Revolution, 1773-5.   7295
B. Donoughue. Oxford D.Phil. 1962.

UNITED STATES OF AMERICA

The influence of Montesquieu upon the American constit- 7296
ution. R.W. Ferguson. London M.A. 1912.
A comparison of the constitutions of the United States 7297
and Australia. B. Jones. Wales M.A. 1924.
Anglo-American relations in the tobacco trade to the   7298
end of the 19th and the beginning of the 20th century. H.
Chasey. Bristol M.A. 1950.
The vice-presidency of the United States: its history   7299
and its political and administrative aspects. S.O. Malick.
London M.Sc. 1959.
The development of a professional service for foreign   7300
affairs in the United States. W.F. Ilchman. Cambridge Ph.D.
1959.
Commercial relations between Great Britain and the   7301
United States of America from 1783 to 1794. W.H. Elkins.
Oxford B.Litt. 1935.
A history of the development of British public opinion 7302
on Anglo-American relations, 1783-94. D.S. Reid. St. Andrews
Ph.D. 1934.
The reception of the American constitution in Britain, 7303
1787-1848. Dorothea H. Pattinson. Birmingham M.A. 1941.
Criticism and defence of the constitution of the   7304
senate of the United States of America during the campaign
for ratification, 1787-9. J.M. Shelat. London M.A. 1933.
Philanthropic reform movements in New York State from   7305
the Revolution to the Civil War. M.J. Heale. Oxford D.Phil.
1967.

7306   British policy in its relation to the commerce and navigation of the United States of America from 1794 to 1807. W.H. Elkins. Oxford D.Phil. 1936.

7307   Henry Wansey: 'The Journal of an excursion to the United States of America in the summer of 1794': critical edition of, with biographical introduction. D.J. Jeremy. Bristol M.Litt. 1967.

7308   The repudiation of state debts by states of the United States of America in the 19th century. G.L. Ridgeway. Oxford B.Litt. 1928.

7309   Racial attitudes in revolutionary and early national America. D.J. Macleod. Cambridge Ph.D. 1969.

7310   A contribution to the study of emigration from North Wales to the United States of America, 1800-50. Ethel K.R.R. Roberts. Liverpool M.A. 1931.

7311   Geographical influences of the exploration of America west of the Mississippi, 1800-50. E.W. Gilbert. Oxford B.Litt. 1928.

7312   Napoleon Bonaparte and the sale of Louisiana to the United States. E.W. Lyon. Oxford B.Litt. 1928.

7313   Barton Stone and the 'Christians' of the West. V.E. Kellems. Edinburgh Ph.D. 1928.

7314   British public opinion on Anglo-American relations, 1805-12. D.R. Currie. St. Andrews Ph.D. 1935/6.

7315   British opinion and the United States of America, 1806-12. R. Horsman. Birmingham M.A. 1955.

7316   The slave trade and Anglo-American relations, 1807-62. A.T. Milne. London M.A. 1930.

7317   The American trade of Liverpool in the early 19th century and the war of 1812. B.H. Tolley. Liverpool M.A. 1967.

7318   American trade restrictions and British commerce, 1808-12. M.G. Knox. Oxford B.Litt. 1938.

7319   The political ideas of John C. Calhoun. R.L. Humber. Oxford B.Litt. 1923.

7320   George Combe and his circle: with particular reference to his relations with the United States of America. A.C. Grant. Edinburgh Ph.D. 1960.

7321   The Anglo-American connection in war-time, 1812-15. B.E. Handren. Edinburgh Ph.D. 1961.

7322   Sir Alexander Cochrane and the conclusion of the American War, 1814-15. B. Humphreys. Liverpool M.A. 1960.

7323   The background and motives of Scottish emigration to the United States of America in the period 1815-61, with special reference to emigrant correspondence. D.L. Jones. Edinburgh Ph.D. 1970.

7324   Agencies for the promotion or facilitation of emigration from England to the United States of America, 1815-61. Mary D. Wainwright. London M.A. 1952.

7325   New Orleans as a port of immigration, 1820-60. A.A. Conway. London M.A. 1949.

7326   The image of American democracy in English politics, 1820-50. D.P. Crook. London Ph.D. 1962.

7327   Richard Cobden and America. K. Fielden. Cambridge Ph.D. 1966.

7328   Religion and society in the early 19th century: a comparative study of church parties within the established churches of Massachusetts and Scotland. Wendy S. Wilson. Aberdeen M.Litt. 1969.

7328A   Andrew Jackson and the <u>Washington Globe</u>. M.J. Debenham. Oxford B.Litt. 1970.

7329   The American Negro faces European immigration in the United States, 1830-1924. W.L. McIntosh. Cambridge Ph.D. 1970.

7330   The Scottish factor in the fight against American slavery, 1830-70. C.D. Rice. Edinburgh Ph.D. 1969.

7331   Relations between British and American abolitionists from British emancipation to the American Civil War. D.M. Turley. Cambridge Ph.D. 1970.

Some connections between British and American reform movements, 1830-60, with special reference to the anti-slavery movement. L. Billington. Bristol M.Litt. 1966. 7332

Some aspects of the railroad history of the south-western states of the American Union, 1830-60. Alison M. Hughes. London M.A. 1950. 7333

British investment in American railways, 1834-98. Mrs. Dorothy R. Adler. Cambridge Ph.D. 1958. 7334

A London merchant banker in Anglo-American trade and finance, 1835-50. J.R. Freedman. London Ph.D. 1969. 7335

Emigration from the United Kingdom to America, 1830-50. Frances Morehouse. Manchester Ph.D. 1926. 7336

Mormon emigration from Great Britain to the United States, 1840-70. P.A.M. Taylor. Cambridge Ph.D. 1952. 7337

British immigration to California before 1870. R.A. Burchell. Oxford B.Litt. 1969. 7338

The idea of political representation in the United States and Great Britain, 1836-56. J.L. Moore. Oxford B.Litt. 1953. 7339

The plough and the loom: attitudes towards the textile mill in South Carolina, 1840-55. P.C.B. Craske. Cambridge Ph.D. 1969. 7340

Anglo-American foreign relations, 1841-61, with special reference to trans-Isthmian communication. G.A. Edwards. Wales M.A. 1951. 7341

Phillip Schaff's concept of the church, with special reference to his role in the Mercersburg movement, 1844-64. T.L. Trost. Edinburgh Ph.D. 1958. 7342

Administrative legislation and adjudication in Great Britain and the United States. E.R. Baltzell. Oxford D.Phil. 1923. 7343

The formation of the Illinois constitution of 1848. C.G. Dilworth. Oxford B.Litt. 1964. 7344

British investment in the United States, 1860-80. J.J. Madden. Cambridge Ph.D. 1958. 7345

The relations of Great Britain and America, especially from 1861 to 1866. Edith E. Baker. Birmingham M.A. 1920. 7346

English opinion and the American Civil War. Emily A. Taylor. Leeds M.A. 1921. 7347

French and Spanish opinion of the American Civil War. E.J. Pratt. Oxford B.Litt. 1925. 7348

The British attitude towards the American Civil War. C.I. Payne. Birmingham M.A. 1928. 7349

Scotland and the American Civil War. R.M. Botsford. Edinburgh Ph.D. 1955. 7350

Birmingham and the American Civil War. Mrs. M. Wendy Corke. Liverpool M.A. 1963. 7351

English sympathy for the Southern Confederacy. S. van Auken. Oxford B.Litt. 1957. 7352

The reaction of Lancashire to the American Civil War. Mrs. Mary L. Arfon Jones, née Ellison. London Ph.D. 1968. 7353

Confederate finance and purchasing in Britain. R.I. Lester. Manchester Ph.D. 1961. 7354

A critical analysis of the part played by the blockade in the defeat of the Confederacy. D.T. Chambers. Wales M.A. 1966. 7355

British attitudes to reconstruction in the United States, 1863-77. Mrs. Christine A. Bolt. London Ph.D. 1966. 7356

Some effects of economic and social changes in American education, 1865-1914. Lilian M. Spencer. London M.A. 1966. 7357

American military policy and civil-military relations, 1865-1904. E. Ranson. Manchester Ph.D. 1963. 7358

American military policy, 1865-80. E. Ranson. Manchester M.A. 1960. 7359

British policy towards a settlement with America, 1865-72. Maureen M. Bullen. London Ph.D. 1956. 7360

7361   The Fenians and Anglo-American relations, 1865-72.
B.A. Jenkins. Manchester Ph.D. 1966.

7362   Congressional radicalism during the presidency of
Andrew Johnson, with special reference to the political ideas
behind it. J.F.S. Russell. Oxford B.Litt. 1952.

7364   A social and economic analysis of Louisiana, 1865-7.
Isobel M. Howells. Wales M.A. 1969.

7365   Northern schemes for agrarian reconstruction in the
South during and after the Civil War in the United States of
America. R.H. Beevers. London M.A. 1950.

7366   A study of the Negro in the southern cities of the
United States in the immediate post Civil War period, 1865-8.
Margaret G. Miles. Wales M.A. 1968.

7367   The effects of the American Civil War on the linen and
wool textile industries of the United Kingdom. O.N. Greeves.
Bristol Ph.D. 1969.

7368   The reconstruction of Georgia. A.A. Conway. Wales
Ph.D. 1964.

7369   The political role of the Southern Unionists during reconstruction. G.C. Atkinson. Manchester M.A. 1952.

7370   The way to Geneva: United States policy and attitudes
towards Great Britain, 1865-72. A.E. Cook. Cambridge Ph.D.
1965.

7371   Investment trusts and investment companies in the United
States and Great Britain since 1868. S.L. Baskin. London
Ph.D. 1966.

7372   The decline of Congressional radicalism during the presidency of Ulysses S. Grant. A.F. Bailey. Manchester M.A.
1967.

7373   The development of city government in the United States
and the United Kingdom, with special reference to the period
since 1870. E.S. Griffith. Oxford D.Phil. 1925.

7374   Middle-class British immigration to the trans-
Mississippi West, 1870-1900. Eve B. Packer. London M.Sc.
1967.

7375   A comparative study of the curriculum and organisation
of secondary education in England and the United States between 1870 and 1900. B.S. Cane. London M.A. 1957.

7376   Scottish capital on the American credit frontier, particularly Texas, 1873-90. W.G. Kerr. Cambridge Ph.D. 1965.

7377   The structure of Pennsylvania, 1876-80. R. Harrison.
Cambridge Ph.D. 1970.

7378   Managerialism in the United States, 1880-1940. D.J.S.
Morris. Oxford B.Litt. 1968.

7379   Christian Socialism in Britain and the U.S.A., 1880-
1914. P.d'A. Jones. London Ph.D. 1964.

7380   Theodore Roosevelt and the politics of the machine
organisations in the United States, 1881-97. E.S.A. Ions.
Oxford B.Litt. 1963.

7381   'The technological challenge': some aspects of the early
development of the electrical lighting industry, with special
reference to England and the U.S.A., 1882-1919. J.P. Brown.
Sheffield M.A. 1964.

7382   Socialism and the American Federation of Labor: 1886-
1903. J.H.M. Laslett. Oxford D.Phil. 1962.

7383   Progressivism and child labour in the United States,
1890 to 1920. A.F. Bailey. Manchester Ph.D. 1970.

7384   Executive-legislative relations in the United States
during the administrations of Grover Cleveland and Benjamin
Harrison. D.S. Porter. London M.A. 1955.

7385   Attitudes towards the Negro in New York City, 1890-1914.
C.S. Greer. London M.A. 1968.

7386   Anglo-American arbitration policies, 1890-1914. O.
Gollancz. Cambridge Ph.D. 1939.

Corruption in American labor organisations: its 7387
origins and development, 1890-1955. J.E. Hutchinson. London
Ph.D. (Ext.) 1963.

Mechanisation in British and American bituminous coal 7388
mines, 1890-1939. C.A. Paull. London M.Phil. 1968.

Anglo-American relations, 1895-1903: a study in British 7389
policy and opinion. A.E. Campbell. Cambridge Ph.D. 1956.

The imperialist controversy in the United States, 1895- 7390
1900. Mary Turner. Manchester M.A. 1953.

The relations of Great Britain and the United States of 7391
America during the Spanish-American War of 1898. H. Holroyde.
Sheffield M.A. 1947.

Aspects of Anglo-American relations, 1899-1906: being 7392
a study in the problem of security. L.M. Gelber. Oxford
B.Litt. 1933.

The Irish question as a factor in Anglo-American rel- 7393
ations, 1899-1921. A.J. Ward. London Ph.D. 1967.

The new liberalism in Great Britain and the United 7394
States - a study in reform thought, with special reference
to the problem of industrial concentration. M.R. Wilson.
Manchester M.A. 1967.

The problem of industrial violence in the United 7395
States, 1899-1909. R. Jeffreys-Jones. Cambridge Ph.D. 1969.

The theology of American protestantism and race rel- 7396
ations. Mrs. Jean DeB. Russell. Edinburgh Ph.D. 1966.

The politics of race under the impact of migration: the 7397
United States (1900-30) and the United Kingdom (1948-68). I.
Katznelson. Cambridge Ph.D. 1969.

The development of education in theological colleges in 7398
the Church of England and in the Protestant Episcopal Church
of America, 1900-50. S.F.D. Walters. Oxford D.Phil. 1957.

Anglo-American relations during the embassy of Sir H. 7399
Mortimer Durand, 1903-6. D. Eden. London M.Sc. 1966.

The politics of women's suffrage in Britain and the 7400
United States of America, 1906-20. D.R. Morgan. Cambridge
Ph.D. 1967.

The political thought and practice of American trade 7401
unionism, 1906-18. I.M. Karson. London Ph.D. 1949.

The embassy of James Bryce in the United States, 1907- 7402
13. P. Neary. London Ph.D. 1965.

The First World War and American progressive public- 7403
ists. J.A. Thompson. Cambridge Ph.D. 1969.

The influence of Colonel House upon Woodrow Wilson's 7404
foreign policy. B. Howe. Sheffield M.A. 1954.

The social and political history of the 18th Amendment 7405
and the Volstead Act. A.A. Sinclair. Cambridge Ph.D. 1962/3.

The United States in the British press from 1914 to 7406
1939. Priscilla A. Johnson. Oxford B.Litt. 1952.

The British press and Anglo-American relations, with 7407
particular reference to the Irish problem, 1916-22. D.W.
Hayward. Manchester M.A. 1966.

Anglo-American relations during the administration of 7408
Herbert Hoover, with particular reference to Europe. Priscilla M. Sheppard. London M.A. 1955.

Fluctuations in investment in housing in Britain and 7409
America, 1919-39. G.P. Braae. Oxford D.Phil. 1960.

Some aspects of the politics of decontrol in Great 7410
Britain and the United States, 1919-21. Mrs. Susan M.H.
Armitage. London Ph.D. 1968.

The Depression, the New Deal and the Left, 1932-40. 7411
G.D. Evans. Cambridge Ph.D. 1965.

Executive leadership and the formulation of a policy 7412
towards Europe during the first administration of Franklin
D. Roosevelt, 1933-7. D.K. Adams. Oxford D.Phil. 1962.

7413   The strength and weakness of Spanish control of the
Caribbean, 1520-1650: the case for the Armada de Barlovento.
R.H. Boulind. Cambridge Ph.D. 1965.

7414   The first settlement of the maritime nations in the
Spanish Antilles. P.W. Day. London M.A. 1916.

7415   The transportation system in the 17th century, with
special reference to the West Indies. A.E. Smith. Oxford
D.Phil. 1932/3.

7416   The sociology of slavery: a study of the origins,
development and structure of Negro slave society in Jamaica.
H.O.L. Patterson. London Ph.D. 1965.

7417   An historical and comparative study of the foundations
of education in the British, Spanish and French West Indies
(up to the end of slavery in the British islands). J.
Latimer. London Ph.D. 1952.

7418   The social, economic and political problems of the
Stuart settlement of Jamaica. R.W. Harris. Bristol M.A.
1943.

7419   The early history of the Bahama Islands to 1730, with a
special study of the proprietorial government. Mrs. Gillian
L. Bain. London M.A. 1959.

7420   The status of French and English in the Neutral Islands,
1635-1763. Gertrude M. Fletcher. London M.A. 1930.

7421   Constitutional and economic development in Barbados,
1641-85. V.T. Harlow. Oxford B.Litt. 1922.

7422   A bibliographical survey of the sources of Jamaican
history, 1655-1838, with particular reference to manuscript
sources. K.E.N. Ingram. London M.Phil. 1970.

7424   The development of executive government in Barbados and
the Leeward Islands, 1660-1783. F.G. Spurdle. London Ph.D.
1931.

7425   The sugar trade of the British West Indies from 1660 to
1756, with special reference to the island of Antigua. R.B.
Sheridan. London Ph.D. 1951.

7426   The constitutional development of Jamaica, with special
reference to the control of the revenue, 1660-1729. Agnes
M. Whitson. Manchester M.A. 1927.

7427   A history of the legal system of Jamaica from 1661 to
1900. E.H. Watkins. Sheffield Ph.D. 1968.

7428   The colonial agents of the British West India islands,
from the first appointment to the close of the 18th century.
Lillian M. Penson. London Ph.D. 1921.

7429   Colonial policy and administration in the West Indies,
1660-85. A.P. Thornton. Oxford D.Phil. 1952.

7430   The struggles of the European Powers for possessions in
Guiana, 1667-1713. Mary Fisher. London M.A. 1926.

7431   The Caribbean in international politics, 1670-1707.
W.G. Bassett. London Ph.D. 1934.

7432   The place of Sir Henry Morgan in the history of Jamaica.
Margaret Hunter. Oxford B.Litt. 1934.

7433   The administration of Sir William Beeston in Jamaica.
A. Walton. Oxford B.Litt. 1958.

7434   The administration of the Leeward Islands, 1699-1721.
W.F. Laws. Edinburgh M.Litt. 1969.

7435   British relations with the Spanish colonies in the
Caribbean, 1713-39. L. Frances Horsfall. London M.A. 1935.

7436   Educational policy in the Bahamas up to 1823 and its
determinants. R.E. Bain. London M.A. 1959.

7437   British administration in Jamaica, 1729-83. G. Metcalf.
London Ph.D. 1963.

7438   The sugar plantations of the heirs of Lady Frances
Stapleton, in Nevis and St. Christopher, 1746-1810. J.R.V.
Johnston. Wales M.A. 1964.

Constitutional struggles in Jamaica, 1748-76. J.W.   7439
Herbert. London M.A. 1927.

West India merchants and planters in the mid 18th cent- 7440
ury, with special reference to St. Kitts. D.W. Thoms. Kent
M.A. 1967.

Protestant missions in Jamaica: a critical survey of   7441
mission policy from 1754 to the present day. J.W. Kilpatrick.
Edinburgh Ph.D. 1944.

Missionary activity in Jamaica before Emancipation.   7442
Mrs. Mary Reckord. London Ph.D. 1964.

Amity Hall, 1760-1860: the geography of a Jamaican   7443
plantation. G.S. Ramlackhansingh. London M.Sc. 1966.

The free port system in the British West Indies, 1766- 7444
1815. L. Frances Horsfall. London Ph.D. 1939.

The development of Creole society in Jamaica, 1770- 7445
1820. L.E. Brathwaite. Sussex D.Phil. 1967/8.

Constitutional developments in Jamaica, 1774-1815.   7446
A.L. Murray. London M.A. 1956.

Spanish colonial administration and the socio-economic 7447
foundations of Trinidad, 1777-97. J.A. Noël. Cambridge
Ph.D. 1966.

The West Indies in the American Revolution. M.J.   7448
Hewitt. Oxford D.Phil. 1937.

Slave society in the British Leeward Islands, 1780- 7449
1800. Elsa V. Goveia. London Ph.D. 1952.

Aspects of the economic history of British Guiana,   7450
1781-1852: a study of economic and social change on the
southern Caribbean frontier. R.E.G. Farley. London Ph.D.
(Ext.) 1956.

Constitutional and political developments in Barbados 7451
and Jamaica, 1783-1815. N.A.T. Hall. London Ph.D. 1965.

The evolution of the present pattern of agricultural 7452
land use in the island of Trinidad, West Indies. Gloria
Young Sing. Belfast Ph.D. 1964.

Land, labour and immigration in Trinidad, 1783-1833. 7453
C.A. Goodridge. Cambridge Ph.D. 1970.

Constitutional development in Trinidad, 1783-1810.   7454
J.C. Millette. London Ph.D. 1964.

British commercial policy in the West Indies from 1783 7455
to 1793. Helen M. Allen. London Ph.D. 1928.

John Bolton, a Liverpool West Indian merchant, 1756- 7456
1837. Beatrice M. Santer. Birmingham M.A. 1955.

The economic development of the British West Indies, 7457
1790-1850, with special reference to the transition from
slave to free labour in Jamaica. D.G.H. Hall. London M.Sc.
1952.

English naval strategy and maritime trade in the Carib- 7458
bean, 1793-1802. M.W.B. Sanderson. London Ph.D. 1969.

The history of education in Trinidad and Tobago from 7459
earliest times to 1900. J.A.R.K. Samarusingh. London Ph.D.
(Ext.) 1964.

Social and administrative developments in British   7460
Honduras, 1798-1843. Narda D. Leon. Oxford B.Litt. 1958.

The economic history of Bermuda in the 19th century. 7461
Mary R.E. Wright. Bristol M.A. 1928.

The emergence of a free-labour economy in the British 7462
West Indies, 1800-50. W.E. Riviere. Glasgow Ph.D. 1968.

The Free Coloured and their fight for civil rights in 7463
Jamaica, 1800-30. Mrs. Sheila J. Duncker. London M.A. (Ext.)
1960.

The convoy system and the West Indian trade, 1803-15. 7464
C. Dowling. Oxford D.Phil. 1965.

The development of the land law in British Guiana.   7465
F.H.W. Ramsahoye. London Ph.D. 1959.

The Baptist Missionary Society and Jamaican emancip- 7466
ation, 1814-45. G.A. Catherall. Liverpool M.A. 1965.

7467   The effect of the slave emancipation in British Guiana and Trinidad. J.R. Maclean. Oxford B.Litt. 1931.

7468   The emancipation of the slaves in Jamaica and its results. W.M. Cousins. London Ph.D. 1928.

7469   The resistance of the planters of Jamaica to the movement for the abolition of slavery. G. Allen. Durham M.A. 1952.

7470   The economic aspect of the abolition of the West Indian slave trade and slavery. E.E. Williams. Oxford D.Phil. 1938.

7471   Church and state in education in British Guiana, 1833 to 1902. Mavis D. Pollard. London M.Phil. 1967.

7472   The history of the Wesleyan-Methodist contribution to education in Jamaica in the 19th century (1833-1900). Mavis E. Burke. London M.A. 1965.

7473   The development of primary education in Jamaica, 1835-65. C.C. Campbell. London M.A. 1963.

7474   The economic development of Jamaica, 1830-1930. Gisela Eisner. Manchester Ph.D. 1956.

7475   The development of education in Barbados, with special reference to social and economic conditions, 1834-1958. A.G. Williams. London M.A. 1964.

7476   Development of secondary education in Trinidad and Tobago. E.A. Furlonge. Sheffield Ph.D. 1968.

7477   Immigration into Trinidad and British Guiana, 1834-71. K.O. Laurence. Cambridge Ph.D. 1958.

7478   The organisation of missionary societies and the recruitment of missionaries in Britain and the role of missionaries in the diffusion of British culture in Jamaica during the period 1834-65. Dorothy A. Ryall. London Ph.D. 1959.

7479   Negro education in the British West Indies: attitudes and policy after Emancipation, 1834-50. R.I. Romain. Cambridge Ph.D. 1962.

7480   The problem of federation in the British West Indies during the 19th century. L.M. Young. Cambridge Ph.D. 1947.

7481   Sugar and the economy of British Guiana, 1838-1904. A.H. Adamson. London Ph.D. 1964.

7482   East Indians and Negroes in British Guiana, 1838-80. R.J. Moore. Sussex D.Phil. 1970.

7483   The social and economic development of the Windward Islands, 1838-65. W.K. Marshall. Cambridge Ph.D. 1964.

7484   Post-emancipation problems in Jamaica, 1838-47. A.V. Long. Oxford B.Litt. 1951.

7485   Jamaican economic development, 1840 to 1865. D.G.H. Hall. London Ph.D. 1954.

7486   The governorships of Sir Henry Barkly in British Guiana and Jamaica. D.D. Rooney. Oxford B.Litt. 1953.

7487   Constitutional problems in Jamaica, 1850-66. C.V. Gocking. Oxford D.Phil. 1955.

7488   Political and constitutional developments in the Leeward Islands, 1854-71. A. de V. Phillips. London M.A. 1964.

7489   The British West Indian sugar industry, 1865-1900. R.W. Beachey. Edinburgh Ph.D. 1951.

7490   Crown colony government in Jamaica, 1865-85. F.R. Augier. St. Andrews Ph.D. 1954.

7491   Trends in the West Indian economy, 1870-1913. W.G. Demas. Cambridge M.Litt. 1956.

7492   The development of the law of succession in the West Indies. N.J.O. Liverpool. Sheffield Ph.D. 1965.

7493   Crown colony government in Trinidad, 1870-97. H.B.D. Johnson. Oxford D.Phil. 1970.

7494   Barbados and the confederation question, 1871-85. A.D.B. Hamilton. London Ph.D. (Ext.) 1947.

7495   The Colonial Office and problems of constitutional reform in Jamaica, Trinidad and British Guiana, 1880-1903. H.A. Will. London Ph.D. 1968.

Indentured immigration into Trinidad, 1891-1916. R. 7496
Shiels. Oxford B.Litt. 1967.
The political development of British Guiana since 1891. 7497
J.W. Harper-Smith. Oxford B.Litt. 1964.
The development of local government and administration 7498
in British Guiana. J.A.E. Young. Oxford B.Litt. 1956.
The rise and development of labour movements in the 7499
British Caribbean, with particular reference to British
Guiana, Jamaica and Trinidad. F.X. Mark. Edinburgh Ph.D.
1959.
The British West Indies in Anglo-American relations, 7500
1895-1940. C.L.McC. Joseph. London M.A. 1965.
The government of the British colonies in the West 7501
Indies. H.H. Wrong. Oxford B.Litt. 1921.
Constitutional and political development of Trinidad, 7502
1898-1925. B. Samaroo. London Ph.D. 1969.
Middle-class colonial politics: a study of Guyana, with 7503
special reference to the period 1920-31. H.A. Lutchman.
Manchester Ph.D. 1967.
Politics and constitution-making in the eastern group 7504
of the British West Indies, 1922 to the present day. C.A.
Hughes. London Ph.D. 1952.
Political change in British Honduras. C.H. Grant. 7505
Edinburgh Ph.D. 1969.
Constitutional development and political change in 7506
Jamaica, 1944-62. T.St.C. Munroe. Oxford D.Phil. 1969.

For Cuba, see under CENTRAL AND SOUTH AMERICA

CENTRAL AND SOUTH AMERICA

The tribes of the Argentine and Paraguayan Chaco: 7507
their history and cultural progress. H.J.L. Norman. Bristol
M.A. 1951.
Sixteenth-century Venezuela. A. Jefferies. Durham 7508
M.Litt. 1955.
The Audiencia of New Galicia in the 16th century: a 7509
study in Spanish colonial government. J.H. Parry. Cambridge
Ph.D. 1939.
The Santa Casa da Misericórdia of Bahia: a social 7510
study, 1550-1750. A.J.R. Russell-Wood. Oxford D.Phil. 1967.
Silver mining and society in Zacatecas, 1550-1700: the 7511
early history of a Mexican mining town. P.J. Bakewell.
Cambridge Ph.D. 1969.
Geographical change in Venezuelan Guayana, 1600-1880. 7512
D.J. Robinson. London Ph.D. 1967.
The attack and defence of Peru in the 17th century. 7513
P.T. Bradley. Leeds Ph.D. 1969.
Letras Anuas de la Provincia del Paraguay de los Anos 7514
de 1626 y 1627. R. Offor. London Ph.D. 1926.
The Company of Adventurers to the islands of Providence 7515
and Henrietta, its foundation and history, 1630-4. A.P.
Newton. London M.A. 1910.
The career of Melchor de Navarra y Rocafull, duque de 7516
la Plata, with special reference to his vice-regency in Peru,
1681-9. J.D. Hilton. Bristol M.Litt. 1967.
The Galeones and Flotas in Spain's American trade, with 7517
special reference to the period 1700-35. G.J. Walker. Cambridge Ph.D. 1964.
Mexico, Manila, Andalusia: consulado rivalry and 7518
American trade, 1704-34. N.P. Cushner. London Ph.D. 1968.
British activities in Yucatan and on the Moskito Shore 7519
in the 18th century. J. McLeish. London M.A. 1926.
The British superintendency of the Mosquito Shore, 7520
1749-87. W.S. Sorsby. London Ph.D. 1969.

7521   Ecclesiastical immunity in New Spain, 1760-1815. Mrs. Nancy M. Marx. London Ph.D. 1965.

7522   Society and administration in late 18th-century Guanajuato, with especial reference to the silver mining industry. D.A. Brading. London Ph.D. 1965.

7523   Pernambuco, 1770-1920: an historical geography. J.H. Galloway. London Ph.D. 1965.

7524   The role of the Spanish peninsular merchants in Oaxaca on the eve of Mexican independence, 1780-1820: a study of the decay of confidence in the Spanish imperial government. B.R. Hamnett. Cambridge Ph.D. 1968.

7525   The intendant system in the Viceroyalty of La Plata, 1782-1810. J. Lynch. London Ph.D. 1955.

7526   The intendant system in Peru, 1784-1814. J.R. Fisher. London M.Phil. 1967.

7527   The development of British enterprise in Argentina, 1806-95. H.S. Ferns. Cambridge Ph.D. 1951.

7528   British influences in the independence of the River Plate provinces, with special reference to the period 1806 to 1816. J. Street. Cambridge Ph.D. 1951.

7529   Britain, Spain and the slave trade to Cuba, 1807-45. D.R. Murray. Cambridge Ph.D. 1967.

7530   Historical study of Anglo-South American trade, with special reference to the period 1807-25. J.S. Jones. London Ph.D. 1934.

7531   Ideas and politics in Chile, 1808-33. S.D.W. Collier. Cambridge Ph.D. 1965.

7532   British interest in the independence of Mexico, 1808-27. W.F. Cody. London Ph.D. 1954.

7533   The relations between Great Britain and the Spanish colonies, 1808-12. A.I. Langnas. London Ph.D. 1938.

7534   The evolution of the Argentine from 1810. H.J. Savory. Manchester M.A. 1937.

7535   Great Britain and the suppression of the Cuban slave trade, 1817-65. L.H. Cawte. London M.A. 1934.

7536   Anglo-Peruvian commercial and financial relations, 1820-65, with special reference to Antony Gibbs & Sons and the guano trade. W.M. Mathew. London Ph.D. 1964.

7537   Anglo-American rivalry in Mexico and South America. E.J. Pratt. Oxford D.Phil. 1928/9.

7538   The part played by Great Britain in the separation of Brazil from Portugal, 1821-5. J.W.W. Liddicoat. London M.A. 1927.

7539   Evangelical worship in Brazil: its origins and development. C.J. Hahn. Edinburgh Ph.D. 1970.

7540   British capital, commerce and diplomacy in Latin America, Independence to 1914 - intervention or abstention? D.C.St.M. Platt. Oxford D.Phil. 1962.

7541   Anglo-Brazilian commercial relations and the evolution of Brazilian tariff policy, 1822-50. A.J. Pryor. Cambridge Ph.D. 1965.

7542   The attitude of France to the South American colonies, 1822-6. W.E. Edwards. Cambridge Ph.D. 1932/3.

7543   Some aspects of Mexican political history, 1824-46. S. Hjartarson. Edinburgh M.Litt. 1968.

7544   British investment in South America and the financial crisis of 1825-6. M.J. Fenn. Durham M.A. 1969.

7545   The evolution of the frontiers and boundaries of Bolivia. Mrs. Joan V. Fifer. London Ph.D. 1964.

7546   Great Britain and the abolition of the Brazilian slave trade, 1830-52. L.M. Bethell. London Ph.D. 1963.

7547   A re-interpretation of the guano age, 1840-80. J.M. Maiguashca. Oxford D.Phil. 1968.

7548   The political career of Bartolomé Mitre, 1852-91. A.J. Walford. London Ph.D. 1940.

7549   Buenos Aires and the Argentine confederation, 1852-61. A.J. Walford. London M.A. 1934.

The mission to Spain of Pierre Soulé, 1853-5, a study   7550
in the Cuban diplomacy of the United States, with special
reference to contemporary opinion. A.A. Ettinger. Oxford
D.Phil. 1929/30.

British relations with Mexico, 1859-62. R.B. Chapman.   7551
Oxford B.Litt. 1936.

The activities of Spain on the Pacific coast of South   7552
America, and her war with the Confederation of the Andes
(Chile, Peru, Bolivia and Ecuador), 1860-86. J.G.S. Ward.
London Ph.D. 1939.

The establishment of Maximilian's empire in Mexico. D.   7553
Dawson. Cambridge M.Litt. 1925.

Anglo-American rivalries in Latin America, 1865-95. J.   7554
Smith. London Ph.D. 1970.

Agricultural colonisation and society in the Argentina   7555
Republic: the province of Santa Fé, 1870-95. E.L. Gallo.
Oxford D.Phil. 1970.

The role of foreign trade and migration in the develop-   7556
ment of the Argentine economy, 1875-1914. V. Vázquez-Presedo.
Oxford D.Phil. 1968.

The Cuban question in Spanish Restoration politics,   7557
1878-98. F.J.D. Lambert. Oxford D.Phil. 1969.

A study of the gold standard with special reference to   7558
Argentina, 1880-1914: its failure and success. A.G. Ford.
Oxford D.Phil. 1956.

The Chilean revolution of 1891: a study in the domestic   7559
and international history of Chile. H. Blakemore. London
Ph.D. 1955.

Aftermath of the War of the Pacific: a study in the   7560
foreign policy of Chile, 1891-6. M.G. Varley. Cambridge
Ph.D. 1969.

Anglo-American relations, 1895-8, with special refer-   7561
ence to the Venezuelan boundary dispute. K. Evans. London
M.A. (Ext.) 1955.

The work and policy of the United States in Panama.   7562
C.B. Wallis. Cambridge M.Litt. 1939.

Anglo-American relations with regard to the Panama   7563
Canal project, 1897-1903. S.P. Kramer. Cambridge M.Litt.
1938.

British policy towards the United States of America,   7564
with special reference to the isthmian question, 1898-1901.
G.W. Barrett. London M.A. (Ext.) 1953.

The Mexican revolution, 1910-14; the diplomacy of   7565
Anglo-American conflict. P.A.R. Calvert. Cambridge Ph.D.
1964.

The social structure of the lower classes in San Sal-   7566
vador, central America; a case study of the social consequences of economic change. A.T. White. Cambridge Ph.D.
1969.

Rural teachers and social and political conflict in   7567
Mexico, 1921-40, with special reference to the states of
Michoacan and Campeche. D.L. Raby. Warwick Ph.D. 1970.

The Chilean radical party and the popular front, 1936-   7568
41. A. Bande. Oxford B.Litt. 1970.

Government policy and the export of manufactures from   7569
Brazil since 1939. J.T. Winpenny. East Anglia M.Phil. 1969.

A U S T R A L I A   A N D   N E W   Z E A L A N D

The pastoral industries of New Zealand - a study in   7570
economic geography. R.O. Buchanan. London Ph.D. 1932.

Criminal transportation, its theory and practice, with   7571
special reference to Australia. G.H. Fairs. Bristol M.A.
1932.

7572   The evolution of settlement in New Zealand: a study in historical geography. J.S. Duncan. London Ph.D. 1960.

7573   The evolution of modern land-settlement policy in Australasia. J.E.F. Jenks. Oxford B.Litt. 1930.

7574   The development of land policy in Australia with special reference to New South Wales (1788-1922). W.H. Wynne. Cambridge Ph.D. 1925/6.

7575   Constitutional development in New South Wales, 1788-1856. A.C.V. Melbourne. London Ph.D. 1930.

7576   The role of government in New South Wales, 1788-1855. N.D. McLachlan. London Ph.D. 1957.

7577   Macquarie, governor of New South Wales, 1809-21. B.H. Travers. Oxford B.Litt. 1949.

7578   Maori land tenure in the 19th century. I.H. Kawharu. Oxford B.Litt. 1958.

7579   New Zealand aspirations in the Pacific in the 19th century. A. Ross. Cambridge Ph.D. 1949.

7580   The influence of the evangelical spirit on a policy of trusteeship towards native races, as illustrated by the records of certain missionary societies dealing with New Zealand (1814-54). A.F. Madden. Oxford B.Litt. 1939.

7581   Early settlement in the South Island of New Zealand, with special reference to the North and East. R.K. Wilson. London M.A. 1947.

7582   The Australian banking and credit system. A.L.G. MacKay. Cambridge M.Litt. 1930/1.

7583   English activities on the north coast of Australia during the first half of the 19th century. Dora Howard. London M.A. 1924.

7584   Britain and the Australian colonies, 1818-31: the technique of government. J.J. Eddy. Oxford D.Phil. 1968.

7585   A study of the development of Catholic education in New South Wales, 1820-36. J.M. Keady. London M.Phil. 1970.

7586   British migration to Western Australia, 1829-50. M. Harris. London Ph.D. 1934.

7587   Geographical influences on the settlement of Swanland, Western Australia. R.A. Hymers. Oxford B.Litt. 1959.

7588   The quality of immigration into Eastern Australia before 1851. R.B. Madgwick. Oxford D.Phil. 1935.

7589   The squatter in New South Wales, 1830-45. C.L. Wilson. Manchester M.A. 1921.

7590   Imperial land administration in Australia, 1831-55. P.C. Burroughs. London Ph.D. 1964.

7591   The foundation of South Australia. R.J. Rudall. Oxford B.Litt. 1911.

7592   England and New Zealand. A.J. Harrop. Cambridge Ph.D. 1925/6.

7593   The colonisation of New Zealand. J.S. Marais. Oxford D.Phil. 1925.

7594   The colonisation of New Zealand by the New Zealand Company (1839 to 1843): a study of the Wakefield system in operation, including some comparison with emigration to other Australasian colonies. M.R.M. Turnbull. Oxford B.Litt. 1951.

7595   Briton and Maori: a comparative study of the relations between the races, 1840-8. S.E. Greville. London M.A. 1910.

7596   The constitutional history of the church in Australia. R.A. Giles. Oxford B.Litt. 1929.

7597   John Bede Polding, archbishop of Sydney. P. McCarthy. Oxford D.Phil. 1960.

7598   The nature and efficacy of the educational aims and policies of the non-Anglican protestant denominations in effecting educational change in New South Wales, 1844-80, set against the background of other operative factors. N.W. Saffin. London Ph.D. 1965.

7599   Radicalism and socialism in Eastern Australia, 1850-1910: a study of political ideas in relation to economic development. R.A. Gollan. London Ph.D. 1951.

The policy of Great Britain regarding Australia, 1850- 7600
1900. W.V. Teniswood. Edinburgh Ph.D. 1936.
The control of native affairs in New Zealand: a con- 7601
stitutional experiment and its consequences, 1855-70. B.J.
Dalton. Oxford D.Phil. 1956.
British migration to Australia, 1860-1914. F.K. Crow- 7602
ley. Oxford D.Phil. 1951.
Sir George Bowen's governorship of Queensland, 1859-67. 7603
N.I. Graham. London M.A. 1962.
The policy of the imperial government towards the re- 7604
cruitment and use of Pacific Island labour with special refer-
ence to Queensland, 1863-1901. O.W. Parnaby. Oxford D.Phil.
1953.
Land policy and the development of settlement in 7605
Queensland, 1868-94. G.P. Taylor. London Ph.D. 1966.
The London capital market and the flow of capital to 7606
Australia, 1870-1914. A.R. Hall. London Ph.D. 1951.
Australian company borrowing, 1870-93: a study in 7607
British overseas investment. J.D. Bailey. Oxford D.Phil.
1958.
Developmental policy and agricultural settlement in 7608
south-eastern Australia. J. Andrews. Cambridge Ph.D. 1936.
British influence on the federation of the Australian 7609
colonies, 1880-1901. B.K. de Garis. Oxford D.Phil. 1966.
The economic depression of Australia in the eighteen- 7610
nineties. E.A. Boehm. Oxford D.Phil. 1960.
A comparison of the constitutions of the United States 7611
and Australia. B. Jones. Wales M.A. 1924.
The working of federalism in Australia. L.C. Wilcher. 7612
Oxford B.Litt. 1933.
British policy to New South Wales, Queensland and 7613
Victoria during the secretaryship of state for the colonies
of the marquess of Ripon, 1892-5. L. Trainor. London Ph.D.
1967.
Anglo-Australian relations, 1901-14: a study at the 7614
official level. Margaret N. Lettice. Cambridge Ph.D. 1967.
Land prices and land valuation in New Zealand (with 7615
special reference to the North Island, 1909-48). H.B. Low.
London Ph.D. 1951.
Social relations between Great Britain and Australia, 7616
1919-39. A.G. Serle. Oxford D.Phil. 1950.
Democratic planning in Australia, 1919-39. C.E. 7617
Fleming. Oxford B.Litt. 1949.

P A C I F I C   O C E A N   A N D   I S L A N D S

The exploration of the South Sea, 1519 to 1644: a study 7618
of the influence of physical factors, with a reconstruction
of the routes of the explorers. Helen M. Wallis. Oxford
D.Phil. 1954.
The occupation of the Falkland Islands. W.C. Down. 7619
Cambridge Ph.D. 1926/7.
European penetration of the South Pacific, 1779-1842. 7620
J.W. Davidson. Cambridge Ph.D. 1942.
Samuel Marsden: a pioneer of civilisation in the South 7621
Seas. S.M. Johnstone. Belfast M.A. 1928.
British missionaries in the south-west Pacific, 1842- 7622
1900: their policies and evaluations with regard to the indi-
genous peoples. J.D. Kesby. Oxford B.Litt. 1963.
The geography of Samoa about 1840. R.F. Watters. Lon- 7623
don Ph.D. 1956.
International relations between Great Britain, Germany 7624
and the United States in the Samoan Islands. Mrs. Lilian M.
Williams. Wales M.A. 1938.

7625   International rivalry in Samoa, 1845-84. Mrs. Sylvia R. Smith. London M.A. 1933.

7626   British policy towards Fiji, 1858-80, with special reference to the evolution, under Sir Arthur Gordon, of indirect rule as a theory and a technique for the government of a native people. J.D. Legge. Oxford D.Phil. 1953.

7627   Racial issues in Fiji. C.A.A. Hughes. Oxford D.Phil. 1965.

7628   The geographical exploration of Papua, 1870-1900. Brenda Hughes. Liverpool M.A. 1958/9.

7629   The Western Pacific High Commission, 1877-88: its creation and problems of administration. J.A. Boutilier. London Ph.D. 1969.

7630   The administration of New Guinea, 1888-1902. R.B. Joyce. Cambridge M.Litt. 1953.

7631   The career of Sir John Thurston, governor of Fiji, 1888-97. J. Millington. London M.A. 1947.

7632   The partition of the Samoan Islands, 1898-9. P.M. Kennedy. Oxford D.Phil. 1970.

7633   British foreign policy, with special reference to relations with America, in the Pacific area, 1903-11. B. Sanders. London M.A. 1964.

I N D E X

References are to numbers, not to pages

(i)

AUTHORS

Ali, A., 6564
Ali, B. Sheik, see Sheik Ali
Ali, M., 6558
Ali, M.M., 6718
Al-Khatrash, F.M., 6025
Al-Khowayter, A.A., 6117
Allan, Bessie B.F., 5049
Allan, D.G.C., 2846
Allan, K., 5232
Allan, Mary B.G., 3836
Allchin, A.M., 5408
Allen, A.T., 4523
Allen, B., 925
Allen, G., 7469
Allen, G.C. (Birmingham M.Com.),
   3975
Allen, G.C. (Birmingham Ph.D.),
   4956
Allen, G.R., 3051
Allen, Helen M., 7455
Allen, J.B.L., 4283
Allen, R. (Belfast M.A.), 3583
Allen, R. (Belfast Ph.D.), 4464
Allerston, Pamela, 443
Allerton, Ethel, 1936
Allin, W.E., 3449
Allison, K.J., 2518
Allison, R. (London M.A.), 422
Allison, R. (London Ph.D.),
   3284
Allmand, C.T., 629
Allmark, K.H., 2584
Allo, Elizabeth M., see Isichei
Allsebrook, W.B.J., 2669
Alpers, E.A., 6209
Alphonso, Violet I., 6714
Altschuler, E.D., 5100
Alty, Winifred, 1372
Al-Wohaibi, A., 5933
Ambrose, G.P., 5971
Ameerali, A.C.L., 6921
Ameller Vacaflor, J., 791
Amenumey, D.E.K., 6387
Amit, M., 165
Andalib-i-Shadani, W.H., 42
Anderson, A.H., 1667
Anderson, Alexander, 5646
Anderson, Annie, 1414
Anderson, B.L., 3933
Anderson, J., 104
Anderson, J.D., 1341
Anderson, Kitty, 2886
Anderson, M.S., 2301
Anderson, M.W., 2218
Anderson, Malcolm, 2092
Anderson, Mary A. (London M.A.),
   2069
Anderson, Mary A. (London
   Ph.D.), 4738
Anderson, Michael, 5284
Anderson, R.D., 2066
Anderson, Sonia P., 5976
Anderson, T.S., 7290
Anderton, Marjorie J., 823
Anderton, N.G., 3716
Andradi, W.M.D.D., 6928

Andrew, C.M., 2086
Andrew, J.D., 3513
Andrews, D.H.B., 5602
Andrews, H.C., 4501
Andrews, J., 7608
Andrews, John H., 3952
Andrews, Julia H., 4542
Andrews, K.R., 2782
Andrews, L.I. (London M.A.),
   5531
Andrews, L.I. (London Ph.D.),
   5533
Andrews, L.S., 3436
Andrews, P.H. (London M.A.),
   5689
Andrews, P.H. (London Ph.D.),
   5561
Andrews, R.M., 2012
Andrews, W.S., 4180
Andritch, Y., 723
Anene, J.C.O. (London M.A.),
   6417
Anene, J.C.O. (London Ph.D.),
   6409
Angles, Judith A.P., 355
Anglin, D.G., 7255
Anglo, S., 3160
Angold, M.J., 540
Angus, F.J.G., 3278
Anis, M.A., 6121
Anjorin, A.O., 6420
Ankawi, A.A., 6113
Ansari, M.A.A., 6562
Ansell, Patricia M., 3652
Anstey, R.T., 6273
Anthony, David W., 2352
Anthony, Douglas W., 7115
Anthony, Ilid E., 342
Anthony-Jones, W.J., 5033
Anwar, M.R., 6762
Applebaum, S.E. (Oxford B.Litt.),
   324
Applebaum, S.E. (Oxford D.Phil.),
   341
Applegate, Nancy, 2277
Appleton, J.H., 5144
Apps, Margaret U., 1533
Apted, M.R., 3227
Araneta, A.S., 7044
Aranya, N., 4906
Arasaratnam, S., 6900
Archer, A.B., 3719
Archer, A.J., 5251
Archer, Elizabeth, 1922
Archer, J.L., 2850
Archer, Margaret (Liverpool
   M.A.), 1317
Archer, Margaret (Oxford
   B.Litt.), 1318
Archibald, F.E., 7193
Arditti, Cynthia I., 4629
Argov, D., 6817
Arhin, P.K., 6354
Aristidou, I., 4961
Arkell, A.J., 6528
Armayor, O.K., 13

292

Armistead, C.D., 4800
Armitage, Susan M.H., 4712
Armour, C., 3946
Armour, W.S., 6460
Armstrong, A., 4176
Armstrong, D.L., 5858
Armstrong, G.G., 4190
Armstrong, H., 2035
Armstrong, N.L., 4902
Armstrong, W.A., 5728
Arnheim, M.T.W., 225
Arnold, H.G., 2127
Asghar, K.G., 6531
Ashby, E.G., 1585
Ashley, Annie, 2151
Ashley, M.P., 2816
Ashman, R.G., 4222
Ashmore, E., 2123
Ashraf, K.M., 6529
Ashton, R., 2809
Ashur, M.S., 6156
Ashworth, G.J., 2500
Ashworth, Margaret M., 3735
Ashworth, W., 5304
Asiegbu, J.U.J., 6062
Aslam, M., 6567
Aspin, Isabel S.T., 1421
Aspinall, A. (Manchester M.A.),
6648
Aspinall, A. (Manchester Ph.D.),
3754
Aspinwall, B., 3826
Aspy, F.C. Walden-, see Walden-
Aspy
Aster, S., 2395
Aston, Margaret E., 865
Atherton, A.J., 2836
Atiya, A.S., 550
Atiyyah, G.R., 6036
Atkin, C.W., 479
Atkin, J.M., 4928
Atkins, Elsie M., 3837
Atkinson, B.J., 4853
Atkinson, Beryl L., 998
Atkinson, G.C., 7369
Atkinson, Patricia B., 1068
Atkinson, T., 3181
Atta, A.M.O., 6200
Atto, C.H., 4302
Auerbach, Erna, 3161
Augier, F.R., 7490
Auld, Muriel, 239
Austen, B., 3385
Austin, M.M., 134
Austin, M.R. (Birmingham M.A.),
5393
Austin, M.R. (London Ph.D.), 4186
Auty, Phyllis, 1350
Avakumović, I. (London M.A.),
1842
Avakumović, I. (Oxford D.Phil.),
1882
Avari, B.J., 4986
Avery, M.D., 4952
Avery, Margaret E., 957
Avi-Yonah, M., 5892

Avrutick, Judith B., 960
Awad, B.A. el L., 40
Awe, Bolanle A., 6389
Axtell, J.L., 4286
Ayandele, E.A., 6401
Ayantuga, O.O., 6388
Aydelotte, J.E., 4127
Aydelotte, W.O., 6066
Ayers, Gwendoline M., 5303
Aylmer, G.E., 2708
Ayres, Elizabeth A., 977
Ayres, G.L., 4922
Ayscough, H.H., 5228
Aziz, K.K., 6853
Aziz, S.M.A., 6767

BABBAGE, S.B., 3057
Baber, F.T., 481
Badger, Stella M., 600
Badian, E., 190
Baggally, J.W., 2206
Bagwell, P.S., 2191
Baha, Lal, 6849
Baig, M.Q., 6565
Bailey, A.F. (Manchester M.A.),
7372
Bailey, A.F. (Manchester Ph.D.),
7383
Bailey, D.S., 2958
Bailey, J.D., 7607
Bailey, M.H., 5440
Bailey, R.N., 1492
Baillie, H.C., 3159
Baily, R.C.J.F., 3299
Bain, A., 5774
Bain, D.S., 2026
Bain, Gillian L., 7419
Bain, R.E., 7436
Bainbridge, T.H., 3337
Baines, Priscilla J., 5216
Bains, Irene, 6402
Bairstow, L., 5289
Bajpai, S.G., 6513
Baker, A.R.H., 409
Baker, Audrey M., 1511
Baker, E.W., 4220
Baker, Edith E., 7346
Baker, F., 4142
Baker, G.F., 5260
Baker, J.A.C., 3372
Baker, J.H., 954
Baker, J.N.L., 7169
Baker, K.M., 1976
Baker, L.G.D., 1347
Baker, N., 7178
Baker, R.F., 3399
Baker, R.L., 6138
Baker, W.J., 5382
Baker-Smith, M.P.D., 1908
Bakewell, P.J., 7511
Bakhiet, G.M.A., 6199
Bakir, A.M., 6095
Bal, S.S., 6740
Balasingham, S.V., 6926
Baldwin, J.R., 2057
Baliga, B.S., 6684

293

Ball, Enid, 3775
Ball, F.E., 4128
Ball, F.J., 3328
Ball, J., 4001
Ball, J.N., 2707
Ball, Marion A.V., 3138
Ball, Nancy (Birmingham M.A.), 5523
Ball, Nancy (Keele Ph.D.), 5582
Balley, E.J., 3035
Ballhatchet, K., 6695
Ballinger, R.B., 3608
Balls, F.E., 5505
Baltzell, E.R., 4587
Bamforth, Winifred, 6006
Bande, A., 7568
Bandyopadhyay, P., 6835
Banerjee, A.C., 6717
Banerjee, T., 6632
Banerji, R.N. (London M.A.), 6597
Banerji, R.N. (London Ph.D.), 6593
Banerji, S., 6550
Banks, J.A., 5285
Banks, Olive L., 5640
Banks, R.F., 4995
Bann, S., 101
Bannerman, J.W.M., 1666
Barber, A.V., 7269
Barber, F.H., 2894
Barber, G.G., 3865
Barber, M.C., 774
Barber, Madeline J., 1094
Barford, Kate E., 2839
Bargman, A., 1747
Bari, A.F.M.A., 6844
Bari, M.A., 6644
Barkakoty, A.K., 6977
Barker, E.E. (London M.A.), 1524
Barker, E.E. (London Ph.D.), 56
Barker, P.A., 1602
Barker, R.S., 5514
Barker, T.C., 5729
Barkley, J.M., 5834
Barlow, F. (Oxford B.Litt.), 1231
Barlow, F. (Oxford D.Phil.), 716
Barmann, L.F., 5375
Barnard, G.L., 3515
Barnard, H.C., 1943
Barnes, Annie M., 1940
Barnes, B., 4525
Barnes, F.R., 1018
Barnes, Marjorie W., 4000
Barnes, Patricia M., 1008
Barnes, S.E., 5696
Barnes, T.G., 3193
Barnett, A.J., 158
Barnett, D.C., 4114
Barnett, R.W., 7140
Barnett, T.R., 1670
Barnett, W.E.R., 6118
Barnsby, G.J. (Birmingham M.A.), 4822
Barnsby, G.J. (Birmingham Ph.D.), 5221

Barnwell, S.B., 2068
Baron, G., 5699
Barooah, N.K., 6675
Barpujari, H., 6964
Barr, P.M., 7102
Barratt, Dorothy M., 2932
Barratt, J.K., 950A
Barrett, Cynthia E., 6706
Barrett, G.W., 7564
Barrett, J.A., 5089
Barron, Caroline M., 1584
Barron, J.P., 147
Barron, T.J., 4727
Barrow, G.L., 5838
Barrow, G.W.S., 1673
Barrow, R.H., 248
Barrow, Winifred M., 4369
Barry, V.A.A., 1939
Bartels, F.L., 6358
Bartle, G.F., 4544
Bartle, R.H., 1432
Bartle, S.H., 291
Bartlett, C.J., 2459
Bartlett, H. Moyse-, see Moyse-Bartlett
Bartlett, J.N., 1575
Bartley, A.J., 4345
Barton, E.W., 4033
Barton, F., 1255
Barty, Elisabeth, 1491
Barua, A.C., 6970
Barua, B., 6956
Basaviah, K., 6709
Basham, A.L., 6465
Bashir, A., 6563
Baskin, S.L., 4909
Bassett, D.K., 6989
Bassett, T.M., 3206
Bassett, W.G., 7431
Bastiampillai, B.E.St.J., 6930
Bastin, J.S., 7004
Bastow, J., 5567
Basu, Anjali, 6580
Basu, Aparna, 6838
Basu, P., 6647
Basu, T., 6449
Batcheler, Lilian E.M., 3934
Bate, F., 3126
Bate, W., 5309
Bater, J.H., 2343
Bates, D.N., 5178
Bates, D.R., 708
Bates, Margaret L., 6268
Bather, L., 5009
Batho, G.R., 2910
Bathurst, R.D., 5974
Battersby, R.J., 5191
Battersby, W.J., 4310
Baugh, D.A., 3897
Baumber, M.L., 2797
Bawden, C.R., 7064
Baxendale, A.S., 6248
Baxter, J.W., 3212
Baxter, R.J., 4704
Baxter, S.B., 3642
Baxter, W.T., 7268
Bayley, C.C., 938

Baylis, B.E., 2567
Baylis, Gertrude, 4939
Bayliss, D.G., 480
Bayliss, G.M., 4689
Bayly, C.A., 6811
Bazeley, Margaret L., 1061
Bazire, Joyce, 1234
Beachey, R.W., 7489
Beacroft, B.W., 5159
Beaglehole, C.H., 4156
Beaglehole, J.C., 3300
Beaglehole, J.H., 6866
Beaglehole, T.H., 6650
Beale, J.M., 2615
Beales, A.C.F., 3805
Beales, D.E.D., 2255
Beamish, Lucia K., 4217
Bean, J.M.W., 1096
Beard, D.L., 7264
Beard, G.W., 4328
Beard, Marie K., 5318
Beard, R., 3791
Beardwood, Alice (Oxford
   B.Litt.), 1131
Beardwood, Alice (Oxford
   D.Phil.), 1130
Beasley, W.G., 7088
Beastall, T.W., 5198
Beattie, J.M., 3673
Beaumont, H., 2735
Beaumont, Olga, 2508
Beavan, Pauline E., 6295
Beavington, F., 5192
Bebb, E.D., 4202
Bebb, W.A., 2514
Bebbington, P.S., 3967
Beck, Joan, 2552
Beck, K.M., 4132
Becket, Edith M., 5542
Beckett, J.C., 4465
Beckles, N.I., 5782
Bedale, Joan E., 1971
Beddard, R.A., 4164
Beddoe, Deirdre, 852
Beddow, J.F.H., 3648
Beebee, Ethel M., 2712
Beech, Elsie, 5749
Beevers, R.H., 7365
Begbie, Cynthia M., 694
Belasco, P.S. (London M.Sc.),
   3854
Belasco, P.S. (London Ph.D.),
   3848
Belham, P., 4314
Bell, A.D., 4846
Bell, E.M., 242
Bell, G.E., 5134
Bell, J.A.M., 5468
Bell, J.B., 7266
Bell, K., 6007
Bell, Margaret H., 729
Bell, P.M.H., 2105
Bellamy, J.G. (Nottingham M.A.),
   975
Bellamy, J.G. (Nottingham Ph.D.),
   951

Bellamy, Joyce M., 5704
Beller, E.A., 2113
Bellord, Joan E.M., 3066
Beloff, M., 3806
Benecke, G., 2115
Benewick, R.J., 4717
Benfield, R.B.I., 595
Ben-Israel, Hedva, 102
Bennell, A.S., 6664
Bennell, J.E.G., 2864
Bennett, D.H.C., 497
Bennett, G.V., 4181
Bennett, H.J.R., 4835
Bennett, J.A.W., 4274
Bennett, J.H., 5454
Bennett, Jennifer A., 4826
Bennett, N.R., 7135
Bennett, R., 3913
Bennett, W.H., 200
Bennison, J., 1106
Benson, E., 3528
Bent, I.D., 888
Bentham, Rosie, 5750
Bentley, G.E., 3166
Bentley, W., 5604
Benyon, J.A., 6305
Berger, Elena L., 6329
Berghahn, V.R., 2175
Berlas, Aquila B., 6712
Bernal, M.G., 7143
Berry, C.A.F., 348
Berry, D., 4366
Berryman, M., 637
Bertie, J., 4785
Bertrand, R., 7233
Beshir, B.I., 5946
Beshir, M.O., 6186
Best, Alice M., 903
Best, G.F.A., 3749
Bethell, D.L.T., 1202
Bethell, J.P., 3377
Bethell, L.M., 7546
Betley, J.A., 1787
Bettey, J.H., 5383
Betts, C.J., 1938
Betts, Marina A.R., 820
Betts, R.S., 2288
Bevan, B.D., 5692
Beyer, J.T., 6673
Beynon, O., 3994
Bhai, H.S., 6771
Bharucha, K.B., 6671
Bhattacharya, B.C., 6781
Bhattacharya, S., 6711
Bhattacharyya, Anima, 6799
Bhattacharyya, Sukumar, 6592
Bhattacharyya, Sureshchandra,
   6485
Bhuyan, S.K., 6962
Bibby, Edna, 2992
Bickerstaffe, D., 4566
Biddiss, M.D., 2056
Bidwell, R.L., 6092
Bienefeld, M.A., 3331
Bier, Elizabeth S., 4266
Bigby, Dorothy A., 1928

Biggs, Winifred, 209
Billingham, P.H., 2748
Billington, J.H., 2348
Billington, L., 4833
bin Ahmat, Sharom, 7028
Bindoff, S.T., 2286
Binfield, J.C.G., 5446
Binford, H.C., 5292
Bingle, R.J., 6690
Binney, J.E.D., 3936
Binns, June R., 3587
Biobaku, S.O., 6382
Birch, Alan (Manchester M.A.),
    5052
Birch, Alan (Manchester Ph.D.),
    3349
Birch, Alison, 1520
Birch, G.C., 4234
Birch, T.W., 470
Birchall, I.H., 110
Birchall, Mary N., 1093
Bird, Ruth, 869
Birdsall, Christine M., 465
Birkhead, E., 5165
Birley, A.R., 292
Birmingham, D.B., 6340
Biro, S.S., 1778
Birrell, Jean R., 1573
Birtles, A., 5566
Birtwhistle, T.M., 3829
Birtwistle, C., 5535
Bishop, A.S., 5518
Bishop, C.D., 326
Bishop, E.W. (London M.A.), 1995
Bishop, E.W. (London Ph.D.),
    3153
Bishop, G.D. (London M.A.), 1411
Bishop, G.D. (London Ph.D.),
    3497
Bishop, J.S., 2517
Bishop, T.J.H., 5272
Bitensky, Maybelle F., 6298
Bivar, A.D.H., 5906
Black, A.J., 755
Black, Alison H., 7065
Black, C.F., 2226
Black, Christine J., 2645
Black, S.F., 2714
Blacker, J.G.C., 1979
Blackett, J.F., 5339
Blackledge, R., 4527
Blackman, G.L., 2965
Blackmore, J.H., 2551
Blackwood, B.G., 3196
Blackwood, R., 5790
Blair, C., 3162
Blake, D.W., 1192
Blake, E.O., 1343
Blake, J.B., 1127
Blake, J.W., 6339
Blake, Mary B., 2425
Blake, W.J., 2661
Blake-Hill, P.V., see Hill,
    P.V.B.
Blakemore, H., 7559
Blance, Thelma, 3575

Blanchard, I.S.W., 1119
Blanchet, J., 5684
Bland, David Edward (Durham
    M.Litt.), 4911
Bland, David Edward (Sheffield
    Ph.D.), 3844
Blanning, T.C.W., 2120
Blatcher, Marjorie, 958
Bleakley, D.W., 5869
Blewett, N., 4685
Blinkhorn, R.M., 2464
Blockley, R.C., 30
Blouet, B.W., 2295
Blumberg, N.B., 2178
Blumenau, R.K., 669
Blundell, D.W., 3386
Blunden, J.R., 1025
Blunden, Margaret A., 4667
Blunt, A.F., 1754
Blutman, Sandra, 4336
Blyton, Mabel H., 54
Boahen, A.A., 6122
Boal, F.W., 513
Boast, W.J., 743
Boden, Caroline E., 3175
Bodonhelyi, J., 3222
Body, G.A., 4109
Boehm, E.A., 7610
Bogomas, E., 2380
Bohn, R.P., 3106
Bolam, C.G., 3466
Bolchini, P., 2258
Bolsover, G.H., 2340
Bolt, Christine A., 7356
Bolton, Brenda M., 1029
Bolton, C.A., 2247
Bolton, Diane K., 1426
Bolton, G.C., 4485
Bolton, P.A., 3592
Bolton, Winifred T.H., 3669
Bolwell, L.H., 4529
Bond, B.J., 4872
Bone, T.R., 5804
Bonine, R.P., 2387
Bonner, Edna R., 6840
Bonsall, B., 3694
Booker, Agatha, 1749
Boon, E.P., 460
Boone, Gladys, 3448
Boorman, D.W., 3089
Booth, Millicent, 1910
Booth, N.H., 5050
Booth, T., 1000
Boothroyd, K.H., 4816
Borpujari, J.G., 6606
Bose, N.S., 6523
Bosher, J.F., 1945
Bosher, R.S., 4155
Bossy, J.A., 3016
Boswell, Katharine C., 401
Bosworth, C.E., 5948
Bosworth, R.J.B., 2264
Botsford, R.M., 7350
Bottomley, A.F., 1586
Boulind, R.H., 7413
Boulton, Helen E., 1066

Boulton-Jones, J.K., 4185
Boultwood, Myrtle E.A., 4268
Bourde, A.J.M.A., 1964
Bourdillon, A.F. Claudine, 1386
Bourne, K., 4751
Boutilier, J.A., 7629
Bowden, P.J., 2521
Bowen, E.M., 4917
Bowen, G., 2556
Bowen, H.G., 3894
Bowersock, G.W., 214
Bowes, Ida, 4492
Bowler, Eileen E.M., 3408
Bowman, H.O., 3261
Bowmer, J.C., 3493
Boyce, D.G., 4707
Boyd, H., 3271
Boyle, L.E., 731
Boyle, T., 4775
Boynton, L.O.J., 2781
Boyson, R. (London Ph.D.), 5061
Boyson, R. (Manchester M.A.),
  5264
Braae, G.P., 5345
Bracewell, C.C., 6630
Bracken, J.R., 2030
Brackenridge, R.D., 3558
Brackwell, C., 5392
Bradburn, W., 3968
Braddock, A.P., 3505
Brademas, S.J., 2463
Bradfield, B.T., 4545
Brading, D.A., 7522
Bradley, Annie, 6617
Bradley, C., 3696
Bradley, Constance V., 3359
Bradley, J., 1865
Bradley, P.T., 7513
Brady, Helen, 2682
Brady, J.D., 1344
Brady, L.W., 4646
Brady, Mary E., 4467
Brailey, N.J., 7015
Brailsford, D.W., 2574
Braithwaite, A.W., 25
Brameld, Nina M., 3171
Brampton, C.K., 579
Bramwell, R.D. (Birmingham M.A.),
  4512
Bramwell, R.D. (Durham Ph.D.),
  5598
Brand, C.P., 4339
Brand, Jeanne L., 5325
Brandon, P.F., 407
Brandon, S.G.F., 311
Brandt, J.A., 2461
Branfoot, Anne I.S., 2346
Branford, W.G., 5760
Brash, W.B., 1450
Brathwaite, L.E., 7445
Bready, J.W., 5246
Brebner, J.B., 7184
Bredahl Petersen, M.A.F., 2396
Breeze, D.J., 283
Breiseth, C.N., 3773
Brennan, E.J.T., 5512

Brennan, Margaret P., 531
Brenner, Y.S., 1141
Brentano, R.J., 1250
Brett, E.A., 6267
Brett, Martin, 1194
Brett, Michael, 35
Brettle, L., 5122
Breuning, Eleonore C.M., 2187
Breward, I., 3037
Brewer, J., 7262
Brewer, R.C., 5846
Brewer, W.D.D., 2133
Brewin, Kathleen A., 2842
Briault, E.W.H., 3444
Brice, I.D., 2732
Bridbury, A.R., 1125
Bridge, F.R., 1869
Bridges, R.C., 6211
Bridges, Shirley F., 1474
Brien, Catherine, 766
Briers, Phyllis M., 1553
Brigg, G.T., 4224
Briggs, E.R., 1953
Brighton, J.T., 2736
Brightwell, P., 2432
Briley, J.R., 3148
Brimson, Blanche E., 1245
Brinkworth, Anne, 706
Brinkworth, E.R.C. (Birmingham
  M.A.), 2545
Brinkworth, E.R.C. (Oxford
  B.Litt.), 3077
Brinton, C., 3870
Briscoe, H.K., 5682
Briscoe, J., 297
Britnell, R.H., 1578
Brittenden, F.H., 2023
Britton, J.A., 5627
Britton, R., 2493
Broadbent, Mary J., 7287
Broadbridge, S.A., 5145
Broadbridge, S.R., 4039
Brock, P. de B., 735
Brock, R.E. (London M.A.), 2632
Brock, R.E. (London Ph.D.),
  2879
Brock, W.R., 3767
Brockbank, J.L., 3197
Brockett, A.A., 3467
Brockett, A.M., 6235
Brocklebank, R.S.G., 4519
Brockway, T.P., 7293
Brodie, Dorothy M., 2630
Brodkin, E.I., 6638
Bromiley, G.W., 98
Bromiley, W.P., 6299
Brook, F.G., 5647
Brook, R., 4877
Brooke, D., 5131
Brooke, P.C., 1213
Brooke, Rosalind B., 767
Brooke, T.H., 2737
Brookfield, G.P., 1505
Brookfield, H.C., 3297
Brookfield, S.H., 2483
Brooks, E., 5058

Brooks, E.C., 3031
Brooks, N.P., 1333
Brooks, P.N., 2967
Broome, Dorothy M. (Manchester M.A.), 1016
Broome, Dorothy M. (Manchester Ph.D.), 1017
Broomfield, F., 1270
Broughton, C.R., 1356
Brown, A.E., 4801
Brown, A.K. Mensah-, see Mensah-Brown
Brown, A.L., 908
Brown, A.M., 2139
Brown, B.F., 3680
Brown, C.K.F. (Leeds M.A.), 2587
Brown, C.K.F. (Oxford B.Litt.), 5578
Brown, C.K.F. (Oxford D.Phil.), 5379
Brown, C.M., 5059
Brown, D., 4854
Brown, F.K., 3875
Brown, G.H., 2772
Brown, G.K., 2232
Brown, G.W., 6368
Brown, H.G., 3867
Brown, H.M., 4140
Brown, J., 5336
Brown, J.C., 956
Brown, J.F., 3731
Brown, J.P., 5093
Brown, Judith M., 6862
Brown, K.D., 4963
Brown, Kathryn V., 2227
Brown, L.H., 3720
Brown, L.T., 3582
Brown, Lucy M., 5114
Brown, M.C., 3063
Brown, R., 5004
Brown, R.A., 989
Brown, S.M., 563
Brown, W.E., 2129
Browne, G.P., 4752
Broxap, Mary, 840
Bruce, I.A.F., 10
Bruce, Sheila M., 2385
Brucker, G.A., 2228
Bruell, Julia L.C., 1098
Brumfitt, J.H., 93
Brunsdon, P.J., 3822
Bryant, F.R., 1889
Bryant, R.W.G., 3394
Bryant, W.N., 1020
Brydon, R.S., 3238
Bryer, A.A.M., 5955
Buchan, Alison M., see Hoppen
Buchanan, R.A., 4978
Buchanan, R.H., 4457
Buchanan, R.O., 7570
Buchan-Sydserff, Marjorie, 4370
Buckland, C.S.B., 1843
Buckland, P.J. (Belfast Ph.D.), 4694
Buckland, P.J. (Birmingham M.A.), 4692

Buckland, Patricia, 2639
Buckler, Georgina G., 537
Buckley, Annie, 946
Buckley, C.T.R., 3675
Buckley, H., 2804
Buckley, Jessie K., 4828
Buckley, K.A.H., 7246
Buckman, J., 5332
Buckner, P.A., 7218
Budd, Susan, 5315
Budge, G.M., 1219
Bünemann, R.J.P., 2155
Bueno de Mesquita, D.M., 591
Buisseret, D.J., 1916
Bull, G.B.G., 2496
Bullen, Maureen M., 7360
Bulley, J.A., 2525
Bulloch, J.B.P., 1675
Bullock, F.W.B., 2542
Bullough, Frances S., 3146
Bulst, C.M., 204
Bunce, M.F., 5199
Bunker, R.C., 4493
Bunnag, T., 7038
Buranelli, V.J., 1931
Burchell, R.A., 7338
Burden, G.H., 430
Burdick, E.L., 5023
Burford, Alison M., 156
Burgess, H.J. (London M.A.), 4321
Burgess, H.J. (London Ph.D.), 5577
Burgess, K.R., 3333
Burgess, M.A.S., 2326
Burgmann, Dorothy M., 163
Burke, G.L., 2271
Burke, Mavis E., 7472
Burke, T., 3580
Burleigh, J.H.S., 732
Burley, G.H.C., 3228
Burley, K.H., 4352
Burley, S.J., 613
Burnes, J.A., 4633
Burnet, G.B., 3556
Burnett, J., 5226
Burney, Elizabeth M., 630
Burns, A.R., 116
Burns, F.P., 5499
Burns, J.H., 3242
Burns, L.P., 4762
Burns, P.L., 7026
Burr, J., 626
Burrell, Elizabeth D.R., 3404
Burroughs, P.C., 7590
Burrow, J.W., 5326
Burstyn, Joan N., 5651
Burtchaell, J.T., 5458
Burtenshaw, D., 406
Burton, Ann M., 4756
Burton, I.F., 3892
Burton, K.G., 3514
Burtt, G.E., 914
Burtt, Lucy M., 4129
Bury, Shirley, 5047
Bush, G.W.A., 5725

Bush, M.L., 2651
Bushell, Dorothy F., 385
Bushrod, Emily, 3480
Bushrod, W.T., 3455
Bussby, F., 2543
Bussey, O., 5367
Butcher, Emily E., 4097
Butler, Barbara J., 5374
Butler, D.H.E., 4705
Butler, J.E., 4777
Butler, J.W. (London M.A.), 5586
Butler, J.W. (London Ph.D.),
   5560
Butler, L.A.S., 1496
Butler, L.H., 1300
Butler, R.M., 296
Butlin, R.A., 449
Butt, Hamida I., 6843
Butt, I.A., 6842
Butt, J., 5784
Butterfield, P.H., 5687
Butterworth, H., 5521
Buxton, T.D., 5630
Buyse, Lorna J., 1110
Byatt, I.C.R., 5092
Byres, T.J., 5817
Byrne, G.H., 5877
Byrne, M.S., 5672
Byrne, P., 2413
Byrne, R.H.D.G., 1942
Byrne, T.W., 944
Bythell, D., 4015

CADOUX, C.J., 5900
Cadoux, T.J., 208
Cadwallader, F.J.J., 920
Caff, W.R.M., 5051
Cain, P.J., 5163
Cairncross, A.K., 4912
Cairns, H.A.C., 6218
Calder, A.L.R., 4718
Caldwell, Sarah J., 4899
Caldwell, T.B., 2084
Callow, H.W. (Liverpool M.A.),
   2922
Callow, H.W. (Manchester M.A.),
   5901
Callus, D.A.P., 1438
Calman, D.A., 7023
Calvert, P.A.R., 7565
Calvert, R.H.B., 5064
Cam, Helen M., 558
Cameron, Anne I., 1696
Cameron, Averil M., 31
Cameron, D., 3258
Cameron, R.H., 4580
Camfield, F.W., 4080
Camm, J.C.R., 3314
Campbell, A.E., 7389
Campbell, A.J., 999
Campbell, C.C., 7473
Campbell, D., 642
Campbell, Eila M.J., 1144
Campbell, F.C., 5638
Campbell, I.B., 2119
Campbell, I.McD., 4450

Campbell, J.J., 6074
Campbell, R.H., 5793
Campbell, W.D., 3570
Campbell, W.McM., 3254
Cane, B.S., 5632
Cane, W.A., 1686
Cannon, J.A., 3693
Cant, Catherine B.H., 2323
Cantle, A., 950
Caplan, G.L., 6312
Caplan, M., 5269
Capp, B.S., 2762
Carberry, Helena P., 4489
Carey, J.V.C., 3082
Cargill Thompson, W.D.J., 2644
Carlin, Mary N., see Birchall
Carlton, D., 4814
Carnell, F.G., 3957
Carnell, P., 1038
Carney, T.F., 21
Carnick, Anne E., 4594
Caroe, Lucy, 4502
Carpenter, Aileen M., 3432
Carpenter, E.F. (London M.A.),
   4182
Carpenter, E.F. (London Ph.D.),
   4165
Carr, A.D., 1646
Carr, J.P., 437
Carr, J.R., 5573
Carr, W., 2131
Carrier, Elsé H., 2027
Carrington, R.C., 235
Carroll, Bridgett G., 1315
Carroll, W.D., 5820
Carrothers, W.A., 4517
Carruthers, S.W., 3097
Carson, Patricia M., 4359
Carsten, F.L., 640
Carter, Alice M.C., 2284
Carter, F.W., 1829
Carter, Felice V., 6250
Carter, J.K., 3235
Carter, Jennifer J., 3631
Carter, P., 4612
Carter, P.N., 1209
Carter, R.B., 3087
Carter, Rosemary, 2007
Cartlidge, Pamela M., 2052
Carus-Wilson, Eleanora M., 1136
Carville, S.A. Geraldine, 1709
Casady, E.R., 3130
Casey, J.G., 2435
Casey, R.P., 679
Cashmore, T.H.R., 6252
Caspari, F.W.E.C., 2641
Cassell, A.J., 5065
Cassidy, Irene, 3047
Cassidy, Ivan, 1719
Cassirer, R., 3740
Casson, J.S., 5407
Catanach, I.J., 6810
Catherall, G.A., 7466
Catto, R.J.A.I., 1464
Caulk, R.A., 6146
Caute, J.D., 2094

Cavendish, Alison E., 1228
Cavendish, P.D., 7152
Cavill, R.J., 469
Cawte, L.H., 7535
Cawthron, D.J., 1263
Cell, Gillian M., 7185
Chaduka, N.L., 6337
Chafer, T.H., 3553
Chakrabarti, H., 6854
Chakravarti, N.R., 7040
Chakravarti, P.C., 6461
Chakravarty, Sasadhar, 6818
Chakravarty, Suhash, 6973
Chaliha, Shanti, 6967
Chalklin, C.W., 2595
Challenger, Sheila B., 622
Challinor, R.C., 5011
Challis, C.E., 2803
Chalmers, C.D., 2991
Chaloner, W.H. (Manchester M.A.),
  5716
Chaloner, W.H. (Manchester
  Ph.D.), 5715
Chamberlain, Muriel E., 4730
Chambers, D.S., 2915
Chambers, D.T., 7355
Chambers, J.D., 4360
Chambers, José F., 5334
Champion, Helen J., 7197
Chan, W.T.K.-K., 7108
Chandaman, C.D., 3922
Chandler, Sylvia L., 4175
Chandler, T.J., 3293
Chandra, L., 6497
Chandra, P., 6645
Chandra, S., 6693
Chandran, M.J., 7039
Chang, K.S., 4206
Chanock, M.L., 6264
Chao, Tang-Li, 7109
Chaplais, P.T.V.M., 609
Chaplin, W.N., 3111
Chapman, B., 2270
Chapman, J., 3433
Chapman, J.K., 4610
Chapman, R.B., 7551
Chapman, S.D. (London Ph.D.),
  4011
Chapman, S.D. (Nottingham M.A.),
  5055
Chappell, D.M., 677
Chappell, Marjorie G., 4748
Chapple, G.F., 1567
Charles, B.G., 1594
Charles, F.W.B., 1506
Charles, R.F., 5027
Charlesworth, S., 2671
Charlton, W.H., 2302
Chasey, H., 7298
Chatfield, D.F., 7265
Chattarji, P.K., 6763
Chatterji, Amiya, 6878
Chatterji, B.R., 6984
Chattopadhyay, A.K., 6624
Chattopadhyaya, B.D., 6479
Chaturvedi, S.N., 6731

Chaudhuri, B., 6966
Chaudhuri, B.B., 6785
Chaudhuri, K.N., 6570
Chaudhuri, P.K., 3942
Chaudhuri, S., 6577
Chaudhuri, Tripti, 6772
Chavda, D.S., 6871
Chavda, V.K., 4726
Checkland, S.G., 3877
Cheetham, Jean, 5117
Cheever, Mary D.F., 6123
Chelliah, D.D., 7002
Ch'en, C.-J., 7090
Chen, C.S., 7111
Chen, T.-L., 7049
Ch'en, Y.S., 7112
Chenevix Trench, Susan M., 1376
Cheng, J.C., 7098
Cheng, K.C., 7160
Cheong, Weng Eang, 7073
Cherry, Althea C., 5495
Chesher, Veronica M., 4051
Cheshire, C.J., 5761
Chesney, H.E., 2754
Chesters, E. Marion, 3128
Chew, E.C.T., 6792
Chew, Helena M. (London M.A.),
  1015
Chew, Helena M. (London Ph.D.),
  1042
Chewter, D.M., 4671
Cheyne, A.C., 4405
Chiang, Pei-Huan, 7107
Chibnall, Joan, 4031
Child, C.J., 2130
Child, J., 4980
Childs, S., 853
Childs, Wendy R., 655
Chilver, G.E.F., 332
Ching, Lin Hsia, 7092
Chiplen, R.F.J., 5188
Chishti, K.A., 6737
Chitnis, A.C., 4439
Chivers, G.V. (Manchester M.A.),
  2770
Chivers, G.V. (Manchester
  Ph.D.), 3207
Chivers, T.A., 7136
Chomchai, P., 1738
Choudhury, D.P., 6791
Choudhury, P.C., 6957
Chow, P.-G., 7085
Chow, T.-K., 7167
Chowdhury, A.M., 6510
Chowdhury, C., 1741
Chrimes, S.B. (Cambridge Ph.D.),
  874
Chrimes, S.B. (London M.A.), 879
Christelow, A., 618
Christian, W.E., 3873
Christiansen, E., 2454
Christie, W., 3557
Christie, W.A., 3527
Christopher, J.W., 7155
Chrysostomides, Julian, 549
Chu, Y.-F., 6958

300

Chughtai, M., 6778
Church, C.H., 2029
Church, L.F., 7276
Church, R.A., 5745
Church, R.J., 6403
Churchill, Irene J., 1217
Churchill, S., 2384
Clack, G.D., 2033
Clanchy, M.T., 931
Clancy, T.H., 3017
Clare, D., 4312
Clark, A.J., 2492
Clark, Cecily, 58
Clark, D.M., 4933
Clark, E.A.G. (London M.A.
  1967), 5581
Clark, E.A.G. (London Ph.D.
  1957), 3378
Clark, G.S., 1103
Clark, Hilda I., 3718
Clark, I.D.L., 4432
Clark, I.M., 2613
Clark, L.A., 4658
Clark, M.N., 2267
Clark, Mary J., 1973
Clark, Millicent E., 2060
Clark, P.L., 5149
Clark, Rosalind B., see Brooke
Clark, W.H., 2470
Clarke, C.A.A., 4030
Clarke, C.P.R., 2447
Clarke, Dorothy P., 4739
Clarke, E., 2570
Clarke, Elizabeth B., 2510
Clarke, G.R., 5851
Clarke, J.F., 4984
Clarke, J.I., 6070
Clarke, Janet M., see Rizvi
Clarke, M., 6173
Clarke, P., 7084
Clarke, P.F., 4675
Clarke, P.L.P., 5530
Clarke, R.D., 1382
Clarkson, L.A., 2537
Clay, C.G.A., 4046
Clayton, A.H.L., 6253
Clayton, J., 4084
Clayton, J.D., 4622
Clayton, K.B., 2072
Clayton, N., 2792
Cleak, K.C., 6004
Cleary, J.M., 3028
Clegg, R.S., 1897
Cleland, D.J., 693
Cleland, I.D., 3492
Clement, E.H., 273
Clement, Mary (Wales M.A.),
  4136
Clement, Mary (Wales Ph.D.),
  4135
Clementi, Dione R., 569
Clements, R.V., 4977
Clementson, J., 6168
Clemoes, P.A.M., 1416
Clerk, D.A., 5823
Clews, S., 5603

Cliffe, J.T., 2912
Clifford, F.A., 968
Clifton, R., 3085
Clinton, D.K., 6282
Clitheroe, T., 4117
Cloke, H., 3518
Clompus, J., 1871
Close, D.H., 4578
Clough, C.H., 80
Clough, Marie, 1095
Clout, H.D., 1969
Clover, V. Helen, 1196
Clubley, C., 1267
Clyde, W.M., 3110
Coates, B.E., 3401
Coates, Winifred D., 1465
Cobb, H.S., 1138
Cobb, Margaret B.B., 1837
Cobban, A.B., 1472
Cobban, A.B.C., 3869
Cobby, G.W.H., 1790
Cochrane, R.A., 4194
Cockburn, J.S. (Leeds LL.M.),
  4363
Cockburn, J.S. (Leeds Ph.D.),
  2484
Cockcroft, W.R., 5299
Cody, W.F., 7532
Coe, W.E., 5856
Cohen, D.W., 6204
Cohen, Sarah (London Ph.D.),
  1012
Cohen, Sarah (Manchester M.A.),
  939
Cohen, Y., 6158
Cohn, H.J., 601
Colaco, Lucy, 6722
Cole, C.R.A., 6433
Cole, D.M., 2875
Cole, H., 881
Cole, J.P., 2262
Cole, Nathalia I.K. Eleady-,
  see Eleady-Cole
Cole, P.D., 6407
Cole, W.A., 3107
Coleman, B.I., 5384
Coleman, D.C., 4351
Coleman, F.L., 6328
Coleman, Olive P., 1139
Coles, Gladys M., 1587
Coles, R., 421
Colgate, H.A., 6992
Collick, R.M.V., 7116
Collie, Frances A., 128
Collier, Frances, 4118
Collier, L.B., 3338
Collier, L.J., 5035
Collier, S.D.W., 7531
Collieu, E.G., 4626
Colligan, J.H., 3475
Collins, A., 4468
Collins, D.C., 3139
Collins, E.J.T., 5171
Collins, H.J., 1798
Collins, Josephine P., 2855
Collins, L.J.D., 2318

Collins, M.F., 5759
Collinson, Marjorie M., 1944
Collinson, P., 2993
Collison, Marjorie M., 5674
Colson, Alice M., 4077
Coltham, S.W., 5478
Coltman, Irene C., 3050
Colvin, J.A., 4779
Colwell, J.J., 1704
Colyer, Muriel M., 2813
Combe, J.C., 4466
Cominos, P.T., 5301
Common, Sarah, 7244
Compton, J.M., 6794
Compton, J.V., 2195
Condon, Mary E.A., 2015
Conn, J.C., 5788
Connell, E.J., 3439
Connell, K.H., 3584
Connell-Smith, G.E., 2415
Consitt, Frances, 1111
Conway, A.A. (London M.A.), 7325
Conway, A.A. (Wales Ph.D.), 7368
Conway, Agnes E., 2627
Conway, J.S., 2201
Conway Davies, J., see Davies,
    J. Conway
Conybeare, C., 4773
Conzen, G., 463
Coogan, Mary F., 1215
Cook, A.E., 7370
Cook, A.F., 5736
Cook, D., 3641
Cook, D.J., 3165
Cook, E., 5202
Cook, G.L., 7249
Cook, W.G.H., 4615
Cooke, A.G.R., 7216A
Cooke, A.J., 2806
Cooke, A.R., 2342
Cooke, B.L., 337
Cooke, D.F., 7008
Cooke, F.E., 5164
Cooke, J.H., 3586
Cookey, S.J.S., 6277
Cookson, J.E., 3766
Coolidge, R.T., 705
Coombs, D.S., 2280
Coombs, P.B., 5404
Coomer, D., 4216
Coontz, S.H., 1729
Cooper, A.E.W., 2412
Cooper, A.J., 2710
Cooper, H., 5961
Cooper, H.H.A., 2697
Cooper, Janet M., 1187
Cooper, M.A.F., 5665
Cooper, M.J., 7059
Cooper, P.K., 293
Cooper, Roslyn L., 2238
Cope, J.A., 3979
Cope, S.R., 3938
Copeland, Jean L., 1387
Copland, I.F.S., 6790
Copley, G.J., 52
Coppenger, R.A., 4242

Coppieters, E.L.X., 4894
Coppock, J.T., 5200
Copson-Niećko, Maria J.E., 1848
Coram, T.C., 7257
Corbett, G.U.S., 777
Corcos, D.F., 2225
Cordingley, Christine, 825
Corke, M. Wendy, 7351
Corley, J.M., 2988
Cormack, W.S., 5811
Corney, C.P., 3068
Cornwall, J.C.K., 2843
Corrigan, H.S.W. (London M.A.),
    1813
Corrigan, H.S.W. (London Ph.D.),
    6020
Corson, J.C., 3861
Cosgrove, J., 2906
Cossons, N., 5133
Costigan, G.M.D.G., 3914
Cottereau, S.R., 1823
Cottis, C.P., 953
Cottle, A.B., 1211
Cotton, Myra K.R., 2933
Cottrell, Ena M.B., 3099
Coughlin, Rose L., 6022
Coulborn, A.P.R., 871
Coull, J.R., 3568
Couper, J.G., 2064
Course, E.A., 5138
Courtemanche, R.A., 7183
Courtman, Moira, 5721
Cousens, S.H., 5854
Cousins, Alice M., 6341
Cousins, W.M., 7468
Couzens, F.C., 3292
Covell, W.R., 5610
Cowan, C.D., 7024
Cowan, I.B., 1684
Coward, B., 1092
Cowell, Phyllis M., 2453
Cowie, L.W. (London M.A.), 4279
Cowie, L.W. (London Ph.D.), 4137
Cowley, F.G., 1601
Cowley, G.O., 2596
Cowper, Christina L.H., 5223
Cox, A.H.G., 3616
Cox, D., 4688
Cox, E.A., 5189
Cox, H., 1247
Cox, Katharine E.C., 2043
Cox, R.C.W. (Leicester M.A.),
    5735
Cox, R.C.W. (Leicester Ph.D.),
    5734
Cox, R.M., 4020
Coxhill, W.T., 4311
Cracknell, B.E., 3409
Cracraft, J.E., 2327
Cragg, D.G.L., 6294
Craig, A.W., 3060
Craig, G.A., 2293
Cramp, A.B., 4891
Cramp, Margaret M., 3695
Cramp, Rosemary J., 1481
Cranfield, G.A., 4303

Craske, P.C.B., 7340
Cratchley, W.J., 5396
Craven, J.W., 4451
Crawford, J.R., 2553
Crawford, Jane A., 1418
Crawford, S.J., 1417
Crawshaw, H.N., 3821
Crellin, J.K., 3516
Cresswell, J., 4062
Crews, C.C., 3924
Criddle, Clara G., 2722
Crimmin, Patricia K., 3908
Crisp, Olga, 1807
Critchley, J.S., 988
Croft, J. Pauline, 2419
Croft, M.J., 4515
Crompton, J., 1294
Cronne, H.A., 829
Crook, D.P., 7326
Crook, J.M., 5466
Crook, L.B.L., 4797
Crosby, A. Essex-, see Essex-
  Crosby
Crosby, G.B., 2561
Crosby, G.E.I., 4470
Cross, J.A., 4793
Cross, M. Claire, 2674
Crotch, W.J.B., 1477
Croton, G.M.D., 1557
Crow, E.P., 4221
Crowder, C.M.D., 1407
Crowe, A.L., 6582
Crowe, Sibyl E., 6408
Crowhurst, R.P., 3900
Crowley, D.W., 4636
Crowley, F.K., 7602
Crowther, D.R. Facey-, see
  Facey-Crowther
Crowther, K.J., 6546
Crowther, P.A., 1090
Crowther, Phyllis M., 3407
Cruickshank, A.A., 6051
Cruickshank, C.G., 2789
Cruickshank, Marjorie A., 5508
Cruickshank, W.W., 130
Cruickshanks, Evelyn G., 1960
Crummett, J.B., 2755
Crummey, D.E., 6134
Crump, Helen J., 3779
Crutchley, Adeline, 1941
Cserenyey, G., 1893
Cuff, P.J., 285
Culcheth, Betty, 4827
Cule, J.E., 4024
Cullen, J.S.B., 4479
Cullen, L.M., 4459
Cumaraswamy, A., 6910
Cumberland, A.G. (Birmingham
  M.A.), 3473
Cumberland, A.G. (London Ph.D.),
  4213
Cumella, S.J., 2745
Cummings, J.R., 192
Cumpston, I. Mary, 4725
Cunliffe, M.F., 4863
Cunningham, A.B. (London M.A.),
  6001

Cunningham, A.B. (London Ph.D.),
  4555
Cunningham, H.St.C., 6016
Cunningham, Mavis, 621
Cunningham, Susan E., 3285
Cunnington, Elisabeth A., 3666
Currie, D.R., 7314
Currie, R., 3491
Curry, J., 2784
Curtin, P.W.E., 2040A
Curtis, C.D., 3633
Curtis, E.L.B., 2216
Curtis, Evelyn E., 771
Curtis, L.P., 4661
Curtis, Margaret, 1019
Curwen, C.A., 7114
Cushner, N.P., 7518
Cuthbert, J.L., 7286
Cuttino, G.P., 856

DAAKU, K.Y., 6343
Dachs, A.J., 6289
Daeley, J.I., 2983
Dakin, D., 1975
Dakin, E., 1155
Dalby, G.R., 5726
Dalby, H.H., 250
Dale, A., 4335
Dale, Marian K., 1137
Dallimore, H., 6385
Dalrymple, Gertrude M., 3707
Dalton, B.J., 7601
Dalton, Heather, 6400
Dalvi, M.A., 5683
Daly, C.B., 6073
Dalziel, J., 6283
Dane, E.S., 3986
Daniel, Barbara J., 557
Daniel, N.A., 536
Daniels, G., 7113
Daniels, G.E., 4651
Daniels, G.W., 4012
Dann, W.S., 2625
Danzig, R.J., 6861
Darby, H.C., 1048
Darby, P.G.C., 6954
Darbyshire, J.A., 1258
Dark, A., 394
Darke, Evelyn B., 674
Darkwah, R.H.K., 6129
Darley, T.C.F., 464
Darlington, R.R., 1422
Darnton, R.C., 1983
Darvall, F.O., 3977
Das, B., 6469
Das, H., 6581
Das, M.N., 6750
Das, S., 6585
Dasgupta, A., 6636
das Gupta, A.R., 6600
Dasgupta, B., 6828
Dasgupta, Sailendranath, 6516
Das Gupta, Uma, 6800
Datta, P., 6789
Datta, Susilkumar, 6649
Datta, V., 6696

Daud, M.A., 6026
Daunton-Fear, R., 3092
Davey, Constance M., 2690
Davey, P.C., 2527
David, E.I., 4697
David, I.W.R., 4539
Davidson, A., 3021
Davidson, D. (Edinburgh Ph.D.), 3217
Davidson, D. (Oxford B.Litt.), 3216
Davidson, J.W., 7620
Davidson, T., 1681
Davie, A.F. (Manchester M.A.), 4381
Davie, A.F. (Manchester Ph.D.), 5724
Davies, A.C., 3325
Davies, A.M.E., 3461
Davies, Alun (Wales M.A. 1911), 2938
Davies, Alun (Wales M.A. 1939), 1993
Davies, Aneurin, 3647
Davies, B.L., 3437
Davies, Brenda M., see Pegrum
Davies, C.C., 6832
Davies, C.E., 4160
Davies, C.S.L., 2778
Davies, Cecily, 886
Davies, Clarice S. (Manchester M.A.), 4072
Davies, Clarice S. (Manchester Ph.D.), 3440
Davies, Clifford, 3323
Davies, D., 3329
Davies, D.E., 5608
Davies, D.H.M., 2547
Davies, David James, 5324
Davies, David John, 4379
Davies, E.I., 4002
Davies, Edith M.E., 5136
Davies, Edward, 3682
Davies, Elwyn, 502
Davies, Emlyn, 1595
Davies, Eulalie M., 1367
Davies, Evan (Oxford D.Phil. 1926), 4066
Davies, Evan (Wales M.A. 1937), 5109
Davies, H.M., 5668
Davies, H.S., 3396
Davies, H.W.E., 4932
Davies, I., 3438
Davies, J., 3414
Davies, J. Conway, 1653
Davies, J.H., 5762
Davies, J.K., 138
Davies, J.M., 493
Davies, J.T., 1658
Davies, J.V., 4178
Davies, James A., 5554
Davies, John A., 3905
Davies, Katharine L., 78
Davies, L.N.A., 5132
Davies, M.E., 3461

Davies, M.H., 212
Davies, M.W., 4614
Davies, N.J., 1295
Davies, P.N. (Liverpool M.A.), 6422
Davies, P.N. (Liverpool Ph.D.), 6435
Davies, Patricia M., 141
Davies, R.G., 1304
Davies, R.H., 1030
Davies, R.R., 1655
Davies, R.T., 2888
Davies, Raymond W., 4788
Davies, Robert W., 2379
Davies, Roy W., 286
Davies, T.W.L., 1662
Davies, V.C., 4521
Davies, W., 7104
Davies, W.H., 178
Davies, W.J., 3948A
Davies, W.S., 1636
Davies, Wendy E., 1620
Davies, William Rhys (Manchester M.A.), 4139
Davies, William Rhys (Manchester Ph.D.), 4145
Davies, William Rosser, 232
Davis, C.T., 585
Davis, D.G., 4143
Davis, Eliza J., 2929
Davis, G.R.C., 211
Davis, Hilda M., 3277
Davis, J.C., 3846
Davis, J.C.W., 3102
Davis, John Frederick (London Ph.D. 1959), 5034
Davis, John Frederick (Oxford D.Phil. 1968), 2921
Davis, R., 3954
Davis, R.W., 3827
Davis, S.G., 7091
Davis, T.B., 11
Davis, W.B.S., 6652
Dawley, P.M., 3032
Dawn, A.F., 5489
Dawson, D., 7553
Dawson, D. Jean, 2701
Dawson, D.W., 4798
Dawson, J.L., 7263
Dawson, M., 6335
Dawson, R.MacG., 7234
Day, P.W., 7414
Day, R.B., 2383
Day, S.R., 3058
Daykin, C.W., 3620
Dé, B., 6633
De, Jatis Chandra, 6482
Dean, A.P., 4589
Dean, D.A., 5703
Dean, D.W., 5516
Dean, K.J., 4676
Dean, Ruth J., 70
Deane, S.F., 1998
Deanesly, Margaret, 1451
de Beer, E.S., 3618
Debenham, M.J., 7328A

Deeley, Ann P., 753
de Garis, B.K., 7609
Deighton, H.S., 1014
de Kalb, Eugenie W., 3141
de Kiewiet, C.W., 6301
de Kiewiet, Marie J., 6230
de la Mare, Albinia C., 818
de la Mare, Kathleen, 1748
De Lange, N.R.M., 5908
de la Perrelle, L.P., 2126
de Madariaga, Isabel, 2331
de Marchi, E.I.R., 3855
Demas, W.G., 7491
de Montgomery, B.G., 1810
Dempsey, Mary, 4635
Denholm, A.F., 4601
Denholm-Young, N., 1082
Dennis, J.M., 2114
Denoon, D.J.N., 6332
Dent, Cynthia A., 1934
Dent, J., 1925
Dent, K.S., 3919
Denton, J.H., 1254
d'Entrèves, A.P., 2678
Deoras, V.R., 6491
Derrett, J.D.M., 6525
Derry, J.W., 3739
Derry, T.K., 2828
Desai, A.V., 2146
Desborough, V.R.d'A., 127
Deshmukh, R.V., 6480
Deshpande, S., 6670
de Silva, C.R. (London Ph.D.
    1932), 6906
de Silva, C.R. (London Ph.D.
    1968), 6898
de Silva, K.M., 6924
de Silva, P.W., 6734
Develin, J.C., 2462
Devereux, F., 574
de Voil, W.H., 5813
de Vorsey, L., 7283
Dewar, A.C., 2279
Dewar, M.W., 3096
Dewar, Mary C., 2658
Dewaraja, Lorna S., 6901
Dewey, J.A., 5605
Dewhurst, K.E., 4102
Dexter, T.F.G., 1495
Dhammavisuddhi, Y., 6892
Dhanda, Pravina, 6953
Dharkar, C.D., 6725
Dickey, Mary C.G., 802
Dickinson, H.T. (Durham M.A.),
    3893
Dickinson, H.T. (Newcastle
    Ph.D.), 3657
Dickinson, J.C., 1346
Dickinson, Joycelyne G., 634
Dickinson, P., 431
Dickinson, R.E., 420
Dickinson, W.C., 3209
Dicks, T.R.B., 2512
Dickson, P.G.M., 3927
Dickson, R.J., 7272
Dietz, B., 2783

Digby, A., 446
Diké, K.O., 6376
Dikigoropoulos, A.I., 524
Dilworth, C.G., 7344
Dilworth, G.M., 2112
Dinwoodie, M.J.C., 5887
Ditchfield, G.M., 3812
Dittmer, B.R., 4063
Dixon, A.A.A., 5925
Dixon, C.W., 2307
Dixon, E.S.H., 5799
Dixon, J.T., 3783
Dixon, K.F., 3937
Dobb, C., 2898
Dobbin, Christine E., 6735
Dobby, E.H.G., 7030
Doble, Evelyn, 5152
Dobson, A., 3611
Dobson, B., 282
Dobson, J.L., 4320
Dobson, R.B., 1393
Dockerill, J.D., 364
Dockrill, M.L., 4799
Dodd, J.A., 155
Dodd, J.P., 5543
Dodds, N., 3654
Dodds, Patricia K., 719
Dodds, W.G., 4032
Dodgeon, M.H., 230
Dodgshon, R.A., 4409
Dodwell, Barbara, 824
Dodwell, C.R., 1498
Doherty, Felicitas M., 7275
Dolbey, G.W., 3489
Dolley, A.H.F., 4923
Dolley, R.C.F., 3622
d'Ombrain, N.J., 4879
Domergue, Françoise, 1826
Don, Y., 1858
Donald, Heather M., 7226
Donaldson, A.G., 5822
Donaldson, Barbara, 1149
Donaldson, G., 3000
Donaldson, R., 1278
Donkin, R.A., 1349
Donnachie, I.L., 3562
Donoughue, B., 7295
Donovan, P.W., 5015
Don Peter, W.L.A., 6897
Dontas, Domna (London M.A.),
    2211
Dontas, Domna (London Ph.D.),
    2215
Dony, J.G., 3371
Doody, W.M., 1296
Doorly, V. Eleanor L., 2256
Doree, S.G., 2266
Dorey, A.J., 4796
Dornier, Ann M., 371
Doty, J.D., 7267
Douch, R., 1159
Dougan, D.J., 3984
Douglas, J., 741
Douie, Decima L., 720
Dove, Constance W., 1100
Dow, A.C., 4407

307

Evans, G.D., 7411
Evans, Gwyneth, 3744
Evans, Hilary A., 5364
Evans, I., 5359
Evans, J.D., 4770
Evans, John Anthony (Birmingham M.A.), 3379
Evans, John Anthony (London Ph.D.), 3296
Evans, K.D., 5637
Evans, Keith, 5119
Evans, Kenneth, 7561
Evans, L.W., 4322
Evans, M.H., 279
Evans, P.C.C., 3268
Evans, R.J.M., 4110
Evans, R.J.W., 1834
Evans, R.W., 4146
Evans, S., 3995
Evans, S.G., 2867
Evans, T., 5660
Evans, T.L., 5447
Evans, T.W., 3607
Evans, W.A., 5452
Everett, B.G., 5607
Everitt, A.M., 3199
Evers, W.K., 1226
Evinson, D., 5467
Ewart, H.J., 4411
Exelby, H.R., 4009
Exley, Margaret, 2793
Eybers, G. von W., 6280
Eyck, U.F.J., 4593
Eyles, D., 6720
Eyre, S.R., 438
Ezera, K., 6441

FABUNMI, L.A., 6126
Facer, P., 3502
Facey-Crowther, D.R., 6159
Fadner, F.L., 2332
Fagan, Eileen H. de L., 912
Fage, J.D., 6327
Fagerstrom, D.I., 7292
Fahmy, A.M., 5920
Fahy, C.F., 2243
Fairbank, J.K. (Oxford B.Litt.), 7101
Fairbank, J.K. (Oxford D.Phil.), 7100
Fairhurst, Herbert, 500
Fairhurst, Horace, 452
Fairless, K.J., 274
Fairlie, Susan E., 2338
Fairs, G.H., 7571
Faith, Rosamund J., 1071
Fanning, J.R., 4682
Farag, Nadia R., 6152
Farley, R.E.G., 7450
Farley, Sarah M., 67
Farmer, D.F.H., 1198
Farmer, D.L., 646
Farmer, H.G., 5915
Farnie, D.A., 5070
Farquhar, M. Marie, see Mont-petit

Farr, D.M.L., 7236
Farr, M.W., 1080
Farrar, L.L., 2171
Farrar, P.N., 5500
Farrell, E. Grace, 2844
Farrell, F.E., 3064
Farrow, W.J., 2734
Fawcett, A., 4426
Fawcett, W.A., 5540
Fear, R. Daunton-, see Daunton-Fear
Fearn, E., 3815
Fearn, H. (London Ph.D.), 6261
Fearn, H. (Sheffield M.A.), 4837
Fearns, J.V., 715
Featherstone, E., 1214
Feaver, E.K., 4134
Feaver, G.A., 4749
Fee, G.W.C., 2468
Feeney, B.J., 1040
Feilding, R.J., 4791
Feinstein, C.H., 4913
Felix, Janina W., 94
Felsenstein, D.R., 5633
Fenlon, D.B., 2233
Fenn, M.J., 7544
Fennell, J.L.I., 2315
Fennell, K.R., 1483
Fennelly, J.M., 6101
Fenwick, Muriel E., 850
Fereday, R.P., 5053
Ferguson, J.T., 880
Ferguson, R.W., 7296
Ferguson, W., 3579
Fergusson, C.B., 3796
Fernando, C., 6925
Fernando, C.N.V., 6907
Fernando, P.T.M., 6937
Fernando, S.T.G., 6913
Ferns, H.S., 7527
Fest, W.B., 1876
Feuchtwanger, E.J., 4616
Fewster, J.M., 4380
ffoulkes, C.J., 1002
Field, A.G., 6946
Field, A. Mary, 7187
Field, R.K., 1070
Fielden, K., 7327
Fielder, G.D., 3465
Fielding, Dorothy D., 313
Fifer, Joan V., 7545
Fikry, A.R., 6150
Finch, Mary E., 2896
Findlay, D.F., 1507
Fines, J.D., 1323
Fingard, Judith J. (London M.Phil.), 7204
Fingard, Judith J. (London Ph.D.), 7205
Finlayson, G.B.A.M., 5739
Finlayson, I.D.B., 5776
Finlayson, W.H., 652
Finn, J.F., 4666
Firminger, W.K., 6608
Firth, C.B., 1305

Firth, J.R., 2011
Fischer, D., 6444
Fisher, D.R., 4582
Fisher, Edward J., 1627
Fisher, Eric J. (Leeds M.A.), 1541
Fisher, Eric J. (Leeds Ph.D.), 1097
Fisher, F.J., 2825
Fisher, H.E.S., 2442
Fisher, J.R., 7526
Fisher, J.W., 6321
Fisher, M.J.C., 1362
Fisher, Mary, 7430
Fisher, N.H., 2937
Fishman, I., 1835
Fitch, Miriam G., 5693
Fitch, T., 3083
Fitter, Hilda E., 2128
Fitton, R.S., 4010
Fitzgerald, Brigid A., 1708
Fitzgerald, W.J., 2660
Fitzhardinge, L.F., 295
Fitzhardinge, Una C., 276
Fitzpatrick, Sheila M., see Bruce
Flajszer, J.L., 712
Flanagan, Lucy, 5709
Fleming, C.E., 7617
Fleming, D.C., 2212
Fleming, J., 51
Fleming, Mary A., 3501
Fletcher, D.J., 1954
Fletcher, Gertrude M., 7420
Fletcher, J.M., 1467
Fletcher, Margery A., 961
Fletcher, N.M., 4309
Fletcher, T.W., 5204
Flight, A.T., 5063
Flinn, M.W., 4914
Flint, J.E., 6404
Flint, Valerie I.J., 799
Flitcroft, J., 1468
Flockhart, Marguerite C., 1967
Florecki, S., 1886
Florescu, R.R.N.A.R., 1844
Floud, R.C., 5068
Fodrio, C., 2042
Fogwill, E.G., 395
Folayan, K., 6079
Foley, D.M., 6393
Foot, M.R.D., 2292
Forbes, A.J. de B., 1744
Forbes, J.D., 1678
Forbes, J.R.M., 757
Ford, A.G., 7558
Foreman, H., 5510
Forester, Alison H., see Hanham
Forey, A.J., 769
Forrest, Jean, 4018
Forrester, D.W.F., 5381
Forrester, E.G., 3649
Forrester, Iris E.V., 4375
Forshaw, Helen P., 1236
Forster, C.A., 5293
Forstner, A.S. Kanya-, see Kanya-Forstner
Forte, S.L., 1459

Fortounatto, M., 704
Foskett, R., 5395
Foss, D.B., 1279
Foster, A.R., 267
Foster, D., 5249
Foster, J.H., 5420
Foster, J.O., 5234
Foster, James, 1200
Foster, John, 7052
Foster, R.T., 5821
Foster, Sarah E., 2814
Foster, W.R., 3244
Foulkes, E.J., 3360
Fouyas, I.M., 688
Fowkes, F.B.M., 1874
Fowler, Elizabeth, 1480
Fowler, J.R., 6951
Fowler, K.A., 862
Fowler, Rachel E., 1904
Fox, A., 4990
Fox, E., 964
Fox, H.G., 2070
Fox, K.O., 4855
Fox, L., 1548
Fox, Leslie P., 4149
Fox, P.W., 1932
Fox, R., 1972
Fozzard, Irene, 2041
Fradin, Jeanne M.B., 1235
Frampton, B.A., 5311
France, J., 59
Francis, M., 4245
Frank, C.N., 210
Frankel, J., 2356
Frankl, M.G. Ekstein-, see Ekstein-Frankl
Frankland, A.N., 1827
Franklin, D.R., 2585
Franklin, Susan M., see Treggiari
Fraser, Constance M., 1252
Fraser, D.E., 3390
Fraser, Derek (Leeds M.A.), 5474
Fraser, Derek (Leeds Ph.D.), 4553
Fraser, Duncan, 4397
Fraser, F., 5360
Fraser, H.M., 118
Fraser, I.H.C., 2695
Fraser, J.D., 4857
Fraser, P., 3764
Fraser, P.M., 174
Fraser, W.H., 4987
Frazer, Beatrice L., 6663
Frazer, N.L., 607
Frechtling, L.E., 6014
Fredericks, R.S., 1688
Freebody, Nina K., 484
Freedman, J.R., 7335
Freeling, Dorothy, 4660
Freeman, Patricia A., 5879
Freeman-Grenville, G.S.P., 6203
Freer, J.L., 1232
Fremantle, Katherine D.H., 2276
French, A.M., 382

French, C.J., 3963
French, R.A., 2320
Frend, W.H.C., 6071
Freund, G., 1821
Friedman, I., 2163
Friend, A.C., 1455
Fries, F.T., 6170
Frischwasser, H.F., 6033
Fritz, P.S., 3678
Froshaug, Ann J., 3459
Frost, M.J., 3434
Fry, G.K., 4596
Fry, H.T., 6607
Fry, M.G., 7168
Fryde, E.B., 1022
Fryer, W.R., 1985
Frykenberg, R.E., 6727
Fu, Lo-Huan, 6960
Fudge, Muriel K., 2538
Fuidge, Norah M., 2681
Fuleihan, D.E.B., 6043
Fuller, A.R.B., 1216
Fuller, G. Joan (London M.A.), 478
Fuller, G. Joan (London Ph.D.), 3387
Fuller, Margaret D., 3456
Fulop, R.E., 2942
Furley, O.W., 3627
Furlonge, E.A., 7476
Fussell, Ethel M., 1340
Fynn, J.K., 6351

GABRIEL, J.R., 1657
Gabriel, R.C., 2687
Gadd, Margaret L., 3158
Gaffney, J.V., 4412
Gailey, R.A., 3561
Gainer, B., 5333
Gair, W.R., 3134
Gairola, C.K., 6476
Galadanci, S.A.S., 6142
Galai, S., 2368
Galal, A.-F.A.K., 6191
Galbraith, Georgina R., 1384
Galbraith, J.D., 1676
Gale, H.P., 6255
Gale, S., 4618
Galea, E.L., 2303
Gallo, E.L., 7555
Gallop, D.F., 3512
Galloway, J.H., 7523
Gallup, S.V., 2085
Galpin, E.T., 4627
Galt, Joan MacC., 5807
Gamble, G.G., 2591
Ganguli, D., 6515
Gann, L.H. (Oxford B.Litt.), 6324
Gann, L.H. (Oxford D.Phil.), 6318
Gannon, F.R., 2200
Gardiner, K.H.J., 7050
Gardiner, Mary A., 317
Gardiner, P.L., 1
Gardiner, Sunray C., 2316

Gardner, J.C., 2608
Gardner, J.R., 810
Gardner, R.D.H., 2217
Garlick, P.C., 3368
Garnett, R.G., 4942
Garnsey, P.D.A., 237
Garrad, K., 2423
Garrard, J.A., 5331
Garrett, A.J., 414
Garrett, Kathleen I., 6736
Garrett, S.K., 6045
Garside, B., 2575
Garside, P.D., 105
Garside, W.R., 5029
Garton, G.D., 4927
Garton, Ida M., 3828
Gary, Anne T., 7281
Gascoigne, Mildred, 4953
Gash, I.J., 6651
Gash, N., 4079
Gaskell, J.P.W., 3997
Gaskin, Brenda P.R., 5783
Gaskin, M., 5806
Gaston, R.W., 778
Gates, Sybil M., 318
Gath, E.R., 7171
Gatherer, W.A., 3240
Gaught, A.S., 3418
Gauld, W.A., 6015
Gauldie, Enid M., 3565
Gavin, Catherine I., 2053
Gavin, R.J., 6061
Gayer, A.D., 4940
Gearing, Eliza A., 1974
Geddes, C.L., 5935
Geduld, H.M., 3998
Gee, E.A. (Birmingham M.A.), 1345
Gee, E.A. (Oxford D.Phil.), 1510
Gee, Olive R., 3727
Gee, S.S., 2080
Gehani, T.G., 6809
Gehl, J.D.W., 1892
Gelber, L.M., 7392
Gelly, M., 4229
Gendall, P.P.W., 2986
Gentles, I.J., 2818
George, K.R.N.St.J. Wykeham-, see Wykeham-George
George, Mary J., 1403
Georgević, I., 1759
Georghallides, G.S., 1873
Gerrish, D., 5888
Gerson, J.J., 7096
Gertzel, Cherry J. (Oxford B.Litt.), 6391
Gertzel, Cherry J. (Oxford D.Phil.), 6423
Getzler, I., 2362
Gharaybeh, A.K.M., 5984
Ghauri, I.A. (London M.A.), 6578
Ghauri, I.A. (London Ph.D.), 6548
Ghorbal, S., 6128

Ghosal, A.K., 6568
Ghose, D.K., 6827
Ghose, N.N., 6509
Ghosh, Bidhukhushan, 6602
Ghosh, Biswanath, 6681
Ghosh, Kamala, 6749
Ghosh, Pansy C., 6833
Ghosh, Sailesh Chandra, 6874
Ghosh, Sankarkumar, 6821
Ghosh, Sureshchandra, 6609
Gibb, H.A.R., 5929
Gibbs, F.W., 1728
Gibbs, G.C., 3782
Gibbs, Marion E., 1227
Gibbs, Mildred E., 4576
Gibbs, N.H., 1116
Gibson, I.F., 5794
Gibson, J.A. (Oxford B.Litt.),
  7235
Gibson, J.A. (Oxford D.Phil.),
  4731
Gibson, Margaret T., 1420
Gibson, S.J.T., 861
Gidden, H.W., 1527
Gidlow-Jackson, A.D., 4588
Gidney, R.D., 7207
Gifford, Daphne H., 1193
Giggs, J.A., 5763
Gilbert, Alison, 3712
Gilbert, E.C., 1486
Gilbert, E.W., 7311
Gilbert, J., 1672
Gilchrist, J.T.I., 710
Gilcriest, Grace H., 3898
Giles, F.J., 6096
Giles, Phyllis M., 4373
Giles, R.A., 7596
Gill, Doris M., 3596
Gillam, S.G., 4289
Gillan, Elizabeth K., 1118
Gillan, I.T., 6072
Gillard, D.R., 2157
Gillespie, R.A., 219
Gillespie, Sarah C., 4981
Gillessen, G.G.M., 2135
Gillett, D.A., 387
Gilling, J.R., 2063
Gillman, Marguerite, 3276
Gillon, R.M., 3243
Gilmore, C.G., 7215
Gilmore, J., 2612
Ginarlis, J.E., 3395
Ginsburg, H.H., 2290
Gintz, Helen, 1736
Girouard, M., 4327
Gittins, L., 3369
Gjurgjevic, T.V., 1872
Gladish, D.N., 2622
Glasgow, E.L.H., 4842
Glass, S.T., 4684
Glasscock, R.E., 1158
Glassman, J.H., 5352
Gleason, J.H., 2341
Gleave, M.B., 3291
Glendon, E.T., 6086
Glover, E.C., 1583

Glover, F.J., 5041
Glunz, H.H., 1413
Glyn-Jones, Eleanor M., 6223
Glynn, J.K., 4573
Goble, Rose U., 737
Gocking, C.V., 7487
Godagé, C., 6922
Goh Yoon Fong, 6594
Gohar, H.M., 6056
Goitein, Ella S., 1923
Golby, J.M., 3777
Goldey, D.B., 2100
Goldfeld, I., 5921
Golding, S.R., 3132
Goldman, S., 32
Goldsmith, R.E., 2122
Goldstein, R., 4792
Goldstrom, M., 5572
Goldthorp, L.M., 1370
Gollan, R.A., 7599
Gollancz, Marguerite E.H.J.,
  959
Gollancz, O., 7386
Gollin, A.M., 5490
Gooch, J., 4875
Gooch, R.K., 2078
Good, Dorothy, 4652
Goodall, G., 1156
Goodall, N., 5377
Gooder, A., 962
Goodfellow, C.F., 6307
Goodison, R.R., 3610
Goodlad, C.A., 504
Goodloe, R.W., 6058
Goodman, A.E., 971
Goodman, D.C., 4318
Goodman, Dorothy B., 1867
Goodman, Phyllis H., 3613
Goodridge, C.A., 7453
Goodridge, J.C., 5046
Goodridge, R.M., 1788
Goodwin, A.K., 4431
Goonewardena, K.W., 6899
Gopal, Krishna K., 6503
Gopal, L., 6502
Gopal, M.H., 6669
Gopal, S., 6813
Gordon, D.I., 5150
Gordon, H., 5653
Gordon, H.G.M., 3241
Gordon, I.A., 3123
Gordon, Jay, 6394
Gordon, John, 2110
Gordon, P. (London M.Sc.), 5504
Gordon, P. (London Ph.D.), 5565
Gordon, R.A., 6870
Gordon, Shirley C., 3534
Gordon-Kerr, F.A., 5897
Gordon Walker, P.C., 4916
Goring, J.J., 2776
Gorodetzky, Nadejda, 2329
Gosden, P.H.J.H., 5235
Gosling, D.K., 2557
Goss, W.A., 4225
Gossage, A.J., 303
Gotlieb, H.B., 2199

Gough, A.G., 2062
Gough, B.M., 7182
Gould, J.D., 2808
Gould, S.C., 1956
Goulden, Cynthia A., see Dent
Gourlay, D.W.F., 6729
Gourvish, T.R., 5130
Goveia, Elsa V., 7449
Gowers, I.W., 3014
Gowland, D.A., 5444
Grace, Helen M., 1005
Grace, J., 88
Grace, W.F.F. (Cambridge Ph.D.), 1857
Grace, W.F.F. (Liverpool M.A.), 2067
Grady, Alison D., 5751
Graham, A.J., 133
Graham, D.S., 7280
Graham, E.H., 943
Graham, G.S., 7200
Graham, J.K., 3266
Graham, Jean M., 517
Graham, Jenny E., 3738
Graham, N.I., 7603
Graham, R.M., 4402
Graham, Sonia F., 6429
Gramolt, D.W., 3406
Gransby, D.M., 2961
Gransden, Antonia, 68
Grant, A.C., 7320
Grant, C.H., 7505
Grant, J.W., 5455
Grant, L.T., 3065
Grant, R.K.J., 1065
Grassi, J.L., 898
Graves, C.L., 2324
Graves, J.T.R., 5642
Graves, N.J. (London M.A.), 2083
Graves, N.J. (London Ph.D.), 2082
Graveson, N., 2449
Gray, D.E., 3757
Gray, Ethel W., 2475
Gray, J.R., 6141
Gray, Kathleen, 4199
Gray, Margaret, 3540
Gray, R.A.R., 5753
Gray, W.B. (Edinburgh Ph.D.), 4392
Gray, W.B. (Oxford B.Litt.), 4391
Gray, W.R.N., 4444
Greaves, B. (Leeds M.A.), 4232
Greaves, B. (Liverpool Ph.D.), 5423
Greaves, Dorothy, 611
Greaves, R.W., 4357
Green, Eleanor M., 176
Green, R.E., 4401
Green, S.M.B., 5106
Green, V., 1364
Greenall, R.L., 5733
Greenberg, M.M., 7077
Greenfield, May, 4949
Greenfield, R.H., 5355

Greenleaf, W.H., 1757
Greenleaves, H., 2767
Greenstreet, D.K., 6936
Greenway, Diana E., 1054
Greenway, W., 1643
Greenwood, H.D., 4196
Greer, C.S., 7385
Greer, Y.C., 3001
Greeves, O.N., 7367
Gregg, Pauline E., 2759
Gregor, R., 2382
Gregory, Alys L. (Manchester M.A.), 935
Gregory, Alys L. (Manchester Ph.D.), 1221
Gregory, D., 5723
Gregory, J.S., 7099
Gregory, M.V., 1021
Gregory, R.G., 4856
Greider, J.C., 2980
Grenville, G.S.P. Freeman-, see Freeman-Grenville
Grenville, J.A.S., 4783
Greville, S.E., 7595
Grewal, J.S., 99
Gribbon, H.D., 518
Grierson, G.H., 3717
Grieve, Muriel J., 6176
Griffin, A.R., 5010
Griffin, C.P., 2524
Griffin, G.J., 4256
Griffin, Kathleen M., 2291
Griffin, W.C., 5037
Griffith, D.G., 3324
Griffith, Dorothi M., 3525
Griffith, E.H., 5194
Griffith, E.S., 5758
Griffith, G.E.H., 4591
Griffith, J.F., 3133
Griffith, Margaret C., 1717
Griffiths, A.R.G., 5845
Griffiths, E.W., 6031
Griffiths, Elnith R., 3452
Griffiths, Elsie M., 1914
Griffiths, J.M., 4534
Griffiths, Naomi E.S., 7196
Griffiths, Olive M., 4203
Griffiths, R.A., 1659
Griffiths, R.L., 4243
Griffiths, R.S., 5634
Griffiths, T.J., 635
Griffiths, W.E., 373
Griffiths, W.W., 263
Grigg, D.B., 3445
Grimble, I., 2611
Grime, A. (Edinburgh Ph.D.), 4205
Grime, A. (Manchester M.A.), 4204
Grimes, W.F., 377
Grimshaw, H.A., 5595
Grimshaw, Mabel I., 7130
Grimshaw, Patricia A., 3550
Grobel, Monica C., 5473
Groenewegen, P.D., 1720
Groombridge, Margaret J., 3189

Handcock, W.D. (Oxford B.Litt.), 2101
Handley, J.E., 4410
Handley, M.D., 5265
Handren, B.E., 7321
Haney, J.V., 2319
Hanham, Alison H., 1173
Hanham, H.J., 4621
Hankey, Ann T., 815
Hanna, A.J., 6227
Hanna, Katharine A., 1272
Hanna, S.G., 4478
Hannam, Una C., 1319
Hannell, F.G., 4508
Hannon, J.S., 4169
Hannon, P.E., 5678
Hans, N., 2333
Hansen, Ann N., 7258
Hansford Miller, F.H., 1289
Hansman, J.F., 5896
Hanson, Julie C., 345
Hanson, L.W., 3674
Haque, S., 5958
Harben, May A., 1868
Harding, A., 932
Hardinge, L., 1592
Hardman, B.E., 5406
Hardman, D.B., 461
Hardy, A., 3704
Hardy, Kathleen E., 2631
Hardy, P., 45
Hardy, S.H., 3366
Hardy, S.M., 3753
Hargrave, Joyce, 5748
Hargreaves, Dorothy, 3776
Hargreaves, J.D., 2090
Hargreaves-Mawdsley, W.N., 636
Hargrove, B., 5220
Harley, J.B., 474
Harley, Rosamund D., 4326
Harlow, V.T., 7421
Harper, Irene M., 7220
Harper, K.J., 2715
Harper, W.P., 2812
Harper-Smith, J.W., 7497
Harran, T.E.A.M., 6039
Harries, N.H., 494
Harris, A. (Hull Ph.D.), 440
Harris, A. (London M.A.), 2506
Harris, B.E. (Nottingham M.A.), 892
Harris, B.E. (Nottingham Ph.D.), 1010
Harris, F.W., 4215
Harris, G.G., 2779
Harris, J.R. (Manchester M.A.), 4368
Harris, J.R. (Manchester Ph.D.), 3344
Harris, J.W., 1730
Harris, L., 6831
Harris, M., 7586
Harris, Margaret F., 499
Harris, Margaret O., 1556
Harris, P.B., 2003
Harris, P.R., 5968

Harris, R.W., 7418
Harris, S.B., 466
Harris, W.H., 1623
Harris, W.J.A., 7156
Harris, W.V., 183
Harrison, B.H., 5240
Harrison, G.A. (London Ph.D.), 2740
Harrison, G.A. (Manchester M.A.), 2741
Harrison, G.B., 3140
Harrison, J.F., 3864
Harrison, J.F.C., 5659
Harrison, Mary M.M., 5347
Harrison, Muriel J., 2022
Harrison, R.J., 4849
Harrison, R.S., 6190
Harrison, Reuel, 5546
Harrison, Robert, 7377
Harrison, W.E.C., 2777
Harrison, Winifred, 4073
Harriss, G.L., 915
Harriss, Irene V., 2893
Harrop, A.J., 7592
Harrop, J., 4966
Harry, I.D., 5580
Hart, C.E. (Bristol M.A.), 1084
Hart, C.E. (Leicester Ph.D.), 483
Hart, Dorothy I., 4607
Hart, G.E., 2960
Hart, Mercy C., 2765
Hart, P.J., 5664
Hart, Teresa A., 548
Harte, R.H. (Belfast M.A.), 139
Harte, R.H. (Belfast Ph.D.), 271
Harting, H.M.R.E. Mayr-, see Mayr-Harting
Hartley, F.D., 5190
Hartley, O.A., 5344
Hartley, T.E., 3186
Hartmann, C.A.H., 2418
Hartridge, R.A.R., 722
Hartridge, R.J., 3306
Hartwell, R.M., 5043
Harvey, Barbara F., 1546
Harvey, D.W., 5172
Harvey, G.E., 6985
Harvey, J., 2109
Harvey, Margaret M., 1406
Harvey, P.D.A., 1552
Harvey, Phyllis G., 910
Hasan, I., 6559
Hasan, M.S., 6011
Hasan, S., 6519
Hasan, S.A., 39
Hasan, S.N., 6527
Hasan, Y.F., 6108
Hasler, P.W., 1006
Haslop, G.S.B., 7172
Hasrat, B.J., 6667
Hassaan, M.R., 6860
Hassaan, Rahmani B.M.R., 6780
Hassall, W.O., 1379
Hassam, S.E., 4687
Hassan, H.I., 6111

Hassan, Parveen, 4631
Hassan, R., 6643
Hassen, Maqbul B., 6875
Hastings, J.M., 1515
Hastings, R.P., 4859
Hastings, W.F., 2564
Hatcher, M.J.J.R., 1589
Hatton, Ragnhild M.R.H., 2282
Haunton, P.R.W., 482
Havill, Ethel E., 2490
Havinden, M.A., 2509
Haward, Winifred I., 1140
Hawgood, J.A., 2136
Hawke, G.R., 5151
Hawkes, G.I., 5539
Hawkins, Eliza B., 6300
Hawkins, Lucy M., 4168
Hawkridge, P.B., 2994
Hawkyard, A.D.K., 1517
Haws, C.H., 3224
Hawtin, J.C., 3917
Hay, Cynthia R. MacL., 9
Haycock, B.G., 6097
Haycock, B.J., 6098
Hayes, A., 1737
Hayes, B.D., 3690
Hayes, J.W., 3895
Hayes-M'Coy, G.A., 3237
Hayward, D.W., 7407
Hazlehurst, G.C.L., 4802
Hazlett, H. (Belfast M.A.), 3279
Hazlett, H. (Belfast Ph.D.),
  3280
Head, P., 4948
Head, P.J., 5001
Head, R.E., 2555
Headlam Morley, Agnes, 1819
Heads, J., 4532
Heale, M.J., 7305
Healy, J.F., 142
Heap, Esther J., 1933
Heard, N., 1576
Hearder, H., 4744
Hearn, G.L., 1781
Hearnshaw, F.J.C., 922
Heasman, Kathleen J., 5368
Heath, P., 1326
Heath, T.G., 2111
Heathcote, Sheila J., 717
Heathcote, T.A., 6769
Heaton, H., 2516
Hedley, R.M., 995
Heeney, W.B.D., 5624
Heigham, Norma (Oxford B.Litt.),
  2403
Heigham, Norma (Oxford D.Phil.),
  2402
Helliar-Symons, Pauline E., 1746
Hembry, Phyllis M., 2931
Hemmant, Mary, 906
Henderson, B.L.K., 3203
Henderson, G.B., 1786
Henderson, G.D.S., 1508
Henderson, H.C.K., 402
Henderson, I., 4780
Henderson, Isabel B., 1664

Henderson, L.O., 5388
Henderson, M.D., 4809
Henderson, Marianne E., 305
Henderson, W.O., 5074
Henderson-Howat, G.M.D., 5666
Henn, K., 4003
Hennessy, C.A.M.S., 2460
Hennings, Margaret A., 899
Hennock, E.P., 5757
Henriques, Ursula R.Q. (Man-
  chester Ph.D.), 4151
Henriques, Ursula R.Q. (Oxford
  B.Litt.), 1257
Henry, J.M., 5832
Henthorn, F., 3507
Hentze, Margot, 2269
Hepburn, A.C., 4679
Heppell, Muriel (London M.A.),
  761
Heppell, Muriel (London Ph.D.),
  762
Hepworth, J.R., 290
Herbert, J., 357
Herbert, J.W., 7439
Herman, N., 2150
Herne, Edith M., 2981
Heron, Audrey H., 2210
Herrick, Helen M., 5463
Herriman, P.A., 7165
Herrington, Elsie I., 6363
Herry, T.W., 154
Herskovits, Jean F., 6367
Hester, J.M., 2177
Hetherington, J.G., 1596
Hettiarachchy, T., 6887
Hewitt, F., 4495
Hewitt, F.S., 4023
Hewitt, H.J. (Liverpool M.A.),
  1383
Hewitt, H.J. (London Ph.D.),
  1571
Hewitt, M.J., 7448
Hewitt, Margaret, 5286
Hewlett, A.D., 3072
Hewson, M.A., 806
Hey, C.G., 5621
Hey, D.G., 3541
Heymann, M., 6038
Heywood, C.J., 5978
Hickey, J.V., 5245
Hickman, Gladys M., 411
Hickmore, Mary A.S., 1134
Hicks, F.W.P., 1529
Hicks, J.B., 1493
Hicks, J.R., 5104
Hiden, J.W., 2186
Higginbotham, Margaret, 4625
Higginbottom, J.B., see Kenyon
Higgins, Donald, 1970
Higgins, Doris, 2051
Higgins, G.M., 4650
Higgins, H., 1599
Higgins, Kathleen, 1751
Higginson, J.H., 3535
Higgs, D.C., 2046
Higham, N., 5482

Highet, T.P., 1147
Highfield, J.R.L., 1286
Higson, P.J., 1172
Hilbert, L.W., 2145
Hilborn, K.H.W., 6028
Hill, A.H., 7075
Hill, A.S.H., 2721
Hill, B.W., 3660
Hill, D.J.F. (Durham M.A.), 121
Hill, D.J.F. (Leeds Ph.D.), 120
Hill, D.R. (Durham M.Litt.), 5912
Hill, D.R. (London Ph.D.), 5922
Hill, H.H., 770
Hill, L.M., 2685
Hill, Mary C., 893
Hill, N.K., 4901
Hill, P.V.B., 259
Hill, R.L., 4946
Hill, Rosalind M.T., 1230
Hillary, H.C., 5537
Hillgarth, J.N., 696
Hilliker, J.F., 6719
Hills, R.L., 3355
Hilton, J.D., 7516
Hilton, Patricia, 1484
Hilton, R.H., 1088
Hilton, T.E., 4531
Hinckley, P., 5847
Hind, R.J., 4764
Hinde, Gladys, 2926
Hinde, R.S.E., 4113
Hindley, D.J.B., 1099
Hindmarsh, Nora M., 2829
Hinds, G.M., 5926
Hine, R.A., 1885
Hines, Jennifer S., 6234
Hinnebusch, W.A., 1381
Hinton, E.M., 3137
Hinton, J.S., 5026
Hinton, M.G., 3756
Hinton, R.W.K., 3950
Hinton, W.J., 3921
Hipkin, Gladys M., 2914
Hirsch, D.K.J. von, Baron, 1850
Hitchcock, R.W. (London M.A.), 3519
Hitchcock, R.W. (London Ph.D.), 3520
Hjartarson, S., 7543
Hjejle, Benedicte, 6625
Hjort, Grethe, 1461
Ho, C.-C., 7154
Hobbs, W.F., 5812
Hobsbawm, E.J.E., 4648
Hodge, C. Esther, 1395
Hodge, H.H., 1210
Hodge, P., 6432
Hodges, T.M., 5126
Hodgett, G.A.J., 2951
Hodgkinson, Gladys R., 5263
Hodgkinson, Lilian A., 2273
Hodgkiss, F.D., 1321
Hodgson, H.B., 5708
Hodgson, J.S., 4947
Hodgson, L.M., 492

Hodgson, S.E., 2955
Hodnett, Dorothy K., 966
Hönigsberg, Sulamith, 5883
Hogan, J.J., 1712
Hogan, T.L., 1385
Hogarth, C.E., 4572
Hogg, C.J., 5747
Hogg, I.W., 3069
Hogg, Sallie, 4955
Holbraad, C., 1785
Holden, Kathleen H., 940
Holder, T., 4803
Holderness, B.A., 4048
Holdsworth, C.J., 1431
Holdsworth, H., 4404
Hole, Winifred V., 5282
Holgate, G., 1530
Holiday, P.G., 2815
Holland, A.J., 3983
Hollenberg, G., 2143
Hollingsworth, L.W., 6242
Hollingsworth, T.H., 3446
Hollingworth, P.D., 1959
Hollis, Patricia L., 5476
Holme, A., 5086
Holmes, Alice M., 244
Holmes, C., 4556
Holmes, C.A., 2744
Holmes, G.A., 1163
Holmes, G.S., 3655
Holmes, J.D., 5461
Holmes, J.E., 5871
Holmes, J.W.N., 605
Holmes, Jessie (London M.A.), 6773
Holmes, Jessie (London Ph.D.), 6677
Holroyde, H., 7391
Holt, Beryl, see Smith
Holt, Caroline L.W., 1177
Holt, J.C., 830
Holt, N.R., 1077
Holt, P.M. (Oxford B.Litt.), 4269
Holt, P.M. (Oxford D.Phil.), 6174
Homeshaw, E.J., 4344
Honda, M., 5956
Honey, J.R. de S., 5620
Honeybourne, Marjorie B., 2928
Hook, A.W., 4299
Hook, Judith A., 2234
Hooley, Joyce, see Moss
Hoon, Bessie E., 3930
Hooson, D.J.M., 4496
Hooson, J., 328
Hope, N.V., 3232
Hope, R.B. (Bristol Ph.D.), 5545
Hope, R.B. (Manchester M.A.), 4116
Hope-Taylor, B.K., 1482
Hopf, C.L.R.A., 2936
Hopkin, N.D., 4107
Hopkins, A., 948
Hopkins, A.G., 6405
Hopkins, A.W., 2366

Hopkins, E., 2849
Hopkins, E.J., 4028
Hopkins, T.G.L., 5101
Hopkinson, G.G., 3341
Hopkirk, D.S. (Edinburgh Ph.D.),
3043
Hopkirk, D.S. (Oxford B.Litt.),
4395
Hoppen, Alison M., 2296
Hoppen, K.T., 5459
Hopper, R.J., 161
Hopwood, D., 5990
Horanszky de Hora, L.E.D., 2480
Horgan, J.T., 6434
Horn, P.L.R., 4996
Hornby, S., 4860
Hornik, M.P., 2138
Hornsby, J.T., 4427
Horsburgh, W., 5809
Horsefield, J.K., 3305
Horsfall, L. Frances (London
M.A.), 7435
Horsfall, L. Frances (London
Ph.D.), 7444
Horsfield, R.A., 1283
Horsley, Lee S., 4304
Horsman, R., 7315
Horton, H., 1564
Horton, J.W., 4581
Horwitz, H.G., 3658
Hoskin, D.G., 4663
Hosking, G.A., 2376
Hoskins, W.G. (London M.Sc.),
4007
Hoskins, W.G. (London Ph.D.),
4043
Hossain, M.A., 6795
Hossain, M.M., 5940
Houghton, Alice M., 1514
Houghton, K.N., 986
Houghton, S.M., 5831
Houlbrooke, R.A., 2919
Houlihan, Catherine, 1466
Household, H.G.W., 4040
Houseman, J.W., 3548
Houseman, R.E., 2162
Houston, G.F.B., 5780
Howard, Dora, 7583
Howard, H.E., 1796
Howard, J., 2098
Howard, J.G.M., 1182
Howard, J.H., 4108
Howard, T.E., 3688
Howard Robinson, Mary F., see
Robinson, Mary F.H.
Howat, G.M.D. Henderson-, see
Henderson-Howat
Howe, B., 7404
Howe, J., 2654
Howell, B., 2592
Howell, Brenda M.. 6949
Howell, D.W. (London Ph.D.),
5176
Howell, D.W. (Wales M.A.), 4058
Howell, E.J., 475
Howell, Margaret E., 1188

Howell, R., 3201
Howells, B.E., 1606
Howells, Isobel M., 7364
Howells, J.M., 3412
Howes, H.W., 658
Howland, R.D., 4648A
Howse, E.M.F., 4191
Hoy, W.I., 3250
Hoyle, Margery L. (Manchester
M.A.), 937
Hoyle, Margery L. (Manchester
Ph.D.), 933
Hozayyen, S.A.S. (Liverpool
M.A.), 5899
Hozayyen, S.A.S. (Manchester
Ph.D.), 6094
Hubbard, C.F.B., 4153
Hubbard, Dorothy G.B., 4273
Hudson, Anne M., 66
Hudson, Mildred E., 3061
Huehns, Gertrude, 3088
Huelin, G., 2930
Huffer, D.B.M., 3309
Hufford, R.A., 4662
Hufton, Olwen H., 1988
Hughes, Alison M., 7333
Hughes, Brenda, 7628
Hughes, C.A., 7504
Hughes, C.A.A., 7627
Hughes, C.F., 5238
Hughes, Carys E., 2773
Hughes, D.B., 5258
Hughes, D.T., 844
Hughes, Dorothy, 863
Hughes, Edward, 2862
Hughes, Evan, 5185
Hughes, G.W., 4189
Hughes, Helen C., 1716
Hughes, J.Q., 2297
Hughes, J.R.T., 4907
Hughes, Kathleen W., 1702
Hughes, Margaret E., 3382
Hughes, Mary C., 6290
Hughes, Mary D.A., 3045
Hughes, Mervyn, 5128
Hughes, Michael, 2116
Hughes, R., 4782
Hughes, Rosemary J.F., 2221
Hughes, S.E., 4701
Hughes, T.O., 4623
Hughes, Thomas Richard, 5590
Hughes, Thomas Rowland, 4325
Hughes, Ursula W., 847
Hughes, W.M., 3320
Hughes-Edwards, W.G., 4228
Huitson, J.A., 3748
Hulbert, N.F., 1108
Hull, F., 2845
Hull, J.E., 4244
Hull, P.L., 1191
Humber, R.L., 7319
Humbert, H.F., 3056
Hume, Anthea M.A., 2923
Humphrey, Bernardine M., 325
Humphreys, B., 7322
Humphreys, Dorothy, 1637

Humphreys, Edith H., 756
Humphreys, I., 4592
Humphreys, K.W., 794
Humphreys, R.A., 3785
Humphries, Muriel, 2876
Hunnisett, R.F., 927
Hunt, C.J., 3342
Hunt, E.M., 3823
Hunt, Elsie M.C., 277
Hunt, F.H., 573
Hunt, H.G., 3423
Hunt, H.J., 2054
Hunt, J.M., 4384
Hunt, K.S., 3804
Hunt, N.C., 3681
Hunt, Noreen, 764
Hunt, R.N.C., 1912
Hunt, R.W., 1454
Hunt, W.K., 4565
Hunter, F., 5349
Hunter, J.M., 3310
Hunter, Margaret, 7432
Hunter, S.C., 7025
Huq, M., 6591
Hurd, D.G.E., 2787
Hurnard, Naomi D., 1470
Hurst, Ellen M.M., 3098
Hurt, B.E., 2353
Hurt, J.S., 5564
Hurt, N.K., 6293
Husain, M., 6539
Husain, M.I., 6674
Husain, S.M. (Manchester M.A.), 6533
Husain, S.M. (Manchester Ph.D.), 6540
Husain, Shahanara (London M.A.), 6504
Husain, Shahanara (London Ph.D.), 6501
Hussaini, A.S., 5960
Hussey, Joan M. (London Ph.D.), 529
Hussey, Joan M. (Oxford B.Litt.), 528
Huston, Thomasina, 2427
Hutchins, E.J., 7217
Hutchinson, J.E., 7387
Hutchinson, J.F., 2371
Hutchinson, J.R., 7288
Hutt, M.G., 1990
Huttman, J.P., 5857
Hutton, C.W., 772
Hutton, Elizabeth M., 2229
Hyam, R., 4794
Hyams, P.R., 926
Hyde, F.E., 4903
Hyde, H.M., 4486
Hyde, J.K., 575
Hyde, Patricia G.M., 1551
Hyman, K., 3939
Hyman, R., 5021
Hymers, R.A., 7587
Hyndman, M.H., 2566

IBRAHIM, H.A., 6202

Iddon, Florence M., 4848
Ifemesia, C.C., 6377
Ijagbemi, E.A., 6217
Ilchman, W.F., 7300
Iliasu, A., 4745
Iliffe, J., 6263
Illingworth, E., 3863
Imam, A., 6798
Imam, Z., 2381
Imlach, Gladys M., 3711
Imlah, Ann G., 2476
Immer, J.R., 3334
Imrie, D.S.M., 4416
Indrapala, K., 6893
Ingham, E., 4197
Ingham, K., 6657
Inglis, K.S., 5370
Ingram, K.E.N., 7422
Ingram Ellis, E.R., 5991
Innes, G.P., 1683
Innes, M.R.H., 423
Instein, H., 849
Inyang, P.E.B., 6380
Ions, E.S.A., 7380
Iqbal, S.J., 6823
Iredale, D.A., 3397
Iredell, G.W., 4390
Irons, R.K., 6077
Irvine, Norah W., 2692
Irvine, R.J., 4709
Irving, R.G., 7241
Irwin, G.W., 7003
Irwin, P.J., 1711
Isaac, D.G.D., 3807
Isaacs, Hilda M., 2987
Ishaq, M., 6710
Isichei, Elizabeth M., 5442
Islam, Kamrunnesa, 6487
Islam, R., 5964
Ismail, O.S.A., 5936
Ismail, Y.A.A., 6115
Isserlin, B.S.J., 5885
Ittyerah, V.M., 6820
Iu, Nancy, 7032
Ives, E.W., 2635
Ives, R.B., 2108
Iwanami, T., 7142

JACK, D.R., 4866
Jack, G.D., 599
Jack, Marian R., see Kent
Jack, R.I., 1162
Jack, Sybil M., 2950
Jacka, Hilda T., 2953
Jackson, A.D. Gidlow-, see Gidlow-Jackson
Jackson, A.H., 132
Jackson, B.H., 5652
Jackson, F., 1539
Jackson, George, 4237
Jackson, Gordon, 4365
Jackson, J.A., 5244
Jackson, J.C., 3400
Jackson, J.M., 5076
Jackson, J.R., 5414
Jackson, Mabel V., 6057

Jacob, E.F., 845
Jacobs, L., 5907
Jacombs, Mary E., 266
Jacques, W., 5841
Jago, C.J., 2436
Jagodzinski, J., 559
Jahan, Bilquis, 6571
Jakobovits, I., 1765
James, G.F., 3885
James, K.I., 389
James, L. (Liverpool M.A.), 6068
James, L. (London Ph.D.), 2125
James, M.G., 4192
James, Margaret, 2913
James, Margaret K. (Oxford
  B.Litt.), 671
James, Margaret K. (Oxford
  D.Phil.), 1126
James, P.G., 6372
James, R.D., 516
James, R.L., 218
James, T.E., 5219
James, Thomas John (London Ph.D.
  1946), 1966
James, Thomas John (Wales M.A.
  1913), 1632
Jameson, Shelagh A., 306
Jamieson, A., 6076
Jamieson, J., 5836
Jamison, W.N., 681
Jaques, Juliette W. (London
  M.A.), 64
Jaques, Juliette W. (London
  Ph.D.), 65
Jarman, T.L., 5472
Jarrett, J.D., 3726
Jarrett, M.G., 319
Jarvis, J.B., 5182
Jasper, J.W.G., 5212
Jasper, R.C.D., 2486
Jayasekera, P.V.J., 6935
Jayawardena, L.R.U., 6920
Jayawardena, V.K., 6932
Jayaweera, C.S.V., 6933
Jayaweera, Swarna, 6448
Jefferies, A., 7508
Jefferson, Margaret M., 6027
Jefferys, J.B., 4905
Jeffreys-Jones, R., 7395
Jeffs, R.M., 919
Jenkins, B., 3871
Jenkins, B.A., 7361
Jenkins, D.T., 4019
Jenkins, D.T.I., 2549
Jenkins, Hester T., 1274
Jenkins, J.E.C., 4510
Jenkins, T.H., 6443
Jenkins, W.A., 4346
Jenkins, Wilfred J., 4170
Jenkins, William J., 2852
Jenks, J.E.F., 7573
Jenks, Margaret H., 5999
Jennett, G.D., 5548
Jennings, B., 2529
Jennings, J.C., 1339
Jennings, J.M., 397

Jennings, J.R.G., 5756
Jennings, J.W., 106
Jennings, M.J., 6976
Jepsen, C.H., 2181
Jeremy, D.J., 7307
Jerman, H.N., 1590
Jessop, J.C., 2614
Jewell, Helen M., 897
Jha, J.C., 6708
Jha, L., 6505
Job, R., 4546
John, A.H., 3327
John, D.G., 3340
John, E., 57
John, E.L.T., 972
John, L.B., 2487
John, Margaret B., 3147
John, Muriel, 4586
John, W.R., 3345
Johnes, E.G., 3770
Johnson, A.M., 3198
Johnson, B.L.C., 3990
Johnson, D.C., 4415
Johnson, D.W.J., 4543
Johnson, Dorothy C., 4562
Johnson, F., 5688
Johnson, G., 6829
Johnson, G.C., 987
Johnson, H.B.D., 7493
Johnson, J.A., 1986
Johnson, J.H., 5826
Johnson, J.R.B., 5519
Johnson, Priscilla A., 7406
Johnson, S.A., 2507
Johnson, W.G., 3603
Johnson, Wilfrid H., 3980
Johnson, William H., 1456
Johnston, C.E., 7181
Johnston, Charlotte S., 3856
Johnston, Edith M., 4474
Johnston, F.R., 1308
Johnston, H.J.M., 4122
Johnston, J.A. (Sheffield
  Ph.D.), 3884
Johnston, J.A. (Wales M.A.),
  3670
Johnston, J.V.R., 7438
Johnston, P.F., 2974
Johnston, R., 7229
Johnston, R.J., 4507
Johnston, S.H.F., 834
Johnstone, S.M., 7621
Jolles, O.J.M., 2158
Jones, A.E., 2349
Jones, Alicia G., 1618
Jones, Alwen I., 2048
Jones, Annie B., 2830
Jones, B.P., 3539
Jones, Benjamin, 7297
Jones, Bridgett E.A. (London
  M.A.), 356
Jones, Bridgett E.A. (London
  Ph.D.), 1207
Jones, Brynmor, 372
Jones, C., 2768
Jones, D.C., 1171

319

Jones, D.C.K., 2192
Jones, D.J.V., 3819
Jones, D.K., 5626
Jones, D.L., 7323
Jones, D.R., 2588
Jones, Douglas Haycock, 4195
Jones, Douglas Henry, 1266
Jones, E.B., 3010
Jones, E.E., 2968
Jones, E.G., 2902
Jones, E.H., 5006
Jones, E.J., 3431
Jones, E.L., 5177
Jones, E.P., 1608
Jones, E.S.P., 689
Jones, E.W., 4306
Jones, Edgar, 5096
Jones, Edith, 6975
Jones, Edward, 367
Jones, Edwin (Cambridge Ph.D.), 89
Jones, Edwin (Wales M.A.), 103
Jones, Eleanor M. Glyn-, see Glyn-Jones
Jones, Emrys, 489
Jones, Ethel, 4125
Jones, F., 5098
Jones, F.C., 7105
Jones, F.W., 5418
Jones, G.E., 2891
Jones, G.F.T., 3593
Jones, G.I.M., 3287
Jones, G. Nesta, 1613
Jones, G.O., 3906
Jones, G.R., 3487
Jones, G.R.J., 1630
Jones, G. Stedman, see Stedman Jones
Jones, Gareth H., 2482
Jones, Gareth W., 5157
Jones, George H., 3645
Jones, George W., 5766
Jones, Geraint L., 5894
Jones, Gilbert A., 4655
Jones, Grace A., 4683
Jones, Griffith W., 615
Jones, Gwilym A., 5553
Jones, Gwilym L., 1631
Jones, Gwladys P., 6274
Jones, Gwynneth M.L., 243
Jones, H.G., 4218
Jones, H.L., 4041
Jones, H.W., 4275
Jones, Helen M., 3462
Jones, Hilda M., 1282
Jones, I.D. Lloyd-, see Lloyd-Jones
Jones, I.G., 84
Jones, Iris M., 6822
Jones, J.B.H., 3091
Jones, J.G.P., 4099
Jones, J.K. Boulton-, see Boulton-Jones
Jones, J.O., 5298
Jones, J.S. (London M.Sc.), 5111
Jones, J.S. (London Ph.D.), 7530

Jones, J.W., 683
Jones, James R., 3624
Jones, John Gordon, 3351
Jones, John Gwynfor, 3191
Jones, John Rowland, 1635
Jones, Kathleen, 3458
Jones, Kathleen M., 2050
Jones, L.S., 5551
Jones, Leslie, 5108
Jones, Llewelyn (Liverpool M.A. 1956), 3778
Jones, Llewelyn (Oxford B.Litt. 1923), 2531
Jones, Llewelyn (Wales M.A. 1915), 2530
Jones, M.A., 4518
Jones, M.C.E., 616
Jones, M.J., 3970
Jones, Madeline V., 2731
Jones, Mansel H., 2076
Jones, Marie, 4938
Jones, Marjorie, 1052
Jones, Mary, 1645
Jones, Mary E., 2488
Jones, Mary K., 6947
Jones, Mary L. Arfon, 7353
Jones, Matthew H., 2723
Jones, Melvyn, 4526
Jones, Morgan, 828
Jones, Morgan H., 4230
Jones, Myrddin, 90
Jones, N.H., 4883
Jones, Nesta, see Lloyd
Jones, O.E., 1621
Jones, P.d'A. (London Ph.D.), 5373
Jones, P.d'A. (Manchester M.A.), 4637
Jones, P.E., 3435
Jones, P.H., 1307
Jones, P.J., 661
Jones, P.N., 4528
Jones, R., 4533
Jones, R.A., 4735
Jones, R.B., 4681
Jones, R.D., 3635
Jones, R. Jeffreys-, see Jeffreys-Jones
Jones, R.L., 7273
Jones, R.O., 2647
Jones, R.P. Duncan-, see Duncan-Jones
Jones, R.T., 3105
Jones, R.W. Lloyd-, see Lloyd-Jones
Jones, Ruth E.A., 2000
Jones, S., 3143
Jones, T.B., 1638
Jones, T.C., 3027
Jones, T.D., 5262
Jones, T.D.M., 5555
Jones, T.E., 3971
Jones, T.I.J., 2821
Jones, T.P. (London M.A.), 5549
Jones, T.P. (London Ph.D.), 5589

Jones, T.R., 4238
Jones, V.B.P., 4577
Jones, Vivian, 6428
Jones, W.G., 1661
Jones, W.J., 2667
Jones, W.J. Anthony-, see
  Anthony-Jones
Jones, W.K. Williams-, see
  Williams-Jones
Jones, W.R., 1104
Jones, W.R.D., 2885
Jones Parry, E. (London Ph.D.),
  2456
Jordan, A., 5843
Jordan, Anita, 5609
Jordan, E.K.H., 5457
Jordan, W.M. (London M.A.), 4006
Jordan, W.M. (London Ph.D.), 2097
Jory, E.J., 269
Jory, J.J., 4021
Joseph, C.L.McC., 7500
Joseph, Constance A., 7274
Joseph, P., 7123
Joshi, Angur B., 5274
Joshi, P.M., 6544
Joy, E.T., 4027
Joyce, R.B., 7630
Jubb, A.J., 2605
Jucker, Ninetta, 3709
Judd, D.O'N., 4759
Judek, S., 5094
Judge, H.G., 1937
Judson, H.I., 1543
Judson, W., 2857
Julian, Elisa A., 6995
Jupp, J., 4861
Jupp, P.J., 4488
Jupp, T.H., 6088
Jwaideh, Albertine (Oxford
  B.Litt.), 6012
Jwaideh, Albertine (Oxford
  D.Phil.), 6013

KABDEBO, T.G., 4590
Kabeer, Rokeya, 6807
Kabir, M., 5945
Kaftal, G., 804
Kagan, R.L., 2414
Kakar, M.H., 6979
Kamen, H.A.F., 2445
Kanapathypillai, V., 6905
Kannangara, P.D., 6914
Kanya-Forstner, A.S., 6155
Kapadia, E.R., 6701
Kararah, Azza M.A.H., 4300
Karim, A., 6595
Karim, K.M., 6576
Karski, T. Kryska, see Kryska-
  Karski
Karson, I.M., 7401
Karugire, S.R., 6206
Kassim, M., 6143
Kates, G.N., 1898
Kathirithamby, Jeyamalar, 6996
Katzenellenbogen, S.E., 6330
Katznelson, I., 5348

Kauffmann, C.M., 800
Kaung Maung, 7013
Kawai, H., 7164
Kawharu, I.H., 7578
Kaye, B.L.B., 5465
Kaye, W.E., 2420
Kayyali, A.-W.S., 6047
Kazi, C.K., 6688
Kazziha, W., 6196
Keady, J.M., 7585
Kean, A.W.G., 2479
Keane, Dorothy, 2694
Keane, P., 5673
Keating, Hilda M. (London M.A.),
  434
Keating, Hilda M. (London
  Ph.D.), 435
Keay, F.E., 6468
Keegan, Kathleen M., 2788
Keeley, K.M., 1394
Keen, M.H., 617
Keeney, G.S., 1518
Keenleyside, T.A., 6873
Keep, J.L.H., 2360
Keet, C.C., 5893
Keil, I.J.E., 1069
Keir, Gillian I., 1324
Kekewich, Margaret L., 1476
Kelham, B.B., 3521
Kelidar, A.R., 6175
Kellas, J.G., 5818
Kelleher, Claire, 785
Kellems, V.E., 7313
Keller, A.G. (Cambridge Ph.D.),
  3120
Keller, A.G. (Oxford B.Litt.),
  551
Kellett, G., 117
Kellett, J.R., 4348
Kelley, F.M.E., 1443
Kelley, Lillian W., 837
Kelly, Christine, 1574
Kelly, J.B., 5994
Kelly, L.E., 7145
Kelly, M.J., 2917
Kelly, S.E., 5612
Kelly, T.H., 4991
Kelly, Thomas (Liverpool Ph.D.
  1957), 5656
Kelly, Thomas (Manchester M.A.
  1945), 1309
Kemm, W.St.J., 3486
Kemnitz, T.M., 4839
Kemp, B.R., 1355
Kendall, Olwen P.F., 336
Kendall, W.F.H., 4710
Kendle, J.E., 4768
Kennedy, B.A., 5839
Kennedy, D.E., 2798
Kennedy, J., 2945
Kennedy, J.R., 5453
Kennedy, P.M., 7632
Kenny, E.J.A., 119
Kent, C.A., 4600
Kent, G.B., 4552
Kent, G.O., 2153

Kent, H.S.K., 2401
Kent, J.H.S., 5436
Kent, J.P.C., 690
Kent, Marian R., 6034
Kent, P.C., 1824
Kent, R.A., 3962
Kent, R.C., 2049
Kenwood, A.G., 4885
Kenworthy, Elizabeth, see
  Teather
Kenworthy, F., 3321
Kenworthy, Pauline F., 459
Kenyon, J.B., 207
Kenyon, J.P., 3628
Kerling, Nelly J.M., 653
Kerr, Barbara M., 5829
Kerr, D.G.G., 7225
Kerr, F.A. Gordon-, see Gordon-
  Kerr
Kerr, M.P.G., 5506
Kerr, Margaret W., 4737
Kerr, Mary A.J.P., 331
Kerr, T.A., 3220
Kerr, W.G., 7376
Kerridge, E.W.J., 2837
Kerrison, S.E., 5740
Kerr-Waller, E., 5492
Kershaw, I., 1085
Kershaw, R.N., 2724
Kesby, J.D., 7622
Kew, J.E., 2835
Kew, N.H., 5449
Kewley, J., 359
Keyserlingk, R.H., 2147
Khan, A.M., 6604
Khan, I.M., 5988
Khan, M., 6978
Khan, M.G.I., 5996
Khan, M.I.R., 6506
Khan, M.J., 6560
Khan, M.Q.H., 6746
Khan, M.S., 36
Khan, Y.M. (London M.A.), 6536
Khan, Y.M. (London Ph.D.), 6561
Khanna, Kahan C., 6730
Khatoon, Latifa, 6768
Khavessian, E., 6030
Khedoori, E., 5951
Khuhro, Hamida, 6738
Kiani, M.-Y., 5963
Kido, T., 1023
Kieran, J.A.P., 6222
Kiernan, R.H., 100
Kiernan, T.J., 2621
Kieve, J.L., 5060
Kilcullen, J., 2250
Kilpatrick, J.W., 7441
Kim, S.H., 4119
Kimball, Elisabeth G., 1043
Kimball, P.C., 3943
Kimble, D.B., 6415
Kimble, G.H., 6338
Kimmich, C.M., 2180
Kindersley, R.K., 2357
King, A.D., 900
King, A.S., 4678

King, Agnes, 2017
King, Alice H.K., 4720
King, D.F., 5125
King, E.J., 1058
King, F.H.H., 7095
King, H.P., 1205
King, K.J., 6270
King, N.Q., 521
King, P., 3090
King, P.D., 555
King, R.G., 561
King, S.H. (London M.A.), 427
King, S.H. (London Ph.D.), 429
King, S.T., 4557
Kings, A.T., 3353
Kingsford, P.W., 4992
Kinnear, M.S.R., 4714
Kinnes, Barbara J., 1521
Kinsey, Elizabeth A.W., 3771
Kinsey, W.W., 3839
Kipkorir, B.E., 6272
Kiralfy, A.K., 2485
Kirby, D.A., 2706
Kirby, D.P., 1663
Kirby, J.L., 1154
Kirby, R.H., 1779
Kirk, M., 3426
Kirkland, Dorothy (Liverpool
  M.A.), 598
Kirkland, Dorothy (Liverpool
  Ph.D.), 606
Kirkland, J., 913
Kirkland, W.M., 4449
Kirkpatrick, R.L., 4761
Kirkus, Agnes M., 3176
Kirwan, L.P., 6106
Kitchen, J.M., 2159
Kitchen, L.W., 1265
Kitching, C.J., 2956
Kitching, J., 3506
Kite, J.C., 4736
Kitshoff, M.C., 4403
Kiwanuka, M.S., 6271
Klein, Helena V., 1733
Klottrup, A.C., 5557
Knapp, R.O., 5207
Knapton, Sheila H., 2757
Knecht, R.J., 2916
Knight, D.M., 5480
Knight, Florence L.P., 3842
Knight, G.R., 7005
Knight, L.S., 3113
Knight, M.J., 831
Knight, Patricia F., 4763
Knightbridge, A.A.H. (Oxford
  B.Litt.), 6164
Knightbridge, A.A.H. (Oxford
  D.Phil.), 6149
Knowles, C.H., 846
Knowles, R., 5719
Knowlson, G.A., 633
Knox, Diana M., 5056
Knox, Eva, 3834
Knox, M.G., 7318
Knox, R.B. (Belfast M.A.), 1706
Knox, R.B. (Belfast Ph.D.), 3274

Knox, R.B. (London Ph.D.), 3275
Knox, S.J., 2969
Koay, S.-C., 7094
Kochan, L.E., 1822
Koenigsberger, Dorothy M., 1753
Königsberger, H.G., 2416
Koeppler, H., 790
Koerner, R.M., 5218
Konishi, H., 15
Konovaloff, S., 1879
Kopsch, H., 5346
Koren, W., 1804
Kornell, K., 668
Kornwolf, J.D., 5487
Kortepeter, C.M., 5966
Kotelawele, D.A., 6903
Kouros, A.K., 2314
Köymen, Oya, 5997
Kraay, C.M., 257
Kramer, M.A., 7
Kramer, S.P., 7563
Krikorian, M.K., 6008
Krishna, B., 6566
Krishna, G., 6865
Krishnamurthy, B.S., 6245
Krishnasawmi, A., 6787
Kryska-Karski, T., 5886
Kuhar, A.L., 697
Kumar, Dharma, 6665
Kumar, S., 6517
Kundu, N. (London M.A.), 6971
Kundu, N. (London Ph.D.), 6500
Kuo, J.-C., 7157
Kup, A.P., 2971
Kurat, Y.T., 1794
Kusseff, M., 699
Kwamena-Poh, M.A., 6210
Kwan, Lai-Hung, 7054
Kwapong, A.O.A., 6099
Kwaw-Swanzy, B.E., 6414
Kyba, J.P., 4815
Kyrris, C.P., 547

LACK, Marguerite E., 896
Ladell, A.R., 4207
Lai, R.C., 6744
Laird, M.A., 6654
Lalaguna Lasala, J.A., 2450
Lall, G., 6668
Lally, J.E., 890
Lamb, H.A., 6666
Lamb, J.G., 4441
Lamb, J.W. (Leeds M.A.), 1190
Lamb, J.W. (Leeds Ph.D.), 1179
Lamb, Phyllis J., 2096
Lamb, R.T.B., 2016
Lamb, W.K., 4617
Lambert, Audrey M., 4075
Lambert, D., 2975
Lambert, F.J.D., 7557
Lambert, M.D., 721
Lambert, R.J., 5312
Lambert, Sheila, 4757
Lambert, W.R., 5241
Lambton, Ann K.S., 5950
Lamont, Claire, 4445

Lamont, Olga F., 1714
Lamont, W.M., 3849
Lamusse, M.J.R., 6950
Lancien, D.P.F., 4818
Landau, J., 6148
Lander, J.R., 917
Lane, D.S., 2361
Lane, H.T., 3959
Lane, Joan, 4104
Lane, Margery, 2399
Lang, Eleanor M., 1399
Lang, R.G., 2871
Langley, J.A., 6427
Langley, S.J., 5091
Langnas, A.I., 7533
Langstadt, E., 684
Langstone, Rosa W., 7224
Langton, J., 2526
Lansberry, H.C.F., 4355
Larcombe, H.J., 5544
Larkin, M.J.M., 2089
Larkin, T.J., 2751
Larner, Christina J., 3214
Lary, Diana C.M., 7151
Lasala, J.A. Lalaguna, see
  Lalaguna Lasala
Laslett, J.H.M., 7382
Latham, A.J.H., 6346
Latham, Lucy C., 1582
Latimer, J., 7417
Lattimore, Margaret I., 1538
Lau, Kit-Ching, 7144
Laurence, K.O., 7477
Laven, P.J. (London M.A.), 2653
Laven, P.J. (London Ph.D.),
  2239
Lavington, Rosalind M., 1415
Law, A., 4413
Law, C.M., 3549
Law, Margaret M., 6136
Lawless, R.I., 322
Lawrence, C.H., 1237
Lawrence, J.F., 4382
Lawrence, Pauline E., see
  Helliar-Symons
Laws, J.H., 2350
Laws, W.F., 7434
Lawson, J., 981
Lawson, J.A., 3888
Lawson, W., 4034
Lawton, H.W., 329
Lawton, R., 4524
Layton, I.G., 2407
Lazenby, W.C., 3547
Lea, J.H., 5445
Leaf, Elfrida, 3182
Leaf, Marjorie, 1109
Leamy, A.R., 3600
Leaning, J.B., 222
Leatherbarrow, J.S., 3024
Leavitt, Mary L.M., 198
Le Breton, J.M.R., 6089
Le Chavetois, G.A., 197
Leddy, J.F., 241
Lee, C.H., 3361
Lee, G.A., 5158

Lee, Hilda I., 2308
Lee, J.M., 3298
Lee, Mong Ping, 1742
Lee, Phyllis, 6326
Lee, Tai Hua, 7047
Lee, Y.-L., 6997
Lee Ngok, 7166
Leech, H.C.L., 5166
Leeming, J.S., 2455
Lees, S.G., 4708
Leese, F.E., 2865
Leese, J., 2629
Le Fevour, E.T., 7093
Leff, G., 1458
Legge, J.D., 7626
Legh, Kathleen L. Wood-, see
    Wood-Legh
Le Goff, T.J.A., 1947
Le Guillou, M., 1875
Lehmann, Pauline M., 1033
Lehmberg, S.E., 2642
Leighton, W.H. (Birmingham M.A.
    1925), 1293
Leighton, W.H. (Birmingham M.A.
    1927), 2934
Le Lièvre, Audrey, 3124
Lello, A.J.E., 3012
Le Marchant, A., 129
Le Mesurier, Alice M.C., see
    Carter
Lenfant, J.H.A.M., 4925
Lenman, B.P., 5868
Lennon, T.W., 3055
Lenton, J.H., 3332
Leon, Narda D., 7460
Leonard, H.H., 2880
Leonard, R.A., 4882
Leonard, S.T., 1777
Le Patourel, J.H., 1563
Lerpinière, D.G., 2959
Leslie, Margaret E., 3868
Leslie, R.F., 1847
Lester, J.R., 2073
Lester, Norah, 1424
Lester, R.I., 7354
Letcher, H.P., 923
Lettice, Margaret N., 7614
Levere, T.H., 5479
Levick, Barbara M., 307
Levick, R.B., 3713
Le Vin, Ann, 1921
Levine, A.L., 4962
Levtzion, N., 6349
Levy, H., 5267
Lewin, Joan, 3115
Lewin, R.A., 3498
Lewinson, G., 1806
Lewis, A., 1401
Lewis, A.H.T., 3393
Lewis, B., 5927
Lewis, Beryl H., 3853
Lewis, D.A., 3384
Lewis, D.G., 2800
Lewis, D.L., 2102
Lewis, D.R., 5019
Lewis, E.A., 1644

Lewis, E.D., 3330
Lewis, E.L., 3352
Lewis, E.R., 1809
Lewis, E.T., 5362
Lewis, Estella M., 3194
Lewis, F.R. (Oxford D.Phil.),
    724
Lewis, F.R. (Wales M.A.), 838
Lewis, G.I., 4520
Lewis, G.J., 4530
Lewis, Gwynne (Manchester
    M.A.), 2045
Lewis, Gwynne (Oxford D.Phil.),
    2044
Lewis, H.V.W., 744
Lewis, J.H., 1616
Lewis, M., 2169
Lewis, M.J.T., 358
Lewis, Mary, 1734
Lewis, N.B. (Manchester M.A.),
    624
Lewis, N.B. (Manchester Ph.D.),
    870
Lewis, O.T., 6215
Lewis, P.W., 5073
Lewis, R.G., 205
Lewis, R.M., 5562
Lewis, Richard A., 5252
Lewis, Roy A., 3991
Lewis, Ruth G., 1906
Lewis, S.E., 2166
Lewis, T., 6083
Lewis, T.E., 947
Lewis, Thomas Harris, 3172
Lewis, Thomas Henry, 2598
Lewis, W.M., 3168
Leyser, Henrietta L.V., 703
Li, Ming-hsun, 3931
Lichtenstädter, Ilse, 33
Liddell, J.R., 3127
Liddell, W.H., 1055
Liddicoat, J.W.W., 7538
Liddle, P., 5587
Liebeschuetz, H., 1428
Liebeschuetz, J.H.W.G., 519
Lightbound, Teresa, 3686
Lightley, J.W., 5895
Lighton, G., 6105
Ligota, C.R., 747
Lilley, Irene M., 5585
Lim, Margaret J.B.C. (London
    M.Sc.), 7041. See also Markey,
    Margaret J.B.C.
Limgard, N., 5671
Lindley, K.J. (Manchester M.A.),
    2749
Lindley, K.J. (Manchester
    Ph.D.), 3086
Lindop, Dorothy E., 2944
Lindsay, J.K., 4664
Lindsay, Jean, 3566
Lindsay, R.R., 759
Lindsay-MacDougall, Katherine
    F., 3125
Linehan, P.A., 751
Lines, C.J., 5077

McArthur, A.A., 676
Macaskill, Joyce, 5186
Macaulay, Janet S.A., 1133
Macauley, J.S., 3078
McBriar, A.M., 4647
McCabe, J.E., 4150
McCallum, Dorothy W., 2599
McCann, Jean E., 4428
McCann, W.P., 5509
McCarthy, E.E., 7253
McCarthy, Lilian P., 2025
McCarthy, P., 7597
McCarty, J.W., 4915
McClain, N.E., 4448
McClatchey, Diana, 3485
McClelland, J.G., 5844
McClelland, J.S., 1801
McClelland, V.A. (Birmingham M.A.), 5464
McClelland, V.A. (Sheffield Ph.D.), 5648
McClure, Elizabeth A., 5488
McClure, S.G., 7149
Maccoby, S., 4830
McCollester, Mary A., 4732
McConica, J.K., 3119
McConville, G., 333
McCord, N., 4898
McCourt, D. (Belfast M.A.), 507
McCourt, D. (Belfast Ph.D.), 508
McCown, Dorothy B., 1780
M'Coy, G.A. Hayes-, see Hayes-M'Coy
McCoy, W.L., 5789
McCracken, Eileen M. (Belfast M.Sc.), 2619
McCracken, Eileen M. (Belfast Ph.D.), 6285
McCracken, J.L. (Belfast M.A.), 4472
McCracken, J.L. (Belfast Ph.D.), 4473
McCracken, K.J., 6228
McCristal, J.F., 1463
McCullagh, C.B., 2
MacCunn, F.J., 2034
McCutcheon, K.L., 1107
McCutcheon, W.A. (Belfast M.A.), 3581
McCutcheon, W.A. (Belfast Ph.D.), 3591
MacDermid, G.E., 4429
McDermott, E.J., 2972
McDermott, J., 5168
MacDonagh, O.O.G.M., 5853
McDonald, A.H., 17
Macdonald, D.F., 3572
Macdonald, E.G., 1832
Macdonald, J., 742
McDonald, J.K., 1957
Macdonald, N., 7198
MacDonald, R.J., 6226
McDonnell, K.G.T., 1554
Macdougall, H.A., 5462
MacDougall, Katherine F. Lindsay-, see Lindsay-MacDougall

MacDougall, N.A.T., 1699
McDougall, T.W., 115
Macdowall, D.W., 258
Mace, Frances A., 1117
McElroy, D.D., 4414
McElroy, Katharine L. (Oxford B.Litt.), 3188
McElroy, Katharine L. (Oxford D.Phil.), 3071
McEwan, J.R., 7068
McEwan, J.W., 3251
McEwen, J.M. (London Ph.D.), 4695
McEwen, J.M. (Manchester M.A.), 4696
MacFadyen, A. (Liverpool M.A.), 2434
MacFadyen, A. (Liverpool Ph.D.), 2437
McFarlan, D.M., 5775
Macfarlane, A.D.J. (London M.Phil.), 4081
Macfarlane, A.D.J. (Oxford D.Phil.), 2905
Macfarlane, D.L., 4434
Macfarlane, Leslie John (London Ph.D. 1955), 1301
Macfarlane, Leslie John (London Ph.D. 1962), 4711
McGehee, E.G., 4290
McGeogh, A., 4985
McGill, P.F., 5880
MacGinley, J.J., 2634
McGlynn, T.R., 1845
McGowan, A.P., 2794
McGrath, J.S.F., 5860
McGrath, P.V., 3956
Macgregor, I.J.G., 2006
McGregor, J.F., 2761
Macgregor, J.J., 5203
MacGregor, Janet G., 3231
MacGregor, M.B., 3260
McGregor, R., 6320
McGuffie, T.H., 3910
McGuinness, T.W., 2528
McGuire, B.P., 711
McGurk, P.M., 781
McHattie, Marjorie D., 3671
Machin, F., 4989
Machin, G.I.T., 3760
McHugh, B.J., 515
McInnes, A.J.D.M., 3662
MacInnes, J., 4399
McIntosh, B.G., 6244
Macintosh, W.H., 5358
McIntosh, W.L., 7329
Macintyre, A.D., 4549
McIntyre, Elizabeth P., 2655
McIntyre, W.D., 4758
McKay, A.I.K., 667
MacKay, A.L.G., 7582
McKay, A.R., 4424
McKay, D.A., 1697
Mackay, D.F., 2254
Mackay, D.L., 3794
McKay, Joan D., 2771
McKeen, D.B., 2904

McKenna, G.P., 260
McKenna, J.W., 873
McKenzie, D.F., 3999
MacKenzie, K., 3831
Mackenzie, Margaret H., 5998
Mackenzie, N.H., 6279
Mackenzie, P.D., 3488
McKeown, M., 5842
Mackerras, C.P., 6959
Mackesy, P.G., 2304
McKibbin, R.I., 4686
Mackie, J.L., 4893
McKie, Muriel, 4595
McKinley, R.A., 1353
Mackinnon, H., 1440
MacKinnon, I.F., 7176
Mackinnon, J.M., 5266
Mackintosh, Mary M., 5814
McKisack, May, 976
Mackoskey, R.A., 2469
Mackrell, J.Q.C., 1965
Mackwell, Christina A., 2673
Maclachlan, A.D., 1774
McLachlan, H.J. (Manchester
  M.A.), 4297
McLachlan, H.J. (Oxford
  D.Phil.), 4154
McLachlan, Jean O., 2448
McLachlan, N.D., 7576
McLane, J.R., 6837
McLaughlin, J.P., 2004
MacLean, A.C., 577
Maclean, A.H., 3858
Maclean, J.N.M. (Edinburgh
  Ph.D.), 4437
Maclean, J.N.M. (Oxford
  B.Litt.), 6635
Maclean, J.R., 7467
McLeish, J., 7519
McLellan, A., 3524
McLellan, N.J., 4836
Macleod, D.J., 7309
MacLeod, M.H., 4255
MacLeod, Marion J., 7231
MacLeod, R.M., 4598
McLeod, W.H., 6545
McLintock, A.H., 7202
McLoughlin, Mary G., 2900
McManus, J.P., 2854
McMaster, J., 7110
MacMillan, D.F., 4864
Macmillan, H.W., 6231
McMillan, William (Edinburgh
  Ph.D. 1925.), 3226
McMillan, William (Manchester
  M.A. 1959), 4463
McMullen, I.J., 7063
Macnab, K.K., 5227
Macnab, T.M.A., 3215
McNally, F.W., 3095
McNaulty, Mary, 4106
McNeill, Barbara A., 4458
McNeill, P.G.B., 2609
McNiven, P., 877
MacNutt, W.S., 7189
Macpherson, H.C., 3252

MacPherson, I.W., 2410
Macpherson, W.J., 6743
McQueen, E.I., 27
Macqueen, Edith E., 3233
Macrae, A., 1677
Macrae, C., 1693
MacSween, M.D., 3560
MacTaggart, R.A., 2481
McWilliam, M.D., 6269
Madan, Annie H., 3615
Madden, A.F. (Oxford B.Litt.),
  7580
Madden, A.F. (Oxford D.Phil.),
  5351
Madden, J.J., 7345
Madden, M., 5017
Maddicott, J.R.L., 858
Maddock, S., 5008
Madge, S.J., 3204
Madgwick, R.B., 7588
Maguire, W.A., 5828
Maher, L.A., 1863
Mahgoub, E.-F., 6195
Mahmood, A.B.M.U., 6618
Mahmood, A.W., 6660
Mahmoud, A.-el H. Hamdy, see
  Hamdy Mahmoud
Mahoney, Florence K.O., 6373
Maiden, J., 383
Maiguaschca, J.M., 7547
Main, A., 3221
Main, J.M., 3841
Mainga, Mutumba, 6311
Mains, Jean A., 2474
Maitland, J.V., 226
Maitland Muller, D.G., 44
Maity, P.K., 6463
Maity, S.K., 6481
Majid-Hamid, Z., 4888
Major, Kathleen, 1220
Majumdar, Amita, 6686
Majumdar, S.C., 6715
Makepeace, R.E., 4193
Makey, W.H., 3948
Malbon, Gladys, 833
Malcolm, C.A., 1669
Malcolm-Smith, Elizabeth F.,
  1852
Malcolmson, Patricia E., 5744
Malcolmson, R.W., 3453
Malcomson, A.P.W., 4469
Male, D.J., 2394
Malhotra, P.L., 6834
Malick, S.O., 7299
Malik, I.Z.-un-N., 6751
Maliwa, Emily N. (London
  M.Phil.), 6238
Maliwa, Emily N. (London
  Ph.D.), 6239
Malkin, H.C., 3904
Mallett, M.E., 593
Malley, Edith, 4070
Mallick, A.R., 6689
Mallier, A.T., 5337
Mallinson, A., 315
Malnick, Bertha, 2325

327

Malone, J.J., 7270
Malone, J.S., 5617
Maltby, A., 5342
Maltby, S.E., 5571
Manbré, S.T., 1275
Mandel, N.J., 6021
Mangat, J.S., 6236
Manley, K.R., 4254
Mann, J.C., 294
Mann, J.G., 662
Manning, B.S., 2753
Manning, F.E., 3752
Manning, W.H., 353
Mansergh, P.N.S., 5870
Mansfield, A.J., 3282
Mansfield, R. (Manchester M.A.), 4198
Mansfield, R. (Manchester Ph.D.), 3483
Maoz, M.M., 6002
Mar, T.T.G., 7127
Marais, J.S., 7593
Maratheftis, F.S., 2298
March, K.G., 4602
Marchant, L.R., 7120
Marchant, R.A., 2996
Marchington, T., 5722
Marcousé, Renée, 1502
Marcus, G.J., 648
Marin, C.A., 6060
Mark, F.X., 7499
Markey, Margaret J.B.C. (London Ph.D.), 6451. See also Lim, Margaret J.B.C.
Markham, S.F., 2207
Marks, L.F. (Oxford B.Litt.), 2223
Marks, L.F. (Oxford D.Phil.), 2222
Marks, Sally J., 2294
Marks, Shula E., 6334
Marriner, Sheila, 5115
Marsden, A., 6082
Marsden, C.A., 2411
Marsden, E.W., 124
Marsden, J.D., 587
Marsden, T.L. (Manchester M.A.), 2582
Marsden, T.L. (Manchester Ph.D.), 2583
Marsden, W.E., 5538
Marsh, J.R.S., 4929
Marsh, P.T., 5417
Marsh, T.N., 7170
Marshall, A.J., 301
Marshall, B.R., 5491
Marshall, Catherine K., 2345
Marshall, D.W.H., 1687
Marshall, Dorothy, 4092
Marshall, G.H., 1027
Marshall, J.D., 3543
Marshall, J.S., 4417
Marshall, P.J., 3797
Marshall, R.M.J., 467
Marshall, Rosalind K., 4389
Marshall, W.K., 7483

Marsot, A.G., 7001
Marston, F.S., 1817
Martell, J.S., 7214
Martin, A.M., 2392
Martin, B.K., 1197
Martin, C.B., 7208
Martin, C.J., 576
Martin, Carola M., 581
Martin, D.A., 4806
Martin, D.G., 7294
Martin, Eveline C. (London M.A.), 6355
Martin, Eveline C. (London Ph.D.), 6357
Martin, F.X., 2220
Martin, G.H., 1129
Martin, J.E., 4951
Martin, J.J.H., 1445
Martin, J.M. (Birmingham M.Com.), 4378
Martin, J.M. (Birmingham Ph.D.), 3425
Martin, Janet D., 4287
Martin, K.L.P. (Manchester M.A.), 4722
Martin, K.L.P. (Oxford B.Litt.), 7212
Martin, M.A., 2446
Martin, Phyllis M., 6345
Martin, R., 5028
Martin, W.S., 5730
Martindale, J.R., 224
Martindale, Jane P., 556
Martindale, L., 4053
Martineau, Erica I.J., 5441
Martinuzzi, L.S., 5142
Marwick, A.J.B., 4702
Marx, Nancy M., 7521
Mary Baptist, Mother, 3290
Mary de Sales, Mother, see Duncombe, Brenda M.
Mary Philomena, Mother, see Forshaw, Helen
Marzari, F.O., 1895
Mason, A., 5031
Mason, B.J., 5357
Mason, H.L., 5849
Mason, J., 3576
Mason, J.F.A., 1031
Mason, M.D., 6361
Mason, R.J., 2949
Massey, F.L., 5695
Masters, D.C., 7228
Mather, D.B., 6104
Mather, F.C., 5250
Mather, W., 1288
Matheson, P.C., 1766
Mathew, W.M., 7536
Mathews, E.F.J., 4367
Mathews, H.F. (Liverpool M.A.), 5563
Mathews, H.F. (London Ph.D.), 5583
Mathias, P., 5225
Mathias, R.G., 3929
Mathias, Stella Y., 3765

Mathur, R.B., 6590
Matthai, J., 6847
Matthew, D.J.A., 1334
Matthew, H.C.G., 4776
Matthews, Hazel, 2686
Matthews, J., 1332
Matthews, J.F., 228
Matthews, Janet H., 643
Matthews, K., 7186
Matthews, T.F.G., 2594
Maude, G.E., 2405
Maule, C.J., 7245
Maung Shein, 7033
Mawdsley, W.N. Hargreaves-, see Hargreaves-Mawdsley
Mawi, N.El-H.H.M.A.El-A., 5973
Mawson, Constance, 1365
Mawson, E.G., 2911
Maxton, G.S., 4430
Maxwell, T., 4398
Maxwell, W.D., 2472
May, A.N., 1075
May, J.M.F., 166
May, T.F., 5618
Maynard, Helen A., 1522
Maynard, W.B., 5443
Mayne, R.J., 709
Mayor, S.H. (Manchester M.A.), 3003
Mayor, S.H. (Manchester Ph.D.), 5363
May-Oung, Mya S., 7036
Mayr-Harting, H.M.R.E., 1189
Mazumdar, Vina, 6855
Mbaeyi, P.M., 6375
Mbye, L.A., 6369
Mead, A.H., 5400
Mead, G.J. de C. (London M.A.), 1013
Mead, G.J. de C. (London Ph.D.), 1950
Meadows, P., 1528
Meads, Dorothy M., 3116
Mealing, S.R., 3748A
Mears, R.A.F., 4223
Measures, G.A., 5769
Medd, P.G., 1183
Medlicott, W.N., 6018
Meebelo, H.S., 6325
Meek, Christine E., 590
Megahey, A.J., 5865
Megaw, Margaret I., 1348
Mehrotra, S.R., 6846
Mehta, M.S., 6691
Mehta, Shobhana K., 6512
Meir, J.K., 3526
Meissner, J.L.G., 1185
Mejcher, H.J.F., 6044
Melbourne, A.C.V., 7575
Meldrum, N., 3257
Mellen, Frances N., 2513
Meller, Helen E., 5320
Mellor, C.M., 1725
Mellor, G.R., 6370
Mellowes, C.L., 4005
Melville, A.M.M., 1105
Ménage, V.L., 48

Mendenhall, T.C., 2872
Mendis, G.C., 6886
Mendis, V.L.B., 6904
Mendl, W.M.L., 2106
Mensah-Brown, A.K., 6360
Menzies, Elizabeth A., 3256
Meredith, D., 6102
Meredith, H.J., 5193
Meredith, J.R., 4096
Meredith, Rosamond, 2874
Merriam, S.H., 5786
Merritt, J.E., 3973
Mess, H.A., 4960
Metcalf, D.M., 645
Metcalf, G., 7437
Metcalfe, B., 3410
Metcalfe, Christine S., see Nicholls
Mettam, R.C., 1935
Meyer, Lilian B., 872
Meynell, Hildamarie, 1814
Miah, M.S., 5939
Michael, J.H., 265
Middleton, C.R., 3899
Middleton, N.G., 5341
Middleton, P.R., 343
Midgley, C., 340
Midgley, Laura M., 839
Midwinter, E., 5248
Midwinter, E.C., 5558
Miers, Suzanne (London Ph.D.), 6067. See also Doyle, Suzanne
Mifsud, G., 1291
Milburn, D., 5717
Milburn, G., 7227
Milburn, G.E., 1223
Mildon, W.H., 3013
Miles, G.J., 7000
Miles, G.S., 471
Miles, H., 3364
Miles, Margaret G., 7366
Miles, Sally A., 568
Miliband, R., 2001
Millar, F.G.B., 28
Millard, Annie M., 2870
Millard, H.I., 1389
Miller, A.B., 4133
Miller, A.T., 3253
Miller, F., 1121
Miller, F.H. Hansford, see Hansford Miller
Miller, H., 5855
Miller, Helen J., 2633
Miller, J.C.MacB., 4219
Miller, J.I., 262
Miller, Margaret S., 2372
Miller, T.B., 4771
Millette, J.C., 7454
Millington, J., 7631
Millor, W.J., 1427
Mills, D.R. (Leicester Ph.D.), 5197
Mills, D.R. (Nottingham M.A.), 3295
Mills, H.H., 789
Mills, Janell A., 7018

329

Mills, L.A., 7010
Mills, M.A., 4680
Mills, Mabel H., 859
Milne, A.T., 7316
Milne, Doreen J., 3626
Milne, J.M., 5477
Milne, R.D., 2183
Milne, T.E., 5156
Milward, A.S., 2204
Milward, W.E., 2659
Mimardière, A.M., 4089
Miner, J.N.T., 1436
Ming, Yui, 1740
Mingay, G.E., 4057
Minio-Paluello, L., 798
Minton, Joyce G., 2502
Mirza, N.A., 535
Mishra, R.C., 5256
Misra, B.B., 6621
Mitcham, P., 7180
Mitchell, A.V. (Manchester
  M.A.), 3820
Mitchell, A.V. (Oxford D.Phil.),
  3768
Mitchell, B.R., 5079
Mitchell, C., 2107
Mitchell, Ena A.E., 82
Mitchell, F., 2790
Mitchell, H., 2018
Mitchell, L.G., 3734
Mitchell, P.K., 2504
Mitchell, R.D., 4436
Mitchell, Rosamund J., 883
Mitchell, W.S., 3255
Mitchiner, Winifred M., 1195
Mitra, B., 6702
Mitter, P., 6537
Mittwoch, Anita, 5898
Moberg, D.R., 4850
Moffat, C.L., 4425
Moffit, L.W., 4361
Moggridge, D.E., 4930
Mohamad, A.M. Rashad, see
  Rashad Mohamad
Mohamed, A.I., 6130
Mohamed, N.E., 6185
Mohan, Krishna, 6524
Mohsin, K.M., 6619
Moir, Esther A.L., 4376
Mojuetan, B.A., 6075
Mojumdar, K., 6806
Mole, D.E.H., 5394
Molla, M.K.U., 6852
Moller, Asta W.R. (Oxford
  B.Litt.), 3981
Moller, Asta W.R. (Oxford
  D.Phil.), 2522
Molloy, Monica, 5575
Moloney, B., 2246
Moloney, T.M., 4753
Molyneux, D.D., 5322
Molyneux, F.H., 5768
Molyneux, M.S., 584
Monaghan, J.J. (Belfast M.A.),
  4483
Monaghan, J.J. (Belfast Ph.D.),
  4487

Monaghan, T.J.A., 4307
Moncreiffe, Sir Rupert I.K.,
  2607
Money, J., 3701
Monger, G.W., 4786
Monteith, Dorothy, 424
Montgomery, A.B., 5796
Montgomery, A.E., 6049
Montpetit, M. Marie, 792
Moody, T.W., 3272
Moon, H.R., 4769
Moore, Claire A.I., 238
Moore, Dorothy I., 3343
Moore, E.B., 1758
Moore, J.L., 4579
Moore, Louise S., 4260
Moore, Margaret F., 1036
Moore, Marjorie G., 5475
Moore, Minnie L., 5140
Moore, P.C., 2550
Moore, Robert J., 7482
Moore, Robin J., 6765
Moorhead, F.J., 816
Mootham, O.H., 1726
Moran, W. (London M.A.), 2562
Moran, W. (London Ph.D.), 1946
Morant, Valerie E., 412
Morehouse, Frances, 7336
Moreton, C.E., 4813
Moreton, H.A.V., 1952
Morewood, Violet, 3721
Morey, G.E. (London M.A.), 1572
Morey, G.E. (London Ph.D.),
  1169
Morgan, B.G., 1504
Morgan, C., 3427
Morgan, D.H.J., 5412
Morgan, D.R., 4852
Morgan, D.T., 5048
Morgan, D.W., 2173
Morgan, E.D., 6260
Morgan, Glyn, 3046
Morgan, Gwenda, 7279
Morgan, H.C., 5649
Morgan, I.J., 5645
Morgan, J.H., 2590
Morgan, J.L., 1695
Morgan, K.O., 4628
Morgan, M.G., 188
Morgan, M.J., 1325
Morgan, Margaret R., 62
Morgan, Marjorie M. (Oxford
  B.Litt.), 1218
Morgan, Marjorie M. (Oxford
  D.Phil.), 1335
Morgan, Monica M., 189
Morgan, P., 4088
Morgan, P.B., 5369
Morgan, P.T.J., 2628
Morgan, R.M., 1619
Morgan, R.P., 1799
Morgan, T.D., 5606
Morgan, Valerie, 4446
Morgan, W.T., 3472
Morgan, W.T.W., 5088
Morgans, H., 4843
Morgans, J.I., 3075

330

Morison, Isabel A., 2281
Moritz, L.A., 122
Morley, Agnes Headlam, see
  Headlam Morley
Morley, C.D., 4499
Morley, F.S., 4774
Morley, R., 5639
Morley, R.D., 851
Morrall, J.B., 857
Morrell, W.P., 4729
Morrice, J.C. (Oxford B.Litt.),
  3142
Morrice, J.C. (Oxford D.Phil.),
  2887
Morris, D.C., 4823
Morris, D.J.S., 7378
Morris, Elizabeth M.D., 4265
Morris, F.C., 1710
Morris, G.E., 807
Morris, G.M. (Nottingham M.A.),
  5430
Morris, G.M. (Nottingham Ph.D.),
  5431
Morris, J.H., 3357
Morris, J.R., 217
Morris, J.T., 1238
Morris, Katharine, 3729
Morris, L.E., 2675
Morris, L.P., 6974
Morris, N., 5890
Morris, Patricia H., 5732
Morris, R.W., 5297
Morris, S.V., 501
Morrish, D.J., 4620
Morrish, P.S., 5402
Morrison, T.V.B., 5534
Morrow, I.F.D., 1795
Mort, Margaret K., 2691
Mortimer, R.S., 3469
Mortimore, M.J., 5707
Morton, D.D.P., 7242
Morton, Ruth G., see Lewis
Morton, W.L., 7201
Mosby, J.E.G., 3419
Moser, W.L., 1268
Moses, J.H., 3651
Moses, N.H., 4874
Mosley, D.J., 148
Moss, J.R., 233
Moss, Joyce, 363
Moss, R., 4226
Mosse, W.E.E., 4741
Moul, Winifred J.E., 4313
Moule, J., 1208
Moulton, Carol H., 229
Moulton, E.C., 6801
Mounfield, P.R., 2539
Mountford, O.E., 5062
Mousley, Joyce E., 2908
Mowat, R.C., 6165
Moyns, Hilda, 801
Moyse-Bartlett, H., 6241
Mudie, Phyllis J., 6639
Muhammad, A., 5938
Muhammadi, R.A., 6579
Muir, Janet W., 980

Muir, R., 506
Muir, T., 3236
Mukherjee, B.N., 6475
Mukherjee, H.N., 85
Mukherjee, Hena, 6742
Mukherjee, Ranjana, 6477
Mukherjee, S., 6642
Mukherji, B.N., 6453
Mulholland, W.J., 7177
Muller, D.G. Maitland, see
  Maitland Muller
Mulligan, R.R.J., 6037
Mullins, Anthea R., 4333
Mullins, E.L.C., 2970
Mullins, Stephanie, 695
Mumford, W.F., 545
Munford, W.A., 5485
Mungeam, G.H., 6249
Munroe, T.St.C., 7506
Munter, R. La V., 4460
Munz, P., 2679
Murdie, Ella, 2305
Muris, C., 4844
Muriuki, G., 6208
Murley, J.T., 2019
Murphy, J., 5576
Murphy, W.P.D., 3187
Murray, A.V., 765
Murray, Alexander L., 7446
Murray, Athol L., 1694
Murray, Audrey M., 1373
Murray, C.H., 675
Murray, Catherine, 4462
Murray, D.J., 3798
Murray, D.R., 7529
Murray, Katherine M.E., 1101
Murray, P.J., 805
Murray, R.G., 2252
Murray, W.G., 6308
Murti, B.S.N., 7027
Musgrave, Clare A., 1160
Musgrave, P.W., 1803
Musson, A.E., 4979
Musson, J.W., 5835
Mustafa, A.A.-R., 6153
Musto, N.M., 445
Musty, J.W.G., 1114
Mutibwa, P.M., 6220
Mutton, Alice F.A., 403
Muztar, A.D., 6534
Mya S. May-Oung, see May-Oung
Myers, A.R. (London Ph.D.), 918
Myers, A.R. (Manchester M.A.),
  982
Myers, J.D., 5773
Myers, J.F., 2637
Mykula, W., 2391
Myres, J.P.H., 2310

NAFF, T., 5989
Nahar, Shamsun, 6808
Naim, M.A., 6963
Nainar, S.M.H., 6507
Naish, M.C., 4055
Naji, A.J., 5943
Namasivayam, S., 6939

O'Kelly, Kathleen M., 4509
O'Kelly, P., 3590
Okonjo, I.M., 6426
Oldfield, M., 1314
Oldham, W., 3705
O'Leary, C., 4563
O'Leary, Ida M., 3623
O'Leary, Mary F.M., 5493
O'Leary, P.K. (Belfast M.A.),
  2249
O'Leary, P.K. (Belfast Ph.D.),
  5882
Oliver, J.K., 5422
Oliver, J.L., 5075
Oliver, R.A., 6219
Oliver, W.H., 3843
Olney, R.J., 4567
O'Loughlin, Carleen, 5195
Olphin, H.K., 3730
Olsen, Constance P.M., 450
Olsen, Marilyn B. MacK., 7203
Olsen, V.H., 2973
Oman, R.J., 3860
Omar, F., 5932
Omar, O.A.-A., 6137
Omosini, O., 6406
O'Neill, J.E., 1700
O'Neill, R.J., 2196
Onek, J., 2185
Onwuka, U., 6439
Oosterhoff, Frederika G., 2274
Opie, D.J., 23
Oppenheimer, Sir Michael B.G.,
  2702
Oppermann, C.J.A. (London M.A.),
  2397
Oppermann, C.J.A. (London
  Ph.D.), 745
Oprey, C., 3912
Oram, H.C., 3358
Orange, A.D., 5471
Orange, G.V., 1357
Orchardson, I.K., 5153
Orme, E.L., 4131
Orme, Margaret, 1212
Orme, N.I., 1446
Orr, J.E., 5366
Orr, J.M., 6732
Orr, R.R., 3081
Orrin, J.E.S., 4535
Osborn, R.R., 4212
Osborne, F.M., 3503
Oschinsky, Dorothea, 1073
Osley, A.S., 20
Osman, M.K., 6193
Osman Abdou, O.M., 6182
Ostergaard, G.N., 4965
Otley, C.B., 4876
Ottrey, F.S., 5718
Otway-Ruthven, Annette J., 907
Ough, Cora J., 1512
Outhwaite, R.B., 2805
Overton, Sylvia E., 1297
Owen, A.T., 309
Owen, A.W., 4231
Owen, C.C., 3307

Owen, D.H., 1647
Owen, E.H., 5230
Owen, E.R.J., 6131
Owen, G., 1612
Owen, G.D., 2831
Owen, G.E., 4831
Owen, H., 1628
Owen, H.G., 2989
Owen, J.B., 3685
Owen, L.A., 2374
Owen, L.H., 2577
Owen, P.E., 5641
Owen, R.H., 3684
Owen, R.J., 5427
Owen, V.T., 2099
Owen, W.T., 4249
Owst, G.R., 1290
Oxley, G.W., 3450
Oxley, J.E., 4319
Özbaran, S., 5965

PACK, L.F.C., 4105
Packer, Eve B., 7374
Pagan, K.V., 379
Page, Frances M., 1079
Page, H.H., 2355
Page, Monica G., 4516
Page, R.A.H., 5123
Page, R.I., 1489
Paisley, Margaret E., 5277
Pal, Arumima, 6845
Palley, Claire, 6317
Palliser, D.M., 3179
Pallister, Anne, 3851
Palmer, A.W., 2358
Palmer, J.J.N. (London Ph.D.),
  625
Palmer, J.J.N. (Oxford B.Litt.),
  1313
Palmer, R.E., 5802
Palmer, R.H., 6319
Palmer, W.C. (London M.A.),
  6444A
Palmer, W.C. (London Ph.D.),
  5972
Paluello, L. Minio-, see Minio-
  Paluello
Panabokke, G., 6884
Pandey, B.N., 6640
Pandey, K.N., 6705
Pandey, M.S., 6458
Panigrahi, D.N., 6683
Panigrahi, Lalita N., 6758
Pankhurst, R.K.P., 3774
Papadopoulos, G.S., 6032
Pape, T., 1532
Papworth, H.D., 5698
Paret, P., 2121
Parham, E.T., 455
Parizeau, J., 7237
Park, J.T., 3715
Parke, Jean, 1083
Parker, D., 1915
Parker, D.O., 3838
Parker, Elizabeth, 1503
Parker, G.H.W., 718

Parker, L.A., 2820
Parker, N.G., 2422
Parker, R.A.C., 3417
Parker, Vanessa S., 428
Parker, W.A., 4115
Parker, W.H. (Oxford B.Sc.), 405
Parker, W.H. (Oxford D.Phil.), 7221
Parkes, J.W., 678
Parkes, M.B., 1448
Parkin, Elizabeth S., 7124
Parkinson, A.J., 3315
Parkinson, Betty J., 1203
Parkinson, C.N., 7079
Parkinson, M.H., 5643
Parks, S.R., 3996
Parnaby, O.W., 7604
Parr, Elizabeth J., 2466
Parris, H.W. (Leeds M.A.), 5146
Parris, H.W. (Leicester Ph.D.), 5147
Parry, B.R., 1605
Parry, Benita, 6776
Parry, Blodwen M., 3872
Parry, C., 4670
Parry, E. Jones (Wales M.A.), 2087. See also Jones Parry
Parry, E.O., 1648
Parry, Eva D., 1222
Parry, J.H., 7509
Parry, O., 4570
Parry, R.I., 5433
Parry, R.J., 1812
Parshad, I.D., 6605
Parsloe, C.G., 3202
Parsons, C.J., 91
Parsons, E.J.S., 2752
Parsons, F.V., 6085
Partington, R.S., 2586
Partner, P.D., 754
Partridge, Monica A., 2335
Pasieka, K.S., 1856
Paterson, Janet, 7190
Pathak, B., 6981
Pathak, V.S., 41
Pathmanathan, S., 6894
Patmore, J.A., 441
Paton, Margaret O. Noël-, see Noël-Paton
Patrick, A.J., 4393
Patrick, J.M. (Oxford B.Litt.), 2729
Patrick, J.M. (Oxford D.Phil.), 3847
Patterson, H.O.L., 7416
Patterson, Sonia, 803
Pattinson, Dorothea H., 7303
Pattison, Ann K., 1123
Pattison, R., 5613
Patton, J.V., 776
Patwari, M.A.S., 6848
Paul, B.C., 6456
Paul, G.M., 18
Paul, J.D.S., 2826
Paul, J.E., 3025
Paul, R.S., 2763

Paull, C.A., 5097
Pavlovsky, G.A., 2365
Pavlowitch, S., 1851
Pay, T.W., 1246
Payne, C.I., 7349
Payne, E.O., 4067
Payne, P.L., 5071
Peach, G.H.W., 5691
Peacock, A.J., 5209
Peake, Margaret I., 882
Pearl, Valerie L., 3200
Pearn, B.R., 2209
Pearson, E., 3311
Pearson, P.C., 5451
Pearson, R.E., 5090
Pearson, S.W., 2907
Pearton, M.G., 1866
Peck, Leonora D.F., 4959
Pecker, Gwendoline F., 3788
Pedley, R., 380
Pedley, W.H., 5217
Peel, A., 2999
Peel, R.A., 352
Peetz, E.A.O., 6224
Pegrum, Brenda M., 3156
Peirce, Elizabeth, 797
Pelham, R.A., 1579
Pelling, H.M., 4640
Pells, E.G., 5323
Pemberton, W.A., 4159
Pemble, J.C., 6694
Pemble, R.J., 5300
Penn, C.D., 2791
Penson, Lillian M., 7428
Percival, J., 330
Percival, Sheila M., 1909
Percy, K.A., 5662
Perkin, J.R.C., 5428
Perkins, J.P., 620
Perkyns, Audrey D., 889
Perren, R., 5206
Perrott, Marjorie E., 3273
Perry, J., 3247
Perry, J.R., 5981
Perry, P.J., 5127
Perry, Reginald (Bristol M.A.), 5625
Perry, Reginald (London Ph.D.), 3356
Persianis, P.K., 2313
Petch, R.B.K., 1299
Petegorsky, D.W., 2760
Péter, L.F., 1854
Peters, J.T., 2118
Petersen, M.A.F. Bredahl, see Bredahl Petersen
Peterson, W.J., 7062
Petherick, C., 1870
Petterson, D.R., 6225
Pettit, P.A.J., 2505
Petty, W.M., 4865
Peyton, S.A., 4354
Pfaff, R.W., 1316
Philips, C.H. (Liverpool M.A.), 3793
Philips, C.H. (London Ph.D.), 3792

Powley, E.B. (Oxford D.Phil.), 3887
Poyser, Elizabeth R., 2237
Prasad, Beni, 6493
Prasad, R.C., 6549
Prasad, Y., 6599
Prashad, G., 6775
Pratt, E.J. (Oxford B.Litt.), 7348
Pratt, E.J. (Oxford D.Phil.), 7537
Preen, Margaret, 1152
Prescot, H.K., 3874
Prescott, Hilda F.M., 827
Prescott, J.R.V., 5876
Presedo, V. Vázquez-, see Vázquez-Presedo
Pressly, H.E., 5350
Pressly, P.M., 2039
Pressnell, L.S., 3304
Prest, W.R., 2688
Preston, A.W., 6804
Preston, R.A., 3643
Prestwich, M.C., 994
Prevelakis, E., 2214
Pribićević, B., 5024
Price, A.R. Rhys-, see Rhys-Price
Price, C.A., 2309
Price, C.D., 4085
Price, D.J., 1473
Price, Dorothea T., 1244
Price, Evelyn M., 1170
Price, F.C., 3692
Price, F.D., 2966
Price, J.L., 2278
Price, Jennie M., 3020
Price, M.G., 2640
Price, M.J., 143
Price, Margaret A., 1175
Price, R.N., 4781
Price, T.W., 5343
Price, W.W., 2541
Prichard, Muriel F. Lloyd, see Lloyd Prichard
Prider, R.R.T., 533
Pridham, G.F.M., 2190
Priest, Margaret, 231
Priestley, C., 3687
Priestley, H.E., 2261
Priestley, Margaret A., 1929
Prince, A.E., 997
Prince, H.C., 3402
Pritchard, Constance, 5184
Pritchard, D.D., 3350
Pritchard, D.G., 3523
Pritchard, E., 5116
Pritchard, E.H., 7072
Pritchard, F.C. (London M.A.), 5568
Pritchard, F.C. (London Ph.D.), 5615
Pritchard, Jean F., 2193
Pritchard, L., 399
Pritchard, W.H., 3094
Proby, J.C.P., 3264

Procter, S.M., 4887
Procter, Zela M., 1359
Pronger, Winifred A., 1471
Prosser, D.S., 4071
Prosser, R.A.E., 157
Prosser, R.F., 472
Prothero, I.J., 4824
Proudfoot, Ann S., 526
Proudfoot, V.B., 512
Prugh, J.W., 3223
Pryce, R., 2265
Pryde, G.S., 2610
Pryor, A.J., 7541
Pugh, D.R.P., 3668
Pugh, F.H., 3029
Pugh, Jennifer, 3545
Pugh, Patricia M., 4163
Pugh, R.K., 5405
Pugh, T.B., 1091
Pugsley, A.J., 3552
Pullan, B.S., 2231
Pulleyblank, E.G., 5928
Pulzer, P.G.J., 1800
Purcell, C.P., 4263
Purcell, Maureen P., 542
Purcell, V.W.W.S., 7082
Purchon, Isabel, 251
Puri, A.A., 6508
Puri, B.N. (Oxford B.Litt.), 6474
Puri, B.N. (Oxford D.Phil.), 6511
Purton, J.A., 5496
Purver, Margery I.N., 4276
Puscariu, A., 1828
Pym, G.W., 552
Pyrah, G.B., 6333

QUAINTON, A.C.E., 1815
Qualter, T.H., 4641
Quentin-Hughes, J., see Hughes, J.Q.
Quested, Rosemary K.I. (London M.A.), 7125
Quested, Rosemary K.I. (London Ph.D.), 6968
Quigley, W.G.H., 1718
Quine, E.K.L., 3468
Quine, W.F., 3736
Quine, W.G., 5030
Quinn, D.B., 3262
Quinn, Mary J., 6748
Quinn, P.L.S., 3500
Quinn, T.J., 14
Quintrell, B.W., 3190
Quirk, Anastasia, 3759
Qureshi, I.H., 6532

RAAB, F., 3845
Rabie, H.M., 6112
Rabinowicz, M.H., 664
Raby, D.L., 7567
Rae, J.M., 4881
Rae, T.I., 3230
Raeside, I.M.P., 76
Rafeq, A.K., 5979

Rafferty, J., 4456
Raffo, P.S., 4808
Raftis, J.A., 1063
Raggatt, F.C., 2520
Rahim, Abdur, 6557
Rahim, M.A., 6552
Rahim, see also Abdel Rahim
Rahman, A.F.M.K., 6596
Rahman, M.F., 6622
Rahman, M.M., 6183
Rahman, Matiur, 6858
Rahman, Mukhlesur, 6464
Rahman, Qamrun, 6814
Rahman, Razia, 6830
Rahman, Z., 6631
Rahtz, P.A., 1485
Rainbow, S.G., 6999
Raine, A., 2573
Raj, J., 6770
Rajaindran, A., 6929
Rajaratnam, S., 6931
Rajkowski, W.W., 5931
Ram, A., 7045
Ram, R.W., 5434
Ramadan, S., 6053
Ramanujam, C.S. (London M.A.),
   6641
Ramanujam, C.S. (London Ph.D.),
   6601
Ramaswami Aiyangar, K.R., 6637
Ramlackhansingh, G.S., 7443
Ramm, Agatha, 1805
Ramsahoye, F.H.W., 7465
Ramsay, Anna A.W., 4747
Ramsay, G.D. (Oxford B.Litt.),
   2851
Ramsay, G.D. (Oxford D.Phil.),
   2838
Ramsay, J.C., 4406
Ramsbotham, R.B., 6626
Ramsden, P., 5861
Ramsey, P.H., 2856
Ranawella, G.S., 6520
Ranft, B.McL., 4870
Ranganayakula, G., 6587
Ranger, T.O., 3269
Ransome, D.R., 3109
Ransome, Gwenllian C., 1352
Ransome, Mary E., 3672
Ranson, E. (Manchester M.A.),
   7359
Ranson, E. (Manchester Ph.D.),
   7358
Rao, A.V., 4305
Rao, B.S., 6850
Raphael, M., 3451
Rashad Mohamad, A.M., 5953
Rashed, Zenab E., 1776
Rashid, M.H., 6472
Rashiduzzaman, M.D., 6872
Ratanapun, Thamsook, see
   Numnonda
Ratanasara, H., 6916
Ratcliffe, K.G.M., 3850
Rath, B.N., 6678
Rathbone, Eleanor, 1419

Rathbone, R.J.A.R., 6442
Ratnayake, Lakshmi K., 6879
Ravenhill, W.L.D. (London
   Ph.D.), 1519
Ravenhill, W.L.D. (Wales M.A.),
   393
Ravetz, Alison, 386
Rawle, W.J., 3976
Ray, A.C., 6611
Ray, Atreyi, 6484
Ray, B.C., 6679
Ray, Hemchandra, 6518
Ray, Parimal, 6796
Raybould, T.J. (Birmingham
   M.A.), 3416
Raybould, T.J. (Kent Ph.D.),
   3415
Raychaudhuri, G., 6489
Raychaudhuri, T., 6573
Raymond, A., 6080
Rayner, Doris, 963
Razzell, P.E., 4100
Rea, K.G., 7243
Read, D. (Oxford B.Litt.), 3840
Read, D. (Sheffield Ph.D.),
   3529
Read, P.W., 3009
Reade, J.E., 5902
Rebbeck, D., 3589
Reckord, Mary, 7442
Redford, A., 4514
Redmond, Mary F., 2603
Redmonds, G., 1153
Reed, F.O., 1762
Reed, J.C., 3157
Reed, M.A., 2600
Reed, R.C., 4654
Reeder, D.A. (Leicester M.A.),
   5291
Reeder, D.A. (Leicester Ph.D.),
   5743
Reedman, J.N., 2534
Reel, C.J., 3040
Rees, A.D., 1593
Rees, A.M., 3824
Rees, D.G., 3964
Rees, D.T., 6010
Rees, D.W., 1629
Rees, F.L., 1625
Rees, Henry (London M.Sc.),
   3551
Rees, Henry (London Ph.D.),
   410
Rees, Herbert, 1609
Rees, L.M. (Wales M.A.), 5701
Rees, L.M. (Wales Ph.D.), 5694
Rees, M., 5702
Rees, Muriel M., 3294
Rees, R., 5321
Rees, R.D. (Reading M.A.), 3511
Rees, R.D. (Reading Ph.D.),
   3746
Rees, W., 1610
Rees, W.H., 2578
Reese, T.R., 7277
Reeves, Marjorie E., 1752

Refai, G.Z., 6583
Regan, G.B., 6310
Reid, A.J.S., 7019
Reid, D.S., 7302
Reid, F., 4603
Reid, F.M., 5174
Reid, H.D.McC., 510
Reid, J.P., 1968
Reid, Marjorie G., 7199
Reid, R.A., 5787
Reilly, H.P., 5680
Reitlinger, G.R., 782
Rempel, R.A., 4921
Renier, G., 2285
Renold, Penelope, 3039
Renshaw, Mary, 929
Revell, Margaret E., 1435
Reynolds, B., 400
Reynolds, C.J., 3135
Reynolds, J.S., 3479
Reynolds, Josephine P., 5305
Reynolds, Kathleen M., 6281
Rhodes, J.N., 3993
Rhodes, W.A., 240
Rhys, W.T., 473
Rhys-Price, A.R., 1896
Riasanovsky, N.V., 2337
Rice, C.D., 7330
Rich, E.E., 5501
Rich, R.W., 5690
Richard, A.J., 1649
Richards, A. Mary, 6353
Richards, D.D., 86
Richards, E.F.T., 3982
Richards, E.S., 5781
Richards, G., 5424
Richards, J.R., 848
Richards, John Hamish, 5283
Richards, John Herbert, 4982
Richards, Margaret, 1124
Richards, Mary A., 4536
Richards, N.F., 1999
Richards, P., 7147
Richards, P.S., 5148
Richards, R.D., 3925
Richards, R.J., 4819
Richards, T., 3103
Richardson, D.J., 5067
Richardson, G.W., 280
Richardson, H.G., 1157
Richardson, H.W., 4924
Richardson, Helen, 1447
Richardson, K.E., 4941
Richardson, N.J.M., 2040
Richardson, P.D., 3965
Richardson, R.C., 2990
Richardson, Sheila J., 5287
Richmond, B.J., 3192
Richmond, C.F., 1001
Rickman, G.E., 254
Ridd, P.M., 2164
Ridd, T., 5712
Riddell, H.G., 6091
Riddell, R.G., 3301
Riddick, S., 3907
Rideout, E.H., 3928

Ridgard, J.M., 1580
Ridgeway, G.L., 7308
Ridout, E.S.F. (London M.A.), 173
Ridout, E.S.F. (London Ph.D.), 152
Rigby, C.J., 5629
Rigby, F.F., 4162
Righton, Norah P., 2289
Riley, K.C., 4500
Riley, P.W.J., 4419
Riley, R.G., 3036
Riley-Smith, J.S.C., 539
Rimmer, P.J., 3317
Rimmington, G.T., 3354
Riste, O., 2409
Ritcheson, C.R., 7282
Ritchie, C.I.A., 1261
Ritter, G.A., 2367
Ritterbush, P.C., 4316
Rive, A., 3960
Riviere, W.E., 7462
Rivlin, Helen A., 6139
Rixon, Mary C., 809
Rizvi, H.A., 6859
Rizvi, Janet M., 6824
Roach, J.P.C., 4608
Roach, W.M., 4454
Roads, C.H., 4868
Roake, Margaret, 3413
Robbins, Ivy C., 3604
Robbins, K.G., 4805
Roberts, A.D.S., 7061
Roberts, A.K. Babette, 1285
Roberts, Agnes E., 730
Roberts, Annie E., 1948
Roberts, B.K., 1059
Roberts, D.A., 5376
Roberts, D.C., 1536
Roberts, D.M., 1634
Roberts, E., 5143
Roberts, E.F.D., 1718
Roberts, E.K., 97
Roberts, Ellen, 934
Roberts, Ethel K.R.R., 7310
Roberts, G.K., 4550
Roberts, Glyn, 2491
Roberts, Gwladys, 4086
Roberts, H.L., 1883
Roberts, H.P., 3504
Roberts, Harry (Leeds M.Comm. 1943), 5764
Roberts, Harry (Manchester M.A. 1928), 941
Roberts, J.A.G., 7078
Roberts, J.C., 2676
Roberts, J.E., 4208
Roberts, J.M., 2248
Roberts, M., 3758
Roberts, M.W., 6923
Roberts, P.R. (Cambridge Ph.D.), 2652
Roberts, P.R. (Wales M.A.), 4049
Roberts, R.F., 3149
Roberts, R.O., 4889
Roberts, R.P., 4022

Roberts, R.S., 2878
Roberts, W.L., 5448
Robertshaw, W., 1542
Robertson, A., 3259
Robertson, Agnes J., 1047
Robertson, Annie S., 344
Robertson, F.W., 1698
Robertson, H.M., 2802
Robertson, L.A., 2473
Robertson, N., 5016
Robinson, A.H.W., 2606
Robinson, C., 4261
Robinson, D.B., 1280
Robinson, D.J., 7512
Robinson, E. Frances, 1853
Robinson, F.C.R., 6857
Robinson, G.B., 5527
Robinson, G.G., 3283
Robinson, H.S., 1808
Robinson, J., 5837
Robinson, L., 312
Robinson, Mary F.H., 1327
Robinson, Olive, 5827
Robinson, Olivia F., 1242
Robinson, R.A.H., 2465
Robinson, R.E., 6247
Robinson, T.H., 4983
Robinson, T.R., 145
Robinson, W.D., 5614
Robinson, W.G., 4257
Robinson, W.R.B., 2832
Robison, O.C., 4240
Robson, A.H., 5579
Robson, Ann P.W., 4943
Robson, E., 3902
Robson, J.A., 1462
Robson, J.L., 5597
Robson, K.J.R., 2565
Robson, R., 3679
Robson, R.J., 3697
Robson, S.T., 2167
Roby, W., 5970
Roche, J.C., 3367
Rockey, O., 7285
Rodden, Judith M., 5469
Roden, D., 419
Roden, R.D., 1735
Roderick, A.J. (London Ph.D.), 1086
Roderick, A.J. (Wales M.A.), 1640
Rodgers, R.J., 5833
Rodgers, W.S., 3422
Rodney, W., 7252
Rodney, W.A., 6344
Roe, E.W.N., 2299
Roebuck, Janet, 5742
Roebuck, P., 4045
Röhl, J.C.G., 2161
Rogan, J., 339
Rogers, A. (Nottingham M.A.), 973
Rogers, A. (Nottingham Ph.D.), 911
Rogers, D.M., 3007
Rogers, F.H., 2824

Rogers, F.R.S., 2563
Rogers, J.G., 3751
Rogers, Margaret S., 1555
Rogers, N.McL., 7254
Rogers, P., 3265
Roker, L.F., 3174
Rokkan, Elizabeth G., 7046
Roland, D., 5593
Rolfe, Eileen M. (London Ph.D.), 5139. See also Pierce
Roll, E., 4025
Rollinson, W., 453
Rollinson, W.W., 4900
Romain, R.I., 7479
Ronchetti, Barbara J., 5470
Rooke, Hilda M., 5082
Rooke, P.J., 5569
Rooney, D.D., 7486
Roos, G.D., 1761
Roper, Margaret, 2918
Roper, Michael, 1180
Rosamond, F.J., 4968
Roscoe, Florence, 2827
Rose, A.G., 5306
Rose, J.H.K., 4301
Rose, M.E., 5239
Rose, Miriam A., 978
Rose, N.A., 6054
Rose, R.B., 2009
Rose, S., 7150
Rosenfield, M.C., 2948
Roseveare, H.G., 3923
Roseveare, Irena M., 1855
Roskell, J.S. (Manchester M.A.), 979
Roskell, J.S. (Oxford D.Phil.), 984
Roskies, Eva F., 6042
Ross, A., 7579
Ross, A.C., 6229
Ross, A.M., 5259
Ross, C., 1724
Ross, C.D., 1168
Ross, D.A., 6365
Ross, D.L., 5308
Ross, E. DeW., 7211
Ross, Elizabeth M., 5290
Ross, Helen M., 3239
Ross, M.A., 3164
Ross, N.S., 4957
Ross, T.A., 3554
Rossell, P.E., 3167
Rosselli, G.A., 2306
Rosser, C.E.P., 354
Rossington, P.G., 5676
Rostow, W.W., 5118
Rotberg, R.I., 6314
Roth, C. (Oxford B.Litt.), 2235
Roth, C. (Oxford D.Phil.), 2236
Rothney, G.O. (London M.A.), 7195
Rothney, G.O. (London Ph.D.), 7179
Rothschild, J.A., 1881
Rothstein, Natalie K.A., 4004
Rothwell, H., 855

Rothwell, Mary M., 942
Rothwell, V.H., 4807
Rotimi, B.O., 6379
Roud, B.J., 2443
Roullet, Anne H.M., 1478
Round, Florence E., 3700
Round, Lucy M., 945
Roussos, J.S., 546
Routledge, F.J., 2807
Rover, Constance M., 4851
Rowdon, H.H., 5438
Rowe, Benedicta J.H., 631
Rowe, D.J., 4825
Rowe, E.A., 4715
Rowe, J.H., 1544
Rowe, Violet A., 2728
Rowe, W.J., 3322
Rowland, E.J., 327
Rowlands, J., 3546
Rowlands, Marie B., 4262
Rowley, R.T., 477
Roxborough, J., 6296
Roxburgh, J.M., 5816
Roy, I., 2799
Roy, J., 167
Roy, W., 5000
Royle, E., 5316
Ruberu, T.R.A., 6911
Rubini, D.A., 3637
Rubinstein, B.D., 4643
Rubinstein, Ruth K., 819
Rudall, R.J., 7591
Ruddock, Alwyn A., 670
Rudé, G.F.E., 2005
Rudkin, Olive D., 3810
Rudsdale, J., 2535
Rueger, Zofia, 734
Ruggles, R.I., 7188
Rumble, G.W.S.V., 2713
Rumney, J., 3457
Rungta, R.S., 6760
Rushton, Jean, 2532
Rusinow, D.I., 2268
Russell, A.J., 5380
Russell, A.K., 4677
Russell, E., 1132
Russell, G.H., 3006
Russell, Ina S. (Manchester
    M.A.), 5987
Russell, Ina S. (Manchester
    Ph.D.), 5986
Russell, J.F.O'N., 1115
Russell, J.F.S., 7362
Russell, Jean DeB., 7396
Russell, Valerie J., 5270
Russell-Wood, A.J.R., 7510
Rust, W.B., 5526
Rutherford, A., 69
Ruthven, Annette J. Otway-, see
    Otway-Ruthven
Rutland, R.A., 381
Rutter, N.K., 180
Ryall, Dorothy A., 7478
Ryan, A.N., 3915
Ryder, A.F.C., 596
Ryder, A.J., 2172

Ryder, J.P., 1783
Ryder, R.F., 5102
Ryder, T.T.B., 168
Ryman, Elizabeth R., 3154
Ryrie, C.C., 681A

SACHAR, A.L., 4583
Sachdeva, D.R., 6756
Sachse, Freda M., 6627
Sachse, W.L., 3195
Sadek, Dawlat A., 5904
Sadeque, Syedah F., 6116
Sadler, R.J., 5731
Saeed, M.M., 6542
Saffin, N.W. (London M.A.),
    5667
Saffin, N.W. (London Ph.D.),
    7598
Safwat, M.M. (Liverpool M.A.),
    6081
Safwat, M.M. (London Ph.D.),
    6084
Saïd, H.C. Abou, see Abou Saïd
Said, Rosemarie J., 6120
Saigh, Eva J.S., 5985
Sainsbury, J.M., 108
Saksena, B.P., 6575
Sakwa, G., 1825
Salem, M.S., 272
Saletan, L., 5162
Saletore, B.A., 6541
Salibi, K.S., 5952
Salim, A.I., 6251
Salmon, E.T., 196
Salmon, J.B., 137
Salmon, J.H.McM., 2677
Salmon, Mary, 832
Salt, J., 5547
Salt, Mary C.L., 610
Salter, J.L., 4183
Saltman, A.A., 1204
Salway, P., 362
Salyer, J.C., 2439
Samaraweera, D.D., 6883
Samaraweera, V.K., 6919
Samaroo, B., 7502
Samarusingh, J.A.R.K., 7459
Sampson, R.V., 1772
Samuel, P., 1739
Samuel, R., 2124
Sandall, P.H., 4315
Sanders, B., 7633
Sanders, I.J. (Oxford D.Phil.),
    1041
Sanders, I.J. (Wales M.A.),
    1369
Sanders, L.J., 16
Sanders, P.B., 6297
Sanderson, F.E., 6237
Sanderson, G.N., 6177
Sanderson, J.M., 3532
Sanderson, Joyce E., 4734
Sanderson, Lilian M. (London
    M.A.), 6192
Sanderson, Lilian M. (London
    Ph.D.), 6187

340

Sanderson, M.W.B., 7458
Sandhu, K.S., 6998
Sandilands, D.N., 2533
Sandison, A.G., 4772
Sandler, S.L., 4871
Sandys, Agnes M., 1388
Sandys-Wood, A., 308
Sangster, P.E. (Oxford B.Litt.), 4308
Sangster, P.E. (Oxford D.Phil.), 4148
Santer, Beatrice M., 7456
Sanyal, N., 6741
Saran, P., 6556
Sargeant, F., 657
Sarkar, K.M., 3800
Sarkar, S.C., 6457
Sarker, R., 6478
Sarkissian, N.K., 5911
Sarson, Gladys M., 4511
Sass, F.W., 6284
Sastri, K.N.V., 6724
Saul, S.B., 5120
Saum, Catherine M., 1405
Saunders, Ann L., 413
Saunders, J.J., 4288
Saunders, Margaret, 1487
Savadge, W.R., 7291
Savage, Donald C., 4665
Savage, Douglas C., 5559
Savidge, A.W.J., 4179
Savigear, P.W.H., 2047
Savill, Audrey L., 1184
Saville, P.V., 5486
Savory, H.J., 7534
Savory, R.M., 5962
Saw Siok Hwa, 7017
Saxton, W.E., 3761
Sayers, Jane E., 1396
Saywell, Ruby J.T., 4120
Scarisbrick, J.J., 2925
Scarre, Anne M., 1705
Schachter, A., 135
Schaffer, B.B., 4559
Schenck, F., 1161
Schenk, H.G.A.V., 1784
Schiefen, R.J., 5460
Schlatter, R.B. (Oxford B.Litt.), 4157
Schlatter, R.B. (Oxford D.Phil.), 4158
Schlenther, B.S., 7271
Schmidt, H.D., 107
Schmitthenner, W.C.G., 289
Schnurman, Josephine E., 659
Schoenbaum, D.L., 2194
Schofield, A.N.E.D., 1408
Schofield, B., 567
Schofield, D.A., 3741
Schofield, P., 1890
Schofield, R.S., 2801
Schove, D.J. (London M.Sc.), 1750
Schove, D.J. (London Ph.D.), 1768
Schoyen, A., 4841
Schram, A.M., 6093

Schreiber, R.E., 2684
Schreuder, D.M., 6313
Schurman, D.M., 4754
Schutmaat, A.L., 2451
Schwarz, G.M., 2156
Schwarz, H.F., 1839
Schwitzer, Joan P., 2079
Scotland, J., 788
Scotney, Phyllis H., 1225
Scott, B.J.V., 5714
Scott, C.F., 2440
Scott, F.R., 2071
Scott, F.S., 826
Scott, Helen, 1713
Scott, Hylton, 4975
Scott, J., 3578
Scott, J.C., 4997
Scott, J.J., 5905
Scott, L., 3698
Scott, Margaret I., 7051
Scott, Richenda C., 1072
Scott, W., 2021
Scott, W.F. (Oxford B.Litt.), 3909
Scott, W.F. (Oxford D.Phil.), 2785
Scotter, W.H., 6371
Scouloudi, Irene, 2901
Scrafton, D., 5160
Scrimiger, Evelyn M., 3784
Scrivens, W., 4362
Scullard, H.H., 288
Scully, F.M. (Bristol M.A.), 3476
Scully, F.M. (Oxford B.Litt.), 5389
Seal, A., 6836
Seaman, W.A.L., 3817
Searle, Dorothy E., 6065
Searle, G.R., 4674
Searle, Joan C., 2002
Sears, J.W., 4812
Seary, E.R., 4895
Seccombe, H.G., 2704
Seckler, Lilian M. (Birmingham M.A.), 650
Seckler, Lilian M. (London Ph.D.), 651
Secret, J.L., 2962
Seddon, P.R., 2698
Sedlo, J., 733
Seed, G., 6704
Sefton, H.R., 4433
Segal, L., 2336
Seikaly, S.M., 6162
Sellars, C.W., 2810
Selleck, A.D., 3471
Sellers, Gabrielle J., 4750
Sellers, I. (Keele Ph.D.), 3490
Sellers, I. (Oxford B.Litt.), 5429
Selley, W.T., 2240
Seltman, P.E.J., 1980
Semple, W., 5874
Sen, Amiya, 6661
Sen, Anu, 6672

Sen, B., 6486
Sen, Kamala, 6764
Sen, S., 6584
Sengupta, K., 6655
Sengupta, Nilakshi, 6455
Serajuddin, A.M., 6614
Serjeant, R.B., 5913
Serle, A.G., 7616
Settar, S., 6526
Severin, G.T., 7057
Sexton, E.L.H., 1701
Seymour, Margaret A., 1390
Seymour, R.E., 4239
Seymour-Ure, C.K., 4673
Shachar, I., 1764
Shadman, S.F., 5992
Shaffner, F.I., 1722
Shah, S.Z. Ahmed, see Ahmed
    Shah
Shaked, H., 6189
Shakoor, A., 5700
Shalaby, A.M.G., 6107
Shanin, T., 2375
Shannon, R.A., 3538
Shannon, R.T., 1862
Shapin, Betty F., 3136
Shapira, I., 4547
Sharadamma, M., 6707
Sharf, A., 523
Sharma, J.P., 6467
Sharma, Krishna, 6543
Sharma, R.S., 6454
Sharp, J.F., 1626
Sharp, L.W., 1679
Sharp, Margaret (Manchester
    Ph.D.), 1570. See also Tout
Sharpe, W., 2858
Shaw, D., 3234
Shaw, G.F., 656
Shaw, J.J.S., 3606
Shaw, Jean Y., 763
Shaw, P.E.O. (Edinburgh Ph.D.),
    5439
Shaw, P.E.O. (Oxford B.Litt.),
    5354
Shaw, S.R., 5135
Shaxby, Joan M., 714
Shead, F.N., 1682
Sheail, J.D.S., 2884
Shearring, H.A., 4383
Sheen, H.E., 5401
Sheik Ali, B., 6612
Shelat, J.M., 7304
Shennan, J.H., 1955
Shepherd, D., 1884
Shepherd, G.W., 4811
Sheppard, F.H.W., 4356
Sheppard, June A., 5175
Sheppard, Priscilla M., 7408
Shere, S.A., 2219
Sheridan, Helen C., 3708
Sheridan, R.B., 7425
Sherman, A.J., 2197
Sherry, D.L.W., 3288
Sherwin-White, A.N., 182
Shewell, M.E.J., 5556

Shibly, A.H., 6783
Shield, I.T., 2964
Shiels, R., 7496
Shiman, R.J., 7132
Shipley, Anne E., 2010
Shirley, F.J.J., 2680
Short, J., 1452
Short, S.H., 2132
Shorter, A.H. (London Ph.D.),
    2515
Shorter, A.H. (Manchester M.A.),
    4937
Shrimpton, C., 4069
Shriver, F.H., 3053
Shukman, H., 2359
Shukry, M.F., 6145
Shutt, R.J.H., 26
Sibbit, Christine, 1526
Siddiqi, A.H., 5916
Siddiqi, Asiya, 6699
Siddiqi, M.H., 6551
Sidey, P.B., 4008
Sidgwick, Rose, 713
Sidhu, J.S., 7034
Sigsworth, E.M., 5042
Silk, W.A., 7121
Sillery, A., 6316
Simkin, A.P., 7129
Simmonds, N.M., 5710
Simmons, Adele D., 6952
Simms, V.H., 3625
Simon, A., 4656
Simons, L.C., 1615
Simpson, A., 3636
Simpson, G.G., 1685
Simpson, Gillian M.L., 5770
Simpson, I.J., 5772
Simpson, M.A., 5798
Simpson, Mary G., 384
Simpson, Morna, 1479
Simpson, R.H., 170
Sims, R.L., 7103
Sinar, Joan C., 1241
Sinclair, A.A., 7405
Sinclair, C., 1665
Sinclair, Marjory S., 7289
Sinclair, Olive W., 1791
Sinclair, W.A., 5121
Sing, Gloria Young, see Young
    Sing
Singer, A.F., 553
Singh, D.N., 6782
Singh, H.K., 6876
Singh, H.L., 6826
Singh, Janardan P., 6462
Singh, Jogendra P., 6490
Singh, R.C.P., 6498
Singh, R.P., 5584
Singh, S., 6777
Singh, S.D., 6459
Singhal, D.P., 6803
Singhal, Devahuti, 6492
Singleton, Betta, 3267
Sinha, B.P., 6488
Sinha, C., 6676
Sinha, D.P. (London M.A.), 6766

342

Sinha, D.P. (London Ph.D.), 6726
Sinha, H., 6494
Sinha, L.P., 6867
Sircar, K., 6721
Siriex, P.H., 4690
Siriweera, W.I., 6889
Sislian, J., 6133
Skelton, Elfreda, 2670
Skidelsky, R.J.A., 4716
Skilling, H.G., 1864
Skilliter, Susan A., 5967
Skinner, F.J., 2257
Skinner, J., 4585
Skinner, K.E., 3460
Skinner, R.F., 3474
Skirrow, P.W., 4418
Skwarczynski, P., 1833
Slack, Margaret, 448
Slade, C.F., 1044
Slade, E.H., 5825
Slade, M.W., 2935
Slade, P., 12
Slade, Ruth M., 6275
Slatcher, W.N., 4029
Slater, A.W., 3374
Slater, Joan E., 1792
Slatter, Mary D., 3074
Slaven, A., 5792
Sliwowski, Z., 1887
Slosser, G.J., 1769
Smail, R.C., 534
Smailes, A.E., 4506
Smalley, Beryl, 1425
Smallpage, E., 3830
Smallpage, P., 4247
Smallwood, Edith M., 310
Smart, Daphne J. Treais-, see Treais-Smart
Smart, Veronica J., 1003
Smith, A.C., 5397
Smith, A.G.R., 2683
Smith, A.H., 2903
Smith, A.J.C., 1442
Smith, Abbot E., 7415
Smith, Ann, 1081
Smith, Anthony, 6266
Smith, Arthur E., 821
Smith, B.H., 4919
Smith, B.R., 3790
Smith, Barbara J., 5601
Smith, Bernice M., 4101
Smith, Beryl, 1338
Smith, C.F., 4447
Smith, C.H.N., 5409
Smith, C.L., 6023
Smith, Constance G., 3833
Smith, D.J., 351
Smith, David Marshall, 3308
Smith, David Michael, 1224
Smith, Donald C., 5797
Smith, Dwight C., 3005
Smith, E., 5644
Smith, E.A., 2406
Smith, E.H., 1549
Smith, E. Lorrain-, see Lorrain-Smith

Smith, Elizabeth E., 1366
Smith, Elizabeth F. Malcolm, see Malcolm-Smith
Smith, F., 5524
Smith, F.B., 4613
Smith, G.E. Connell-, see Connell-Smith
Smith, H. (London M.A.), 3336
Smith, H. (London Ph.D.), 5275
Smith, H.B., 3443
Smith, H.C., 2179
Smith, H.G., 4829
Smith, H.J., 1924
Smith, H.K. (Sheffield M.A.), 5391
Smith, H.K. (Sheffield Ph.D.), 5413
Smith, I.R., 6172
Smith, J., 7554
Smith, J.B., 1614
Smith, J.N., 6378
Smith, J.S.C. Riley-, see Riley-Smith
Smith, J.T., 1534
Smith, J.W.A., 4280
Smith, J.W. Harper-, see Harper-Smith
Smith, L.A.H., 7210
Smith, L.C., 177
Smith, M.B., 5233
Smith, M.P.D. Baker-, see Baker-Smith
Smith, M.W., 417
Smith, Mildred Wretts (Wales M.A.), 2317. See also Wretts-Smith
Smith, N.M., 87
Smith, Nancy E.V., 2140
Smith, P., 5319
Smith, Phyllis Woodham, see Woodham Smith
Smith, R., 5083
Smith, R.A., 1375
Smith, R.A.L. (Cambridge Ph.D.), 1337
Smith, R.A.L. (London M.A.), 1050
Smith, R.B., 2892
Smith, R.E.F., 639
Smith, R.E.G., 592
Smith, R.J. (Nottingham M.A.), 891
Smith, R.J. (Nottingham Ph.D.), 5746
Smith, R.S., 2523
Smith, S.B., 4017
Smith, S.G.D., 7250
Smith, Sidney (Manchester M.A. 1940), 874A
Smith, Sidney (Reading Ph.D. 1937), 1007
Smith, Sylvia R., 7625
Smith, T.A., 5675
Smith, Vera, 5805
Smith, W.A., 3992
Smith, W.E.L., 1277
Smith, W.H.C., 2457

Smith, W.J., 990
Smithers, P.H.B.O., 3667
Smithson, R.J., 1763
Smoldon, W.L., 786
Smout, T.C., 2398
Smythe, B.H., 4138
Snead, G.A., 619
Snell, L.S., 2947
Snidvongs, Neon, 7016
Snodgrass, A.McE., 131
Snow, Dorothy M.B., 5398
Snow, W.G.G., 3248
Soar, J.R., 5679
Sobhy, H.M.H., 6090
Softley, P., 5288
Solberg, C.T., 4668
Somaratna, G.P.V., 6895
Sommer, Eleonore, 1444
Sommerlad, M.J., 4292
Somper, S., 5663
Soni, S.K., 6753
Soper, D.O., 1920
Soper, T.P., 3573
Sorrenson, M.P.K., 6254
Sorsby, W.S., 7520
Soule, Vivian J., 7163
Southall, Evelyn J., 3737
Southern, A.C., 3008
Southgate, D.G., 4575
Soward, F.H., 7206
Spagnolo, J.P., 6009
Sparks, H.J., 3881
Spate, O.H.K., 5706
Spaul, J.E.H., 321
Speak, Joan E., 2756
Speake, J.G., 1535
Speake, R., 3544
Spear, T.G.P., 6589
Spears, W.E., 4210
Speck, W.A., 3653
Speed, P.F., 5588
Speight, M.E., 4541
Spellman, J.W., 6496
Spence, R.T., 2909
Spencer, F. (Manchester M.A.), 3706
Spencer, F. (Manchester Ph.D.), 3786
Spencer, H., 692
Spencer, K.M., 5705
Spencer, Lilian M., 7357
Spencer, Lois M.G., 2718
Spencer, R.A., 6019
Spendlove, Jean M., 3689
Sperber, D., 316
Sperling, J.G., 3932
Spiegler, J.S., 6438
Spiers, M., 5271
Spiller, M.R.G., 4271
Spiro, R.H., 4035
Splevins, A., 24
Spooner, F.C., 1900
Spooner, R.T., 4669
Spratt, J., 2847
Spray, W.A., 6943
Spring, D.W., 6041

Springall, Lillie M., 5179
Springhall, J.O., 4787
Spruill, C.P., 3303
Spufford, H. Margaret (Leicester M.A.), 2498
Spufford, H. Margaret (Leicester Ph.D.), 2881
Spufford, P., 672
Spungin, M.F., 2494
Spurdle, F.G., 7424
Squire, K.A.J., 1371
Squire, P.S., 2339
Sreenivasachar, P., 6522
Stadler, K.R. (London M.A.), 1888
Stadler, K.R. (Nottingham Ph.D.), 1894
Stafford, D.A.T., 2075
Stafford, G.W., 2241
Stager, J.K., 7194
Stainton, D.C., 4999
Stambrook, F.G., 1820
Standen, J.D., 5737
Stander, S.S., 3373
Standing, Christine, 1707
Stanford, M.J.G., 2889
Stankiewicz, W.J., 1918
Stanley, G.F.G. (Oxford B.Litt.), 7238
Stanley, G.F.G. (Oxford D.Phil.), 7239
Stanley, Mary, 758
Stannard, Gillian I., see Keir
Staples, A.C., 6948
Starmer, Gladys, 4505
Starr, A.J., 5124
Statham, J., 5036
Stauffer, D.A., 2560
Staveley, E.S., 185
Staveley, M., 1525
Stayt, J.R., 4065
Stedman, A.R., 2571
Stedman Jones, G., 4958
Steele, E.D., 5863
Steele, I.J.D., 5570
Steele, I.K., 3780
Steele, M.C., 6323
Steer, K.A., 366
Steer, Lesley A., 660
Steinberg, J., 2141
Stephan, J.J., 7076
Stephen, D.A.V., 6366
Stephen, J.F.M.D., 5416
Stephen, J.S., 3577
Stephens, A.E. (London M.Sc.), 1143
Stephens, A.E. (London Ph.D.), 3880
Stephens, G.H.A., 3969
Stephens, J.E., 3151
Stephens, M., 2576
Stephens, W.B. (Exeter M.A.), 5655
Stephens, W.B. (London Ph.D.), 3951
Stephenson, A.M.G. (Oxford B.Litt.), 5403

344

Stephenson, A.M.G. (Oxford
  D.Phil.), 5415
Stephenson, E., 3084
Stephenson, G.G., 1434
Stephenson, H.W., 4093
Stephenson, J., 416
Stern, J.A., 1816
Stern, Patricia A., 4323
Sterne, E.C., 4795
Stevens, C.E., 691
Stevens, J.R., 5154
Stevenson, G., 3588
Stewart, A.T.Q. (Belfast M.A.),
  4484
Stewart, A.T.Q. (Belfast Ph.D.),
  4693
Stewart, Barbara J., 7014
Stewart, C.C., 6348
Stewart, J., 5910
Stewart, J.D., 4329
Stewart, R.M., 4904
Stigant, E.P., 4241
Stilliard, N.H., 6342
Stitt, F.B., 1559
Stojanović, M.D., 1861
Stokes, A.D., 560
Stokes, E.T., 6700
Stokes, Kathleen E., 7284
Stone, E., 1062
Stone, S.M., 5425
Stone, Thora G., 6350
Stones, E., 3533
Stones, E.L.G., 955
Storey, R.L., 1320
Storrs, Constance M., 1199
Stoye, J.W., 4083
Strachan, A.J., 5808
Stradling, R.A., 2438
Strain, R.W.M., 4480
Stranks, C.J., 3073
Stranz, W.J., 4558
Straukamp, J.E., 2421
Straw, F.I., 3289
Streatfeild, F., 1899
Street, Fanny, 1233
Street, J., 7528
Stretton, Grace, 1167
Stribley, F.U., 5307
Strick, H.C., 5018
Strong, C.F. (London M.A.),
  1793
Strong, C.F. (London Ph.D.),
  2251
Strong, R.C., 3163
Stroud, L.J., 5622
Stuart, D.G., 3599
Stuart, Esmé R. Pole, see Pole
  Stuart
Stuart, F.C., 3832
Sturdy, D.A.M., 1588
Sturge, C., 2650
Sturgess, G., 3714
Sturgess, R.W., 5170
Sturgis, J.L., 4733
Sturman, R.H., 5623
Sturman, Winifred M. (London
  M.A.), 1360

Sturman, Winifrid (Winifred) M.
  (London Ph.D.), 1336
Stuttard, J.C., 4042
Sudbury, P.G., 1607
Suleiman, A., 5884
Sullivan, J.J., 4481
Sullivan, J.P., 5525
Sully, G.H., 4167
Summers, D.E., 3389
Summers, D.F., 5371
Summerton, N.W., 2168
Sumner, L.V. (Manchester M.A.),
  3733
Sumner, L.V. (Manchester Ph.D.),
  3769
Sun, Mary Man Yue, 7126
Sundaram, Lanka, 6569
Suntharalingam, R., 6819
Supple, B.E., 2868
Sutcliffe, Dorothy, 1248
Sutcliffe, G., 7007
Sutcliffe, Gillian H., see
  Nicolson
Sutherland, D.W., 949
Sutherland, Gillian R., 5594
Sutherland, Nicola M., 1911
Sutton, G.B., 5038
Sutton, G.M., 5771
Sutton, J.H., 5738
Sutton, J.S., 3803
Sutton, K., 2032
Swainson, Beatrice M., 396
Swaisland, H.C., 6063
Swales, R.J.W., 2646
Swales, T.H. (Leeds M.A.), 3430
Swales, T.H. (Sheffield Ph.D.),
  2954
Swallow, Mary A., 3391
Swaminathan, K.D., 6880
Swan, C.M.J.F., 2977
Swann, Brenda A.S., 4060
Swann, D., 3955
Swanton, M.J., 1488
Swanwick, Aileen E., 5173
Swanzy, B.E. Kwaw-, see Kwaw-
  Swanzy
Swartwout, R.E., 780
Sweet, Jennifer M., 1229
Sweetinburgh, Florence E., 1243
Sweetland, A.J., 144
Sweetman, E., 4554
Swiderska, Halina-Maria, 1831
Swift, E.M., 1178
Swift, Eleanor, 1074
Swift, Marion J., see Waller
Swinbank, Brenda, 388
Swinburne, J.S., 6232
Swinfen, D.B., 4721
Sydenham, M.J., 2013
Syder, S.N., 3972
Sydserff, Marjorie Buchan-,
  see Buchan-Sydserff
Sykes, N. (Leeds M.A.), 4174
Sykes, N. (Oxford D.Phil.),
  4173
Symons, L.J., 514

345

Symons, Pauline E. Helliar-,
see Helliar-Symons
Syrett, D., 3903

TADESSE TAMRAT, 6114
Taffs, Winifred A. (London M.A.), 2700
Taffs, Winifred A. (London Ph.D.), 2149
Tai, E.C., 7162
Tailby, Nicola G., 227
Tamrat, see Tadesse Tamrat
Tamuno, S.M., 6430
Tangri, R.K., 6240
Tann, Jennifer, 2519
Tanner, J.I., 3079
Taplin, E.L., 5003
Targett, A.B., 1560
Tarling, P.N., 7009
Tarn, J.N., 5281
Tasie, G.O., 6395
Tata, M.A., 6797
Tate, Merze, 4767
Tate, R.B. (Belfast M.A.), 740
Tate, R.B. (Belfast Ph.D.), 77
Tate, W.E., 3420
Taverner, R.L. (London Ph.D.), 3537
Taverner, R.L. (Wales M.A.), 3499
Taylor, A.F. (Birmingham M.A.), 5599
Taylor, A.F. (Leicester Ph.D.), 5503
Taylor, A.J., 4014
Taylor, Aileen A., 854
Taylor, B.K. Hope-, see Hope-Taylor
Taylor, Barry, 1913
Taylor, Bessie, 3290
Taylor, E.S., 7086
Taylor, Emily A., 7347
Taylor, F. (Manchester M.A.), 73
Taylor, F. (Manchester Ph.D.), 74
Taylor, G., 4016
Taylor, G.E., 2624
Taylor, G.P., 7605
Taylor, Gloria C., 4834
Taylor, J.E., 201
Taylor, J.G., 2559
Taylor, J.R., 2020
Taylor, Lilias, 71
Taylor, Louise B., 3218
Taylor, P., 4497
Taylor, P.A.M., 7337
Taylor, R., 4867
Taylor, T.S., 2985
Taylor, W., 3245
Taylour, W.D., Lord, 126
Teale, W.N., 447
Teather, Elizabeth, 426
Teba, P.F., 6398
Tebby, Dorothy M., 588
Tejón, G., 2424

Temkin, S.D., 4634
Temple, A., 5215
Temple, Nora C., 1949
Templeman, G., 1306
Tengey, J.G.K., 2378
Teniswood, W.V., 7600
Tenkorang, S., 6352
Terpstra, C., 4248
Terrett, I.B., 1026
Terry, C.W., 2750
Terry, Janice J., 6197
Tesh, Elsie, 749
Teviotdale, D.A., 5800
Thaikoodan, J., 6658
Than Thun, 6986
Thapar, Romila, 6471
Thaper, K.S., 6739
Themelis, T.P., 1755
Theobald, A.B., 6839
Thet, M.K., 6994
Thet Tun, 6761
Thio, Eunice, 7029
Third, Betty M.W., 4408
Thirlby, P.L., 3070
Thirsk, I. Joan, 4047
Thomas, A.W., 2569
Thomas, Annie L., 3987
Thomas, Barbara J., see Kinnes
Thomas, Brinley, 603
Thomas, Brynmor, 1992
Thomas, C., 498
Thomas, C.M., 2739
Thomas, D.A., 3030
Thomas, D.N., 3447
Thomas, David (Liverpool M.A. 1928), 5169
Thomas, David (Wales M.A. 1957), 4064
Thomas, David Hopkin, 5681
Thomas, David Hubert (London Ph.D.), 5511
Thomas, David Hubert (Wales M.A.), 5685
Thomas, David Hywel, 884
Thomas, Edgar, 1045
Thomas, Elizabeth, 1642
Thomas, Emlyn, 3944
Thomas, Emlyn G., 4082
Thomas, Esmée M. (Oxford B.Litt.), 304
Thomas, Esmée M. (Wales M.A.), 245
Thomas, Evan G., 5875
Thomas, F.N.G., 3882
Thomas, G., 1253
Thomas, G.F., 3683
Thomas, G.H., 6125
Thomas, G.I., 3326
Thomas, Gillian R., see Sutherland
Thomas, Gwyn R., 2743
Thomas, H., 3375
Thomas, I.D., 2742
Thomas, J.D., 2711
Thomas, J.G.T., 4295
Thomas, J.H., 3177

346

Thomas, J.I., 1591
Thomas, James, 5552
Thomas, James E., 5296
Thomas, Jean F., see Pritchard
Thomas, Joan L., 2861
Thomas, John (London Ph.D. 1934), 3370
Thomas, John (Wales M.A. 1925), 5105
Thomas, John Alun (Liverpool M.A. 1951), 4184
Thomas, John Alun (London Ph.D. 1926), 4561
Thomas, John Alun (Sheffield Ph.D. 1955), 7175
Thomas, John Emlyn, 5257
Thomas, L., 2939
Thomas, Laetitia J., 2738
Thomas, Mary W., 6988
Thomas, Maurice W., 4945
Thomas, P.D.G. (London Ph.D.), 3722
Thomas, P.D.G. (Wales M.A.), 3676
Thomas, P.J. (Oxford B.Litt.), 6586
Thomas, P.J. (Oxford D.Phil.), 6779
Thomas, P.W., 2716
Thomas, R.G., 4540
Thomas, S.E., 4892
Thomas, Shirley M., see Walker
Thomas, Susan P., 2088
Thomas, T.G., 275
Thomas, W.C., 3033
Thomas, W.P., 4296
Thomas, W.S.G., 491
Thomas, W.S.K., 3169
Thomason, May B., 543
Thomasson, H.W., 6955
Thomis, M.I. (London M.A.), 4880
Thomis, M.I. (Nottingham Ph.D.), 3813
Thompson, A.N., 7216
Thompson, A.R., 5777
Thompson, B., 4964
Thompson, Beatrice M.H., 3034
Thompson, C.A., 3129
Thompson, C.E., 175
Thompson, C.H., 864
Thompson, D.M., 5365
Thompson, Derek, 433
Thompson, Donald, 5669
Thompson, E., 2008
Thompson, F.F., 2091
Thompson, F.M.L., 5187
Thompson, G.L.S., 4442
Thompson, I.A.A., 2417
Thompson, J.A., 7403
Thompson, James, 199
Thompson, John, 2244
Thompson, P.R., 4653
Thompson, W., 6064
Thompson, W.D.J. Cargill, see Cargill Thompson
Thoms, D.W., 7440

Thomson, A.G., 3564
Thomson, D., 3866
Thomson, Edith E.B., 4394
Thomson, F.J., 5353
Thomson, I., 817
Thomson, J., 686
Thomson, J.A.F., 1298
Thomson, K.J.T., 586
Thomson, L.D., 5032
Thomson, M.A., 3630
Thomson, W.S., 952
Thorley, J., 298
Thorn, Gwendolen A., 63
Thorn, L.S., 612
Thorne, C.G., 736
Thorne, Elizabeth H., 4111
Thorne, K.C.P., 5536
Thornley, Isobel D., 2638
Thornton, A.P., 7429
Thornton, Dorothy, 6634
Thornton, Gladys A., 1581
Thorogood, A. Jean, 822
Thorp, J., 4372
Thorpe, E., 5014
Thorpe, H., 432
Thraves, Laura H., 3728
Thrupp, Sylvia L., 1135
Thurston, H.S., 415
Tibbo, G.K., 1004
Tickner, F.J., 2275
Tickoo, Champa, 6745
Tidmarsh, K.R.S., 2344
Tierney, B., 750
Till, R.D., 3542
Tillakaratne, M.P., 6902
Timings, F.L., 5054
Timms, A.A.F., 1994
Timothy, J.R.W. Gwynne-, see Gwynne-Timothy
Timson, R.T. (London M.A.), 1329
Timson, R.T. (London Ph.D.), 1374
Tin Ohn, 7043
Tinker, H.R., 6452
Tite, C.J.C., 2703
Titow, J.Z., 1076
Tobias, A., 663
Tobias, J.J., 5229
Todd, A.C., 3742
Todd, D.K.C., 4294
Todd, G.F., 4908
Todd, Mary, 4377
Toft, Jean, 5254
Tokmakoff, G.B., 2373
Tolley, B.H., 7317
Tolley, Ivy H., 1437
Tomkinson, F., 5889
Tomlinson, H.E., 647
Tomlinson, J.L., 2028
Tomlinson, J.R.G., 3710
Toms, Elsie, 1087
Tonkinson, E., 2536
Tooley, C.W., 7122
Tooley, Marian J., 578
Topham, A.J., 5040

347

Topham, W., 2452
Topley, D.N., 1775
Topping, C.J.H., 921
Tordoff, W., 6412
Tough, D.L.W., 3229
Toulmin, Rachel M., 522
Toussaint, Marie M.A., 6944
Tout, Margaret (Manchester
  M.A.), 1569. See also Sharp,
  Margaret
Towlson, C.W., 4235
Townley, W.E., 5253
Towse, M.W., 2764
Toy, H.S., 4374
Toye, E.C., 3825
Toynbee, Margaret R., 727
Tracy, J.N., 6993
Trafford, Evelyn E., 2689
Trainor, L., 7613
Tranter, N., 4094
Trapido, S., 6303
Trautmann, T.R., 6483
Travers, B.H., 7577
Treadgold, D.W., 2363
Treadwell, V.W., 3270
Treais-Smart, Daphne J., 7133
Treanor, D.V., 4147
Treble, J.H., 5243
Treggiari, Susan M., 247
Tregonning, K.G.P., 7031
Treharne, R.F. (Manchester
  M.A.), 841
Treharne, R.F. (Manchester
  Ph.D.), 842
Trench, Susan M. Chenevix, see
  Chenevix Trench
Trevor, Daphne, 6304
Trickett, A.S., 2165
Trigg, E.B., 2540
Tripathi, A., 6659
Tripathi, R.S., 6499
Trood, Stella M.E., 2719
Tropp, Eluned H., 487
Trost, T.L., 7342
Trott, A.L. (Wales M.A.), 5591
Trott, A.L. (Wales Ph.D.), 5592
Trott, C.D.J., 495
Trotter, D.J.B., 4760
Trotter, Eleanor, 4341
Troust, J.C., 2471
Trowell, B.L., 1176
Trueman, B.E.S., 3988
Truscott, M.J., 4056
Tsuzuki, C., 4638
Tuck, J.A., 866
Tuck, P.J.N., 7035
Tucker, Anne D., 2657
Tucker, D.R., 5713
Tucker, G.N., 7222
Tucker, G.S.L., 3302
Tucker, H.F.G., 3799
Tucker, M.G., 1838
Tuckwell, R.H., 5110
Tugwood, Ruth M.S., 2780
Tulloch, W.J., 1674
Tumelty, J.J., 2208

Tunsiri, V., 4571
Tunstall, D., 5611
Turberville, A.S., 3638
Turley, D.M., 4832
Turnbull, Alma C., 3646
Turnbull, Constance M., 7022
Turnbull, M.R.M., 7594
Turner, A.C., 4723
Turner, B.H.P., 4918
Turner, C.E.A., 4272
Turner, D.A., 5574
Turner, D.J., 3699
Turner, D.R., 4713
Turner, Dorothy M., 3496
Turner, H.A., 4371
Turner, H.D., 4091
Turner, Hilary L., 1494
Turner, J.M., 3495
Turner, J.S.T., 3598
Turner, Margaret, 5661
Turner, Margaret E., 1391
Turner, Mary, 7390
Turner, Mary E., 2444
Turner, Olga, 2429
Turner, St.J.A., 5419
Turner, W.G., 6140
Turpin, K.C., 3661
Turton, B.J., 5137
Turton, E.R., 6214
Twaddle, M.J., 6258
Tweed, R.B., 3249
Twelvetrees, B.L., 4330
Twitchett, D.C., 7053
Tyack, G.C., 2581
Tyack, N.C.P. (Bristol M.A.),
  7259
Tyack, N.C.P. (London Ph.D.),
  7261
Tyacke, N.R.N., 3054
Tylecote, Mabel, 5658
Tyler, A. Elizabeth, 1903
Tyler, P. (Oxford B.Litt.),
  2997
Tyler, P. (Oxford D.Phil.),
  2998
Tyler, W.E., 5779
Tyman, J.L., 7192
Tyson, J.C., 3522
Tyson, M. (Manchester M.A.),
  60
Tyson, M. (Manchester Ph.D.),
  928
Tyson, R.E., 5072

UDAGAMA, P.P., 6881
Ukpabi, S.C., 6424
Ullman, R.H., 2377
Underdown, D.E., 2766
Underdown, P.T. (Bristol M.A.),
  3691
Underdown, P.T. (London Ph.D.),
  3723
Underhill, Kathryn V., see
  Brown
Underwood, V.P., 1449
Upasak, C.S., 6470

348

Ure, C.K. Seymour-, see
  Seymour-Ure
Urry, W.G., 1550
Usher, G.A., 1273
Ussishkin, Ann N., 6055
Utechin, S., 2388
Utley, Winifred, 685
Uzoigwe, G.N., 6419

VACAFLOR, J. Ameller, see
  Ameller Vacaflor
Vaidya, N.L., 6713
Vakil, C.N., 6788
Vale, M.G.A., 627
Vamplew, W., 5803
van Auken, S., 7352
van den Driesen, I.M., 6918
Van der Esch, Patricia A.M.,
  2467
van der Poel, J., 6315
van der Sprenkel, Sybille M.,
  7066
van Lohuizen, J., 6615
van Straelen, H.J.J.M., 7106
Varley, Joan, 4343
Varley, M.G., 7560
Varley, W.J., 458
Varma, J.N., 6588
Vaughan, R., 61
Vázquez-Presedo, V., 7556
Veale, E.W.W., 1568
Veale, Elspeth M., 1113
Veitch, Janet (Liverpool M.A.),
  3763
Veitch, Janet (Liverpool Ph.D.),
  3762
Veliz, C., 4068
Vella, A.P., 1441
Verghese, K.E., 6723
Vermeule, C.C., 256
Verney, D.V., 2408
Vernon, Helen R., 4672
Veverka, J., 4886
Veysey, A.G., 3595
Vickers, D.W., 1721
Vickery, A.V., 5214
Vierck, H.E.-F., 1490
Villers, Milda, 1727
Villiers, J.F.H., 2441
Vince, S.W.E., 4490
Vincent, E.R.P., 4126
Vincent, H.M., 2253
Vincent, J.R., 4604
Vincent, W.A.L. (Oxford
  B.Litt.), 3152
Vincent, W.A.L. (Oxford
  D.Phil.), 4281
Vivian, D.W. Frances St.C.
  (Cambridge M.Litt.), 4112
Vivian, Frances St.C. (London
  Ph.D.), 4331
Virgoe, R., 985
Voigt, J.H., 113
von dem Knesebeck, G.-L., 5213
Vorzimer, P.J., 5484

WADDELL, D.A.G., 3632
Wade, Anthea, 970
Wade, Margaret M., 843
Wadman, D.C., 1811
Wadsworth, G.C., 3246
Wagle, N.K., 6466
Wagstaff, E., 3935
Waheeduzzaman, A.M., 6698
Wahlstrand, Janet M., 3634
Wainwright, Mary D., 7324
Waites, B.F., 1351
Wake, W.C., 160
Wakefield, G.S., 2546
Walden-Aspy, F.C., 1328
Wales, A.E., 4317
Waley, D.P., 565
Walford, A.J. (London M.A.),
  7549
Walford, A.J. (London Ph.D.),
  7548
Walker, A.S., 1797
Walker, D.G., 1562
Walker, E.C., 1771
Walker, Enid, 3392
Walker, F., 451
Walker, F.B., 3725
Walker, F.X., 3023
Walker, G.J., 7517
Walker, G.S.M., 1703
Walker, I. Kathleen, 6623
Walker, J.C., 7191
Walker, J.H., 5815
Walker, James (Edinburgh Ph.D.
  1928), 2618
Walker, James (Manchester Ph.D.
  1931), 3602
Walker, Joan, 768
Walker, Lorna E.M., 924
Walker, O.H., 3219
Walker, P.C. Gordon, see Gordon
  Walker
Walker, R.B., 2940
Walker, R.F. (Oxford D.Phil.),
  993
Walker, R.F. (Wales M.A.), 836
Walker, S.J., 5328
Walker, Shirley M., 1174
Walker, W.H.T., 2662
Walkley, G., 4337
Wall, D., 3732
Wall, J., 360
Wall, R., 5754
Wallace, D.E., 4443
Wallace, M.W., 511
Wallace, R.G., 6078
Wallace, W.V., 1836
Wallach, J.L., 2170
Wallas, May G., 1961
Wallbank, Annie M.M., 3002
Waller, B., 2152
Waller, D.K., 7158
Waller, E. Kerr-, see Kerr-
  Waller
Waller, Elizabeth M.L., 589
Waller, J., 3080

Waller, Marion J., 4277
Wallick, C.C., 5785
Wallis, C.B., 7562
Wallis, E.W., 3213
Wallis, Helen M., 7618
Wallwork, Kenneth (Manchester M.A.), 3318
Wallwork, Kenneth L. (Leicester Ph.D.), 3319
Walmsley, F.S., 2312
Walpole, Kathleen A., 7209
Walsh, H.G., 7232
Walsh, J.D., 4236
Walsh, M.J., 6392
Walsh, Nora, 3442
Walshe, A.P., 6336
Walters, D.E., 3104
Walters, S.F.D., 5654
Walters, W.E., 6035
Walthew, C.V., 261
Walton, A., 7433
Walton, J., 4974
Walton, K., 3559
Walton, Mavis, see Cunningham
Walvin, J., 3816
Wang, Gung Wu, 7056
Wang, Ling, 7048
Wang, S.-T., 7117
Wang, T.-T. (Cambridge M.Litt.), 7134
Wang, T.-T. (Cambridge Ph.D.), 7074
Wangermann, E., 1841
Wanklyn, M.D.G., 2746
Wansbrough, J.E., 673
Warburg, G., 6184
Warburton, W.H. (Birmingham M.Com.), 4820
Warburton, W.H. (Oxford B.Litt.), 4973
Ward, A.J., 7393
Ward, Christine, 5317
Ward, David, 442
Ward, Dora, 1617
Ward, F.M., 3743
Ward, J.G.S., 7552
Ward, J.R., 4037
Ward, Jennifer C., 1053
Ward, John Towers, 4944
Ward, John Trevor, 5196
Ward, L.O., 5507
Ward, M.F.C., 1745
Ward, P.G., 1402
Ward, Pamela W.U., 3597
Ward, Phyllis J., 2037
Ward, S.G.P., 3918
Ward, Sibyl, 5840
Ward, W.E.F., 564
Ward, W.R., 3926
Wardle, D., 5542A
Ware, Helen R.E., 5295
Ware, Jean E., 5483
Warhurst, P.R., 6246
Wark, K.R., 3026
Warmington, J., 220
Warnapala, W.A. Wiswa, see Wiswa Warnapala

Warne, A. (Leeds M.A.), 725
Warne, A. (Leeds Ph.D.), 4152
Warner, M., 4649
Warner, T.E., 4477
Warner, W.J., 4141
Warren, A.E., 2982
Warren, J.C.P. (London Ph.D.), 2142
Warren, J.C.P. (Sheffield M.A.), 1859
Warren, J.D.A., 1846
Warren, Lucy M., 3405
Warren, W.L., 1292
Warriner, Doreen, 2189
Warrior, Valerie M., 194
Washington, J.H., 6286
Wason, Margaret O., 140
Wastell, R.E.P. (London M.A.), 4896
Wastell, R.E.P. (London Ph.D.), 6216
Wasti, S.R., 6856
Waterhouse, Rachel E., 3464
Waters, S.H., 3185
Waters, W.H. (Cambridge M.Litt.), 1651
Waters, W.H. (Wales M.A.), 1598
Waterson, Nellie M. (Birmingham M.A.), 5236
Waterson, Nellie M. (Oxford B.Litt.), 3644
Watkin, E.E., 5107
Watkins, D., 81
Watkins, D.H., 392
Watkins, E.H., 7427
Watkins, K.W., 4817
Watkinson, Amy E., 1032
Watkinson, C.D., 4605
Watkinson, Mary H., 5340
Watson, A.F., 4121
Watson, A.G., 3155
Watson, C., 1354
Watson, D.H. (Sheffield M.A.), 3789
Watson, D.H. (Sheffield Ph.D.), 3703
Watson, E., 509
Watson, G.R., 284
Watson, J.B., 2890
Watson, J.E., 3530
Watson, P.H.P., 3441
Watson, Paula K., 3891
Watson, T.J., 3571
Watt, D.E.R., 1691
Watt, J.A., 779
Watters, A.C., 5450
Watters, R.F., 7623
Watts, A.H., 5903
Watts, A.McK., 3062
Watts, D.G., 1078
Watts, M.R., 5456
Waugh, Mary, 5755
Wayper, C.L., 1860
Wearing, J., 7223
Wearmouth, R.F. (Birmingham M.A.), 3494

350

Wearmouth, R.F. (London Ph.D.), 5435
Weatherhead, J.F., 4972
Weatherill, Lorna M., 3985
Weaver, F.J., 1902
Weaver, Jean A., 5550
Weaver, P.R.C., 246
Webb, A.N., 1361
Webb, A.W., 6416
Webb, D.J., 5155
Webb, J.G., 2859
Webb, Margaret G., 969
Weber, E.J., 2093
Webster, G.A., 375
Webster, J.B., 6413
Webster, J.R., 5616
Webster, Mabel G.A., 349
Webster, R.A., 370
Webster, V.R., 2579
Wedlock, Gladys H., 5720
Weeks, D.C. (London M.A.), 6029
Weeks, D.C. (London Ph.D.), 6171
Weerawardana, I.D.S., 6940
Weetch, K.T., 3347
Weheba, A.F.M.M., 6110
Wei, Y.-S., 6278
Weiner, A., 649
Weinroth, H.S., 4790
Weinstock, Maureen, 3208
Weir, A.J., 3795
Weir, T.E., 4387
Weisheipl, J.A., 1453
Weiss, R., 1469
Weissbruth, Alice, 281
Weitzman, Sophia (Manchester M.A.), 6682
Weitzman, Sophia (Manchester Ph.D.), 6629
Welch, C.E. (Liverpool M.A.), 1259
Welch, C.E. (Southampton Ph.D.), 1201
Welch, P.J. (London M.A.), 1773
Welch, P.J. (London Ph.D.), 5387
Welles, Judith B., 3067
Wellesz, Emmy F., 795
Wells, A.R., 2198
Wells, C.M., 213
Wells, Edith N., 1537
Wells, Evelyn B., 2727
Wells, F.A., 3363
Wells, R.J., 4250
Welsby, P.A., 3059
Welton, L.J.F., 2272
Wenzel, Marian B., 796
Were, G.S., 6207
Werff, L.L. Vander, 6446
Wertimer, S., 4537
West, F., 3536
West, F.J. (Cambridge Ph.D.), 895
West, F.J. (Leeds Ph.D.), 887
West, H.W., 5361
West, J., 1056
Westall, Elsie, 1917

Westcott, Margaret R., 2822
Western, J.R., 3911
Westmarland, B.T., 2604
Weston, G.A., 3482
Westworth, O.A., 4026
Whale, Gwendolyn B.M., 3808
Whale, Joyce M., 760
Wharfe, L., 439
Wharhirst, Gwendolen E., 2957
Wharton, N.M.L., 8
Wheatley, P. (London M.A.), 1037
Wheatley, P. (London Ph.D.), 6983
Wheatley, R.R.A., 2203
Wheaton, J., 4873
Wheeler, P.T., 3569
Wheeler, R.G.G., 4845
Whelan, Margaret E., 3019
Whetter, J.C.A., 4350
Whibley, Mildred, 2311
Whileblood, Stella M., 1398
Whisker, R.F., 3210
Whitaker, E.H., 1789
Whitaker, G.R., 1363
Whitaker, P., 4606
Whitaker, R.H., 1181
Whitaker, S.P., 2717
Whitaker, W.B. (Bristol M.A.), 2963
Whitaker, W.B. (London Ph.D.), 4095
Whitcomb, E.A.L., 2031
Whitcomb, J.D., 6292
Whitcombe, Elizabeth M., 6757
White, A., 2568
White, A.N. Sherwin-, see Sherwin-White
White, A.T., 7566
White, A.W.A., 3989
White, B.R., 3004
White, Cynthia L., 5224
White, Edna F., 2623
White, G.D., 6265
White, J.W., 5356
White, L.F.W., 5529
White, O., 5686
White, P., 901
Whiteford, D.H., 4400
Whitehand, J.W.R., 418
Whitehead, E., 5528
Whitehouse, Muriel D., 202
Whitehouse, W.J., 1368
Whiteman, E. Anne O., 4161
Whiteside, D.T., 4284
Whitfield, D.W., 1392
Whitfield, J.H., 2597
Whitford, F.J., 5872
Whitlaw, J.A.G., 4476
Whitmore, P.J.S., 1919
Whitney, J.C., 5891
Whitson, Agnes M., 7426
Whittaker, M.B., 4258
Whittam, J.R., 2260
Whitter, J., 4347
Whittington, G.W., 1046

Whittle, G., 5141
Whitty, R.G.H. (London M.A.), 2601
Whitty, R.G.H. (London Ph.D.), 3170
Whitworth, E.C., 2699
Whomsley, D., 1256
Whyatt, G.K., 4054
Whyte, J.H. (Belfast Ph.D.), 5878
Whyte, J.H. (Oxford B.Litt.), 5859
Wickenden, H.J., 7260
Wickenden, J.N., 83
Wickramasinghe, Sirima, 6890
Wickremeratne, L.A., 6927
Wickremeratne, U.C., 6909
Wicks, Margaret C.W., 5279
Wickwar, W.H., 4324
Widdows, E.J., 4
Wightman, Edith M., 338
Wightman, Evelyn M., 5247
Wightman, W.E., 1148
Wightman, W.R., 444
Wijetunga, W.M.K., 6888
Wilcher, L.C., 7612
Wilcock, C.M., 3811
Wild, J.P., 252
Wilde, P.D., 5044
Wilder, J.S., 4435
Wilding, P.R., 5338
Wiliam, A.I.R., 1624
Wiliam, U., 4278
Wilkes, J.J., 300
Wilkes, Julia M., 476
Wilkins, Mira S., 4639
Wilkins, Phyllis M., 4076
Wilkinson, B. (Manchester M.A.), 904
Wilkinson, B. (Manchester Ph.D.), 905
Wilkinson, Ethel M., 4123
Wilkinson, J.C., 5975
Wilkinson, J.F., 4233
Wilkinson, J.K., 302
Wilkinson, J.T., 4209
Wilkinson, J.W., 1600
Wilkinson, Joyce M., 1322
Wilkinson, Mary K., 5498
Wilkinson, P., 5329
Wilks, I.G., 6347
Wilks, M.J., 572
Wilks, W.I., 5210
Will, H.A., 7495
Willan, T.S. (Oxford B.Litt.), 3205
Willan, T.S. (Oxford D.Phil.), 3945
Willatts, E.C., 5183
Willcock, B.G., 6450
Williams, A.F., 5167
Williams, A.G., 7475
Williams, A.H., 3478
Williams, A.H.N., 368
Williams, A.J., 4038
Williams, Ann, 775

Williams, Beryl, 6017
Williams, C.M., 2725
Williams, C.R., 4936
Williams, D.M., 5113
Williams, D.M.E., 3601
Williams, D.R.A., 3508
Williams, D.S.M., 6980
Williams, Daniel T., 1240
Williams, David, 3724
Williams, David T., 570
Williams, Donovan, 4743
Williams, E. Ann, 1035
Williams, E.E., 7470
Williams, E.R., 2774
Williams, F., 3517
Williams, G.A. (London Ph.D.), 1566
Williams, G.A. (Wales M.A.), 1565
Williams, Glanmor, 3011
Williams, Glyndwr, 3896
Williams, H.G., 3112
Williams, H.M., 4538
Williams, I., 1641
Williams, J.D., 4334
Williams, J.G., 3614
Williams, J.H., 346
Williams, J.M., 6322
Williams, J.R., 5007
Williams, J.S., 3118
Williams, James, 6160
Williams, James E. (Leeds M.A.), 3376
Williams, James E. (Sheffield Ph.D.), 5013
Williams, John, 787
Williams, John Alan, 4897
Williams, John Anthony, 4259
Williams, John E., 4644
Williams, L.A., 5129
Williams, L.F.R., 1331
Williams, L.J., 5081
Williams, Lilian M., 7624
Williams, Lillian, 5242
Williams, Lionel H., 2882
Williams, Louis H., 5635
Williams, M.J., 3901
Williams, Mabel, 5278
Williams, Margaret F., 3470
Williams, Michael, 5208
Williams, Moelwyn I. (Leicester Ph.D. 1967), 4050
Williams, Moelwyn I. (Wales M.A. 1939), 4513
Williams, Myfanwy, 4838
Williams, N.J., 2860
Williams, Nellie, 3755
Williams, P.H., 2672
Williams, P.T., 4935
Williams, Patricia M., 5327
Williams, R.T., 153
Williams, Reginald A., 5697
Williams, Richard, 150
Williams, Roger A., 1743
Williams, T.H., 4890
Williams, T.L., 992

Williams, T.S., 3594
Williams, V.E.N., 376
Williams, W.O., 3180
Williams, W.P., 3818
Williams, W.T., 2626
Williams, Winifred S., 1656
Williams-Jones, W.K., 4364
Williamson, C.F., 2705
Williamson, Dorothy, 1400
Williamson, F., 967
Williamson, J.A., 1926
Williamson, Margaret T., 4087
Willis, D.P., 505
Willis, G.G., 687
Willis, J.R., 6132
Willis, P., 4332
Wills, Stella R., 5650
Wills, W.D., 5386
Willson, F.M.G., 4560
Wilmer, R.H., 1756
Wilson, A.E., 278
Wilson, A.J., 6938
Wilson, A.J.N., 299
Wilson, A.M., 1958
Wilson, Alexander, 5801A
Wilson, Allan, 365
Wilson, Barbara M., 3184
Wilson, Barbara N., 2943
Wilson, C.L., 7589
Wilson, D.J., 5410
Wilson, D.K. (London Ph.D.),
  6915
Wilson, D.K. (Oxford B.Litt.),
  6908
Wilson, D.R., 123
Wilson, Eleanora M. Carus-, see
  Carus-Wilson
Wilson, F.H., 234
Wilson, F.L., 5830
Wilson, Frances M., 19
Wilson, G.A., 4471
Wilson, H.S., 4869
Wilson, I.M., 1927
Wilson, Jean S., 2693
Wilson, K., 868
Wilson, K.P., 1128
Wilson, M.R., 4858
Wilson, R., 1731
Wilson, R.G., 3961
Wilson, R.K., 7581
Wilson, S., 114
Wilson, T.G., 4699
Wilson, Wendy S., 5795
Winawer, H.M., 2351
Winchester, Barbara, 2899
Windsor, G., 2544
Windsor, R., 594
Wink, C.A.S., 5231
Winnett, A.R., 2548
Winnicki, T.Z., 4810
Winpenny, J.T., 7569
Winter, E.P., 2558
Winter, J.M., 4691
Winters, R.L., 1901
Wirszubski, C., 206
Wise, H.B.A., 5596

Wiseley, W.C., 2202
Wiseman, T.P., 195
Wiskemann, Elizabeth M., 2259
Wiswall, F.L., 4862
Wiswa Warnapala, W.A., 6941
Witcombe, D.T. (Manchester
  Ph.D.), 3609
Witcombe, D.T. (Oxford B.Litt.),
  3617
Witherick, M.E., 4503
Withycombe, R.S.M., 5421
Wolffe, B.P. (Oxford B.Litt.),
  876
Wolffe, B.P. (Oxford D.Phil.),
  875
Wolfson, Freda, 6384
Wollaston, E.P.M., 4659
Wolters, O.W., 6982
Wong, Ellie L., 7071
Wong, F.H.K., 7006
Wong, O.H.-L., 7118
Wong Hoy Kee, F., 7081
Wong Lin Ken, 7012
Wood, A.H., 1310
Wood, A.J.R. Russell-, see
  Russell-Wood
Wood, A.S., 4246
Wood, A. Sandys-, see Sandys-
  Wood
Wood, Alfred C. (Oxford
  B.Litt.), 5977
Wood, Alfred C. (Oxford
  D.Phil.), 5969
Wood, Anthony C., 4342
Wood, D.P.J., 3121
Wood, E.R.G., 4522
Wood, J., 902
Wood, J.D., 4453
Wood, J.R.T., 3664
Wood, K.W., 3890
Wood, Katherine, 1271
Wood, Margaret E., 1497
Wood, Marguerite, 3211
Wood, N., 3117
Wood, O., 3316
Wood, P.D. (Reading Ph.D.), 486
Wood, P.D. (Wales M.A.), 485
Wood, Priscilla J., 1251
Wood, R.J., 2786
Wood, T., 1689
Woodall, Ethel M., 728
Woodard, C., 5314
Woodcock, B.L., 1260
Woodcock, N.E., 1410
Woodham Smith, Phyllis, 4267
Woodhead, J.R., 4349
Woodhouse, M.G., 5025
Wood-Legh, Kathleen L. (Cam-
  bridge Ph.D.), 1281
Wood-Legh, Kathleen L. (Oxford
  B.Litt.), 965
Woodruff, S.A., 4421
Woodruff, W., 5057
Woods, C.J., 5866
Woods, F.U., 3750
Woods, J.F., 6003

SUBJECTS OF THESES

(Note: Subjects like canals, forests, heresies, industries,
schools are not necessarily arranged under a general heading
but may be indexed under a particular name)

Administration (<u>cont.</u>)
  judicial, in India, 6530, 6621, 6628, 6684, 6702; in ancient
    Rome, 301
  local, <u>see</u> Local government
  military, in ancient Greece, 169; in India, 6841
  naval (medieval), 995, 1002; (17th cent.), 2792; (17th–19th
    cent.), 3879–919A <u>passim</u>; in ancient Greece, 169
  Roman imperial, 211, 246
  rural, in the U.S.S.R., 2387, 2393
Administrative families (medieval), 894, 898
Administrative personnel, <u>see</u> Officials, government
Admiralty (18th–19th cent.), 3908; lords commissioners (17th–18th
  cent.), 3885
Admiralty jurisdiction (17th cent.), 3779; (19th–20th cent.),
  4862
Adult education, 5655–63; in Ghana, 6431
Adulteration of food, 5226
Adur valley, Sussex, 402–3
Aehrenthal, Count Alois Lesca von (1854–1912), 1870
Aelfric, called Grammaticus (fl. 1006), 1416
Aelred of Rievaulx (1109–66), 1371
<u>aes</u> coinage, 257–8
Aethelweard (d. 998?), 56
Aetolian League (323–189 B.C.), 172
Afghanistan, 6955–81 <u>passim</u>; and India, 6449
Afghans, 6701; in India (16th–17th cent.), 6552
Afif, Muslim historian (medieval), 45
Africa, 4763, 4794, 6056–69; (Roman), 236, 317–24; central, 6203–
  72 <u>passim</u>; east, 6061, 6203–72 <u>passim</u>; north, 6070–93; north-
  east, 6094–202 <u>passim</u>; southern, 6068, 6279–337; west, 4758,
  6061, 6338–442
African Lakes Company, 6231
African National Congress, 6336
Africans, as Christian ministers, 6383; in civil service, 6369,
  6440; education of, 6059, 6226, 6262; liberated, 6366–7;
  political awareness of, 6325; taxation of, 6302
Agathias (<u>c</u>. 536–82), 31
Agha Khan (1800–81), 6728
Agrarian conditions, in United Provinces, 6757
Agrarian distress (18th–19th cent.), 4109
Agrarian problem, in Rumania (20th cent.), 1883
Agrarian reform, in Denmark (18th cent.), 2403; in Egypt (20th
  cent.), 6200
Agrarian system, Mughal, 6555
Agrarian unrest (16th–17th cent.), 2846; (19th cent.), 4077–9
Agricultural change (18th cent.), 4056; (18th–19th cent.), 4072,
  4074, 5171; (19th cent.), 5172; (19th–20th cent.), 4520; in
  Scotland, 4409
Agricultural co-operation, 5201; in India, 6810, 6847
Agricultural engineering industry, 5077
Agricultural imports and exports (17th–18th cent.), 3957
Agricultural interest groups, 5216; in France, 2081
Agricultural labour, 4996, 5017, 5171, 5178–80, 5205, 5217; in
  Scotland, 5780; in Wales, 5185; in Madras Presidency, 6665
Agricultural labourers' revolt, 4077–8
Agricultural policies (20th cent.), 5214; in India (19th–20th
  cent.), 6835
Agricultural rents, 5195–6
Agricultural revolution, <u>see</u> Agricultural change
Agriculture
  in British Isles, 389–518 <u>passim</u>; in England (medieval), 1045–
    99 <u>passim</u>; (15th–17th cent.), 2819–49 <u>passim</u>; in England and
    Wales, 2497, 2501, 2506–7, 2511–12; (17th–20th cent.), 3400–45;
    (17th–19th cent.), 4041–79 <u>passim</u>; (19th–20th cent.), 4515,
    5168–218; in Ireland, 5857–8; in Scotland, 4410, 4446; in
    Wales (medieval), 1606; (16th–17th cent.), 2501, 3173; <u>and</u>
    <u>see above</u>

Agriculture (cont.)
  in Argentina, 7555; in Australia, 7608; in Canada, 7192, 7231;
    in Ceylon, 6921; in Cyrenaica (ancient), 324; in Denmark, 2402;
    in Egypt, 6110, 6125, 6139; in France, 2081; in Gaul, 330; in
    India, 6453, 6785, 6797; in Roman empire, 238-40; in Russia,
    2365; in Trinidad, 7452
  see also Plantations
Agronomes, 1964
Ahmad of Sarhind, Shaikh (1564-1624), 6565
Ahmed Khan, Sir Syed (1817-98), 6755, 6780
Aids (14th cent.), 1015
Ailly, Pierre d' (1350-1420), cardinal, 730
Air power, strategic, 4883
Air raid shelters, 5347
Aircraft industry, 5102
Aire and Calder Navigation, 4029
Airedale, W.R. Yorks., 448
Ajivikas, 6465
Akbar, Jalāl-al-dīn (1542-1605), Mughal emperor, 6562-3
Akuapem state, 6210
Akwamu, 6347
Alabaster carving, 1513
Al-Amin (d. 813), caliph, 5934
Alary, Pierre-Joseph (1689-1770), 1953
'Alawi dynasty, 6075
al-Bakri, b. Abi 'L. Surūr (d. 1619), 50
Albanians, history of (10th cent.), 55
Albany, duke of, see Stewart, John
Albert (1819-61), prince consort, 4593
Albigensians, 725
Albion Steam Flour Mill, 4026
Alciston, Sussex, 1558
Aldgate, see London
Aleppo, Syria, 5947, 5968
Alexander (1888-1934), king of Jugoslavia, 1893
Alexander, William Lindsay (1808-84), 5785
Alexander Neckham (1157-1217), 1454
Alexandria, Egypt, 6100-1; patriarchate of, 741
Alexandria-Cairo-Suez railway, 6137
Alfred (849-901), king, 1415
Alfreton, Derbys., 5769
'Alī b. Abī Tālib (d. 660), 5924
'Alī Dīnār (c. 1865-1916), sultan of Darfūr, 6839
Aliens (medieval), 831, 1130-1; (16th cent.), 2882-3; (16th-17th
    cent.), 2901; (19th-20th cent.), 5331-3; in Wales (16th cent.),
    2882
Aliens Act (1905), 5333
Alkali industry, 3375
Allahabad, India, 6811
Allen, William (1532-94), cardinal, 3017
Allen and Hanbury, 3373
Alliance High School, Kenya, 6272
Alliances, European (19th cent.), 1805
All-India Muslim League, 6859
Allotment schemes (18th-19th cent.), 4114
All-Union Leninist Communist League of Youth, 2389
al-Malik al-Zāhir Baibars, see Baybars I
Al Ma'mūm, caliph (813-33), 5934
Almoner, see King's almoner
Al-Mu'ayyad fi' d-Dīn ash-Shīrāzi (d. 1077), 37
'Al-Musqtataf, 6152
Al Mu'tasim, caliph (833-42), 5936-7
Al-Mutawakkil, caliph (847-61), 5938-9
Alpujarras rebellion (1568-71), 2423
Alrewas, Staffs., 1574
Alsace-Lorraine, 2292
Altan Tobci, 7064

Altars, in Roman Britain, 359
Al-Turi, 'Al-Hājj 'Umar b. Sa'īd al-Fūtī (c. 1794-1864), 6132
Alum trade, 2535
Aluminium industry, 5101
Amalgamated Society of Engineers, 4983
Amalgamated Society of Railway Servants, 4994
Amampondo, 6294
Amarna period, in Egypt, 6096
America, colonial, 3789-90, 3899, 3903, 3905-6, 7169-83, 7257-95
America, see also North America; South America; United States of
    America
American Civil War (1861-5), 7347-68 passim
American Federation of Labor, 7382
American independence, idea of, 7286
American Loyalists, 7288-9
American Papers, Committee of Whole House, 3790
American Revolution, 7287-90, 7292-5, 7448; and Ireland, 4475
American War of Independence (1775-83), 2331, 3903, 3905-6, 4448
Amir Khusrau (1253-1325), 45
Amity Hall, Jamaica, 7443
Amlwch, Anglesey, 3546
Amman valley, 3329
Ammianus Marcellinus (4th cent.), 30
Ampthill, 1st Baron, see Russell, Odo William Leopold
Amsterdam, Holland, 2276
An Lu-Shan (8th cent.), 5928
Anabaptists, 1763, 4195
Analogy, role of, 1753
Anarcho-syndicalist movement, in Spain, 2463
Anatolia, 6008
Anchiennes cronicques de Pise, Les, 76
Ancona, Italy, 2224
Andalusia, Spain, 7518
Andes, Confederation of the, 7552
Andhra region, India, 6477
Andrew Salus, Saint (d. c. 948), 701
Andrewes, Lancelot (1555-1626), bishop, 3059-60
Aneirin, see Book of Aneirin
Angell, Sir Norman (1847-1967), 4791-2
Angers, France, 2039
Anglesey, 3431, 3778, 4540, 5238
Anglesey, 1st marquess of, see Paget, Henry William
Anglicanism, 2960, 3092, 3218, 3495, 4156
Anglo-Austrian alliance (1748-56), 1837
Anglo-Chinese treaties, 7092
Anglo-Congo treaty (1894), 6278
Anglo-Egyptian treaty (1936), 6202
Anglo-French Entente (1904), 2087, 2091
Anglo-German conventions (1898), 2164
Anglo-Japanese alliance, 7135-9, 7142, 7148
Anglo-Norman Chronicle (Trivet's), 69-70
Anglo-Norman language, 921, 1447
Anglo-Russian Agreement (1903-7), 2366
Anglo-Saxon Chronicle, 52-3, 56
Anglo-Saxon Church, 1182
Anglo-Saxon language, see Old English
Anglo-Saxon settlement, 1484, 1518-26 passim
Anglo-Saxons, 1024, 1047, 1145, 1183-4, 1414, 1481-93; in Ireland,
    1705
Anglo-Spanish Treaty (1667), 2439
Anglo-Welsh wars (13th cent.), 993
Angola, 6340
Angus, 2614
Anna Comnena (b. 1083), 537
Annals of Merton, 60
Annals of Southwark, 60
Annals of Winchcombe, 57

Armament, nuclear, 2306
Armaments industry, German, 2204
Armenian Church (5th cent.), 5911
Armenian question, 6029
Armenians, in Anatolia and Syria (19th-20th cent.), 6008
armes parlantes, 647
Arminianism, 3053-4; in Scotland, 4403
Armour (14th cent.), 662; (14th-17th cent.), 1509; (16th cent.),
    3162; in ancient Greece, 131
Armourer, 1002
Arms, succession to, in Scotland, 2607
Arms traffic, in West Africa, 6398
Army, armed forces (medieval), 990, 992; (16th cent.), 2778; (16th-
    17th cent.), 2790; (17th cent.), 2746, 2799, 2818, 3279-80;
    (17th-19th cent.), 3879-918 passim, 7178; (19th cent.), 6375;
    (19th-20th cent.), 4862-84 passim; Scottish (17th cent.),
    4392; Arab, 5912; Chinese (8th-9th cent.), 7055; of Delhi
    sultans, 6536; Egyptian, 6168; French (medieval), 595; (19th
    cent.), 6155; German, 2196; Indian, 6783, 6859; Jacobite,
    4428; Roman, 282-96, 377, 383; Spanish, 2422, 2454
Army of the Ten Thousand, 159
Army officers (18th cent.), 3895; German (19th-20th cent.), 2159
Arnim, Count Harry Karl Kurt Eduard von (1824-81), 2153
Arnold of Brescia (d. 1155), 564
Arnot, William (1808-75), 5786
Arnulf of Lisieux (d. 1184), bishop, 716
Arras, congress of (1435), 634
Arsenian controversy, 546
Art and artists (medieval), 777-804 passim; English (medieval),
    1478-517 passim; French, 1898, 1909, 2063-4, 4124; Indian,
    6537; see also Painting
Arthuna, 6515
Artificial silk industry, 5096
Artillery (ancient), 124
Artists' colours (17th-19th cent.), 4326
Arts and crafts, in Scotland, 3576
Arun valley, Sussex, 403
Arundel, Sussex, college of Holy Trinity, 1299
Arundel, Thomas (1353-1414), archbishop, 865
Arwystli, 3173
Asceticism, in ancient India, 6452
Ascham, Roger (1515-68), 2888
Ashanti, 6351, 6354, 6412
Ashton-under-Lyne, Lancs., 3321, 5658
Ashworth, Henry (1794-1880), 5061
Asia Minor, Greek cities of, 162; Roman colonies in, 301, 307
Aske's Hoxton Hospital, 4096
Asoka, 6471
Assam, 6675, 6956-81 passim
Asser (d. 909?), bishop, 1415
Assiento, 3934
Assize rolls, 931-2, 952, 1563
Assizes (16th-18th cent.), 2484
Association Internationale Africaine, 6273
Association of the Friends of the People, 3822
Athanasius, Saint (293-373), bishop, 741
Atheism, in France (18th cent.), 1968
Athens (ancient), 138-81 passim
Attorney (18th cent.), 3679
Attwood, Thomas (1783-1856), 4941
Auckland, 1st earl of, see Eden, George
Auditors, 4906
Audley End, Essex, 4334
Augustine, Saint (354-430), bishop of Hippo, 587
Augustinian canons, 1346
Augustinus Triumphus (1243-1328), 572
Augustus (d. 14 A.D.), Roman emperor, 208, 212-15

Aumale, countess of, see Fortibus, Isabella de
Aurangzib (1618-1707), emperor of Hindustan, 6579-81
Australia, 7570-617 passim
Austria (17th cent.), 5978; (18th cent.), 1838; (19th cent.), 1841,
    1846, 1850; (19th-20th cent.), 1800, 1859; (20th cent.),
    1871-2, 1885, 1888, 1892, 1894, 2268; and Britain, 1837, 1839,
    1843, 2140
Austria-Hungary, 1804, 1870; and Britain, 1860, 1869
Authority, political (14th cent.), 857; (17th cent.), 3848, 3860;
    (20th cent.), 5378; problem of (medieval), 572
Autun, Honorius of, see Honorius Augustodunensis
Aviation, see Civil aviation
Avvakum (1620-82), Russian priest, 2323
Axis Powers, 2466
Aylesbury, Bucks., 5761
Ayrshire, 4431, 5819
Azevedo, Jeronimo de (fl. 1594-1612), 6896
'Azm Pashas, 5979

BABEUF, François Noël (1760-97), 1980
Babylon, 5883-4, 5907
Back to the land movement, 5210
Bacon, Francis (1561-1626), Viscount St. Albans, 3154
Bacon, Roger (d. 1294), 1456
Bactria (3rd-4th cent.), 5906
Bagehot, Walter (1826-77), 5481
Baghdad, Iraq, 6012
Baginton, Warwicks., 1493
Bagot, Richard (1782-1854), bishop, 5400
Bahamas, 7419, 7436
Bahia, Brazil, Santa Casa da Misericórdia, 7510
Baines, Sir Edward (1800-90), 4609
Baji Rao II, peshwa (1796-1818), 6662
Baking (ancient), 122
Baking industry, 4995
Balance of payments (19th cent.), 3942; Indian, 6850
Baldwin (d. 1190), archbishop, 1207
Baldwin, George (d. 1826), 6120
Bale, John (1495-1563), bishop, 2968
Balfour, Arthur James (1848-1930), 1st earl of Balfour, 4682, 4759
Balkan peninsula (12th-14th cent.), 645
Balkan states, 1828-95 passim
Balkan Wars (1912-14), 1873
Ballistics (17th cent.), 3879
Ballycastle, co. Antrim, 4471
Balmes, Jaime Luciano (1810-48), 2451
Baltic powers, 1819, 2398-9
Baluchistan, 6769
Bancroft, Richard (1544-1610), archbishop, 3057-8
Bandino, Domenico di (c. 1340 - c. 1413), 815
Banerjea, Surendranath (1848-1925), 6817
Bangor, co. Down, 4458
Bangor Normal College, Caern., 5701
Banjarmasin, 6594
Bank notes, circulation of, 4894; issue of, 5806
Bank of England, 3305, 3925
Bank rate (19th cent.), 4891
Banking system, Australian, 7582; Canadian, 7181; French, 2042;
    Irish, 5838; of the U.S.A., 7181
Bankrupts, 920
Banks, Sir Joseph (1743-1820), 3794
Banks, banking, 3925; (18th-19th cent.), 3304; (19th cent.), 4902;
    joint stock, 4892; merchant (18th cent.), 3938; savings, 4887;
    in Scotland, 5806
Bantam, 6989
Baptism, 675; (19th-20th cent.), 5428
Baptist Missionary Society, 7466

Baptists (16th-17th cent.), 2558; (17th cent.), 3042, 3093, 4210,
    7262; (17th-19th cent.), 3474; (18th cent.), 4238; (18th-19th
    cent.), 3482, 3530, 4237, 5425; (19th cent.), 5445; (19th-20th
    cent.), 5428; in Scotland, 3578, 4436; in India, 6656; see
    also Particular Baptists
Baragan, Rumania, 1845
Barante, Prosper de (1782-1866), 101
Barbados, 7421, 7424, 7451, 7475, 7494
Barbaro, Daniele (1513-70), 2239
Barbary states, 6077; Britain and, 6078
Bardi, 1132
Bardic order, 1662
Barère, Bertrand (1755-1841), 2010
Barham, 1st Baron, see Middleton, Charles
Baring, Evelyn (1841-1917), 1st earl of Cromer, 4762, 6165-7
Baring, Thomas George (1826-1904), 1st earl of Northbrook, 6801
Barking abbey, Essex, 1336
Barkly, Sir Henry (1815-98), 7486
Barnes, Robert (1495-1540), 2937
Barnett, Samuel Augustus (1844-1913), 5330
Barni, see Zia-ud-din Barni
Barnsley, W.R. Yorks., 5537
Barnton, Ches., 3397
Baron Hill, Anglesey, 1171
Baronial reform, 845
Baronial tenure, Welsh, 1646
Baronies, ecclesiastical (13th-14th cent.), 1042
Barons, baronage (13th cent.), 830, 833, 853; (14th cent.), 866;
    (15th cent.), 1168
Barons' Wars, 841-6
Barotseland, 6312
Barracks Act (1890), 4877
Barrington, Cambs., 1484
Barrington, Shute (1734-1826), bishop, 4190
Barrow-in-Furness, Lancs., 454
Barry, Glam., 5552, 5763
Barry Dock and Railways Company, 5132
Barton, Edward (1562?-1597), 5967
Basel, Council of (1431-49), 738, 1408
Basford, Notts., 5269
Basil the Great (c. 330-379), bishop of Caesarea, 686
Basra, Iraq, 5918, 5943, 6012
Basses-Pyrénées, department of, France, 2061
Basutoland, 6295, 6305-6
Bath, Som., 4170, 4821, 5339, 5545, 5588
Bath and Wells, bishops of, 2931
Bath and Wells, diocese of (medieval), 1295, 1312; (18th-19th
    cent.), 3486
Bath-houses, in Roman Britain, 350
Batley, see Greenwood and Batley
Battersea, see London
Bauernfeld, Eduard von (1802-90), 1846
Bavaria, 2125, 2139; (20th cent.), 2190
Baxter, Richard (1615-91), 4207-9
Baybars I (1223-77), Mamluk king of Egypt, 6116-17
Bayeux, France, 1988
Beacons (16th-17th cent.), 2786
Beaconsfield, 1st earl of, see Disraeli, Benjamin
Beale, Dorothea (1831-1906), 5506
Béarn, 557
Beaumaris, Anglesey, 1633
Bec-Hellouin abbey, France, 1335
Bechuanaland, 6289, 6304, 6316
Beckenham, Kent, 3290
Becket, Thomas, see Thomas à Becket
Becon, Thomas (1512-67), 2958
Bedford, 3202

362

Bedford, duke of, see John of Lancaster; 4th duke of, see Russell, John

Bedford Level, 3405

Bedfordshire, 5192; (medieval), 961, 971; (16th-17th cent.), 2834; (17th-18th cent.), 4094; south, 4067

Bee-Hive, 5478

Beekeeping (ancient), 118

Beer, adulteration of, 5226

Beeston, Sir William (1660-1702), 7433

Béjar, house of (17th cent.), 2436

Bek, Antony (1283-1310), bishop, 1252-3

Belfast, 4483, 4487, 5843, 5869, 5874; Queen's Island, 3589

Belfast Charitable Society, 4480

Belgian Revolution (1830), 1787

Belgium (19th cent.), 1787, 2292; (19th-20th cent.), 2288, 6276; (20th cent.), 1811, 2294; and Britain (19th cent.), 2289

Bellay, Guillaume du (1491-1543), 79

Bellay, Martin du (d. 1559), 79

Bellum Iugurthinum (Sallust's), 18

Belorussia, Western (16th cent.), 2320

Benedictines (medieval), 1424, 1465; (16th-17th cent.), 3041

Benevento, Italy, St. Peter's abbey, 797

Benfield, see Boyd, Benfield & Co.

Bengal, 6509; (early), 6469, 6500-1; (medieval), 6485-7, 6510; (17th cent.), 6576; (17th-18th cent.), 6577, 6580-1, 6591; (18th-20th cent.), 6592-868 passim; south-east (early), 6472; west, 6799; partition of, 6851

Bengal legislative council, 6869

Benguela Railway, 6330

Benin, Bight of, 6371

Benson, Joseph (1749-1821), 4251

Bentinck, Lord William Cavendish (1774-1839), 2306, 6680, 6704-6

Bentinck, William Henry Cavendish (1738-1809), 3rd duke of Portland, 3699

Bentivoglio, Giovanni II, of Bologna (1443-1508), 2217

Bereford, Sir William de (d. 1326), 953

Berkenhead, Sir John (1616-79), 2716-17

Berkshire, 416, 4494; (medieval), 931, 934-5, 1071, 1582; (18th-19th cent.), 3514; (19th cent.), 4079; east (16th-17th cent.), 2842; northern (early), 1525

Berlin West African Conference (1884-5), 6408

Bermondsey, see London

Bermuda, 7461

Bernard, Saint (1090-1135), 765, 1348

Berridge, John (1716-93), 4147

Berwick upon Tweed, Northumb., 998

Berwickshire, 4409

Betchworth, Surrey, 5605

Béthune, Anonyme de, 65

Bethune College, Bengal, 6672

Beust, Count Friedrich Ferdinand von (1809-86), 1849

Beverley, E.R. Yorks., 1576

bhakti, doctrine, 6543

Biafra, Bight of, 6371

Bible (medieval), 1413; commentators on (medieval), 1425

Bibles, copying of (medieval), 659

Biblical inspiration, theories of, 5458

Biddulph, Thomas Tregenna (1763-1838), 4149

Bigod, house of, 1156

Bihar, 6458, 6576, 6689

Bijapur, kingdom of, 6544, 6548

Biography, English (pre-1700), 2560; (19th-20th cent.), 5328; in ancient Rome, 205

Birkbeck, George (1776-1841), 5656

Birmingham, 2532, 3365, 3367, 4002, 4991, 5054, 5148-9; (18th cent.), 4039; (18th-19th cent.), 3334, 3480, 3967, 4106, 4153, 4379; (19th cent.), 4828-9, 5322, 5394, 5503, 5757, 7351;

Birmingham (cont.) (19th–20th cent.), 4956, 4990, 5440, 5556, 5599; (20th cent.), 4859, 4929; Hazelwood School, 5621; King Edward VI grammar school, 3522
Birmingham, bishopric of, 5402
Birth-rate, French (18th cent.), 1979
Bishoprics, English (19th–20th cent.), 5402
Bishops (6th cent.), 695; in England (medieval), 1188, 1191, 1214, 1225-6, 1276-7, 1304, 1419, 1673; (16th cent.), 2925; (18th–19th cent.), 4115; (19th–20th cent.), 5412; in Wales (15th cent.), 1304; in France (18th cent.), 1987; in politics (18th cent.), 3654; trials of (16th–18th cent.), 2555
Bismarck, Prince Otto Eduard Leopold von (1815-98), 2147, 2151-3, 6066
Bisticci, Vespasiano da (15th cent.), 818
Bithynia, 123
Black Country, 3473, 4571, 4822, 4956, 4990, 5221
Black Death, 1089, 1164; in Wales, 1656
Black Sea (19th cent.), 1795; remilitarisation of, 2350
Blackburn, Lancs., 4611
Blackburn hundred, 4611, 5535
Blackmore vale, 5188
Blackwell, George (d. 1613), 3039
Blackwood, Frederick Temple Hamilton-Temple (1826-1902), 1st marquess of Dufferin and Ava, 7241
Blackwood's, 6060
Blair Atholl, Perths., 3575
Blanket manufacture, 5041
Blantyre, Nyasaland, 6229
Blathwayt, William (1649-1717), 3643
Bleaching industry, in Scotland, 3565
Blomfield, Charles James (1786-1857), bishop, 5387
Blyden, Edward Wilmot (1832-1912), 6396
Blyth priory, Notts., 1374
Board of Agriculture, 4073
Board of Education, 4672
Board of Trade (17th–18th cent.), 3929; (18th–19th cent.), 3780; (19th cent.), 5114, 5147
Board of Works, Irish, 5845
Bockleton, Worcs., 5184
Body, George (1840-1911), 5419
Boeotia, 135
Boer War (1899-1902), 4781-2
Boethius (c. 480-524), 1426
Bogomilism, 700
Bogue, David (1750-1825), 4248
Bohemia (15th cent.), 668; (16th–17th cent.), 1835; (19th cent.), 1864
Bohemian question (20th cent.), 1874
Bohemond I (c. 1058-1111), 531
Bohun lordship, in Wales, 1655
Boldon, Uthred of (c. 1315-1396), 864
Bolingbroke, 1st Viscount, see St. John, Henry
Bolivia, 7545
Bolshevism, in Austria, 1885
Bolton, Lancs., 3359-60, 5014
Bolton, John (1756-1837), 7456
Bolton priory, W.R. Yorks., 1085
Bombay, 6688; (17th cent.), 6583; (18th–19th cent.), 6646; (19th cent.), 6782, 6812; (19th–20th cent.), 6790, 6797, 6810; (20th cent.), 6452, 6864, 6871
Bombay City, 6735
Bombing, aerial, 1827, 4882
Bonar, Andrew Alexander (1810-92), 5802
Boniface of Savoy (d. 1270), archbishop, 1240
Bonner, Edmund (d. 1569), bishop, 2924
Bonnet, Georges (1889-1973), 2104
Book of Aneirin, 1641

Book of Llandaff, 1620
Book production (16th-17th cent.), 2823
Book trade, bookselling (12th-14th cent.), 659; (16th-17th cent.),
    2823; (17th cent.), 3157; (17th-18th cent.), 3996; (18th
    cent.), 4000
Bookbinding, Scottish (15th-17th cent.), 3255
Book-keeping, military (Roman), 284
Books, private collections of (medieval), 1432; provision of, in
    religious orders, 794
Booth, Abraham (1734-1806), 4242
Bordeaux, France, 1948, 1982
Border, Scottish (14th cent.), 1689; (16th-17th cent.), 3229-30
Borneo, 6990, 6997, 7003; North, 7021, 7031
Borough administration, see Local government
Borough franchise (17th cent.), 2699-700
Borough representation, see Parliamentary representation, borough
Boroughs, and the Crown (15th cent.), 916
Borrowing
  company, in Australia, 7607
  government (16th-17th cent.), 2804-5, 2809, 2812; (20th cent.),
    4926; see also Debt, national; Government finance
Bosanquet, Bernard (1848-1923), 5488
Bosco, John, Saint (1815-88), 2250
Bosley, Ches., 1545
Bosnia (medieval), 796
Bossuet, Jacques (1627-1704), 1939
Boston, Lincs., 5768
Boston, Thomas (1677-1732), 4423
Boston, Thomas (1713-67), 4421
Bothwell, 5th earl of, see Hepburn, Francis Stewart
Bouchardon, Edmé (1698-1762), 1962
Boulainvilliers, Henry de (1658-1722), 88
Boulanger, Georges Ernest Jean Marie (1837-91), 2080
Boulton, Matthew (1728-1809), 4024
Boulton and Watt, 4025-6
Bourbon, Indian Ocean, 6944
Bourbon monarchy, conspiracy against, 2047; restoration of, 2051
'Bourgeois', in French political thought, 1997
Bourke, Sir Richard (1777-1855), 4720
Bourke, Richard Southwell (1822-72), 6th earl of Mayo, 6795
Bournemouth, Hants, 3288
Bowen, Sir George Ferguson (1821-99), 7603
Bowes, John, and Partners, 5062
Bowet, Henry (d. 1423), archbishop, 1313
Bowood circle, 3726
Bowring, Sir John (1792-1872), 4544
Boxer movement, 7131
Boyd, Benfield & Co., 3938
Boyle, Richard (1566-1643), 1st earl of Cork, 3269
Brabant (medieval), 1110
Bradford, W.R. Yorks., 1543, 4568, 4997, 5600, 5707-9
Bradford, John (c. 1510-1555), 2974
Bradford dale, 1542
Bradley, Staffs., 3992
Bradwardine, Thomas (d. 1349), archbishop, 1458
Brāhmī script, 6470
Braid, James (d. 1860), 5231
Bramber, Sussex, 3695
Bransford, Wolstan de (d. 1349), bishop, 1284
Brantingham, Thomas (d. 1394), bishop, 1263
Brass trades, 4991
Brasses, memorial, 1509, 3158
Bray, pays de, France, 1969
Braybrooke, Robert (d. 1404), bishop, 1300
Brazil, 7538-9, 7541, 7546, 7569
Bread, adulteration of, 5226
Brechin, diocese of, 3557

Breckland, 3403, 5194
Brecon, 5549
Brecon, lordship of, 1610
Breconshire, 5636
Breedon priory, Leics., 1353
Brent, upper, 414
Breviarium (Festus's), 29
Breviate of a life of Margaret Charlton (Baxter's), 4209
Brewing industry, 5056
Brick, in building, 2579
Brick industry, 5035
Bridgeman, Charles (d. 1738), 4332
Bridges (18th cent.), 4359
Bridget, Saint (1302-73), 1308
Bridgewater, 3rd duke of, see Egerton, Francis
Bridgewater, 1st earl of, see Egerton, John
Bridgewater Canal, 4038
Brigantes, 380
Brigg, Lincs., grammar school, 3507
Bright, John (1811-89), 4585, 4733-4
Brighton, Sussex, 4839, 4964
Bristol, 1108, 3469, 3958, 5544, 6353; (medieval), 981, 1122,
     1136, 1568; (16th-17th cent.), 2824, 7171; (17th cent.), 2741,
     7259; (17th-19th cent.), 4097; (18th cent.), 3691, 3723,
     3964-5, 4224-5, 4251, 7291; (18th-19th cent.), 3552; (19th
     cent.), 1788, 5154, 5725; (19th-20th cent.), 5155, 5320;
     (20th cent.), 4701, 5164; east, 4495; Redcliffe, 1530; St.
     James's church, 1529; church of SS. Philip and Jacob, 2557;
     St. Thomas's church, 2557
Britain (Roman), 253, 274, 296, 340-88
British Auxiliary Legion, 2455
British Columbia, 7251
British Fisheries Society, 3381
British Guiana, 7450-99 passim
British Honduras, 7460, 7505
British Isles, and ancient Greeks, 144
British North America Act (1867), 4752
British North Borneo Chartered Company, 7031
British Somaliland Protectorate, 6235
British South Africa Company, 6321, 6324
British Southern Africa, 6063
British West Africa, 6063, 6357, 6369, 6375
British West Sumatra, 6996
Brittany, 1913; duchy of, 615-16, 633
Brodley, Matthew (1586-1648), 3502
Brokage book (15th cent.), 1139
Bromley, Kent, 1554, 3290
Bromsgrove, Worcs., 1540
Bromyard, John of (fl. 1390), 1466
Bronescombe, Walter (d. 1280), bishop, 1242
Brooch, saucer, Anglo-Saxon, 1487
Brooke family, Barons Cobham, 2904
Brougham, Henry Peter (1778-1868), Baron Brougham and Vaux,
     3754-5, 5575
Broughton, Great (Flints.?), 5265
Brousse, Paul Louis Marie (1844-1912), 2075
Brown, John (1610?-1679), 4386
Brown, John (1784-1858), 5789
Browne, Maximilian von (1705-57), 2117
Browne, Robert (1550?-1633?), 3004-5
Bruce, Archibald (1746-1816), 4440
Bruce, Victor Alexander (1849-1917), 9th earl of Elgin, 6834
Bruges, Belgium, 652
Brunei, Borneo, 7021
Brunner, Mond & Co., 5082
Brunus Longoburgensis (fl. 1280), 811
Brush-making industry, 1779

366

Brussels Anti-Slave Trade Act (1890), 6067
Brut, 1449
Brutus (Marcus Junius Brutus) (d. 42 B.C.), 19
Bryce, James (1838-1922), Viscount Bryce, 7402
Bubwith, Nicholas (d. 1424), bishop, 1319
Bucer, Martin (1491-1551), 2936
Buchan, 11th earl of, see Erskine, David Steuart
Buchan, John (1875-1940), 1st Baron Tweedsmuir, 4772
Buchanan, George (1506-82), 3225, 3240
Buckfield, Adam of (fl. 1300?), 1457
Buckingham, archdeaconry of, 2545, 3077
Buckingham, 1st duke of, see Stafford, Humphrey; 3rd duke of, see
    Stafford, Edward; 1st duke of the 2nd creation, see Villiers,
    George
Buckingham, James Silk (1786-1855), 4557
Buckinghamshire, 4031; (medieval), 936-7, 971; (16th-17th cent.),
    2834; (17th cent.), 3198; (17th-19th cent.), 3621
Buddhism, in Burma, 6986; in Ceylon, 6883-5, 6892
Buddle, John (1773-1843), 4023
Budgetary system, of the U.S.S.R., 2379
Budleigh, East, Devon, 2889
Buenos Aires, 7549
Buganda kingdom, 6271
Building, house, see Housing and house-building; monastic, 1375
Building trades (17th cent.), 3982; (20th cent.), 5104
Builth, Radnors., 1611
Bukedi, Uganda, 6258
Bulgaria (medieval), 700; (20th cent.), 1881; and Jugoslavia
    (20th cent.), 1884; and Russia (10th cent.), 560
Bulgarian atrocities, 1862
Bulkeley family, 1171
Buller, Charles (1806-48), 4554
Bullinger, Henry (1504-75), 2985
Bulmer wapentake, 3426
Bulwer, Sir Henry (1801-72), 6007
Bunting, Jabez (1779-1858), 5443
Burgesses, parliamentary, see Parliamentary representation, borough
Burgh, Elizabeth de (14th cent.), Lady of Clare, 1160
Burgh, Hubert de, see Hubert de Burgh
Burghley, Baron, see Cecil, William
Burghs, Scottish, 1668
Burgundy, 581, 1476
Burgundy, duke of, see Louis of France
Burial rites, in Scotland, 1688
Burke, Edmund (1729-97), 3723, 3739, 3869, 4150
Burma, 6982-7046 passim; and see (19th cent.), 7083; (20th cent.),
    6452
Burma-China boundary, 6447
Burnell, Robert (d. 1292), bishop, 847
Burry estuary, 488
Burscough priory, Lancs., 1361
Burslem, Staffs., 5603
Burton Charity, 2568
Burton-upon-Trent, Staffs., 436, 3307
Bury, Lancs., 3540, 5675
Bury St. Edmunds abbey, Suffolk, 1503
Bury St. Edmunds Chronicle, 68
Business corporations, in India, 6760
Business organisation (19th-20th cent.), 4905
Busoga, Uganda, 6204
Bute family, 3414
Butler, James (1665-1745), 2nd duke of Ormonde, 4470
Butlers Marston, Warwicks., 4104
Buwayhid dynasty, 5944-5, 6519
Buxton, Derbys., 5722
Buxton, Sir Thomas Fowell (1786-1845), 3832
Byland abbey, N.R. Yorks., 1350

Byrhtferth, 1417
Byzantine Church, see Eastern Church
Byzantium, 519-52 passim, 743

CABINET (18th-19th cent.), 3733; (19th cent.), 4576, 4618; (19th-
    20th cent.), 4619; 'shadow', 4713
Caecilius Metellus family, 188
Caernarvon boroughs (19th cent.), 4540
Caernarvonshire, 3427-8; (16th cent.), 3180; (16th-17th cent.),
    2902; (17th cent.), 3191; (19th cent.), 3778, 4540, 5045,
    5298; (19th-20th cent.), 5238; (20th cent.), 5641
Caerwent, Mon., 376
Caesar, Sir Julius (1558-1636), 2685
Cahors, France, 571
Calabar, 6346
Calais, France, 611-14, 2628-9
Calcewaith deanery, Lincs., 2508
Calder basin, Yorks., 4525
Calder-Darwen valley, 3318-19
Calhoun, John Caldwell (1782-1850), 7319
Calico trade, Indian, 6586
California, U.S.A., 7338
Caliphate, Persian, 5916; western, 642
Calonne, Charles-Alexandre de (1734-1802), 1986
Calvin, John (1509-64), 2470
Calvinism, 1719, 1762, 3034, 4221
Cambodia, 6984, 7020
Cambridge, 2963, 3641
Cambridge University (15th-17th cent.), 1907; (16th-17th cent.),
    2977-8; (17th-19th cent.), 3641; King's Hall, 1472
Cambridge University Press (17th-18th cent.), 3999
Cambridgeshire, 425, 2499; (medieval), 938-40, 1586; (16th-17th
    cent.), 2498, 2881; (17th-19th cent.), 3641; (18th-19th cent.),
    3441; (19th-20th cent.), 5203
Camer, Kent, 3413
Camisards, 1933
Campbell, George (1719-96), 4424
Campeche, Mexico, 7567
Canaan, 5887
Canada, 7168, 7177, 7181, 7184-256
Canada Act (1791), 7206, 7210
Canada West, 7223
Canals, 3394, 3397-8, 4037-40
Candellas, 6523
Canfield, Benedict (1563-1611), 3040
Canning, George (1770-1827), 3762-3
Canonisation, process of, 727
Canonists, canon law, 719, 750, 752; in England, 925, 1439
Canonsleigh abbey, Devon, 1358
Cantacuzenus, see John VI, Cantacuzenus
Canterbury, Kent, 1498, 1550; cathedral priory, 1081; Christ
    Church priory, 1051, 1093, 1218, 1333, 1337, 1385; St.
    Gregory's priory, 1373
Canterbury, archbishopric of, 1217-18, 2917
Canterbury, archbishops of (13th cent.), 1251
Canterbury, diocese of (medieval), 1260
Canterbury, province of, 1259; court, 1201
Canton, China, 7073
Cape Breton, Nova Scotia, 4429
Cape Colony, 4720, 6290, 6293
Cape of Good Hope, 3804, 6280, 6296, 6303
Capital, in Lancashire (18th cent.), 3933; import of, 1731
Capital development, of India, 6787
Capital investment, see Investment
Capital issues (20th cent.), 4922
Capital ship, 4871
Capitalism, in Oldham (19th cent.), 5234

Capodistrias, Johannes Antonius (1776-1831), 2212
Car industry, 5084-6
Caracalla, Roman emperor (211-17), 222
Caravan routes, in the Sudan (19th cent.), 6127
Caravanserai, Iranian, 5963
Carbery, 2nd earl of, see Vaughan, Richard
Cardiff, Glam., 4592, 5126, 5245, 5270
Cardigan, 1612
Cardigan Bay, 3382
Cardiganshire, 490, 2530, 3461, 3994
Cardwell, Edward (1813-86), Viscount Cardwell, 4750, 4874
Career patterns, Chinese (17th-18th cent.), 7067
Cargill, Donald (d. 1681), 3249
Caribbean (16th-17th cent.), 7413; (17th-18th cent.), 7431; (18th
    cent.), 7435; (18th-19th cent.), 7458
Carlisle, 5141
Carlisle, diocese of, 4176
Carlist movement, 2464
Carlo Emanuele I (1562-1630), duke of Savoy, 2244
Carlyle, Thomas (1795-1881), 4450
Carmarthen, 1634
Carmarthenshire, 3172, 3393, 4136, 4508, 5212
Carmelites, 1378, 1391
Carnarvon, 4th earl of, see Herbert, Henry Howard Molyneux
Carnwyllion, commote of, 2590
Carolingian empire, 558, 643
Carpenter, John (d. 1476), bishop, 1325
Carpenter (medieval), 638
Carrier, Jean-Baptiste (1756-94), 2027
Cartae Baronum (1166), 1040
Cartel des Gauches, 2100
Cartmel, Lancs., 5747
Cartography, 1144, 2604-5, 3147, 4028; marine, 1143, 2606, 6943;
    of Canada, 7188, 7203; of West Africa, 6338
Cartularies, lay, 1298; monastic, 1329-95 passim
Cartwright, John (1740-1824), 3809
Cartwright, Thomas (1535-1603), 2963
Carucage, 1006
Cary, John (d. 1720?), 3959
Casaubon, Meric (1599-1671), 4271
Caslon, William (1693-1766), 4001
Cassius Dio Cocceianus (c. 155-235?), 28
Caste, in Bengal, 6500
Castelar, Emilio (1832-99), 2461
Castell, Edmund (1606-85), 4385
Castile (medieval), 77, 618, 655, 667; (15th-16th cent.), 2412;
    (16th cent.), 2413; (17th cent.), 2430, 2436
Castle Lyons, Holt, Denbighs., 377
Castlereagh, Viscount, see Stewart, Robert
Castles, 989, 999; in Wales, 1628; in Spain, 2412
Casual labour, 4958
Catalonia (9th-10th cent.), 644; (17th cent.), 2430; (18th cent.),
    3893
Catapult (ancient), 124
Catering industry, 5067
Cathedral clergy (14th cent.), 1262
Cathedral schools (12th cent.), 802
Catholic Apostolic Church, 5439
Catholic emancipation, see Emancipation, Catholic
Catholic Homilies (Aelfric's), 1416
Catholic Mission, 6380
Catholicism, Roman, see Roman Catholicism
Cattaneo, Carlo (1801-69), 2252
Caulfield, Edward (18th cent.), 3577
Cavalry, Roman, 291
Cawley, Ralph (d. 1777), 4311
Caxton, William (1422?-1491), 1476-7

Cecil, Edgar A.R. (1864-1958), 1st Viscount Cecil of Chelwood,
    4808
Cecil, Lord Robert, see Cecil, Edgar A.R., above
Cecil, Robert A.T. Gascoyne- (1830-1903), 3rd marquess of Salisbury,
    2157, 2358, 6176, 6419
Cecil, William (1520-98), Baron Burghley, 2806
Cecil family (16th-17th cent.), 2683; (18th-19th cent.), 3298
Cefalonia, Greece, 2210
Celtic Church, 1185, 1592; in Scotland, 1670
Celtic monks, 759
Celts, 357, 1479-80, 1663, 2611
Cely family, 1173
Cemeteries, Anglo-Saxon, 1483-4
Cennick, John (1718-55), 4478
Censorship, government (16th-17th cent.), 3136
Central Society of Education, 5580
Cetswayo (c. 1836-1884), king of the Zulu, 6310
Ceylon, 4727, 4797, 6448, 6722, 6879-941
Chaco, Argentina, 7507
Chadderton, Lancs., 5749
Chadwick, Sir Edwin (1800-90), 5252
Chain-stores, in France (20th cent.), 2088
Chaitanya, see Srikṛṣṇa-Chaitanya
Chalcedon, Council of (451), 5911
Chalmers, Thomas (1780-1847), 4449
Chalukyas, 6489
Chamberlain, Joseph (1836-1914), 4656
Chancery (medieval), 904-5; (16th-17th cent.), 2667; court of
    (medieval), 957
Chancery, of earls of Chester, 1561
Chandravati, 6515
Channel Islands, 570, 921, 1029, 1563
Chantries, 1215, 2955-6
Chantry lands, in Wales, 2831
Chapel Royal (medieval), 888
Chapels, proprietary, 4170
Chaplains, army, 4407; naval, 2784-5
Charcoal iron trade (17th-18th cent.), 3990
Charities, 2482, 5220, 5368
Charity, Reformation influence on (16th cent.), 2894
Charity Commission, 4560
Charity Organisation Society, 5314
Charity schools, 3519-20; in Wales, 4135
Charlemagne (c. 742-814), Holy Roman emperor, 698
Charles VI (1685-1740), Holy Roman emperor, 2116
Charles I (1600-49), king, 2718, 2752, 3281
Charles II of Navarre (b. 1332), called Charles the Bad, 588
Charles XII (1682-1718), king of Sweden, 94
Charles, duc de Bourbon (1490-1527), constable of France, 1902
Charles Albert (1798-1849), of Sardinia, 2310
Charlett, Arthur (1655-1722), 4289
Charlton, Margaret (d. 1681), 4209
Chartered companies, in Nigeria, 6404
Charters, in Book of Llandaff, 1620; of Canterbury, 1550; of Kent,
    1523; royal (10th cent.), 885; Saxon, 1047; of Somerset, 1524;
    of Southampton, 1527; town (17th cent.), 3203
Chartier, Alain (c. 1385 - c. 1433), 597-8
Chartism, 4835-9; in Scotland, 5801, 5801A; in Wales, 4838
Chateaubriand, François René, vicomte de (1768-1848), 108
Chatham, 1st earl of, see Pitt, William
Chatham Chest, 2911
Chaundler, Thomas (d. 1490), 1474
Chauny, France, 1897
Chauvelin, Germain-Louis de (1685-1762), 1958
Cheddar, Som., 1485
Chefoo, Convention of (1876), 7117
Chemical manufacturing industry, 3374

Chemistry (18th-19th cent.), 3516; (19th cent.), 5479-80; teaching
    of (19th cent.), 5672
Chertsey abbey, Surrey, 1087
Cheshire, 458, 460; (medieval), 1383, 1569-71; (16th-17th cent.),
    3026; (18th-19th cent.), 3440; east, 459, 4072; north, 461-2
Chester, 463; (Roman), 373-5; (medieval), 948, 1128; (14th-16th
    cent.), 1266; (16th-17th cent.), 2863; (17th cent.), 3189;
    (17th-18th cent.), 3946; (19th cent.), 5265
Chester, archdeaconry of, 1288
Chester, diocese of, 2990
Chester, earls and earldom of, 1560-1, 1570
Chesterfield, Derbys., 3292, 5562, 5610
Chhatrapati, Shahu, Bhonsla raja (1708-49), 6598
Ch'i Chung-min Kung jih-chi, 7061
Ch'i Piao-chia (1602-45), 7061
Ch'iang people, 7051
Chichele, Henry (1362?-1443), archbishop, 1314-15
Chichester, Sussex, 378-9; Oliver Whitby School, 3515
Chichester, diocese of, 1189
Child, Sir Josiah (1630-99), 6582
Child labour, 5180, 5579; in the U.S.A., 7383
Children, handicapped, 5277, 5844; law relating to, 5219; legal
    rights of, in Scotland, 2608; mentally deficient, 5584; under
    poor law, 5258-61; in public care, 5341; social welfare of,
    5223
Chile, 7531, 7559-60, 7568
Chilean Revolution (1891), 7559
Chillenden, Thomas of (d. 1411), 1302
Chillingham, Northumb., 3411
Chillingworth, William (1602-44), 3080-1
Chilterns, 418-19, 3402, 4519, 5190, 5200; southern, 3282
China, 6447, 6450-1, 7020, 7032, 7047-168 passim; and Iran (13th
    cent.), 7058; and Tibet (17th cent.), 7060
Chinese, in south-east Asia, 7000-1
Chinese Communist bases, 7166
Chinese Nationalist party, 7152
Chinese Revolution (1911), 7144-5
Chinese Soviet Republic, 7158
Ch'ing government, 7090
Chippenham, Wilts., 3693
Chirk, Denbighs., 1645
Chisti movement, 6527
Chittagong, India, 6614
Chiu Chang Suan Shu, 7048
Chiu T'ang Shu, 7053
Chivalry, at English court (14th cent.), 1161
Chobham, Thomas de (d. 1327), 1270
Choiseul, Étienne François de (1719-85), 1973
Chola, 6888
Cholmley, Sir Hugh (1600-57), 2737
Chorley, Lancs., 5536
Christian missions, see Missions, Christian
Christian Schools, Brothers of the, see La Salle Brothers
Christian Socialism, 5359-61, 5372-4
Christian Unity movements, 1769
Christian year, 676
Christianity, early, 279-80, 360, 1593, 1595; in Alexandria, 6101;
    in Asia Minor, 5901; in Britain, 360, 1178; in North Africa,
    6071-3; and Roman empire, 279-80
Christians, martyrdom of (177 A.D.), 333
Christians (American protestant denomination), 7313
Chronicles (medieval), 51-78 passim, 855
Chrysostom (St. John Chrysostom) (345-407), bishop, 688
Church, Sir Richard (1784-1873), 2211
Church
    early, 181, 776-7, 1595; of Jerusalem, 5905; see also
        Christianity, early

Church (cont.)
    medieval, 100, 530, 675-740, 786; in England, 1178-328 passim;
        in Scotland, 1681, 1684; in Wales, 1642, 1658
    in Australia, 7596; in Basutoland, 6295; in China, 7052, 7097;
        Eastern, see Eastern Church; in Ethiopia (13th-16th cent.),
        6114; in Massachusetts, 7328; in Shetland (16th-17th cent.),
        3213; in Wales (19th cent.), 5551; Western (16th-18th cent.),
        1755; (16th-17th cent.), 1756
Church, mission of (16th cent.), 2470
Church and state (11th cent.), 1190; (16th cent.), 2644; (17th
    cent.), 3052, 3848; (19th cent.), 3749, 5389, 5391, 5491;
    in Ireland, 5878; in Byzantine empire, 522; in Ceylon, 6929;
    in France, 1899, 2089
Church briefs, 2552
Church Building Commission, 5385
Church councils, see Councils, church
Church courts, see Ecclesiastical courts
Church discipline (17th cent.), 3089; in Scotland, 2613; (16th
    cent.), 3223; (17th-18th cent.), 4402
Church doctrine (16th-17th cent.), 1756, 2976, 3004; (17th cent.),
    3062-3; Congregational (19th-20th cent.), 5455
Church extension (19th cent.), 5384, 5386
Church Missionary Society, 6380, 6759, 7216
Church of England, 2541, 2548; (16th-18th cent.), 2543; (16th-17th
    cent.), 2544, 2916-3105 passim; (17th-19th cent.), 3644, 4154-
    94; (19th cent.), 4836, 5349, 5577-8, 5624, 6005; (19th-20th
    cent.), 4139-40, 5379-422; (20th cent.), 5515, 5654; in
    America, 7175, 7204-5, 7216, 7266; see also Anglicanism
Church of England Zenana Missionary Society, 6759
Church of Ireland, 3585, 5416, 5862
Church of Scotland, 2612; (15th-16th cent.), 1697; (16th-17th
    cent.), 2616, 3043, 3209-61 passim; (17th-19th cent.), 4384-
    455 passim; (19th cent.), 5795-6; (19th-20th cent.), 5797,
    5809; in New Brunswick, 7193
Church of Scotland Mission, 6229
Church Pastoral-Aid Society, 5404
Church schools, 5591
Church screens, painted, 1511
Church unity (early), 680-1, 686
Churches (19th cent.), and the working class, 5363, 5370; polit-
    ical influence of, 4615
    African, 6413; Anglo-Saxon, 1486
    of Devonshire, 1511; of Leicestershire, 5365, 5370; of Norfolk,
    1511; of North Wales, 1596; of Stour valley, 1512; of Surrey,
    2587
Churches of Christ, 5450
Churchill, Lord Randolph (1849-95), 4635
Church-Papists, 3025
Cicero, Marcus Tullius (106-43 B.C.), 198, 301-2
Cilicia, province of, Asia Minor, 301-2
Cinque ports, 1101-2
Cistercians, 766; in England, 1068, 1348-50, 1371, 1431; in Ire-
    land, 1709
Citizenship, Roman, 182
City-state, Greek, 148, 181
Civic movement, in Italy (medieval), 564
Civil aviation, 5165-7
Civil procedure, in Supreme Court, 4633; in Bengal, 6632
Civil service, British home (19th-20th cent.), 4596; in British
    West Africa, 6369; of Canada, 7234; of Ceylon, 6914, 6941; of
    East India Company, 6568, 6673; of India, 6762; of Nigeria,
    6440
Civil War (1640-60), 1928, 2714-72 passim, 2796-9, 3051, 3086;
    in Wales, 2738-9
Civilians, in Roman Britain, 361-2
civitas christiana, conception of, 684
Clamanges, Nicholas de (b. 1360), 729

Clapham sect, 4191-2
Clare, co., 4489
Clare, Suffolk, 1581
Clare, Lady of, see Burgh, Elizabeth de
Clare family, 1053
Clarendon, 1st earl of, see Hyde, Edward; 4th earl of, see
    Villiers, George William Frederick
Clark, C. & J., 5038
Clarke, Adam (d. 1832), 4250
Clarke, William (fl. 1598-1602), merchant, 5968
Class meeting, Methodist, 3488
Class structure (medieval), 1533, 1603; (17th cent.), 4088; in
    Bengal (early), 6500; in Nazi Germany, 2194; see also Middle
    classes; Working classes
Class-consciousness, in Oldham (19th cent.), 5234
Classical movement, puritan, 2993-4
Classics, teaching of, in Scotland, 5771
Claudius (10 B.C. - 54 A.D.), Roman emperor, 216
Clausewitz, Karl von (1780-1831), 2170
Clement, Saint (d. 916), metropolitan of Bulgaria, 699
Clement of Alexandria (c. 160 - c. 220), 679
Clenard, Nicolas (c. 1495-1542), 2272
Clergy, 2563, 5410; (medieval), 1014, 1164, 1257, 1262, 1280,
    1287, 1306, 1346, 1387; (14th-16th cent.), 1269, 1278, 1298;
    (15th-16th cent.), 1326; (16th cent.), 2918, 2933, 2970; (16th-
    18th cent.), 2543; (16th-17th cent.), 2932, 2975, 2989, 3047;
    (18th-20th cent.), 3481; (18th-19th cent.), 3485; (19th cent.),
    5379-80, 5411; Welsh (medieval), 1657; Scottish, 3224, 3232,
    4447; French (18th cent.), 1991; in Normandy (15th cent.), 629;
    Venetian (16th-17th cent.), 2230; see also Ministers
  Catholic (18th-20th cent.), 3481; in Wales, 3028
Clerical order, French (18th cent.), 1990
Clerkenwell, see London
Cleveland, N.R. Yorks., 4492; west, 2504
Cleveland, archdeaconry of, 1280
Cleveland, rural deanery, 5410
Cleveland, Stephen Grover (1837-1908), president of the U.S.A.,
    7384
clientelae, in Roman politics, 190
Clifford, John (1836-1923), 5456
Clifford, Thomas (1630-73), 1st Baron Clifford of Chudleigh, 3606
Clifford family, 2909
Climate, 1750; in Roman times, 115
Clinton, Henry Fiennes (1720-94), 2nd duke of Newcastle, 3687
Clinton, Henry Pelham Fiennes Pelham (1785-1851), 4th duke of
    Newcastle, 3777
Clinton, Henry Pelham Fiennes Pelham (1811-64), 5th duke of New-
    castle, 4746
Clodius (93?-52 B.C.), 202
Cloth industry, see Woollen and worsted industries
Cloth trade, Flemish and Brabantine (medieval), 1110
Clothing manufacture, in Roman empire, 252
Club de l'Entresol, 1953
Clubs, of Scotland (18th cent.), 4414; French political (18th
    cent.), 2006
Cluniacs, 764, 1340
Clwyd, vale of, 3429
Clydach, river, 4071
Clyde ports, 2618
Clydeside, 4672
Coal mining, coal industry, coalfields, 2525, 3317, 3337, 3340,
    5135; (16th-18th cent.), 2522, 2524, 2526; (17th cent.), 3981;
    (17th-18th cent.), 3989; (18th-20th cent.), 3316; (18th-19th
    cent.), 3320, 3341, 4020-1, 4023; (19th cent.), 4512, 5048-50,
    5063, 5065, 5222; (19th-20th cent.), 4493, 4526-7, 4989, 5013,
    5034, 5064, 5079, 5081, 5097; (20th cent.), 4856, 4969, 5024,
    5029-31; in Ireland, 3581, 4471; in Scotland, 5792, 5810;

Coal mining, coal industry, coalfields (<u>cont.</u>)
  in Wales, 3338-40, 4022, 4528-9, 5005, 5012, 5025, 5033, 5058,
  5105, 5132, 5283, 5661; in Japan, 7116; in north-west Europe,
  1802; in the U.S.A., 7388
Coal trade, English (19th cent.), 5049, 5116; Irish (17th-18th
  cent.), 3948; Welsh (17th-18th cent.), 3947; world (20th
  cent.), 1738
Coasting trade (17th-18th cent.), 3945
Cobbett, William (1762-1835), 3834
Cobden, Richard (1804-65), 7327
Cobham, Barons, <u>see</u> Brooke family
Cobham, Lord, <u>see</u> Oldcastle, Sir John
Cochin China, 7020
Cochrane, Sir Alexander (1758-1832), 7322
Cod fisheries, in North America, 7179
Coffee industry, in Ceylon, 6918
Coin hoards, of Roman Britain, 344
Coinage and currency, in England (Saxon), 1003; (medieval), 1004;
  (16th cent.), 2803; (17th cent.), 3921, 3931; in Balkan penin-
  sula (medieval), 645; of Canada, 7181; of China (19th cent.),
  7095; of ancient Greece, 136, 142-3; Hellenistic, 180; of
  Illyria, 166; in south India, 6479; of Indo-Greeks, 146; in
  Massachusetts (17th-18th cent.), 7269; of Paeonia, 166; of
  Palestine (Roman), 315-16; of Roman Britain, 385-6; of ancient
  Rome, 256-9; of the U.S.A., 7181; <u>see also</u> Mint, Islamic; Money
  bronze, 143; electrum, 142; gold and silver, 1900; limitation of,
  1723; literature on (16th-17th cent.), 2807
Coke family, 3417
Colbert, Jean-Baptiste, marquis de Torcy (1665-1746), 1936
Colchester, Essex, 1578, 3174, 4541
Colchester graduale, 820
Cole, Sir Galbraith Lowry (1772-1842), 3804
Coleraine, co. Londonderry, 3271
Collectivism, 4658
Colleges, planning of (16th-17th cent.), 3138
Collegia, members of (4th-5th cent.), 685
Collings, Jesse (1831-1920), 5210
Collins, Anthony (1676-1729), 3862
Collins, Michael (1890-1922), 5879
Colne valley, 3314
Cologne, province of (13th cent.), 724
Coloma, Carlos, marqués de la Espina (1567-1637), 2429
Colon, Joseph (1420-80), 664
Colonial administration, <u>see</u> Administration, colonial
Colonial agents, in British West Indies, 7428
Colonial and imperial policy, 6247; (17th cent.), 7174, 7429;
  (17th-19th cent.), 3779-806 <u>passim</u>; (18th cent.), 7200-1, 7277;
  (18th-19th cent.), 3300, 6639, 6641; (19th cent.), 6061-2,
  6066, 6287-8, 6296, 6370, 6372, 6391, 6404, 6667, 6681, 6700-1,
  6703, 6730, 6740, 6773, 6794, 6827, 7003, 7217, 7228, 7626;
  (19th-20th cent.), 4719-819 <u>passim</u>, 6393; (20th cent.), 6264,
  6267, 6333, 6855, 7212
Colonial development, German (19th cent.), 2154
Colonial governors (18th-19th cent.), 3300
Colonial Laws Validity Act, 4721
'Colonial marriage', Anglo-German, 2155
Colonial Office (19th cent.), 3798, 3801, 4721, 4727, 7218, 7236;
  (19th-20th cent.), 7495; (20th cent.), 4797; Dominions Depart-
  ment, 4793
Colonial rivalry, Anglo-French (18th-19th cent.), 1984
Colonies, British, <u>see</u> Crown Colony administration, Plantation
  colonies; Greek (ancient), 133
Colonisation, French (19th cent.), 2079; of ancient Greece, 12;
  of ancient Rome, 196; Welsh (16th-17th cent.), 2514, 2774;
  puritan ideas on, 3066; Quaker experiment in, 3860
Columban, <u>Saint</u> (543-615), 1703
Combe, George (1788-1858), 7320

Combination, see Trade unions
comes sacrarum largitionum, 690
Comité d'Études du Haut-Congo, 6273
Commerce, see Economic relations; Trade
Commercial law, of ancient Athens, 152
Commercial policy, see Economic policy
Commercial travellers, 4986
Commission for Sick and Wounded Seamen, 3891
Commission for Transport, 3891
Commission for Victualling the Navy, 3891
Commission of Eastern Enquiry, 6919
Commissioners for India, 6645
Commissions, administrative, 4560; in France, 2078
Committee for Trade, 3796
Committee of Imperial Defence, 4879
Committee of Public Safety, 2023-4
Committee of Union and Progress, in Turkey, 6040
Commodus, Lucius Aelius Aurelius (161-92), Roman emperor, 292
Common lands, of Lancashire, 457; of Sussex, 407
Commons, house of (14th cent.), 963; (15th cent.), 982; (17th
    cent.), 2702, 3600-1, 3609, 3859; (18th cent.), 3653, 3671,
    3689; (19th cent.), 3764, 3775, 4561, 4723; (20th cent.),
    4695; leadership of, 4577; members of, see Parliament, members
    of; membership of (19th cent.), 4573-4; standing committees,
    4650
Commonty, division of, 3563
Commonwealth, British, and Irish Free State, 5877
Commonwealth, idea of, in India, 6846
Commonwealth of Nations, development of, 4774
Commonwealth party, 4718
Communications (17th-20th cent.), 3385-99; (18th cent.), 3987;
    in Wales (medieval), 1598; (18th-19th cent.), 3392
Communications, imperial (18th cent.), 3783
Communist bases, Chinese, 7166
Communist movement, German, 2178
Communist party, of Bulgaria, 1881; of Canada, 7252; of Czecho-
    slovakia, 1880; of France, 2094; of Great Britain, 4710-11;
    of Jugoslavia, 1882; of the Philippines, 7044
Companies, investment, 4905, 4909; joint stock, 4908, 4910
Company of Adventurers, 7515
Compendium (Gaguin's), 78
Composition fines, royalist, 2815
Compostela, James of, see James, Saint
Comuneros revolt (1520-1), 2413
Concert of Europe, 1784-6
Concessions, in China, 7128
Conciliar movement, 729
Concordats, with England (14th-15th cent.), 1403
Condorcet, Jean Antoine Nicolas de Caritat, marquis de (1743-94),
    1976
Condottieri, 592, 674
Confederación Española de Derechas Autonomas, 2465
Confederacy, American Southern, 7352, 7354-5
Confederation, see Federation
Conferences, colonial and imperial, 4768
Confessions of Faith, Baptist, 3093
Congo Free State, 6274-5
Congo question, 6277
Congregation of the Assumption, 1789
Congregationalism (17th cent.), 3042, 7265; (17th-19th cent.),
    3474; (18th-20th cent.), 3524; (18th-19th cent.), 3483; (19th-
    20th cent.), 5454-5; in Ireland, 5832; in Scotland, 4442-4
Congressional radicalism, 7362, 7372
Conrad, Joseph (1857-1924), 4772
Conscientious objectors, 4881
Conservative party (19th cent.), 4582, 4616, 5319; (19th-20th
    cent.), 4918; (20th cent.), 4681, 4695, 4708, 5346, 6874

Consistory courts, of St. Davids, 3472
Constance, Council of (1414-17), 737, 1407
Constantine I (274-337), Roman emperor, coinage of, 385
Constitution, American, 7296-7, 7303; Australian, 7611; Canadian,
    7229; of Ceylon, 6938, 6940; Weimar, 2182-3
Constitutional crisis (1297), 851-2
Constitutional-Democratic party, Russian, 2369, 2386
Contarini, Gasparo (1483-1542), cardinal, 1766
Continuous voyage, 1726
<u>Contra Petrobusianos</u> (Peter the Venerable's), 715
Conventiclers, 4396
Convention, French, 2013
Convention parliament (1660), 3607; (1688-9), 3636
Convocation (15th cent.), 1314; controversy about (18th cent.),
    4174
Convoys (18th cent.), 3900; (19th cent.), 7464
Conway, Henry Seymour (1721-95), 3718
Conway valley, 3324
Cook, Arthur James (1883-1931), 5030
Cooke, Henry (1788-1868), 5836
Cooper, Anthony Ashley (1621-83), 1st earl of Shaftesbury, 3605,
    3627
Cooper, Anthony Ashley (1671-1713), 3rd earl of Shaftesbury, 3864
Cooper, Anthony Ashley (1801-85), 7th earl of Shaftesbury, 5246-7
Cooper, Thomas (1517-94), bishop, 3012
Co-operation, consumers', 4957; Owenite, 4942; <u>see also</u> Agri-
    cultural co-operation
Co-operative organisations, 5509
Co-operative party, 4629
Copenhagen expedition (1807), 3915
Copleston, Edward (1776-1849), bishop, 5396
Copper mining, copper industry, 3344, 3975, 5046; of Wales, 3344-5;
    of Rhodesia, 6328-9
Copts, 6162
Corbet, John (1620-80), 4205
Corinth (early), 137, 143
Cork, co., 3580
Cork, 1st earl of, <u>see</u> Boyle, Richard
Corn laws, 4890, 4898
Cornhill family, 894
Cornish, Sir Samuel (d. 1770), 6993
Cornovii, 381
Cornwall, 390, 487, 3322; (early), 1519; (16th cent.), 2661, 2947;
    (16th-17th cent.), 2527; (17th cent.), 4054, 4350; (18th
    cent.), 4223; (18th-19th cent.), 4140; (19th cent.), 3835,
    4902, 5046, 5432; central, 4503; west, 391, 2528, 4051
Cornwall, duchy of (medieval), 1589
Cornwall, earl of, <u>see</u> Gaveston, Peter of; Richard (1209-72); 2nd
    earl of, <u>see</u> Edmund (1250-1300)
Cornwallis, Charles (1738-1805), 2nd Earl Cornwallis, 6648
Coromandel (17th cent.), 6573, 6593
Coroner (medieval), 927
Corruption, at British elections, 4563; in American labour organ-
    isations, 7387
Corstopitum, 352
Costs, in Roman empire, 236
Costume, academic, 636, 2563; on brasses, 1509; clerical, 2563;
    legal, 636
Côte d'Or, department of, France, 2052
Cotswolds, 4065, 5039
Cottington, Francis (d. 1652), Baron Cottington, 2710
Cotton, John (1584-1652), 3067
Cotton, William (d. 1621), bishop, 3047
Cotton, marketing of, in Uganda, 6257; production of, in Egypt,
    6131; in the Sudan, 6144
Cotton famine, 5074

Cotton industry, 3317, 4012, 4014; (18th cent.), 4011, 4016; (18th-19th cent.), 3359-61, 4013, 4015, 4018, 4118; (19th cent.), 5070, 5083, 5286; (19th-20th cent.), 5014, 5061, 5098; in India, 6586-8, 6606, 6670-1, 6864; in South Carolina, 7340
Council, royal, 889, 910, 913; in Ireland, 1717
Council in the Marches of Wales (16th-17th cent.), 2672
Council of India, 6777
Councils, church, 750; (5th cent.), 692; (15th cent.), 755, 909, 1406
Counter-Reformation, 3017-18; in Wales, 3027; in Italy, 2233; in Sweden, 2397
Counter-Revolution, French, 1986, 2020
Country houses, 2581, 4336
Country party, 3609, 3616, 3637
County councils, 5713-14
County government (16th-17th cent.), 3169-208 passim
Coupar Angus abbey, Perths., 1695
Court, English royal (12th cent.), 890; (14th cent.), 1161; (16th cent.), 3124; (18th cent.), 3673; French royal (18th cent.), 1960
Court leet, 922
Court life, in ancient India, 6480
Court of aldermen (17th cent.), 4349
Court of Arches (17th cent.), 4163
Court of common council, 4349
Court of requests (16th-17th cent.), 2669
Court of session, 4438
Court rolls (14th cent.), 1574
Courtier (16th cent.), 2879
Courts
    borough, 2601; burgh, 1667; county (medieval), 924; criminal, 2481; justiciar's, 1715; mayor's (17th cent.), 3195; portmote, 548; private (medieval), 924; sheriff's, 948, 3209; see also Chancery; Ecclesiastical courts; King's bench; Sewers; Supreme Court
    Carolingian, 558; in Ghana, 6360; Muslim, 6530; West Saxon, 558
Couthon, Georges (1755-94), 2026
Covenanting movement, 3249-52
Coventry, Warwicks., 472, 3364, 5337, 5740
Coventry, Henry (1619-86), 3617
Coventry, Sir William (1628?-1686), 3616-17
Coventry and Lichfield, diocese of, 1323, 2944
Cowper family, 4046
Cox, Richard (1500-81), bishop, 2965
Crafts, of Roman Britain, 352
Craftsmen (17th-18th cent.), 4328
Craig, John (1512-1600), 3220
Craigie, Sir Robert (1883-1959), 7163
Cranborne, Dorset, 2510
Cranmer, Thomas (1489-1556), archbishop, 1268, 2927, 2967
Crassus, Marcus Licinius (c. 115-53 B.C.), 20, 199
Crawshay family, 3348
Credit (14th cent.), 1022; (18th cent.), 3933; in Australia, 7582
Creole society, in Jamaica, 7445
Creuddyn peninsula, 3324
Crewe, Ches., 5715-16
Cricklade, Wilts., 3693
Crime (19th cent.), 5227, 5229
Crimean War (1854-6), 1795-6
Criminal law, 2481, 3772; in Bengal, 6632
Croft, Sir James (1518-91), 2673
Crofting, 3568-9
Croker, John Wilson (1780-1857), 3773
Cromer, 1st earl of, see Baring, Evelyn
Cromwell, Henry (1628-74), 2768
Cromwell, Oliver (1599-1658), 1926, 2763
Cromwell, Ralph (d. 1456), 4th Baron Cromwell, 1170, 1517

Cromwell, Thomas (1485?-1540), earl of Essex, 2649
Cross, Richard Assheton (1823-1914), 1st Viscount Cross, 4623-4
Crosswood House, Cardigs., 3412
Crosthwaite, Sir Charles (1835-1915), 7036
Crowland abbey, Lincs., 1079
Crowley, Robert (1518?-1588), 2888
Crown, English (medieval), 833, 916, 1013, 1061, 1286, 1404, 1584;
    (17th cent.), 3272; (19th cent.), 4626-7, 4581, 5388; Scottish
    (medieval), 1671
Crown Colony administration, 4727, 6951, 7490, 7493
Crown lands (15th cent.), 875-6; (16th-17th cent.), 2805, 2818
Croydon, Surrey, 5734-5
Cruger, Henry (1739-1827), 3723
Crusades, 38, 532-52 passim
Cuba, 7529, 7535, 7550, 7557
Cubbon, Sir Mark (1784-1861), 6724
Cults, of Boeotia, 135; Teutonic, in Roman Britain, 357
Cultural activities, organised (19th-20th cent.), 5320
Cumberland, 2497, 3337; (early), 1518; (Saxon), 1492; (18th cent.),
    3694; (19th cent.), 5129; west (Roman), 368; (18th-20th cent.),
    3316; (20th cent.), 4971, 5340
Cumberland, earls of, 2909
Cunliffe-Lister, Philip (1884-1972), 1st earl of Swinton, 4706
Cunningham, Sir Alexander (1814-93), 6798
Cure of souls, see Pastoral ministry
Curial class, 237
Currency, see Coinage and currency; Money
Curtius Rufus, Quintus (fl. 41-54 A.D. ?), 27
Curzon, George Nathaniel (1859-1925), Marquess Curzon of Kedleston,
    6841-3
Customs and excise (medieval), 1128; (17th cent.), 3924; (17th-18th
    cent.), 3930; in Ireland (17th cent.), 3270; in China, 7100-1;
    in South Africa, 6315
Custos pacis, 930
Custumal, 1272
Cutlery trade, 3368
Cuxham, Oxon., 1552
Cyfeiliog, 3173
Cymmrodorion, Honourable Society of, 3462
Cynon, river, 4071
Cyprus, 524, 2300, 2312-14
Cyrenaica (ancient), 324
Cyrurgia Magna (Brunus Longoburgensis'), 811
Czech Brethren, see Unity of the Czech Brethren
Czechoslovak problem, 1875
Czechoslovakia, 1819, 1826, 1879-80
Czechs (18th cent.), 1836; (18th-19th cent.), 1840; (19th cent.),
    1864; (19th-20th cent.), 1865; (20th cent.), 1877-8

DACCA, India, 6627
Dahomey, 6356, 6365
Dahomey-Niger hinterland, 6411
Dalderby, John de (d. 1320), bishop, 1267
Dalhousie, 9th earl of, see Ramsay, George; 1st marquess of, see
    Ramsay, Sir James Andrew Broun
Dalip Singh, 6739
Dall, Robert (1745-1828), 4247
Dalmatia (Roman), 299-300
Dalradian highlands, 514
Dalrymple, Alexander (1737-1808), 6607
Dalrymple, John (1673-1747), 2nd earl of Stair, 3664
Damascus, province of (18th cent.), 5979
Dambedeniya, 6891
Dame schools, 3535
Danby, 1st earl of, see Osborne, Sir Thomas
Dante Alighieri (1265-1321), 584-5
Danube and Danubian region, 1820, 1828, 1863

Danubian wars (2nd cent.), 292
Danzig, 2180, 2202, 2858
Dardanelles expeditions (1807), 3916
Darfur, Sudan, 6528
Darien scheme, 4406
Darley Abbey, Derbys., 4018
Dartford, Kent, 5560, 5586
Dartmoor, 395
Dartmouth, Devon, 2780, 2853
Darwen, Lancs., 3318-19
Darwin, Charles Robert (1809-82), 5484
Datin family, 669
Daucleddau, Pemb., 3339
Davenant, Charles (1656-1714), 3632
David, Saint (d. c. 601), 1638
Davidson, John (1549-1604), 3243
Davies, John (d. 1644), 3149
Davies, Richard (d. 1581), bishop, 3011
Davies, William (d. 1593), 3030
Day, John (1522-84), 3131-2
Deaf, education and welfare of, 3571, 5276, 5844
Dean, Forest of, 481-3; (medieval), 1061, 1084; (17th cent.), 4042;
    (17th-19th cent.), 3508; (19th-20th cent.), 5034
De Anima (Aristotle's), 1457
Deans, rural (12th-13th cent.), 1200
Death practices, in Scotland, 1688
De balneis Puteolanis (Petrus de Ebulo's), 800
Debentures market, 2818
Debt, national (17th-18th cent.), 3927; (18th-19th cent.), 3303; (19th-
    cent.), 4889; redemption of, 4916; see also Borrowing, government
Debt, public, in India, 6789
Debtors, 920
Debts, state, in the U.S.A., 7308
De Burgh family, 1714
De Causa Dei (Bradwardine's), 1458
Deccan states, 6561
Dechristianisation movement, 2016
De Claris Jurisconsultis (Diplovatatius's), 790
De Consolatione Philosophiae (Boethius's), 1426
Decontrol, politics of (20th cent.), 4712
Decourt, Jehan (16th cent.), 1909
Decretals, 1397, 1402
Dee, basin, 1591; estuary, 3377, 3946
Defence, imperial, 4754, 4879, 7249
Defence policy and strategy, 4785, 4798, 6954; in France, 2106;
    see also Military policy; Naval policy
Defences and fortifications, in Roman empire, 296; of Malta, 2296;
    of towns in England and Wales, 1494
Defoe, Daniel (1661?-1731), 3863
De formatione corporis humani in utero (Giles of Rome's), 806
de Hoghton family, 1064
De Invectionibus (Giraldus Cambrensis'), 1636
Deistic thought, in France (17th-18th cent.), 1938
de la Fléchère, see Fletcher
de la Pomerai family, 1146
Delcassé, Théophile (1852-1923), 2086-7
Delhi, sultanate of, 6532-6
Delhi Territory, 6677
Delinquents (17th cent.), 4047
De Mandatis Divinis (Wyclif's), 1463
Demetrius I of Macedonia, surnamed Poliorcetes (337-283 B.C.), 177
Democracy, American, image of (19th cent.), 7326
Democratic Association, 4826
Democratic party, Roman, 239
Demonology, Scottish (16th-17th cent.), 3214
Denbigh, lordship of, 1647
Denbighshire, 5182

Denmark, 2396, 2399, 2402-3
De Pauperie Salvatoris (Richard Fitzralph's), 1716
Depopulation, of rural Wales, 4521, 4533
Depression
    agricultural, 5199, 5205-6
    economic (20th cent.), 4966; in Scotland (19th cent.), 5817; in
        Australia (19th cent.), 7610; in the U.S.A. (20th cent.), 7411
Deptford, see London
Derby, 3815, 4572, 5393, 5737
Derby, earl of, see Henry IV; 4th earl of, see Stanley, Henry;
    14th earl of, see Stanley, Edward George Geoffrey Smith; 15th
    earl of, see Stanley, Edward Henry
Derbyshire, 438-9, 3400, 5013, 5135; (medieval), 975, 1119; (16th
    cent.), 2645; (17th cent.), 2736; (17th-18th cent.), 3466,
    3597, 4198; (18th cent.), 4008; (18th-19th cent.), 3483, 3513,
    3815, 4186; (19th cent.), 4572, 5430; north, 3341; south, 2524
De Rebus Gestis (Paulus Aemilius's), 78
Derelict villages, of co. Durham, 5215
De Sancto Thoma Archiepiscopo Cantuariensi, 1210
Despenser, Henry (d. 1406), bishop, 871
De Tribus Processionibus (Richard St. Victor's), 1674
De viris claris (Domenico di Bandino's), 815
Devlin, Joseph (1871-1934), 5872
Devolution, and Northern Ireland, 5870; and Wales, 4628
Devon, earls of (15th-16th cent.), 2822
Devonshire, 393; (early), 1519; (medieval), 1025, 1117; (16th
    cent.), 2661, 2676, 2835, 2946-7; (16th-17th cent.), 3014;
    (17th-18th cent.), 4043, 4132; (18th cent.), 4152; (18th-19th
    cent.), 3380; (19th cent.), 4902, 5046, 5713; south, 1511;
    west, 3471
Devotion, popular (medieval), 768; Puritan, 2546
D'Ewes, Sir Simonds (1602-50), 3155
Dewsbury, W.R. Yorks., 5041, 5703
Diaries (17th cent.), 4087
Dictum de Kenilworth, 933-46
Dieulacres abbey, Staffs., 1362
Digger movement, 2760
Dindaethwy, commote of, 1633
Dinefwr, house of, 1660
Diocletian (284-305), Roman emperor, 226, 280
Diodorus Siculus (fl. 60-57 B.C.), 16, 3122
Dion Cassius, see Cassius Dio Cocceianus
Dionysius of Halicarnassus (d. c. 7 B.C.), 198
Diplomacy (medieval), 856, 880; (17th cent.), 5978; Florentine
    (15th-16th cent.), 2221; German, 2171; of Greek city-states,
    148; Mughal (16th-17th cent.), 6557; open, 4795; Ottoman
    (18th-19th cent.), 5989
Diplomatic policy, Diplomatic relations, see Foreign policy;
    Foreign relations
Diplomatic service, of Britain (19th-20th cent.), 4735; of China,
    7074; of France (18th-19th cent.), 2031; of the U.S.A., 7300
Diplomatic vocabulary, Russian (15th-17th cent.), 2316
Diplovatatius (Thomas Diplovatatzis) (1468-1541), 790
Directory, French, 1778, 2029
Disarmament, 1746, 2191, 4814-15; movement for (19th cent.), 4767
Disestablishment, 5357-8; in Ireland, 5862; in Wales, 4628
Disinherited, 846
Disraeli, Benjamin (1804-81), 1st earl of Beaconsfield, 4607
Dissenters and dissent, religious (17th-19th cent.), 4195-258;
    (18th cent.), 3652, 4297; (19th cent.), 5757; see also Non-
    conformity
Distribution, theory of (17th-18th cent.), 1720
Ditchfield grant (1628), 3194
Diversorum patrum sententiae (Humbert of Silva Candida's), 710
Divorce, 2549, 5288-9
Divorce Act (1857), 5289
Dixon coal mines, 5792

Diyala region, 5884
Dock companies, 5123
Docks and dockyards, 3880, 3955, 4866, 5154
Dockyard schools, 4866
Doddridge, Philip (1702-51), 4215
Dodwell, Henry (1641-1711), 4169
Domesday Book, 1024-44 passim
Domestic labour, 5287
Dominic (12th cent.), prior of Evesham, 1339
Dominicans, 809, 1370, 1381-2, 1384
Dominion status, 7230
Dominions, 1743-4, 4537, 4809, 4816, 7135
Domitian (52-96 A.D.), Roman emperor, 219
Donaghadee, co. Down, 4458
Donaldson, Frederick Lewis (1860-1953), 5374
Donatist schism, 6071
Donoughmore constitution, of Ceylon, 6940
Dorchester group, 7258
Dormer family, 2834
Dorset, 399; (medieval), 400, 1035-6; (16th cent.), 2676; (18th-
    19th cent.), 3421, 4109; (19th-20th cent.), 5127
Douai, France, seminary, 3028
Doubs, department of, France, 2052
Douglas, Neil (1750-1823), 4449
Douglas, Thomas (1771-1820), 5th earl of Selkirk, 7208
Doukai family, 527
Dover, Kent, 3383
Dover, Thomas (1662-1742), 4102
Dover, treaty of (1670), 3615
Dowlais, Glam., 3347
Down, co., 512-13, 3582
Downshire, 3rd marquess of, see Hill, Arthur Blundell S.T.
Downton, Wilts., 3693
Dowry, in ancient Greece, 128
Drainage and reclamation, of fens and marshland, 488, 3405, 3407,
    5175, 5208
Drake, Sir Francis (1540?-1596), 2788
Drapers' Company, 2873
Dravidian settlements, in Ceylon, 6893
Dress, see Costume
Droitwich, Worcs., 1118
Druids, Irish, 1707
Dual System, 5508
Dubrovnik, Jugoslavia, 1829
Dudley, Worcs., 2852, 4003
Dudley, 2nd earl of, see Ward, William
Dudley, Lords, 3415-16
Dudley, Dud (1599-1684), 2852
Dudley, Edmund (1462?-1510), 2630
Dudley, John (1504?-1553), duke of Northumberland, 2650
Dudley, Robert (1532?-1588), earl of Leicester, 2273-4
Dufferin and Ava, 1st marquess of, see Blackwood, Frederick T.
Duguit, Léon (1859-1920), 2101
Duma (1907-14), 2376
Dumbarton Glass Work Company, 3574
Dumbleton, John of (fl. 1340), 1453
Dunbar, E. Lothian, 4420
Dunbar, William (1465?-1530?), 3212
Duncan, Jonathan (1756-1811), 6603
Dundas, Henry (1742-1811), 1st Viscount Melville, 6633-4
Dundee, 5782, 5820
Dunkers, 2118
Dunkirk, France, 1926
Dunster castle, Som., 1036
Dunton, John (1659-1732), 3996
Durand, Sir Henry Mortimer (1850-1924), 7399

Durham, 366, 3620, 4377, 4569; cathedral, dean and chapter of,
    1231-2; cathedral priory, 1057, 1393, 3048; song school, 2561
Durham, county, 432, 3418, 4975, 5215; (early), 1518; (Saxon),
    1486; (medieval), 430-1; (16th cent.), 2943; (17th-19th cent.),
    3620; (19th-20th cent.), 5050, 5477; (20th cent.), 5031
Durham, diocese of, 1213-14, 1278, 4156
Durham Miners' Association, 5029
Dutch, in Ceylon, 6899-900, 6903, 6905; in Colchester (16th-17th
    cent.), 3174; in Coromandel (17th cent.), 6573; in Malaya, 7009
Dutch East India Company, 2275, 6615, 6999
Dutch Reformed Church of South Africa, 6284
Dutch Republic, 2280-1; and Britain, 2282; see also Holland
Dutch Wars (1652-4), 2279
Dutch West India Company, 6341
Dyeing, 1724-5
Dyer, Sir Edward (1543-1607), 3135
Dyke, Thomas Jones (fl. 1865-1900), 5311
Dynasts, in Asia Minor, 162

EAST AFRICA, see Africa
East Africa Protectorate, 6249, 6252-4
East Anglia, 420, 5077; (medieval), 1169, 1512; (16th cent.),
    2860; (17th cent.), 7261; (18th-19th cent.), 3442; (19th
    cent.), 4502; (19th-20th cent.), 5195
East Anglian Railways Company, 5150
East Bergholt, Suffolk, 2566
East India Company, 6568-70, 6608, 6651, 6962, 6989; (17th cent.),
    5972, 6577, 6582; (17th-18th cent.), 6591; (18th cent.), 3788,
    3791, 6592-3, 6597, 6621, 6635; (18th-19th cent.), 6625, 6645,
    6647; (19th cent.), 6694, 6720, 6763; see also Dutch East
    India Company
East India Company interest, 3792-3
East Indian Railway, 6742
East Indians, in British Guiana, 7482
East Indies (15th-16th cent.), 6443; (16th cent.), 6987; (17th
    cent.), 6988; (17th-18th cent.), 6444A; (19th-20th cent.),
    7010; (20th cent.), 5122
East Indies squadron, 6992
East Pakistan, 6571, 6844, 6848
Eastern Association, 2744
Eastern Bengal and Assam, 6852
Eastern Church, 529, 743, 1755, 5353-4; and Anglican Church, 2541
Eastern Counties Railway, 5152
Eastern question, 2340, 6005, 6015-16, 6030, 6138
Eastland (17th cent.), 3950
Easton, Adam (d. 1397), cardinal, 1301
Eastry, Henry of (d. 1331), 1385
Ebbw Vale, Mon., 3328
Eccles, Lancs., 5767
Ecclesfield, W.R. Yorks., 3541
'Ecclesia', concept of (medieval), 718
Ecclesiastical administration, see Administration, ecclesiastical
Ecclesiastical Commission (16th-17th cent.), 2998; (19th cent.),
    4560
Ecclesiastical courts, 2997; (medieval), 1201, 1259-61; (16th
    cent.), 2919; (16th-18th cent.), 2545, 2995; (16th-17th cent.),
    2996, 3047; (17th cent.), 4159, 4163; (17th-19th cent.), 3472
Ecclesiastical history, 97
Ecclesiastical immunity, in New Spain, 7521
Ecclesiastical life, see Religious life
Ecclesiastical policy, in France (19th cent.), 2074; in Ireland
    (17th cent.), 3278; in Scotland (12th-13th cent.), 1673; (17th
    cent.), 3260; see also Religious policy
École unique, 2077
Economic controls, war-time, 4931
Economic crisis (1825-6), 7544; (1857), 4907; in France (1859),
    2070

382

Economic depression, see Depression, economic
Economic enterprise, British overseas, see Investment, British
    overseas
Economic enterprise, western, in China, 7093, 7108
Economic policy (17th cent.), 2816-17, 2913; (18th cent.), 7455
Economic relations
    British, with Brazil, 7541; with Canada, 7237; with China, 7085;
        with France, 2072; with Germany, 2127-8; with Hamburg, 2158;
        with Hungary, 1858; with Italy, 2258; with Middle and Far
        East, 6445; with Peru, 7536; with Portugal, 2442; with Russia,
        2338; with Scandinavia, 2401; with South America, 7530, 7540;
        with Spain, 2448; with the U.S.A., 7301, 7318, 7335; with the
        U.S.S.R., 2392
    English, with Castile (medieval), 655; with East Indies (16th-
        17th cent.), 6987-8; with Flanders (medieval), 651; with France
        (17th cent.), 1929; (17th-18th cent.), 1930; (18th cent.),
        1948; with Gascony (medieval), 657, 671; with Guinea (16th cent.),
        6987; with Holland (medieval), 653; with India (17th-18th
        cent.), 6566; with Ireland (16th cent.), 3263; (17th-18th cent.),
        4459; (18th cent.), 4476; with Italy (16th-18th cent.), 2237;
        with the Mediterranean (15th-16th cent.), 670; with Russia
        (16th cent.), 2317; with Spain (16th-17th cent.), 2415, 2419-
        20, 2439; with Turkey (17th cent.), 5977; with Venice (medi-
        eval), 656; with Zeeland (medieval), 653
    Scottish, with Poland (16th-18th cent.), 1832; with Scandinavia
        (17th-18th cent.), 2398
    Venetian, with Egypt (15th-16th cent.), 673; with England (medi-
        eval), 656
Economic thought (17th cent.), 2808; (17th-19th cent.), 3302; in
    Ireland (18th cent.), 4468
Économies royales, Les (Sully's), 1917
Ecumenical movement, 5356
Eden, George (1784-1849), 1st earl of Auckland, 6726
Edeyrnion, barons of, 1646
Edgar (944-75), king, 885
Edinburgh, 4413, 4416, 4445, 4450, 5808; Canongate, 1667; univer-
    sity, 4439
Edmondes, Sir Thomas (1563?-1639), 1921
Edmund, Saint (d. 1240), archbishop, 1236-9
Edmund (1250-1300), 2nd earl of Cornwall, 839
Education, 1410-77 passim, 2560-76 passim, 3109-57 passim, 3496-
    535 passim, 4265-323 passim, 5491-562; and see (17th cent.),
    4085; (19th cent.), 5433; (19th-20th cent.), 4628, 5064; (20th
    cent.), 5340
    in Ireland, 2425; (18th-19th cent.), 4481-2; (19th-20th cent.),
        5822-82 passim
    in Scotland, 2614-15, 3576, 5771-2, 5814-16; (16th-17th cent.),
        1719, 2616; (18th cent.), 4413
    in Wales (15th-16th cent.), 3113; (17th cent.), 3152; (17th-18th
        cent.), 4278, 4281; (18th cent.), 4184, 4296; (18th-19th cent.),
        3517, 4322; (19th-20th cent.), 5491-562 passim
    in Assam, 6967; in Athens (ancient), 154; in the Bahamas, 7436;
        in Barbados, 7475; in Bengal, 6654, 6692, 6710, 6714, 6719,
        6766, 6845, 6868; in British Guiana, 7471; in Burma, 7013; in
        Ceylon, 6448, 6897, 6908, 6910-12, 6916, 6922, 6925, 6927, 6929,
        6933; in China, 7083; in Cyprus, 2313-14; in East Africa, 6270;
        in East Pakistan, 6844; in Egypt, 6160, 6191, 6198; in Europe
        (medieval), 776-820 passim; and see (19th cent.), 1791; (19th-
        20th cent.), 1789, 1803; in France, 2077; (16th cent.), 1905;
        (16th-17th cent.), 1719; (18th cent.), 1951, 1966; (18th-19th
        cent.), 1946, 1994-6; (19th cent.), 2039, 2082; (19th-20th
        cent.), 2083-4; in Gaul, 334; in Gold Coast, 6358; in India,
        6590, 6838, 6843; (ancient), 6468; (18th-19th cent.), 6622;
        (19th cent.), 6688, 6696, 6726, 6749, 6780; (19th-20th cent.),
        6748; in Italy, 2249-50; in Jamaica, 7472-3; in Jammu and
        Kashmir, 6745; in Jersey, 2562; in Kerala, 6658; in Madras,
        6747; in Malaya, 7006-7; in the Maltese Islands, 2303; in

383

Education (cont.)
 Mysore, 6709; in New England, 1719; in New South Wales, 7585,
 7598; in Nigeria, 6380, 6392, 6428-9; in Orissa, 6678; in the
 Philippines, 6448; in Prussia, 2123; in the Punjab, 6710, 6746;
 in Rhodesia, 6322; in Russia, 2333; in Sierra Leone, 6359; in
 Spain, 2414, 2462; in the Straits Settlements, 7002; in the
 Sudan, 6185-7, 6192-3, 6195; in Switzerland, 2475; in Tanganyika, 6266; in Tobago and Trinidad, 7459; in Uganda, 6250; in
 the United Provinces, 6731; in the U.S.A., 7357; in the U.S.S.R.,
 2385; in Upper Canada, 7207; in the West Indies, 7417, 7479
 African, 6059, 6226, 6262; Buddhist, 6883; Catholic, 2564,
 3505-6, 4481-2, 5567, 5613, 5617, 6747, 7585; commercial,
 5683; of the deaf, 3571; industrial, 4323; Jewish, 1835, 5890;
 medical, 3464; Muslim, 6107, 6689, 6710; Negro, 7479; pauper,
 5258-61; physical, 2574; Quaker, 4273; religious, 154, 4243,
 4308, 5318, 5685-6, 5775
Education Acts (1872), 5814; (1902), 5530; (1906, Provision of
 Meals), 5531-2; (1918), 5533
Education Department, 5519
Edward I (1239-1307), king, 848-9, 994
Edward III (1312-77), king, 588, 1132, 1161
Edward, prince of Wales (1330-76), 1570, 1654
Edward ap Roger (d. 1587?), 3133
Edwardian settlement, of Wales, 1650-1
Edwards, Edward (1812-86), 5485
Edwards, Jonathan (1629-1712), 4214
Edwards, Lewis (1809-87), 5447
Edwards, Thomas (1599-1647), 3094
Egba state, 6382
Egbert (d. 839), king of Wessex, 822
Egerton, Francis (1736-1803), 3rd duke of Bridgewater, 4070
Egerton, John (1579-1649), 1st earl of Bridgewater, 2849
Egerton, Sir Walter (1858-1947), 6430
Egidio (Antonini) da Viterbo (d. 1532), patriarch of Constantinople,
 2220
Egypt, 6094-202 passim; and see (ancient), 1478; (15th-16th cent.),
 673; (19th cent.), 4762, 5993
Eifion, Caern., 4243
Eire, 5877-8, 5881-2
Eisteddfod, 1597
Elbe-Saale frontier, 1745
Eleanor de Montfort (1215-74), 843
Eleanor of Castile (d. 1290), queen of Edward I, 850
Electioneering, 3649, 3651, 3777; in Wales, 4539
Elections, parliamentary, 4563; (1625, 1626, 1628), 2711; (17th-
 18th cent.), 3639; (18th cent.), 3655; (1705), 3666; (1710),
 3672; (1784), 3737; (1806, 1807), 3756; (1818), 3769; (1835,
 1837), 4578; (1868), 4621; (1880), 4645; (1886), 4665; (19th-
 20th cent.), 4620; (1906), 4677; (1910), 4685; (1922), 4714;
 (1929), 4715
 in Anglesey (1830, 1831, 1832), 3778; in Blackburn and Blackburn
 hundred (19th cent.), 4611; in Bradford (19th cent.), 4568; in
 Bristol (1918), 4701; in Caernarvonshire (1830, 1831, 1832),
 3778; in Clare (1828), 4489; in Cumberland (18th cent.), 3694;
 in Derby (19th cent.), 4572; in Derbyshire (17th-18th cent.),
 3597; (19th cent.), 4572; in Durham (19th cent.), 4569; in
 Essex (18th cent.), 3702; in Glamorgan (19th-20th cent.), 4538;
 in Ireland (1832, 1835, 1837), 5846; (1852), 5859; in Kent
 (18th cent.), 3677; in Lancashire (17th-18th cent.), 3634; in
 Leicestershire (17th-18th cent.), 3597; in Newcastle (19th
 cent.), 4569; in Northamptonshire (17th-19th cent.), 3649; in
 North and South Northumberland and Tynemouth (1852), 4594; in
 north-west England (20th cent.), 4675; in Oxfordshire (1754),
 3697; in Somerset (1918), 4701; in South Wales (1918), 4701;
 in Staffordshire (17th-18th cent.), 3597; in Walsall (20th
 cent.), 4676; in Westmorland (18th cent.), 3694; in York City
 (18th cent.), 3692

Elections, parliamentary (<u>cont.</u>)
  in Canada, 7223
Electoral law and procedure, in Scotland, 3579
Electoral system (20th cent.), 4705
Electorate (20th cent.), 4675
Electrical industry, 5019, 5092, 5095
Electrical lighting industry, 5093
Electrical Trades Union, 5019
Electricity industry, 5094
Elementary education, 5323, 5563-614
Elementary Education Act (1870), 5501-2, 5593
Elephant, in Hellenistic warfare, 175
Eleusinian mysteries, 139
Elgin, 9th earl of, <u>see</u> Bruce, Victor Alexander
Elgin treaty (1854), 7228
Elias of Cortona (<u>c</u>. 1180-1253), 767
Eliot, Sir John (1592-1632), 2707
Élites, African, 6272; in Ceylon, 6937; in Egypt, 6196; in Lagos,
  6407; army (19th-20th cent.), 4876; political, in revolutionary
  Paris, 2012
Elizabeth I (1533-1603), queen, 103, 2666
Ellenborough, 1st earl of, <u>see</u> Law, Edward
Elliot, Sir Gilbert (1751-1814), 1st earl of Minto, 3800, 6686
Elliot, Gilbert John Murray Kynynmond (1845-1914), 4th earl of
  Minto, 6856
Elliot (Elliott), Sir Henry George (1817-1907), 6010
Elliott, Ebenezer (1781-1849), 4895
Elmham, Thomas (d. 1440?), 74
Elmsall, South, W.R. Yorks., 5760
Ely, diocese of, 1323, 3089
Ely cathedral priory, Cambs., 1343
Elyot, Sir Thomas (1490?-1546), 2642-3, 2888
Emancipation, Catholic, 3700, 3759-60, 4548
Emancipation, slave, <u>see</u> Slavery, abolition of
Embassies, English (medieval), 610
Emigration, <u>see</u> Migration
Emigration policies, British (19th cent.), 4122
Emigrés, French (18th-19th cent.), 2017, 4123; <u>see also</u> Refugees
Emin Pasha Relief Expedition, 6172
Empire, British (16th-17th cent.), 2514; (17th-19th cent.), 3779-
  806 <u>passim</u>; (19th cent.), 4733, 4760, 5351; (19th-20th cent.),
  4759, 5119; (20th cent.), 4924; <u>see also</u> Imperialism
  attitudes to, 5351
Empire Settlement Act (1922), 4537
Empiricism, in political reasoning (16th-17th cent.), 1757
Employer, capitalist (18th-19th cent.), 3968
Employment, industrial (19th-20th cent.), 4932-71 <u>passim</u>, 5142,
  5286; <u>see also</u> Labour; Workers
Enclosure, 457, 2507, 2511, 2819-20; parliamentary, 3420-6, 3430;
  in Wales, 2821, 3427-9, 3431
Encyclopaedists, 1966
Endowed schools, in Jersey, 2562
Endowed Schools Act (1869), 5504-5
Engineering industry, 3354; (18th-19th cent.), 3333, 3353; (19th
  cent.), 4983-4; (19th-20th cent.), 5076-7; (20th cent.), 5024,
  5026, 5104; in Ireland, 5856; in Scotland, 5811
English language, in Ireland, 1711-12; in Scotland, 1679
English Revolution (1688), 3861, 3886
Enlightenment, 1772, 1968, 1998
<u>Enragés, Les</u>, 2009
Entertainment, popular, <u>see</u> Recreations
<u>Entheticus de dogmate philosophorum</u> (John of Salisbury's), 1429
Enthusiasm (18th cent.), 1771; reaction against (17th cent.), 4277
Eperqueries (fish tithes), 1029
Epidaurus, Greece, 156
Epirus, despotate of, 541
Episcopal appointments (medieval), 1277

Episcopal constitutions, 1214
Episcopal elections (13th cent.), 1226
Episcopal vacancies (medieval), 1188
Episcopate, see Bishops
Equatorie of the Planetis, 1473
Equites, order of, 197
Erbery (Erbury), William (1604-54), 3075
Eremetical movement, 703
Erewash valley, 3311
Erghum, Ralph (d. 1400), bishop, 1297
Eritrea, 6103
Erskine, David Steuart (1742-1829), 11th earl of Buchan, 4441
Erskine, John (1721?-1803), 4421
Erskine, Thomas (1788-1870), 5787-8
Escouchy, Mathieu d' (1420-c. 1483), 75
Essex, 1509, 4082, 5674; (Saxon), 1521; (medieval), 941, 970, 1051,
    1094; (15th-16th cent.), 3112; (16th cent.), 2844, 3022; (16th-
    17th cent.), 2833, 2840, 2845, 2905; (17th cent.), 3190, 4081;
    (17th-18th cent.), 4352; (18th cent.), 3702; (18th-19th cent.),
    4069; (19th cent.), 5189; (19th-20th cent.), 5601; east, 3406;
    metropolitan, 4949; northern, 3285; south-east, 421; south-west,
    422, 3284
Essex, earl of, see Cromwell, Thomas
Estates and estate management (medieval), 1045-99 passim; (15th-
    16th cent.), 2822; (16th-17th cent.), 2832-4, 2836; (17th
    cent.), 2849; (19th cent.), 5206; in Ireland (19th cent.),
    5828; in Scotland (18th-19th cent.), 3573; (19th cent.), 5781;
    see also Landownership
Estienne, Robert (1530-70), 1903
Estonia (20th cent.), 2186
Ethics (medieval), 808
Ethiopia (13th-16th cent.), 6114, 6118; (19th cent.), 6134-6,
    6146; (20th cent.), 1742-3
Etruria (Roman), 183
Eugenius III (d. 1153), pope, 749
Euphrates expedition, 5996
Euphrates valley, 6006
European Danube Commission, 1863
Eustache le Moine (d. 1217), 63
Evangelicals, evangelical party, evangelical revival (18th cent.),
    4143-4, 4146-9, 4236, 4308; (18th-19th cent.), 3479, 4237;
    (19th cent.), 5350-1, 5368, 5406-7; in Ireland, 3585; in Scot-
    land, 4451; (17th-18th cent.), 4399; (18th cent.), 4425-6;
    (19th cent.), 5791
Evangelism, North American (19th-20th cent.), 5356
Evans, Griffith (1835-1935), 5483
Evans, John (1814-76), 5448
Evening education, see Adult education
Evesham, vale of, 5193
Evolution, Darwinian, 5484; in social theory, 5326
Ewe people, 6387
Ewing, Greville (1767-1841), 4444
Excavation, scientific, see Archaeology
Exchequer (14th cent.), 1016-17; (17th-18th cent.), 3642; Scottish
    (15th-16th cent.), 1694; of the Jews, 1012
Exchequer Chamber, 906
Exclusion contest, 3625-6
Exe estuary, 3378
Exeter, Devon, 1516, 3467, 3951, 5710-11; cathedral, 1099, 1507
Exeter, diocese of (medieval), 1192, 1263, 1287; (16th cent.),
    2920; (19th cent.), 5383
Exeter Book, 1418
Exiles, Czech (18th cent.), 1836; English Catholic (16th-17th
    cent.), 2426; English protestant (16th cent,), 2472, 2923,
    2971; Italian (19th cent.), 5278; see also Emigrés; Refugees
Expenditure, government (18th cent.), 3936; (19th cent.), 4886;
    (19th-20th cent.), 4917; military, 4748

Experiment, in modern thought, 1753
Exploration, of East Africa, 6211; and the empire (18th cent.),
    3794; of Papua, 7628; of the South Sea, 7618; of western
    U.S.A., 7311; see also Northwest passage; Voyages
Ex-service men, organised, 4700
Extra-territoriality, in Japan, 7105
Eye, Northants., 3182, 3538
Eyre, bills of, 921
Eyre, forest, 1084
Eyre family, 2874
Eyre rolls, see Assize rolls
Ezo, 7076

FABIANISM, 4647-8, 4648A
Fabric rolls, 1507
Fabrics, see Textile fabrics
Factory Acts, 4939; see also Legislation, factory
Factory controversy, 4943
Factory councils, Italian (20th cent.), 2267
Factory movement, 4944
Factory system, 4939
Fairs and markets, 1105-7
Falkland Islands, 7619
Falls family, 4420
Family
    economy of (18th-19th cent.), 4118; size of (19th cent.), 5285;
        structure of (19th cent.), 5284-6
    in ancient Athens, 138, 163; Roman imperial, 228; in Roman
        politics, 192
Family Compact (1761), 2450
Family history, English (medieval), 1145-77 passim; English and
    Welsh (15th-17th cent.), 2874-914 passim
Famine, see Great Famine
Famine policy, in India, 6835
Far East, 5899, 7047-168
Fardle House, Devon, 2889
Farington, William (1537-1610), 2836
Farm size, in Carmarthenshire, 5212
Farming, see Agriculture
Farrar, Frederic William (1831-1903), 5414
Fascists, British, 4717
Fashoda crisis (1898), 6177
Fastolf, Sir John (d. 1459), 1517
Fatawa-i-Jahandari, 46
Fatimid caliphate, 5942, 5944, 5946, 5951, 6111
Faversham abbey, Kent, 1356
Feckenham, Forest of, 1056
Federal Republican party, Spanish, 2460
Federalism, in Australia, 7612; in India, 6878
Federalist revolt (1793-4), 2021
Federation, in Australia, 7609; in British West Indies, 7480,
    7494; of Canada, 7235
Federations, ancient Greek, 173
Feet of fines, 1556-7
Felkin, William (1795-1874), 5055
Fellenberg, Philipp Emanuel von (1771-1844), 2475
Feminist movement, 4120-1
Fenians, 7361
Fenland, 1048-9; see also Drainage and reclamation
Fergusson, Sir James (1832-1907), 6812
Ferrara-Florence, Council of (1439), 739
Festus (4th cent.), 29
Feudal tenures, in Scotland, 1680
Feudalism, 1024-44 passim; in ancient China, 7047; in northern
    India, 6503; in French political thought, 1965
Ffestiniog, Merioneth, 3351
Ffraid, I.D., see Evans, John

Fichte, Johann Gottlieb (1762-1814), 2130
Field systems, of Chilterns, 419; of Kent, 409; see also Open
    fields
Fife, 2615, 3209
Fifth Monarchy men, 2762
Figgis, John Neville (1866-1919), 5378
Fiji, 6721-2, 7626-7, 7631
Film industry, British, 5103
Filmer, Sir Robert (d. 1653), 2719
Final concords, 1555
Finance (medieval), 1003-23, 1142; (16th cent.), 2241-2; (16th-
    17th cent.), 2801-18; (17th cent.), 3207; (17th-19th cent.),
    3920-44; (19th-20th cent.), 4885-931; Scottish burgh, 2610;
    military (medieval), 994, 1022; of royal household (medieval),
    903, 915; of shipping industry (17th cent.), 3954; see also
    Government finance
  Anglo-American, 7335; in ancient Athens, 169; in Bengal, 6659;
    in Canton, 7073; in Castile, 2436; Confederate, 7354; in Egypt,
    6147, 6151; in Florence, 2222-3; in India, 6715, 6771, 6788;
    of Mysore state, 6669; in Russia, 2372; of T'ang dynasty, 7053
Finances, of Durham priory (17th cent.), 3048; of James VI, 3238
Financial administration, see Administration, financial
Financial institutions, Canadian, 7233
Financial interests, British, in Bombay, 6646; in Canton, 7073; in
    Tigris-Euphrates valley, 6006
Financial system, of Egypt (medieval), 6122; of India, 6779
Financiers, Italian (15th-16th cent.), 2241-2
Finch, Daniel (1647-1730), 2nd earl of Nottingham, 3658-9
Finland, and Britain (19th-20th cent.), 2405; and the U.S.S.R., 2384
Finnian of Clonard, Saint (c. 470-548), 1702
Firle, Sussex, 2907
Firmin, Thomas (1632-97), 4093
First International, 1798-9
Firth of Forth, 4384
Fís Adamnám, 1704
Fiscal autonomy, Canadian, 7228
Fiscal policy (18th-19th cent.), 3940; (19th-20th cent.), 4885-931
    passim
Fish tithes, 1029
Fish trade (16th cent.), 2854
Fisheries, Newfoundland, 7186; Shetland, 504
Fishing industry, 1103, 3380-1
Fitch, William, see Canfield, Benedict
Fitnat al Qayrawan, 35
Fitzmaurice, see Petty-Fitzmaurice
Fitzralph, Richard (d. 1360), archbishop, 1716
Fitzroy, Augustus Henry (1735-1811), 3rd duke of Grafton, 3711
Fiume, Jugoslavia, 2266
Five Dynasties, in North China, 7056
Flanders (medieval), 651, 1110; (16th-17th cent.), 2422; (18th
    cent.), 3894; and England (17th cent.), 2277
Flavel, John (1630-91), 4206
Flavian emperors, 218
Fleets, Roman, 295; Spanish, 7517
Fleetwood, Lancs., 5738
Fleming, Richard (d. 1431), bishop, 1318
Flemings (16th-17th cent.), 3174
Fletcher, John William (1729-85), 4144-5
Flint, 1648
Flint glass industry, 2533
Flintshire, 1626, 4935-6
Flixton, South Elmham, Suffolk, 1580
Florence, Italy (15th cent.), 593, 674; (15th-16th cent.), 2221-3;
    (16th cent.), 2235-6; (18th cent.), 2246; convent of San Marco,
    771
Fonts, Norman, 1502

Food, adulteration of, 5226; marketing of (17th cent.), 3956;
    world supply of, 7169
Footwear manufacture, 2539, 5037-8
fora, 251
Forbes, Patrick (1564-1635), bishop, 3248
Ford, John (1801-75), 5622
Foreign Office (19th cent.), 4742, 6234; (19th-20th cent.), 4735
Foreign policy (17th cent.), 1923, 3953; (17th-19th cent.), 3779-
    806 passim; (18th cent.), 2328; (18th-19th cent.), 1999, 5991,
    7306; (19th cent.), 1793, 1851, 2135-293 passim, 2453, 2456,
    2458, 5994-6030 passim, 6065, 6080, 6082, 6087, 6138, 6140,
    6171, 6173, 6176, 6273, 6277-8, 6201, 6686, 6769, 6791, 6800,
    6831-2, 6965, 6972, 7009, 7020-1, 7035, 7037, 7094, 7099, 7119,
    7122, 7124, 7134, 7228, 7360; (19th-20th cent.), 1863, 4719-
    819 passim, 6027, 7029, 7121, 7126, 7131; (20th cent.), 1813,
    1876, 1889-90, 2264, 2294, 2377, 2395, 6035, 6038, 6043, 6046,
    6450, 7140, 7159, 7165
  of Austria-Hungary, 1804, 1870; of Canada, 7249, 7255; of Chile,
    7560; of Czechoslovakia, 1826; of Holland (18th cent.), 2284;
    of France (18th cent.), 1958, 1973, 2445; (19th cent.), 2043,
    6155; (19th-20th cent.), 1804, 2086-7; (20th cent.), 1815,
    1826, 2098, 2103-4; of Germany (19th cent.), 2152, 6065; (19th-
    20th cent.), 1804; (20th cent.), 1815, 2180, 2186-7, 2195,
    2201; of India, 6873; of Italy (19th cent.), 2260; (19th-20th
    cent.), 1804; of Japan, 7150, 7153, 7156; Mughal, 6560-2; of
    ancient Rome, 190; of Russia, 1804, 2341; of Sardinia, 2310;
    of the U.S.A., 2468, 7370, 7404, 7412; of the U.S.S.R., 2380-2
Foreign relations, British (19th-20th cent.), 4719-819 passim;
    with Afghanistan, 6963, 6973; with the Agha Khan (19th cent.),
    6728; with Austria (18th cent.), 1837, 1839; (19th cent.),
    2140; with Austria-Hungary, 1860, 1869; with China (18th cent.),
    7072; (18th-19th cent.), 7071, 7074; (19th cent.), 7032, 7087,
    7096, 7104, 7107, 7109, 7120; (19th-20th cent.), 7127; with
    Dutch Republic (18th cent.), 2282; with Egypt (18th cent.),
    6120-1; (19th cent.), 6137; (19th-20th cent.), 6126; with
    Finland, 2405; with France (18th cent.), 2030; (19th cent.),
    2057-9, 2069, 2253, 2455, 4747, 6177; (19th-20th cent.), 2076,
    2087, 6425, 7039; (20th cent.), 2090, 2099, 2105, 2185, 6045,
    6052; with Germany (19th cent.), 2148-9, 2157, 2164, 4747,
    7025, 7624; (19th-20th cent.), 2145, 2165-6; with Haidar Ali
    (18th cent.), 6612; with Iran, 5992, 5995, 6004; with Italy,
    2263, 2266, 6170; with Japan, 7149, 7163-4; with Kuwait, 6025;
    with Latin America, 7540; with the Mediterranean (18th cent.),
    2301; with Mexico, 7551; with Montenegro (19th cent.), 1842;
    with the papal states (18th-19th cent.), 1777; with the Persian
    Gulf (19th-20th cent.), 6026; with Portugal, 2451, 6246; with
    Rumania, 1844; with Russia (18th cent.), 2331; (19th cent.),
    2340, 2342, 2349, 2358, 6804, 6972, 6974-6; (19th-20th cent.),
    2352, 2355, 7129; (20th cent.), 2366, 6041-2; with Sardinia,
    2311; with Scandinavia (18th cent.), 2401; with Serbia, 1853;
    with Siam, 7027, 7042; with Spain (18th cent.), 2446, 2448;
    (19th cent.), 2459, 7023; with Spanish colonies (19th cent.),
    7533; with Switzerland (19th cent.), 2476; (20th cent.), 2477;
    with Turkey, 5997, 6019, 6023; with the U.S.A., 7129, 7168,
    7296-412 passim, 7500, 7537, 7554, 7561, 7564-5, 7624, 7633;
    with the U.S.S.R., 2381, 6863; with Zanzibar, 6215
  English, with Flanders (17th cent.), 2277; with France (medieval),
    607-35; (16th cent.), 1910; (16th-17th cent.), 1914; (17th
    cent.), 1924, 1926, 1928; with Germany, 2113; with the Mughals,
    6583; with the Palatinate, 2114; with Portugal (17th-18th
    cent.), 2444; with Spain (16th cent.), 2421; (17th cent.),
    2434, 2437-8, 2440; with Swiss Protestants (17th cent.), 2473;
    with Turkey, 5977
  of Great Powers, in Far East, 7123, 7130, 7167
  For foreign relations of countries other than Great Britain see
  under name of individual country
Forestry Commission, 4560

Forests (medieval), 1045-99 _passim_; (16th-18th cent.), 2505
Forests policy, in New England, 7270
Forster, Sir John (1520?-1602), 2654
Fort Edmonton, Canada, 7220
Fort William presidency, 6684, 6702
Fortibus, Isabella de (d. 1293), countess of Aumale, 1082
Fortification, _see_ Castles; Defences and fortifications; Manor-
    houses, fortified
Foster, John (1770-1843), 5426
Foster, John, & Son, 5042
Foster family, 4469
Fountains abbey, W.R. Yorks., 1347
Four Hundred, uprising (411 B.C.), 158
Fourier, François-Marie-Charles (1772-1837), 1980, 2038
Fox, Charles James (1749-1806), 3734, 3739
Foxe, John (1516-87), 2973
France, 1779, 1896-2106; _and see_ (medieval), 567, 578, 581, 595,
    597, 662, 665, 787-9; (15th-16th cent.), 1754; (16th cent.),
    79, 1759, 2677; (16th-17th cent.), 1719, 3016; (17th cent.),
    4090; (17th-18th cent.), 4280; (18th cent.), 2284, 2445, 3874,
    7070; (18th-19th cent.), 4123; (19th cent.), 1780, 1790, 2452,
    3913, 4124-5, 6009, 7020, 7348; (19th-20th cent.), 1804, 6020;
    (20th cent.), 1826, 2184-5, 6089; northern (12th cent.), 802
  and Britain (18th cent.), 2030; (19th cent.), 2057-9, 2069,
    2253, 2455, 4747, 6177, 6411; (19th-20th cent.), 2076, 6425,
    7039; (20th cent.), 1811, 2090, 2099, 2105, 6045, 6052; and
    Egypt, 6133, 6142; and England (medieval), 607-35; (16th
    cent.), 1910; (16th-17th cent.), 1914; and Germany (19th-20th
    cent.), 2076; and Italy (19th-20th cent.), 1809; (20th cent.),
    1824; and Japan, 7103; and Morocco, 6088, 6092-3; in Neutral
    Islands (17th-18th cent.), 7420; and Poland, 1825; and Russia,
    1807-8; and Scotland (medieval), 582; (16th cent.), 3228; and
    Siam, 7027, 7035; and South American colonies, 7542; and Tunis,
    6083
Franchise (13th cent.), 1075
Franchise, borough, parliamentary, _see_ Borough franchise; Parlia-
    mentary franchise
Francis, Sir Philip (1740-1818), 6682
Franciscans, 767-8, 770, 813, 1363-5, 1369-70
Franciscans Conventual, 1392
Franciscans Observant, 770
Franco, Francisco (1892-1975), 2466
Franco-Russian Alliance, 1807-8
Frank almoign, 1043
Frankfort, Germany, 2110, 2136
Franklin, William (1731-1813), 7275
Franks, 1024
Fraser, James (1639-99), 4397
Fraternity, concept of (18th cent.), 2003
Fraticelli, 720
Free Church Council, 5457
Free Churches, 5685
Free Coloured, 7463
Free labour, in West Indies, 7457, 7462
Free port system, in West Indies, 7444
Free trade, free trade movement, 3976, 4899-900, 4921; in France,
    1944-5; in the Netherlands, 2287
Free trade treaties, 4745
Freedmen, in Rome and the empire, 246-7, 249
Freedom of speech (17th cent.), 2702; (20th cent.), 5489
Freiburg im Breisgau, Germany, 2111
Freikorps, 2175
French and Indian War (1754-60), 3899
French chronicles, 51-78 _passim_
French Church (15th-17th cent.), 1899; (17th-18th cent.), 1934;
    (20th cent.), 2089; _see also_ Gallican Church
French language, in England (13th-15th cent.), 1433

French Revolution, 102, 1967, 1990, 1996, 2000-30 <u>passim</u>; and
    Scotland, 4449; and Wales, 3818
Frere, Sir Bartle (1815-84), 6310
Freud, Sigmund (1856-1939), 1801
Friars, 1367-8, 1372, 1387, 1437; in Wales, 1639
Friedjung, Heinrich (1851-1920), 1872
Friendly societies, 3455-6, 4114, 5235
Frisia, East, 2116
Frith, John (1503-33), 2942
Froebelian doctrines, 5585
Fronde, 1924
Fukien, China, diocese of, 7097
Fulanis, 6364
<u>Fulk Fitzwarine</u>, 1434
Fur trade, of London (medieval), 1113; Canadian, 7211
Furness, Lancs., 453, 3543, 5129, 5747
Furnishings, domestic (medieval), 1150; ecclesiastical, 677
Furniture, Welsh, 2588
Furniture industry, 4027, 5016, 5075
Fylde, Lancs., 5604

GAGE FAMILY, 2907
Gaguin, Robert (1433-1501), 78
Gainsborough, Lincs., 3553
Galatia, 2410
Galerius, Roman emperor (305-11), 227
Gallican Church, 1939
Gallicanism, 1920
Galloway, 3562
Galt, John (1779-1839), 4455
Gambia, 6069, 6373
Gambia, river, 6350
Gandhi, Mohandas Karamchand (1869-1948), 6862
Gaol delivery (15th cent.), 959
Garbett, Samuel (1717-1803), 3967
Gard, department of, France, 2044-5
Gardening (18th cent.), 4332; landscape, 3402; market, 5191-3
Gas industry, 4901
Gascoigne, Thomas (1403-58), 1471
Gascony, 583, 627, 657, 671; and England (13th cent.), 608-9
Gascoyne-Cecil, Robert A.T., <u>see</u> Cecil, Robert A.T. Gascoyne-
Gases, thermal properties of, 1972
Gaston VII de Béarn (<u>c</u>. 1229-90), 608
Gauīyad Vaisnavas, 6585
Gaul, 274, 296, 325-35, 1595
Gaveston, Peter of (d. 1312), earl of Cornwall, 854
Gawdy family, 4085
Gāzī Girāy (1554-1608), khan of the Tatars, 5966
Geld rolls, 1035
Gell, Sir John (1593-1671), 2736
Gemistos, George, surnamed Plethon (d. 1452), 551
General Assembly, of Church of Scotland, 3233-4, 3246, 3257
General Staff, 4875
General strike, 4976; (1926), 5030-2
Geneva, Switzerland, 2470-2
Genlis, Stéphanie Félicité de (1746-1830), 2037
Gentiles, Jewish attitude to (early), 5891
Gentry (15th-17th cent.), 2874; (16th cent.), 2890; (16th-17th
    cent.), 2903, 2906, 2908; (17th cent.), 2912, 3199; (17th-
    18th cent.), 4089; (19th cent.), 5564; in Wales (16th-17th
    cent.), 2891, 2895, 2902, 4049, 4058
Gentry democracy, in Shanghai, 7141
Geographers (medieval), 5507; Arab, 5933
Geography, teaching of, 5664; in France, 2083
George III (1738-1820), king, 3699
George, David Lloyd (1863-1945), 1st Earl Lloyd-George, 4802
George, Henry (1839-97), 4637

Georgia, U.S.A. (19th cent.), 7368; colonial, 7276-7
Germain, George Sackville (1716-85), 1st Viscount Sackville, 3898
German Church (13th cent.), 724
German Protestant Church, 2176
German Revolutions (1848-9), 2137; (1917-20), 2172
Germania (Roman), 336-9
Germanophiles, British, 2143
Germans, in Bohemia (19th cent.), 1864; Christian, in Palestine
    (20th cent.), 6055
Germany, 2107-204; and see (medieval), 643, 702, 1460; (19th
    cent.), 106, 1799, 6065, 7025, 7624; (19th-20th cent.), 1785,
    1800, 1803-4, 6020, 6243, 6276; (20th cent.), 1736, 1746,
    1819, 1892, 1894, 2097, 4814, 6089, 6263; north-east (medieval),
    640
  and Britain, 2145, 2148-9, 2157, 2164-6, 4747; and England (17th
    cent.), 2113; and France, 1778, 2076; and Italy, 1820; and
    Russia, 1806; and the U.S.S.R., 1821-2
Gerson, Jean Charlier de (1363-1429), 734
Gesta Henrici Quinti, 74
Gezira scheme, 6179
Ghana, 6069, 6414-15; (17th-18th cent.), 6343; (18th cent.), 6352,
    6355; (18th-19th cent.), 6358; (19th cent.), 6372, 6374, 6384;
    (19th-20th cent.), 6360, 6378, 6383, 6399-400, 6410, 6431,
    6442; western, 6436
Ghaznavid rule, 5948
Gibbon, Edward (1737-94), 97
Gibbs, Antony, & Sons, 7536
Gibraltar, 2447
Gibson, Edmund (1669-1748), bishop, 4173-4
Giffard family, 3411
Gilbert, Davies (1767-1839), 3742
Gild system (Saxon), 1100
Gilds (medieval), 1112; (16th-17th cent.), 2824; (17th cent.),
    2825; of Roman empire, 304
Giles of Rome (1247-1316), 806, 1441
Gill, John (1697-1771), 4239
Giraldus Cambrensis (1146?-1220?), 1636-8
Girls, education of, 3116, 3534, 4265, 5506; in Bengal, 6672; in
    the Sudan, 6192
Girondin party, 2013, 2022
Gladstone, William Ewart (1809-98), 2292, 4622, 4757, 4770-1,
    4903, 5416-17, 6065, 6164, 6313
Glamorgan, 2487, 3390, 3449, 4529; (medieval), 1615, 1652; (16th-
    17th cent.), 2891; (17th cent.), 2738-9; (17th-19th cent.),
    3470; (17th-18th cent.), 4050, 4278; (18th-20th cent.), 3414;
    (18th-19th cent.), 3392, 3460; (19th cent.), 3775; (19th-20th
    cent.), 4538; west, 3465, 5257
Glamorgan, lordship of, 1613-14
Glamorgan, vale of, 494, 4513
Glanvill, Joseph (1636-80), 4277
Glanville, Gilbert (d. 1214), bishop, 1208
Glas, John (1695-1773), 4427
Glasgow, 5798, 5816, 6064; constituency, 5800
Glasgow, diocese of, 1682
Glass, painted (medieval), 1499-500
Glass industry, glassworks, 2533-4, 5059; in Scotland, 3574
Glastonbury abbey, Som., 1069
Glebe terriers, 2508
Glendower, see Glyndwr
Gloucester, diocese of, 2932, 2966
Gloucester, duke of, see Woodstock, Thomas of
Gloucester, Robert of (fl. 1260-1300), 66
Gloucester, vale of, 4970
Gloucester Technical College, 5676
Gloucestershire, 468, 2519-20; (medieval), 921, 1446; (17th cent.),
    2741; (17th-19th cent.), 3509; (18th cent.), 4376; (18th-19th
    cent.), 3356; (19th-20th cent.), 4501, 4523

Glove trade, 2538
Glyndwr, Owen (1359?-1416?), 1657-8
Gobineau, Joseph Arthur, comte de (1816-82), 2056
Godolphin, Sidney (1645-1712), 1st earl of Godolphin, 3932
Godwin, William (1756-1836), 3874-5
Golconda, 6548
Gold Coast, see Ghana
Gold money, in France (15th-17th cent.), 1900
Gold movements, international, 1722
Gold standard, and Argentina, 7558
Gold thread monopoly, 2811
Golden Horde, 2318
Goldsmith bankers, 3925
Gonzaga family, 589
Goodman, Christopher (1520?-1603), 2969
Goodwin, Thomas (1600-80), 3087
Gordon, Arthur Hamilton (1829-1912), 1st Baron Stanmore, 4610,
    7626
Gordon, George Hamilton (1784-1860), 4th earl of Aberdeen, 2057-8,
    4730
Gordon Riots, 3728-9
Gospel-books, 781
Gosport, Hants, 3882
Gothic style, 810
Goulburn, Henry (1784-1856), 4558
Governing class, see Ruling class
Government, idea of (17th cent.), 2720
Government, in India (ancient), 6493; (19th-20th cent.), 6775
Government finance (16th cent.), 2241-2; in France (20th cent.),
    2100
Government of India Act (1935), 6877
Governor-generalship, of Canada, 7230, 7241
Gower, 4022, 4340, 5181
Gower family, see Leveson-Gower
Gracchus, Caius Sempronius (d. 121 B.C.), 197
Grace, controversy on (18th cent.), 4138
Gracehill, co. Antrim, 4478
Grafton, 3rd duke of, see Fitzroy, Augustus Henry
Graham, Sir James Robert George (1792-1861), 4543
Grain trade (19th cent.), 2127, 2338; (20th cent.), 1737; see also
    Wheat trade
Grammar, teaching of (medieval), 1436
Grammar schools, 2576; (17th-18th cent.), 4281-2; (19th-20th
    cent.), 5667; (20th cent.), 5638, 5640; in Wales, 4281; of
    Ontario (19th cent.), 7227
Grampound, Cornw., 2486
Granada, Spain, sultanate of, 587
Grand Alliance (1701-3), 1773
Grand tour, in Italy, 2229
Grandes Chroniques de France, 67
Grandisson, John (d. 1369), bishop, 1263, 1283
Grange, monastic, 1067-8
Grant, Ulysses Simpson (1822-85), president of the U.S.A., 7372
Grants, to Scottish Church (medieval), 1681
Granville, 2nd Earl, see Leveson-Gower, Granville George
Granville, George (1667-1735), Baron Lansdowne, 3663
Great Famine, 5845, 5853-4
Great Horde, 2318
Great Ouse, 3389
Great Schism, 729, 1405
Great Tew circle, 3079
Greece, 2205-70 passim; (20th cent.), 1873; and Turkey (20th
    cent.), 2216
    ancient, 12, 115-25 passim, 126-81, 214; and Rome, 297
Greek works, quotations from, in Anglo-Saxon, 1414; translation
    of (medieval), 798
Greenfield, William (d. 1315), archbishop, 1271

Hallum, Robert (d. 1417), 1321-2
Hamburg, and Britain (19th-20th cent.), 2158
Hamilton, Lord George Francis (1845-1927), 6835
Hamilton family, 4389
Hammersmith, see London
Hammond, Edmund (1802-90), Baron Hammond, 4738
Hamoaze, see Plymouth
Hampshire, 5201; (medieval), 901, 1582; (16th cent.), 2945; (16th-
    17th cent.), 3013, 3025; (17th cent.), 3192; (18th-19th cent.),
    4055; (19th cent.), 4077; (19th-20th cent.), 5559; north-east,
    3287
Hampton Charles, Herefs., 5184
Hampton Court Conference (1604), 3056
Hampton-upon-Thames, Middx., 2575
Hanbury, see Allen and Hanbury
Hancock, house of, 7268
Handboc (Byrhtferth's), 1417
Handicapped, education and services for, 3523, 5277, 5844
Handloom weaving industry, 4015-16; in Scotland, 5783
Hankampu, 7069
Hanley, Staffs., 5253
Han-Lin Academy, 7067
Hanover, and Britain (18th-19th cent.), 2119
Hanseatic League, 649-50, 2857
Hanson, Joseph Aloysius (1803-82), 5468
Harbours, see Ports and harbours
Hardie, James Keir (1856-1915), 4603
Harewood House, W.R. Yorks., 4333
Harley, Robert (1661-1724), 1st earl of Oxford, 3608, 3660-2,
    3668-9
Harling, West, Norfolk, 4085
Harney, George Julian (1817-97), 4841
Harold (1022?-1066), king, 1030
Harris, Howell (1714-73), 4230-1
Harris, James Howard (1807-89), 3rd earl of Malmesbury, 4744
Harris, William Wade (fl. 1865-1915), the 'Prophet Harris', 6436
Harrison, Benjamin (1833-1901), president of the U.S.A., 7384
Harrison, Frederic (1831-1923), 4599-600
Harrogate, W.R. Yorks., 441
Harrow School, Middx., 5618
Harsa (d. c. 650), Hindu emperor, 6492
Harsnett, Samuel (1561-1631), archbishop, 3069
Hartlepool, West, co. Durham, 5557
Hartley, Henry Robinson (1777-1850), 5646
Harvest technology, 5171
Harwich, Essex, 2513
Haslingfield, Cambs., 1484
Hassop, Derbys., 2874
Hastings, Francis Rawdon- (1754-1826), 1st marquess of Hastings,
    6690
Hastings, Henry (1535-95), 3rd earl of Huntingdon, 2674
Hastings, Selina (1707-91), countess of Huntingdon, 4244-5
Hastings, Warren (1732-1818), 3797, 6627-30
Hatfield Chase, 3410
Hatteclyff family, 914
Haute-Marne, department of, France, 2052
Haverfordwest, Pemb., 2488
Haweis, Thomas (1734-1820), 4246
Head, Sir Edmund Walker (1805-68), 4731, 7225
Headington, Oxon., 1547
Health visiting service, 5310
Heanor, Derbys., 5769
Heath, Sir Robert (1575-1649), 2695
Heathenism (Saxon), 1184; see also Paganism
Heber, Reginald (1783-1826), bishop, 4193
Hebrew, study of (17th cent.), 4270
Hebrews (early), 5887

<u>Historia Francorum</u> (Raymond of Aguilers'), 59
<u>Historia Langobardorum</u> (Paul the Deacon's), 54
Historians, 10-114 <u>passim</u>
Historical explanation, 1-2, 6
Historical knowledge, 3
Historiography, 10-114; Maronite, 5952
History, conception of, in the Enlightenment, 1772; teaching of
    (15th-17th cent.), 3115; (17th-19th cent.), 3498; (19th cent.
    5665-6
<u>History of the Crusades</u> (Ibn al-Athir's), 38
Hitchin, Herts., 3531
Hitler, Adolf (1889-1945), 2198
Hobbes, Thomas (1588-1679), 1927, 3156
Hog, James (1658-1734), 4425
Hogg, Quintin (1845-1903), 5688
Holgate, Robert (1481?-1555), archbishop, 2962
Holiday industry, 5087-90
Holkham, Norfolk, 3417
Holland, 1779; (medieval), 653; (19th cent.), 7003; <u>see also</u>
    Dutch Republic
Holland, Henry Scott (1847-1918), 5420
Holles, Thomas Pelham-, <u>see</u> Pelham-Holles
Holme valley, 3314
Holstein, Baron Friedrich von (1837-1909), 2138
Holt, Denbighs., 377
Holt, John (d. 1915), 6423
Holy Alliance, 3802
Holy Ghost Fathers, 6222
Holy Roman Empire, 2115-16, 2316
Holyhead road, 5128
Holyoake, George Jacob (1817-1906), 5316
Home demand, in economic growth (18th cent.), 3962
Home Office (19th cent.), 3748A, 3771-2, 4624
Home Rule movement, 4660, 4662-3; <u>see also</u> Irish Home Rule Bills
Homicide, law of, 2479
<u>honestiores</u>, 337
Hong Kong, 7086, 7091
Honorius Augustodunensis (d. <u>c</u>. 1130), 799
Hooker, Richard (1554?-1600), 2678-80, 2980
Hoover, Herbert Clark (1874-1964), president of the U.S.A., 7408
<u>Horrea</u>, 254
Horsfall, Thomas Coglan (1841-1932), 5305
Horsham, Sussex, 408
Horton, Sir Robert John Wilmot (1784-1841), 3770, 3803
Hosiery trade, 3363
Hospital (medieval), 1390; (19th-20th cent.), 5302-3; in Wales,
    3465
Hough-on-the-Hill, Lincs., Loveden hill, 1483
House, Edward Mandell (1858-1938), 7404
Household, archiepiscopal, 1220; of the Black Prince, 1570; of
    Elizabeth de Burgh, 1160; of John, lord of Ireland, 1152;
    queen's (14th cent.), 903; royal (medieval), 885-919 <u>passim</u>,
    990; (19th-20th cent.), 5274; of T'ang dynasty, 7055
Housing and house-building (18th-19th cent.), 4037; (19th cent.),
    5225, 5291-4; (19th-20th cent.), 5281-2, 5337; (20th cent.),
    5338, 5344-5; in Scotland, 5798, 5820; in Wales, 5283; in the
    U.S.A., 7409; <u>see also</u> Country houses; Manor-houses
Housing standards, 5282
Howard, Henry (1517-47), earl of Surrey, 3130
Howard, William (1626?-1694), 3rd Baron Howard of Escrick, 3613
Howard League for Penal Reform, 5306
Howards, chemical manufacturers, 3374
Howdenshire, 898
Howe, Richard (1726-99), Earl Howe, 7290
Howe, Sir William (1729-1814), 5th Viscount Howe, 7290
Howell, George (1833-1910), 4845
Hoysalas, 6525-6

Hsuan-Tung regency, 7145
Hubert de Burgh (d. 1243), 833-5
Huddersfield, W.R. Yorks., 5658
Hudson's Bay Company, 7216, 7216A
Hübmaier, Balthasar (1485-1528), 2469
Hügel, Friedrich von (1852-1925), 5375
Hugh (1024-1109), abbot of Cluny, 764
Hugh of Wells (d. 1235), bishop, 1223-4
Huguenots, in England, 4167, 4285; in Ireland, 4466; in France,
    1912
Huish, Mark (1808-67), 5130
Hull, E.R. Yorks., 1103, 5293; (medieval), 1104; (16th cent.),
    2886; (17th cent.), 3948A; (18th cent.), 4365; (19th cent.),
    5004, 5704; (19th-20th cent.), 5158
Humanism, 1908, 2218; in England (12th cent.), 1428; (15th cent.),
    1469; (16th cent.), 3118-19, 3122; in Germany (15th-16th
    cent.), 2111; (19th-20th cent.), 2126; in Italy, 77, 2233
Humanist movement, 5315
Humanitarianism, 4141, 6418
Humanities, teaching of (19th-20th cent.), 5667
Humayun, 6550
Humber warplands, 3283
Humbert of Silva Candida (d. 1061), cardinal, 709-10
Humboldt, Wilhelm von (1767-1835), 2122-3
Hume, Joseph (1777-1855), 3833
Hūnas, 6484
Hundred Years War, 607-35 passim, 1022
Hungary, 1794, 1854, 1858
Hungerford family, Lords Hungerford, 1072, 1154
Hunslet, W.R. Yorks., 2591
Huntingdon, countess of, see Hastings, Selina
Huntingdon, 3rd earl of, see Hastings, Henry
Huntingdonshire, 426
Hus, John (1373-1415), 732-3
Husbandry, in Russia (medieval), 639
Huskisson, William (1770-1830), 3753
Hussey, Thomas (1741-1803), 4479
Hussites, 668
Huxley, Thomas Henry (1825-95), 5670
Hyde, Edward (1609-74), 1st earl of Clarendon, 86-7, 3607, 3611
Hyde, Laurence (1641-1711), 1st earl of Rochester, 3612
Hyderabad, India, 6687
Hydraulics (ancient), 119
Hyndman, Henry Mayers (1842-1921), 4638
Hypnotism, 5231
Hyria, Greece, 180
Hywel Dda (d. 950), 1623

IBADAN, 6389
Iberian peninsula (Roman), 253
Ibn al-Athir (d. 1234), 38
Ibn al-Azraq al-Fāriqī (1116-76), 40
Ibn Hajar al-'Asqalānī (d. 1448), 47
Ibn Taimiya (1263-1328), 5958
Iceland, 2404
Iddesleigh, 1st earl of, see Northcote, Sir Stafford Henry
Ijebu people, 6388
Ile de France, see Mauritius
Illinois, U.S.A., 7344
Illumination, manuscript, 781, 784-5, 792, 800, 812, 820, 1498,
    1508, 1514
Illyria (ancient), 166
Image of Governaunce (Elyot's), 2643
Image-worship, controversy over, 1294
Immigration, see Migration
immunes, of Roman army, 283

Imperial affairs, in parliament (19th cent.), 4755; views on
    (19th cent.), 4764
Imperial British East Africa Company, 6230
Imperial Continental Gas Association, 4901
Imperial government, Roman concept of, 220
Imperial Land Regulations, 7198
Imperial Ottoman Railway, 6003
Imperial policy, see Colonial and imperial policy
Imperial preference, 4929
Imperialism, 4765, 4776; attitudes to, 4778, 4780-1; economic,
    4789; problem of, 4779; see also Empire, British
Imperialist controversy, in the U.S.A., 7390
Imperialist sentiment (19th cent.), 4763; in fiction, 4772-3
Impey, Sir Elijah (1732-1809), 6640
Inauguration rituals, royal (medieval), 562
Inbā' Al-Ghumr, 47
Incendium amoris (Richard Rolle's), 1451
Income, landed (16th cent.), 2892; (18th-19th cent.), 3320
Income tax, 4923; Indian, 6786
Independent Labour Party, 4640, 4668, 4702-3, 4860
Independent Social Democratic party, German, 2172-3
Independents (16th-18th cent.), 4198; (16th-17th cent.), 2558,
    3002, 4195-6; (17th cent.), 3087, 4197; (18th cent.), 3466,
    4215; (18th-19th cent.), 4257; in Wales (19th cent.), 5433
India, 6453-878; and see 99; (medieval), 41-2, 45, 6984; (15th-
    16th cent.), 6443; (18th cent.), 3787; (18th-19th cent.),
    5991; (19th cent.), 4726, 4762; (19th-20th cent.), 113, 6446;
    (20th cent.), 2381, 6450-2; and Afghanistan, 6449; and ancient
    Greeks, 145; and Iran, 6449; and Nepal, 6806; and Tibet, 6666
India, north-west frontier, 6729, 6831-2
India Board, 6763
India Office (19th cent.), 4743, 6763
Indian Central Legislative, 6872
Indian Guaranteed Railways, 6743
Indian migrant labour, to Ceylon, 6722; to Fiji, 6721-2; to Malaya,
    6722, 7023; to Mauritius, 6721, 6953; to Natal, 6721
Indian Mutiny, 6638
Indian National Congress, 6821-2, 6833, 6865, 6870
Indian native states, 6639, 6691, 6705, 6842
Indian Ocean, 6942-3, 6948, 6954
Indians, American (18th cent.), 7283
Indians
    in Africa, 6068; in Burma, 7040; in East Africa, 6236; in Malaya,
    6998; in the Transvaal, 6331; see also Indian migrant labour
    in civil service, 6762
Indirect rule, in Fiji, 7626
Individualism, economic (16th-17th cent.), 2802
Indochina, 7001
Indo-Greeks, 146
Indology, 6642
Indonesia, 6982
Indus, lower (early), 6475
Industrial arbitration, 4988
Industrial change, 4141, 4948, 4962; see also Industrial Revol-
    ution; Technological change
Industrial disputes, 4975, 5005; in Canada, 7254
Industrial relations (19th-20th cent.), 4972-5033
Industrial Revolution, 3322, 3335, 3358-9, 3370, 3398, 3968, 3971,
    4009, 4015, 4021, 4119; in Scotland, 4447; in Wales, 3327,
    4322
Industrial violence, in the U.S.A., 7395
Industry, in England (medieval), 1100-44 passim; in England and
    Wales (15th-17th cent.), 2823-52 passim; (17th-19th cent.),
    3945-80 passim, 3981-4027; (18th-20th cent.), 3293, 3302-36
    passim, 3337-84, 3392, 3394; (19th cent.), 4360, 4497, 5496,
    5579, 5748; (19th-20th cent.), 4932-71, 5034-110, 5123-67
    passim; (20th cent.), 4535, 4858; and see 470, 4103, 4505,

Industry (cont.)
  5677; in Ireland, 3562, 5881; in Scotland, 5817, 5819; in
  France, 2042, 2082; in Germany, 2189; in Italy, 2262; in
  Mughal empire, 6554; in Russia, 2343, 2372; in the U.S.S.R.,
  2393
Industry, rural, 475, 4515
Infant schools, 2614
Infanticide, 6625, 6758
Infantry, Bengal native, 6661; Prussian (18th-19th cent.), 2121
Infectious diseases, 5303
Ingolstadt, Germany, 2111
Ingram, Sir Arthur (d. 1642), 2810
Inheritance taxation, 3920
Injuries, claims for (19th cent.), 5275; workmen's (18th-19th
  cent.), 3336
Innocent I (d. 417), pope, 742
Inns of Court (16th-17th cent.), 2688
Inoculation, see Smallpox inoculation
Inquisition (medieval), 719; Lisbon, 3225
Inscriptions, Anglo-Saxon, 1489, 1491; in Bengal, 6486; Celtic,
  in Gaul, 335; at Epidauros, 156
Inspectorate
  in the Punjab, 6751
  mines, see Mines inspectorate
  schools, 5522-3; in Scotland, 5804
Intellectuals (medieval), 791; French (20th cent.), 2094
Intelligence service (16th-17th cent.), 2675
Intendants, in France (18th cent.), 1950; in Spanish America,
  7525-6
Interest (money), 3302
Interests, in English political thought (17th cent.), 3852
International, see First International; Second International
International law, in England and France, 1780
Internationalism, 4770, 4811
Intolerance, religious (17th cent.), 3050; see also Toleration,
  religious
Invasion of Britain, German plans for (20th cent.), 2203; planning
  against (19th-20th cent.), 4769
Invasions, of England by the French, 1896; of Roman Britain by the
  Irish, 371; of Wales, 1599-600
Investiture contest, 747
Investment
  British home (19th-20th cent.), 4885, 4905, 4912-13; Canadian,
  7246; French, 2042
  British overseas, 7257, 7540, 7606; (19th cent.), 4901, 6743,
  7334, 7345, 7527, 7544; (19th-20th cent.), 4885, 4912-15,
  6003, 6802; (20th cent.), 4924-5, 4928; Scottish overseas,
  7376; see also Financial interests
Ionian Islands (19th cent.), 2207-9
Ipswich, Suffolk, 1129, 2859, 3126, 5124
Iran (medieval), 39, 5916, 5949, 5960; (17th cent.), 5972; (18th
  cent.), 5988; (18th-19th cent.), 5991; (19th cent.), 5992,
  6022; (20th cent.), 6024, 6041-2; and Britain, 5995, 6004; and
  China (13th cent.), 5956; and India (20th cent.), 6449; and
  Russia (19th cent.), 5995; and Turkey (19th cent.), 5995
Iraq, 5917, 5926, 5931; (early), 5896; (9th cent.), 5937; (10th
  cent.), 5942-3; (13th-16th cent.), 5957; (19th cent.), 5996;
  (19th-20th cent.), 6011; (20th cent.), 6036, 6043-4; lower,
  6013
Ireland, 507-18, 2619-21; (early), 1595; (medieval), 783, 991,
  1149, 1700-18, 2627; (15th-17th cent.), 3262-81; (16th-17th
  cent.), 3237; (17th cent.), 3043; (17th-20th cent.), 3580-91;
  (17th-19th cent.), 4456-89; (17th-18th cent.), 3948; (18th-
  19th cent.), 3521, 3740; (19th cent.), 5367, 5416; (19th-20th
  cent.), 4659-707 passim, 5369, 5822-82, 7272; (20th cent.),
  4679, 7393, 7407; and Spain (16th-17th cent.), 2427
Irish community, in England, 5243-4; in Cardiff, 5245

Irish Home Rule Bills (1886), 4662; (1914), 4682, 4693
Irish parliamentary party, 4549
Irish Society (17th cent.), 3273
Iron and steel industry (18th-20th cent.), 3346; (18th-19th cent.),
    3349; (19th-20th cent.), 1803, 5080; (20th cent.), 1736, 4969,
    5109; of Scotland, 3570, 5794; of Wales, 5080; of Germany,
    1736, 1803; of the U.S.A., 1736
Iron industry, trade, ironworks, 1124; (17th cent.), 2852; (17th-
    18th cent.), 3990; (18th cent.), 3991-2; (18th-20th cent.),
    3316; (18th-19th cent.), 3341, 3347; (19th cent.), 5052-3; in
    Scotland (19th cent.), 5794
Iron ore mining, 4914; in Sweden, 2406
Ironside, Isaac (19th cent.), 5547
Ironwork, in Roman Britain, 353
Iroquois, and Europeans (17th cent.), 7173
Irrigation, and population movements, 7169
Irvingite Church, 5439
Isabella of France (1292-1358), queen of England, 861
Isami, Muslim historian (medieval), 45
Isauria (early), 5901
Isis, cult of, in Italy, 272
Islam, western concept of and attitudes to (medieval), 532, 536;
    see also Arabs; Muslims
Islamic reformist movement, 6132, 6644
Isle St. John, Canada, 7197
Islington, see London
Islip, Oxon., 1546
Ismā'īl b. 'Abd Al-Qādir (d. 1897), 6189
Ismaīl Pasha (1830-95), ruler of Egypt, 6145
Ismailis, 535, 5927
Israel (early), 5888; see also Palestine
Italian question, 2253, 2255, 2261
Italianate fashion (19th cent.), 4339
Italians, in London (19th cent.), 5278; see also Financiers
Italy, 2217-70; and see (5th cent.), 744; (medieval), 591, 662,
    1120; (15th-16th cent.), 1754; (19th cent.), 6170; (19th-20th
    cent.), 1804; (20th cent.), 1742-3, 1816; south (9th-10th
    cent.), 760; and Britain, 2263, 2266; and France, 1809, 1824;
    and Germany, 1820
ius Latii, 187
ius municipii, 187
Ivory Coast, 6436

JACKSON, Andrew (1767-1845), president of the U.S.A., 7328A
Jacobinism, 1970; in Austria, 1841
Jacobitism, 3645-7, 3678, 4400, 4428
Jaffna, kingdom of, 6893-4
Jahangir, Nūr-al-dīn Muhammad (1569-1627), Mughal emperor, 6562
Jamaica, 7413-506 passim
James, Saint (d. 44 A.D.), Santiago, 658, 1199
James I (1566-1625), king, 2244, 3053, 3145, 3238
James II (1633-1701), king, 4467
James III (1451-88), king of Scotland, 1699
James, John Angell (1785-1859), 5453
Jandun, John of (fl. 1323), 578
Jansenism, 1952
Japan, 7047-168 passim; and China, 7153; France and, 7103; and the
    U.S.A., 4788
Jaunpur, sultanate of, 6542
Java, 7005
Jay, William (1769-1853), 5350
Jean IV, duke of Brittany (d. 1399), 616
Jean V, duke of Brittany (d. 1442), 533
Jeanbon Saint-André (1749-1813), 2033
Jefferson, Thomas (1743-1826), president of the U.S.A., 7285
Jejākhabhukti, 6523
Jenkins, Sir Richard (1785-1853), 6685

Jenkinson, Charles (1727-1808), 1st earl of Liverpool, 3709, 3727, 3796
Jenkinson, Robert Banks (1770-1828), 2nd earl of Liverpool, 3765-7, 6288
Jersey, 1028, 2562
Jerusalem, church of (1st cent.), 5905; pilgrims to (15th cent.), 665
Jervis, John (1735-1823), earl of St. Vincent, 3909
Jesuits, in Ceylon (17th cent.), 6897; and council of Trent, 1767; mission of (1580), 3019
Jet objects, in Roman Britain, 354
Jewel, John (1522-71), bishop, 3009-10
Jewellery trade, 3367
Jewish Agency, 6054
Jewish Antiquities (Josephus's), 26
Jewish Bund, 2359
Jewish disabilities, relief of, 4547
Jewish illumination, 812
Jewish Revolt, 324
Jewish schooling systems, of London, 3500
Jewish stereotype, 1764
Jews (early), 265-6, 310-11, 678, 5891, 5907-8; (16th cent.), 1765; in England (13th cent.), 1011-12, 1155; (17th-20th cent.), 3500; (18th-19th cent.), 3457; (19th-20th cent.), 1800, 5331; in central Europe (17th-18th cent.), 1835; in Ottoman empire (16th-17th cent.), 5961; in Palestine (early), 5894; (19th-20th cent.), 6021; in Russia (19th-20th cent.), 2351, 2356; in Yemen (17th-19th cent.), 5973
Joachim of Fiore (d. 1202), 1752
John XXII (1249-1334), pope, 753
John VI, Cantacuzenus (c. 1292-1383), Byzantine emperor, 548
John (1167?-1216), king, 830-1; as lord of Ireland, 1152
John (fl. 1210), abbot of Ford, 1431
John de Gray (d. 1214), bishop, 1219
John of Lancaster (1389-1435), duke of Bedford, 631, 879
John of Salisbury (d. 1180), bishop, 1427-30
Johnson, Andrew (1808-75), president of the U.S.A., 7362
Johnson family, 2899
Johnston, Archibald (1611-63), Lord Warriston, 3258
Johnston, Nathaniel (1627-1705), 4287
Jones, Sir Alfred Lewis (1845-1909), 6422
Jones, Griffith (1683-1761), 4295
Jones, John (d. 1658), 3143-4
Jones, Philip (1618-74), 3595
Jones, Sir William (1746-94), 6642-3
Jordan, Sir John Newell (1852-1925), 7144
Joseph ibn Leb (c. 1500-80), 5961
Josephus Flavius (37-95 A.D. ?), 26
Journal of an excursion to the United States of America (Wansey's), 7307
Journalism (16th-18th cent.), 2493; (18th cent.), 4304; (20th cent.), 5018; German (20th cent.), 2193
Journeymen (16th cent.), 2827
Judea (Roman), 312-13
Judicial administration, see Administration, judicial
Judicial precedent, doctrine of, 947
Judiciary, 906, 2634, 2697, 2714; in Bengal, 6676
Jünger, Ernst (b. 1895), 2192
Jugoslavia, 1819, 1882, 1893; and Bulgaria, 1884
Julian, Saint (d. 690), bishop of Toledo, 696
Julian of Eclanum (d. c. 455), 689
Jury reform, in India, 6830
Just rebellion, Knox's doctrine of, 3221
'Just war', 1761
Justices of the peace (16th-17th cent.), 2897; (17th cent.), 3191-2; (18th cent.), 4376; (18th-19th cent.), 4375
Justiciar, 887, 895; court of, in Ireland, 1715

Juvenal des Ursins, Jean (1400-72), 606
Juxon, William (1582-1663), archbishop, 3076

KABĪR, 6543
Kaffir War (1834-5), 6293
Kaggwa, Sir Apolo (d. 1927), 6271
Kairouan, Tunisia, 35
Kałankatuaçi, Movsēs (10th cent.), 55
Kanauj, 6499
Kandyan kingdom, 6901-2
Kantemír, Antiokh (1709-44), 4110
Karelia, East, 2384
Karīm Khān Zand (d. 1779), 5981
Kashmir (medieval), 6517, 6524; (19th cent.), 6759, 6827
Katanga, Congo, 6330
Kaunitz, Prince Wenzel Anthony (1711-94), 1838
Kautilīya Arthaśāstra, 6483
Kaye, John (1783-1853), 5395
Kaye, Sir Richard (1736-1809), 4187
Kay-Shuttleworth, Sir James (1804-77), 5524, 5691
Keach, Benjamin (1640-1704), 4210
Kedah, Malaya, 7028
Kellawe, Richard de (d. 1316), bishop, 1279
Kelsall, John (1683-1743), 4218
Kempis, Thomas à (d. 1471), 736
Ken-Chü-Ti (Chinese Communist bases), 7166
Kenfig, Glam., 1616
Kenilworth, Warwicks.: abbey (formerly priory), 1354, 1537;
    castle, 1537; see also Dictum de Kenilworth
Kennedy, see M'Connel and Kennedy
Kennedy, James (1406?-1465), bishop, 1696
Kennett, White (1660-1728), 4181
Kensington, see London
Kent, 409; (early), 1523; (medieval), 946, 1039, 1081, 1094; (16th-
    19th cent.), 2604; (16th-17th cent.), 3186; (17th cent.),
    2731, 3199, 4351; (17th-19th cent.), 3385; (17th-18th cent.),
    3952; (18th cent.), 3677; (19th cent.), 4078, 4542, 5172;
    (20th cent.), 5560; north-west, 3408, 5755
Kenya, 6207, 6260; (19th-20th cent.), 6244, 6251; (20th cent.),
    6256, 6261-2, 6270, 6272; northern (19th-20th cent.), 6214
Kerala, kingdom of, 6658
Kesteven, Lincs., 3295, 4354
Ket, Robert (d. 1549), 2662-3
Kettering, Northants., 5752
Khan, Saiyid Muhammad Reza (c. 1717-91), 6604
Khitan empire, 6960
Khuzistan, Iran, 5896
Kidwelly, Carm., 1649
Kiev, Russia, Pechersky monastery, 761-2
Kikuyu, 6208, 6265
Kilkenny, Confederation of, 3281
Kilwardby, Robert (d. 1279), archbishop, 1444
Kimberley, 1st earl of, see Wodehouse, John
Kineton hundred, 474
King, Henry (1592-1667), bishop, 3082
'King William's War' (1688-9), 3887
King's African Rifles, 6241
King's almoner (13th-14th cent.), 896
King's bench, court of (15th cent.), 958
King's lieutenants, in France (14th cent.), 621
King's Lynn, Norfolk, 428, 1583
King's master masons, 1504
King's messenger service (medieval), 893
King's secretary (15th cent.), 907
King's Works (15th-16th cent.), 3109
Kingsbridge, Devon, 394

Labour representation, direct, 4855
Labour unrest (20th cent.), 4857
La Bourdonnais, Mahé, comte de (1699-1753), 1959
Labrador (18th cent.), 7195
Lacy family, 1148-9
Ladies' Sanitary Association, 5310
Lagos, 6367, 6394, 6397, 6405, 6407
Laissez faire, 1792
Laity (14th-16th cent.), 1298
Lajpat Rai (1865-1928), 6817
Lake District, 464, 823, 2826, 4366
Lamb, William (1779-1848), 2nd Viscount Melbourne, 4580
Lambe, Sir John (c. 1566-1646), 3074
Lambert, Francis (1487-1530), 1901
Lambeth, see London
Lambeth Conference (1867), 5415
Lanark, New, 5574
Lanarkshire, 5814
Lancashire, 2552, 3317, 3344, 5011, 5207; (medieval), 921, 950,
    964, 979, 1215; (16th cent.), 2841, 2890, 2941, 2949; (16th-
    17th cent.), 2897, 2906, 2975, 3024; (17th cent.), 2749, 3051,
    3196, 4041, 4162; (17th-18th cent.), 3634; (18th cent.), 3933,
    4361; (18th-19th cent.), 3343, 3532, 4257, 4362, 4381; (19th
    cent.), 3839, 4565, 4836, 4847, 5074, 5083, 5232-3, 5248,
    5284, 5286, 5445, 5558, 5644, 5658, 5723-4, 7353; (19th-20th
    cent.), 5541; (20th cent.), 4683, 5612; east, 5204; north,
    369, 1564; north-east, 5264; south, 457, 461, 2586, 5444;
    south-west, 451, 2526
Lancashire and Yorkshire Railway, 5145
Lancashire Public School Association, 5626
Lancaster, duchy of (13th-15th cent.), 1072
Lancaster, 1st duke of, see Henry of Lancaster; earl of, see
    Thomas
Lancaster, house of, 874A
Lancaster, John of, see John of Lancaster
Lancaster, lordship of, in Wales, 1655
Lancaster, shrievalty of (14th cent.), 900
Lancastrian schools, 5573
Land
  capital and rental values of, 5196; in political theory (19th
    cent.), 5186; income from, 2892, 3320; market in (medieval),
    1071; (16th cent.), 2835; sales of (16th-17th cent.), 2805;
    (17th cent.), 2815, 2818, 4047
  in Nyasaland, 6245; in Trinidad, 7453
Land administration, in Australia, 7590; in Iraq, 5917, 6013
Land law, 2483; in Ireland, 5864; in British Guiana, 7465
Land Nationalisation Society, 5209
Land policy, in Australasia, 7573; in Australia, 7574; in East
    Africa Protectorate, 6254; of East India Company, 6591;
    imperial (18th-19th cent.), 3301; in Oudh, 6770; in Queensland,
    7605; in Rhodesia, 6319
Land prices, in New Zealand, 7615
Land reform, 5209; Irish, 5863
Land Restoration League, 5209
Land resumption, in Bengal, 6698
Land revenue, in India, 6618, 6626, 6676, 6684, 6699, 6702
Land settlement, in England (19th-20th cent.), 5213
Land systems, of Isle of Man, 502; in the Punjab, 6752; in south
    India (medieval), 6514
Land tax (1412), 1094; (17th-18th cent.), 3926; (18th-19th cent.),
    4066-7
Land tenure, 498; (medieval), 1024-44 passim; Babylonian, 5883-4;
    Maori, 7578
Land use, 460, 480, 2504; (medieval), 474; (17th-20th cent.),
    3400-45 passim; (17th-19th cent.), 4041-79 passim; (19th-20th
    cent.), 5168-218 passim; in Ireland, 511, 513; in Wales, 491;
    in France, 1969, 2032

Landed interest, 4006

Landownership, 491; in England (medieval), 1045-99 <u>passim</u>; in England and Wales (17th-20th cent.), 3400-45 <u>passim</u>; (17th-19th cent.), 4041-79 <u>passim</u>; (18th-19th cent.), 3320; (19th-20th cent.), 5168-218 <u>passim</u>; in Italy (medieval), 560; <u>see also</u> Estates and estate management

Landowning classes (16th-17th cent.), 2834; (18th-19th cent.), 4069; (19th cent.), 5207

Landscape parks, gardens, 3401-2

Lanfranc (d. 1089), archbishop, 1196, 1420

Langley, Thomas (d. 1437), bishop, 1320

Langton, Stephen (d. 1228), archbishop, 1220-2, 1423

Langton, Walter (d. 1321), bishop, 1256

Lansdowne, Baron, <u>see</u> Granville, George

Lansdowne, 5th marquess of, <u>see</u> Petty-Fitzmaurice, Henry Charles Keith

Laos, 7015

La Plata, viceroyalty of, 7525

La Rochelle, France, 1915

la Salle, St. Jean Baptiste de (1651-1719), 1946, 4310

La Salle Brothers (Brothers of the Christian Schools), 1946, 4310, 7081

Lasco, John a (1499-1560), 2935

Lateran decrees, enforcement of, 1399

Latimer, Hugh (1485?-1555), bishop, 2888

Latin America, 7507-69

Latitudinarians, 4138

Latvia (20th cent.), 2186

Laud, William (1573-1645), archbishop, 3070-2

Lauderdale, 1st duke of, <u>see</u> Maitland, John

Laudian party, 4155

Laurier, Sir Wilfrid (1841-1919), 4779

Lavernock, Glam., 5552

Law, Edward (1790-1871), 1st earl of Ellenborough, 6736

Law, William (1686-1761), 4220

Law (medieval), 920-60; (19th-20th cent.), 4634; common (16th cent.), 2637; homicide, 2479; private, 2478; relating to charities, 5220; relating to children, 5219; in Ireland (medieval), 1715; in Malawi, 6238; in Nigeria, 6426; Roman, 682-3; of Southern Rhodesia, 6317

  <u>see also</u> Commercial law; Criminal law; International law; Land law; Succession, law of; Welsh laws

Law and order, in England (13th cent.), 930; in ancient Rome, 193

Law courts, <u>see</u> Courts

Law reporting (16th cent.), 2636

Lawrence, John Laird Mair (1811-79), 1st Baron Lawrence, 6971

Lay, Horatio Nelson (fl. 1849-65), 7096

Lay preaching (16th-18th cent.), 2551; Methodist, in Scotland (18th cent.), 4435

Lay subsidy (1332), 1019; (1524/5), 2884

Layard, Sir Austen Henry (1817-94), 6017

Lea valley, 5751

Lead mining, lead industry, 2529, 3320, 3341-2; in Wales, 2530-1, 3993-4; in Roman empire, 253

League of Nations, 1739, 1741-2, 4808

Learning (medieval), 1410-77 <u>passim</u>; revival of, in Byzantium, 525, 528

Leasehold tenure (17th cent.), 4041; (19th cent.), 5291

Leather industry, 2536-8

Lebanon, 6000-1, 6009, 6050

Le Bon, Gustave (1841-1931), 1801

Lecale, barony of, co. Down, 4457

Leckwith, Glam., 5552

Leclerc, Jean (1657-1736), 1940

Leeds, W.R. Yorks., 442; (18th cent.), 4312; (18th-19th cent.), 3332, 3484, 3961; (19th cent.), 4553, 5254, 5427; (19th-20th cent.), 5332; city council, 5765

Leet jurisdiction, 922
Leeward Islands, 7424, 7449, 7488
Left-wing movement, 4818, 4860-1; in India, 6867; in the U.S.A.,
    7411
Legal costume, 636
Legal profession (15th-16th cent.), 2635; (16th cent.), 2636
Legal relations, British, with Hanover (18th-19th cent.), 2119
Legal system, institutions, in China, 7066; in Jamaica, 7427; in
    Lagos, 6394; in Malawi, 6238
Leghorn, Italy, 2237
Legislation
    administrative, 4587; against Catholics, 2620, 3020, 3023, 3055;
        colonial, 4721; educational, 5515, 5584; factory, 3752, 4939,
        4945, 4960; housing, 5294; labour, 1810; lunacy, 3458; mining,
        5063; on monopolies, 4959; moral, 3091; social, 5237, 5336,
        5343; see also Law
    in East Africa Protectorate, 6254; French (18th cent.), 2008;
        in ancient Rome, 197, 241; Visigothic, 555
Legislative commission, Russian (1767), 2330
Legitimism, French (19th cent.), 2062
Leicester, 1115, 3354, 4505, 4974; (medieval), 1549; (17th-19th
    cent.), 4357; (17th-18th cent.), 4346; (19th-20th cent.),
    4948; (20th cent.), 4688
Leicester, earls of, see Simon de Montfort; Dudley, Robert
Leicester, honor of, 1548
Leicestershire, 2524, 2579, 4504; (medieval), 969, 1044, 1088,
    1556; (15th-17th cent.), 2820; (16th cent.), 2950; (16th-17th
    cent.), 2991; (17th-18th cent.), 3466, 3597; (18th-20th cent.),
    3293; (18th-19th cent.), 3423, 4237; (19th cent.), 5197, 5365;
    (19th-20th cent.), 4511
Leighton, Robert (1611-84), archbishop, 4395
Leintwardine area, Herefs., 480
Leith, 4417
Leith, Concordat of (1572), 3218
Leng, Sir William Christopher (1825-1902), 4602
Lenin, Vladimir Ilyich (1870-1924), 2382
Lennox, Charles (1735-1806), 3rd duke of Richmond, 3712
Lépine, Stanislas (1836-92), 2064
Letter-books, ecclesiastical (13th cent.), 1230-1
Lettere Storiche, Le (Luigi da Porto's), 80
Letters describing the Character and Customs of the English and
    French Nations (Muralt's), 1956
Lettice Dykes Educational Charity, 2566
Leucosia, Cyprus, 2298
Levant (early), 134
Levant Company, 5969-71, 5986-7
Levellers, 2756-9
Leveson-Gower, Granville George (1815-91), 2nd Earl Granville,
    2292
Leveson-Gower family, 4052
Lewes, Sussex, 3695
Lewis, William Thomas (1837-1914), 1st Baron Merthyr, 5005
Lewisham, see London
Leyland hundred, 1539
Li Hsiu-ch'eng (c. 1825-1864), 7114
Libanius (314-93), 519-20
Liber Responsalis, 1344
Liberal movement, liberalism, 3740, 4575, 4636, 4642, 4858; in
    France, 2040A; in Germany, 2167; in the U.S.A., 4858
Liberal party (19th cent.), 4604-5, 4622, 4643-4, 4663, 6028;
    (19th-20th cent.), 4591, 4606, 4658, 4775, 4777, 5335; (20th
    cent.), 4678-9, 4687, 4696-9, 4794, 6333; in Scotland (19th
    cent.), 5818
Liberal Unionist party, 4664
Liberals (19th cent.), 4765-6, 5863; (19th-20th cent.), 4776,
    5331; (20th cent.), 4796
Liberated Africans, 6366-7

Liberation movement, Russian, 2368
Liberation Society, 5358
Liberia, 6069, 6368, 6393
Libertas, idea of, in ancient Rome, 206
Libraries (16th–17th cent.), 3127; (17th cent.), 3155; circulating
    (18th cent.), 4298; public, 5485; in Scotland, 5778–9
Libya, western (20th cent.), 6190
Libyans (early), 6099
Lichfield cathedral, Staffs., 1274; see also Coventry and Lichfield
Lidgett, John Scott (1854–1953), 5511
Liège, Belgium, 669
Life of Alfred (Asser's), 1415
Lightfoot, Joseph Barber (1828–89), 5410
Ligue (1576), 1913
Lilburne, John (1614?–1657), 2759
Limoges, France, 1975
Lincoln, 3550, 5719; cathedral, 1223–4, 1317
Lincoln, archdeaconry of, 2940
Lincoln, diocese of, 1318, 1323, 2918, 2957, 4160
Lincolnshire, 429, 4201, 5090; (medieval), 952, 1027, 1049, 1555;
    (16th cent.), 2951; (16th–18th cent.), 2508; (19th cent.),
    4567; (20th cent.), 5344; south, 3176, 3445; Holland Division,
    2914
Lindsey, 898, 2507, 3430, 4048
Linen textile industry, 7367
Lingard, John (1771–1851), 103
Lintot, Bernard (1698–1758), 4000
Lippe, 2115
Lisbon, Portugal: earthquake (1755), 2449; inquisition, 3225
Lisieux, France, diocese of (18th cent.), 1991
Lisle, Viscount, see Plantagenet, Arthur
Lister, Philip Cunliffe-, see Cunliffe-Lister
Literacy (medieval), 789; (16th–17th cent.), 2881; (19th cent.),
    5273; in Ghana, 6431
Literary life (medieval), 788
Liturgia Sacra (Poullain's), 2110
Liturgy (medieval), 768, 1316; (17th cent.), 4128; reform of, by
    Charlemagne, 698
Liverpool (18th cent.), 3966, 3973, 4312, 4369–70; (18th–20th
    cent.), 3490; (18th–19th cent.), 3972, 4371, 7456; (19th
    cent.), 3974, 5113, 5225, 5299, 5309, 5321, 7317; (19th–20th
    cent.), 4646, 5008; (20th cent.), 4704, 5376; constituency,
    4565; Corporate Estate, 5225; Corporation schools, 5576
Liverpool, 1st earl of, see Jenkinson, Charles; 2nd earl of, see
    Jenkinson, Robert Banks
Livery companies, in Ireland (19th cent.), 5827
Lives (Plutarch's), 19–23, 177
Livestock, in Ireland, 5852; marketing of (17th cent.), 3956
Living standards, middle-class, 5285; rural, 5324
Livingstonia Mission, 6228
Livy (Titus Livius) (59 B.C. – 17 A.D.), 17, 198
Llandaff, see Book of Llandaff
Llandaff, diocese of, 2939, 2952, 2987, 3029, 5386
Llandough juxta Penarth, Glam., 5552
Llanelly, Carm., 5066
Llanwonno, Glam., 5609
Llewelyn Bren (d. 1317), 1652
Lloyd-George, 1st Earl, see George, David Lloyd
Llwchwr valley, 3329
Llyfr Coch Asaph, 1621
Llynan, Caern., 4243
Llywelyn ab Rhys, see Llewelyn Bren
Loanga coast, 6345
Loans, British, to China, 7111
Local councils, of Roman Africa, 320
Local government, 2592, 2597; (medieval), 1518–89 passim; (15th–
    17th cent.), 3169–208 passim; (17th–20th cent.), 3536–53

Local government (<u>cont.</u>)
  <u>passim</u>; (17th-19th cent.), 4340-83 <u>passim</u>; (19th cent.), 5731,
    5733, 5742; (19th-20th cent.), 5440, 5753, 5758, 5764; <u>see</u>
    <u>also</u> Parish government
  in Ireland (17th-19th cent.), 4456-89 <u>passim</u>; in Wales, 2598,
    2602, <u>and see entry above</u>
  African, 6256; in American colonies, 7177; in Assam, 6977; in
    British Guiana, 7498; in Burma, 6452; in France (medieval),
    567; (18th cent.), 1949; in India, 6452, 6754, 6756, 6814;
    in Sierra Leone, 6433; in the U.S.A., 7373
Locarno treaties (1924-5), 4813
Loch, James (1780-1855), 5781
Locke, John (1632-1704), 1927, 3627, 3855-8, 4286
Locke, Richard (fl. 1795-1805), 3743
Lodi dynasty, 2219
Loharas, 6524
Lollardy, 1293-5, 1323, 2929; in Scotland, 3215
London, 3500; (medieval), 869, 882, 921, 981, 1013, 1111, 1113,
    1135, 1565-7, 1584, 2928; (14th-16th cent.), 1298; (15th-16th
    cent.), 3159; (16th cent.), 2854-5, 2858, 2864, 2866, 2886,
    2929, 2948, 2970; (16th-17th cent.), 2878, 2898, 2901, 2989;
    (17th cent.), 2764, 2812, 2850, 2870-1, 3194, 3200, 3207-8,
    3272, 3956, 4348-9; (17th-18th cent.), 3963; (18th cent.),
    3703, 4004, 4027, 4060, 4111; (18th-19th cent.), 3306, 3459,
    3937, 4006; (19th cent.), 4383, 4824-6, 5047, 5279-80, 5291,
    5294, 5384, 5476, 5573, 5581, 5663, 5688, 5706, 5827; (19th-
    20th cent.), 4653, 5036, 5056, 5069, 5244, 5297, 5602, 5606,
    5689, 5697, 7606; (20th cent.), 4922, 5122, 5561, 5638-9;
    north-east, 3551, 4951; south-east, 4952, 5139; south-west,
    4953
  Aldgate, Holy Trinity priory, 2948; Battersea, 2559, 5742;
    Bermondsey, 4952; Blackfriars bridge, 4359; Clerkenwell
    nunnery, 1379; Deptford, 411, 2779; East End, 4958, 5770;
    Hackney, 1554; Hammersmith, St. Mary's College, 5627; Isling-
    ton, 4030; Kensington, 5744; Lambeth, 5292, 5742; Lewisham,
    5602; Marylebone, 4030, 4356; Regent's Park, 413; St. Paul's
    cathedral, 1216; St. Stephen's, Coleman St., 2706; St. Clement
    Danes Holborn Estate grammar school, 2572; Southwark, 60,
    2928, 4952; suburbs, 5741, 5743; Tyburn, 413; University,
    5647; Wandsworth, 5742; Whitechapel, 1554
London, Conference of (1828-31), 2212
London, see of (15th cent.), 1319
London and Birmingham Railway, 5148
London basin, 5183
London Lead Company, 3993
<u>London Magazine</u>, 4325
London Missionary Society, 5377, 6282, 6314
London Transport Board, 5140
Londonderry, 3272
Londonderry, co., 5824-6
Long, James (1814-87), 6733
Long Parliament, 2724-6, 2748
Longland, John (1473-1547), 2957
Longley, Charles Thomas (1794-1868), archbishop, 5403
Lonsdale, 4933
Lopez de Ayala, Pedro (1332-1407), 71-2
Lord chancellor (17th cent.), 2693
Lord lieutenant, in Ireland (18th cent.), 4472
Lords, house of (16th-17th cent.), 2668; (17th cent.), 2701, 2765,
    3600; (17th-18th cent.), 3638; (19th cent.), 4583, 4626, 4644
Lotharingia, 561
Loughborough, Leics., 2568, 5720; Burton Charity, 2568; grammar
    school, 2568
Loughborough, 1st Baron, <u>see</u> Wedderburn, Alexander
Louis IV (1287-1347), Holy Roman emperor, 752
Louis IX, <u>Saint</u> (1215-71), king of France, 543, 727
Louis XIV (1638-1715), king of France, 1931-5

Madras, 6587; (18th cent.), 6597, 6636; (18th-19th cent.), 6617, 6650; (19th cent.), 6665, 6680, 6782, 6819; (19th-20th cent.), 6747, 6754
Magadha kingdom, 6488, 6505
Magazines, 4416, 5224
Magic, 2540
Magna Carta, in political thought, 3851
Maha Mongkut, ruler of Siam (1851-68), 7016
Maharashtra, kingdom of, 6491
Mahāvamsa, 6886
Mahdi (Mohammed Ahmed) (1844-85), 6189
Mahdist revolution (1881-5), 6157
Mahmúd of Ghazna (971?-1030), Afghan emperor, 6521
Mahrattas, 6584, 6623
Maidstone, Kent, 412
Maine, Sir Henry James Sumner (1822-88), 4749
Maintenon, Françoise d'Aubigné, marquise de (1635-1719), 1941-3
Mainz, Electorate of (18th cent.), 2120
Maitland, John (1616-82), 1st duke of Lauderdale, 4393-4
Maitland, Sir Thomas (1759-1824), 2209, 2307
Major-generals (17th cent.), 2767
Makerfield district, Lancs., 452
Malabar, 6600
Malatesta family, 661
Malawi, 6228, 6238-40
Malaya, Malay peninsula, 4758, 6722, 6982-7046 passim
Malmesbury, 3rd earl of, see Harris, James Howard
Malplaquet campaign (1709-11), 3894
Malta (16th-18th cent.), 2295-7; (19th cent.), 2308-9; (19th-20th cent.), 2302; Royal University, 2299
Maltese Islands (19th-20th cent.), 2303
Malvern Hills, 467
Malwa, India, 6515-16
Mamluks, 5951, 6113, 6115
Man, Isle of, 502
Managerialism, in the U.S.A., 7378
Manasā, cult of, 6463
Manchester, 462, 4323, 4629; (18th cent.), 4312; (19th cent.), 3841, 4585, 5571, 5658; (19th-20th cent.), 4606, 5009, 5159, 5671; (20th cent.), 4968; Free School, 5626; Victoria Park, 5271
Manchester School (political organisation), 4897
Manchuria, 7125, 7142
Manchurian question, 1741-2, 7159-60
Mandate of heaven, concept of, 7065
Mandates, in Iraq, 6044; in Middle East, 6045; in Palestine, 6047
Manichaeans, see Neo-Manichaean heresy
Manila, 6993, 7518
Manitoba, 7192
Manning, Henry Edward (1808-92), 5464
Manning constitution, of Ceylon, 6938
Manor, in Gower (17th cent.), 4340
Manor-houses, fortified, 1517
Manorial system, decay of (15th cent.), 1582
'Manorial' system, German, 640
Manors, administration of, 1045-99 passim
Mansell family, 2875
Mansfield, Notts., 3549, 5756
Mantua, Italy, 589
Manuel II Palaeologos (d. 1425), Byzantine emperor, 549
Maoris, 7578, 7595
Mapledurham, Oxon., 4059
Maps, mapping, see Cartography
Maqrizi (1364-1442), 49
March, 1st earl of, see Mortimer, Roger
Marchland, Welsh (19th-20th cent.), 4530
Marchmont, Berwicks., 4430

Marcus Antonius (83?-30 B.C.), 210
Marcus Aurelius (121-80), Roman emperor, 292
Margam, Glam., 2875
Margaret, Saint (d. 1093), queen of Scotland, 1670
Margarit y Pau, Juan de (1421-84), cardinal, 740
Margary affair, 7117
Marie Antoinette (1755-93), queen of Louis XVI, 2000
Marie de Lorraine, see Mary of Guise
Maritime activity (16th-17th cent.), 2774, 2777
Maritime power, see Sea power
Maritime rights, belligerent, 4740
Marius, Gaius (155-86 B.C.), 21
Market gardening, 5191-3
Market towns, of Sussex, 2596
Markets, see Fairs and markets
Marlborough, Wilts.: grammar school, 2571; St. John Baptist
    hospital, 2571
Marlowe, Christopher (1564-93), 3141
Maronites, 5952
Marprelate controversy, 3038
Marriage, 2548-9, 3446-7; (17th cent.), 4081; (19th cent.), 5285;
    in ancient India, 6455-6; in Norway (18th-19th cent.), 2400;
    St. Augustine's treatises on, 687
Married women's property controversy, 5288
Mars, cult of, 273-4
Marsden, Samuel (1764-1838), 7621
Marseille, France, 1788, 2021
Marshal, Richard, see Richard Marshal
Marshland, 3406, 3409; see also Drainage and reclamation
Marsilius of Padua (1270-1342), 577-9, 586
Marten, Henry (1602-80), 2725
Martin V (d. 1431), pope, 754
Martinelli, Vincenzo (1702-76), 4111
Martov, Julius (1873-1923), 2362
Martyr, Peter (1457-1526), 2930
Marvell, Andrew (1621-78), 3604
Marwānidi dynasty, 40
Marx, Karl (1818-83), 4843
Marxism, 'legal', in Russia, 2357
Mary II (1662-94), queen, 3644
Mary, of Guise (1515-60), queen of James V of Scotland, 3211
Mary, queen of Scots (1542-87), 3240
Mary legends (12th cent.), 1209
Maryland, colonial, 7287
Marylebone, see London
Masaryk, Thomas Garrigue (1850-1937), 1865
Mascarene Islands, 6944
Masons, king's master, 1504
Mass behaviour, theory of, 1801
Massachusetts, U.S.A., 7269, 7328
Massachusetts system, 5500
Massawah, Eritrea, 6170
Materialism, in France (18th cent.), 1968
Mathematical schools (17th-18th cent.), 4283
Mathematics (medieval), 1412; (16th-17th cent.), 3121; (17th
    cent.), 4284; Chinese, 7048
Matlock, Derbys., 5722
Matthew Paris (d. 1259), 61, 1372
Mauretania Caesariensis, 322
Mauretania Tingitana, 321
Maurice, Frederick Denison (1805-72), 5397
Mauritania, Southern, 6348
Mauritius, 3804, 4797, 6721, 6944-53 passim
Mauryas, 6470-1
Maxentius, Roman emperor (306-12), 227
Maxim the Greek (d. 1556), 2319
Maximilian (1459-1519), Holy Roman emperor, 3162

Maximilian (1832-67), emperor of Mexico, 7553
Maximus (d. 388), Roman emperor, 387
May, John, see Mey
Mayo, 6th earl of, see Bourke, Richard Southwell
Mbundu people, 6340
Meat market (20th cent.), 5110
Meaux abbey, E.R. Yorks., 1357
Mechanical engineering industry, 3353
Mechanics' Institutes, 5657-8, 5660
Mechanisation, in coal mines, 5097
Mecklenburg (18th cent.), 2116
Medical profession (18th cent.), 4101; (18th-19th cent.), 3464;
    (19th-20th cent.), 5325; in the Roman empire, 255
Medical services, of poor law, 5263
Medici, Cosimo de (1389-1464), 602
Medici, Lorenzo de (1448-92), 603
Medicine, 4098; (16th-17th cent.), 2878; (18th-19th cent.), 3464;
    in Wales (18th cent.), 4099; Arab (medieval), 642; Greek
    (ancient), 160; Jewish (16th cent.), 1765; Roman (ancient),
    242
Mediterranean region, 1748; (early), 117; (15th-16th cent.), 670;
    (18th cent.), 2301; (19th cent.), 2304
Medway towns, 410
Meeting-house, dissenting, 3487
Mehemet Ali (1769-1849), 6128, 6138-40
Mekong river, Indochina, 7039
Melbourne, 2nd Viscount, see Lamb, William
Melchett, 1st Baron, see Mond, Alfred Moritz
Melton, William (d. 1340), archbishop, 1016, 1280
Melton Mowbray, Leics., 2593
Melville, 1st Viscount, see Dundas, Henry
Melzi d'Eril, Francesco (1752-1816), 2248
Memoirs of the reign of King George III (Walpole's), 3706
Mendicant orders, 1437; see also Friars
Mendoza, Bernardino de (c. 1540-1604), 2424
Menelik II (1844-1913), emperor of Ethiopia, 6146
mens rea, in law of homicide, 2479
Mentally deficient children, 5584
Mercantile interests (18th cent.), 3671, 3703
Mercenaries (13th cent.), 990; Scottish (16th-17th cent.), 3237
Mercersburg movement, 7342
Merchant Adventurers, 2856
Merchant service, 4985, 5116, 5161-2
Merchants, English (medieval), 1116, 1123, 1128-9, 1135, 1140,
    1549; (16th-17th cent.), 2858-9, 2867, 2871, 5968; (18th
    cent.), 5984, 7291, 7440, 7456; (18th-19th cent.), 3961;
    (19th cent.), 5113; Scottish (medieval), 652; foreign, in
    medieval England, 1130-1; Italian (medieval), 1120; Spanish,
    in Mexico, 7524
Mercia, 821, 1033
Mercoeur, Philippe-Emmanuel de Lorraine, duc de (1558-1602), 1913
Mergers, industrial, in Canada, 7245
Merioneth, 498, 3352, 3427; (16th-17th cent.), 2602; (17th-19th
    cent.), 4049; (18th cent.), 4364; (18th-19th cent.), 3970
Merseyside, 4605
Merthyr, 1st Baron, see Lewis, William Thomas
Merthyr Tydfil, Glam., 5262, 5311
Merton priory, Surrey, 60
Mesopotamia, see Iraq
Metallurgy, metal industry, 2527, 2532; in Israel (early), 5888
Metalwork, Anglo-Saxon, 1493; Celtic, 1480; see also Ironwork
Metcalfe, Charles Theophilus (1785-1846), 1st Baron Metcalfe,
    6683
Methodist Missionary Society, 6380
Methodists, Methodist movement, 4195-258 passim, 5423-57 passim;
    and see 3474, 3488, 3491, 4171; (18th-19th cent.), 3489, 3495,
    4139-40; (19th cent.), 5349, 5563, 5615; (19th-20th cent.),

Methodists, Methodist movement (cont.)
5583; (20th cent.), 5022; in Ireland, 3586-7; in Scotland,
4435; in Wales, 4227-30; in Ceylon, 6915; world, 1730; see
also Primitive Methodism; Wesleyan Methodism
Metropolitan Asylums Board, 5303
Metternich, Clemens Wenzel Nepomuk Lothan, Prince von (1773-1859),
1843
Mewar, India, 6490
Mexican Revolution (1910-14), 7565
Mexico, 7537; (18th cent.), 7518; (18th-19th cent.), 7524; (19th
cent.), 7532, 7543, 7551, 7553; (20th cent.), 7567
Mey, John (d. 1456), 1718
Michael VII Ducas, Byzantine emperor (1071-8), 533
Michoacan state, Mexico, 7567
Middle classes, 4825, 5285, 7374; in Scotland, 5798
Middle East, 5883-6005 passim
Middleham, lordship of, 1587
Middlesbrough, N.R. Yorks., 5293, 5730
Middlesex, 2496; (11th cent.), 1034; (17th cent.), 3204; (17th-
18th cent.), 4053, 4353; (18th-19th cent.), 4375; (19th cent.),
5573; (19th-20th cent.), 5702
Middleton, Charles (1726-1813), 1st Baron Barham, 3907
Middlewich, Ches., 4343
Midhurst, Sussex, 3695
Midlands, 2533, 2536; (medieval), 1500; (17th cent.), 3982; (17th-
18th cent.), 3990; (18th cent.), 3991, 4011; east, 1496, 3308,
5133-4; north-east, 5199; south-east, 466, 5035; west, 3372,
3386, 3438, 3701, 4378
Migration
British, 4122, 4977; to America, 4518; to Australia, 7586, 7588,
7602; to the Dominions, 4537; to New Zealand, 7594; to South
Africa, 6292; to the U.S.A., 7324, 7336-8, 7374; English, to
New England (17th cent.), 7260-1
Irish, 5853; to colonial America, 7272; to England and Wales,
5244-5, 5829-30
Scottish, to Nova Scotia, 4429; to the U.S.A., 7323
Welsh, to the U.S.A., 7310
Indian, 4725, and see Indian migrant labour; Jewish, 5331, 6021;
Maltese, 2309
in England and Wales, 4119, 4514, 4532, 5211, 5324; in Ireland,
5848; in Scotland, 3567; in central Africa, 6237; in Dalmatia
(Roman), 299; in western Libya, 6190; among Luo peoples, 6205;
in the Sudan, 6104; in Tunisia, 6070
to Britain, 5331-3, 5348; to the Argentine, 7556; to British
Guiana, 7477; to British North America, 7209; to colonial
America, 7272; to New England, 7260-1; to Nova Scotia, 4429;
to Palestine, 6021; to Trinidad, 7453, 7477, 7496; to Uganda,
6259; to the U.S.A. (19th cent.), 7310, 7323-5, 7336-8, 7374;
(19th-20th cent.), 7329; (20th cent.), 7397
Mikhailovsky, Nicolas Konstantinovitch (1842-1904), 2348
Milan, Italy (11th cent.), 563; (19th-20th cent.), 2262
Milanese insurrection (1848), 2252
Milburga, Saint (d. 722?), 1342
Miles Platting, Manchester, 5401
Miletus, 149
Milford, Pemb., 3379
Military activity, English royal (medieval), 991, 994, 998; in
Wales (medieval), 1629-30; Roman, in Britain, 367, 371, 382,
384
Military administration, see Administration, military
Military attachés, British and German, 2145
Military conversations (20th cent.), 1811
Military expeditions (16th-17th cent.), 2789; (18th-19th cent.),
6999
Military expenditure, colonial, 4748
Military forces, see Army
Military obligations (16th cent.), 2775-6

414

Military opinion (20th cent.), 7136
Military organisation (medieval), 534, 988-90, 993, 997; (16th-
    17th cent.), 2781; of the Khitan empire, 6960; of the Mahrattas,
    6584
Military planning (20th cent.), 2168
Military policy and strategy (19th cent.), 4807, 6690, 6804; (19th-
    20th cent.), 6159; in Scotland (medieval), 1678; in France
    (20th cent.), 2103; of the U.S.A., 7358-9
Military service (20th cent.), 4880-1
Military supplies, see Supplies, military
Military terms (12th cent.), 987
Militia, Canadian, 7242
Mill-Hill Fathers, 6255
Milling, flour, 4026; in antiquity, 122
Milne, Sir Alexander (1806-96), 7183
Milyukov, Paul (1857-1943), 2386
Mine Adventurers of England, 3995
Miners and mining, 2528, 3343, 3980; (16th cent.), 2826; (16th-
    17th cent.), 2527; (19th cent.), 5053, 5063, 5065; overseas,
    4915; in Spain (ancient), 125; see also Coal mining; Copper
    mining; Iron ore mining; Lead mining; Silver mining
Miner's bond, 4975
Mines inspectorate, 5064-5
Minims, order of, 1919
Ministerial inquiries (medieval), 850, 863
Ministers, African Christian, 6383; Huguenot, in Ireland, 4466;
    Scottish (16th-17th cent.), 3232
Minorca, 2305
Minoresses, order of, 1386
Minorities, in southern Asia, 6866
Minstrels, 1175
Mint, Islamic (medieval), 5914
Minto, 1st earl of, see Elliot, Sir Gilbert; 4th earl of, see
    Elliot, Gilbert John Murray Kynynmond
Mir Jafar Khan (1691-1765), 6611
Mir Qamaruddin Nizam ul Mulk Asaf Jah I, nizam of Hyderabad
    (1724-48), 6599
Mirabeau, Honoré Gabriel Riquetti, comte de (1749-91), 1985, 2007
Miracles, 1209; controversy about (17th-18th cent.), 4134
'Mirror of fools', 713
Miskawaih (951-79), 36
misr, 5918
Missal (12th cent.), 797
Mission schools, 6653, 7008
Missionaries, recruitment of, 7478
Missions, Christian, 5377; in Africa, 6058-401 passim; in Ceylon,
    6907-8, 6924-5; in China, 7080-1; in India, 6651-8, 6718,
    6732-4, 6759, 6772, 6809; in Jamaica, 7441-2, 7478; in
    Madagascar, 6224; in Malaya, 7008; to the Muslims, 6446; in
    New Zealand, 7580; in the south-west Pacific, 7622
Mitcham, Surrey, 5605
Mithila, 6505
Mitre, Bartolomé (1821-1906), 7548
Mixed-monarchy debate, 2745
Moderatism, in Church of Scotland, 4432-3
Modernist crisis, 5375
Modijeras, Christian attitudes to, 580
Modus Tenendi Parliamentum, 966
Moffat, Robert (1795-1883), 6291
Mohair manufacture, 1727
Mohammad V, sultan of Granada (14th cent.), 587
Moiun, barony of, 1036
Mole basin, 3434
Monarchy (medieval), 562; limited (16th cent.), 3242; mixed (17th
    cent.), 2745; French, 1915-2052 passim; Sicilian (12th cent.),
    714; Spanish (15th cent.), 604
    see also Crown; Habsburg monarchy

Monasteries, monasticism, 756-75 <u>passim</u>, 780; in England, 1329-95;
    in Ireland, 1706; in Scotland, 1671, 1673; in Wales, 1601;
    Norman, 763, 1334
Monasteries, dissolution of, <u>see</u> Religious houses, suppression of
Monastic lands and property, disposal of, 2946, 2948-50, 2952,
    2954, 2956; in Wales, 2831
Mond, <u>see</u> Brunner, Mond & Co.
Mond, Alfred Moritz (1868-1930), 1st Baron Melchett, 4689
Monetary experience, of Ceylon, 6917
Monetary policy (early), 116; British international (20th cent.),
    4930; in the Netherlands (15th cent.), 672
Monetary reconstruction, in Czechoslovakia, 1879
Monetary reform (1821), 3943
Money (early), 116; paper, 3925; theory of (17th-18th cent.),
    1721; <u>see also</u> Coinage and currency
Money market (18th-19th cent.), 3937; (20th cent.), 4922
Money stock, Canadian, 7232
Moneyers, Anglo-Saxon, 1003
Mongols, 44, 5956, 7057-8, 7064
Monmouth boroughs, 2490
Monmouth rebellion (1685), 3633
Monmouthshire, 2490, 2576, 2592; (17th cent.), 2738, 2749; (18th-
    20th cent.), 3391; (18th-19th cent.), 3971; (19th cent.),
    4570; (19th-20th cent.), 5081, 5258, 5608; south-east, 496
Monmouthshire and South Wales Coal Owners' Association, 5081
Monopolies (16th-17th cent.), 2862; (17th cent.), 2806, 2811;
    (19th-20th cent.), 4959
Mont St. Michel abbey, France, 784
Montacute, Richard, <u>see</u> Montague
Montagne, in French Revolution, 2022
Montagu, John (1718-92), 4th earl of Sandwich, 3786, 3901
Montague, Richard (1575-1641), bishop, 3078
Montague, William (1301-44), 1st earl of Salisbury, 1159
Montenegro, and Britain (19th cent.), 1842
Montesquieu, Charles de Secondat, marquis de (1689-1755), 1957,
    7296
Montfort, John de, <u>see</u> Jean IV, duke of Brittany
Montfort, Simon de, <u>see</u> Simon de Montfort
Montgomerie, Sir James (d. 1694), 4388
Montgomery, lordship of, 1617
Montgomeryshire, 4934, 5554, 5635
Mont-Tonnerre, department of (19th cent.), 2033
<u>Monumentum Ancyranum</u>, 212
Monymusk, Aberdeenshire, 3573
Moor, Sir Ralph Denham Rayment (1806-1909), 6430
'Moral revolution', in France (20th cent.), 2103
Moravians, 4221, 4234-5; in Ireland, 4478
Moray, Sir Robert (1608-73), 3259
More, Hannah (1745-1833), 4313-14
More, Sir Thomas (1478-1535), 2647-8, 2888, 3128-9
Morel, Edmund Dene (1873-1924), 4789
Morgan, Evan (<u>c</u>. 1574-1643), 3046
Morgan, Sir Henry (1635?-1688), 7432
Morgan, Sir Thomas (1604-79), 2800
Morley, John (1838-1923), Viscount Morley, 4600, 4630, 4760
Mormons, 7337
Morocco (17th cent.), 6075; (19th cent.), 6085; (20th cent.),
    6086-93
Morpeth, Northumb., 4380
Mortality, in British peerage, 3446; of clergy (medieval), 1164
Mortimer, Roger (d. 1330), 1st earl of March, 861
Mortimer family, 1604
Morton, John (1420?-1500), cardinal, 2916
Mosaics, Roman, 323, 351
Moseley, Humphrey (d. 1661), 3157
Moshoeshoe I (d. 1870), 6297
Mosquito Shore (18th cent.), 7519-20

Mother Goddess, cult of, 6464
Mount Stephen, 1st Baron, see Stephen, George
Mousket, Philippe (13th cent.), 64
Mowbray family, 1054
Much Wenlock, see Wenlock
Mughal empire, 6552-63, 6583
Muhammad (570-632), 5921
Muhammad bin Tughluq, sultan of Delhi (1325-51), 6539
Muhammad ibn Habîb (d. 860), 33
Mundella, Anthony John (1825-97), 4625
Münejjim Bāshi (d. 1702), 39
Municipal aristocracies, of Roman Africa, 319
Municipal Corporations Act (1835), 4362, 5739-40
Municipal government, see Local government
Munro, Sir Thomas (1761-1827), 6650
Muralt, Béat Louis de (18th cent.), 1956
Murray, Sir James (1751?-1811), 3902
Murray, Sir John (1768?-1827), 5988
Murray, Sir Robert, see Moray
Murshid Qulī Khān (d. 1727), nawab of Bengal, 6595
Murshidabad district, Bengal, 6619
Muscovy (16th cent.), 2319
Muscovy Company, 2322
Musculus, Wolfgang (1497-1563), 2108
Music (medieval), 786; in England (medieval), 1176; (15th-16th
    cent.), 3159; (17th cent.), 3168; in Scotland (18th cent.),
    4415; Arab (medieval), 5915
Muslims, 6107; in Africa, 6056, 6105, 6183, 6349, 6362; in India
    and Pakistan, 6446, 6508, 6530, 6538, 6540, 6565, 6567, 6622,
    6689, 6755-859 passim; in Near East, 6446; in Spain, 32, 554,
    587, 641; see also Arabs; Islam; Modijeras
Mutaoarrifiya, Lebanon, 6009
Mycenean culture, 126
Myddelton, Sir Thomas (1586-1666), 2743
Mysore, 6615, 6669, 6709, 6724, 6815
Mysticism, 736, 1450-2
Mystra, despotate of, 551
Mytilene, 142

NĀDIR SHĀH (1687-1747), king of Iran, 5980
Nagpur, 6685
Nail trade, 4002-3
Nānak (1469-1539), Indian gurū, 6545
Nanking regime, Japanese puppet government in China, 7152
Nannau family, 1605
Nannau Hall, Merioneth, 4049
Nant Ffrancon valley, Caern., 492
Napatan-Meroitic kingdom, 6098
Napier, Sir Charles James (1782-1853), 2210
Naples (ancient), 180; kingdom of (15th cent.), 596
Napoleon Bonaparte (1769-1821), 2035-6
Napoleon III (1808-73), French emperor, 1797, 2059-60, 2067,
    2070-1
Narodnik movement, 2346
Narrative history, 7
Natal, 6298-9, 6326, 6334, 6721
National Association for the Promotion of Social Science, 5300
National Bolshevists, German, 2192
National Education League, 5503
'National efficiency', 4674
National Liberals, German, 2147
National Minority movement, 5028
National revival, Czech (18th-19th cent.), 1840; French (20th
    cent.), 2093
National schools, 5590, 5843
National Socialist party, 2188, 2190, 2196
National Society, 4321, 5589

Neville, Ralph (d. 1244), bishop, 1235
Nevis, Windward Islands, 7438
New Deal, 7411
New England, 1719, 7260-2, 7265, 7270
New Galicia, Mexico, 7509
New Guinea, 7630
New Orleans, U.S.A., 7325
New Science (17th cent.), 4271
New South Wales, 4720, 7574-7, 7585, 7589, 7598, 7613
New Spain, 7521
New Testament criticism, 2218
New York City, U.S.A., 7385
New York State, U.S.A., 7305
New Zealand, 7570-617 passim
New Zealand Company, 7594
Newark, Notts., 3696; area, 434
Newbury, Berks., 5534
Newcastle, 1st duke of, see Pelham-Holles, Sir Thomas; 2nd duke of,
    see Clinton, Henry Fiennes; 4th duke of, see Clinton, Henry
    Pelham Fiennes Pelham; 5th duke of, see Clinton, Henry Pelham
    Fiennes Pelham
Newcastle and Carlisle Railway, 5141
Newcastle Commission (1861), 5499
Newcastle Emlyn, Carm., 1632
Newcastle-under-Lyme, Staffs., 1532
Newcastle-upon-Tyne, Northumb., 1127, 2869, 3201, 4569
Newdigate family, 3989
Newfoundland, 7185-7, 7190, 7195, 7201-2, 7219, 7247
Newman, Henry (fl. 1708-43), 4137
Newman, John Henry (1801-90), cardinal, 5461-3, 5860
Newport, Mon., 3539, 5136, 5608
News (16th-17th cent.), 3139
Newspapers, see Press, newspaper
Nicaean empire, 540
Nice, France, 2071
Nicholas I (1796-1855), tsar of Russia, 2339
Nicolson, William (1655-1727), bishop, 4177
Nicopolis, crusade of (1396), 550
Nicosia, Cyprus, 2298
Nidderdale, W.R. Yorks., 4507
Niger, 6376-7, 6390, 6395, 6416
Nigeria, 6069, 6380-1, 6390, 6401, 6404, 6409-10, 6426, 6439-41;
    Northern, 6420, 6428-9; Southern, 6385, 6417, 6430; western,
    6379, 6434
Nikon (Nikita Minin) (1605-81), patriarch of Moscow, 2324
Nile (19th cent.), 6124, 6177
Nine Power Treaty (1922), 1740
Nishapur, Iran, 5930
Nithsdale, Dumfries., 4453
Nkore, kingdom of, 6206
Nobility (Saxon), 1145; (14th cent.), 1163; (15th-16th cent.),
    1172; Castilian (17th cent.), 2436; Frankish, 1024; French
    (18th cent.), 1950, 1987, 1992; Indian (13th cent.), 6531;
    Piedmontese (18th cent.), 2245; Roman (medieval), 746; Russian
    (18th cent.), 2330; see also Aristocracy; Peerage
Nobility of service, Frankish, 1024
Nola, Italy, 180
Nomads, in Tunisia, 6070
Nonconformity, 3466-95 passim, 4195-258; and see (17th cent.),
    3603; (17th-19th cent.), 3504; (17th-18th cent.), 3853, 4132;
    (18th cent.), 4296; (19th cent.), 2045, 5357, 5551; (19th-20th
    cent.), 5423-57, 5510; in Wales, 4249, 5424, 5452
Nonjurors, 4168
Non-resistance, doctrine of (17th-18th cent.), 3861
Norfolk, 1511, 2517, 3419; (medieval), 972, 1038, 1051, 1305,
    1572; (16th cent.), 2662-3, 2954; (16th-17th cent.), 2518,
    2903; (17th cent.), 2847; (18th-19th cent.), 3454, 3690; (19th
    cent.), 5179; west, 427

Noricum, 337
Normandy, 628-30, 1054, 1148-9
Norrbotten county, Sweden, 2406
Norris, Sir William (1657-1702), 6581
Norsemen, 823, 1594
North, Frederick (1732-92), Lord North, 3719-20
North Africa, see Africa
North America (18th cent.), 3899; (19th-20th cent.), 5356
North Carolina, colonial, 7273
North of England, problem of (16th cent.), 2671
Northampton, 5037, 5759
Northamptonshire, 466; (medieval), 942-4, 968; (16th-18th cent.),
    2505; (16th-17th cent.), 2834, 2896; (17th-19th cent.), 3649;
    (19th-20th cent.), 4499
Northbrook, 1st earl of, see Baring, Thomas George
Northcote, Sir Stafford Henry (1818-87), 1st earl of Iddesleigh,
    4916
North-Eastern Railway, 5131
Northern Ireland, 516, 5855-80 passim
Northern Reform Union, 4844
Northumberland, 449, 4975; (early), 1518; (Saxon), 1486; (16th
    cent.), 2943; (18th-19th cent.), 3320, 3748, 4032; (19th
    cent.), 4848; (19th-20th cent.), 5050, 5477; (20th cent.),
    5031; north, 450
Northumberland, duke of, see Dudley, John; 9th earl of, see
    Percy, Henry
Northumberland, dukes of (19th cent.), 5187
Northumberland, North and South, constituency, 4594
Northumbria, 1187, 1663
Northumbria, earl of, see Waltheof
North-west, Canadian, 7238, 7243
North-West Frontier Province, 6849
Northwest passage, search for (18th cent.), 3896
Northwest Rebellion (1885), 7239
North-Western Provinces and Oudh, see United Provinces
Norway (20th cent.), 2409
Norwich, Norfolk, 981, 3183, 3195, 3362; cathedral priory, 1062
Norwich, diocese of, 1323, 2919, 3089
Notaries, papal (15th cent.), 1409
notarii, Roman imperial, 229
Notary, office of, 956
Notre Dame de Namur, Sisters of, 5494, 5541
Nottingham, 3289, 3310, 3813, 5542A, 5745-6; Catholic diocese,
    5567; High School, 2569
Nottingham, archdeaconry of, 3036, 4159
Nottingham, 2nd earl of, see Finch, Daniel
Nottinghamshire, 435, 5010, 5135; (medieval), 898, 975, 977; (16th
    cent.), 2645; (16th-17th cent.), 2523; (17th-18th cent.),
    3466; (18th cent.), 4360; (18th-19th cent.), 3651; (19th-20th
    cent.), 4515, 5431, 5542, 5682
Nova Scotia, 7184, 7189, 7196, 7204, 7214
Novgorod, Russia, 568, 605
Nubia, Lower, 6106
Nuclear armament, 2306
Numidia (Roman), 318
Numismatic art, Roman, 256
Nuneaton, Warwicks., 5717
Nunneries, 1380, 2953
Nupe kingdom, 6361
Nut and bolt industry, 3372
Nyanza, Kenya, 6233, 6261
Nyasaland, 6226-7, 6237, 6245, 6309

OAKENGATES, Salop, 4500
Oates, Titus (1649-1705), 3622
Oaxaco, Mexico, 7524
Obedientiary rolls, 1338

O'Brien, James Bronterre (1805-64), 4840

Overton, Richard (fl. 1642-63), 2756
Owen, Sir Isambard (1850-1927), 5553
Owen, John (1616-83), 3102
Owen, Robert (1771-1858), 3842, 4942, 5237, 5360, 5574
Oxford, 1505, 1588, 2589, 2752, 3479; region, 2580
Oxford, archdeaconry of, 2545
Oxford, diocese of, 2932, 5405
Oxford, 1st earl of, see Harley, Robert
Oxford Movement, 5399-401, 5625
Oxford University (medieval), 801, 803, 813, 1438, 1441-3, 1458-9,
    1462; (14th-16th cent.), 1510; (15th-16th cent.), 1467; (16th
    cent.), 3125; (16th-17th cent.), 2977; (17th cent.), 3072;
    Brasenose College, 4311; Christ Church, 3126; Corpus Christi
    College, 3127; Merton College, 1089, 1453
Oxfordshire, 4534; (16th-18th cent.), 2509; (16th-17th cent.),
    3021; (17th-19th cent.), 3420; (18th cent.), 3697; (18th-19th
    cent.), 3485; (19th cent.), 4075; west, 5178
Oxwich, Glam., 2875
oyer and terminer, 960

PACIFIC ISLANDS, 7604
Pacific Ocean region, 4758, 7579, 7618-33
Pacifism, see Peace movement
pacta conventa (1573), 1833
Padua, Italy, 575; region, 660
Padua, Marsilius of, see Marsilius
Paeonia, Greece, 166
Paganism, survival of, 1593; see also Heathenism
Pageantry (16th-17th cent.), 3163; see also Public spectacle
Paget, Henry William (1768-1854), 1st marquess of Anglesey, 3778
Pagula, William (d. 1350?), 731
Pahang, 7012, 7026
Pahlen Report (1908-9), 6980
Painted decoration, domestic (16th-17th cent.), 3227
Painting (19th cent.), 5486; in Scotland (14th-17th cent.), 3227;
    theories of (15th-16th cent.), 1754; Tuscan (14th-16th cent.),
    804
Pakistan, 6767, 6774, 6778, 6823, 6859; see also East Pakistan;
    West Pakistan
Pāla empire, 6504
Palatinate, 601, 2114
Paléologue, Maurice (1859-1941), 2095
Palestine (early), 314-16, 5885, 5888, 5892-5, 5897; (3rd cent.),
    5908; (19th cent.), 6002; (19th-20th cent.), 6021; (20th
    cent.), 6033, 6047, 6054-5; see also Judea
Pāli canon, 6466
Pallavicino family, 2241-2
Palm oil trade, 6342
Palmer, William (1811-79), 5353
Palmer Company, 6690
Palmerston, 3rd Viscount, see Temple, Henry John
Pamphlets, news (16th-17th cent.), 3139; royalist (17th cent.),
    2732
Pamphylia, see Lycia and Pamphylia
Pan-African movement, 4784, 6427
Panama, 7341, 7562, 7564
Panama Canal, 7563
Pan-Slavist thought (19th cent.), 2332
Paoli, Pascal (1725-1807), 4112
Papacy (medieval), 542, 577, 714, 741-55; and England, 1396-409
Papal states (18th-19th cent.), 1777
Paper money, 3925
Paper-making industry, 2515, 4018, 5073; in Scotland, 3564; in
    Wales, 5073
Paphlagonia, 123
Papua, 7628
Paraguay, 7507, 7514

Parākramabāhu I of Ceylon (1164-97), 6890
Paramara dynasty, 6515-16
Paris (14th-15th cent.), 594; (18th cent.), 1955, 2005, 2011-12;
    (19th cent.), 2039; university (medieval), 801, 803, 813
Paris, Matthew, see Matthew Paris
Paris, Peace of (1763), 1776
Paris Peace Conference (1919), 1817, 1888-90, 7157; see also
    Versailles, treaty of
Paris Peace Congress and Treaty (1856), 2067, 4741
Parish, in North Riding (17th cent.), 4341; origin of, 1186
Parish clerk, Scottish (medieval), 1697
Parish government, 3538; (14th cent.), 1288; (17th cent.), 3188
Parish life (15th-16th cent.), 1585; (16th cent.), 2944; (16th-
    17th cent.), 3036
Parish overseer, 4082
Parish registers, Bristol, 2557
Parker, Matthew (1504-75), archbishop, 2981-4
Parker Chronicle, 52-3
Parkes, Sir Harry Smith (1828-85), 7113
Parkes, Joseph (1796-1865), 4828
Parkyns, Sir Thomas (1664-1741), 4330
Parlement, of Bordeaux (18th cent.), 1982; of Paris (medieval),
    594; (18th cent.), 1955
Parliament (medieval), 966; (14th cent.), 1020; (15th cent.), 976;
    (1449-50), 985; (1545), 2657; (17th cent.), 2694, 2703; (1640-
    60), 2724-6, 2748; (1659), 2770-1; (17th-18th cent.), 3884;
    (18th cent.), 3652, 3782, 3787-8; (19th cent.), 3750-1, 4550,
    4576, 4617, 4737, 4755, 4757, 5388, 5498; (19th-20th cent.),
    4562, 5633; (20th cent.), 1818; of Ireland (medieval), 1713;
    of Scotland (17th-18th cent.), 4390; see also Commons, house
    of; Lords, house of
  members of (15th cent.), 980; (1422), 984; (1563-7), 2681; (1571),
    2682; (1584-5), 2686; (1586-7), 2687; (1593), 2689; (1597),
    2690; (1601), 2691; (1659), 2771; (17th-18th cent.), 3597;
    (1701), 3648; (1784-90), 3737; see also Parliamentary repre-
    sentation
  opening address (14th-15th cent.), 967
  French (19th-20th cent.), 2078; (20th cent.), 1818, 2092, 2098;
    Polish (20th cent.), 1891
Parliamentarians, French (19th cent.), 2065
Parliamentary constituencies, geographical aspects of (19th-20th
    cent.), 4651; new (1832), 4564
Parliamentary debates (18th cent.), 3650, 3722; (19th cent.), 4662,
    4666; in France (18th cent.), 2006
Parliamentary elections, see Elections, parliamentary
Parliamentary franchise, 4615
Parliamentary government, in Austria, 1871; in Egypt, 6148, 6201;
    in Italy, 2269; in Japan, 7150; in Sweden, 2408
Parliamentary history, of Bristol (18th cent.), 3691; of North
    Wales boroughs, 2491; of Reading (18th-19th cent.), 3299; of
    Tamworth (17th-19th cent.), 3599
Parliamentary opposition, 4680
Parliamentary petitions (medieval), 978, 982
Parliamentary privilege, 4673
Parliamentary reform movement, 3806-43 passim
Parliamentary representation (16th cent.), 2625; (19th-20th cent.),
    4564; of Ireland (19th cent.), 4488; concept of, 3876, 4589
  borough (16th cent.), 2640; of Bristol (15th cent.), 982; of
    Cambridge (17th-19th cent.), 3641; of Durham (17th-19th cent.),
    3620; of Grampound, 2486; of Haverfordwest (16th-18th cent.),
    2488; of Kent (17th cent.), 2731; of London (15th cent.), 982;
    of Manchester (19th cent.), 4585; of Monmouth, 2490; of Newark
    (18th cent.), 3696; of Norwich (15th cent.), 982; of Pembroke,
    2488; of Pontefract (18th cent.), 3696; of East Retford (18th
    cent.), 3696; of Southampton (15th cent.), 982; of Sussex
    (18th cent.), 3695; of Wiltshire (15th cent.), 983; (18th
    cent.), 3693; of York (15th cent.), 982; of Yorkshire (19th
    cent.), 3592

423

Parliamentary representation (cont.)
    county (medieval), 965, 986; of Bedfordshire (medieval), 961,
    971; of Buckinghamshire (medieval), 971; of Cambridgeshire
    (17th-19th cent.), 3641; of Derbyshire (15th cent.), 977;
    (16th cent.), 2645; of Devon (16th cent.), 2676; of Dorset
    (16th cent.), 2676; of Durham (17th-19th cent.), 3620; of
    Essex (medieval), 970; of Glamorgan (16th-19th cent.), 2487;
    of Hertfordshire (medieval), 970; of Kent (18th cent.), 3677;
    of Lancashire (medieval), 964, 979; of Leicestershire (medi-
    eval), 969; of Monmouthshire, 2490; (16th cent.), 2656; (19th
    cent.), 4570; of Norfolk (medieval), 972; of North Wales (18th
    cent.), 3676; of Northamptonshire (medieval), 968; of Notting-
    hamshire (15th cent.), 977; (16th cent.), 2645; of Pembroke-
    shire, 2488; of Radnorshire, 2489; of Rutland (medieval), 968;
    of South Wales (18th-19th cent.), 3746; of Suffolk (medieval),
    972; of Surrey (medieval), 973; of Sussex (medieval), 973;
    (16th cent.), 2646; of Wales (16th cent.), 2656; (19th cent.),
    4570; of Warwickshire (medieval), 969; (17th cent.), 2748; of
    Worcestershire (medieval), 974; of Yorkshire (14th-16th cent.),
    962
Parliamentary surveys (17th cent.), 3204-5
Parliamentary system, of the United Kingdom, deviations of (20th
    cent.), 4690
Parry, William John (1842-1927), 5007
Parsons, Robert (1546-1610), 3017-18
Parthia, 308-9
Particular Baptists, 4240, 4254
Parties, political, 3592-778 passim, 4538-718 passim; and see
    (14th cent.), 869; (18th cent.), 4175; (19th cent.), 4753,
    5497; (19th-20th cent.), 5507; (20th cent.), 5516
  in Athens (ancient), 157; in Austria, 1859; in Bombay Presidency,
    6871; in Canada, 7250; in Egypt, 6148; in France, 2043; in
    Germany, 2181; in Holland, 2290; in Russia, 2363
Party, political, concept of (18th cent.), 3866
Passfield, Baron and Baroness, see Webb, Sidney James and Webb,
    Beatrice
Pastoral custom (medieval), 1105
Pastoral ministry (17th cent.), 3065; in Scotland (17th cent.),
    4387; (18th cent.), 4421
Patañjali, 6474
Paterikon of the Kievan Monastery of Caves, 762
Pathans, 6681
Patriotism, French (medieval), 787
Patronage
  art (16th cent.), 3161; (18th cent.), 4331; by medieval popes,
    810, 819
  ecclesiastical, 1241, 1277-8, 1376; in Scotland, 1683
  educational, 2562, 4268
  political (17th cent.), 2698; (18th-19th cent.), 3742
Paul the Deacon (740-95), 54
Paulus Aemilius of Verona (d. 1529), 78
Pauperism, 2499
Peace, attitudes to (19th cent.), 4732; idea of, in ancient
    Greece, 168
Peace movement (20th cent.), 4790-2, 4805-6
Peace negotiations (1914-17), 2171
Peaceful settlement of disputes, 1747
Peak district, 437, 4498
Pearce, Zachary (1690-1774), bishop, 4180
Peasant agriculture, in Ceylon, 6921
Peasant movement, Russian (20th cent.), 2374
Peasantry (medieval), 1070-1; of Ireland (19th cent.), 5847; of
    Russia, 2354, 2375, 2387
Peckham, John (d. 1292), archbishop, 1245-8
Pecock, Reginald (1395?-1460?), bishop, 1309
peculium, of Roman slave, 245
Pedro (1334-69), king of Castile, 71

Petrucci family, 2225
Petrus de Ebulo (fl. c. 1195), 800
Petty, Sir William (1737-1805), 2nd earl of Shelburne, 3784-5
Petty-Fitzmaurice, Henry Charles Keith (1845-1927), 5th marquess
    of Lansdowne, 6830
Pharmaceutical industry, 3373
Phelps-Stokes commissions, 6270
Philanthropic reform movements, in New York State, 7305
Philip II (1527-98), king of Spain, 2416-18, 2431
Philippines, 6448, 6995, 7044
Phillack, Cornw., 1544
Philopoemen (253-183 B.C.), 179
Philosophy (medieval), 798, 1410-77 passim
Phrygia (early), 5901
Physical recreation, physical education (16th-18th cent.), 2574;
    (19th cent.), 5321-2
Physically handicapped, see Handicapped
Physics (14th cent.), 1453; teaching of, 1411, 3497
Pi y Margall, Francisco (1824-1901), 2460
Pickering, vale of, 3424
Pickering district, N.R. Yorks., 443
Picts, 1664
Piedmont (18th cent.), 2245
Piers Plowman, 1461
Pilgrims, pilgrimages, 658, 1294; English (medieval), 1199;
    French (medieval), 665-6; in Mamluk period, 6113; Muslim
    (19th cent.), 6362
Pilsudski, Joseph (1867-1935), 1891
Pindaris, 6681
Pipe roll, of bishop of Winchester, 1077
Pipe rolls, 1005, 1007-10
Piracy, 2773, 2780, 2787
Piraeus (ancient), 165
Pirivena education, 6916
Pisa, Italy, 76, 593
Pisan War (15th cent.), 593
Pistoia, synod of (1786), 2247
Piteå, Sweden, 2407
Pitt, William (1708-78), 1st earl of Chatham, 3707, 3713, 3716-17,
    3721, 3899
Pius II (Aeneas Sylvius Piccolomini), pope (1458-64), 819
Pizolpasso, Francesco (c. 1380-1443), 599
Place, Francis (1771-1854), 4320
Place-names, of Kentish charters, 1523
Plainsong music-drama, 786
Planning, democratic, in Australia, 7617
Plantagenet, Arthur (1480?-1542), Viscount Lisle, 2629
Plantation colonies, 3798
Plantations, 6269, 6920, 6931, 7005, 7011, 7440, 7443
Plant-motives, in manuscripts, 1514
Plea rolls (16th-18th cent.), 2485; see also Assize rolls
Pleas coram rege, 928
Pliny, the Younger (61-c. 113), 271
Plotting (17th cent.), 3085, 3603
Plumpton family, 1174
Plundering, in ancient warfare, 132
Plurality of forms, 1438
Plutarch (c. 46-120), 19-23, 177
Plymouth, Devon, 1143, 1538, 3471; Hamoaze, 3880
Plymouth Brethren, 5437-8, 6314
Pococke, Edward (1604-91), 4269
Poillevillain de Clémanges, Nicholas (d. 1437), 816
Poincaré, Raymond (1860-1934), 2184
Poland (15th cent.), 737; (16th cent.), 1833; (16th-18th cent.),
    1832; (19th cent.), 1787, 1847-8, 1855-7; (20th cent.), 1886,
    1889-91; and Britain (19th cent.), 1848; and France (20th
    cent.), 1825; and the Ukraine (20th cent.), 1887

Portland, 3rd duke of, see Bentinck, William Henry Cavendish
Portmote courts, 948
Porto, Luigi da (1486-1529), 80
Portraiture (16th cent.), 3161; (17th-18th cent.), 4329
Ports and harbours, 1104, 2513, 2860, 3376-9, 3383-4, 3398, 3951,
    3955, 5123-5, 5127, 5136, 5155, 5164; in Ireland, 4458, 5840;
    in Scotland, 2618, 5782; in Wales, 3379, 5126
Portsmouth, Hants, 3881-2, 4866
Portugal, 2410-68 passim, 6246, 6340, 6402, 7538; and Britain
    (17th-18th cent.), 2444; (19th cent.), 2457
Portuguese, in Ceylon, 6896, 6898; in East Indies, 6443; in India,
    6443, 6546; in Persian Gulf, 5965
Portuguese revolution (1826-34), 2453
Positivists, 4849
'Possessors' and 'Non-possessors' in Russia (15th-16th cent.),
    2315
Post Office, 3783, 4036, 5142
Postal service, 3385
Potter, George (1832-93), 5478
Pottery, in Roman Britain, 364, 377; (medieval), 1115, 1602
Pottery industry, 4973; (medieval), 1114; of north Staffordshire,
    3370, 3985-8, 4226
Pottinger, Eldred (1811-43), 6729
Poullain, Valérand (1515-c. 1560), 2110
Poulton-le-Fylde, Lancs., 2876
Poussin, Nicolas (1594-1665), 1754
Poverty, doctrine of (medieval), 712, 721
Powell, Vavasor (1617-70), 3104-5
Power, in Thucydides, 15
'Power of the sword', 2713
Powys (medieval), 1625
Prairie provinces, of Canada, 7244, 7250
Praja Socialist party, 6876
Prazos, 6212
Preachers, order of, see Dominicans
Preaching (medieval), 1229, 1290; see also Lay preaching; Sermons
Prefectoral Corps, French (19th cent.), 2040
Prehistory, idea of, 5469
Prene, John (d. 1443), archbishop, 1718
Preparatory schools, 5568
Presbyterian Church, of Ghana, 6378; in Western Canada, 7191
Presbyterianism (16th-17th cent.), 2999-3000; (17th cent.), 3042,
    3087, 4197; (17th-19th cent.), 3474; (17th-18th cent.), 3466,
    4203; in Ireland, 3583, 4463-5, 4484, 5833-4; in Scotland,
    3043, 3231, 3254, 4398, 4429; in America, 7264, 7271; in
    Canada, 7193; in India, 6809; in South Africa, 6283
Press
    control of, 3111; freedom of (15th-17th cent.), 3110; (19th
        cent.), 4324; (20th cent.), 5489
    newspaper (18th cent.), 4303, 4312; (18th-19th cent.), 3512-14,
        3529; (19th cent.), 3799, 5474-6, 5478; (19th-20th cent.),
        2162, 5477; (20th cent.), 1812, 2200, 4673, 5018, 6091, 7160,
        7406-7; in Ireland (17th-18th cent.), 4460; in Wales, 3511;
        in British West Africa, 6437; on China coast, 7084; in France
        2006, 2022, 2041; in Germany, 2147, 2174; international, 1734
    periodical, in Wales, 3510
    printing (18th cent.), 3997; in France (16th cent.), 1903
Pressure groups, 4700, 4709, 4860, 6418
Preston, Lancs., 5675, 5705
Price, Richard (1723-91), 3871-2
Prices (12th-14th cent.), 646; (15th-16th cent.), 1141; (19th
    cent.), 5170; in Ireland (20th cent.), 5874; in Wales (16th
    cent.), 2830; in Palestine (3rd-4th cent.), 316; of land, 7615;
    of oil, 6828; of wool, 1732
Pridi Banomyong (fl. 1932), 7046
Priesthood of All Believers, 2553-4
Priestley, Joseph (1733-1804), 3868

Public order (17th cent.), 2764; (17th-18th cent.), 3806; (18th-19th cent.), 3747-8; (19th cent.), 3977, 5250
Public ownership, 4965
Public passenger transport, 5140, 5160; in Wales, 5143, 5157
Public schools, 5620
Public service, and Quakerism (19th cent.), 5441
Public spectacle (15th-16th cent.), 3160; see also Pageantry
Publication, registration for, in Scotland, 2617
Publishing (17th-18th cent.), 3998-9; subscription (18th cent.), 4302
Pulsford, John (1815-97), 5449
Pulszky, Francis (fl. 1849-60), 4590
Punishment, criminal, 2481; school, 5569
Punjab, 6506; (early), 6497; (19th cent.), 6668, 6740, 6744; (19th-20th cent.), 6746, 6751-3, 6756
Punti, 7078
Purchase system, abolition of, 4874
Puritanism, 2546-7, 2721, 2990-4, 2996, 3013-14, 3049, 3053, 3057, 3064-6, 3083, 3091, 3106, 3168, 4272
Pusey, Edward Bouverie (1800-82), 5381
Pym, John (1584-1643), 2712

QADIRIYYA, 6348
Qarmati movement, 5927
Quadrilogue invectif (Chartier's), 598
Quakers, 3106-7, 3468-9, 3471, 3474, 3854, 4211, 4217, 4273, 5440-2, 5622, 6224, 7281; in Ireland, 4461; in Scotland, 3556; in Wales, 3470; in America, 7281
Quarrying, see Slate-quarrying
Quarter sessions, 2600, 4353-4, 4363, 5713-14; in Wales, 2598, 3180, 4364
Queen Anne's Bounty, 4179
Queensland, 7603-5, 7613
Quesnel family, 1909
Quincy, Roger de, see Roger de Quincy
Quo warranto proceedings, 949-50

RABBINATE (14th-17th cent.), 663
Race relations, in Central Africa, 6218; in Fiji, 7627; in Natal, 6334; in New Zealand, 7595; in Northern Rhodesia, 6318, 6324; in the U.S.A., 7309, 7396-7
Rachanuphap, Prince Damrong (fl. 1892-1915), 7038
Radical party, of Chile, 7568
Radical theory, evolution of, 2492
Radicalism (17th-19th cent.), 2706, 3806-43 passim, 3853; (19th cent.), 4320, 4626, 4766; (19th-20th cent.), 4778, 4820-61 passim; in Australia, 7599; in Russia (19th cent.), 2348; (20th cent.), 2370; see also Congressional radicalism
Radnorshire, 1619, 2489, 2577, 5634
Radstock, Som., 2525
Raetia (Roman), 336
Raffles, Sir Thomas Stamford (1781-1826), 7004
Ragged School Union, 5581
Railway Commissioners, 5147
Railway interest, 4550, 4632
Railway rates, 5163
Railway works, 5677
Railways (19th cent.), 4992, 5292; (19th-20th cent.), 4993-4, 5123-67 passim; (20th cent.), 5024; in Ireland, 3591; in Scotland, 5803; in Wales, 5151; in Egypt, 6137; in India, 6741-3; in Northern Rhodesia and Katanga, 6330; in Russia, 2353; in South Africa, 6315; in Turkey, 6003; in the U.S.A., 7333-4; in West Africa, 6403
Rajshahi, India, 6618
Ralegh family, 2889
Ramsay, George (1770-1838), 9th earl of Dalhousie, 7215
Ramsay, Sir James Andrew Broun (1812-60), 1st marquess of Dalhousie, 6749

Ramsey abbey, Hunts., 1063
Rangoon, Burma, 6761
Rank-and-file movements, 5025-6
Ranters, 2761
Rapin de Thoyras, Paul (1661-1725), 92
Rašid al-din Fadl Allah (d. 1318), 44
Rathbones, of Liverpool, 5115
Rational Protestants, 3808
Rawdon-Hastings, Francis, see Hastings, Francis Rawdon-
Rawlinson, Richard (1690-1755), 4291
Raymond of Aguilers (11th cent.), 59
Raynal, Guillaume François (1713-96), 1967
'Reactionary' writers, in Russia (19th cent.), 2344
Reading, Berks., 1116, 3299, 5736; abbey, 1355
Reading habits (19th cent.), 5777
Rearmament (20th cent.), 4815
Rebecca riots, 5278
Rebellions and risings (1233-4), 836; (1549), 2661-3; in north of
    England (1403-8), 877
Rechenberg, Freiherr von, governor of Tanganyika (1906-11), 6263
Reciprocity treaty (1854), 7228
Reclamation, see Drainage
Recoinage (17th cent.), 3931
Reconstruction, in the U.S.A., 7356, 7365, 7368-9
Recreations (16th-18th cent.), 2574; (18th-19th cent.), 3453; (19th
    cent.), 5232-3, 5320-2
Recruitment, military (18th cent.), 3911; naval (18th-19th cent.),
    3912; (19th cent.), 4867; of Roman legionaries, 285
Recusants (16th-17th cent.), 2874, 2906-7, 3006, 3008, 3020-6,
    3051; (17th-18th cent.), 4132, 4259; Welsh, 2038-9
Red River Rebellion (1869-70), 7238
Redemption, theology of (12th-13th cent.), 711; (17th cent.), 4397
Reform
    administrative (19th cent.), 4588; in Bengal, 6648; in Spain
        (18th cent.), 2443
    ecclesiastical, in Russia (18th cent.), 2327
    judicial (19th cent.), 4999; in Bengal, 6648
    municipal, 5739-40, 5757
    parliamentary, see Parliamentary reform movement
    penal, see Prison reform
    social (18th cent.), 3873; in Wales, 5242
Reform Acts (1832), 4565, 5846; (1867), 4612-16; (1884-5), 4654-5
Reform League, 4846-7
Reform movements (19th-20th cent.), 4820-61 passim; in Scotland,
    4454; in Turkey (19th cent.), 6002; (20th cent.), 6035, 6039-
    40
Reform policy, British, in India (20th cent.), 6861
Reformation, 733, 2470; in Denmark, 2396; in England, 2644, 2893-4,
    2921, 2930, 2934-7, 2940-3, 2958, 2964, 2985, 3119; in France,
    1901; in Ireland, 3264; in Italy, 2232; in Scotland, 3215-17,
    3223-4; in Wales, 2938-9; attitudes to (19th cent.), 5382;
    Wesley's views on, 4222; writing on (17th-18th cent.), 89
Reforms, in Russia (1801-3), 2334; (1856-66), 2345
Refugees, anti-Nazi, 2197; French (17th cent.), 4090; French and
    Italian (16th-17th cent.), 2471; Hungarian (19th cent.), 1794;
    see also Exiles
Regency crisis (1788), 3739
Regensburg, colloques of (1541), 1766
Regionalism, in Italy, 2270
Re-insurance treaty (1887), 1806
Relieving officer (19th-20th cent.), 5256
Religion, 2540; (17th cent.), 3196; (19th cent.), 1788; in Wales
    (17th cent.), 3045; in ancient Greece, 129; and see Ecclesi-
    astical history in Table of Contents
Religions (Roman), 268-81 passim, 355-7; see also Cults
Religious controversies (16th cent.), 1759; (16th-17th cent.),
    2978, 2988

Religious houses, 1329-95 *passim*, 2928; in Ireland (16th cent.),
  3265; suppression of, 2945-7, 2951
Religious inquiry (19th cent.), 5411
Religious leaders (medieval), 791
Religious liberty, see Toleration, religious
Religious life (18th-19th cent.), 4153, 4214; in Scotland (medi-
  eval), 544; (17th cent.), 3260; (17th-18th cent.), 4400; (18th-
  19th cent.), 4429, 4449
Religious movements (18th cent.), 7276; in Wales (17th cent.),
  3104; in Georgia, 7276
Religious orders, 756-75 *passim*, 794; in England, 1329-95 *passim*;
  in Venice (16th-17th cent.), 2230
Religious policy, in Ceylon, 6927; see also Ecclesiastical policy
Religious revival (18th cent.), 4141-2; (19th cent.), 5366-7,
  5408; (19th-20th cent.), 5369; in Wales, 4146
Religious settlement (16th cent.), 2970, 2979-81; (16th-17th
  cent.), 2977; (17th cent.), 3102, 4155
Religious thought, in Scotland, 5787
Religious toleration, see Toleration, religious
Religious uniformity (16th cent.), 3117
Religious wars, French, 2677
Remonstrances au roy (Juvenal des Ursins), 606
Renaissance, 551, 1898, 2218, 2220, 2641, 3123
Renan, Joseph Ernest (1823-92), 110
Rents, agricultural, 5195-6
Reparations, French (1818), 2049
Repingdon, Philip (d. 1424), bishop, 1318
Representative government, in Germany, 2181; in India, 6818
Repression, political (18th cent.), 3820; in France (17th-18th
  cent.), 1933
Reprobationes (Giles of Rome's), 1441
Republican institutions, in ancient India, 6467
Republicanism, in England (17th cent.), 2725, 3602
Requesens, Luis de (d. 1576), 2431
Resistance, doctrine of (17th-18th cent.), 3861
Responsible government, 4739, 7223-4
Restoration, French (1814), 2051; (1830), 2052
Resumption, acts of (15th cent.), 875-6
Retail trade (19th cent.), 5112; in France (20th cent.), 2088
Retford, East, Notts., 3696; King Edward VI Grammar School, 3114
Reunion, Indian Ocean, see Bourbon
Revenue, public, 3920-44 *passim*; Scottish crown (15th-16th cent.),
  1694; Scottish public (17th cent.), 4392; see also Land
  revenue
Revenue administration, of Chittagong (18th cent.), 6614; of East
  India Company, 6570; in Jamaica (17th-18th cent.), 7426
Revenue policy, in Guntur district (19th cent.), 6727
Revivalist movements, see Religious revival
Revolution, theories of, 1980
Revolutionaries, European, in London (19th cent.), 5280
Revolutionary and Napoleonic Wars (1793-1802), 2015, 2019, 3940,
  6999
Revolutionary movement, Chinese (19th-20th cent.), 7126
Revolutions (1848), 1791, 1793, 2136-7, 2252
Revue Britannique, 2050
Rewards, in schools, 5569
Rheims, France, 792
Rhetoric, study of (12th cent.), 802; in Roman empire, 270
Rhodes, Hellenistic, 174
Rhodesia, 6304, 6319, 6321, 6323; north-eastern, 6227, 6309;
  Northern, 6314, 6318, 6324-5, 6328-30; Southern, 6317, 6320,
  6327, 6337
Rhondda valley, 3330, 5022, 5661
Rhys family, 1660
Ribblesdale, 446
Ricasoli, Baron Bettino (1809-80), 2260
Ricci, Scipio dei (1741-1810), 2247

Rice industry, of Burma, 7017
Rich, Edmund, see Edmund, Saint
Rich, Sir Richard (1496?-1567), 1st Baron Rich, 2655
Richard I (1157-99), king, 827
Richard II (1367-1400), king, 866, 870, 872
Richard (d. 1184), archbishop, 1207
Richard (1209-72), earl of Cornwall, 837-8
Richard Marshal (d. 1234), 3rd earl of Pembroke, 836
Richard St. Victor (d. c. 1173), 1674
Riche, Barnabe (1540?-1617), 3137
Richer, Edmond (1559-1633), 1920
Richmond, 3rd duke of, see Lennox, Charles
Riel, Louis (1844-85), 7238-9
'Rifā 'ah Rāfi 'al-Tahtāwī (1801-73), 6142
Rifle, breech-loading, 4868
Right wing, British, 6860; French, 2092; Spanish, 2465
Rimini, Italy, 661
Riots, anti-Protestant, in the Gard (19th cent.), 2045
Ripley, Derbys., 5769
Ripon, diocese of, 5403
Ripon, 1st marquess of, see Robinson, George Frederick Samuel
Ripon cathedral, W.R. Yorks., 1265
Rippon, John (1751-1836), 4254
Risorgimento, 2254, 2257
River Plate provinces, 7528
Road haulage industry, 5106
Road-book, 4028
Roads, 4034; (18th-19th cent.), 3387-8, 3395; (19th cent.), 5128-9;
    in Scotland (18th-19th cent.), 3577, 4431; in Wales, 3390, 3393
Robert, Saint, of Knaresborough (d. 1235?), 1234
Robert de Bethune (d. 1148), bishop, 1203
Robert de Chesney (d. 1166), bishop, 1205
Roberts, John (1749-1817), 4243
Roberts, Owen Owen (1793-1866), 5230
Roberts, Samuel (1763-1848), 4117
Robertson, William (1721-93), 96
Robes, see Costume
Robespierre, Maximilien de (1758-94), 2028
Robinson, George Frederick Samuel (1827-1909), 1st marquess of
    Ripon, 4601, 6813-14, 7613
Roby, William (1766-1830), 4257
Rochester, diocese of, 1208
Rochester, 1st earl of, see Hyde, Laurence
Rockingham, 2nd marquess of, see Watson-Wentworth, Charles
Rodney, George Brydges (1719-92), 1st Baron Rodney, 3904
Rodrigues, João (17th cent.), 7059
Roger (d. 1179), bishop, 1206
Roger de Quincy (d. 1265), 2nd earl of Winchester, 1685
Rohana, 6520
Rohilkhand, India, 6638
Rohillas, 6596
Rolle, Richard (1290?-1349), 1450-1
Rolls Royce, 5085
Romaine, William (1714-95), 4143
Roman Catholic Church (19th cent.), 5355; in Ireland (19th cent.),
    5866
Roman Catholicism, 3505; (16th cent.), 3019, 3039; (16th-17th
    cent.), 2426, 2544, 2564, 2977, 3007, 3015-16; (17th cent.),
    2749, 3055, 3085-6, 3098-100; (17th-19th cent.), 3411, 4259-64;
    (18th-20th cent.), 3481; (18th-19th cent.), 3506; (19th cent.),
    5567; (19th-20th cent.), 5458-64, 5648; (20th cent.), 5613; in
    Ireland (16th-17th cent.), 2620; (18th-19th cent.), 4481-2;
    (19th cent.), 5243, 5833, 5842, 5862, 5866; in Wales, 2556,
    3030, 4264; see also Recusants
  in Bavaria, 2190; in Bombay province, 6716; in Ceylon, 6925; in
    France, 2062, 2074, 2089, 2102; in Madras, 6747; in New South
    Wales, 7585; in Nigeria, 6392; in Spain, 2451; in Uganda, 6255

Roman d'Eustache le Moine, 63
Roman empire, 182-296 passim, 297-388
Roman empire, eastern, see Byzantium
Romano-Austrians, 553
Romantic movement, Romanticism, in England, 3870; in France, 2054;
    in Russia, 2336
Rome (ancient), 115-25 passim, 182-296 passim
Rome (medieval), 810; (19th cent.), 2259; idea of, in Dante, 585;
    papal court (16th cent.), 2915; sack of (1527), 2234; see of,
    1178; seminary, 3028; see also Vatican palace
Romulus, 198
Rondelet, Guillaume (16th cent.), 1906
Ronquillo, Don Pedro (fl. 1674-91), 2440
Roosevelt, Franklin Delano (1882-1945), president of the U.S.A.,
    7412
Roosevelt, Theodore (1858-1919), president of the U.S.A., 7380
Roscher, Wilhelm (1817-94), 2133
Roscoe, Sir Henry Enfield (1833-1915), 5671
Roscoe, William (1753-1831), 3738
Rose, Hugh James (1795-1838), 5398
Rosebery, 5th earl of, see Primrose, Archibald Philip
Rosmini-Serbati, Antonio (1797-1855), 2249
Ross, Alexander (1590-1654), 3068
Rossendale, Lancs., 465, 4199
Rossetti, Gabriele (1783-1854), 4126
Rosslyn, 1st earl of, see Wedderburn, Alexander
Rotherham, W.R. Yorks., 5546, 5680
Rotherham, Thomas (1423-1500), archbishop, 1327
Rothwell, William (13th cent.), 1445
Rotterdam, Holland, 2278
Rouen, France, archbishops of (11th-12th cent.), 706
Roumania, see Rumania
Roumeliot campaign (1827-9), 2211
Rous, Francis (1581-1659), 2715
Rousseau, Jean-Jacques (1712-78), 1970-1
Roxburghshire, 4409
Royal Academy Schools, 5649
Royal Air Force, 4883-4
Royal entry, 1177, 2411
Royal family (12th cent.), 891
Royal Flying Corps, 4884
Royal Geographical Society, 6211
Royal inauguration (medieval), 562
Royal Institution of South Wales, 5668
Royal Society, 4275-6
Royal Welch Fusiliers, 3906
Royalism (17th cent.), 2733
Royalist party (17th cent.), 2766
Royalists, English (17th cent.), 2719, 2721, 2732, 2740-1, 2799,
    2815; French (18th cent.), 2017-18; (19th cent.), 2046
Ruanda-Urundi, 6276
Rubber cultivation and industry, 6931, 5057, 7011
Rudolf II (1552-1612), 1834
Rug, Merioneth, 4049
Ruhr, 2134
Ruling class, Roman, 185; in the U.S.S.R., 2388
Ruling eldership, Presbyterian, 5834
Rumania, 1844-5, 1866, 1883
Rundale system, 507-8
Rune stones, 1489
Rupert's Land, Canada, 7216
Ruskin, John (1819-1900), 5307
Russell, Sir Henry (1783-1852), 6687
Russell, John (1710-71), 4th duke of Bedford, 3682-4
Russell, Lord John (1792-1878), 1st Earl Russell, 4576-7, 4584
Russell, Odo William Leopold (1829-84), 1st Baron Ampthill, 2149

Russia, 2315-76; and see (medieval), 639, 704, 762; (19th cent.),
    1844, 4726; (20th cent.), 6037; in Asia, 6968-9, 6972, 6974-6,
    6980, 7125, 7129; see also Union of Socialist Soviet Republics
    and Britain (18th cent.), 2331; (19th cent.), 2340, 2342, 2349,
    2358; (19th-20th cent.), 2352, 2355; (20th cent.), 2366,
    6041-2; and Bulgaria (10th cent.), 560; and France, 1797,
    1806-8; and India, 6804; and Iran (19th cent.), 5995
Russia Company, 2321
Russian Church (17th cent.), 2324
Russian Revolution (1905), 2368; (1917), 1815
Russo-Japanese War (1904-5), 7140
Rutherfurd, Samuel (1600-61), 3254
Rutherwyk, John de (fl. 1307-47), 1087
Rutland, 968, 2583
Rycaut, Sir Paul (1628-1700), 5976
Rye, Sussex, 3695
Rye House plot (1683), 3626
Ryle, John Charles (1816-1900), bishop, 5407

SACKVILLE, 1st Viscount, see Germain, George Sackville
Sacraments, doctrine of, 2967; theory and practice of, 2558
Sadler, Michael Thomas (1780-1835), 3776
Safawids, 5962-4
Saffārid dynasty, 5940
Saffron Walden, Essex, 424
Sahara (18th-19th cent.), 6122
Sailors, in coal trade (19th cent.), 5049
St. Albans, Herts., 415, 4355; abbey, 1331, 1395
St. Albans, Viscount, see Bacon, Francis
St. Andrews, Fife, 5812
St. Andrews, Glam., 5552
St. Asaph, Flints., 1621
St. Asaph, diocese of, 1626, 4183-4
St. Catherine's monastery, Mt. Sinai, 5951
St. Christopher, Leeward Islands, 7438, 7440
St. Cyr, France, 1943
St. Davids, diocese of, 3472, 4178
St. Davids cathedral, Pemb., bishops and chapter of, 1643
St. Helena, island, 6444A
St. Helens, Lancs., 4368, 5540, 5729
St. John, Henry (1678-1751), 1st Viscount Bolingbroke, 1954, 3657
St. John of Jerusalem, knights of (medieval), 539, 775; (16th-18th
    cent.), 2295-7
St. Just, Louis Antoine Léon de Richebourg de (1767-94), 2024-5
St. Kitts, see St. Christopher
St. Omer abbey, France, 785
St. Petersburg, Russia, 2343
St. Vincent, earl of, see Jervis, John
Sainte-Marthe, Abel Louis de (1620-97), 1937
Saints, 1197-8; Celtic, 1593; Irish, 1197; Tuscan, 804
'Saints' in parliament, 3750
Saint-Simon, Claude-Henri de Rouvroy, comte de (1760-1825), 1980-1
Saladin (d. 1193), 538
Salamanca, Spain, Irish College, 2425
Salaries, teachers', 5696, 5698
Salford, Lancs., 455, 4629, 5733
Salisbury, Wilts., 1233; cathedral, 1262; College of Sarum St.
    Michael, 5692
Salisbury, bishops of, 1233
Salisbury, diocese of, 1297, 2964
Salisbury, 1st earl of, see Montague, William; 3rd marquess of,
    see Cecil, Robert A.T. Gascoyne-
Saljūqid empire, 39, 5948-50
Sallust (86-34 B.C.), 18, 203
Salomonid kings, 6118
Salt industry, trade, 1118; (medieval), 1125; (16th-17th cent.),
    2862; Indian, 6602

Salvation Army, 5317-18
Salvian of Marseilles (d. <u>c</u>. 484), 232, 693
Samoa, 7623-5, 7632
Samos, 147
Sampson, Richard (d. 1554), bishop, 2959
San Salvador, 7566
Sanā, Arabia, 5935
Sancroft, William (1617-93), archbishop, 4164
Sanctuary, 677
Sanderson, Robert (1587-1663), bishop, 4160
Sandwich, 4th earl of, <u>see</u> Montagu, John
Sandys, Edwin (1516?-1588), archbishop, 2979
<u>sangha</u>, Buddhist, 6884-5, 6892
Sanitary administration, <u>see</u> Public health
Sanitation, town (16th cent.), 3177; <u>see also</u> Public health
Santa Fé province, Argentina, 7555
Santiago, order of, 566
Sarawak, 7021
Sardinia (Roman), 191; (19th cent.), 2310; and Britain, 2311
Sassanians, 5906
Satavahana dynasty, 6476
Sati, 6625, 6707
Satire (16th cent.), 3129; (16th-17th cent.), 3136; (19th cent.),
    4319
Sa'udi state, 5982
Savile, Sir George (1726-84), 3686
Savoy, 2071, 2244
Savoy Conference (1661), 4127-8
Saxons, <u>see</u> Anglo-Saxons
Saxony (20th cent.), 2187
Scandinavia (medieval), 783; (17th-18th cent.), 2398; and Britain
    (18th cent.), 2401
Scarbrough, earls of (19th cent.), 5198
Schaff, Phillip (1819-93), 7342
Scheldt (19th cent.), 2286
Schism, <u>see</u> Donatist schism; Great Schism
Schleswig-Holstein (19th cent.), 2131-2
Schlieffen, Count Alfred von (1833-1913), 2170
Schönerer, Georg, Ritter von (1842-1921), 2142
Scholarship, attacks on (17th-18th cent.), 4294
Scholarship, <u>see also</u> Antiquarian scholarship; Learning
School boards, 5599-610 <u>passim</u>, 5663; in Scotland, 5816
School books (18th-19th cent.), 4315; (19th cent.), 5572
School managers, 5565, 5582
Schools, English, in Ireland (17th-18th cent.), 4462
Schools of industry, 2614
Science (16th-17th cent.), 3154; (17th cent.), 3146, 3156; (18th-
    19th cent.), 4317; (19th cent.), 4318; (19th-20th cent.),
    5465-90 <u>passim</u>
Science, teaching of, 3496; (17th cent.), 4272; (19th-20th cent.),
    5664-89 <u>passim</u>; in Ireland and Scotland, 3521
Science and Art Department, 5520-1
Scientific research, 5684
Scientists, Czech (18th-19th cent.), 1840
Scilly Islands, 2594
Scipio Africanus (<u>c</u>. 235-183 B.C.), 288
Scotland, 500, 1663-99, 2607-18, 3209-60, 3554-79, 4384-455,
    5771-821; <u>and see</u> (medieval), 544, 652, 2627; (16th cent.),
    1909; (16th-18th cent.), 1832; (16th-17th cent.), 1719, 2112,
    3000; (17th cent.), 2323, 3043, 7265; (17th-18th cent.), 2398;
    (18th-19th cent.), 3521; (19th cent.), 3583, 4645, 4987, 5492,
    6732, 7323, 7330, 7350, 7376; north-east, 506; south-west, 365,
    501; and England (17th cent.), 3256; (17th-18th cent.), 4405;
    and France (medieval), 582
Scots Confession (1560), 3236
Scotsmen (medieval), 1691
Scott, David (1786-1831), 6675

Scott, Mackay Hugh Baillie (1865-1945), 5487
Scott, Sir Walter (1771-1832), 104-5
Scott, William Bell (1811-90), 5805
Scottish Mission, in Kenya, 6244
Scottish Typographical Association, 4981
Scottish wars (1327-35), 1690
Scraptoft, Leics., 484
Screens, see Church screens
Screw propellor, 4865
Scribism, 5895
Scriptorium, of Bury St. Edmunds, 1503
Scripts (14th-15th cent.), 1448; in India, 6470, 6485
Scrope, Sir Geoffrey Le (d. 1340), 955
Sculpture, alabaster, 1513; English (12th cent.), 1501; Hoysala,
    6526; Irish (early), 1701; monumental, 1496; Oxford school,
    2589; on Roman altars, 359; Saxon, 1492
Scuole Grandi, Venice, 2231
Scutages (14th cent.), 1015
Sea, and Roman empire, 233
Sea charts, 1143
Sea power, Egyptian (medieval), 5920, 6109; Spanish (16th cent.),
    2418; and Wales (17th cent.), 2795
Seafaring industry (18th-19th cent.), 3382
Seamen, Welsh (16th-17th cent.), 2774
Sea-people, of ancient Athens, 165
Second International, 1814
Secondary education, 1790, 5615-43, 5665-6, 5693, 5698-9; in
    Ireland, 3588; in Wales, 5615-43 passim; in Assam, 6981; in
    Bombay province, 6716; in France, 1790, 2035, 2066; in Germany,
    2109, 2126; in Nigeria, 6434; in the Sudan, 6195; in Trinidad
    and Tobago, 7476; in the U.S.A., 7375
Secret committee, in Russia, 2334
Secretaries of state (16th-17th cent.), 2665; (17th cent.), 2696;
    (17th-18th cent.), 3629-30; in France (16th cent.), 1911; see
    also Under-secretaries of state
Secretary at war (18th cent.), 3892
Secretary hand, Tudor, 1448
Secularist movement, 5316
Security, English government (16th cent.), 2664; French national
    (20th cent.), 2097; international, 1744, 1823
Segregation, native, in Southern Rhodesia, 6320
Selangor, 7012, 7026
Selby abbey, W.R. Yorks., 1338
Select committee on colonial military expenditure (1861), 4748
Self government, in Nova Scotia, 7214
Seljuqs, see Saljūqid empire
Selkirk, 5th earl of, see Douglas, Thomas
Senate, in Northern Ireland, 5880; Roman, 195, 208-9, 216-17, 225;
    of the U.S.A., 7304
Senchus Fer nAlban, 1666
Senegal (17th-18th cent.), 6350
Separatists, 2558, 3003-5, 3050
Sequestration of estates (17th cent.), 2754
Serbia (19th cent.), 1851-2, 1861; and England (19th cent.), 1853
Serbian Church, 723, 1830
Serge industry, 4007
Serjeants, in Domesday Book, 1032
Serjeants at law, order of, 954
Sermons (medieval), 1291; Welsh, 3046
Service book, of Marian exiles, 2472
Servitudes, in Scottish law, 3554
Servius Tullius (578-534 B.C.), 198
Settlement, 389-518 passim, 3282-97 passim; in Scottish Highlands,
    3561; in Wales, 2501, 3294; in Borneo, 6997; in Dalmatia
    (Roman), 299; in East Africa, 6236, 6254; among Luo peoples,
    6205; see also Anglo-Saxon settlement
Settlement, religious, see Religious settlement

Seven Years War (1756-63), 1775, 3900, 6993
Severn valley, 470, 3436
Severus, Alexander, Roman emperor (208-35), 223
Severus, Lucius Septimius (146-211), 221-2
Sewers, courts of (16th cent.), 3176
Sexton, Thomas (16th cent.), London merchant, 2858
Sextus V (1521-90), pope, 2240
Sexual relationships (17th cent.), 4081
Seymour, Edward (1506?-1552), duke of Somerset, 2651
Seymour, Edward (d. 1621), earl of Hertford, 3187
'Shadow cabinet', 4713
Shaftesbury, 1st earl of, see Cooper, Anthony Ashley (1621-83);
    3rd earl of, see Cooper, Anthony Ashley (1671-1713); 7th earl
    of, see Cooper, Anthony Ashley (1801-85)
Shah Jahan, Khurram Shibāb-al-dīn Muhammad (d. 1666), 6562, 6574-6
Shaikh Ahmed, Khan of the Golden Horde (fl. 1500), 2318
Shaikh Sidiyya, 6348
Shanghai, 7141; International Settlement, 7112
Shantung, question of, 7147, 7157
Sharp, James (1613-79), archbishop, 3253
Sheep-farming (medieval), 1068
Sheffield, W.R. Yorks., 4098; (18th cent.), 4312; (18th-19th
    cent.), 3368, 3821; (19th cent.), 4625, 4827, 5547-8; (20th
    cent.), 4969
Shelburne, 2nd earl of, see Petty, Sir William
Sheldon, Ralph (1623-84), 4290
Shen Pao-Chen (1820-79), 7089
Shen-Ts'e armies, 7055
Sheppey, John (d. 1360), bishop, 1291
Sherbrooke, 1st Viscount, see Lowe, Robert
Sheriffs (medieval), 892, 899-902, 919; (16th-17th cent.), 3186;
    in Scotland, 1669; (16th cent.), 3209
Sherlock, Thomas (1678-1761), bishop, 4182
Sherwood Forest, 1066
Shetland, 503-4, 3213
Shidehara, Kijuro, Baron (1872-1951), 7153
Shields, South, 2599
Shī-'ism, 5924, 5927, 5931, 6111
Shipbuilding industry, 3983-4; (15th cent.), 1134; (17th cent.),
    2793; (18th-20th cent.), 3316; (19th cent.), 4984; (19th-20th
    cent.), 5078; (20th cent.), 5108; in Ireland, 3589; in Scot-
    land, 5811
Shipmoney, 2814
Shippen, William (1673-1743), 3675
Shipping, in Ireland, 1700
Shipping industry (17th cent.), 3948A, 3954, 7263; (19th cent.),
    3974, 5154, 5156, 5169; (20th cent.), 6435
Ships, Greek (ancient), 153
Shirt industry, of Londonderry, 5825
Shoa, kingdom of, 6129
Shore, Sir John (1751-1834), 1st Baron Teignmouth, 6660
Shorncliffe Camp, Kent, 4877
Short service, army, 4872
Shrewsbury, Salop, 478, 1534; (medieval), 1535; (17th cent.),
    2735, 2872-3
Shrewsbury, earls of, 1166
Shropshire, 475; (13th cent.), 932; (17th cent.), 2734; (17th-19th
    cent.), 3474; (19th cent.), 5543; (19th-20th cent.), 5555;
    north, 2849; southern, 476-7
Shuttleworth, Sir James Kay-, see Kay-Shuttleworth
Siam, 7035, 7037-8, 7046; and Britain, 7016, 7027, 7042; and
    France, 7016, 7027
Siamese Forward Movement, 7015
Sibbes, Richard (1577-1635), 3064
Siberia, 2354, 7149
Sicily (Roman), 305; (early), 16; (12th cent.), 569, 714; (16th
    cent.), 2416; (19th cent.), 2306

Sidmouth, 1st Viscount, see Addington, Henry
Siena, Italy, 2225
Sierra Leone, 4727, 6359, 6366, 6370, 6433
Sierra Leone Frontier Police, 6421
Signet office (15th cent.), 907
Sikhs, 6667, 6701, 6730
Silk industry, 4004-6, 4888, 5044
Silk-ribbon industry, 3364
Silva Candida, see Humbert
Silver mining, in Wales, 2531; in Mexico, 7511, 7522
Silver money, in France, 1900
Silver standard, in China, 7154
Silver thread monopoly, 2811
Silversmithing trade, 5047
Simcoe, John Graves (1752-1806), 3748A
Simon de Montfort (c. 1208-1265), earl of Leicester, 843-6
Sinclair, Sir John (1754-1835), 4073
Sind, 6506; (8th-10th cent.), 6508; (16th cent.), 6551; (19th
     cent.), 6737-8
Sindhia family, 6641
Sinking Fund, 4916
Sino-Japanese War (1937-45), 7161-2, 7166
Sion Lleyn, see Roberts, John
Sīra, 37
Skelton, John (1460?-1529), 3122-3
Skinners' Company, 1113
Skoropadsky, Pavel Petrovich (1873-1945), 2390
Slate-quarrying, in Wales, 3350-2, 5007, 5045
Slave Coast, 6352
Slave compensation, 4896
Slave emancipation, see Slavery, abolition of
Slave trade, 6353, 7316, 7529; (17th-18th cent.), 3963; (18th
     cent.), 3964-5, 3973, 6352; (19th cent.), 6947; abolition of,
     3830-1, 3972, 6067, 6363, 7470, 7535, 7546
Slavery, in British Leeward Islands, 7449; in India, 6625; in
     Jamaica, 7416, 7457; in Pharaonic Egypt, 6095; in ancient Rome,
     245-6, 248; in South Africa, 6287; in the Sudan, 6145;
     abolition of, 6222, 7466-8, 7470
Slavophiles, 2337
Slovaks (20th cent.), 1877
Slovenes, conversion of, 697
Smallpox inoculation, 4100; movement against, 5308
Smirke, Sir Robert (1781-1867), 5466
Smith, Sir Harry George Wakelyn (1787-1860), 6300
Smith, Joseph (1682-1770), 4331
Smith, Richard (1783-1868), mines manager, 5053
Smith, Sir Thomas (1513-77), statesman, 2658
Smith, Sir Thomas (1558?-1625), merchant, 2867
Smith, William (1728-83), American Loyalist, 7289
Smith, William (1756-1835), politician, 3826-7
Smithson family, 4327
Smyrna, Turkey (ancient), 5900; (17th cent.), 5976
Smyth, John (d. 1612), 3004
Smythe, Thomas (1522-91), 2866
Snowdonia, 4509
Soap manufacture, 1728, 3369
Social change (19th-20th cent.), 4648A; in India (19th cent.),
     6695-6
Social conditions, in Ireland (17th-18th cent.), 4461
Social Credit movement, 7253
Social criticism, in the Scottish Church (19th-20th cent.), 5797
Social democracy, in Austria, 1885; in Germany, 1799; in Russia,
     2360-2
Social Democratic party, German, 2150; Russian, 2359
Social history, see Economic and Social History in Table of
     Contents
Social institutions, in Ceylon (early), 6882

Social life (18th cent.), 4152; (19th cent.), 5357, 5365, 5392,
    5394; in Wales (medieval), 1606, 1637, 1657; (17th-18th cent.),
    4050; (18th cent.), 3818, 4227; in Ceylon (17th cent.), 6902;
    in India, of English (18th cent.), 6589, 6609; in India, of
    Portuguese (16th-17th cent.), 6546; in Portugal (17th-18th
    cent.), 2441
Social mobility (19th cent.), 5207; in Iceland, 2404; in Roman
    empire, 250; in Russia, 2375
Social movements, in Georgia, 7276
Social origins, of army officers (18th cent.), 3895; of bishops
    (19th-20th cent.), 5412; of city councillors, 5765; of
    political leaders (19th-20th cent.), 4657
Social policy (17th cent.), 2913; (19th-20th cent.), 4708, 5219-348
    passim; in Ceylon, 6923-4; in India, 6695
Social problems and questions (16th cent.), 2888; (17th cent.),
    4157-8; (17th-18th cent.), 4202; (19th cent.), 5319; (19th-
    20th cent.), 5335
Social science, 8; in England (19th cent.), 5300; in France, 1976,
    2038
Social services, 4917
Social thought, 5418, 5422; in Bengal (19th cent.), 6781; in Egypt
    (20th cent.), 6194
Social welfare (19th-20th cent.), 5219-538 passim; ideas on (18th-
    19th cent.), 4114
Socialism, socialist thought (19th cent.), 1782; in England, 3842,
    4586, 4637-9, 4691; in Wales, 4670; in Australia, 7599; in
    China, 7143; in France (18th cent.), 2002; (18th-19th cent.),
    1989; (19th cent.), 2054; in Russia, 2356; in the U.S.A., 7382
Socialist Labour Party of Great Britain, 4671-2
Socialist League, 4860
Societies, democratic (18th cent.), 3816-17; literary (16th-17th
    cent.), 3134; (18th cent.), 4306; religious (16th-18th cent.),
    2542; (17th-19th cent.), 3503; (17th-18th cent.), 4171; (18th
    cent.), 4172; Methodist, 4229; see also Clubs
Society, in political thought (18th cent.), 3873
Society for Promoting Christian Knowledge, 4135-7
Society for the Diffusion of Useful Knowledge, 5472-3
Society for the Encouragement of Learning, 4302
Society of Arts, 3463
Society of the Sacred Heart, 5493
Socinianism, 3079, 3101, 4154
Soderini, Piero (1452-1522), 2238
Sokemen (11th cent.), 824
Soldiers (medieval), 807, 992
Sologne, France, 2032
Solomon, 5888
Somaliland, 6235
Somerset, 396, 1108; (early), 1524; (11th cent.), 1036-7; (17th
    cent.), 2750, 3187, 3193; (17th-18th cent.), 4132; (18th-19th
    cent.), 3358, 4314; (19th cent.), 4382, 5260; (19th-20th cent.),
    5034; (20th cent.), 4701; north central, 397
Somerset, duke of, see Seymour, Edward (1506?-1552)
Somerset, Lord Charles Henry (1768-1831), 6290
Somerset, Henry (1577-1646), 5th earl and 1st marquess of Worcester,
    2742
Somerset Levels, 5208
Song school, 2561
Songs, Anglo-Norman political, 1421; soldiers' (medieval), 807
Sorby, Henry Clifton (1826-1908), 5482
Soulé, Pierre (1801-70), 7550
South Africa, 4777, 6279-337 passim
South African confederation, 6307
South African Dutch republics, 6301
South African General Mission, 6314
South America, 7507-69
South Australia, 4721, 7591
South Carolina, U.S.A. (19th cent.), 7340; colonial, 7273

South China Sea, 6991
South Pacific (19th cent.), 4758
South Sea (16th-17th cent.), 7618
South Sea Company, 3934-5
Southampton, Hants, 401, 1527; (medieval), 922, 981, 1138-9;
    (15th-16th cent.), 670; (16th cent.), 2861, 3175; (17th cent.),
    4080; (17th-19th cent.), 3983; (19th cent.), 5732; Hartley
    Institution, 5646
Southport, Lancs., 5538
Southwark, see London
Southwell, Notts., 5269
South-West Africa, 6065-6
Sovereignty, concept of, 1927, 2721; doctrine of, 2101; in ancient
    Indian polity, 6494; of the people (18th cent.), 2008; theory
    of, 5, 2144
Spain, 2410-68 passim; and see 2647; (Roman), 125; (medieval), 32,
    554, 604, 641, 658, 751, 795; (16th-17th cent.), 7413; (18th
    cent.), 7435, 7517-18; (19th cent.), 7025, 7348, 7391, 7529,
    7550, 7552, 7557; (20th cent.), 4817-18; and Britain (18th
    cent.), 2446, 2448; (19th cent.), 2459; and England (16th
    cent.), 2421; (17th cent.), 2434, 2437-8, 2440; and the U.S.A.
    (19th cent.), 7391
Spanish Armada, 2428
Spanish Civil War (1936-9), 2466-8, 4817-18
Spanish marriages (1841-6), 2456
Spanish Nationalists, 2466
Spanish Republic (1873), 2461; (1931-6), 2465
Spanish-American War (1898), 7391
Sparta (ancient), 140, 176
Spear, Anglo-Saxon, 1488
Speculum Ecclesie (St. Edmund's), 1236
Speed, John (1552?-1629), 3147
Spence, Thomas (1750-1814), 3810
Spencer, Robert (1640-1702), 2nd earl of Sunderland, 3628-9
Spencer, business house, 5071
Spencer family, 2834
Spice trade, Roman, 262
Spinola family, 2241-2
Spirituality (14th-15th cent.), 1460
Spitalfields Acts, 4006
Spofforth, W.R. Yorks., 1541
Spottiswoode, John (1565-1639), archbishop, 3247
Spouses, legal rights of, in Scotland, 2608
Sprat, Thomas (1635-1713), bishop, 4275
Squatter, in New South Wales, 7589
Squires, see Gentry
Srikrsna-Chaitanya (1485-c. 1534), 6547
Srivijaya, Indonesia, 6982
Stafford, Edward (1478-1521), 3rd duke of Buckingham, 1517
Stafford, Humphrey (1402-60), 1st duke of Buckingham, 881
Staffordshire (medieval), 975, 1037, 3986; (17th cent.), 2733;
    (17th-18th cent.), 3597, 3985, 4262; (18th cent.), 3987;
    (19th cent.), 4524, 4551, 5170; north, 3370; south, 3346,
    4511-12
Stahlhelm, 2175
Stair, 2nd earl of, see Dalrymple, John
Stamford, Lincs., 2819, 3298; nunnery, 1360
Stamp Act crisis, 3789
Stamp duty, 5475-6
Standing committees, of house of commons, 4650
Standish, (? Lancs.), 456
Stanley, Edward George Geoffrey Smith (1799-1869), 14th earl of
    Derby, 4751, 4904
Stanley, Edward Henry (1826-93), 15th earl of Derby, 2292
Stanley, Henry (1531-93), 4th earl of Derby, 2900
Stanley, Sir Henry Morton (1841-1904), 6274
Stanley family, 1092

Stanmore, 1st Baron, see Gordon, Arthur Hamilton
Stapeldon, Walter de (1261-1326), bishop, 1016, 1263
Staple, 1140; of Calais, 614; at Westminster, 1133
Stapleton, Thomas (1535-98), 2972
Stapleton plantations, 7438
Star chamber, 2670, 2709
Starkey, Thomas (1499?-1538), 2888
State, conception of (16th cent.), 2641; role of (17th-19th cent.), 3844
State authority, in ancient India, 6495
State intervention, in education (17th cent.), 3150-2; (19th cent.), 5517; in merchant service (19th-20th cent.), 5161-2; in public health (19th-20th cent.), 5325
Stationers' Register, 3140
Statistical Accounts, 4446-7
Status, in Nazi Germany, 2194; in Roman empire, 237; see also Women, status of
Statute of Artificers, 2828-9
Statutory authorities, 4595
Steam engine, 5051
Steel industry, see Iron and steel industry
Steel pen trade, 5054
Stephen (1097?-1154), king, 829
Stephen, George (1829-1921), 1st Baron Mount Stephen, 7226
Stephen, Sir James (1789-1859), 4727
Stephen, Sir James Fitzjames (1829-94), 4608
Stepney, Middx., 1554
Stewart, Francis, see Hepburn, Francis Stewart
Stewart, John (1481-1536), duke of Albany, 3210
Stewart, Robert (1769-1822), Viscount Castlereagh, 3802, 3831, 4486
Stipends, of Scottish ministers (16th-17th cent.), 3232
Stirlingshire, 5774
Stockport, 4016, 4372-3, 5570
Stoke-upon-Trent, Staffs., 5603
Stolypin, Peter Arcadievich (1863-1911), 2373
Stone, Barton Warren (1772-1844), 7313
Stone building materials, in Roman Britain, 346
Stoneleigh hundred, 474
Storey, Edward (1422-1503), bishop, 1328
Stow, archdeaconry of, 2940
Strafford, 1st earl of, see Wentworth, Thomas
Straits Settlements, 7002, 7010, 7019, 7022
Strategy, see Defence policy; Military policy; Naval policy
Stratford-on-Avon, Warwicks., 1112
Strathmore, 1672
Strathnaver, 2611
Stratton, Adam de (fl. 1265-90), 1080
Straw industry, 3371
Strecche, John (fl. 1407-25), 73
Strip lynchets, 1046
Strutt, W.G. and J., 4010
Stuart, James (1843-1913), 5653
Stubbe, Henry (1632-76), 4275
Stukeley, William (1687-1765), 4293
Sturm, John (1507-89), 2109
Styal, Ches., 3547
Subject, rights of, 2480
Subscription controversy, 4463-4
Subsidies (14th cent.), 1021; see also Lay subsidy
Subversion, popular (16th cent.), 2664
Succession, law of, in Scotland, 2067-8; in West Indies, 7492
Sudan, 6094-202 passim; northern, 6127; southern, 6141; western, 6122, 6132, 6155
Sudbury, Simon (d. 1381), archbishop, 1292
Sudeten crisis (1937-8), 1826
S'ūdras, 6454

Suetonius (70-121?), 25
Suez Canal, 6143, 6445
Suffolk, 2517, 2597; (medieval), 972, 1051, 1572; (16th-17th cent.),
    2840; (17th cent.), 2847, 4196; (19th cent.), 4837; (19th-20th
    cent.), 5454; Sandlings, 3404
Sugar beet industry, 5100
Sugar cane industry, of British Guiana, 7481; of Mauritius, 6949-50;
    of West Indies, 7425, 7438, 7489
Sugar taxation, 4893
Sugar trade, of Bristol, 3958
Suhrawardi movement, 6527
Sulla, Lucius Cornelius (138-78 B.C.), 201
Sullivan, Robert (1800-68), 5837
Sully, Maximilien de Béthune, duc de (1559-1641), 1916-17, 5552
Sulu question, 7025
Sumatra, 6996, 7019
Summa confessorum (Thomas de Cobham's), 1270
Summa de Ente (Wyclif's), 1462
Summa Summarum (William of Pagula's), 731
Sun Mill Co., 5072
Sunday observance (18th cent.), 4095; in Scotland, 3235, 3558
Sunday school movement, 3525-7
Sunderland, 2nd earl of, see Spencer, Robert
Sundial, 1751
Superannuation schemes (17th-19th cent.), 3451; see also Pensions
Supernaturalism (17th cent.), 3146
Supplies
    military (16th cent.), 2778; (16th-17th cent.), 2790; (18th
    cent.), 7178; in ancient Greece, 130
    naval (16th-17th cent.), 2790
Supreme Court of Judicature, 4633
Surnames, of the West Riding, 1153
Surrey, 2500; (medieval), 945-6, 973, 1094; (17th-18th cent.),
    3598; (19th cent.), 4076, 4078, 5255, 5573
Surrey, earl of, see Howard, Henry
Sussex, 405-7; (medieval), 927, 946, 973, 1094, 1105, 1579; (16th
    cent.), 2646; (16th-18th cent.), 2596; (16th-17th cent.),
    2843, 2908; (17th-18th cent.), 3952; (19th cent.), 4078, 5180;
    coast of, 3297; east, 1095, 3444, 4061, 4683; South Downs,
    5173; south-east, 3443; west, 5202
Sutherland, 3569
Sutherland, dukes of, estates of, 5206, 5781
Sutri, Italy, 184
Sutton, Thomas (fl. 1290-1311), 1443
Suzdal, princes of, 568
Swahili-speaking communities, 6251
Swaledale, N.R. Yorks., 2529
Swan, William (15th cent.), 1409
Swanland, Western Australia, 7587
Swansea, 3169, 3345, 3465, 5550, 5591, 5712
Swansea valley, 493, 3340
Swarajya party, 6870
Sweden, 2397; (medieval), 745; (17th cent.), 2399; (19th-20th
    cent.), 2408
Swift, Jonathan (1667-1745), 90-1
Swindon, Wilts., 5677
Swinton, 1st earl of, see Cunliffe-Lister, Philip
Switzerland, 2183, 2469-77; and Britain, 2476-7
Sykes, Sir Mark (1879-1919), 6046
Symington, William (1795-1862), 5790
Syndicalism, 5022-3
syndicats, agricultural, 2081
Syracuse (early), 178
Syria, 5985; (medieval), 534-5, 538-9, 5949, 5954; (18th cent.),
    5984; (19th cent.), 5990, 6002; (19th-20th cent.), 6008; (20th
    cent.), 6050; and Turkey (20th cent.), 6039

TACITUS, Cornelius (c. 55-120), 24
Taine, Hippolyte Adolphe (1828-93), 110-11, 1801
Taiping rebellion (1850-64), 7098-9
Talbot, Richard (1630-91), earl of Tyrconnel, 4467
Talbot family, 1166
Talmud, Babylonian, 5890
Tamworth, Staffs., 3599
T'ang dynasty, 7052-5
Tanganyika, 6243, 6263, 6266, 6268; coast of (medieval), 6203
Tangier (17th cent.), 6076
Tanjore (18th cent.), 6601
Tanner, Thomas (1674-1735), bishop, 4292
Tanzimat, Turkish reforming decree, 6002
Tariff policy, of Brazil, 7541
Tariff reform movement, 4918-20
Tariffs (19th cent.), 5114
Tārīkh Al-Mausil, 34
Tarkhans, 6551
Tatars, Crimean, 5966
Taunton, Som., 2601, 3170, 7260
Taxation (14th cent.), 1020; (17th cent.), 2813; (19th-20th cent.),
    4917; clerical (13th-14th cent.), 1014; income, 4923; inherit-
    ance, 3920; lay (14th cent.), 1019; (15th-16th cent.), 2801;
    (16th cent.), 2884; sugar, 4893; wool (14th cent.), 1018; see
    also Land tax; Subsidies
  of Africans, 6302; in Ceylon, 6913; Indian, 6602; Roman, 264
Tayler, John (d. 1534), 2632
Taylor, Jeremy (1613-67), bishop, 3073
Tea, adulteration of, 5226
Tea industry, in Ceylon, 6931; in East Africa, 6269; in India,
    6572
Teachers, training of, in England and Wales (19th-20th cent.),
    5690-701 passim; in Ireland, 5835; in India, 6711-13
Teaching profession, 5000, 5690-701; in Scotland, 5773; in Wales,
    5690-701 passim; in Mexico, 7567; in Nigeria, 6379, 6439
Technical education (19th-20th cent.), 5664-89 passim; (20th
    cent.), 2096; in Belgium, 2288; in France, 2096
Technological change, in industry, 1736, 1803, 3333-4; see also
    Industrial change; Industrial Revolution
Tees-side, 3315, 4492
Teify valley, 489
Teign estuary, Devon, 3378
Teignmouth, 1st Baron, see Shore, Sir John
Telegraph industry, 5060
Telford, Thomas (1757-1834), 3577
Telugu country, 6522
Temne people, 6217
Temperance question, 5240-1
Templars, 769, 774, 1388-9
Temple, Henry John (1784-1865), 3rd Viscount Palmerston, 2251,
    5998, 6061, 6138
Temple, Sir Richard (1826-1902), 6793
Temples, in Roman Britain, 358
Tenant-right, in Ireland, 5839
Tenantry (18th-19th cent.), 4065-6
Tenbury, Worcs., 5184
Tenison, Thomas (1636-1715), archbishop, 4165
Tennant, Smithson (1761-1815), 4317
Terror, in France, 2027; White, in France, 2044
Terrorism, in Bengal, 6854; in France (18th cent.), 2014
Teutonic Hanse, see Hanseatic League
Teutonic knights, 737
Tewkesbury, Glos., 2585, 2603
Texas, U.S.A., 7376
Textile fabrics (medieval), 1109; Islamic, 5913
Textile industry, see Cotton industry; Linen textile industry;
    Woollen and worsted industries

444

Textile technology, 3355
Thagi, 6625
Thailand, see Siam
Thames and Severn Canal, 4040
Thames estuary, 3408-9
Thames Navigation Commission, 3396
Thames-side (18th-20th cent.), 3399
Thanet, Isle of, Kent, 5088
Theatre (16th-17th cent.), 3164-5; (17th cent.), 3166; in Russia
    (17th-18th cent.), 2325; (18th cent.), 2326
Theatre of the Empire of Great Britain (Speed's), 3147
Thegns, 1024, 1032
Theobald (d. 1161), archbishop, 1204
Theodore of Tarsus (602?-690), archbishop, 1181
Theodosius (c. 346-395), Roman emperor, 228, 521
Theodosius II (401-50), Roman emperor of the east, 231
Theological colleges, 5654
Theological writings (14th-16th cent.), 1269
Theophanes (750-817), 526
Thessaly (early), 150-1
Thévet, André (1502-90), 1904
Third Department, 2339
Third estate, in France (18th cent.), 1993
Third Sacred War (355-346 B.C.), 171
Thirty, uprising (403 B.C.), 158
Thirty Years War (1618-48), 1836, 2113, 2432
Thomas (1277?-1322), earl of Lancaster, 858
Thomas à Becket, Saint (d. 1170), archbishop, 1210-12, 1430
Thomas Aquinas, Saint (c. 1227-1274), 573-4
Thomas, William (d. 1554), 2653
Thomason tracts, 2718
Thomism, 1443
Thompson, William (1785?-1833), 3774
Thomson, Andrew Mitchell (1779-1831), 4451
Thomson, William (1819-90), archbishop, 5413
Thomson, William, & Co., 5156
Thoresby, Ralph (1658-1725), 4288
Thring, Edward (1821-87), 5629
Thucydides (d. c. 401 B.C.), 11, 14-15
Thurston, Sir John Bates (1836-97), 7631
Tiberius (d. 37 A.D.), Roman emperor, 108
Tibet, and China (17th cent.), 7060; and India (19th cent.), 6666
Tientsin, treaty of (1858), 7109
Tierney, George (1761-1830), 3730
Tigris-Euphrates valley (19th cent.), 6006
Tikhon, Saint (1724-83), of Voronezh, 2329
Timber production, 483
Timber-framed construction, 1112, 1506, 2579, 2584-5
Tin industry, in Malaya, 7012
Tinplate industry, 5006; in Wales, 5066, 5107
Tiptoft, John (d. 1470), earl of Worcester, 883
Tipu Sultan (1749-99), 6649
Tirpitz, Alfred von (1849-1930), 2141
Tiruvālīśvaram, 6880
Titchfield abbey, Hants, 1078
Tithe disputes (16th-17th cent.), 2961
Tobacco industry and trade, 3960, 5099
Tobago, 7459, 7476
Tocqueville, Alexis de (1805-59), 2055
Tocwith priory, W.R. Yorks., 1352
Todd, Anthony (1738-98), 4036
Tokugawa government, 7076
Toleration, Locke's theory of, 3855
Toleration, religious (17th cent.), 3052, 3081, 3094, 4129-31;
    (17th-18th cent.), 4133, 4261; (18th-19th cent.), 3826, 4151;
    in America (18th cent.), 7273; in France (17th cent.), 1918;
    see also Intolerance

445

Toleration Act (1689), 4213
Tombstones (medieval), 796, 1496
Tonbridge, Kent, 2595
Tongking, Indo-China, 7020
Tonson, Jacob (1656?-1736), 3998
Tooley, Henry (d. 1551), 2859
Tory party (18th cent.), 3657, 3669, 3674; (18th-19th cent.),
    3735; (19th cent.), 3762, 3837, 4946
Toryism (18th cent.), 3688; (19th cent.), 4545; liberal, 3767
Totnes, Devon, 394, 2853
Toulouse, France, 2046
Tournay, Jehan de (fl. 1488-9), 666
Town planning, 5304-5
Town-country relations, 1578, 5268
Towns, see Urban development; administration of, see Local govern-
    ment
Towy valley, 3437
Toynbee Hall, 5330
Tractarians, 5354-5; pre-Tractarians, 4185
Tractatus Eboracenses, 1423
Trade, 470; (medieval), 1100-44 passim; (15th-17th cent.), 2853-73;
    (17th cent.), 3921; (17th-19th cent.), 3945-80 passim; (19th
    cent.), 7317; (19th-20th cent.), 5111-22, 5136, 5496; of
    Ireland (17th cent.), 3270, 3277; of Scotland (medieval), 652;
    (19th-20th cent.), 5782
  in Africa, 6209, 6273, 6422; in Ancona (15th-16th cent.), 2224;
    to Asia (16th-17th cent.), 6444; (18th cent.), 6600; in
    Banjarmasin (18th cent.), 6594; in Bengal, 6577, 6659; in
    Borneo, 6990; in Burma, 7033; in the Caribbean, 7458; in
    China, 7073, 7077; in eastern seas (19th cent.), 7073, 7079;
    in Ethiopia (19th cent.), 6135; in France (19th cent.), 2082;
    on Gold Coast, 6343; of Indian Ocean (19th cent.), 6948; of
    Indonesia (early), 6982; in Japan, 7110; on the Niger, 6376-7;
    in Russia (20th cent.), 2372; in South America, 7517-18; in
    South China Sea (17th-18th cent.), 6991; in the Sudan (19th
    cent.), 6127; in the West Indies, 7464; in western Europe
    (20th cent.), 2179
  overseas, external (17th-18th cent.), 6990-1; (18th-19th cent.),
    7458; (19th cent.), 3942, 7073, 7077, 7079, 7110; (19th-20th
    cent.), 4870; (20th cent.), 2398, 2618; of Scotland, 2618; of
    the Argentine, 7556; of Brazil, 7569; of Ceylon, 6934; of Gold
    Coast, 6410; of ancient Greece, 136, 161; of India, 6605, 6796;
    of Iraq, 6011; of the Loanga coast, 6435; of Nigeria, 6410; of
    Poland, 1832, 1886; of the Roman empire, 263, 298; of Spain,
    7517-18
  see also Economic relations
Trade cycle (19th cent.), 3979, 5121; (20th cent.), 4927
Trade routes, of Asia Minor (early), 5903; to China (19th cent.),
    7083; of the Syrian desert, 5904
Trade union official, 5001
Trade unions, in England and Wales, 3333, 3975, 3980, 4972-5033
    passim, 5509; in Ireland, 5869; in Germany, 2189; in Japan,
    7116; in Russia, 2364; in the U.S.A., 7401
Traders, see Merchants
Trades councils, 4987, 5008-9; in Ireland, 5869; in Scotland, 4987
Traffic, street, 5159
Trajan, Marcus Ulpius (b. 53 A.D.), Roman emperor, 220
Tramp shipping, 5154
Tramways, 5158
Transhumance, 517
Translators (medieval), 798
Transmundus (12th cent.), papal notary, 717
Transoxiana, 5929
Transport, in England and Wales, 3385-99, 5123-67; and see (medi-
    eval), 1598; (18th cent.), 3987; (19th-20th cent.), 4515; in
    Ireland, 3590; in Scotland, 5821; in Burma, 7033; in India,
    6723; land, in the Mediterranean (early), 117; in the Roman
    empire, 260; in the Sudan, 6182

Transport service, in Revolutionary War, 2015
Transport system, mineral, 5058
Transport workers (20th cent.), 5020
Transportation, criminal, 7571; (17th cent.), 7415; (18th cent.),
    3705
Transvaal, 6308, 6313, 6331-2
Travancore, 6820
Travel and travellers (medieval), 1167; (17th cent.), 4083; to
    France (18th cent.), 1978; to India (16th-17th cent.), 6549;
    to North America (18th-19th cent.), 7180; to Switzerland
    (18th-19th cent.), 2474; to Syria, 5985; and see below
Travel literature, South African, 6279
Travellers, European, in medieval Asia, 7057; French, in England,
    4125
Treason, 950A; (medieval), 951; (17th cent.), 2692; legislation
    relating to, 2638, 2660
Treasury (17th-18th cent.), 3596, 3642; (18th cent.), 7178; (19th
    cent.), 3757, 4597, 4756
Treatise on the Miracles of the Virgin (William of Malmesbury's),
    1209
Treaty of 1921, 5879
Trebizond, 5955
Trecothick, Barlow (c. 1719-1775), 3789
Tremenheere, Hugh Seymour (1804-93), 4556
Trent, Council of (1545-63), 1767
Trent valley, 2582
Trevecka, Brecon, 4230-1
Tribal administration, in Iraq (19th-20th cent.), 6013
Tribal policy, of Muhammad, 5921
Tribal unrest, in Bengal, 6708
Tribunate, Roman, 189
Trier, Germany (Roman), 338
Trincomalee, Ceylon, 6992
Trinidad, 4727, 7447-502 passim
Trinity House, Deptford, 2779
Triple Alliance (1668), 1770
Tripoli, 6079
Triumphal procession, 2411
Triumvirs, 202
Trivet, Nicholas (1258-1328), 69-70
Trojan War, 127
Tropical development, in West Africa, 6406
Trotsky, Leon Davidovitch (1879-1940), 2383
Trotternish, Isle of Skye, 3560
Truant schools, 5606
Truro, Cornw., bishopric of, 5402
Trusteeship, policy of, 7580
Trust(s), charitable, 2482; imperial, 6247; investment, 4909; law
    of, 3680
Ts'ai Yung (133-92), 7049
Tucker, Abraham (1705-74), 4299
Tucker, Josiah (1712-99), 3857
Tudhaliyaš IV (c. 1260-1230 B.C.), 5886
Tübingen, Germany, 2111
Tunis (19th cent.), 6080-4
Tunisia, 6070
Tunstall, Cuthbert (1474-1559), bishop, 2926
Turanians, 6955
Turf working, 3582
Turgot, Anne Robert Jacques (1727-81), 1974-5
Turkey, 1830; (18th-19th cent.), 5987; (19th cent.), 6029; (19th-
    20th cent.), 6003, 6020; (20th cent.), 6035, 6040, 6049, 6051,
    6053; and Britain, 5997, 6019, 6023; and England (16th cent.),
    5967; (17th cent.), 5977; and Greece, 6048; and Iran, 5995;
    and Syria, 6039; see also Ottoman empire
Turkish question (20th cent.), 6038
Turkish Straits, 6027, 6031, 6037

Turkish tribes (medieval), 44
Turks, in Arabia (19th cent.), 5993; in Asia (6th-7th cent.), 6958;
    in India (13th cent.), 6531; in Iraq (9th cent.), 5937; in
    Palestine (19th-20th cent.), 6021; in the Persian Gulf (16th
    cent.), 5965
Turner, Francis (1638?-1700), bishop, 4166
Turnpike roads, trusts, 3390, 4030-2, 4356; in Wales, 4033
Tuscany, 804-5, 2257
Tutbury, honour of, 1573
Tutorial appeal (13th cent.), 1251
Tweedsmuir, 1st Baron, see Buchan, John
Tyndale, William (d. 1536), 2922
Tyndall, John (1820-93), 5669
Tynemouth, Northumb., 5607; constituency, 4594
Tyneside, 3836, 5049
Type-founding (18th cent.), 4001
Tyrannies, in Asia Minor. 162; Athenian, 140-1; Spartan, 140
Tyrconnel, earl of, see Talbot, Richard
Tyrolese marriage (1341-2), 586
Tyrone, co., 515; east, 3581
Tyrone, 2nd earl of, see O'Neill, Hugh
Tyrwhitt, Thomas (1730-86), 4307
Tytler, Alexander Fraser (1747-1813), Lord Woodhouselee, 4445
Tytler, William (1711-92), 4445

'UBAID PERIOD, in Iraq, 5942
Udaipur, India, see Mewar
Uganda, 6204, 6206; (19th cent.), 6221, 6248; (19th-20th cent.),
    6250, 6255; (20th cent.), 6257, 6259; eastern, 6258
Uighur empire, 6959
Ukraine (20th cent.), 2390-1; and Poland (20th cent.), 1887
Ukrainian people (medieval), 559
Ullerston, Richard (d. 1423), 1310, 1406
Ulster, 518, 5844; (18th cent.), 7273; (18th-19th cent.), 3588;
    (19th cent.), 5836, 5839, 5868; (20th cent.), 4693; north,
    514
Ulster, earls of, 1714
Ultra-royalist movement, French (19th cent.), 2046
Umayyad caliphate, 5925; in Spain, 554
Umbria (Roman), 183
Unauthorised Programme, 4656
Under-secretaries of state (18th cent.), 3698
'Undertakers' in Ireland, 4472
Unemployed labour, 4709
Unemployment, 4716, 4940, 4963, 4967-9, 5334
Unfree classes (medieval), 1151
Ungava, Canada, 7216A
Union, with Scotland and Ireland, see Act of Union
Union Bill (1822), 7217
Union of Socialist Soviet Republics, 1746, 2377-95; and Britain,
    2381, 6863; and Finland, 2384; and Germany, 1821-2; and India,
    2381, 6863; see also Russia
Unionist party, 4682
Unionists, 4692, 4694-5, 4921
Unionists, in southern U.S.A., 7369
Unitarianism, 3466, 3480, 3812, 5429
United Brethren, Church of, 3477
United Nations, 1747
United Provinces, 6452-3, 6731, 6758, 6857
United States of America, 7181; (19th cent.), 2136, 7624; (19th-
    20th cent.), 7102, 7296-412, 7550, 7562; (20th cent.), 1736,
    1741, 2177, 2195, 2468, 6270; and Barbary states, 6077; and
    Britain (19th cent.), 7537, 7554, 7561; (19th-20th cent.),
    7500, 7563-5, 7624; (20th cent.), 7633; and China, 7132-3,
    7155; and Far East, 7129, 7168; and Germany, 7624; and Japan,
    4788; and Philippines, 6448; and Russia, 2378
Unity of the Czech Brethren, 735

Universal supremacy, claims to (14th cent.), 577
Universities (medieval), 801, 808, 814; in England (medieval),
     1465, 1468, 1691; (15th-17th cent.), 2562; (16th-17th cent.),
     3138; in Ireland, 5860-1; in Scotland, 1692; in Wales, 5645;
     in Germany, 2111, 2156; in India, 6764; in Pakistan, 6767; in
     the Sudan, 6161
Universities Mission to Central Africa, 6314
University extension movement, 5653
Unrest, see Agrarian unrest; Labour unrest; Political unrest;
     Tribal unrest
Unskilled labour, 5015
Upper Canada, 7207, 7213
Urabi Pasha (d. 1911), 6158
Urban development, settlement (early), 5896; in Ceylon, 6879; in
     Egypt (20th cent.), 6191; in Mughal empire, 6554; in the
     Netherlands, 2271; in Roman empire, 261
Urban leadership, in India, 6735
Urquhart, David (1805-77), 5999
Ushaw, co. Durham, 5617
Ushinski, Konstantin (d. 1871), 2347
Ussher, James (1581-1656), archbishop, 3274-5
Usury (medieval), 1157; (16th-17th cent.), 2877
Utbī states, 5983
Utilitarianism, 6700
Utopia (More's), 3129
Utopianism (17th cent.), 3846-7
Utrecht, treaty of (1713), 1775
Uwchgwyrfai, Caern., 3435

VACCINATION, see Small-pox inoculation
Vagrancy, 2499; (16th cent.), 2886
Vaisnava schools, 6585
Valence, Aymer de (d. 1324), earl of Pembroke, 860
Valencia, Spain, 2435, 3893
Valle Crucis abbey, Denbighs., 1627
Value, theory of (17th-18th cent.), 1720
Vandals, in North Africa, 6074
Vane, Sir Henry (1589-1655), 2727
Vane, Sir Henry (1613-62), 2728-30
Van Mildert, William (1765-1836), bishop, 4194
Vannes, France, 1947
Vasić, Serbian informer, 1872
Vatican palace, Italy (15th cent.), 819
Vaughan, Charles John (1816-97), 5619
Vaughan, Sir John (1603-74), 3614
Vaughan, John (1663-1722), 4136
Vaughan, Richard (1606-86), 2nd earl of Carbery, 3594
Vaughan, Robert (1592?-1667), 3143
Vauvenargues, Luc de Clapiers, marquis de (1715-47), 1961
Vendée, France, 2027
Venezuela, 7512; (16th cent.), 7508; (19th cent.), 7561
Venice, Italy, 656, 673, 2230-1
Verney family, 2834
Verona, Guarino da (1374-1460), 817
Versailles, treaty of (1919), 1816, 1818; see also Paris Peace
     Conference (1919)
Vespasian (d. 79 A.D.), Roman emperor, 25
Veterans, Roman, 294
Vettori, Francesco (1474-1539), 2221
Veysey, John (d. 1554), bishop, 2920
Via media (17th cent.), 4162
Vicarage system (13th-15th cent.), 722
Vice-presidency, of the U.S.A., 7299
Victoria, Australia, 7613
Victoria College, Jersey, 5628
Vienne, France (Roman), 333
Vijayanagara empire, 6541

Vili people, 6345
Village community, in the U.S.S.R., 2394
Village school (19th-20th cent.), 5596
Villas, in Roman Britain, 347-50
Villeinage, 926, 1582
Villiers, George (1592-1628), 1st duke of Buckingham, 1923, 2794
Villiers, George William Frederick (1800-70), 4th earl of Claren-
    don, 2455
Vilna, Russia, see Wilno
Vincent de Paul, Saint (1576-1660), 1922
Vintners Company, 2855
Violence, in ancient Rome, 193; industrial, 7395; politics of
    (19th cent.), 1781
Virginia, colonial (17th cent.), 7259, 7264; (18th cent.), 7273,
    7279
Vischer, Sir Hanns (1876-1945), 6429
Visconti, Filippo Maria (1391-1447), duke of Milan, 592
Visconti, Giangaleazzo (d. 1402), duke of Milan, 591
Visigoths, 555
Vita divi Vespasiani (Suetonius's), 25
Vita domini Roberti de Bethune (William de Wycumba's), 1203
Vita Sancti Andreae Sali, 701
Vita Wulfstani (William of Malmesbury's), 1422
Vitelli, Paolo (d. 1499), 674
Vivarium monastery, Italy, 758
Viviani, René (1863-1925), 2085
Vladimir, Saint (d. 1015), of Kiev, 704
Vocation, ministerial (18th cent.), 4217
Vocational training, 2565
Volstead Act (1919), 7405
Volta basin, 6349
Voltaire, François-Marie Arouet de (1694-1778), 93-5
Voluntary authorities, 4595
Voluntary controversy, 5796
Voluntary schools, 5611-12
Vosges, department of, France, 2052
Vossius, Gerard Johann (1577-1649), 83
Voyages, to America, 7170-1
Vyvyan, Sir Richard Rawlinson (1800-79), 4545

WADE, Sir Claude Martine (1794-1861), 6701
Wade, George (1673-1748), 3577
Wage-earning classes (18th-19th cent.), 3939; (19th cent.), 4514;
    of Paris (18th cent.), 2005; see also Working classes
Wages, 4991; (15th-16th cent.), 1141; (18th cent.), 3969; (18th-
    19th cent.), 3332; (19th-20th cent.), 5005; agricultural
    (19th cent.), 5185; regulation of (16th cent.), 2829; in
    Ireland (20th cent.), 5874; in Wales (16th cent.), 2830; in
    Germany (19th-20th cent.), 2146
Wahhabi doctrines, 6644
Wakefield, W.R. Yorks., 3185, 5750
Wakefield, Henry (d. 1395), bishop, 1296
Wakefield colonial system, 4722, 7594
Walden, Roger (d. 1406), archbishop, 1319
Wales, 81, 485-99, 2556, 2588, 3452, 3510, 4033, 4249, 5143;
    (Roman), 372, 384; (medieval), 992-3, 1340, 1494, 1590-662;
    (15th-17th cent.), 3169-208 passim; (15th-16th cent.), 2626,
    2652, 3113; (16th cent.), 2830, 2938; (16th-18th cent.), 2531,
    2598; (16th-17th cent.), 2514, 2773-4, 2887, 3027-8, 3046;
    (17th cent.), 2795, 2872-3, 3045, 3103-4, 3142, 3601, 3623;
    (17th-19th cent.), 3504; (17th-18th cent.), 3947; (18th cent.),
    3818, 4099, 4135, 4146, 4296; (18th-19th cent.), 4322, 4831;
    (19th cent.), 4533, 4570, 4838, 4890, 5241, 5278, 5424, 5433,
    5592, 5645; (19th-20th cent.), 4521, 4628, 4855, 5073, 5157,
    5185, 5324, 5631; south-east, 4539; south-west, 2512, 2895,
    5762

Wales (<u>cont.</u>)
  North, 3294, 3344, 3350, 3352; (Roman), 373, 377; (medieval),
    1630-1, 1644; (16th-17th cent.), 2501; (17th-18th cent.),
    3993; (18th cent.), 3676; (19th cent.), 5452, 7310; (19th-20th
    cent.), 5007; (20th cent.), 4670
  South, 3511, 5012, 5132; (Roman), 376; (15th-17th cent.), 2821;
    (18th-19th cent.), 3327, 3338, 3478, 3517, 3746, 3819, 4264;
    (19th cent.), 5242, 5660; (19th-20th cent.), 4528, 5005, 5015,
    5058, 5080, 5283; (20th cent.), 4701, 5025, 5033, 5105, 5107
  Marches of, 2578, 2672
Walker, <u>see</u> Wormalds and Walker
Wall decoration, early Christian, 778
Wallasey, Ches., 2567
Waller, Sir William (1598-1668), 2747
Walpole, Horace (1717-97), 4th earl of Orford, 3706-7
Walsall, Staffs., 2536, 4344, 4676, 5587
Walthamstow, Essex, 5754
Waltheof (d. 1076), earl of Northumbria, 826
Walwyn, William (fl. 1649), 2756-7
Wandsworth, <u>see</u> London
Wang Fu-chih (1619-92), 7065
Wansey, Henry (1752?-1827), 7307
War, attitudes to (19th cent.), 4732; plans to end, 1735; problem
    of (16th cent.), 1760; <u>see also</u> Peace movement
War, in the eastern seas (1803-10), 7079
War, usages of (14th cent.), 617
War of Devolution (1667-8), 1770
War of 1812, 3919, 3919A, 7317, 7321-2
War of France and Spain (1622-59), 2436
War of Intervention in Russia (1917-20), 2377, 7149
War of Jenkins' Ear (1739-48), 3897
War of the Holy League (1684-99), 5978
War of the League of Augsburg (1689-97), 3888-9
War of the Spanish Succession (1701-14), 2280, 2444-5, 3892-4
Ward, Sir Henry George (1797-1860), 6926
Ward, Seth (1617-89), bishop, 4161
Ward, Thomas Asline (1781-1871), 5548
Ward, William (1817-85), 2nd earl of Dudley, 5053
Ward, William George (1812-82), 5459
Wardrobe accounts, 1167
Wardship, royal, 929
Warfare, in ancient Greece, 130, 132; Hellenistic, 175; in ancient
    India, 6459-61; Indian mountain (19th cent.), 6693
Warham, William (1450-1532), archbishop, 2631, 2917
Warrington, Lancs., 5655
Warriston, Lord, <u>see</u> Johnston, Archibald
Wars of the Roses (1455-85), 882, 1693
Wartheland (20th cent.), 2202
Warton, Lancs., 3544
Warwick, 473
Warwick, countess of, <u>see</u> Greville, Frances Evelyn
Warwickshire, 471, 2581, 3425; (Saxon), 1522; (medieval), 969,
    1556; (17th cent.), 2748; (17th-18th cent.), 4089; (19th cent.),
    4524, 5470; (19th-20th cent.), 4493; east, 4511
<u>Washington Globe</u>, 7328A
Water power (18th-19th cent.), 3360; in Ireland, 518
Water supply, in Roman Britain, 345; (19th-20th cent.), 5297
Water utilisation, in Khuzistan and Iraq, 5896
Watercourses (17th cent.), 4342
Waterford, Ireland, 1710
Waterhouse charity, 4084
Waterways, inland, in Ireland, 3591; <u>see also</u> Navigation
Watson, Richard (1781-1833), 4253
Watson-Wentworth, Charles (1730-82), 2nd marquess of Rockingham,
    3699, 3703, 3713-14, 3731-2, 3789
Watt, <u>see</u> Boulton and Watt
Watts, Isaac (1674-1748), 4301

Waverley Novels, 105
Weald, 1124, 2848, 3387; western, 404
Wealth (medieval), 1157-8; (16th cent.), 2884; (16th-17th cent.),
    2896-7
Weapons, in ancient Greece, 131
Weardale, 5049
Wearside, 3836
Weaver valley, 5082
Weavers' Company, 1111
Webb, Beatrice (1858-1943), Baroness Passfield, 4649, 5512
Webb, Sidney James (1859-1947), Baron Passfield, 4649, 5512
Wedderburn, Alexander (1733-1805), 1st Baron Loughborough and 1st
    earl of Rosslyn, 3708
Wedgwood, Josiah (1730-95), 3988
Wednesbury, Staffs., 4345, 5091
Weimar constitution and republic, 2174, 2177, 2181-3
Welded tube trade, 5091
Welfare, social, see Social welfare
Welfare policy, in Ghana, 6432
Welfare State, 5314
Wellesley, Arthur (1769-1852), 1st duke of Wellington, 2048, 3805,
    3918
Wellesley, Richard Colley (1760-1842), Marquess Wellesley, 6663-4
Wellington, Salop, 4500
Wellington, 1st duke of, see Wellesley, Arthur
Wells cathedral, Som., 1228; see also Bath and Wells
Welsh border, 1533, 1603-4, 4064
Welsh language, 2577-8
Welsh laws, 1622-4
Welshpool, Mont., 1618
Wenlock, Salop, Much Wenlock priory, 1342, 1345
Wensleydale, 4507
Wentworth, Charles Watson-, see Watson-Wentworth
Wentworth, Sir John (1737-1820), 7284
Wentworth, Thomas (1593-1641), 1st earl of Strafford, 3276-8
Wenvoe, Glam., 5552
Wesley, John (1703-91), 4138, 4171, 4219-22, 4224-5, 4244, 4477
Wesleyan Methodism, 3492-4, 3518, 5443, 5451, 6293-4; in Scotland,
    4434; in Wales, 3478; in India, 6734; in Jamaica, 7472
Wessex, 389, 558, 822, 1183
Wessington, John (d. 1451), 1393
West Africa, see Africa, west
West African Frontier Force, 6424
West Derby hundred, 3450
West Ham, Essex, 5679
West Indies, 7413-506 passim; and see (17th cent.), 7174; (18th
    cent.), 7178; (19th cent.), 7183
West of England, Friendly societies in, 3456; woollen industry in,
    2839, 3357
West Pakistan, 6751
West Penwith, Cornw., 392
West River province, China, 7120
Westbury, Wilts., 3693
Western Australia, 7586
Western Canada, 7188, 7191
Western Pacific High Commission, 7629
Westminster, Middx., 1133; bridge, 4359; St. Margaret's parish,
    4342; St. Stephen's chapel, 1515
Westminster Assembly, 3096
Westminster Committee, 3761
Westminster Confession, 3097
Westminster Directory, 3095
Westmorland, 369-70, 1518, 3694, 5129
Wharfedale, 448
Wharton, Philip (1613-96), 4th Baron Wharton, 3593
Wheat trade, European, 1749
Whethamstede, John (d. 1465), 1395

Whig Junto, 3665
Whig party (17th cent.), 3624-5, 3627; (18th cent.), 3656, 3670, 3734, 3739, 3745; (19th cent.), 3754, 3758, 3768
Whiggism, 4575
Whigs (17th cent.), 3640; Rockingham, 3699, 3713-14; Scottish, 4438
Whitbread and Co., 5056
Whitchurch, Salop, grammar school, 2570
White, Sir William Arthur (1824-91), 6023
White Horse, Vale of, 417
White settlers, in Cape of Good Hope, 6303; in Natal, 6299, 6334; in Northern Rhodesia, 6324; in South Africa, 6285, 6291; in Tropical Africa, 6225
Whitechapel, see London
Whitefield, George (1714-70), 7278
Whitehaven, Cumb., 3376, 3948
Whitgift, John (1532-1604), archbishop, 3031-5
Whitstable, Kent, 5753
Wid basin, 2502
Wielopolski, Alexander (1803-77), 1855
Wigan, Lancs., 4854
Wight, Isle of, 1526, 2605, 2945, 3013
Wilberforce, Samuel (1805-73), bishop, 5405
Wilfrid, Saint (634-709), bishop, 1180
Wilkins, William (1778-1839), 4337
William I (1027-87), king, 825, 1030
William III (1650-1702), king, 3640; as William of Orange, 3635
William (c. 1130-c. 1190), archbishop of Tyre, 62
William de Braose (d. 1211), 828
William de Montibus (d. 1213), 1440
William de Wycumba (fl. 1160), 1203
William of Corbeil (d. 1136), archbishop, 1202
William of Malmesbury (d. 1143?), 1209, 1422
William the Marshal (d. 1219), 1st earl of Pembroke, 832
Williams, Edward (1750-1813), 4249
Williams, John (1582-1650), archbishop, 3061
Willison, John (1680-1750), 4421-2
Willoughby family, 2523
Wills (medieval), 1122, 1302
Wilno, Russia, 2351
Wilson, Florens (1504-47), 1908
Wilson, Sir Robert Thomas (1777-1849), 3914
Wilson, Woodrow (1856-1924), president of the U.S.A., 7404
Wiltshire (medieval), 983, 1072, 1080, 1582; (16th-17th cent.), 2837-8; (17th cent.), 2740, 3187; (17th-18th cent.), 4259; (18th-19th cent.), 4009; north-west, 4063
Winchcombe abbey, Glos., 57, 1330
Winchelsea, Sussex, 3695
Winchelsey, Robert (d. 1313), archbishop, 1254-5, 1442
Winchester, Hants, 1528, 3181, 4105; cathedral, 1272; College, 5272
Winchester, bishopric of (medieval), 1072, 1074, 1076-7, 1083
Winchester, 2nd earl of, see Roger de Quincy
Wind and pressure observations, 1768
Windham, William (1717-61), 2020
Windle, Sir Bertram (1858-1929), 5873
Windsor, Berks., St. George's chapel, 1285
Windward Islands, 7483
Wine trade (medieval), 657, 671, 1126; (18th cent.), 1948
Wingate, Sir Francis Reginald (1861-1953), 6197
Wingfield, Sir Richard (1469-1525), 2639
Wingfield, Sir Robert (1464?-1539), 2639
Winkworth, Catherine (1827-78), 5652
Winkworth, Susanna (1820-84), 5652
Wirksworth, Derbys., 5718
Wirral, Ches., 5265
Wisbech Stirs, 3039

Wishart, George (c. 1513-1546), 3219
Witchcraft (16th-17th cent.), 2905; in Scotland, 2612
Witney, Oxon., 1551; grammar school, 3501
Wodehouse, John (1826-1902), 1st earl of Kimberley, 4758
Woking, Surrey, 5605
Wollaston, William Hyde (1766-1828), 4318
Wollaton, Notts., 2523; Wollaton Hall, 3167
Wolsey, Thomas (1475?-1530), 3126
Wolverhampton, Staffs., 2751, 3309; borough council, 5766
Wolverton, Bucks., 5721
Women
   education of (15th-17th cent.), 3116; (17th cent.), 4267; (17th-
     18th cent.), 4266; (19th cent.), 5650-1; (19th-20th cent.),
     5506; in France (16th cent.), 1905; in India, 6590, 6672,
     6714, 6845
   in ancient Rome, 243-4; in the early church, 681A; magazines for,
     5224; and poor law, 5290; property of, 5288; religious life
     for (12th cent.), 1359; social life of, in medieval Bengal,
     6501; in trade unions, 4997; travellers to Switzerland (18th-
     19th cent.), 2474; writers (18th cent.), 4121, 4309
   status of (19th cent.), 5288; in Italy (16th cent.), 2243; in
     Malawi, 6239; in Muslim Spain, 641
Women workers (18th-19th cent.), 3335; (19th cent.), 5286; (19th-
   20th cent.), 4954-5; in agriculture, 4074, 5180; in textile
   industries (15th cent.), 1137
Women's suffrage movement, 4851-2
Wood, Anthony (1632-95), 4290
Wood, Sir Charles (1800-85), 1st Viscount Halifax, 6764-6
Wood, Sir Richard (1806-1900), 4555, 6081
Woodard, Nathaniel (1811-91), 5625
Woodard schools, 5624
Woodford, William (c. 1330-c. 1397), 1464
Woodhouselee, Lord, see Tytler, Alexander Fraser
Woodlands, 492, 3282, 3296; in Ireland, 2619; in Wales, 3296
Woodlands Estate, Dorset, 1090
Woodstock, Thomas of (1355-97), duke of Gloucester, 867-8
Wool (14th cent.), 1022; prices of (19th-20th cent.), 1732; supply
   of (16th-17th cent.), 2518; taxation of (14th cent.), 1018
Wool textile industry, see Woollen and worsted industries
Wool trade, English, 2520; (medieval), 1105, 1120-1; (16th-17th
   cent.), 2521; Welsh (17th cent.), 2872-3; international, 1733;
   see also Cloth trade
Woollen and worsted industries, 2516-17, 2519-20, 3358; (medieval),
   1137; (15th-17th cent.), 1581; (16th cent.), 2841; (16th-17th
   cent.), 2518, 2838-40; (18th cent.), 4008, 4011; (18th-19th
   cent.), 3356-7, 3362, 3961, 4009, 4019; (19th cent.), 5040-3,
   7367; (19th-20th cent.), 4972, 5039; in Scotland, 3555
Wootton Basset, Wilts., 3693
Worcester, 3178
Worcester, diocese of, 1264, 1295, 2932, 4088, 4183
Worcester, earl of, see Tiptoft, John
Worcester, earls of (16th-17th cent.), 2832
Worcester, 1st marquess of, see Somerset, Henry
Worcestershire, 468; (medieval), 469, 974, 1070, 1506; (19th-20th
   cent.), 4522-3; (20th cent.), 5614; east, 2511; north-east,
   3312
Worden Hall, Lancs., 2836
Workers, injured and deceased, 3336; social conditions of, 3342-3,
   3371, 5048-9
'Workers' Control', 5024
Workers' Union, 5021
Workhouses (18th cent.), 4103
Working classes (18th-19th cent.), 4118, 4241; (19th cent.), 4820,
   4825, 4847, 5232, 5273, 5319, 5364, 5370, 5435; (19th-20th
   cent.), 4781, 5282; in Scotland, 5777; see also Wage-earning
   classes
Working classes, union of, 3843

Working hours, 3331, 4947, 5050
Working-class associations, German (19th cent.), 2137
Working-class movement, 4653, 4672, 4820-61 **passim**, 5359, 5363,
    5433; see also Labour movement
Works schools, in Wales, 4322
World Disarmament Conference (1932), 2191
World War I (1914-18), 2170, 2265, 2409, 2477, 4801-4, 4807, 7403
World War II (1939-45), 1827, 1895, 2170, 2203-4, 2395, 5346-7
Wormalds and Walker, 5041
Worship, Calvinist public, 1762; cathedral, 2550; of English
    Puritans, 2547; Scottish (16th-17th cent.), 3226
Worsted industry, see Woollen and worsted industries
Wrangle, Lincs., 3536
Wraysbury, Bucks., 5597
Wren, Matthew (1585-1667), bishop, 3089-90
Wrexham, Denbighs., 5048
Writtle, Essex, 1531
Württemberg (Roman), 339
Würzburg abbey, Germany, 2112
Wyatt, Sir Henry (1460?-1537), 2627
Wyatt, James (1746-1813), 4335
Wyatville, Sir Jeffry (1766-1840), 4338
Wyclif, John (d. 1384), 1268, 1293, 1462-3, 2934
Wymondley, Great and Little, Herts., 1559
Wynn, Charles Watkin Williams (1775-1850), 3744
Wynne, Sir John (1553-1626), 4086
Wyse, Sir Thomas (1791-1862), 5580

XENOPHON (fl. 430-357 B.C.), 159
Xerxes (d. c. 464 B.C.), 155

YAHYA BIN AHMAD SIHRINDI, 45
Yangtze river province, China, 7120
Yao people, 6209
Yarmouth, Great, Norfolk, 1577, 3384
Ya'-rubi dynasty, 5974
Yemen (9th-11th cent.), 5935; (17th-19th cent.), 5973
Yeomanry (17th cent.), 4044
Ynysymorengwyn, Merioneth, 4049
Yonne, department of, France, 1949
York, 3550, 5293; (medieval), 981, 1423; (14th-16th cent.), 1575;
    (16th cent.), 3179; (16th-17th cent.), 2775, 3184; (17th
    cent.), 3197; (18th cent.), 3692; (18th-19th cent.), 3528;
    (19th cent.), 5728; (19th-20th cent.), 5727; St. Peter's
    School, 2573
York, archbishops of, 1187, 1249-51
York, diocese of (medieval), 1241, 1261, 1271; (16th cent.), 2956;
    (16th-17th cent.), 2961, 2996; (17th cent.), 3049, 3069
York, dukes of, 1091
York, house of, 884
York, province of, 1249, 1271, 2997-8; court, 1201
York, vale of, 4507
York von Wartenburg, Hans David Ludwig (1759-1830), 2121
Yorke, Charles (1722-70), 3715
Yorkshire, 962, 1107, 2516, 5144-5; (medieval), 897, 1068, 1370;
    (15th-17th cent.), 1097; (16th cent.), 2956; (16th-18th cent.),
    2995; (17th cent.), 2737, 2767, 2815, 2912, 3592; (17th-18th
    cent.), 4045; (18th cent.), 3811, 4236; (18th-19th cent.),
    3291, 4232-3; (19th cent.), 4847, 5041, 5043, 5423, 5522,
    5657-9; (19th-20th cent.), 4972
east (17th cent.), 3044; (18th-19th cent.), 4107; (19th cent.),
    5175; north, 3433; north-east (medieval), 1351; north-west,
    448; south, 4020; (18th-19th cent.), 3341; (19th cent.),
    4526-7; (19th-20th cent.), 4989; south-west, 5218; west, 5160
East Riding, 440, 2506, 2565, 3401; (19th cent.), 5434
North Riding, 3020; (17th cent.), 3205, 4341; (18th cent.),
    4363

Yorkshire (cont.)
  West Riding, 1153, 3401; (16th cent.), 2892; (17th cent.), 3151;
    (18th-19th cent.), 3422, 4019; (19th cent.), 3838, 5040, 5239,
    5434, 5748; (19th-20th cent.), 5764
Yorkshire County Association, 3811
Yorkshire Philosophical Society, 5471
Yoruba tribes, 6385-6, 6389
Yorubaland, 6413
Yoshida Shōin, 7106
Young, Arthur (1741-1820), 4068
Young, James (1811-83), 5784
Young Irelanders, 5851
Youth (20th cent.), 4787; in the U.S.S.R., 2389
Youth movements, uniformed, 5329
Yüan, Shih-K'-ai (1859-1916), 7144
Yucatan, 7519
Yu'firid dynasty, 5935
Yugoslavia, see Jugoslavia
Yūsif Mikhāīl (b. c. 1865), 6154
Yusuf, Shayk Ali (1889-1913), 6175
Yusuf Pasha Qaramanli, of Tripoli, 6079

ZACATECAS, Mexico, 7511
Zambesi, 6212
Zanzibar, 6215, 6242
Zeeland (medieval), 653
Zia-ud-din Barni (fl. 1356), 45-6
Zionism, 2163, 6047; Gentile, 6054
Zulus, 6310
Zwingli, Ulrich (1484-1531), 1758